11547

Teaching Music through Performance in Band
Volume 3

Also available from GIA Publications, Inc:
Teaching Music through Performance in Band, Volume 1
Teaching Music through Performance in Band, Volume 2

G-5333

Teaching Music through Performance in Band

Volume 3

Larry Blocher
Eugene Migliaro Corporon
Ray Cramer
Tim Lautzenheiser
Edward S. Lisk
Richard Miles

Compiled and Edited by Richard Miles

GIA Publications, Inc.
Chicago

G-5333

Copyright © 2000 GIA Publications, Inc.
7404 S. Mason Ave.
Chicago, IL 60638
www.giamusic.com
ISBN: 1-57999-092-4
Printed in the United States of America

Table of Contents

PART II: The Band Conductor as Music Teacher

ACKNOWLEDGEMENTS

The following research associates are gratefully acknowledged for outstanding scholarly contributions to the "Teacher Resource Guides":

Mike Alexander
University of Wisconsin • Milwaukee, Wisconsin

Kenneth Ayoob
Humboldt State University • Arcata, California

Diane M. Bargiel
Director of Instrumental Music and Artist Series
Juniata College • Huntingdon, Pennsylvania

Dennis Beck
Unionville High School • Markham, Ontario, Canada

John Cody Birdwell
Director of Bands
Texas Tech University • Lubbock, Texas

Sheryl A. Bowhay
Board of Education
Lambton County • Sarnia, Ontario, Canada

Gordon R. Brock
Director of Bands
University of North Dakota • Grand Forks, North Dakota

Marcellus Brown
Boise State University • Boise, Idaho

Robert Cameron
Director of Bands
Duquesne University • Pittsburgh, Pennsylvania

John C. Carmichael
Director of Bands
Western Kentucky University • Bowling Green, Kentucky

Patrick F. Casey
Director of Bands
Central Missouri State University • Warrensburg, Missouri

Jeff Cranmore
Director of Bands
Dowell Middle School • McKinney, Texas

Susan Creasap
Assistant Director of Bands
Morehead State University • Morehead, Kentucky

Wayne F. Dorothy
Visiting Assistant Professor
Morehead State University • Morehead, Kentucky

Mark Duker
Indiana University • Bloomington, Indiana

Jeff Emge
Texas A & M University • Commerce, Texas

Bradley P. Ethington
Associate Director of Bands
Syracuse University • Syracuse, New York

Sean Flanigan
Instructor of Trombone
Bowling Green State University • Bowling Green, Ohio

Otis French
Associate Conductor
United States Army Field Band • Washington, DC

Cheryl Fryer
Doctoral Conducting Associate
University of North Texas • Denton, Texas

Brad Genevro
Assistant Director of Wind Studies
University of North Texas • Denton, Texas

Jay W. Gilbert
Director of Bands and Chair, Music Department
Doane College • Crete, Nebraska

Nancy M. Golden
Masters Conducting Associate
University of North Texas • Denton, Texas

Richard A. Greenwood
Director of Bands
University of Central Florida • Orlando, Florida

Lawrence Dale Harper
Director of Bands
Carroll College • Waukesha, Wisconsin

Edward Harris
Director of Bands
California State University/Stanislaus • Turlock, California

Glen J. Hemberger
Director of Bands
Southeastern Louisiana University • Hammond, Louisiana

Leslie W. Hicken
Director of Bands
Furman University • Greenville, South Carolina

Paul R. Hinman
Director of University Bands
East Tennessee State University • Johnson City, Tennessee

Paula Holcomb
Director of Bands
State University of New York College • Fredonia, New York

Winona Holsinger
Masters Conducting Associate
University of North Texas • Denton, Texas

Diane Janda
Conductor of the Concert Band
Lycoming College • Williamsport, Pennsylvania

Keith Kinder
Associate Professor of Music
McMaster University • Hamilton, Ontario, Canada

James L. Klages
Professor of Trumpet
Ft. Lewis College • Durango, Colorado

Kenneth Kohlenberg
Director of Bands, Professor of Music
Sinclair Community College • Dayton, Ohio

Brian Lamb
Director of Instrumental Studies
Southwest Baptist University • Bolivar, Missouri

Alan Lourens
Lecturer in Music
Conductor, Wind Ensemble
Western Australian Conservatorium of Music

Rich Lundahl
Assistant Director of Bands
Delta State University • Cleveland, Mississippi

John P. Lynch
Associate Director of Bands
Northwestern University • Chicago, Illinois

Matthew Mailman
Director of Bands and Associate Professor of Music
Oklahoma City University

Victor A. Markovich
Professor of Music
Director of Bands and Winds/Percussion Studies
Wichita State University • Wichita, Kansas

Jennifer McAllister
Saskatoon, Saskatchewan, Canada

Keelan McCamey
Heritage of American Band
Langley Air Force Base • Hampton, Virginia

Matthew McInturf
Sam Houston State University • Huntsville, Texas

Sarah McKoin
Director of Bands
University of Buffalo • State University of New York • Buffalo, New York

Robert Meunier
Director of Bands
Drake University • Des Moines, Iowa

Joseph P. Missal
Director of Bands
Oklahoma State University • Stillwater, Oklahoma

Ryan Nelson
Doctoral Conducting Associate
University of North Texas • Denton, Texas

Paul Nickolas
Indiana University • Bloomington, Indiana

Doug Norton
American School in London • London, United Kingdom

Craig Paré
Director of University Bands
DePauw University • Greencastle, Indiana

Douglas A. Peterson
Director of Instrumental Music
Daytona Beach Community College • Daytona Beach, Florida

James Popejoy
Doctoral Conducting Associate
University of North Texas • Denton, Texas

Edwin C. Powell
Director of Bands
McLennan Community College • Waco, Texas

Jeffrey H. Renshaw
Director of Bands
University of Connecticut • Storrs, Connecticut

R. Mark Rogers
Director of Publications
Southern Music Company • San Antonio, Texas

Darin Schmidt
Indiana University • Bloomington, Indiana

Rodney C. Schueller
Northern Illinois University Bands • DeKalb, Illinois

Kevin L. Sedatole
Associate Director of Bands
The University of Texas at Austin • Austin, Texas

Kenneth Singleton
Director of Bands
University of Northern Colorado • Greeley, Colorado

Courtney Snyder
Graduate Conducting Assistant
Baylor University • Waco, Texas

Tony Spano, Jr.
Academy of Visual and Performing Arts
Culver City High School • Culver City, California

Gary A. Speck
Wind Ensemble Conductor
Miami University • Oxford, Ohio

Jack Stamp
Professor of Music
Indiana University of Pennsylvania • Indiana, Pennsylvania

Scott A. Stewart
Director of Instrumental Music
Emory University • Atlanta, Georgia

Yoshiaki Tanno
Doctoral Associate
Indiana University • Bloomington, Indiana

Ibrook Tower
Wind Ensemble Director
Pennsylvania Academy of Music • Lancaster, Pennsylvania
Instrumental Music Instructor
Milton Hershey School • Hershey, Pennsylvania

Frank C. Tracz
Director of Bands
Kansas State University • Manhattan, Kansas

Thomas Martin Wubbenhorst
Associate Professor of Music
Georgia State University • Atlanta, Georgia

Introduction

Larry R. Blocher

Commercials. They are everywhere these days. Sometimes they are hard to ignore. Sometimes they just won't go away. Sometimes I wonder why "sophisticated musicians" (that would be us) find ourselves humming the "tunes" or even singing the words to such "classics" as Meow Mix, Kit Kat Bars, Band-Aids, etc.

A few years ago I taught with a music colleague who had written a number of very successful commercial "jingles," including Kentucky Fried Chicken "We Do Chicken Right!" (my apologies to all of you who thought you had finally forgotten that one). One day I asked Jay what his formula was for writing a successful commercial jingle. He replied that the single most important ingredient for success was finding what he called the "hook" – a line, a phrase, a big idea – that would "hook" the listener. He suggested that once the hook was "in," it was likely to be stuck there for a long time.

As music conductors/teachers we have the opportunity to "hook" our students/performers/listeners in positive ways that have the potential to last a lifetime. For those of us who teach music through performance in band, some of our best opportunities to "get the hook in" occur during our music rehearsals.

Volume III of the *Teaching Music through Performance in Band* series serves as one of a growing number of resources designed to assist music teachers/conductors in selecting music, materials, and techniques for getting the hook "in." Like the other two volumes in the series, the text is divided into two parts. Part I contains a number of independent but related chapters. Each chapter addresses issues and/or techniques basic to teaching music during the band rehearsal. Part II contains resource guides for one hundred band works, grades two through six. Each resource guide includes analytical and historical information about the selection. This information is provided as a starting point for enriching the performance experience for both the conductor and the performer.

The project continues to be a team effort. We are indebted to the many fine music teachers who demonstrate an incredible passion for teaching music through performance every day. Their enthusiasm is infectious. It is our collective hope that once the music hook is indeed in, it will remain stuck for a lifetime.

PART I

THE TEACHING OF MUSIC

CHAPTER 1

Making Connections

Larry R. Blocher

"It's what you learn after you know it all that counts."
··· John Wooden ···

Introduction

At this writing, a new school year is about to begin. Each year as I watch music students getting ready to get ready to learn all the "music stuff" that causes the words **music major** to appear by their names on class lists, I am reminded that in many cases the core music education major curriculum – music theory, aural skills, music history, class piano, applied music, conducting, various music education methods, and ensembles – consists of separate and seemingly unrelated courses (at least on paper). Band is where you do band, and music theory is where you do music theory, and music history is.... You get the idea. As an undergraduate music student, I spent a good deal of time in what I now call "survival mode." As a result, I often failed to make the connection that each of these areas could be related not only to each other but also to the world beyond school.

Music history was a special problem. (I have had several wonderful music history teachers, so I accept responsibility for my special problem.) As an undergraduate, I spent a good bit of my time in music history class reading about and memorizing important facts about important people, and placing these people and facts into important blocks of time. Sometimes (especially around test time) I would even do the separate "required listening" outside of music history class. I was good at the memory part, and so at least for awhile, I knew music history, especially when I was in music history class. For me, music history stopped at the music history classroom door.

When I went to graduate school, I took a series of diagnostic entrance examinations and, as a result, had the opportunity to relearn the music history facts that I had "learned" earlier. Once again, music history was something that serious graduate music students studied in music history class.

After several years of teaching music, I returned to graduate school and took another series of diagnostic entrance exams that confirmed the fact that I was indeed music history "challenged." This time, however, the process used to "fix" my problem was different. While the important facts and important people and important blocks of time were still important, my focus this time around (thanks to a wise music history teacher) was not on memorizing isolated facts that seemed useful only in the music history classroom. The focus was on making connections between music history and the rest of the world. For me, music history no longer existed in a music history vacuum. I began to consider the importance of *making connections* – of making transfers – to my own learning process. *It was a Kodak moment.*

The Process of Education

The idea that **"making connections"** has the potential to affect the learning process is not new. Forty years ago, Jerome Bruner, writing about the process of education in an important book with the same name, stated that "the best way to create interest in a subject is to render it worth knowing, which means to make the knowledge gained useable in one's thinking beyond the situation in which the learning has occurred."[1] For our purposes in this chapter, we will refer to making knowledge/skills useable, meaningful, and applicable in different situations as *transfer.*

Bruner considered transfer to be fundamental to the educational process. He was also quick to point out that knowledge or skills acquired without an understanding of the fundamental principles of a subject would likely be forgotten.[2] Bruner called these fundamental principles the underlying *structure* of a subject. "The teaching and learning of structure, rather than simply the mastery of facts and techniques, is at the center of the classic problem of transfer.... If earlier learning is to render later learning easier, it must do so by providing a general picture in terms of which the relationships between things encountered earlier and later are made as clear as possible."[3] For our purposes in this chapter, we will refer to any attempt to make connections between things learned earlier and things learned later as **teaching for transfer.**

Let's review for a moment. According to Bruner, to improve the process of education in any subject, we need to identify the fundamental principles – the structure – the "big ideas" – of the subject, and then teach these ideas in a sequential way that will assist students in seeing and understanding the relationships between them. Understanding these relationships – making transfers – has the potential to improve both student long-term memory and comprehension of new information. Michael Mark states that Bruner's work, and the work of many others who found new meaning in his ideas, sparked interest in a new movement in the 1960s called "conceptual learning."[4]

Concepts

A concept may be thought of as a "group or cluster of related phenomena."[5] A "concept consists of a person's organized information about…objects, events, ideas, or processes…that enables the individual to discriminate the particular entity…and also to relate it to other entities and classes of entities. A concept has a recurring quality that gives it generalizability."[6]

In a recent conversation, Bentley Shellahamer provided the following illustration of what a concept is and why teaching concepts may be important to the teaching/learning process in music:

> You can improve your band's performance level by at least 200% if you apply the techniques of **Hioneephonicism** by the second week of each school year. As you apply the three components of **Hioneephonicism** to your band, you will notice that your band's levels of **Intraprecture, Omnolamnon,** and **Uloty** will increase significantly. Each time that you review the techniques involved in **Hioneephonicism,** you will notice a faster recovery time that will lead to a much keener awareness of **intonation, balance,** and **blend.**

By now, you should be scratching your head and saying, "What in blazes is he talking about?" When you heard the term *Hioneephonicism* the very first time, your brain began looking for the place where you had filed the concept called *Hioneephonicism*. When you didn't find it (I'm assuming that you did not find it because I made it up), your brain tried to find the closest thing possible. As you continued listening, your brain kept trying to find a place to "plug in" what you were hearing. Your search got really frantic when you heard the words *Intraprecture, Omnolamnon,* and *Uloty* (perhaps you even tried to relate these concepts to other concepts that you have acquired having to do with Middle Eastern breathing techniques or yoga). It wasn't until I got to *intonation, balance,* and *blend* that your brain could finally draw upon some acquired knowledge and make sense out of what you were hearing. Your brain had a place for *intonation,* but it did not have a place for *Hioneephonicism.* (Now you have a place for *Hioneephonicism* – which is in the place where you store nonsensical words!)

In a similar manner, when you sit down at your computer and prompt the computer to find a particular *file,* the computer looks for the file and then opens it. In that file will be everything that you have stored in memory relating to the subject indicated by the file name. Some files may be so large that you choose to set up a file *directory* on your hard drive for just that topic. In this case, when you want to access information about the particular topic, you would go to that directory first and then go to an individual file corresponding to the information you wanted. As you acquire more information on the main topic, you would open additional files.

A *concept* is much like both of these examples. A concept is a category where we store knowledge about similar and related information. A concept is an organizer. Unlike a fact, which is specific to an item, a concept allows generalizing to occur. Just like your computer hard drive, when you want to deal with information on a specific topic, your brain must open that file. And just like your computer, as you gain more information on a particular topic, you may have to add more files.

When you hear the word *sonority*, for example, you immediately open the file (concept) called *sonority*. In that file is everything you currently know about sonority. In that file, you may have references to other concepts, like balance, blend, intonation, tone quality, harmonic series, acoustics, tone production, etc. The more you know about sonority, the more references to other concepts you will have stored in that file.

When you take the time to teach the students in your band musical concepts in a sequential way, the effect of adding each new concept to their musical memory (hard drives) has the potential to be compounded many times because each new concept has many reference points that lead to *related* concepts. When you teach a new musical concept to your students in band, teaching that concept increases your students' potential to deal with new musical experiences in the future.

The time that we as music teachers or band directors spend *teaching* music concepts seems worth the investment, because over time, our students will acquire the background (fundamental principles) needed to relate those concepts to new situations more easily *if* we help them make those connections – *if we teach for transfer.*

Volume II of *Teaching Music through Performance in Band* suggests that teaching musical concepts may involve teaching for student **awareness** of any musical idea (skill or knowledge), some type of **understanding** of the idea, and opportunities for students to **apply** the information learned in similar situations.[7] The potential for transfer in the music teaching/learning process may be dependent on the acquisition of musical concepts.

Making Research Connections: Looking at Band Directors in Rehearsal

Almost eight years ago, Bentley Shellahamer, Richard Greenwood, and I began a long-term project designed to look at what band directors do in band rehearsals. Knowing that band directors (ourselves included) spend a great deal of time preparing ensembles for public performance, we realized that during the rehearsals for those performances, band directors had the opportunity to teach students about music through band. Given the importance attached to teaching musical concepts, we had a special interest in the amount of time

that band directors spent in teaching concepts during typical band rehearsals. For the purposes of these studies, we defined conceptual teaching as *any verbal attempts by band directors in band rehearsals to make students aware of, have an understanding of, and/or be able to transfer any musical concept.*

We started our look at band director behaviors by asking selected middle school and high school band directors in Florida to send us videotaped recordings of two or three of their entire band rehearsals during a one-week period. At the same time, we began to look at previous research in the area of sequential patterns of music teaching.

Teaching Cycles

What began as a method of teaching labeled *direct instruction* in other academic areas appeared to have application for music rehearsals as a three-step process, described first as a teaching unit and then refined to a teaching cycle and sequential patterns of instruction as shown in figure 1.

Band directors using this **teaching cycle**, sequenced as director task presentation (*instruction*), student performance (*response*), and related director *feedback*, were effective in producing good performances while maintaining a high level of student attentiveness and positive student attitudes. This teaching cycle model became the basis for analyzing band director "behaviors" in rehearsals.

Band Director Behaviors

Building on the teaching cycle model, our initial videotape analysis showed band directors delivering *instruction* in three ways: (1) verbally (directions or instructions), (2) nonverbally (directions or instructions), and (3) conceptually (as defined earlier). Band directors delivered *feedback* in two ways: (1) verbally and (2) nonverbally. We observed a third type of band director behavior, which involved no director proactive conducting, no eye contact, and no visual feedback. We labeled this type of band director behavior *non-interactive listening.* A final category involved all nonmusical behaviors of band directors.

The specific band director behavioral categories used to analyze what band directors did on the rehearsal tapes follows:

NONMUSICAL:
- Teacher disciplines students
- Downtime (getting ready; teacher performs administrative tasks)
- Nonmusical directions ("Close the door," "Take your hat off," "Listen to the announcements")

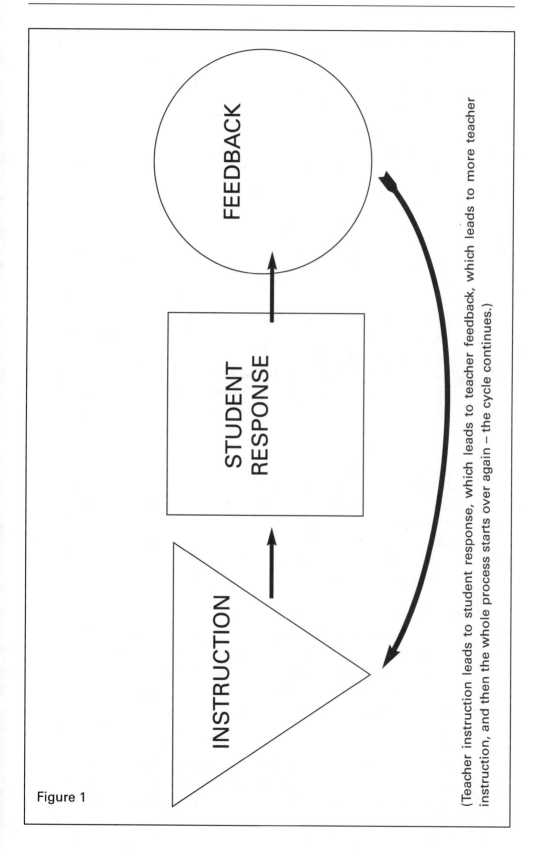

Figure 1

(Teacher instruction leads to student response, which leads to teacher feedback, which leads to more teacher instruction, and then the whole process starts over again – the cycle continues.)

- Announcements
- Interruptions from the office, messengers, visitors

NONVERBAL INSTRUCTION (DIRECTIONS):
- Teacher gives instruction through proactive conducting (attentive, helpful gestures, eye contact)
- Teacher's facial expressions, body language, and other non verbal cues instruct or elicit responses

VERBAL INSTRUCTION (DIRECTIONS):
- Teacher gives verbal instructions or directions that deal with specific musical attributes of the performance at hand ("Take the repeat at letter D," "Third trumpets, play louder in measure 42")

NON-INTERACTIVE LISTENING:
- Teacher purposely listens to student performance but takes no active part in the performance
- Students play with no visible or aural teacher interaction
- Teacher beats time but does not attend to musical performance through conducting gesture, facial response, eye contact, or verbal response

NONVERBAL FEEDBACK:
- Teacher provides nonverbal reaction that is based on student response that reinforces, shapes, or changes further student responses
- Teacher responds in a nonverbal manner to something students do in such a way that the teacher lets the students know something about their performance

VERBAL FEEDBACK:
- Teacher provides verbal reaction to student response that reinforces, shapes, or changes further student performance
- Teacher verbally responds to something that students do in such a way that the teacher lets the students know something about their performance

CONCEPTUAL TEACHING:
- Teacher reinforces or introduces a concept in such a way that students are given opportunities for awareness and understanding with a potential for transfer ("Whenever we

see tenuto markings, they indicate that we must give them full value with a sustaining quality.")

- Teacher asks questions in such a way that the answers contribute to the formulation of relationships, new ideas, or expansion of categories ("Now that we have played through the piece several times, can anyone name the compositional style being used and explain how it differs from the Bach we played earlier?")
- Teacher answers questions in such a way that the answers relate to a broader array of instances than the one at hand ("Yes, that is a cadence, but in this instance it is a deceptive cadence. In a deceptive cadence, the dominant chord is followed by something other than the tonic.")[8]

Initial Results

Randomly ordered 20-minute segments (beginning, middle, and end) from each videotape were analyzed using the behavioral categories outlined previously. Results indicated that overall, middle school and high school band directors were teaching musical concepts less than 3 percent of the total time in rehearsals. We decided to take another look.

The Next Steps in the Project

Over time, our project grew to include (1) videotapes of middle school and high school student teachers from seven states, (2) videotapes from a national sample of band directors identified as "outstanding" by their peers, and (3) videotapes from college and university band directors. For each sample, the instructions to band directors, videotape format used, and videotape analysis procedures remained consistent with the original Florida band director study.

Having looked at hundreds of hours of band rehearsals, the results of our additional studies indicated that band directors at all levels spent very little time teaching musical concepts in rehearsal. Student teachers spent less than 1 percent of rehearsal time teaching musical concepts, outstanding band directors spent less than 1 percent of rehearsal time teaching musical concepts, and college and university band directors spent just over 3 percent of the time teaching musical concepts. Looking at all groups together, our four sample populations spent less than 2 percent of their total rehearsal time – roughly 19 seconds out of a 20-minute rehearsal segment – teaching musical concepts in band rehearsals.[9]

Stop and think for a moment. In a typical band rehearsal, how much time

do you spend introducing or reinforcing musical concepts? If you were asked to describe what is supposed to happen during a band rehearsal, "rehearse the music" would probably be included in your answer. You would not be wrong! We all face situations where "we have a performance in two weeks," and "the music has to be ready," and "the band has to sound like a band"! However, in addition to getting the music ready, or perhaps as a part of getting the music ready (teaching music through performance), we must also teach our students to play their instruments better, and we must teach them about music.

Making More Connections

How could you use conceptual teaching in a band rehearsal? Perhaps you could start with a part of your daily rehearsal, the warm-up. What if you used the first five minutes of every band rehearsal to teach your students a musical concept as a part of your warm-up? Think about how much you could teach your students each year if you used this approach. And what if you connected the warm-up concept to the music to be rehearsed later in the rehearsal? The idea has transfer written all over it. What follows is an example of one of these five-minute warm-ups.[10]

A. OBJECTIVE:
    Students will be able to describe, identify, and play the style indicated by the term *dolce*.

B. STRATEGIES:
    1. Have the students play Chorale #1. Conduct it very straight, with no variation in tempo or dynamics.
    2. Play the chorale again, but this time in a march style, quick tempo, many accents. Discuss the appropriateness.
    3. Play the chorale again, but this time very slowly and majestically. Use loud dynamics and much emphasis on the beat. Discuss the effect and appropriateness.
    4. Have the students sing the chorale as sweetly, lightly, and expressively as possible.
    5. Write the word *dolce* on the board. Say the word.
    6. Define dolce.
    7. Have students suggest ways in which they can produce *dolce* sounds on their instruments.

C. EVALUATION:
    Play the chorale in *dolce* style.

D. TRANSFER TO MUSIC REHEARSAL:
   1. Band director plays a recording of the beginning of the second
      movement of Malcolm Arnold's *Prelude, Siciliano,* and *Rondo.*
   2. Students play the first phrase of this movement in *dolce* style.

Our warm-up example could easily become part of a regular rehearsal.
The example could take either five minutes (as designed) or as much time as
you wish – you decide. The example provides the opportunity to teach student
awareness and understanding, and has the potential to add to what students
know and are able to do with music. The conceptual model makes a connection to what comes next in a regular rehearsal ("We needed to rehearse this
movement anyway") and *teaches for transfer.*

Comprehensive Musicianship

"Comprehensive musicianship may be defined as 'performance with
understanding.' It is theory applied to practice; it is knowledge and skill
applied to practical music making."[11] There appears to be a very real connection between this definition of comprehensive musicianship and conceptual
teaching and teaching music through performance as described in this chapter. "Proponents of comprehensive musicianship offer numerous arguments in
favor of the approach, including broadened education for students and
improved curricular status for music, but critics often counter that such gains
might come at the expense of performance quality and student interest. On
the contrary, research suggests that learning is enhanced with no appreciable
loss in performance quality at the individual or ensemble level. Moreover,
students appear to enjoy the challenge and variety of comprehensive activities."[12]

It is difficult to argue against teaching music through performance in
band as part of our regular rehearsals.

What the Teacher Does Is What the Students Get[13]

"What people say, what people do, and what they say they do
are entirely different things."
– Margaret Mead –

Band directors have the potential to affect what students have the opportunity to learn in a performance setting. "It is the teacher [band director],
through his or her behaviors, who has the opportunity to present the subject
matter involved in the study of music in rehearsals in ways that will enable

students to develop not only the performance skills they will need to be successful on the next performance, but also assist students in understanding and generalizing the concepts necessary to become independent performers and consumers of quality music."[14]

Teaching the music while teaching about music (teaching concepts) requires band director desire (passion), planning (organization), materials, and techniques. Stop for a moment and think about real students who either are in your band right now or will be in your band. Make one final connection, this time thinking about those students. Ask yourself:

What do I want my students to know and be able to do as a result of their time in band with me?

Notes

1　Jerome S. Bruner, *The Process of Education* (Cambridge, MA: Harvard University Press, 1960), 31.

2　Ibid., 24.

3　Ibid., 12.

4　Michael L. Mark. *Contemporary Music Education*, 3rd ed. (New York: Schirmer Books, 1996), 69.

5　Harold Abeles, Charles Hoffer, and Robert Klottman, *Foundations of Music Education* (New York: Schirmer Books, 1984), 178.

6　Larry Blocher, Richard Greenwood, and Bentley Shellahamer, "Teaching Behaviors of Middle School and High School Band Directors in the Rehearsal Setting," *Journal of Research in Music Education* 45, no. 3 (Fall 1997): 458.

7　Richard B. Miles, ed., *Teaching Music through Performance in Band*, Vol. II. (Chicago: GIA Publications, 1998), 9.

8　Blocher, et al., 461-462.

9　Larry Blocher, Richard Greenwood, Bentley Shellahamer, and Frank Tracz, "Band Is More Than a Four Letter Word," paper presented at the Biennial Meeting of the Music Educators National Conference, Phoenix, AZ, April 1998.

10　Bentley Shellahamer, Assistant Dean, Florida State University, interview with the author, Tampa, FL, 5 January 1995.

11　James R. Austin, "Comprehensive Musicianship Research: Implications for Addressing the National Standards in Music Ensemble Classes," Update: *Applications of Research in Music Education* 17, no. 1 (Fall-Winter 1998): 25.

12　Ibid., 30.

13　Clifford Madsen and Cornelia Yarbrough, *Competency-Based Music Education* (Raleigh, NC: Contemporary Publishing, 1985), 8.

14　Blocher, et al., 465.

CHAPTER 2

Silence and the Space of Time

Edward S. Lisk

Quite spontaneously I have used silence as a means of expression.
It is perhaps the only means of bringing into relief the emotional value of a phrase.
··· Claude Debussy ···

Introduction

Individuals have a variety of ways to express themselves when communicating with others. Poets and authors convey their innermost feelings and impressions through words placed on paper; sculptors choose a variety of materials such as metals, stone, wood, or clay to convey their expression through objects; visual artists choose canvas, paper, or other surface to convey their expression through colors. As musicians, our means for communicating musical expression is presented through an imaginary "canvas of silence." Silence permeates our musical world. We interpret the composer's innermost thoughts, impressions, and feelings by "painting" the sounds of melody, harmony, and rhythm moving in and out of silence.... *Silence is the conductor's canvas for musical expression!*

Music, moving in and out of silence, has far-reaching implications for artistic thought and performance. We often overlook the importance of space and the duration of silence. Silence is as equally important as sound! Various combinations of sound and silence (melody, harmony, and rhythm) must be accurately placed within this space if music is to have value and meaning for those listening. Silence is quite difficult to measure or evaluate. Consequently, we become impatient waiting for the next musical entrance or have difficulty acknowledging its correctness.

The musical considerations for silence are critical ingredients for artistic expression and performance. The way we perceive and respond to the measurement of melody, harmony, and rhythm within this space of silence affects the quality and musicality of a performance. The quality of silence that precedes or succeeds any musical activity (entrances, notes, rhythms, articulation, etc.) determines the quality of that musical event. The slightest

unintended change of silence can vary tempi and rhythmic patterns. The measurement of sound and its duration requires a precise mental and physical response to silence and pulse. It is not the sound or tap of the beat (metronome), but the accuracy or measurement of silence between the beat that establishes a consistent pulse.

Measuring the Space of Time

The finest architects work with absolute precision in the measurement of materials and objects when designing a new building or structure. When we view an architectural design or building, we can see beauty, harmony, and rhythmic proportions that obviously express the architect's innermost feelings and impressions for strength, authority, poise, grace, or motion, to name a few. As notable composer Stephen Melillo states, "A building is architecture in space...music is architecture in time. Music is a 'Time Art.'" He further states, "Musical architecture is as detailed and specific as the physical structure is in space...but its evolution happens in more than just space. It manifests itself in the lapse of Time. This is where the composer and conductor merge, in the Time Art. The entire subtlety and beauty of music lies in its evolution in Time."

To better perceive *silence* before and after the beat, I introduce to you the *Ruler of Time*, an instructional graphic that accurately represents the measurement of silence or the invisible space between pulses or beats. By using a traditional measuring device (a standard ruler or yardstick) and placing it in a musical context and referring to it as a *Ruler of Time*, students immediately create an awareness and understanding for the precise division of space and the placement of notes within this space (rhythm). The image provides a "mental boundary for exactness" with time and rhythm.... Measurement is basic and is necessary when producing any product of quality or value. The measurement of space, its divisions and subdivisions must be mentally synchronized within the entire ensemble while developing internal pulse for rhythmic accuracy and clarity.

The Ruler of Time

1. The *length* and *width* of the *Ruler of Time* are determined by *tempo*.
   a. The *slower* the tempo, the *longer* and *wider* the space of subdivided silence.
   b. The *faster* the tempo, the *shorter* and *narrower* the space of subdivided silence.

2. The *lower* and *upper* horizontal lines represent the *downbeats* and *upbeats*.

3. The three horizontal lines between the *lower* and *upper* horizontal lines represent sixteenth and thirty-second note subdivision.

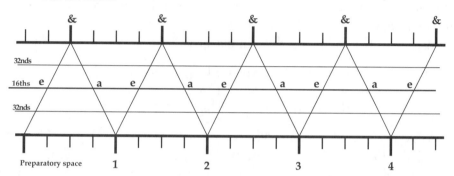

The *Ruler of Time* illustration, used with a metronome, will reinforce the importance of measured time within the space of silence. To expand the students' awareness to this space of silence, set the metronome at quarter note = 60 and have students focus their attention and listen carefully to the duration of silence *between* the beat. When listening in this manner, we discover how many unconnected thoughts can occur in our mind within this space or silence between the beats. If intelligence is being able to "read between the lines," then is musical intelligence found in the "silence between the beats"?

Applying the Ruler of Time

When presenting this illustration, demonstrate tempo variations by holding a pencil in a horizontal position above the top edge of the music stand. The top edge of your music stand represents the *downbeat* (bottom horizontal line) and the pencil represents the *upbeat* (upper horizontal line). The space between these two lines represents the *silence* between the beat, in which *time* (and thought) must travel or move through.

Use your baton (between stand and pencil) to indicate tempo/pulse as you tap the bottom horizontal line (stand edge) and upper horizontal line (pencil). Students can respond with the syllable "ta" or "da" either at the down or up beat as you tap the stand edge and pencil. Recognize and hear how precise their response is to the down or up beat. Now conduct a four-beat pattern and have students respond in the same manner and compare the difference with the horizontal lines of the stand and pencil ("a picture is worth a thousand words").

Draw the *Ruler of Time* on the blackboard (or make a transparency) and tap through the subdivision of a beat (four parts of 1-e-&-a) to emphasize the need for ensemble members to respond with "timed-thinking" with rhythm patterns. Next, have the students respond with "ta" or "da" on a specific subdivision such as the "e" or the "a" of the beat as you tap through the four parts of a beat. When students become comfortable with this simple exercise, continue tapping through each syllable (four parts of the beat) and vary student responses with the following rhythm patterns:

1. An eighth and two sixteenths (1-&-a, 2-&-a, etc.)
2. Two sixteenths and an eighth (1-e-&, 2-e-&, etc.)
3. A sixteenth rest, three sixteenths (1-e-&-a, 2-e-&-a, etc.)

As you continue teaching various rhythm patterns, clarify each pattern by using the *Ruler of Time* illustration. When students make rhythmic errors, write the problem rhythm pattern over the *Ruler of Time*. Indicate a rest with an open note (hollow head of a quarter, half, eighth, etc.) as illustrated.

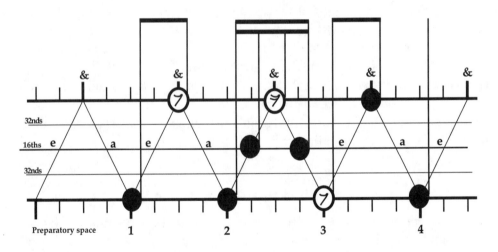

Tempo Variations and the Ruler of Time

The following two illustrations represent the subdivision of time and silence when tempo increases or decreases. The space and its division increase or decrease proportionately to ensure rhythmic accuracy and clarity. The students create an image of this measurement and respond accordingly.

Ritard, Rallentando

Increase the space between the stand edge and pencil for a slower tempo (baton has greater distance to travel between beats). As tempo decreases or slows down, the *Ruler of Time* increases in size, both horizontally and vertically. The space of silence increases proportionately.

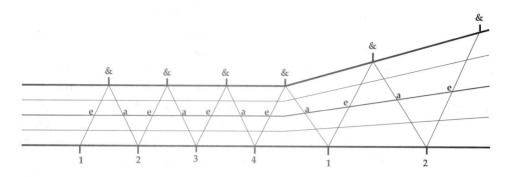

Accelerando

Decrease the space between the stand edge and pencil for a faster/quicker tempo (baton has less distance to travel between beats). As tempo increases or speeds up, the *Ruler of Time* decreases in size both horizontally and vertically. The space of silence decreases proportionately.

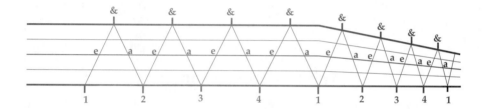

An excellent teaching approach is to have students play a passage that may indicate an *accelerando* or *ritard*. With your baton, tap the tempo between the two horizontal lines (stand and pencil) while the students play the passage with an *accelerando* or *ritard*. Play the passage two or three times before conducting the passage normally. You will notice a significant improvement with the students' rhythmic response. This is the result of the mental picture of time and its boundaries that control rhythmic accuracy (again, "a picture is worth a thousand words").

Teaching the "Up" or "And" of a Beat

Traditional instructional techniques often use the "foot tap" in the early stages (and often beyond) when teaching an "up" or "and" of a beat. During my early years of teaching, I spent considerable time with my beginner students emphasizing this steady beat (foot tap) and how to play accurate rhythms while tapping their feet. Little did I know that most of the students' early rhythm problems happened because of the inconsistencies with foot tapping, frequently creating many variations with tempo and rhythm patterns. Did you ever think of a young child's shoe size? I'm sure this sounds ridiculous and you are wondering what this has to do with counting or beating time. During the early part of my career when teaching beginners, I discovered that one must consider the student's shoe size. This significantly affects the size and speed of the downbeats and upbeats and the student's reaction to tempo and rhythm patterns. When considering a smaller shoe size (size 4) versus a larger shoe size (size 10), the smaller shoe size arrives at the downbeat or upbeat much quicker than a larger shoe size (try this with your students). Just as Suzuki took into consideration the need for small violins for small students, perhaps we should take into consideration the students' physical attributes that may affect their musical results. If you are experiencing tempo or rhythmic inaccuracies, perhaps you may need to adjust your instructional methods. By using the *Ruler of Time* as presented in the previous section, you no longer have any problems with students understanding the accurate placement of the "up" or "and" of a beat.

Now that I have shared with you some concepts and instructional techniques dealing with silence and its measurement for rhythmic accuracy, let us investigate some other ways to perceive music moving in and out of our "canvas of silence."

The Space of Silence

Throughout my musical career, I had many questions that went beyond the unadorned markings of musical notation in search of musical expression. I present these questions for your consideration. The intent of the questions is to trigger deeper thought of what it is we are teaching students as they make music and, hopefully, more than just notes and rhythm patterns. The questions are as follows:

1. How large are rests?
2. How much silence will a quarter rest consume?
3. Does the sound of a note stop precisely on a given beat?
4. Will any part of the sound spill into the rest? If so, how much?
5. Does a phrase end?
6. What happens to the right side of a note?
7. What is a cut-off?
8. What is a release?

Do the questions have anything to do with artistic considerations? You hold the answers. The answer to each question will be the result of your artistic interpretation of the literature being studied or performed. The considerations play an important role in the musical development of student musicians. The interpretation can be literal, producing a contrived result, or be treated as an artistic expression.

Musicians devote considerable practice time in their quest to develop flawless entrances or releases of notes and phrases. Occasionally, we use incorrect words to describe a musical expectation. In this case, the word *release* means *to let go*, and to let go of something means we no longer have control of what is to be released. Furthermore, the way we use the word *release* may also indicate an ending or stopping of a particular note and imply less importance for *what is to come*. When this occurs, the term *release* eliminates any form of interpretation of *how* a note or phrase moves into silence (usually a rest, or when taking a breath for the next phrase). I believe the term intrudes upon artistic considerations with the flow or lyricism of a musical phrase.

I found the concept, *the start or beginning of silence*, was essential when teaching phrases and musicianship. The start or beginning of silence is an important concept that places the mind in a position with *what is to occur* and *what happens **after** it occurs!* This thoughtful action is created after an entrance and throughout the duration of a particular note, followed by how that note moves into silence. The concept directs the mind to focus on the horizontal flow of sound moving to the right side of a note's duration. This is a powerful concept indicating thought-thinking energy moving to an approaching point that occurs simultaneously through musical decisions, not a series of separate events...*a fine musical detail for artistic expression.*

The following exercises demonstrate a reaction and feel for the differences between the meaning of the word *release* and *how silence begins*. The instructional techniques opened the doors to a beautiful world of musical expression that my students and I enjoyed as we performed the wind masterworks. I am certain that you will experience new insights with this concept and its application to musical expression.

EXERCISE 1: Sing a pitch for 5 counts. While singing, silently process the 5 counts (1-2-3-4-5) in a slow tempo (quarter note = 60) and think about how you will *release* the note as you arrive at count 5. Do not tap your foot, as it would destroy the purpose of this process. Do this several times to become aware of the *feel of releasing* the tone precisely on the fifth beat. You will feel a definite abruptness when arriving at the *release* on count 5. As you become aware of the feeling of release, move to the next exercise.

EXERCISE 2: Sing a pitch for 5 counts, think and feel *how silence will begin* as you arrive at count 5. Do not tap your foot, as the beat/pulse is a silent, internal process. Close your eyes (to remove any visual disturbance) and focus thinking and feeling on the subtlety and gentleness of arriving at this point at which silence begins. Do this several times to become aware and acquainted with the *feeling of silence* beginning. A difference should be immediately evident. The result is a thoughtful, gentle, artistic response not intruding upon or offending the silence as it begins. The treatment and perception of silence becomes an artistic result and eliminates any mechanical or contrived occurrence. The thoughtful consideration is given to arriving at the right side of the tone being produced. The mind moves *through and into* silence instead of abruptly releasing or ending on a specific count. The process has created new meaning for the silence that follows any sound...*a new dimension in perceiving sound and silence!*

EXERCISE 3: Apply the same procedures with an instrument while sustaining a tone for 5 counts.

To take this concept to the next level of musicianship, I would like to suggest the following:

Play a long, extended pitch (no designated beats), and while sustaining the pitch, think about how this note moves and tapers into infinity...*a point beyond any end or cut-off!* Close your eyes as you sustain and imagine this pitch moving along a tapering line. Do this several times to become aware of the feeling of moving into the space of silence. The power of your imagination and thoughtful flow of sound creates a beautiful, flawless taper, similar to an artist's brush being lifted off the canvas. The subtlety and gentleness of moving into this distant point should be immediately evident. It is a result of a thoughtful, gentle, artistic response to sound moving and disappearing into the silence of infinity. This removes any physical or mental restrictions and again focuses thought and care to the right side of the tone being produced.

Once your ensemble experiences this concept and responds accordingly, be very careful how you use the term *cut-off* for a fermata or other extended note or chord. The interpretation and experience of sound moving into infinity develops an intensely unified focus within an ensemble. The conducting movements and patterns that traditionally indicate the end or cut-off require some modification. As you will quickly note, any return to such cut-off movements may become offensive to the ensemble and imply little or no intellectual involvement from ensemble members. No longer will you have to treat your ensemble members as being passive by cutting them off (think about this statement).

Lifting the Stroke of Sound off the Canvas of Silence

A musical performance should not be similar to a picture painted by numbers by sacrificing personal expression in fear of *spilling* over the indicated lines (or what an adjudicator may say). The next musical exercise will allow the ensemble and director to experience the beautiful sounds that exist beyond the line or boundaries of musical notation…a new dimension in playing phrases and musical considerations dealing with artistic responses. The musical exercise provides artistic opportunities for students to step outside the boundaries of line rigidity and abruptness and to discover the beauty that lies beyond the "line." *If an artist is able to control the beauty and color of a brush stroke being lifted off the white canvas surface, or the color disappearing into the white canvas of silence…shouldn't the musician have similar control of sound moving into the white of silence (a rest or the end of a composition)?*

Expanding the start or beginning of silence concept provides artistic consideration for resonance and decay of notes moving into the space of silence indicated by a rest. Apply this concept where a space of silence (rest or breath mark) follows a phrase, fermata sign, end of a composition, or any similar point in music.

Note that the following musical example does not have a time signature or bar lines. The process does imply 4/4, 3/4, and 2/4 time followed by a whole note with a fermata sign. The exercise is as follows:

STEP 1: The students are to count the exercise in the following manner with a pulse of quarter note = 60 or less:

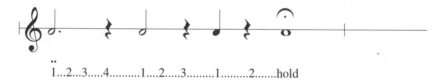

1...2...3.....4..........1...2....3.........1........2......hold

STEP 2: Play the exercise through several keys using major chords while silently counting in the normal or traditional way (use the Circle of 4ths found in *Teaching Music through Performance in Band, Volume 2*, Chapter 2).

STEP 3: After playing the following example in the usual conducted way, eliminate the counting of the quarter rest on beats 4, 3, and 2. Consider the two statements on the next page very carefully to gain the musical benefits with this departure from any conventional approach.

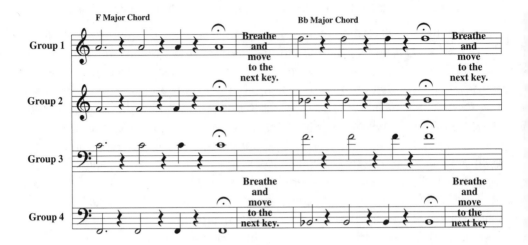

- The beat-number syllable before the rest is now extended and tapers or decays into the rest.
- The rest is implied and felt in tempo, but not counted by the beat number.

The entire ensemble carefully speaks the process as follows:

1 - 2 - threeeee…the "eeeee" tapers/decays into the "felt" fourth beat into silence.
1 - twoooooo…the "ooooo" tapers/decays into the "felt" third beat into silence.
1-onennnnnn…the "nnnn" tapers/decays into the "felt" second beat into silence.
Hollllllllddddd….the "lllldddd" tapers decays into silence (unmeasured duration).

The illustration below will further clarify the counting process and the tapering of the beat:

(4)Implied   (3)Implied   (2) Implied
1 - 2 - threeeeeeeeeee…..1 - twoooooooooo…..Onennnnnnnnnn…Holddddddddd

This teaching process again gains control of the right side of the note as it decays into silence (a performance skill not addressed in any method books). The ensemble should practice counting the sequence several times in tempo. The word "hold" is extended and provides a natural duration and taper for the whole note into silence (as in the ending of a composition). After the hold, the students breathe and sense together the next natural entrance of the sequence. Emphasize the importance of implying the *felt* beat of the rest. You now can extend or abbreviate the decay of sound as it moves into the silence of the rest.

It is important to emphasize to students that this timed spoken feeling and thinking energy is the same response (mind-body connection) that must be projected through the instrument to achieve the musical result! This process establishes a unified ensemble interpretation of the counting process and controlled decay of sound that can be applied to literature. You now have complete control of a note's duration as it diminishes into the silence of a rest!

Play the exercise and continue through the Circle of 4ths using major chords. To start the ensemble, the director must count aloud (quarter note = 60) the process as indicated above, with the extended decay of the number and hold; then take a preparatory breath, in tempo, with the students to indicate their entrance for the exercise. Once students become comfortable with the concept and process, *do not conduct…trust the timed "ensemble thought" and they will naturally breathe together.* The results will be flawless.

As the students become comfortable with the exercise, repeat and have the students close their eyes while playing. The musical results improve significantly by using imagery. Playing with their eyes closed will intensify their thinking and remove any visual distractions that inadvertently may shift or change focused concentration.

The success of this counting and thinking process is determined by *how* the sound of counting the extended beat (before the rest) tapers or diminishes into the quarter rest of silence in order to control the musical result. This same feeling and response are projected through the instrument! I understand the concern this will create with any traditional response to rests and our need to be specific and accurate with notation. Understand that *the time and pulse are still in place!* This rehearsal technique allows you to control the length of decay for tonal sonority and resonance…the natural characteristics of all musical sounds.

Many traditional techniques dealing with articulation or conducting often disturb or clip the natural resonance, or decay of sound... This concept and exercise takes you beyond such unmusical reactions (and beyond the "paint by number" approach). This is another area where I believe the beauty of expression is hidden within a musical performance. This process is similar to the analogy presented earlier...*an artist is able to control the beauty and color of a brush stroke being lifted off and disappearing into the white canvas of silence...musicians are now able to control the beauty of sound moving in and out of silence!*

This process should become a part of your rehearsal when shaping an artistic response to the natural decay of notes, chords, phrases, fermatas, or endings. I reemphasize the controlling factor again and that it is the energy of thought moving with sound into silence and *feeling* this spoken decayed beat into silence. This does not require a cut-off and should not be conducted. The ensemble becomes unified through timed thinking, the key to precision (the accuracy will surprise you). It is important to understand that the exercises are a natural occurrence with all musical sounds (unless the composer indicates the note should be abruptly cut off). Anything you do to change such a natural occurrence will be detrimental to the quality of your musical performance.

Room Acoustics and Performance Considerations

The previous exercises set up another important listening situation when shaping overall ensemble sonority. Rehearsal room acoustics can be perfect, too dead, too much reverberation, or simply unacceptable in some form. We find similar conditions in a theater, auditorium, ballroom, or school gymnasium. The *ring* or *echo* that follows any type of sound produced in a room can become a part of the musical performance. This process expands an ensemble's listening dimension by playing into and along the diminishing line of "echo." Surprisingly, this provides the ensemble with an opportunity to control the length of reverberation within the room or hall. In fact, where acoustical conditions are less than desirable, we are able to create and extend the ring or echo in such situations. This is an opportunity to expand the range or scope of listening for ensemble tonal sonority.

The listening awareness and connection can be made by clapping your hands, whistling, or shouting short, abbreviated words loudly in a room. The short, loud sound projects and amplifies a ring or echo that follows the sound. Simply apply the thought and feeling of the spoken decay as presented in the previous exercise to extend the ring or echo of the room. Thoughtful consideration is again given to the right side of the tone being produced by keeping the mind/thought moving in the direction of sound diminishing along the line of "echo" in the room or hall. The consideration for room acoustics extends and enhances the *sound into silence* performance concept.

The sound and silence concepts presented in this chapter provide you with many opportunities and interpretive considerations when preparing literature. They may include final note of a phrase, fermata, *sforzando*, grand pause, *crescendo* leading to a *fortissimo* followed by silence, *decrescendo* leading to a *pianissimo* followed by silence, last note of a march, isolated staccato notes, and short, fragmented and punctuated rhythms to name a few. The musical opportunities will continue to unfold and become obvious with various styles of literature.

Conclusion

A musician's mind constantly moves in time, synchronized with other members, creating an "ensemble" of musical expression through the lyricism of melodic, harmonic, and rhythmic sounds moving in and out of silence. This musically timed-thinking energy (mind-body connection) is what elevates the musician to that mysterious summit experience and continues to bring us back repeatedly to create and become part of a beautiful music making experience.

The rehearsal considerations I provided for you in this chapter can be applied to all of the selected literature found in this three-volume publication. They are musical awareness exercises that will immerse your students into the fine art of musical performance. Such rehearsal techniques are not often addressed and may be one of the many mysteries of musical expression. Perhaps (with this chapter), this particular mystery has been solved.

Your responsibilities as a band director are immense when teaching music through band performance. You must provide students with appropriate learning experiences so they will become active participants and decision-makers in their pursuit for musical excellence based upon the masterworks of wind literature. This is best accomplished through the wind literature presented in this text along with Volumes 1 and 2.

Notes

Some of the concepts and musical examples found in this chapter were taken from *The Intangibles of Musical Performance* and used with permission from Meredith Music Publications, 170 N.E. 33rd St., Ft. Lauderdale, FL 33334.

CHAPTER 3

Podium Personality

Ray Cramer

Introduction

Since the first time a baton was used to "lead" musicians in rehearsals and performances, there has been a fascination with conductors and how their personalities impact music making. We all have a personality that directly affects how we relate to people every day of our lives. Regardless of the profession in which we are engaged, the success of our work directly reflects the nature and passion of our personalities.

When I was a relatively new teacher (many years ago), I attended a conference that was being held for hundreds of teachers who were being honored for each having received an outstanding young educator award. The guest speaker was the president of 3M. It was an inspiring speech, and certainly he said many things that I have remembered over subsequent years. The main topic of his presentation was to encourage people to utilize the power of personality to ensure success in any field of endeavor. He shared information that he had read from a doctoral study pertaining to the importance of personality in assessing one's success.

According to the information shared in his speech, there are three basic ingredients that contribute to one's success in any work. There is the need for *intelligence, knowledge of subject matter* and, of course, *personality*. If you were to attach to each of these a percentage of importance as they relate to success, the response would probably be like mine; it seemed logical and clearly apparent to me that each was an equally important component of success.

As the president continued his speech, all of us in attendance were astonished as he finished relating the information found in this document. The paper revealed that intelligence has a very low percentage assigned to it. People in any chosen field will have the basic intelligence to be successful, or they will choose another field. For example, if I do not have an I.Q. to be able to achieve the skills necessary to become a research scientist, I will direct myself toward another profession where I know my basic intelligence will allow me to be successful.

People proceed through a training program designed to give information necessary to allow them to attain success because of the knowledge gained through study and application. So no matter what the chosen field, either there is the intelligence to complete the requirements for that program or another field is chosen. However, regardless of the level of intelligence and amount of knowledge one has, unless a dynamic personality is added to the mix, success will not be achieved at its highest level.

I am sure you will be astonished, as I was, when it was related to us that in this doctoral study only 7 percent of success in any field of work could be attributed to *intelligence* and *knowledge* concerning the chosen field. It was made abundantly clear in this dissertation that 93 percent of one's success is directly related to the *power of personality*.

Concert Components

The Audience

When an audience is gathering for a concert performance of any kind, there is a level of anticipation and expectation that accompanies the waiting crowd. Without question, there will be a great difference between the level of expectation of the audience assembling in Carnegie Hall and those assembling in the gymnasium of a local school. Yet there are certain elements present that will always remain the same. The members of the ensemble all desire to perform (or at least we hope they do) to the best of their ability. The ensemble and the conductor believe in the music, have worked diligently in preparation, and are excited about the opportunity to exhibit their musicianship through performance. The concert will ultimately demonstrate the ability of the performers to benefit from the process of preparation as individual players and the ensemble as a unit. The concert attendees will listen to the concert and determine the success of the program as being the direct result of the leadership the group has had from the person standing on the podium. There is no getting around the fact that, after the performance, the preconcert expectation affects whether the audience praises or criticizes the conductor. After all, it was the job of the conductor to have the players prepared for the concert.

The Conductor

Despite the many ingredients that are part of the recipe for performance success, a conductor must never forget the importance of making good impressions even before the downbeat takes place. From the moment the ensemble

is finished tuning, the audience waits for the entrance of the conductor to begin the program. As the conductor enters, the audience begins to make mental notes as they evaluate the presence of the conductor. Does the conductor walk slowly or quickly? Is there a smile or an expressionless stare? Does the conductor make eye contact with the audience or ignore their presence? What is the posture of the conductor walking to the podium? Does the conductor acknowledge the ensemble and the audience or merely step on the podium to begin the first number?

This first contact with the audience speaks volumes about the personality of the conductor and his/her approach to the performance. A good conductor will:

- Walk with spirit (a bounce in his or her step) and be confident, assured, and poised to portray an image of positive control.
- Make that all-important eye contact with the audience and give them a reassuring smile that shows appreciation for their being present to take part in the musical presentation about to begin.
- Acknowledge the ensemble on stage by having them stand.
- Have the performers turn to face the audience when they stand and share a smile of their own.
- Shake hands with the concertmaster or concertmistress which, by this simple act, expresses appreciation to the entire ensemble for preparing the program.

All of these pre-performance protocols are very important in helping to establish a positive rapport with the audience. There are enough "barriers" already in place that tend to create a wall between the performers and the audience. Barriers create a feeling of separation and tend to reduce the musical impact of the performance. For example, the conductor and the members of the ensemble are in formal attire; the audience is not. The ensemble is performing in a brightly-lit environment while the audience sits mostly in the dark. The ensemble is above the audience on a raised stage and you, the conductor, are even higher, standing on the podium. There are so many things to consider – and the downbeat has yet to be given.

The previous paragraphs have focused mainly on the perception of the audience as they wait for the start of a program. They have anticipated this concert in a wide spectrum of emotion ranging from those of nervous parents there to support their children (and thank you to those important folks) to people who paid high-ticket prices to hear their favorite symphony or watch their favorite conductor.

The Performers

A few lines must be added regarding the thoughts and expectations of the performers who sit on stage waiting for the concert to finally become a reality. The veteran professional musician and a young student musician performing for the first time have very different expectations for what is about to take place. Obviously, their feelings will vary greatly in a wide spectrum of anticipation (perhaps, also, in the number of last-minute trips to the restroom). For the sake of discussion and since *Teaching Music through Performance in Band* is geared to those of us in the education of young musicians at the secondary and university level, I direct the following comments to non-professional musicians.

Young musicians are generally so nervous before a performance that, more often than not, nerves get in the way of their best effort. I had a college band director who used to say, "If the music is well rehearsed and basic fundamentals carefully observed, then the performance will be maintained at a high level of proficiency." If the student members feel the music has been well prepared and they are confident of their own performance level, then confidence overcomes nerves. With younger groups, it pays to follow a few sound principles just prior to a performance:

1. Allow for adequate warm-up time with the full ensemble.
2. Utilize the same materials and tuning procedures you employ in a regular rehearsal.
3. Keep the ensemble focused but without tension.
4. Don't give ensemble members a lot of free time just prior to taking the stage, as this usually creates situations that can lead to faulty mental and physical preparation.
5. Don't let the ensemble sit in the performance area for an undue length of time prior to starting the performance. This just creates added stress and tension among the musicians.
6. Make the students feel at ease and relaxed through your confidence and attitude in the warm-up room.
7. After acknowledging the audience and having the ensemble stand and be seated, do not wait too long before you give the downbeat.
8. Just before you give the downbeat, make sure you give the band a warm, confident smile that says you have complete confidence in their ability to perform well.
9. Maintain eye contact with the ensemble prior to the downbeat and well into the first phrase before you look at the score.
10. Finally, make sure you have mentally sung the opening phrase to yourself so you have the tempo well in mind before you give the preparatory beat.

Path to the Podium

All of us have a story to share of our "path to the podium." For most, it is one of careful planning and progression through an approved course of study in music education that led to our work as conductors. Somewhere along the line our paths crossed with a teacher and/or conductor who inspired, motivated, and instilled in us a desire to consider a career in music.

For others, however, the path to the podium came after working in some related music field or as a member of a professional orchestra. There are numerous examples in our orchestral heritage of conductors who emerged from the ranks of the orchestra membership to become quite famous conductors: Toscanni, Monteux, Ormandy, Barbiralli, and Wallenstein, to name just a few. Some who decide on a conducting career may have arrived at this decision through a deepening desire to explore the profession or, in some cases, by sheer accident. On the other hand, most of us in the band conducting field grew up playing in a band and proceeded through a degree program which eventually led us to a conducting position in an educational institution. Music has been an integral part of our existence for all of time and will continue in that capacity for as long as there is life on our planet. I cannot imagine life without music. So as we begin the new century – and millennium – we must continue to strive for excellence in teaching. We must constantly evaluate our role as music educators and conductors. Music enriches lives, so we must continue to build positive musical connections with people at every age level.

Productivity through Personality

Expectations

Does the band that you stand in front of on a regular basis understand your expectations for them as an ensemble? The students certainly sit in front of you with *their* expectations, so you must first determine if you are both on the same page. I have been in front of some bands where it was pretty apparent my expectations did not match those of the students. The matter at hand, then, is how to establish a common ground so that in the end everyone will feel a sense of satisfaction in what has been accomplished. It doesn't hurt to let students know your goals for them as an ensemble. This can be done in a variety of ways, but certainly you can just simply state your objectives. These objectives may be long range or short range, but the most important criterion is the manner in which you go about attaining these goals. Make sure you are honest and reasonable relative to the age, ability, and potential of the players in your band.

During the past thirty years I have had the opportunity, and the great pleasure, to guest conduct many different bands throughout the United States and in several foreign countries. One of the things I often find interesting and enjoyable is when three or four small schools join together for some type of festival which combines the talents of several bands. These are wonderful events which give the students and communities involved a unique musical experience. Often, when discussing literature selection for these "festival bands," the directors involved select music quite above the ability of their individual bands. I fully understand their rationale. Each of the participating schools probably has a small ensemble, many times without a complete instrumentation. When they combine forces, there is a full instrumentation and an increased number of players. It is, therefore, logical to be drawn into the belief that music of a much higher grade level can be performed. While each of the schools primarily perform grade three material, for example, there is now the false assumption that this bigger ensemble, with all instrumental parts covered, can choose music from a much higher grade level. And of course, the guest conductor is to accomplish this feat with a short one-day rehearsal schedule! We all know, however, that no matter what people think, there is no *magic* in the little white stick!

Each of us in our own programs, regardless of the level, must be realistic in what our students can successfully achieve. Of course, there are many factors involved: the individual ability of the performers, the amount of rehearsal time available prior to each performance, and the difficulty of the music selected for the program. The key words for me are "successfully achieve." There must be a sense of musical satisfaction at each juncture of the road for programs to move from one level to the next.

Preparation

In any given situation, it goes without saying that the better the preparation for the rehearsal the more productive it will be. The psychology involved in the approach to a rehearsal can be a tremendous advantage for the conductor. After all, the conductor is the one who has studied the score; made decisions on balance, dynamic subtleties, phrasing, tempo, and timbre; and anticipated potential problems in technique and rhythmic complexity. Using a "bull's-eye" approach, everything from the warm-up to the final selection in the rehearsal is carefully thought out and planned. Therefore, at the end of the rehearsal everyone involved will feel as though the intended goals of the day have been met.

I cannot stress enough that all too often we forget we are dealing with young students who have their own likes and dislikes, loves and hates, and good and bad habits. Sometimes all of the best preparation and effort seems to be for naught. We must not allow ourselves to become so agitated and frustrated during the rehearsal that we lose our control and vision for that particular day. The worst thing you can do is begin to react and say things in such a negative manner that not only will that day be lost but it may also take a

long time to get attitudes and positive feelings flowing once again.

The conductor certainly has a broad spectrum of approaches from which to choose in creating the atmosphere desired for a rehearsal. One can be either tyrannical in his/her approach or the other extreme of completely passive. Conductors have found success at both ends of this spectrum. However, every conductor must have an approach in this sensitive area that best represents each individual personality.

I once attended a conducting workshop given by Frederick Fennell when he was still conducting the Eastman Wind Ensemble. I was exhilarated, motivated, and inspired to become a Fennell clone (long before the infamous sheep). So I rushed home to my aspiring Class B high school band and attempted to employ everything I had learned. I assumed it would enable my ensemble to respond in the same manner I observed in this select college band under the baton of Mr. Fennell. For the next several rehearsals, what actually transpired with my band was the group became less proficient and focused while our next concert was fast approaching. During a private lesson with a sophomore contrabass clarinet player (Richard Hansen, now the Director of Bands at St. Cloud State University), I mentioned how frustrated I was becoming at the poor progress of the band and that, in fact, I felt the group was quickly losing ground. In the most innocent way, Mr. Hansen told me, "You know, Mr. Cramer, you just haven't been yourself lately." With all due respect to my good friend and colleague Mr. Fennell, it hit me like a slap in the face that I can *only* be effective as I work through my *own* personality. This is a valuable lesson for every conductor to learn; be yourself and utilize, to the full potential, *your personality* and not that of someone else.

With a focused and positive approach to the music, the ensemble and the individual members will obtain a much more satisfying result. There seems to be a general consensus of opinion that conductors, through the force of individual personalities, make things happen. The music making under their leadership becomes convincing and meaningful. Here is what Leonard Bernstein had to say on this subject:

> "Almost any musician can be a conductor, even a pretty good one, but only a rare musician can be a great one. The qualities that distinguish great conductors lie far above and beyond technique alone. These are the tangibles of conducting, the mysteries, and the feelings that conductors strive to learn and acquire. If they have a natural perception, it will increase and deepen as they mature. But, even the pretty good conductor must have this attribute in their personality and that is the power to communicate through arms, face, fingers and whatever vibrations may flow from them."

Work Ethic

Are you a diligent person? Is there a persistence and urgency about your rehearsal technique with which the students can readily identify? A conductor who possesses these traits will instill in his or her students a similar work ethic, one that will produce positive results in a timely manner. In each rehearsal there needs to be a feeling of accomplishment. Nothing builds success like success. So even if you begin with the most conservative goals, if these goals are met the ensemble will feel good about the time and energy invested. Perhaps one of the greatest assets we need to cultivate in working with young musicians is patience. We need to take to heart the phrase that is often found written on restaurant menus: "Please be patient; quality food takes time to prepare." While we all have experienced young students who seem to make giant strides overnight, it usually follows that most young musicians advance at a slower rate, and we need to respect their differences. Losing our patience slows down progress. One of my Indiana University colleagues, Eugene Rousseau, is the ultimate example of persistent patience. His even disposition and patience never seem to waiver when working with his students. Yet his expectations remain high. He continues to be encouraging with all his students as they develop to their full potential.

Help your students become diligent workers as you demonstrate your willingness to be diligent in your work with them. They will identify this outstanding characteristic of your personality and respond to your motivation and example.

Discipline

Nothing productive can ever be accomplished if there is chaos and uncontrolled behavior. Teaching/learning cannot take place without order and control. All of us can cite examples of programs and conductors at every level who emphasize control techniques using harshness and the old "iron fist" approach to discipline. Some have successful programs. There are, however, many others no longer teaching because this technique did not work for them. I know the subject of discipline and control continues to elicit extensive writing. I have no intention of getting too deeply into this area for fear of traveling an already well-worn path, but a few comments are appropriate.

The handling of discipline is uniquely individual. So much of what we do or say is directly connected to the way we were "controlled" as young children by our parents and teachers. My personal experience was growing up in a home where there were expectations of how I was to act and treat other people. My parents never hesitated to discipline when they felt my actions deserved punishment. However, one of my sisters enjoys teasing me by saying that if I got spanked it was with a broom straw and that she got the handle. Now, I know that was not true, but the point is there was a line to be towed and we were expected to follow the rules. Likewise, in school I had my share

of strict teachers as well as those who maintained a fairly lax classroom. It seemed to me that I learned more, and felt greater satisfaction about my work, when the class was well organized, focused, and the teacher set expectations for the class to follow and achieve.

I firmly believe students need, desire, and welcome direction in their lives. Teachers who helped to shape and formulate my future direction and goals in music had a wide range of discipline techniques. There is of course *discipline*, and then there is *discipline*. Some people may become mean-spirited, vindictive, and insensitive in their approach and seem to have little success. Yet others can be strict disciplinarians and still achieve successful and lasting results. The key is the manner in which discipline is administered. It must be carried out in such a way that students know the teacher really cares for them and believes in what is being taught. When students sense they are not respected as individuals who can contribute to the program, all is lost. Work your own special "magic" by carefully evaluating how you can be the most effective using *your personality* in the way you want to approach your students. Genuinely care for your students and instill in them a sense of personal pride in what they are doing. You will be rewarded far beyond your expectations.

Consistency

As teachers, this area keeps us constantly scrutinizing our handling of students. We need to be consistent in all that we do and say, but this is so difficult to carry out. Yet we must strive for this in the most honest and forthright manner that we can.

I once commented to a respected colleague that he always appeared to be so consistent in how he treated people on and off the podium. (Even though it has been over thirty years since he made the following statement, it is still firmly etched in my mind.) He said, "I am the same person whether I am on the podium or not. Why should I deceive my students into thinking I am two different people? If my personality doesn't work in one place, why would it work in the other?" Through consistency in our actions and expectations, we can maintain uniformity and accountability in dealing not only with students in rehearsal but in all of our professional and personal relationships.

Verbal Communication through Personality

Things to Avoid

I am sure we could all write a book filled with the "things" we wished we had *not* said in the rehearsal room. There are things I have said in the heat of a tense rehearsal that I wish I could take back. The frustration level can become very intense at times, and we let thoughtless words slip out. Usually the moment we express ourselves this way we know it is going to cause pain to someone. Verbal barbs can cause deep wounds though they seem small at the time, but they rarely work in any shape or form. We must guard against this kind of overreaction.

The only recourse you have when you realize there has been a serious error in your choice of words is to go to the person and offer an apology. The best course of action is to say "I'm sorry" when you have caused pain to an individual student or even the entire ensemble. Students will understand and accept this. When you don't let your pride get in the way of a sincere apology, the students' respect for you will deepen. Using humiliation, fear, cruelty, name calling, sarcasm, or any form of unkind behavior is neither necessary nor effective. These negative approaches will only produce ineffective results.

Psychological Perceptions

There are many in the teaching profession who studied psychology extensively. I wish I had paid closer attention and worked harder in the required psychology courses I had in undergraduate school, for they contained a great deal of "perfectly sensible" ways to deal with students. However, like many students at that age, I just did not see the importance of these non-music-related courses. If I had paid more attention to the subject matter, it just might have saved me from some avoidable, early bruises to my ego – not to mention embarrassing moments.

Do you allow your negative attitudes to show? If you are like most people, then you are probably guilty of harboring a negative attitude from time to time. If you are experiencing problems with attitude, then you must leave them at the door of the rehearsal room. So often attitudes are shaped by situations that have nothing to do directly with the rehearsal and the students. Avoid a condescending attitude or manipulative and demeaning conversation when speaking with students. Everyone wants and needs to feel respected as individuals, regardless of age. Couch your criticisms carefully and offer positive encouragement in liberal doses. A good rule to follow is to use many positive comments for every negative comment that you make.

I am sure every conductor when stepping to the podium desires to be "liked" by the entire ensemble. There are, of course, those who at least on the surface give the impression they couldn't care less if anyone liked them. Nevertheless, inwardly we all want to be liked by our students and people we deal with on a regular basis. Conductors who want to be "buddies" or one of the "gang" and allow themselves to be called nicknames will find control and attention hard to come by in the rehearsal room. Very few directors have the ability to pull off this kind of rapport. More often than not it fails. Not every student is going to like you (hopefully more will than not), but the important thing is they must respect what the program represents and what you represent. Remember, respect is a two-way street, so develop a sincere respect for

students and they will want to respect you as well. Even those students who do not necessarily like you can respect you deeply for your knowledge, your vision, your diligence, your enthusiasm, your exuberance and, most assuredly, your love for music and music making.

Effective Participation through Personality

Motivation

Every great teacher/leader/conductor must possess the ability to motivate and inspire young people. Students who are motivated and excited will consistently perform at a higher level of execution than students of perhaps even greater ability but without the advantage of inspired leadership. We must always keep in mind that our students look to the podium for confident and knowledgeable direction. A major factor of motivation is our own personal attitude. Students must know, without a doubt, that we are sincere in what we are trying to achieve. Even though we show determination and diligence, it will be our sincerity, enthusiasm, and positive attitude that produce concentrated effort from our students.

Self-Esteem

The more I read about youth today, the more I realize that one of the most important aspects of their daily lives is the need for self-esteem. Self-esteem can be shattered very easily, so we must be careful in dealing with this issue. Many students feel intuitively that their teachers like them, but it is equally or perhaps more important that they feel respected by their teachers. I often tell my own students preparing for a teaching career, "You must like your students to work with them." We need to become perceptive teachers capable of "reading" our students. In doing so we can better cope with situations in the classroom before possible confrontational situations occur. How do students look when they walk in the door? What is their posture? Do they make eye contact with you or their peers? Listen to what they are saying to their friends. If the morale of your membership is high, then positive things will transpire in your program.

Students will work effectively if they are having fun. It is important to understand that having fun while accomplishing musical goals is critical; it's not just chasing the notes. The higher the level of accomplishment, the greater the satisfaction. Tireless effort will come forth if students are enjoying the challenge placed before them. As conductors, a keen sense of humor is necessary for enjoyable rehearsals. I'm not suggesting that you should tell an endless stream of jokes from the podium, but certainly any rehearsal is ripe with opportunities to develop your "podium side" manner.

Non-Verbal Communication through Personality

Posture

As I was growing up, my mother reminded me on a fairly consistent basis to "stand up straight." She was doing her best to establish good posture habits, but I am sure she also knew that a person who tends to "slump" could project a negative image. If we want to portray a positive personality, a correct posture will visibly add to that image. Don't shuffle but walk with a brisk, powerful stride that projects confidence and strength. Perhaps one of the most enjoyable and informative conducting sessions I ever attended was taught by a mime. I learned so much about using my body and face to express many different emotions, all without saying a word. The importance of posture and how posture can project strong images to the audience was eye opening. Stand tall and use your physical presence to the fullest as you exhibit power and strength in your conducting.

Face and Eyes

It is pretty difficult to mask emotions when all people have to do is look at the face and into the eyes. The face and eyes usually express one's true feeling. It was probably a parent who first said, "I can read you like a book," referring to the facial expression of a conscience-stricken child.

As conductors, we must learn to take full advantage of our faces and eyes. We can "say" so much without saying anything at all. Avoid using inappropriate faces that might humiliate a student in front of his or her peers. This never results in anything except frustration and discouragement. Following is a rehearsal situation that happens quite often. Which reaction would you choose to use?

A student has been working diligently in rehearsal, not goofing off, but makes an incorrect entrance in a piece being rehearsed. The student is one of the better musicians in the band and a leader. The conductor now has a couple of choices: (1) stop the rehearsal for an opportunity to once again exhibit your power and position by making this error an example of poor practice habits and lack of concentration or (2) recognize the student's facial expression (which says, "I feel bad about the error."), catch the student's eye, and give the student a reassuring smile and a nod of the head that says, "I understand what happened and I know it won't happen again." The music making does not stop.

Everyone in the ensemble knows what happened and who made the mistake, but by choosing the second option, you have helped turn what could

have been an embarrassing situation for the student and an uncomfortable feeling for the band into a positive experience. You have gained more respect from your students because you demonstrated not only insight and control but also kindness. A smile has a strength that can far surpass the sneer and look of anger. Use smile muscles frequently, and show the group how enjoyable making music can be.

Leadership through Personality

Throughout the history of mankind we have had men and women with character, competence, integrity, and skill step forward to provide outstanding leadership in every aspect of our society. There are others who have shown only one or two of the attributes mentioned above and failed in leadership. Strength of *leadership through personality* must involve all four of these elements to ensure positive results.

Strong leadership *sees* what needs to be done and *takes action* to ensure success. Conductors must not turn away from tasks that seem below their station. If a task needs to be done to make the program more efficient and you have the means to carry it out, then do it; leaders serve!

Outstanding conductors influence others not because of their position or power but because the quality of their relationships with people has gained their trust and confidence. In the past I have asked students to write down their thoughts addressing the question, "What makes a great leader?" Amazingly to me, many of the answers turn out to be the same time after time. Here are a few of these shared thoughts describing effective leadership: "they supported me," "they had the courage to do the right thing," "they challenged me," "they listened," "they acted as mentors to others," "they recognized outstanding work," "they followed through on commitments," and perhaps the one shared most often, "they exhibited humility at all times." What a tremendous checklist for all of us to gauge the quality of our leadership skills.

Leadership demands that we are *learners*. We live in an ever-changing world. If someone would have told me twenty years ago that I would be doing this kind of work on a word processor small enough to sit on my lap, I would have smiled and, shaking my head in disbelief, said, "I don't think so." It is difficult to remain current with every new development, but we must continue to grow. Without growth comes stagnation. No one ever has enough knowledge, so continue to learn and grow through every form of communication. Teachers and conductors in our profession have a tremendous advantage because everyone is so cooperative and willing to share information. What a great profession we have chosen. I feel sorry for the millions of people who go to work every day wishing they did not have to go.

Conclusion

Bruno Walter states in his book, *Of Music and Music-Making*, "It is far better for a conductor to build their own style and traits through their own character and personality. The more powerful the personality of the conductor, the more they can demand."

Your students need your energy, your creativity, your courage, your vision, and especially your love of music. There is another aspect I have not yet mentioned, which is that the students need you to *stay* in the profession. The profession needs you to *stay in the profession*. At a presentation I was giving a few years ago at the Midwest clinic, I asked to see the hands of people who were about to embark upon a teaching career. It was a good-sized audience, including a large number of young "soon-to-be-graduated" college students, who quickly raised their hands. I continued by inquiring as to how many had been teaching for five years or less. Again a good number of hands flew into the air. As can be expected, as I progressed through the years in five-year increments the number of hands raised at each level declined dramatically as the number of teaching years increased.

Every precaution must be taken to avoid the all-too-familiar "band director burn-out." Pace yourself and your program. So many programs and teachers keep such demanding schedules that both the teachers and the students begin to lose their motivation and vision for the real music making goals. Stay in good health; exercise on a regular basis; and above all else, save time in your busy schedule for yourself and your family. The music profession needs your strength of character, your powerful personality, and your musical maturity.

I have always enjoyed this pointed statement made by William Steinberg when he said, "I think mainly that every conductor develops their own method with which they express themselves after their own nature and that the only factor that counts is the power of their personality."

Through the *power of personality* and the shared love for music, we can exalt, enlighten, and encourage our students in such a manner as to have a positive impact on them and all future generations of music makers.

CHAPTER 4

Teaching Music with an Emphasis on Form and Structure

Richard Miles

Skills in analysis, evaluation, and synthesis are important
because they enable students to recognize and pursue excellence
in their musical experiences and to understand and enrich their environment.
Because music is an integral part of human history,
the ability to listen with understanding is essential
if students are to gain a broad cultural and historical perspective.
The adult life of every student is enriched by the skills, knowledge,
and habits acquired in the study of music.

··· The National Standards for Arts Education[1] ···

Introduction

The purpose of this chapter is to provide an overview of the basic elements of musical structure or construction as related to compositions and how these elements may be used to enhance the teaching and development of musicianship. Most all musical compositions are a result of an organization of various musical ideas expressed in some formal type of classification or design. Music itself is no randomization of sounds; rather, music is generally agreed to be a collection of sounds *set* and *arranged* in an orderly manner to express something. The structural organization, for lack of a better description, is most often referred to as the *form* or *design* in music.[2]

Through the study and analysis of music structure (the tonal center) and design (the melodic intent), we may better understand the musical essence that the composer intends to be expressed through the creative process of composing. So why bother and be concerned with sharing and teaching information regarding these elements in performing arts classes – classes where we strive to primarily *perform* music? As presented in Chapter 4, Volume 2, of *Teaching Music through Performance in Band* (see pages 37-40), "academic accountability" is enhanced in the performing ensemble when *comprehensive*

musicianship concepts are presented. Therefore, "a greater musical literacy, accountability, and alignment with current educational direction can be achieved."

The National Standards for Arts Education, as addressed in Content Standard 6, outline the responsibility of music teachers to actively involve students in comprehensive music learning. Below are the established Achievement Standards recommended for every course in music, including performance courses, for Grades 9 through 12 and Grades 5 through 8 involving Content Standard 6.[3]

CONTENT STANDARD 6:
Listening to, analyzing, and describing music.

Grades 9-12:
Achievement Standard, *Proficient:*
Students

    a. Analyze aural examples of a varied repertoire of music, representing diverse genres (e.g., fugal entrances, chromatic modulations, developmental devices) and cultures, by describing the uses of elements of music and expressive devices

    b. Demonstrate extensive knowledge of the technical vocabulary of music

    c. Identify and explain compositional devices and techniques used to provide unity and variety and tension and release in a musical work and give examples of other works that make similar uses of these devices and techniques

Achievement Standard, *Advanced:*
Students

    d. Demonstrate the ability to perceive and remember music events by describing in detail significant events (e.g., fugal entrances, chromatic modulations, developmental devices) occurring in a given aural example

    e. Compare ways in which musical materials are used in a given example relative to ways in which they are used in other works of the same genre or style

    f. Analyze and describe uses of the elements of music in a given work that make it unique, interesting, and expressive[4]

Grades 5-8:
Achievement Standard:
Students

    a. Describe specific music events (e.g., entry of oboe, change of meter, return of refrain) in a given example, using appropriate terminology

    b. Analyze the uses of elements of music in aural examples representing diverse genres and cultures

    c. Demonstrate knowledge of the basic principles of meter, rhythm, tonality, intervals, chords, and harmonic progressions in their analyses of music[5]

This chapter presents a basic student-oriented introduction to form analysis through descriptions of basic form types and mapping procedures which outline the overall structural design. Also presented are musical compositions, which serve as examples for analysis study and listening. For an extensive review of the analysis of musical form and structure, readers should consult the following sources, which are credited for all of the information included in this chapter:

Apel, Willi. *Harvard Dictionary of Music*. Cambridge, MA: The Belknap Press of Harvard University Press, 1972.

Berry, Wallace. *Musical Structure and Performance*. New Haven: Yale University Press, 1989.

Cone, Edward T. *Musical Form and Musical Performance*. New York: W.W. Norton & Company, Inc., 1968.

Consortium of National Arts Associations. *National Standards for Arts Education - What Every American Should Know and Be Able to Do in the Arts*. Reston, VA: Music Educators National Conference, 1994.

Ericksen, Connie M. *Band Director's Curriculum Resource*. West Nyack, NY: Parker Publishing Company, 1998.

Green, Douglas M. *Form in Tonal Music*. Second Edition. Orlando, FL: Harcourt Brace & Company, 1993.

Holoman, D. Kern. *Masterworks: a Musical Discovery*. Upper Saddle River, NJ: Prentice-Hall, 1998.

Kohs, Ellis B. *Musical Form*. Boston, MA: Houghton Mifflin Company, 1976.

Labuta, Joseph A. *Teaching Musicianship in the High School Band*. Revised edition. Ft. Lauderdale, FL: Meredith Music Publications, 1997.

LaRue, Jan. *Guidelines for Style Analysis*. Second edition. Warren, MI: Harmonie Park Press, 1992.

Meyer, Leonard B. *Explaining Music*. Berkley and Los Angeles, CA: University of California Press, 1973.

Miles, Richard, ed. *Teaching Music through Performance in Band*, Volumes 1 and 2. Chicago, IL: GIA Publications, 1996, 1998.

Morton, Peggy Klein. *Harmony, Form and Expression*. St. Louis, MO: McDonald Publishing Company, 1990.

Thomson, William. *Introduction to Music as Structure*. Reading, MA: Addison-Wesley Publishing Company, 1971.

Spring, Glenn, and Jere Hutcheson. *Musical Form and Analysis*. Dubuque, IA: Wm. C. Brown Communications, Inc., 1995.

The Building Blocks of Music and the Musical Architecture

If we were to consider the process needed to build a home, we would most likely begin by establishing a plan for construction. Many fundamental decisions would be necessary. Note the similarities to building a home and composing a musical composition.

In either case, we would likely decide the following. First, we would need to decide upon the basic style of the house (e.g., ranch, two-story, brick, or log home). We might hire an architect or purchase ready-made architectural plans to establish the floor plan. In constructing a musical composition, we would likely decide on the formal style and approach to the music.

Second, the size of the home would need to be determined. Likewise, the composer would need to outline the length of the work and likely determine if there were to be additional elements to the basic form (such as an introduction and a coda).

Third, the foundation of the home would need to be constructed. In the composition, the tonal centers would need to be established.

Fourth, the walls of the home would be built. Likewise, compositions would require the creation of themes, subjects-countersubjects, etc.

Fifth, the ceilings would be built. In the musical composition, phrases, cadences, and harmonic movement would be constructed.

Sixth, the roof would be attached. In the composition, the tempo would be determined.

Seventh, the fixtures, windows, doors, etc., would be installed. Such refinement aspects for the composer would include determining the required articulations and expressive markings for stylistic interpretation.

The building blocks, whether architectural or composing aspects, all relate. Most require planning and sequential development in the creative process.

Form and Structure in Musical Compositions

Creating the structural foundation of a composition requires two primary elements in music: 1) the tonal relationship or the *tonal structure* and 2) the layout outline or *structural design*. "*Design* is the organization of those elements of music called melody, rhythm, cadences, timbre, texture, and tempo. The harmonic organization of a piece is referred to as its *tonal structure* .... *Form* is an inclusive term which refers both to the *design* of a composition and to its *tonal structure*."[6]

Since the form is the structural outline, several general types or descriptions, which serve as the foundations for study, are presented in this chapter. These formal types may be expressed in two primary classifications: 1) *single forms*, such as binary, rounded binary, ternary, variation, sonata, rondo, and

imitative forms (or genres, such as the fugue) and 2) *compound forms*, which involve more than one movement (instrumental forms such as the concerto and the suite).[7]

In most aspects of music composition, there are exceptions to note, and caution is needed when applying "formula" procedures for analysis. As presented by Douglas Green in *Form in Tonal Music*, it is important to note that "the works of the great composers rarely seem to have been created by pouring musical ideas into a preconceived mold. On the contrary, great music shapes itself into whatever form is most fitting to make explicit the particular concept in the mind of the composer. Consequently, it is a mistake to think of the study of form as a process by which we familiarize ourselves with a certain number of standard 'blueprints,' then proceed to label each composition accordingly. To approach a composition with an open mind, ready to discover what the composer has in store for us, is a safer procedure than to assume in advance that any particular pattern will be in evidence. This does not mean that we cannot attempt a systemization of forms. A perusal of the great musical literature of the past shows that certain broad formal categories tend to appear again and again. Thus we speak of 'standard forms' and give them names."[8]

The Analysis Process

Our first goal in the analysis process is to identify and/or discover the division of parts in a composition. The parts are then divided into sections, subsections, and subdivisions. It is possible that some works may have no characteristics of division at all; thus, they would be labeled "one-part" forms.[9]

Most standard form types present the tonal structure of a composition through harmonic development. When a *part* of a composition ends with an incomplete harmonic conclusion (non-original tonic key), the part is referred to as being tonally "open." A continuation of the composition is expected and, thus, is termed "continuous." If the part ends with a complete cadence that is harmonically complete and a separate section, the part is labeled "sectional," or tonally "closed."[10]

Most standard forms are divided into the *single-form* category of either one-part forms, two-part forms (binary), three-part forms (ternary), five- to seven-part forms (rondo), variation forms (*sectional* forms such as theme and variation), ostinato forms (*continuous* forms such as the basso ostinato, chaconne, and passacaglia), and imitative forms or genres (fugue). As is true in most all aspects of music, there are possible exceptions to most compositional construction rules, and other unique forms are possible (see resources for further in-depth descriptions and examples).[11]

Numerous analysis procedures exist. Douglas Green in *Form in Tonal*

Music presents the following "Six-Step Method of Analysis" to assist with developing a systematic method. Consider using these analytical techniques:

STEP 1:
Consider the successive phrases, note their cadences, and come to a conclusion regarding the tonal structure of the piece, deciding whether it exhibits a single, double, triple, or other harmonic movement. If single, is the harmonic movement complete, interrupted, or progressive? In a double harmonic movement, of which type is each?

STEP 2:
Consider the design from the cadential point of view, noting the presence or absence of any divisive conclusive cadence.

STEP 3:
Consider the design from the motivic and melodic point of view, noting the presence or absence of contrasting phrases and phrases that are restatements of other phrases. (A restatement differs from a repetition in that the former is a recurrence after contrast while the latter is an immediate recurrence. Restatements are important elements of form; repetitions are not.) Represent the design graphically by means of letter: A-BA, A-B-A, A(ll)A', and so on.

STEP 4:
In light of steps 1, 2, and 3, come to a conclusion regarding the number of parts into which the piece will separate.

STEP 5:
Considering steps 1 and 4, decide whether the form is continuous, sectional, or (if there are three or more parts) full sectional.

STEP 6:
Decide whether or not the piece coincides in a general way with any of the commonly used standard forms ...[12]

Basic Form Mapping Procedures

The overall design of many compositions can be notated or illustrated with *schematic drawings* of the form. These drawings may help introduce several basic procedures for analysis and mapping examples, and may help present a visual outline of the design, tonal structure, instrument voicing, and possible dynamic intent of the composition.[13] The following listing of eight basic form mapping procedures, as presented by Connie Ericksen in *Band Director's Curriculum Resource*, presents concepts to help map the form and assist with the music analysis process.

ANALYSIS AND MAPPING CONCEPT STATEMENTS:

1. All the elements of music combine to give compositions *form*.

2. All compositions are based on the principles of *unity* and *variety*. Form analysis is determining how and where compositions employ these principles.

3. A diagram outlining a composition's unity and variety can be called a *form map*, which shows the composition's overall shape.

4. Many compositions have followed generally similar shapes. Groups of similarly shaped compositions are categorized as particular form types, some of which are *rondo*, *binary* and *ternary*, *sonata allegro*, and *fugue*.

5. All compositions use procedures of *repetition*, *contrast*, *variation*, or *development*. Through listening for these procedures and the placement of final cadences, large sections of a composition can be identified.

6. A form map uses a horizontal arc to represent each large section of a composition, as shown below:

7. Where two arcs meet, the measure number is given and the cadence is identified. Under each arc, there are descriptions of that particular section. Sections are identified with letters to illustrate unity or contrast:

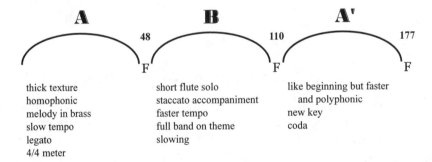

A	**B**	**A'**
48	110	177
F	F	F

thick texture
homophonic
melody in brass
slow tempo
legato
4/4 meter

short flute solo
staccato accompaniment
faster tempo
full band on theme
slowing

like beginning but faster
   and polyphonic
new key
coda

8. More detailed analysis shows smaller sections, phrases, keys, and specific measures: [14]

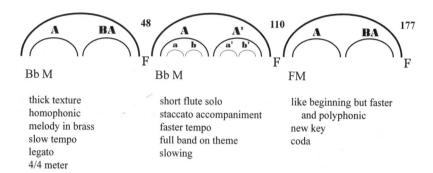

thick texture	short flute solo	like beginning but faster
homophonic	staccato accompaniment	and polyphonic
melody in brass	faster tempo	new key
slow tempo	full band on theme	coda
legato	slowing	
4/4 meter		

Please refer to the additional mapping ideas and options presented at the end of this chapter (see pages 69–71). There are many ways to be creative with the visual descriptions and drawings of the musical events and architectural layout of a composition.

The mapping layout on the next page appears in Volume 2 of *Teaching Music through Performance in Band*, page 537. This example, contributed for Volume 2 by Jeffrey Renshaw, portrays Section A (of three sections) of *and the mountains rising nowhere* by Joseph Schwantner. Notice the detailed inclusion of options regarding the construction design, tempi, time signatures, events, and motives. Again, there are many possibilities for visual portrayal of the form and musical events.

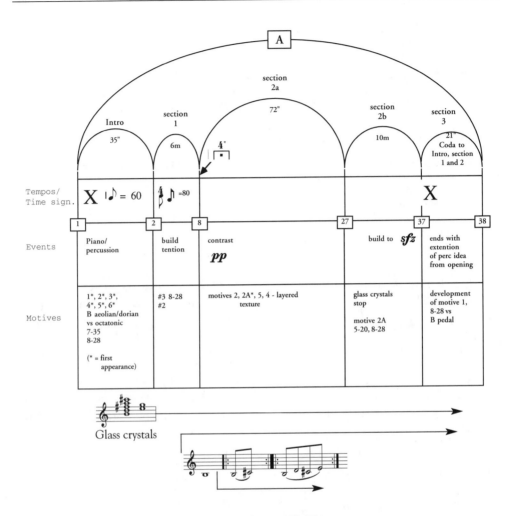

Single or "Small" Forms

Single or "small" forms are those forms that are made up of one movement or an independent large section. Forms that involve multiple movements and large sections, often including varying types of smaller formal types, are referred to as "compound" forms. The *single-forms* category (one-movement forms) includes forms that often repeat sections and are referred to as variation, binary, ternary, sonata, rondo, etc., forms. *Compound forms* include instrumental types such as the concerto, suite, and sonata.[15]

Two-Part Forms

As presented earlier, forms may be divided into various categories. This section introduces the two types of single forms. These two types include *continuous* and *sectional* divisions; within each division there may be smaller units.

Continuous binary forms (or divisions) are divided by the design and involve a single harmonic movement with a conclusive cadence. This type of binary form can be further analyzed to fall within three categories: *simple (continuous) binary, rounded (continuous) binary,* and *balanced (continuous) binary form.*[16]

Sectional binary forms (or divisions) involve "double harmonic movement, that is, two complete or interrupted harmonic movements."[17] This type of binary form can also be further analyzed to fall within three categories: *simple (sectional) binary, rounded (sectional) binary,* and *bar form.*[18] Each of these larger divisions of both continuous and sectional forms often contain smaller phrase units.

Basic Mapping Concepts

Throughout the varied forms and sections of binary form, the same or similar material is used. These sections of similar or same material can often be charted with various graphic descriptions. The basic charting or *mapping* possibilities of two-part forms are demonstrated in the following representations:

1. In the most simplistic visual form for reference to young students, some refer to this two-part form as the "cheese and cracker" form. This form, then, would be described as a *section of same material* (the cheese) and a *section of different material* (the cracker).

2. Many major resources refer to this form with the following visual letter labeling and representation indicating two distinctly different sections:

$$\text{A (section) B (section)}$$

3. Often, the binary form is represented and mapped with the use of arc lines to distinguish the two separate sections, as shown below:

4. Some sources refer to the form with bar lines and repeat signs:

$$\|: \underline{\quad\quad}^{\text{A}}\underline{\quad\quad} :\| \quad \|: \underline{\quad\quad}^{\text{B}}\underline{\quad\quad} :\|$$

5. In music appreciation and general music texts, binary form is often represented with various geometric designs with different shapes used to distinguish the two primary parts:

Traditional Mapping of Two-Part Forms

CONTINUOUS SIMPLE BINARY FORM:

Simple binary form is made up of two independent sections in which no similar material is presented in each section. *Continuous simple binary form* is distinguishable from other types because the first part of the form (A) is separated from the second part (B) with a harmonically *open* cadence, often "an emphatic conclusive cadence on a nontonic chord."[19]

This form could be displayed in the following manner: AB or AA´

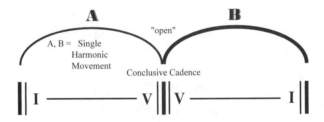

Note: It is important to note that other options are possible.

CONTINUOUS ROUNDED BINARY FORM:

Rounded binary form consists of two harmonically separate sections in which one section is completely harmonically independent while the other section consists of two combined designs and tonal cadences and harmonic movement. *Continuous rounded binary form* involves two conclusive cadences outlining the two parts; however, there are three melodic divisions with two melodic divisions found within the first section, which leads continuously to the other tonally and melodically independent section. Thus, the two-part continuous rounded binary form would be mapped in the following manner: (AB) (A´) or AB ll A´

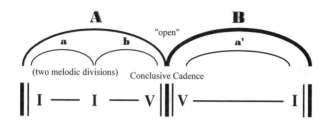

Note: Other harmonic movement options are possible.

Continuous Balanced Binary Form:

Balanced binary form involves two similar sections in which the closing section or particular passage of part one is repeated for the close of the second section. The part two section or passage usually appears transposed.[20] Balanced binary form could be mapped in the following manner: AA´

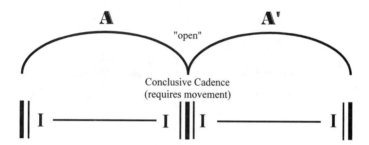

Note: "Part 2 closes with a transposed restatement of the passage that ends part one."(Green, 93)

Sectional Simple Binary:

Two independent and complete harmonic sections (or harmonic movements within the sections) in which the first section is harmonically *closed* from the second is referred to as *sectional simple binary form*. The division is the *tonal structure*.

If the melodic material in the two sections is similar, the design would be labeled as follows: A-A´. If the second section contrasts the first melodically, the design would appear as follows: A-B. The following outlines each option:

A-A´

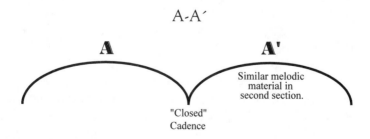

A-B

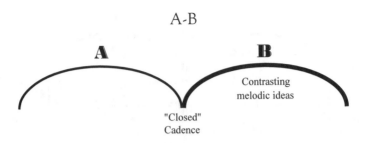

SECTIONAL ROUNDED BINARY FORM:

This form is the opposite or *counterpart* of the rounded continuous binary form. The difference is the "first part completes a harmonic movement."[21] *Sectional rounded binary form* "consists of sections A and B, but within B there is a return of material from A. Section B is not completely independent; it serves as a bridge between the original A and the return of A material."[22] The sectional rounded binary form would be mapped with the following design: A-BA

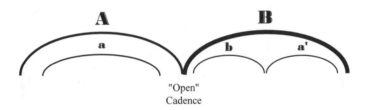

SECTIONAL BINARY BAR FORM:

The design of this form is A-A-B. What distinguishes this form with three divisions is that the tonal structure involves only *two complete harmonic movements:* (A A) and (B). Notice that part one (A A) is simply repeated and part two (B) is not. It is not unusual to find the repeat part of section A to vary somewhat. The mapping of sectional binary bar form is as follows: A-A-B

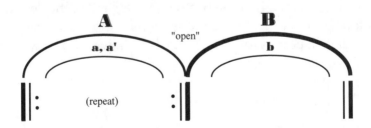

The repetition of section B of the above would be defined as *sectional inverted bar form* and would be mapped as follows: A-B-B

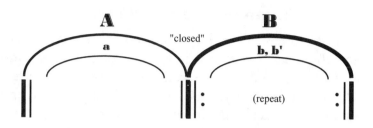

One-Part Forms

One-part forms are constructed using one tonal harmonic movement, but the movement may be separated into smaller subdivisions or parts. These parts do not interrupt the harmonic movement. The primary factor that divides the sections in most forms is the tonal independence or tonal movement of one section to the next. This movement is usually generated by tension and/or release created by conclusive cadences or by the use of other texture contrasts.

One-part forms primarily involve one single theme or musical idea and texture. Modulation is possible, not to the extent to express other keys, but rather temporarily with the entire form remaining in a single key.[23]

Mapping of One-Part Forms

One-part forms can be presented to younger students as the "cracker" form. There is only one part, with no "cheese" to accompany as in the illustrative description of two-part forms (the "cheese and cracker" form).

GEOMETRIC MAPPING OPTIONS:

TRADITIONAL MAPPING OPTIONS:

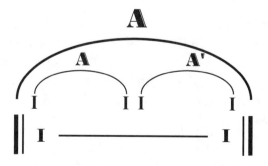

One-part form uses primarily a single theme and texture involving double harmonic movement within a single period.

Three-Part Ternary Forms

It is important to remember that *form* is distinguished and identified by the *design* and the *tonal structure* or movement of the composition. What makes *ternary form* unique is that the construction of this form involves the use of three distinct and usually large sections, with each section or part being "independent and thematically important."[24] Ternary form can be found as a complete movement of a larger work or as a section of a larger form.[25] Many options of length, repetition, and symmetry are possible with this form. "Within each large section of a ternary form, there will be a one-part form or a binary form."[26] The design of these three unique and independent sections can vary according to the contrast and similarities to other sections. It is important to note that there are several tonal options for the division of the three sections:

$$A \text{ (I-V)} \quad B \text{ (V-V)} \quad A \text{ (I-I)}$$
$$A \text{ (I-I)} \quad B \text{ (V-V)} \quad A \text{ (I-I)}$$

Mapping of Three-Part Ternary Forms

The mapping of ternary form can appear with many visual options. As with two-part form, young students may be able to relate to the form by simply describing the form as the "Oreo cookie" form. The form could then be described as having a *section of same material* (the outer layer of the cookie), a *section of different material* (the middle filling), and a *closure section of the same or similar material* (the outer layer of the cookie).

GEOMETRIC MAPPING OPTIONS:

"same"   "different"   "same"

TRADITIONAL MAPPING OPTIONS:

As with binary form, several types of ternary forms are possible. The harmonic movement (although still sectional and independent) could involve *double movement* – the second section could be contrasted and the design would appear as follows: (A) (B A) or A-BA. This type would be recognized as *sectional ternary form*.

SECTIONAL TERNARY FORM:

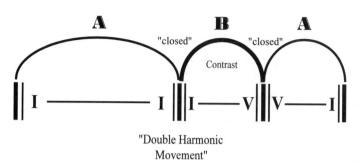

"Double Harmonic
Movement"

When the sections of ternary form are defined with three separate, complete, or interrupted harmonic movements, the type would be *full sectional ternary form*. This would be recognized as the traditional and most recognized type: (A) (B) (A) or A-B-A.

FULL SECTIONAL TERNARY FORM:

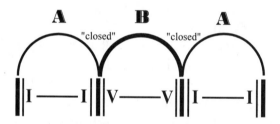

"Triple Harmonic Movement" (Can be complete or interrupted movements)

If one of the sections were to have an interrupted harmonic movement still including a conclusive cadence and contrast, the design would be (A B) (A) or AB ll A and would be considered *continuous ternary form*.

CONTINUOUS TERNARY FORM:

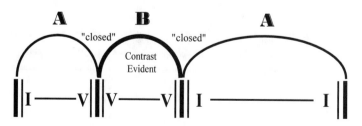

"Single Interrupted Harmonic Movement"

There are many possible types of binary and ternary forms. One notable ternary example that is not presented is "Da Capo" ternary form because of

the limited representation in band music. For clarification, readers are encouraged to consult *Form in Tonal Music*, Chapter 8, "The Ternary Forms."

Five- to Seven-Part Forms

Rondo Form

Rondo form, portrayed as (ABACA), (ABACABA), (ABACDA), etc., is a sectional form that is considered by many to be an extension of the ternary design ideas of three-part form (ABA…). This form involves a theme or section (A), referred to as a *refrain*, and alternates with contrasting themes or sections (B, C, or D), referred to as *episodes*.[27] "The 'A' section keeps coming around again and again, with different sections between."[28] The episodes introduce new material and modulate to closely related tonal centers or *keys*.[29] The rondo form is often found to be a movement of larger *compound* forms of composition, such as the instrumental *sonata*, *suite*, and *concerto*, serving as the final conclusion movement.[30]

Mapping of Rondo Form

As with several other forms, young students may remember and recognize this form by referring to it as the "Big Mac" form. This form could be described as a *section of same material* – A (the outer layer of the bread), a *section of different material* – B (upper-level filling "burger/cheese"), a *section* of the *same or similar material* – A (the middle layer of bread), *another section of different material* – C (lower-level filling "burger/sauces, etc."), closed by the return of the *same material again* – A (the outer layer of the bread).

GEOMETRIC MAPPING OPTIONS:

5-Part Rondo "Traditional"	A	B	A'	C	A'	
7-Part Rondo "Classical"	A	B	A'	C	A'	B	A'

Traditional Mapping Options:

Five-Part Rondo Form:

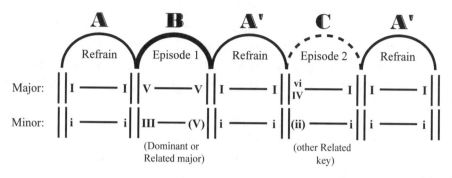

Classical Rondo Form (Seven-Part):

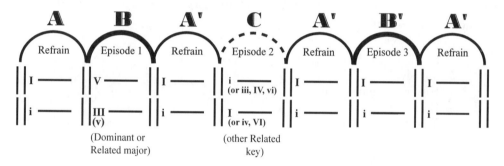

It is important to note that many classical composers used a special hybrid form that combined the rondo and sonata form to create a unique *sonata rondo* form. Using the above classical rondo form design, the sonata form's "development section" is substituted for the second episode (C) of the classical rondo form. This compositional aspect is found mostly in finale movements of larger works, particularly in the classical period.[31]

Theme and Variation Form

Variation form involves the statement of an idea, a thematic sentence (*theme*), and then repeats that theme in a succession of altered transformations (*variations*). This form of music is found as an independent composition and frequently as a movement of a larger work in an instrumental suite or sonata.[32] Often, transitions, bridges, and extensions are found between the variations to provide contrast for needed modulations and to add variety and development of larger section grouping.[33]

Theme and variation form can be divided into two primary categories or types: using either *continuous* or *sectional* variations. As defined by Green,

"*Sectional* variations are those based on a theme that consists of one or more periods with, usually, a pause or clear caesura at the end of the theme and each variation. *Continuous* variations are those based on a theme comprising only a phrase or two (usually covering a total of from four to eight bars), the variations following each other uninterruptedly. The former are represented by the theme and variations (or variations on a theme) and the eighteenth century doubles; the latter by the ground bass (basso ostinato), chaconne, and passacaglia."[34] This section addresses the *sectional* variations category of theme and variation forms.

In sectional variation form, the theme length and form is normally the same throughout, while other musical elements are used to provide the contrast. It is important to note that the next to the last variation is usually presented in a minor key.

Joseph Labuta, in *Teaching Musicianship in the High School Band*, presents ten musical elements and materials that are used to create alteration in the variations. These include the following:

1. Rhythm and tempo
2. Melody
3. Bass line or inner parts
4. Harmony
5. Texture
6. Dynamics
7. Instrumentation
8. Key
9. Mode
10. Form (design or length)[35]

Green suggests that the most common musical elements and materials that are altered to provide the variations are the "melody, the bass, the texture, and the precise harmonic sequence."[36]

The following presents Connie Ericksen's listing, found in the text of the *Band Director's Curriculum Resource*, of eight possible ways that sectional variations may differ:

1. *Melodically oriented* variations maintain melodic content similar to that of the original theme.
2. *Harmonically oriented* variations follow the harmonic progressions of the theme.
3. *Simplified* variations eliminate notes from the original theme and maintain only the theme's general outline.
4. Variations in the *opposite mode* are those written in a major key if the original theme is in a minor key, and vice versa.
5. *Double* variations are those wherein a variation serves as a theme and is, therefore, varied.

6. *Contrapuntal* variations introduce new thematic material before the variation is completed, or vary the original theme using fugal devices.

7. *Character* variations manipulate the theme to take on the qualities of a recognizable genre, such as a minuet, gigue, march, and so on.

8. In *free* variations, any changes can be made to the theme so long as it remains remotely recognizable.[37]

Mapping of Theme and Variation Forms

Younger students may refer to this form as the "pizza" form. The fundamental part of all pizzas is the crust (the *theme*) with multiple options for toppings, e.g., sausage, cheese, pepperoni, mushrooms, etc. (the *variations*).

GEOMETRIC MAPPING OPTIONS:

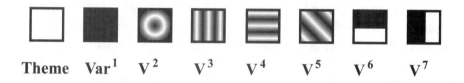

There are numerous options for portraying the variation sections. Some refer to the sectional forms in the following manner: (A A1 A2 A3 A4 A5 A6 A7, etc.).

TRADITIONAL MAPPING OPTIONS:

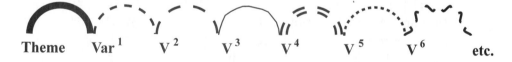

Continuous Variation Forms

Ostinato Forms (Passacaglia and Chaconne)

An *ostinato* is a short musical section, segment, or phrase that persistently repeats over and over again throughout a section or often an entire composition. Since the Baroque period, composers have used this technique to create compositional variety by using a short musical section, segment, or phrase (usually in one voice) and writing variations around these fixed melodic ideas (with the exception of the *chaconne*, where the variation is harmonic). This variation is *continuous*, with the repetition throughout the work. If the ostinato were to appear in the lowest voice and constantly be repeated

there, this would be referred to as a *basso ostinato form*. Some refer to this lowest bass voicing as the "ground bass" or *cantus firmus* – a technique used often by the famous Baroque composer, J.S. Bach.

Two additional ostinato variation forms are found in compositional writing, and the differences of the two forms have been the source of academic debate since the time of Handel. These two are the *passacaglia* and *chaconne* variation forms. The *Harvard Dictionary of Music* defines the differences of the two as follows: "a *passacaglia*...is a continuous variation based on a clearly distinguishable ostinato that normally appears in the bass but that may occasionally be transferred to an upper voice, as in Bach's passacaglia. A *chaconne*, on the other hand, is a continuous variation in which the 'theme' is a scheme of harmonies (e.g., I-VI-IV-V) usually treated so that the first and last chords are fixed whereas the intervening ones can be replaced by substitutes.... The characteristic trait of the chaconne is, therefore, a regularly recurrent harmonic structure without a clearly recognizable ostinato."[38]

The same principles of mapping with letter identification for theme and variation form, as well as the use of arcs and graphic notation for the sectional variation forms, apply equally for these continuous variation forms.

Sonata Form (Sonata-Allegro Form or First Movement Form)

The *sonata form* has been referred to by many as the *first movement form* or the *sonata-allegro form* (fast/slow/fast form) for hundreds of years. Since the classical and romantic periods and continuing today, this form has been found in many overtures and the first movements of many larger compositional forms, such as the symphony.

The sonata form consists of three main sections: (1) the *exposition* (A), (2) the *development* (B), and (3) the *recapitulation* (A). It is the complexity of construction and the organizational and developmental aspects that involve the movement of tonality, which especially distinguishes this form.

Labuta describes the form as follows: "In the exposition, two or more contrasting themes are presented. In the development section, the themes are manipulated and tension is built. Usually the climax of the work occurs here. The themes are restated and resolved in the recapitulation in the tonic key. The design and tonal structure of the sonata-allegro form is an elaboration of the rounded binary principle."[39]

In the text of *Form and Tonal Music*, Green further describes the unique function of this form: "The sonata form, like the continuous binary forms from which it evolved, is in its very nature rooted in tonality. Tension set up by sharply defined key centers is possible only to tonal music and it is this tension that constitutes the foundation of sonata form. A key center is established (first theme), undermined (transition), and a new key center set up (second and closing themes). The establishment of a second key center causes a tense situation demanding a reconciliation, which comes about after a period of harmonic fluidity (development) when the original key center dominates (recapitulation). More briefly, the tonal structure of the normal sonata form can be explained as a progressive harmonic movement (exposition) that is prolonged (development) and finally begun again and completed (recapitulation)."[40]

It is important to note that many composers, especially in the classical and romantic periods, incorporated optional components to modify the sonata form. These components have included the use of an introduction (a section which normally uses a slow tempo that leads into the sonata form), and a coda (a section that follows the basic sonata form – some sections short, some long – whose role is to prolong the tonic chord to add closure to the composition). If an introduction is used, the coda is usually also included. These optional modifications to sonata form are found primarily in most overtures and symphonies.

Mapping of Sonata Form (sonata-allegro form)

The mapping of sonata form can also appear with many descriptive options. Young students may remember this form by referring to the process of making a "club sandwich." The sandwich has basically three primary bread parts (outside, middle, outside) and is stuffed (or "developed") between sections in creative ways.

Other visual displays may also assist in understanding the design aspects of this form.

GEOMETRIC MAPPING OPTIONS:

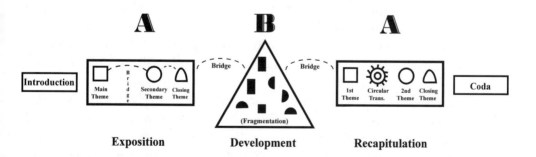

TRADITIONAL MAPPING OPTIONS:

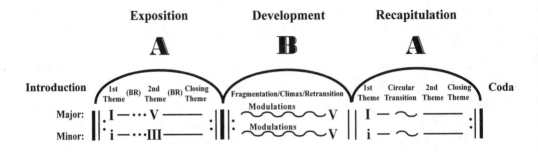

The Fugue

Although considered by most music theorists to be more a *compositional style, genre, process,* or *texture* rather than a *form,* the *fugue* has developed since the late seventeenth century into a frequently used procedure of imitative counterpoint and harmonic organization. The fugue, with its illusive construction features that are most difficult to describe in a "standard formula," has been used as a primary compositional procedure from J.S. Bach, to Hindemith, to present composers.[41]

The fugue, which involves a polyphonic style of composing, is usually made up of three or four imitative parts or voices. The style of composing involves an *open continuous* growth and development unlike the *closed* or *sectional* forms presented earlier. The basic structure alternates *expositions* and *episodes.*

As described by Labuta, "The fugue is a monothematic form (or more correctly, technique) in which a theme (fugue subject) is extended and developed by imitation. As illustrated...(in the design that follows), the fugue begins with a statement of the subject in one voice part alone. The subject is 'answered' by another voice part at the interval of a fourth or fifth while the original voice plays a countersubject against it. In an exposition of a four-voice fugue, there are two sets of such statements and answers as the subject is restated in a series of successive entrances. Expositions and episodes alternate until the fugue ends. As the fugue moves toward its climax, the composer often uses "stretto" to build intensity. Stretto refers to the overlapping (*imitation*) of subject entrances in close succession."[42]

Mapping of the Fugue

Fugue

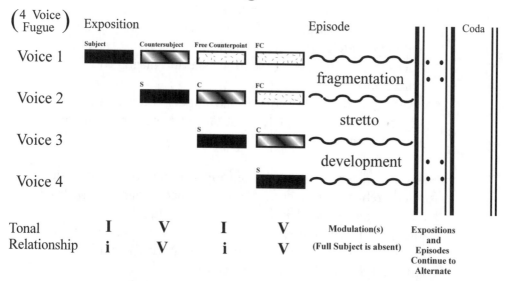

*Adapted from Labuta (p. 98), Ericksen (p. 184), Apel (p. 336)

Note: Rarely does an exposition present subjects in voice order (e.g., 1, 2, 3, 4).

Teaching Ideas and Strategies

There are many creative ways to integrate information about form and structure into the daily rehearsal. The following listing serves as an introduction of ideas for the innovative music educator:

1. Select band literature that you can specifically use to teach about the form and structure. Consider selecting one work for each concert preparation period to study in detail. Develop a three- or four-year cyclic plan to present all "standard forms." This curricular approach could be easily integrated into other cyclic instructional plans. For additional curricular ideas, please refer to Chapter 7, Volume 1, of *Teaching Music through Performance in Band.*

2. When rehearsing *all* band works, refer to the form parts, sections, themes, variations, etc., rather than the rehearsal numbers, letters, or measures. This daily rehearsal technique will assist with the awareness of form divisions and will

stimulate students' listening for the development and
compositional variety aspects.

Here are some rehearsal examples:
- "Please begin at the development."
- "Clarinets, be careful to avoid rushing the reprise of the
  second theme in the recapitulation."
- "Let's try a softer mallet on the bass drum during the third
  variation."
- "Restart at the coda. This time trumpets, softer and more
  detached. Also flutes, excellent articulation improvement on
  the restatement of the first theme."

3. Make sure all students mark the form structure on their music
    for daily rehearsal reference. Pass out a special handout with all
    major aspects outlined and listen to a recording of the work
    while marking the parts. Listen to each division separately as
    the students mark their individual parts. With the marking
    completed during the first rehearsal of the new work, the
    director can refer to each division as suggested above for each
    of the following rehearsals.

    You can save rehearsal time by having the major sections
    marked (identified) with colored markers on each part (before
    the music is passed out). It just takes advance planning and a
    few interested librarian helpers.

4. When purchasing new band works or reusing works in your
    library, order two additional music scores to use as visual
    displays in the band room by marking the *form and structure*.
    Use color highlighters to outline the many divisions, sections,
    variations, and/or themes. Consider separating the pages and
    posting the score in consecutive page order all around the walls
    of the band room. Chances are great that your students will
    show their curiosity by following their parts throughout the
    score. They will likely be able to see and better understand the
    form when outlined on the score, especially when they find
    their part and identify how all of the form divisions and other
    relationships interact in the construction of the music.

5. Create a music listening area in your band room for special
    student enrichment. Provide the opportunity for students to
    listen to recordings and review scores of all of the works that
    you are preparing for the next concert. These listening and

enrichment opportunities can be made available whenever convenient for the director or the students (e.g., before and after school, or possibly during study hall, lunch, and other times). Some directors provide the opportunity for students to check out the recordings and scores to take them home for study and review.

6. Include instructional resources in the rehearsal to help portray the design aspects. Refer to form aspects by using the chalkboard, transparencies on the overhead projector, or slides, or by creating a special PowerPoint (or other similar) computer presentation.

7. Create special illustrative handouts for distribution to each student. Describe and visually portray various musical aspects to improve the performance as well as accentuate the form and structure.

8. Create a special resource and reference area for students to have the opportunity to read and research about the music you are performing. Books, articles, and videos placed on display and available for students to review may encourage them to do additional creative enrichment on aspects of music form and structure. Here are several outstanding book sources to consider in addition to those listed at the start of this chapter:

Blueprint for Band by Robert Garofalo, Ft. Lauderdale, FL: Meredith Music Publications, 1983.

The Conductor's Anthology, Volume 6, Northfield, IL: The Instrumentalist Publishing Company, 1989.

Guides to Band Masterworks by Robert J. Garofalo, Volumes I & II, Ft. Lauderdale, FL: Meredith Music Publications, 1992.

Instructional Designs for Middle/Junior High School Band by Robert J. Garofalo, Volumes I & II, Ft. Lauderdale, FL: Meredith Music Publications, 1995.

Listening Guides for Band Musicians by Roland Stycos, Portland, MA: J. Weston Walch Publisher, 1991.

Music in the Middle/Junior High School: Syllabus/Handbook by The University of the State of New York, The State Education Department, Bureau of Curriculum Development, Albany, NY: New York State Education Department.

Teaching Musicianship in the High School Band by Joseph A. Labuta,
    Revised Edition, Ft. Lauderdale, FL: Meredith Music
    Publications, 1998.
Teaching Music through Performance in Band, Volumes 1, 2, and 3,
    Chicago: GIA Publications, 1996, 1998, 2000.

For additional creative instruction and enrichment strategies,
please review the text from *Scheduling and Teaching Music*,
published by GIA Publications, Chicago, Illinois, 2000.

Conclusion

To earn a degree in music education, one must study many elements and
areas of music in great detail (in the United States, for four to five years). Not
only do we study an instrument and demonstrate performance competency, we
must study music theory (in most colleges, two to three years), history, appreciation, conducting, and many other music and education classes. Why study
all of these subjects? Wouldn't it be just as well to focus only on *band directing
skills*?

There has been much debate among music scholars as to what works best
to stimulate and create outstanding music teachers (band directors).
Ultimately, the most successful music educator (band director) seems to have
competency and proficiency in *all* of the areas above as well as *dedication, curricular direction*, mastery of *classroom control and motivation*, and an *enthusiasm
for teaching*.

If becoming informed and aware of all of the above comprehensive musicianship areas leads to better informed teachers, then it seems only reasonable
that the study of all of these music elements and how these elements relate to
the performance of music is important and vital for all students as well.
Through this process of *comprehensive musicianship* development, we become
better *musicians* and we become more capable of relating to what composers
intend for performers to project in and with their music. At the same time, we
most likely will experience a deeper *response* to the innate expressive qualities
of music.

The Benefits in the World of Education

As we search for continued accountability in our music teaching, it is
important to remember the many benefits of studying music and all of the
Arts. The National Standards for Arts Education present the following as a
guide for our justification:

Arts (music) education benefits the *student* because it cultivates the whole child, gradually building many kinds of literacy while developing intuition, reasoning, imagination, and dexterity into unique forms of expression and communication. This process requires not merely an active mind but a trained one. An education in the arts (music) benefits *society* because students of the arts (music) gain powerful tools for understanding human experiences, both past and present. They learn to respect the often very different ways others have of thinking, working, and expressing themselves. They learn to make decisions in situations where there are no standard answers. By studying the arts (music), students stimulate their natural creativity and learn to develop it to meet the needs of a complex and competitive society. And, as study and competence in the arts (music) reinforce one another, the joy of learning becomes real, tangible, and powerful.[43]

Form Mapping Options

Here are additional design ideas for creating visual diagrams. Directors and students are encouraged to develop visual diagrams and portrayals to assist in the understanding of compositional construction and architecture.

Form Design Options

ONE-, TWO-, AND THREE-PART FORM OPTIONS:

VARIATION FORM OPTIONS:

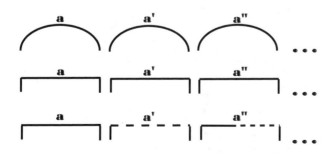

RONDO FORM OPTIONS:

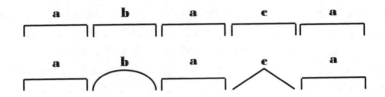

FUGUE DESIGN OPTIONS:

MELODIC OR THEME DESIGN OPTIONS:

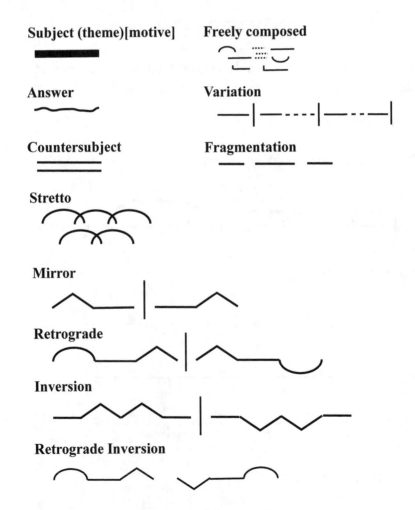

Tonal Answer

Real Answer

Augmentation

Diminution

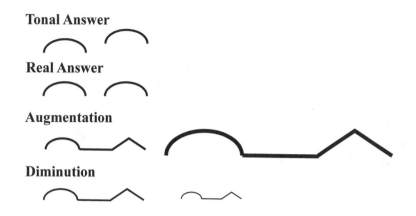

Form and Structure

Music Compositions of "Basic Forms"

The following listing presents band compositions divided into "basic form" groups. This listing is a selected compilation of information obtained from the Teacher Resource Guides of Volumes 1, 2, and 3 of *Teaching Music through Performance in Band*, Robert Garofalo's *Guides to Band Masterworks* and *Instructional Designs for Middle/Junior High School Band*, Joseph Labuta's *Teaching Musicianship in the High School Band*, Connie Ericksen's *Band Director's Curriculum Resource*, and Roland Stycos's *Listening Guides for Band Musicians*. Please note that these works are listed as references for study and may or may not meet all specifications of the referred-to "basic forms." Listed forms may be based on compositional aspects of the "basic forms."

Binary Forms

Air and March	Henry Purcell/Gordon	Bourne
Blessed Are They	Johannes Brahms/Buehlman	Ludwig Music
Brazilian Folk Dance Suite II. Movement	William Rhodes	Kjos Music
Caccia and Chorale	Clifton Williams	Barnhouse
Chorale and Shaker Dance	John Zdechlik	Kjos Music
Fanfare and Allegro	Clifton Williams	Southern Music
First Suite in E-Flat II. Intermezzo	Gustav Holst	Boosey and Hawkes
Incantation and Dance	John Barnes Chance	Boosey and Hawkes
The Leaves Are Falling	Warren Benson	Hal Leonard
Overture for Band, Op. 24 Andante	Felix Mendelssohn-Bartoldy/Boyd	Ludwig Music Publishing Co.
Second Suite in E-Flat "Song of the Blacksmith"	Gustav Holst	Boosey and Hawkes

Soundings	Cindy McTee	Magnamusic-Baton
II. "Gizmo"		
III. "Waves"		
The Stars and Stripes Forever	John Philip Sousa/ Brion and Schissel	C.L. Barnhouse
Suite Provençale	Jan Van der Roost	De Haske
Movement I.		
Three Chorale Preludes	William Latham	Warner Bros.
"O Sacred Head Now Wounded"		

Rounded

A Solemn Music	Virgil Thompson	Schirmer
Ancient Voices	Michael Sweeny	Hal Leonard Corp.
Blue Shades	Frank Ticheli	Manhattan
Brazilian Folk Dance Suite	William Rhoads	Kjos
Movement I.		
Canzona	Peter Mennin	Carl Fischer
Carpathian Sketches	Robert Jager	Hal Leonard
Divertimento	Vincent Persichetti	Theodore Presser
II. Song		
Down a Country Lane	Aaron Copland	Boosey and Hawkes
Emblems	Aaron Copland	Boosey and Hawkes
English Folk Song Suite	Ralph Vaughan Williams	Boosey and Hawkes
II. Intermezzo - "My Bonny Boy"		
III. March - "Folk Songs from Summerset"		
Exaltations, Op. 67	Martin Mailman	Boosey and Hawkes
Fanfare, Ode, and Festival	Bob Margolis	Manhattan Beach
Movement I.		
Movement III.		
Four French Songs	Robert Hanson	Southern Music
Movement I.		
Movement III.		
Four French Songs	Robert Hanson	Southern Music
Movement III.		
Jupiter Symphony	Wolfgang Mozart/Bake	ProArt
"Minuet and Trio"		
Linz Symphony	Wolfgang Mozart/Beeler	Rubank
"Minuet and Trio"		
Masque	W. Francis McBeth	Southern Music
Mini Suite	Morton Gould	Hal Leonard
I. "Birthday March"		

Orient et Occident 　Grande March	Camille Saint-Saëns	Maecenas
Overture for Winds	Charles Carter	Bourne
Portrait of a Clown	Frank Ticheli	Manhattan Beach
Postcard	Frank Ticheli	Manhattan Beach
Renaissance Suite 　"La Mourisque"	Tielman Susato/Curnow	Jenson
Satiric Dances 　Movement I. 　Movement II.	Norman Dello Joio	Associated
Sea Songs	Ralph Vaughan Williams	Boosey and Hawkes
Shadows of Eternity	Thomas Stone	Daehn Publications
Symphony No. 3 　II. Adagio	Vittorio Giannini	Warner Bros.
Symphony #3 "Shaker Life"	Dan Welcher	Theodore Presser
Symphony #3 "Slavyanskaya" 　Movement II.	Boris Kozhevnikov/ 　Bourgeois	Wingert-Jones
Three on the Isle 　I. 　II.	Hugh Stuart	TRN Music
Tocatta Marziale	Ralph Vaughan Williams	Boosey and Hawkes

Ternary Forms

Ballad	Morton Gould	Schirmer
Cajun Folk Songs 2 　Movement 1 　Movement 2	Frank Ticheli	Manhattan Beach
Chant Rituals	Elliot Del Borgo	Warner Bros.
Dreamcatcher	Walter Mays	Rental (composer)
Fantasia in F	Wolfgang Mozart	Shawnee
Four Scottish Dances 　Movement I.	Malcomb Arnold/Paynter	Carl Fischer
Jedermann	Paul Whear	Ludwig Music
New World Symphony 　"Largo"	Antonin Dvorak	Kalmus
Piece of Mind 　Movement I 　Movement III	Dana Wilson	Ludwig Music
Sea Songs	Ralph Vaughan Williams	Boosey and Hawkes
Second Suite in F 　Movement I: March	Gustav Holst	Boosey and Hawkes

Sinfonia Noblissima	Robert Jager	Elkan-Vogel
Sinfonietta	Ingolf Dahl	Broude
Movement III.		
Spectrum	Herbert W. Bielawa	Shawnee Press
Suite Divertimento	Jay Gilbert	Southern Music
Movement II. Pastorale		
Symphony No. 1	Robert Jager	Volkwein Bros.
Movement I.		
Trauermusik	Richard Wagner/Votta/Boyd	LudwigMusic

Rondo Form

Balladair	Frank Erickson	Bourne
Concerto for Twenty-Three	Walter Hartley	Accura Music, Inc.
Winds		
Movement III.		
Movement IV.		
Crown Imperial	William Walton/Duthoit	Boosey and Hawkes
Dance of the Jesters	Peter I. Tchaikovsky/	Curnow Press
	Cramer	
Fanfare and Rondo	Purcell/Gardner	Staff
Fanfare and Rondo	John Velke	Shawnee Press
Gazebo Dances for Band	John Corigliano	G. Schirmer Music
Greenwillow Portrait	Mark Williams	Alfred
Mini Suite	Morton Gould	Hal Leonard
II. "A Tender Waltz"		
Prelude and Rondo	Burnet Tuthill	Summy-Birchard
Prelude, Siciliano, and Rondo	Malcomb Arnold	Carl Fischer
I. Prelude		
II. Siciliano		
III. Rondo		
Rondo and Minuet	Wolfgang Mozart/Paulson	Mercury
Rondo for Band	Barton McLean	Shawnee Press
Rondo Giocoso	Frank Erickson	Bourne
Rondo Marziale	Arthur Frankenpohl	Shawnee
Royce Hall Suite	Healey Willan/Teague	Associated
Finale		
Sandy Bay March	Brian West	Yamaha
Second Suite in F	Gustav Holst	Boosey and Hawkes
Movement I.		
Sinfonia No. 4	Walter Hartley	Wingert-Jones
II. Adagio		

III. Vivace
IV. Allegro Molto

Symphony for Band	Vincent Persichetti	Elkan-Vogel
Symphony No. 3 "Slavyanskaya" Movement III.	Boris Kozhevnikov/ Bourgeois	Wingert-Jones
Third Suite for Band Movement III. Rondo	Robert Jager	Volkwein
Tunbridge Fair	Walter Piston	Boosey and Hawkes
With Quiet Courage	Larry Daehn	Daehn

Theme and Variation Forms

American Salute	Morton Gould	Warner Bros.
Chester Overture for Band	William Schuman	Merion
Chorale and Shaker Dance	John Zdechlik	Kjos Music
Dance Variations	John Zdelchlik	Kjos Music
Diamond Variations	Robert Jager	Volkwein
Enigma Variations	Sir Edward Elgar/Slocum	Shawnee
Fantasy on "Yankee Doodle"	Mark Williams	Alfred
Fantasy Variations on a Theme by Niccolò Pagannini	James Barnes	Southern Music
Fantasy Variations on George Gershwin's Prelude II for Piano	Donald Grantham	Warner Bros.
First Suite in E-Flat I. Chaconne	Gustav Holst	Boosey and Hawkes
Four Scottish Dances Movement II.	Malcomb Arnold/Paynter	Carl Fischer
Konzertmusik, Op. 41	Paul Hindemith	Schott Publishers
A Little French Suite Movement III.	Pierre La Plante	Bourne Publications
Masquerade for Band	Vincent Persichetti	Elkan-Vogel
Mini Suite III. "Bell Carol"	Morton Gould	Hal Leonard
Scenes from "The Louvre" II. "Childrens Gallery"	Norman Dello Joio	Hal Leonard
Surprise Symphony Movement II.	Joseph Haydn/Kiser	Hal Leonard
Symphonic Variations	Cesar Franck/Arlen	Kendor
Theme and Variations, Op. 43a	Arnold Schoenberg	Schirmer
Theme and Variations	Ludwig van Beethoven/Reed	Mills

Variants on a Medieval Tune	Norman Dello Joio	Hal Leonard
Variation Overture	Clifton Williams	Ludwig Music
Variations for Wind Band	Ralph Vaughan Williams/ Hunsberger	Boosey and Hawkes
Variations on a Hymn by Louis Bourgeois	Smith	Jenson
Variations on a Korean Folksong	John Barnes Chance	Boosey and Hawkes
Variations on a Theme by Haydn	Norman Dello Joio	Marks
Variations on a Theme by Mozart	Anne McGinty	Hal Leonard
Variations on "America" for Band	Charles Ives	Theodore Presser
Variations on "Joy to the World"	James Christensen	Kendor
Variations on "Scarborough Fair"	Calvin Custer	Hal Leonard
Variations on a Shaker Melody	Aaron Copland	Boosey and Hawkes
William Byrd Suite III. "John Come Kiss Me Now"	William Byrd/Jacob	Boosey and Hawkes
Wycliffe Variations	Paul Whear	Ludwig Music

Sonata Form (Sonata-Allegro Form)

Al Fresco	Karl Husa	Schirmer
American Overture for Band	Joseph Jenkins	Presser
Awayday	Adam Gorb	Maecenas
Concert Overture in G	Florian Mueller	Bourne
Concerto for Twenty-Three Winds Movement I.	Walter S. Hartley	Accura Music, Inc.
Dedicatory Overture	Clifton Williams	Edward Marks Music
A Downland Suite "Prelude"	John Ireland	G & M Brand Publishing
Egmont	Ludwig van Beethoven/ Winterbottom	Boosey and Hawkes
Festive Overture	Dmitri Shostakovich/ Hunsberger	MCA
Korean Folk Rhapsody	James Curnow	Hal Leonard
London Symphony	Joseph Haydn/Isaac	Belwin
Lyric Dance	Frank Bencriscutto	Shawnee
Marriage of Figaro	Wolfgang Mozart/Slocum	Mills
Minuet and Allegro Allegro	Wolfgang Mozart/Whitney	Alfred
Overture for Band Allegro Vivace	Felix Mendelssohn/Boyd	Ludwig Music

Overture in C	Charles Simon Catel/ Goldman/Smith	Mercury
Overture in C	Francois Gossec/Goldman	Mercury
Overture in Classical Style	Charles Carter	Bourne
Paradigm	Sol Berkowitz	Frank
Polly Oliver	Thomas Root	Kjos Music
Russlan and Ludmilla	Mikhail Glinka/Henning	Carl Fisher
Satiric Dances Movement III.	Norman Dello Joio	Schirmer
Sinfonietta Movement I.	Ingolf Dahl	Hal Leonard
Suite Francaise I. "Normandie" III. "Ile de France"	Darius Milhaud	Hal Leonard
Symphonie for Band	Louis E. Jadin	Shawnee Press, Inc.
Symphonie Pour Musique d'Harmonie	Paul R. Marcel Fauchet/ Gillette/Campbell-Watson	Witt Mark
Symphony in B-Flat Movement I.	Paul Hindemith	Schott Music
Symphony No. 3 I. Allegro Energico IV. Allegro con brio	Vittorio Giannini	Warner Bros.
Symphony No. 3 "Slavyanskaya" Movement I. Movement IV.	Boris Kozhevnikov/ Bourgeois	Wingert-Jones
Symphony No. 5 Movement I.	Ludwig Beethoven/Godfrey	Chappell
Symphony No. 6 Movement I.	Vincent Persichetti	Elkan-Vogel
The Tzar's Bride	Rimsky-Korsakov/Harding	Kjos Music
Third Symphony Movement I. Movement IV. (modified sonata form)	James Barnes	Southern Music
Titus Overture	Wolfgang Mozart/Moehlman	Fitz Simmons
Tocatta for Winds	Joseph Jenkins	Hal Leonard
Unfinished Symphony	Franz Schubert/Cailliet	Carl Fischer

Fugue

Symphony in B-Flat Movement III. (double fugue)	Paul Hindemith	Schott Music

Cantus Firmus and Fugue	François Couperin/Scott	Pro Art
Fughetta	John Stainer/Righter	Schmitt
Fugue a la Gigue	J.S. Bach/Holst	Boosey and Hawkes
Fugue in d minor	J.S. Bach/Moehlman	Fitz Simmons Press
Fugue in g minor	J.S. Bach/Kimura	Curnow Press
Hymn and Fuguing Tune No. 1	Henry Cowell	Belwin
Little Fugue in g minor	J.S. Bach/Boyd	Cole
Passacaglia and Fugue in c minor	J.S. Bach/Hunsberger	Schirmer
Passacaglia and Fugue in c minor	J.S. Bach/Falcone	Southern Press
Prelude and Fugue	Vaclav Nelhybel	Frank Press
Prelude and Fugue in b-flat minor	J.S. Bach/Moehlman	Fitz Simmons
Prelude and Fugue in b-flat minor	J.S. Bach/Moehlmann	Warner Bros.
Prelude and Fugue in f minor	J.S. Bach/Moehlman	FitzSimmons
Prelude and Fugue in f minor	Houston Bright	Shawnee Press
Prelude and Fugue in g minor	J.S. Bach/Moehlman	FitzSimmons Press
Tocatta and Fugue in d minor	J.S. Bach/Leidzen	Carl Fischer
Variations and Fugue	Vittorio Giannini	Columbo

Ostinato Forms

Caucasian Passacaglia	Vaclav Nelhybel	G. Schirmer
Chaconne with Four Variations	Marcel Frank	Fox
Chaconne	Henry Purcell/Gardner	Staff
First Suite in E-Flat I. "Chaconne" (passacaglia form)	Gustav Holst	Boosey and Hawkes
Fourth Symphony Finale	Johannes Brahms/Foote	Kendor
La Fiesta Mexicana "Mass"	H. Owen Reed	Summy Birchard
Passacaglia	Alfred Reed	Frank
Passacaglia	Cyril Scott/Leist	Galaxy
Passacaglia and Fugue	Harold Johnson	Carl Fischer
Passacaglia and Fugue in c minor	J.S. Bach/Hunsberger	G. Schirmer
Passacaglia (Homage on B-A-C-H)	Ron Nelson	Ludwig Music
Passacaglia in c minor	J.S. Bach/Chidester	Belwin-Mills
Passacaglia in E-Flat	Marcel Frank	Bourne
Passacaglia in g minor	Houston Bright	Shawnee
A Solemn Music (passacaglia)	Virgil Thomson	G. Schirmer Music

Notes

1   Consortium of National Arts Associations. *National Standards for Arts Education - What Every American Should Know and Be Able to Do in the Arts*. Reston, VA: Music Educators National Conference, 1994, 59.

2   Joseph A. Labuta. *Teaching Musicianship in the High School Band*. Ft. Lauderdale, FL: Meredith Music Publications, Revised, 1997, 80.

3   Consortium of National Arts Associations. *National Standards for Arts Education*, 42.

4   Ibid., 61.

5   Ibid., 44.

6   Douglas M. Green. *Form in Tonal Music*. Second Edition. Orlando, FL: Harcourt Brace & Company, 1993, 4-5.

7   William Apel. *Harvard Dictionary of Music*. Second Edition, Revised. Cambridge, MA: The Belknap Press of Harvard University Press, 327-328.

8   Douglas M. Green. *Form in Tonal Music*. Second Edition. Orlando, FL: Harcourt Brace & Company, 1993, 73.

9   Ibid., 74.

10 Ibid., 74.

11 Ibid.

12 Ibid., 93-94.

13 Labuta, 84.

14 Connie M. Ericksen. *Band Director's Curriculum Resource*. West Nyack, NY: Parker Publishing Company, 1998, 175-176.

15 Apel, 327-328.

16 Ibid., 93.

17 Ibid.

18 Ibid.

19 Ibid., 76.

20 Ibid., 78-79, 93.

21 Ibid., 81.

22 Ericksen, 178.

23 Spring and Hutcheson, 98.

24 Labuta, 90.

25 Ellis B. Kohs. *Musical Form: Studies in Analysis and Synthesis*. Boston: Houghton Mifflin Company, 1976, 107.

26 Ericksen, 181.

27 Labuta, 90.

28 Peggy Klein Morton, *Harmony, Form and Expression*. St. Louis: McDonald Publishing Company, Inc., 1990, 13.

29 Labuta, 90.

30 Apel, 740.

31 Green, 232, 233.

32 Green, 99.

33 Kohs, 141.

34 Green, 98.

35 Labuta, 91.

36 Green, 101.

37 Ericksen, 192.

38 Apel, 141-142.

39 Labuta, 93.

40 Green, 218.

41 Kohs, 177.

42 Labuta, 97.

43 "Summary Statement," *National Standards for Arts Education*. Reston, VA: Music Educators National Conference, 1994, 5-6.

CHAPTER 5

Fervor, Focus, Flow, and Feeling: "Making an Emotional Connection"

Eugene Migliaro Corporon

Fervor and Creativity

As I begin my thirtieth year of teaching, I have come to realize how fascinated I am with the musical learning process in all of its manifestations, especially rehearsing and performing. All of the elements of musicing are in and of themselves intriguing, but the one that holds the most interest for me is the day-in and day-out metamorphosis that the artwork and the musicers go through as their interaction grows to maturity. From the outset it is important to acknowledge that great musicing can happen anywhere and at any time. For this to transpire, it is crucial that the musicians feel, first and foremost, a sense of *fervor* from the conductor/teacher. The performers must be convinced that the leader deeply believes in all aspects of the interaction: the composer, the music, the musicians, and the value of the experience. There should be no room for doubt in the minds of the musicers that the conductor is taken over by the feelings and values found in the work of art. While it would be wonderful if all of our musical successes came in the presence of witnesses, it is well known that that doesn't always happen. I believe that we should be appreciative of any emotionally fulfilling moment that evolves in the process wherever and whenever it appears. The fact that those moments don't materialize in front of an audience makes them no less valuable or meaningful. Being fervent about the music implies having great passion for what we do and being consumed while we are doing it. This is not possible unless we have great respect for and emotional connection with the music. As a conductor/teacher, it's not enough to identify and experience the emotion yourself; you must also be able to transmit it to others.

In addition to fervor, a crucial catalyst in the process is *creativity*. The entire issue of creativity has been profoundly explored by Mihaly

81

Csikszentmihalyi in his book entitled *Creativity*. There is much to be learned by a careful study of his work. Creativity is an illusive concept that defies definition; it does, however, reveal itself through observation and evaluation. One thing is certain: *without creativity, true musicing cannot proceed.* Perhaps the greatest challenge one faces while musicing is to avoid being lured into mindless, repetitive drill in order to attain technical mastery. While technique is required to achieve expressive and creative performances, pursuing technique for its own sake often erects effective barriers which prevent creativity and expression from ever getting through. Technique must have a musical purpose and be approached through creative expression. In the relentless pursuit of perfection, we must not forget to be inventively creative about telling the stories and portraying the emotions that are contained in the work of art.

To develop an environment that fosters and promotes creativity, we must come to understand not only what we think but, most importantly, how we feel. We must inject the thinking and feeling aspects of ourselves into the music throughout the course of the musical process. We must feel the music before we can become advocates for the music. To remain creative, we must be willing to live "forever in the question" and not become content with finding one – and only one – answer. Remaining open to all the musical possibilities that a great work offers is essential. It is important to understand and accept that the current reality of a piece, no matter how well founded, will become obsolete. Each new performance of a work redefines the meaning of that work and presents new opportunities for creative exploration. Our success is dependent upon three conditions that are constantly interacting: *intellect, intuition,* and *insight.*

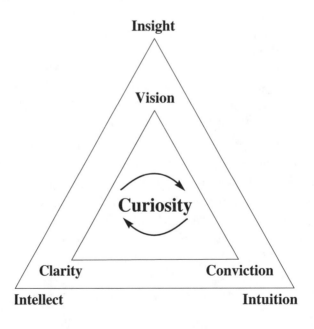

Intellect is a condition of the conscious mind, while *intuition* is a condition of the subconscious mind. *Insight* leads to musical ideas, actions, and feelings that are new and deemed valuable. *Curiosity* drives the process like a rotary engine. The goal of creativity is clearly to amplify and expand human potential. Music is the embodiment and expression of our humanity in sound. It brings richness and meaning to our lives especially when intellect and intuition lead to new insights. Mihaly Csikszentmihalyi tells us that a truly creative act changes or adds to some part of the culture. A creative idea must also be understandable to others. He says:

> "Creativity occurs when a person using the symbols of a given domain has a new idea or sees a new pattern that is acknowledged and accepted by the field who decide that the idea should be included in the domain or discipline."

He concludes that creativity is the result of a system that contains, first, the individual performing the creative act (the musicer); second, the domain or discipline (music); and third, the field, others in the discipline who act as gatekeepers or "evaluators" of proposed creative ideas (colleagues and critics). This leads us to criticism.

Surprisingly, an important component of creativity is criticism. If one is to grow professionally and personally, one must be prepared to submit his or her work to intense scrutiny. For me, this can best be illustrated through the process of a recording session. Following several weeks of careful preparation, a production team of at least six people, led by a big-eared producer, show up with scores in hand to listen critically to every musical move that is made. In addition to detecting error, their charge is to discover possibilities that may have been missed or to challenge musical decisions when they see other options that they believe represent better choices. On occasion I find myself having to defend a position. In that moment I must rely on my intellect, intuition, and insight to decide whether to hold my ground or follow a newly offered and potentially better path. In these collaborative tests of will, my *clarity*, *conviction*, and *vision* help me to make what I perceive to be the best possible choice for the composer, the work, the project, and the ensemble.

One of the wonderful things about the recording environment is that you can explore a new idea instantaneously and incorporate it on the spot if deemed appropriate. A recording production team is akin to the world's most watchful festival evaluation panel with one big difference: the team has a vested interest in the outcome. They are, in effect, co-conspirators in the process. They share the responsibility for the end product and, therefore, become an integral part of the creative act.

As the recording sessions proceed, the conductor and ensemble have the opportunity to pursue a variety of emotions, concepts, and suggestions as time

and patience permit. Rehearsing and performing are both crucial components of recording. What is wonderful about the experience is that you have the opportunity to take a Polaroid of the choices that are made, an aural photo of the very instant when you say, "There, that's it, that's exactly what we want." As a snapshot or documentation of a very specific point in time, the recording does not permanently eliminate all other possibilities that are not on the tape or in the picture. It simply allows one to capture a perfected moment, or thought, or feeling – one of several that may have equal merit.

Exposing emotion and meaning while experiencing value is the goal of a creative musicing process. This goal cannot be reached without music that embodies these three essential qualities: *emotion, meaning,* and *value.* Programming is one of the most crucial and delicate issues that we face. There are instances when we are tempted to choose music because of its *impressive* qualities rather than because of its *expressive* qualities. Expressive value must be the overriding qualifier for the choices we make if we are to contribute to the musical well-being of the ensemble and, most importantly, to the individuals within it. Playing quality music is the only way to add to the complexity of the musicians and to develop more complete musicers. By the way, it's not enough to play "good music"; one must select a workable program that is diverse and suits the ensemble in order to achieve success. Undoubtedly, performing and listening to music of substance builds character and elevates the human experience. Playing great music exposes the musicers and listeners to great minds. A well-structured interaction allows one to develop more sensitive and interesting human beings. To accomplish this, a great conductor/teacher must:

1. Choose appropriate and substantive music.
2. Set clear goals.
3. Inspire action.
4. Give positive feedback.
5. Acknowledge accomplishment.
6. Strengthen the self-worth of the musicians.
7. Nourish creativity and encourage individuality.

There is no doubt that musicing can lead to growth of the self and has the power to develop and increase self-awareness and self-esteem in the musicers. For this to happen, we must make our teaching electrostatic, charged with energy, ideas, and emotions. The musicians must be convinced that the activity is worth their investment of psychic and physical energy. They must become engaged and enrolled in order to grow.

Creativity often results when we value the quality of the experience over the perfection of the performance. The ability to set clear and attainable goals gives purpose to our actions. Any great musicing that I have been a part of as participant or observer balanced *activity* with *reflection*. Focusing the musicers' attention through the prudent use of these two endeavors will yield great achievement. The chart below illustrates steps we can follow to stay connected during the reflective moments.

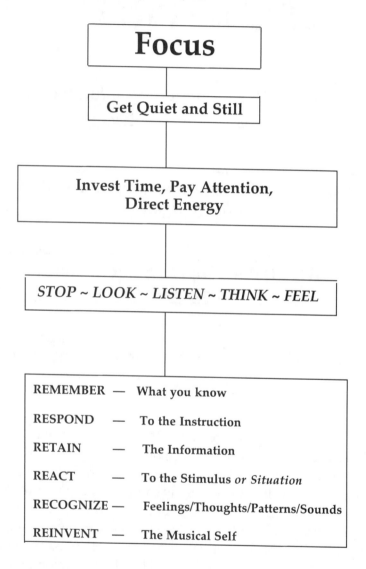

Undoubtedly, a key component of creativity is growth! We live in the "Age of Information." Just about anyone has access through personal computers to more information than can be digested in numerous lifetimes. Simply possessing the information does not guarantee it will be used effectively. In fact, we sometimes mistake having the information with being able to apply it creatively. I conceive of growth as being the result of four stages of interaction: (1) "acquiring" information through research increases *awareness*; (2) "internalizing" information through study produces *knowledge*; (3)

"applying" information through experience yields *wisdom*; and (4) "contributing" information through ingenuity creates *revelation*.

GROWTH!!!

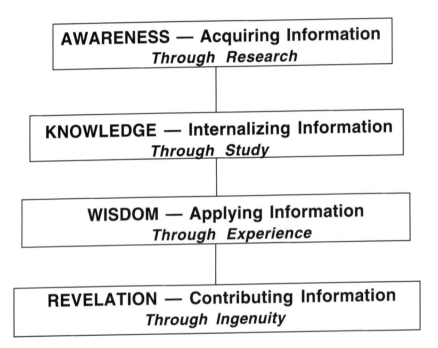

AWARENESS — Acquiring Information
Through Research

KNOWLEDGE — Internalizing Information
Through Study

WISDOM — Applying Information
Through Experience

REVELATION — Contributing Information
Through Ingenuity

I am not convinced that creativity can be passed from one person to another. Nonetheless, we do have a responsibility to set up the conditions which allow creativity to develop within each person. While we may not be able to teach creativity directly, we surely can guide people to their intuitive, creative selves. Creativity is something one discovers from within. It seems to work from the inside out and be evaluated from the outside in. When we encourage someone to think creatively, we are in fact giving them permission to be original, to do one-of-a-kind things. Therefore, developing individuality should be a primary goal of musicing. It is imperative to realize that we are not just responsible for teaching our musicians what to do. We must be sure to teach them how to make musical decisions for themselves. Great musicing begins with unique individual contributions.

The conductor/teacher lives in the duality of complete knowing and complete unknowing. Creative music making requires ideas and plans. It is equally important to allow discovery and invention to interact with and influence those ideas and plans.

Admittedly, reason and order are important; however, one must be careful not to pursue these ideals to the exclusion of everything else. It is paramount to follow the mysteries contained in the work as well. A composition seeks to create a mystical journey that takes the listeners somewhere they did not expect to go. A condition of great musicing is that nobody, not even the composer, really knows where that journey is going to lead or what will happen as a result of the trip. It is the unexpected events along the way that make musicing one of life's great adventures.

Optimal Experience and the Inner Game of Music

In recent years, the work of Mihaly Csikszentmihalyi and Barry Green have influenced me greatly. Their theories of *Optimal Experience* and the *Inner Game of Music*, respectively, have helped me solidify my approach to studying, rehearsing, and performing music. While explaining his ideas of optimal experience, Mihaly Csikszentmihalyi says:

"The best moments in our lives usually occur when a person's body or mind (or both) is stretched to its limits in a voluntary effort to accomplish something difficult and worthwhile."

Is this not a perfect description of musicing at its best? It seems clear that the most memorable musical moments are not made up of passive, inactive, or relaxing times. Optimal experiences in our musicing require insight, intuition, intent, interaction, and intelligence. Creating memorable experiences for ourselves and others is not something we can leave to chance. We must develop a blueprint for action! We have to become aware of the process and learn to manage the various stages which contribute to achieving our goals. It goes without saying that we must gain a sense of mastery in our discipline in order to determine the content and quality of our musical lives. Mastery, however, is not enough. We need a philosophical foundation, a well-developed thought process which allows us to proceed knowingly, thoughtfully, and with feeling. If we are to guide others to optimal musicing, we must be able to create experiences that involve structured challenge and lead all involved to serious fun.

We are in the business of developing bodies, minds, and spirits through the use of action, memory, and emotion. The body takes action, the mind creates memory, and the spirit is revealed through our emotions. It is clear that the act of musicing brings people joy and a sense of purpose. Spending your life's energy in pursuit of an ideal greater than yourself and developing personal dedication to a discipline far grander than any self is a sure way of designing musical lives worth living. We must be willing to give ourselves over

and let go to the power of the music. Pursuing our art for its own sake allows music to function as an end in itself rather than being used as a means to an end. I am convinced that these ideas are integral to developing honesty, creativity, and expressiveness in one's musicing.

If achieving the optimal musical experience is a philosophical ideal, then the Inner Game of Music could well be the best and most pragmatic approach to that ideal. The Inner Game provides the pedagogical tools to help us build the optimal musical experience. In its most fundamental sense, the Inner Game seeks to have our achievement be equal to our potential. An additional aim of the Inner Game is to create the optimal musical or emotional experience while eliminating anything and everything that restricts or blocks that goal. The four basic elements of the Inner Game – *will*, *awareness*, *trust*, and *potential* – align themselves surprisingly well with the four basic elements of optimal experience – *attention*, *focus*, *flow*, and *expression*. If you begin the process with *will* and follow the elements one after the other as they interact you can, I believe, create a successful growth system which connects the two approaches in a seamless and consistent manner. These combined systems not only encourage but allow creativity and expression to emerge.

In this chapter I will explore the synergy that exists between these two dynamic disciplines and offer some thoughts which may help conductors/teachers achieve greater levels of expression in their musicing and teaching. I believe that there are strong parallels between these two systems of observation and that both theories are accurately descriptive of what is occurring during the creative process we call musicing. A flow chart follows, which will function as an overview of this proposed comparison. I will deal with the ideas in pairs, traversing the ideological terrain from left to right.

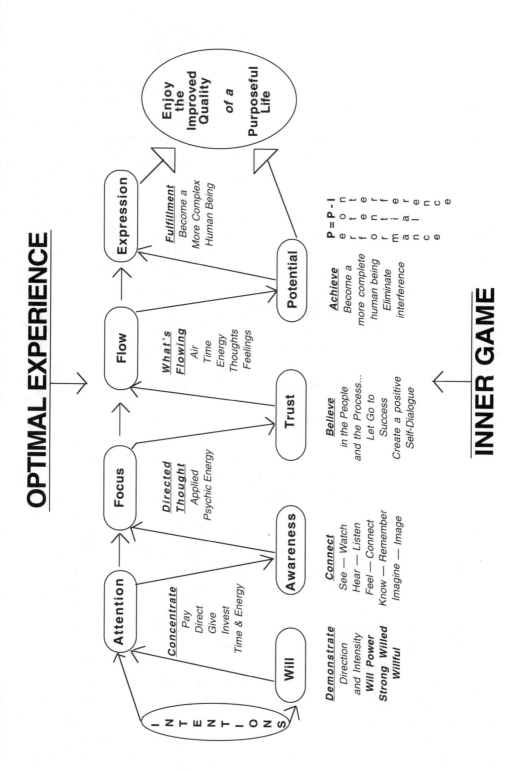

Will and Attention

At the outset of our sojourn, it must be assumed that everyone has the best of intentions as well as the desire to participate and contribute. No one comes to the process intending to fail or interfere. The challenge we face is to turn good intentions into tangible results. The most important factor in ensuring a successful journey is *will*. *Will* refers to *the determination of the individual to succeed*. Commitment is the result of will. The presence of will allows us to take action and achieve. *Will* is defined by Barry Green as "the direction and intensity of your intent." This definition infers that you intend to accomplish something substantive and significant and that you are directing energy towards that goal. We often assign strength to those who exhibit will. We speak of them as being strong willed or willful and admire their will power. It is the energy created by exerting our will that commands attention in others and allows one to concentrate and excel. Will is the driving force behind our intentions that creates accomplishment through action. Determination is a by-product of will and allows us to direct our psychic energy or intensified thought towards the task at hand whether it be studying, practicing, rehearsing, or performing. Once our will has been engaged and is well directed, we are able to move forward, build momentum, and turn our thoughts toward attention.

Attention requires intention. If we are going to succeed, we must capture the attention of the musicers. Every musician has the same three things to contribute to the process: their time, energy, and attention. Often we ask musicians to "pay attention," "direct their attention," or "give us their attention." All of these requests are about getting the musicians to concentrate on and contribute to the project. Being attentive implies being open to the possibility of interaction and being willing to exert effort to create and be a part of an environment filled with success. Making a difference requires complete and undivided attention. It is impossible to be an active and contributing participant when musicing without paying attention and taking action. If you don't have the musicians' attention, it is pointless to proceed until you do.

The performers and conductor/teacher must come to understand that the process provides unlimited opportunities to act upon their good intentions. The musicers must treat every interaction as though it were an audition, an opportunity to demonstrate their level of preparation and depth of commitment. Musicing provides all involved multiple chances to "live their word." Musicers must demonstrate that they are willing to give their time, energy, and attention. There is real power in the concept of these three elements working together, for the good of the composer, the work of art, and each other. In the theory of optimal experience, developing attention or the ability to concentrate is a key ingredient to success. So, too, in music. The goal when musicing must always be to create the optimal emotional experience.

Musicians have long known that this is impossible without concentration. Concentration infers being completely conscious of and present to sights, sounds, and sensations as well as thoughts, feelings, and images.

For the conductor/teacher, the ability to organize information is key. Thoughts must follow one another in a logical progression. Organized thought is a prerequisite to a productive process. It is most important to bring order and logic to bear while still leaving room for expression and creativity to emerge. Great musicing is about revealing expression through ordered thought. Even though consciousness is infinitely expandable, there are human limits to the amount of information that can be comprehended in one sitting. The skilled teacher/conductor has a real sense of how much information to offer at any particular point in time. For example, style is created in a work by matching events in the music to an already known and accepted class of events which define a particular practice and reveal existing traditions. With the proper amount of study and experience, we are able to identify, evaluate, and classify the incoming information. Once the information is collected and compared to our imaged ideal, it becomes painfully clear that our choices and changes can't be disseminated all at once, especially if we are to maintain a balance between activity and reflection. If we overload a musician's circuits with too much information packed into too small a time frame, the breaker switches in the mind automatically shut the process down.

I believe it is attention that allows us to select and prioritize the relevant bits of information that should be incorporated into our performance from the potential millions of bits that are available. Attention allows us to retrieve information, compare information, evaluate information, and decide which information is appropriate and most meaningful. We must develop the ability in ourselves as well as in our ensembles to focus attention at will, to be oblivious to distraction, and to concentrate singularly and completely. Attention allows us to order consciousness and to put it in the service of our emotional goals. The quality of the experience is totally dependent upon our ability to exert our will, invest energy, command attention, and focus concentration.

Concentration allows us to develop consistency in the performance and to collectively adhere to our stylistic decisions. If we can get control of the experience through directing, giving, and paying attention, we can impact the situation for the better. By exerting and focusing our psychic energy, we can eliminate psychic disorder which includes things like fear, tension, anxiety, guilt, and anger. All of these negative feelings do nothing more than divert attention away from the true purpose of the interaction: connecting with the music and the people who are experiencing it.

Awareness and Focus

Assuming that we have been successful at engaging *will* to create *attention* and have established a high level of *concentration*, we can move ahead to the next pair of objectives: *awareness* and *focus*. It is through our awareness that we create focus. Awareness is developed and deepened by monitoring and paying attention to what we see, hear, feel, know, and imagine. Literally every instruction we give or follow during the course of the process comes from one of these five sub-skills of awareness. We ask people to watch, listen, connect, remember, and image as we work to broaden their sphere of awareness and direct their thoughts toward the goals. It is most important to understand that directed thought or psychic energy sustains physical energy. Being engaged helps one to transcend time and fight fatigue. It is not enough to develop attention; we must also be able to apply our psychic energy in very detailed and precise ways.

The goal is to develop the ability in ourselves and others to use attention to zero in on one element of the music at a time. Being able to pay specific attention to a single issue, no matter how minute, until it is just the way it needs to be is a necessary skill for someone intending to accomplish great things in rehearsal and performance. Great musicers are able to focus attention at will and eliminate interference. It becomes impossible to distract them from their goal. To solve a single problem, you must be able to ignore many other problems. It is important to prioritize problems and to develop the ability to distinguish between those problems that need immediate attention and those that will be taken care of by the musicians. Given the opportunity, the performers can and should solve many issues on their own. My greatest success comes when I deal with one issue at a time, understand that all problems can be dealt with in due time, and encourage and allow the other musicers to collaborate in the problem solving.

When focused, we are able to retrieve information, access ideas, compare sounds, evaluate feelings, and make decisions about what is relevant. Achieving a state of *focus* allows us to make exciting and memorable choices that create lasting solutions which reveal emotion and meaning in the music. When focused, we are able to impact the quality of the experience. Focus allows us to control and direct consciousness and put it in the service of our goals. We must make every individual in the ensemble acutely aware of the partnership and sub-skills I have been discussing. The more focused we become the more likely we are to release the spirit of the composer from the page and connect with the emotions stimulated by the work. Those who are able to become one with the composer's intentions and emotions are using their *will* to direct *attention*, increase *awareness*, and bring the composition into *focus*.

Trust and Flow

The next set of objectives are very difficult to separate because each is actually a condition of the other. It is important to introduce *trust* into the process and to let go to the success that trust fosters. Trust can only occur in a positive setting. The musicers must be able to trust the conductor/teacher as well as each other with their feelings. Everyone is responsible for creating an environment which nurtures trust. Trust is something that evolves. It is something that grows slowly and takes time to develop. You cannot demand trust; you must earn it. Patience is an important factor in this process. All of the musicians must feel that, as the leader, you are willing to do whatever it takes for as long as it takes to ensure that they experience positive success. You have to put your trust in something, and very often it is one another. When trust is high, musicians are willing to take chances. Being willing to put one's self at risk usually results in greater spontaneity, and spontaneity is a key condition of creative expression. We must learn to trust in our own ability and in the ability of others.

As an ensemble member, it is important to understand that no single musicer can ensure success, but any single musicer can prevent the group from experiencing total success. One of the mystical things about musicing is that the collective has far greater power and is able to accomplish much more than any single individual within it. Time and again ensembles rise to heights of achievement that don't seem attainable. Trust makes it possible for the impact of the whole to be greater than the sum of its parts. The conductor/teacher, the composer, the work of art, and the musicians all share the responsibility for creating an atmosphere of trust. Confidence and humor are often by-products of trust. (To return to the recording analogy for just a moment, it is interesting and revealing to note that the best takes almost always follow praise or laughter.)

Flow is a word used in almost every discipline when describing an event that is naturally purposeful and has direction. As musicians we often use the term to describe a condition of effortlessness and timelessness. In this state things seem just right and absolutely everything works. We can do no wrong. It's fair to ask, what's flowing? While I have no scientific proof, my personal experience has revealed that what's flowing is psychic energy. The energy I am speaking of is full of feeling, purpose, thought, and direction. It is not to be mistaken for an uncontrollable burst of energy, which is very well meaning but most often too diffuse to have much impact on the target. One must learn to develop the ability to use beams of energy in very subtle ways. It is energy that connects the various and diverse moments in music into a seamless and cohesive whole. A work is literally welded together with energy. The amount of energy needed to make the connections varies. At times it must be applied sparingly, while in other instances it takes every bit that you can muster. In any event, energy is a required component of flow. According to Mihaly

Csikszentmihalyi, there are eight major conditions of flow. I have paraphrased them below. These are very familiar to musicians. In fact, they are very descriptive of a well-structured musicing process.

1. Confront a task you have a chance of completing.
       (Select the right music.)
2. Concentrate on what you are doing.
       (Employ will, attention, awareness, and focus.)
3. Provide clear goals.
       (Know and communicate what you want to
       accomplish.)
4. Provide opportunity for immediate feedback.
       (Use equal amounts of positive criticism
       and sincere praise.)
5. Operate with a deep but effortless involvement that
    removes the worries and frustrations of everyday life from your
    awareness.
       (Let go to trust. Play the Inner Game.)
6. Create an enjoyable experience which allows people to
    exercise a sense of control over their actions.
       (Be a good teacher.)
7. Let concern for the self disappear and a better sense of self
    emerge following the flow experience. Improve self-esteem.
       (Be a great teacher!)
8. Alter the sense of time.
       (Transcend the moment.)

Mihaly Csikszentmihalyi believes quality experiences can be achieved by allowing *flow* to guide the way. Barry Green believes that using the skills of *awareness*, *will*, and *trust* will allow us to fulfill 100 percent of our potential and achieve our expressive goals. The concepts below are descriptive of what we admire in a great teacher and can serve as a guide to successful musicing for the novice as well as for the most experienced.

1. Develop realistic and achievable goals for your ensembles.
2. Bring order and direction to the process.
3. Get individuals to invest their time, energy, and attention.
4. Overcome seemingly insurmountable challenges with well-
    directed energy.
5. Pursue what you do for its own sake.
6. Create a meaningful pattern out of the experience.
7. Control consciousness so that you may exert influence over the
    quality of the experience.

Potential and Expression

The sounds of music are, for all intents and purposes, invisible. As David Whitwell points out in his book, The Art of Conducting, "music is the only art you cannot see." I like to think of music as a sort of perpetual mobile made up of feelings, thoughts, and energy that moves too fast to be seen. The expressive movements we create in space, our "designs in the nowhere" as Frank Zappa called them, portray the constantly changing perspectives and relationships of those three elements. In fact, we can make the invisible quite visible by incorporating the emotions we experience as well as the ideas we have into the motions we make. The symbols of music are put down on the page in black and white. When musicing, you don't see the color; you hear the color. Imagination plays an integral role in conceptualizing the colorization of the aural work of art. The conductor must learn to use movement and space in a myriad of ways in order to realize their imaged timbral and stylistic concepts.

Music has been called the language of emotions. The conductor's movement creates the visual syntax within that language and is what connects the musicers' and listeners' emotions to the sounds and symbols. In addition to aural memory, musicers must experience the music as physical memory if their work is to become consistent and have impact. Our movement must be instinctively expressive. We must develop a tactile sense of where the sounds are located in the space in front of us and how the music feels in the muscles in order to sculpt sound in space. Several other refining elements, which include *shape*, *direction*, *emphasis*, and *scoring* as well as *balance*, *blend*, and *clarity*, can be revealed through our kinesthetic space forming.

I have been present at numerous performances led by master pedagogues who had accomplished a great deal but had not yet fulfilled their own or the group's expressive potential. In fact, their worst nightmare had come to pass.... They had become the last and only obstacle between the musicers and their ability to play expressively. Their lack of skill in providing the visual syntax was failing their ensemble. They could verbally describe what they wanted when stopped, but because the performance takes place in a moving silence that does not allow for simultaneous verbal description, they were ineffective in leading the music making at the exact moment of inception when it mattered most! It is somewhat ironic but true nonetheless: conducting is a silent art. Not having the facility to show how the music should sound eliminates the ability to be spontaneous, and that indirectly stifles the emotive character of the music.

A primary role of the conductor is to make the performers' jobs easier; another is to help all involved access their emotions. Conductors should be facilitators of feeling and execution, as well as revealers of emotion. It is possible for conductors to create interference in this process no matter how well meaning they may be. To keep this from happening, our technical and expressive skills need to be as developed as our players' skills. It is unfair and

unreasonable to expect our musicians to be more artistic and expressive than we are. We must realize that telling them how to play the piece isn't enough. If words could aptly describe music, there would be no need for music. Great artistry involves being able to show how the music goes as it is unfolding. Music happens in the present. It is about what's going on right now! It can't be about what should happen, what could happen, or what might happen.

Musicing puts one as close to the act of creation as one can get. What I am speaking of here is the primary difference between coaching and conducting. Coaching, of course, has its place and is completely appropriate as the primary method of instruction if we plan to send the musicians out on stage without a conductor. You cannot stand in front of an ensemble and move without having impact on their playing! There is no neutrality; your skill level will determine whether that impact will be positive or negative. Verbal instruction can help others to find the way on their own. However, if one is going to participate visually at the exact moment of recreation, one must develop the facility to become an equal partner in the music making. The consummate conductor/teacher is a composite of three important facets, all of which contribute to success.

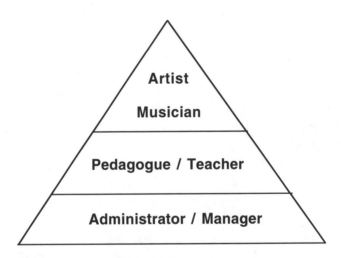

All too often we continue to grow as administrators and teachers without looking after the key ingredient that leads to expression...our artistry. I have placed the artist musician at the top of the pyramid because I believe it is the most important factor in discovering and transmitting expressiveness. While our work is much more broad based when all three skills are in place, you will notice that the artist musician part of the diagram remains complete as a pyramid even if extracted from the larger pyramid. There are countless examples of great musicians who are not gifted as teachers or administrators who still have incredible impact when musicing. Management and teaching skills contribute to our success; however, when it comes to conducting there can be no doubt that action truly does speak louder than words. The ability to *show* what you mean and feel – not just *say* what you mean and feel – is paramount in communicating musical expressiveness. In this "age of musical diversity," the gestures must be as spontaneous and varied as the sounds. An artist conductor is *part coach*, developing attention and focus so the players can achieve; *part director*, making sense of the symbols and their story; and *part choreographer*, designing motion and stillness using time, space, distance, speed, and resistance in a way that is both expressive and helpful. It is impossible to "explain" or "administrate" a piece totally and completely into existence. Music is much too spontaneous for that. When you speak about music, you are "talking music" not "making music." Through gesture we depict the sounds and their meaning in advance of their appearance. An artistic conductor remains pro-active throughout the process and avoids becoming reactive as much as possible. Great conductors in action are able to predict the future with their motions as they time travel through the work.

We must establish a sense of flow to achieve our goals. For me, the true purpose of conducting is to help others fulfill their expressive potential as they capture and reveal the composer's soul. The theories of the Optimal Experience and the Inner Game converge on this essential issue. Additionally, if our achievement is to be equal to our potential, we must do all that we can to eliminate internal and external interference. A great place to start is with the interferences that we ourselves create. Ultimately our goal should be to improve the quality of the human experience by developing lives filled with feeling and purpose through performance in band.

The artist conductor is a conduit through which creative energy and spontaneous expression flows. We must conduct with compelling conviction in order to project the truth that is in the music. To do this, we create a balance between respect for the composer's ideas and freedom of expression. It is just not enough to be competent; we must become contagious. Expressiveness is an elusive component of that condition. We cannot infect people without it. In the absence of expressiveness the music becomes meaningless; with too much, the composer's ideal can be buried in exhibitionism.

There are a number of factors we must pay attention to in order to improve our ability to be "responsible expressionists." *Shape, direction, emphasis,* and *scoring* are among the most important. *Shape* deals with the vertical aspects of music, the rise and fall of the line created by phrase and melodic contour. *Direction* deals with the horizontal aspects of music, the expansion and contraction created by moving toward or away from perceived or implied goals. *Emphasis* deals with the sagittal aspects of music, the weight and stress of the various moments of impact. *Scoring* deals with the diagonal textures and layers of activity that are created by instrument choices which are integral to the colorization of the music. All of the elements above contribute significantly to the experience and help us understand the structure and

architecture as well as the form and function of the sounds. Paying close attention to these factors helps us discover where, when, and how to attach our feelings to the music.

Three additional conditions which must be present to ensure our connection are *balance*, *blend*, and *clarity*. *Balance* refers to adjustments of volume which make it possible to hear all of the ideas that are present. *Blend* refers to adjustments of timbre which facilitate the combining and mixing of individual sounds into new instrument hybrids. *Clarity* refers to establishing transparent textures which allow the ear to hear absolutely everything that the eye sees in the score.

Expressive Elements

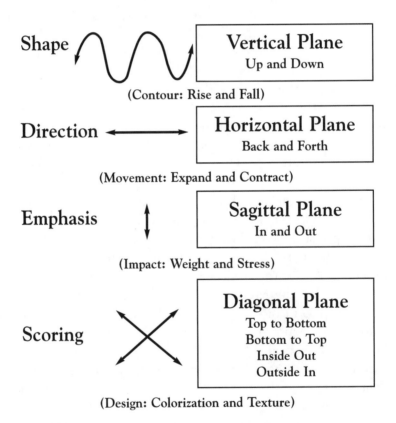

Another group of factors that amplify the expressive qualities of a work are *suspense*, *transformation*, and *journey*. An important aspect of holding the listener's attention is *suspense*. Suspense creates expectation and keeps the listener engaged in the process. Anticipation is the result of not knowing what comes next. The magic in the music is very often revealed by the illusive *transformation* that a work seems to go through as it unfolds. Transformation quite often leads to surprise. The written symbols remain the same for all time, but the expressive values found in great music allow for the implied meanings to shift and be perceived differently. When one experiences expressive music making, there is always a sense of *journey*. You feel as though you have been transported from where you were to someplace new. In music very often the journey is just as interesting (if not more so) than the destination. In other words, it's not where you ended up, but how you got there.

We don't always understand these expressive qualities in a piece of music right away. Not being able to understand a composition upon first hearing may not be a negative. It may, in fact, be a virtue of the work, for it compels one to listen deeply and repeatedly to discover emotion and meaning. Before one can truly know a piece, one must perform the piece. There is an ancient Chinese proverb:

> I Hear and I Forget.
> I See and I Understand.
> I Do and I Remember.

The process of learning a work often begins with listening to it. What follows next involves a great deal of looking at the symbols to determine the implied meaning behind them. The final stage requires physical interaction or doing to assume ownership.

To achieve expressive performances, the conductor must also be sure the musicians have multiple opportunities to hear, see and, most importantly, do. Every rehearsal and performance presents opportunities for action. The challenge, of course, must be equal to the capabilities of the players. Great musicing is about experiencing the expressive qualities of the music every time we recreate the work.

When we play with expression, it is important to understand what's being expressed...memories of feelings and ideas. Music functions as a memory activator and an emotion stimulator. When musicing, we rely heavily on memory and recollection. We draw upon our past experiences to make a connection to the work. Life experiences therefore become very important in the music making process. Paul Hindemith offers some wonderful insight regarding this issue in his book, *A Composer's World*. He says,

> "Music does not express feelings but merely releases images of feelings. It is only with the memory of feelings in our mind that we can have any feeling like reaction caused by music. The reactions music evokes are not feelings, but they are the images, memories of feelings."

Hindemith believes "it is impossible to keep music from uncovering the memory of former feelings" and "if music did not instigate us to supply memories of feelings kept in the storage rooms of our mind, it would remain meaningless." I believe this premise is one of the clearest explanations of emotion and meaning that I have read. It explains a great deal about the individual responses we have to music. Because each listener brings his or her own feelings and life experiences to the interaction, the impact of a given work will vary with each and every individual perceiving it. Making an expressive connection requires creativity which leads to invention. Above all, one must be willing to be patient and do the work that allows revelation to occur. I have found great wisdom and guidance in the words of Confucius regarding the expressive qualities of music.

> "Music rises from the human heart when the human heart is touched by the external world. When touched by the external world, the heart is moved, and therefore finds its expression in sounds. These sounds echo, or combine with one another and produce a rich variety....
>
> ...Therefore when the heart's chord of sorrow is touched, the sounds produced are somber and forlorn; when the heart's chord of satisfaction is touched, the sounds produced are (languorous) and slow; when the chord of joy is touched, the sounds produced are glowing and expansive; when the chord of anger is touched, the sounds are harsh and strong; when the chord of piety is touched, the sounds produced are simple and pure, and when the chord of love is touched, the sounds produced are sweet and gentle...."

Confucius suggests that human nature is made up of seven emotions – joy, anger, sorrow, fear, love, hate, and desire – all of which do not have to be learned because they are natural instincts common to all humans. While we have come to understand that emotions are very complex and much more varied than those offered by Confucius, imagine how effective and affective our work would be if we simply followed our natural instincts and incorporated these seven basic emotions into our musicing on a daily basis. Consider the impact the music would have if we allowed the music to "rise from the human heart." The concept appears quite obvious; nonetheless it is critical to identify the emotion that the music invokes and not hesitate to express it.

Musicians are truly magicians who translate messages from the past, some ancient and some more recent. The encrypted mysterious symbols we call *notation* contain the memories, thoughts, and feelings of peoples, cultures, and civilizations. This miracle translation is accomplished with the help of decoder mechanisms, better known as instruments, that are fueled by an invisible substance called air. Music, just like air, is not an illusion. It is real. The mystery remains: while neither can be seen, its presence surely can be heard and felt.

Individual expression is the magic ingredient that turns sounds into music. Every composition of value provides the musicers with the opportunity and responsibility to express something. What we express is unique to each individual and will be perceived in many different ways. The countless types of responses that each person experiences are the true miracles of the process. The art of musicing connects souls one to the other. Its power and significance moves us, transports us, and carries us away. As artist conductors/teachers, we are charged with the responsibility of preserving and bettering humanity. Performing music is like holding a mirror up to the soul. It reflects the very best that humankind has to offer. The next time you make music, determine to create a journey of the heart. Make memories, make mysteries, make miracles, make magic, make music!

CHAPTER 6

The Band Director as a Leader

Tim Lautzenheiser

Introduction

Successful band programs are a reflection of a successful band director. It is rare to find one without its predictable counterpart. Higher education continues to search for the ideal preparatory curriculum that offers the expectant music educator the necessary library of knowledge required to create and nurture a quality band program; however, the development of the leadership personality of the band director continues to be an equal challenge. We know that teaching context is equally as important as the curriculum content. With that in mind, this chapter is devoted to a bird's-eye view of two leadership styles as they impact the teaching/learning environment.

The Band Director as a "Leader"

We would all agree that the responsibilities of a successful band director extend far beyond the podium. Aspiring young music educators are required to study all aspects of music history, theory, form and analysis, composition, rehearsal techniques, orchestration, curriculum development, acoustics, and a host of related subjects. The development of the band director as a "leader" is often overlooked or discounted as an area outside the realm of musical expertise needed to be a professional success.

Times have changed. The inner desire to participate and contribute to a quality ensemble is still a high priority of young music makers; however, the process to achieve this end has shifted dramatically over the last three decades. In the past, students were expected to be obedient, focused, and dedicated to excellence. If they did not oblige, strong disciplinary measures were often brought to bear. Such extrinsic, imposed control became the admired standard as a requisite for musical success. An all-or-nothing approach is not as well received by today's more worldly students. Although the quest for musical excellence is still at the forefront of their desired goals, the journey (process) is equally as important as the destination (product). There is a shift from the authoritarian band director to the music educator who is concerned about the overall welfare of each musician while maintaining the group's high artistic standards, both on and off the podium.

There is an important difference that exists between the *demand* for excellence and the *desire* for excellence. While both avenues may produce the same results, the impact on the participants often dictates their future commitment to the ensemble/band. For example, a director-enforced rehearsal atmosphere can (and often does) produce an outstanding ensemble; the demand for excellence is recognized by the students/members and they behave accordingly; often this is to avoid any negative reprimands generated by the director. The second example is a student-imposed disciplined atmosphere leading to a similar quality performance; however, the rehearsal environment is a reflection of both the musicians' and the director's agreed-upon intent. Moreover, the desire for excellence shifts more of the responsibility back to the members of the group.

In reviewing these two examples, we (as music educators) must ask, "Which environment develops the lifelong musician?"

A Demand for Excellence

Noted author/psychologist, Dr. Abraham Maslow, points to survival as the primary human need on his Scale of Hierarchy. When an individual is confronted with a perceived threat, the initial reaction is to survive at all costs. In other words, the person chooses whatever path ensures ongoing survival. Based on this premise, behavior modification can be determined or controlled by pain, shame, guilt, and/or blame. Submission takes precedence over confrontation; the follower simply submits to the pressure rather than risk the consequences of challenging the authority figure and the outcome associated with insubordination. In a classroom setting, we can extrinsically (and expediently) motivate students by employing management/leadership tactics that threaten perceived survival (e.g., avoidance of pain, embarrassment, etc.).

A Desire for Excellence

A desire for excellence finds the source of motivation within the followers/students. Rather than the director being responsible for the rehearsal climate, the students determine the organization's level of expectation. They are given more freedom concerning appropriate behavior, individual commitment, disciplinary standards, and so forth. Generally, it takes more time to achieve the same level of musical performance as a director-controlled ensemble since time-consuming group choices now become a part of the learning process. For many directors, the benefits gained by sharing the ownership of

the program are more important than the satisfaction of having ultimate control.

Arguably, there are merits to both styles of leadership, classroom management, and teaching philosophies. To suggest there is only one acceptable route to musical excellence is short-sighted; however, by understanding the extremes of the teaching/leadership processes, we increase our options for creating the best atmosphere to support our educational/musical goals.

As a reference point, let us label our two teaching styles as follows:

1. Demand for excellence (director control-oriented)
2. Desire for excellence (student control-oriented)

(Author's note: To avoid being caught in the semantics of the words desire and demand, we all know every fine music educator teaches from a position of desire; we also know every successful student is demanding in his/her personal learning habits. Demand and desire stand as equal partners in the growth/success journey. We are focusing on the source of application: is it director generated or student generated? Or what combination will best serve the journey/process and the destination/product?)

A *demand* for excellence reflects a more traditional style of leadership. The focus is on "finding and fixing" what is wrong, and the extremes justify the means in accomplishing the desired results. A *desire* for excellence is a more contemporary style of teaching/leadership. The focus is on an agreed alignment of the members to contribute to the purpose and vision of the organizational goals, with the means often taking a higher precedent over the extremes.

The consummate leader/teacher/director does not necessarily prescribe to one particular style, but blends both to accommodate the given situation(s). By reviewing the characteristics of *demand* and *desire*, we can gain a better perspective of what will best serve our programs.

Comparison of Teaching Styles

FINDING SOLUTIONS:
Director A is answer/tell-oriented:
Director A feels the need to answer every question and give specific instructions to the members of the ensemble. This guarantees the situation outcome and avoids the confusion associated with lack of direction. It can also thwart creative problem-solving and decision-making offered by the students.

Students become accustomed to the director "being in charge," and they wait obediently for the next directive.

Positive value:

It offers quick, instructive directions for problem-solving.

Negative potential:

Students rely totally on the director and avoid personal initiative.

Director B is question/listen-oriented:

Director B does not feel a need to "have all the answers," but focuses the students on finding their own solutions. While this leadership style develops group responsibility, it can consume an inordinate amount of time. Many possible solutions will be tried before an acceptable idea surfaces. The director must offer guidance and structure for the students.

Positive value:

A source of creative ideas comes forth and the students learn and understand the pros and cons of decision-making.

Negative potential:

Forward momentum can be lost because of a lack of unified direction. Without proper coaching, students can become frustrated because they simply don't know what to do, how to do it, or why they should do it.

DECISION-MAKING:

Director A makes all decisions:

Director A looks at every choice with a careful analysis of how it will impact the organization. Top-down decision-making is the overall mode of operation. Even though there may be various student leaders/officers, etc., the "final call" is made by the director. In truth, this style of leadership is a combination of leader-manager; assigning, doing, and evaluating is a function of the director.

Positive value:

There is total control and complete understanding of every programmatic detail.

Negative potential:

An excessive amount of time is spent micro-managing, checking and re-checking every choice/decision while being the only answer source for the group.

Director B empowers students to make decisions:

Director B assigns given tasks to the students in an effort to develop a sense of organizational ownership while tapping the creative thoughts of the participating students. Members are challenged to resolve their own problems and are encouraged to learn by trial and error. The director monitors the

progress of the students as they explore choices and seek solutions; ongoing assessment and course correction is required.

Positive value:

This method of leadership helps access the wealth of knowledge and creative energy within the ensemble.

Negative potential:

Some students take action before having proper data; their unbridled enthusiasm can take the group off course. Communication can become easily fragmented.

MOTIVATION:

Director A pushes the ensemble for results:

Director A gets behind the organization and drives the members forward as they move to a higher standard of musical performance. When the group does not respond, the *demand* for excellence becomes the primary focal point and the leader/director counters by pushing with more force. The power source is the director; the emphasis is on the hard issue – the musical product.

Positive value:

When there is progress slow-down, the director can take immediate steps to quickly reverse the cycle.

Negative potential:

Students are only motivated to perform at the request/demand of the director. Extrinsic motivation is often seen as required for musical success.

Director B pulls the ensemble toward a vision:

Director B is postured in front of the program, ensemble, and students to create a visionary goal. When the group does not respond favorably, the *desire* for excellence becomes the primary focal point and the leader/director counters by focusing the attention of the group members on their chosen goal. The emphasis is on the soft issue – the people rather than the product. The students are challenged to rise to the occasion and urged to understand their responsibility to take charge of their musical destiny.

Positive value:

The source of energy lies within the students; goal achievement is attained as a result of their contribution; intrinsic motivation is developed. Director-student communication is expanded, enhanced, and creates group synergy.

Negative potential:

If the students do not recognize their need to assume this responsibility, forward momentum is halted. An excessive amount of valuable time can be lost.

PROGRAM PACING:

Director A has definite opinions:

Director A maintains forward progress by relying on the tried-and-true ideas and thoughts that have stood the test of time. While there is always room for growth, there is a certain black-and-white approach that keeps the program and the students well within the dictated, approved boundaries of the director. The future of the program is predictable since it reflects the opinions and thoughts of the director.

Positive value:

People know what behavior is appropriate and they usually adapt quickly. There is no second guessing or wondering how to interpret the directions of the leader/director/teacher.

Negative potential:

Opinions are not challenged or questioned; thus, alternative options are rarely explored. People simply wait for instructions and obey without going through a detailed thought process for themselves.

Director B is open minded and invites new data:

Director B also has opinions, but they exist as an avenue to further exploration of possibilities. "Either/or" gives way to "How can we make it work?" The line of right or wrong is flexible, and the thoughts and opinions of Director B are always in transition. Having an open ear encourages students to express their ideas without fear of appearing inferior or unknowing.

Positive value:

Students eagerly share their thoughts and ideas, realizing they can contribute to the texture of the program. Rather than repress concerns, students bring them to an open forum where there can be discussion and resolution.

Negative potential:

Students who need clear and concise directions are often confused by the ongoing shifts in program adjustments. They can easily be discouraged and frustrated by the lack of direction-definition if the director does not communicate the given changes and the reasons for those changes.

LEADERSHIP POSTURE:

Director A demonstrates a mode of self-protection:

As part of the control posture, Director A never allows a situation where there will be any kind of threat to his/her position or leadership stance. The system is designed to maintain the security of the director and to avoid any questioning of the dominance of the leader. There is a clear-cut division between student, teacher, administrator, parent, etc.

Positive value:

Although this may be interpreted as a self-serving characteristic, it can help directors/leaders move ahead without fear of being undermined by others in the organization.

Negative potential:

Students/members begin to reflect the self-protection theme and start building their own walls of defense to guard their personal interests. Honest communication begins to decrease between director and students.

Director B is more relaxed in the interpretation of position importance:

Director B avoids self-protection to demonstrate a higher level of self-confidence. Time and energy that might be spent protecting the position of director is devoted to the inclusion of others to share the various responsibilities connected with decision-making and program mission.

Positive value:

The students connect to a common vocabulary and interpret the director's open style as a pathway to mutual growth for everyone.

Negative potential:

If the director doesn't maintain a professional posture, the lines between student and teacher become blurred and many students cannot decide what is and what isn't acceptable behavior.

PROBLEM IDENTIFICATION AND CORRECTION:

Director A focuses on problems and is quick to correct them:

Director A has a radar-keen sense when it comes to identifying problems. The never-ending goal of solving every problem to attain perfection is at the top of the priority list. The ability to analyze every minute infraction and give specific directions for correction ensures ongoing improvement.

Positive value:

The director can use knowledge, experience, and a library of solutions to push the ensemble forward at a very fast pace. Veteran teachers can even predict problems before they occur and help the students avoid potential breakdowns.

Negative potential:

The emphasis is always in a "fix and repair" mode. If there are no evident problems, some must be created to accommodate this style of teaching/leadership. Rarely is there the opportunity to feel a sense of personal satisfaction and enjoy a group celebration.

Director B highlights building strengths by learning from mistakes:

Director B recognizes problems but encourages, leads, and demonstrates "how" to fix them and "why" the correction needs to happen. Instead of

giving the students the answer, Director B will go through an educational exchange allowing the students to contribute to the improvement pattern while offering creative counsel to find the solution.

Positive value:

The members of the group begin to model self-responsibility and share the responsibility of critical correction. The director can now dedicate more energy to other aspects of musical growth.

Negative potential:

The director may assume the students have proper information to complete the correction process while the members of the group either may be waiting for instructions or simply do not know what to do or how to do it, which leaves the ensemble at a musical standstill.

A Template for Success

As we examine today's most successful directors/leaders, there are some obvious key characteristics that serve as the foundation's cornerstones that we can highlight and adapt to our own situations:

1. Present an inspiring and compelling mission:

Instead of merely "working to get better," outstanding directors constantly communicate the group's shared goals. While elevating the musical standards, they create an ongoing awareness of various ways to support the ensemble's vision. The long-range goals are always at the forefront of their communication, thus allowing the students to focus on the self-imposed behaviors required to achieve the organizational mission.

2. Demonstrate proven disciplines necessary to create group synergy:

The emphasis is on the "power of the people" rather than the strict authoritarian rule of the director. The energy of the students serves as the fuel for forward motion. Discipline is an outgrowth of the commitment of the group members; instead of "being told what to do," the students are challenged to develop their own parameters of behavior that will support the program from bottom to top.

Positive discipline renewal comes from an ongoing series of group questions such as:

- "What is working well for us and why is it working?"
- "How could we better serve the people, the group, the goals?"
- "What behavior will best support those around us?"
- "What behaviors are counterproductive? How can we alter them?"

Blame is discouraged; solution options are encouraged.

3. Put people first:
    The young musicians, students, members of the group are the source of unlimited growth and development. It becomes the director's responsibility to unleash the knowledge, creativity, and talent inherent in every member. This requires an ongoing interaction among everyone associated with the program; an open and honest line of communication confirms the director's concern for the welfare of the musicians.

4. Model a high degree of self-responsibility:
    The "Do as I say, not as I do" theme is not as effective in today's educational setting. It is important for the director to take responsibility for mistakes and share credit for successes. Modeling is still the most potent method of teaching/leading; therefore, it is imperative that the successful director demonstrates trust, appreciation, caring, and concern. The master teacher/educator understands that it is not necessary to have the answers to all questions, but that strength often comes from saying, "I don't know. Let's find the answer together."

5. Have high expectations for results:
    The modern-day successful band directors are both people-oriented and results-oriented. They focus on the dual task of "taking care of people" and "creating results through those people." While accepting who people are, they do not accept behavior that does not support the goal of quality. This delicate balance is an ongoing learning process for the director and the ensemble; it is constantly changing, shifting, becoming.

Creating a Culture of Quality through Leadership/Modeling

One of the most difficult challenges directors face has little to do with the actual teaching of music; it concerns the establishment of a positive learning atmosphere that encourages the members of the group to contribute without fear of embarrassment, reprimand, pain, etc. If the students assume a defensive posture to protect themselves, it becomes impossible to access their creative potential; however, if the director consistently models a forward-focused discipline, a remarkable shift in attitudes, energy, and performance can be felt. There will be a dramatic improvement recognized in every facet of the rehearsal climate and performance achievement.

Conclusion

The style of teaching we choose is a very personal decision; it usually is an outgrowth of our own educational background. "We don't teach as we're taught to teach; we teach as we are taught." We tend to replicate the style of our most influential mentors as well as draw on our own learning experiences as the foundation of our teaching approach.

As we add more data to our collection of teaching tools, it becomes advisable to expand our leadership skills accordingly. Yet this area of personal growth seems to be the most difficult, the most challenging and, often (unfortunately), the most ignored. It takes an open mind, a willing spirit, and an accepting attitude; it is simply easier and less threatening to add more curriculum content without shifting the teaching context. However, if we expect our students to reach a higher level of musical expertise, we are responsible for modeling the characteristics needed to achieve this end – and this involves change.

We all know what changes need to be made to advance our band programs, whether it is larger budgets, better schedules, more administrative support, greater community awareness, or a host of other possible factors. However, these changes will not take place until we change. If, in fact, the band program is a reflection of the band director, then to manifest changes in the program we must first manifest changes within ourselves. And it is more than changing the surface behavior; it involves a rigorous identity review and a constant evolutionary improvement of our teaching philosophies.

In Stephen Covey's popular book, *The Seven Habits of Highly Effective People*, he writes, "Change – real change – comes from the inside out. It doesn't come from hacking at the leaves of attitude and behavior with quick fix personality ethic techniques. It comes from striking at the root – the fabric of our thought, the fundamental, essential paradigms, which give definition to our character and create the lens through which we see the world."

In other words, the responsibility for creating an environment that supports ongoing positive growth and development is squarely on our shoulders. We must provide and model the positive disciplines we expect of our students and supporters. When we do so, the group begins to change; more and more people begin to follow the leader (the band director), and a noticeable transformation takes place.

Perhaps the most important question we must ask is, "What do I want the band to be?" Whatever answers are generated by this question can be transferred to the correlating question, "What are the characteristics of the band director who can create this envisioned program?" It is not enough to simply answer these introspective questions; we must become our answers.

Whether a *demand* for excellence or a *desire* for excellence; there is one very obvious commonality: *excellence*. The journey to excellence requires a delicate balance of demand and desire. If the destination is reached at the

expense of the group members, we must re-evaluate our leadership style. If excellence is experienced throughout the learning process, the benefits enjoyed by everyone are immeasurable.

In the words of Carl Jung, distinguished psychologist/philosopher, "The human is doomed to make choices." As directors, teachers, leaders, the choices we make shape the lives of every musician in the band.

Strike up the band....

PART II

THE BAND CONDUCTOR AS MUSIC TEACHER

Teacher Resource Guides

Grade Two

Teacher Resource Guide

All the Pretty Little Horses
Anne McGinty
(b. 1945)

Unit 1: Composer

Anne McGinty is one of the most prolific woman composers in the field of concert band literature today. Her compositions and arrangements extend to all levels and consist of approximately 150 titles, all of which are currently published. McGinty began her education at Ohio State University, where she studied with Donald McGinnis. She left Ohio State University to pursue a career in flute performance; she played principal flute with the Tucson (Arizona) Symphony Orchestra, the Tucson Pops Orchestra, and the Tucson Symphony Orchestra Woodwind Quintet. She later returned to complete her Bachelor of Music Degree, summa cum laude, and master's degree from Duquesne University, Pittsburgh, Pennsylvania, where she concentrated on flute performance, music theory, and composition. In addition to being a member of the American Society of Composers, Authors and Publisher (ASCAP), McGinty has received annual composition awards since 1986. She received the Golden Rose Award from the Women Band Directors National Association and the Outstanding Service to Music Award from Tau Beta Sigma, a national honorary band sorority. She is listed in Who's Who of American Women and the International Who's Who in Music. McGinty is also active as a guest conductor, clinician, and speaker throughout the United States and Canada.

Unit 2: Composition

All the Pretty Little Horses, written in 1998, is an American folk lullaby in minor mode. It was dedicated to McGinty's best friend, Paulette, who was diagnosed with cancer. Writing this arrangement provided McGinty with a sense of hope during this difficult time and served as an honest expression of her feelings surrounding this personal tragedy. The folk song, possibly English in origin, has a plaintive quality and serves as an excellent continuation of the folk song tradition. The words of the song are as follows:

> Hushabye, don't you cry, go to sleepy little baby,
> When you wake, you shall have all the pretty little horses,
> Blacks and bays, dapples and grays, coach and six a little horses,
> Hushabye, don't you cry, go to sleepy little baby.

Consequently, Paulette has fully recovered from the cancer. McGinty recently presented her with a special gift: a crystal horse.

Unit 3: Historical Perspective

Composers have written and collected folk songs for centuries, and it is in this tradition that McGinty continues to write folk arrangements for young band. Composers such as Holst, Vaughan Williams, and Grainger were all avid collectors of folk material and have contributed many popular settings of folk songs. McGinty believes that the tradition of children singing and playing folk tunes in America may die out in the next few generations. In writing at least one folk song arrangement per year, it is her hope that the tradition of folk song collecting and arranging will not only survive, but also prosper through music education in the twenty-first century.

The formation and growth of Queenwood Publications has undoubtedly contributed to the success of McGinty's music as well. She and her husband, John Edmondson, founded the business in 1987 with one simple goal: to publish quality music. In the company's twelve years of existence, they have been involved in the writing, recording, production, and engraving of music at all levels.

Unit 4: Technical Considerations

All the Pretty Little Horses is modal in conception; however, some related scales that the students will be utilizing while performing this piece include B-flat major, G minor, E-flat major, and C minor. The tempo indications in the different sections are McGinty's own markings, but it is her hope that every director uses these tempi as a reference in developing his/her own interpretation of the piece.

The instrumentation is flexible, allowing for either a few players on a part or a full concert band. The piece is written in such a way so as to provide flexibility without sacrificing clarity of line, even when a larger number of bass instruments are used. The percussion instruments utilized in the arrangement provide instrumental color, including orchestra bells, finger cymbals, suspended cymbal, and triangle. The entire band must breathe together in m. 32 for ensemble purposes, and the trumpets should raise their bells slightly in m. 38 to project the melody.

Unit 5: Stylistic Considerations

The presentation of this folk tune must reflect the characteristic quality of the human voice. The students must know and be able to sing the words to the song in order to learn the necessary shape of the tune. Throughout the arrangement, the students should play to the rest with a slight taper, avoiding the habit of chopping the ends of phrases. Careful consideration concerning this point involves McGinty's use of percussion. The students must listen to the decay of the percussion instruments in order to comfortably shape releases. In addition, every repetition of the folk song is slightly different, lending itself to differences in orchestration, tempo, meter, and dynamics. Therefore, careful consideration by the conductor to teach the students subtle differences in each repetition of the melody should be a definite goal. The initial statement of the theme is melancholy and provides a plaintive, sorrowful beginning to the composition. Each subsequent statement of this solemn, hymn-like tune should contain a reflective and beautiful quality throughout.

Unit 6: Musical Elements

The song presented in this arrangement is modal; however, there are moments in the work where the composer has chosen denser harmonies. Two examples include the re-transition (mm. 46-50), as well as what the composer has referred to as a harmonic "closeness" (mm. 57-58). These harmonies are chosen carefully by McGinty, and it should be noted that while she has utilized chord progressions with parallel motion and/or suspended seconds, she is attempting to depict specific feelings with these brief harmonic instabilities.

The melody in this arrangement has a narrow range and is presented a total of six times, each with subtle changes in instrumentation and/or meter. The melody is accompanied by an eighth note line that should support the melody. The rising/falling nature of this accompaniment, an intentional decision by the composer, offers a subtle shape to this line and provides an appropriate background for the tune.

Unit 7: Form and Structure

SECTION	MEASURE	EVENT AND SCORING
A		
Introduction	1-4	Folk-like accompaniment introduced in the clarinet
Theme 1x	5-12	Flute, oboe, saxophone present melody
Theme 2x	13-21	Solemn, hymn-like statement in the low brass and woodwinds; phrase is elongated one bar
B		
Theme 3x	22-29	Melody in cornet/trumpet and flute/oboe
Theme 4x	30-37	"Crux" of the piece in m. 34
Theme 5x	38-45	Melody in brass with upper woodwind accompaniment
Retransition	46-50	"Weeping" transition
A′		
Theme 6x	51-58	Melody in low brass/woodwinds
Codetta	59-61	Brief "reflective" closing

Unit 8: Suggested Listening

Anne McGinty:
> *Athenian Festival*
> *Atlantica*
> *Bach: Air*
> *Centennium*
> *Choros*
> *Once to Every Man and Nation*
> *Shepherd's Dream*
> *The Red Balloon*

Unit 9: Additional References and Resources

Dvorak, Thomas L., Cynthia Crump Taggart, and Peter Schmaltz. *Best Music for Young Band.* Brooklyn, NY: Manhattan Beach Music, 1986.

Kreines, Joseph. *Music for Concert Band.* Tampa, FL: Florida Music Service, 1989.

McGinty, Anne. Interview by the author, Hampton, VA, 24 February 1999.

Queenwood Publications, Scottsdale, AZ.

Contributed by:

Keelan McCamey
Heritage of American Band
Langley Air Force Base
Hampton, Virginia

Teacher Resource Guide

Along the Caney Fork

John Hosay
(b. 1965)

band setting by James Hosay
(b. 1959)

Unit 1: Composer

James Hosay is a native of Nashville, Tennessee, but he has spent most of his life in his adopted state of Virginia. Growing up in Norfolk, he began arranging for his school band at age thirteen. He eventually wrote his first original composition two years later. After graduating from high school, Hosay joined the military as a trumpet player and attended the U.S. Armed Forces School of Music. After graduation, he served as a music copyist for the U.S. Army Band. During this time he developed his composition and orchestration skills by studying the techniques used by top-quality arrangers. In 1991, after competing against a large field of civilian and military writers, Hosay obtained his current position of Arranger/Composer for the U.S. Army Band (Pershing's Own), in Washington, DC. Since that time he has become successful as a published composer. He currently resides in Reston, Virginia, where in the spring of 1995 he began writing music for concert band and brass band exclusively for Curnow Music Press.

Unit 2: Composition

Along the Caney Fork is a band setting of a folk-like tune that was originally written by John Hosay, James Hosay's brother. John Hosay originally conceived the tune while walking along the Caney Fork River in eastern Tennessee on an early summer morning with his bride to be. This simplistic tune serves as a beautiful setting for young band, as it captures the essence and natural splendor of the Caney Fork River and its surroundings.

Unit 3: Historical Perspective

Military composers have contributed immeasurably to the repertoire of concert bands for many years. This is due to the growing number of performances of military composers' music by school ensembles at every level. The increasing popularity of wind recordings has also bridged the gap between military and school ensembles. More composers are having their music played and recorded by high school and junior high bands throughout the country. Writing for a professional ensemble on a daily basis gives the military composer a unique opportunity to utilize the tone colors of the concert band.

Unit 4: Technical Considerations

The scales of B-flat major, E-flat major, and F major are required for the ensemble. Accidentals occur primarily in transitions. Rhythmic concerns are straightforward, containing mostly quarter and eighth note movement. The range utilized in this arrangement is not extreme. The percussion instruments used in the arrangement include orchestra bells, bell tree (wind chimes may be substituted if so desired), and suspended cymbal.

Unit 5: Stylistic Considerations

Along the Caney Fork should have a lyrical and expressive quality throughout. The piece contains a beautiful melody that is folk-like in character, and the accompaniment, while it requires careful shaping, should never overpower the *legato* line. Where appropriate, the players must play to the rest, avoiding the habit of clipping the ends of notes. The sustained tones in this arrangement must contain a beautiful tone quality throughout while remaining subordinate to the melody. In the middle section, it is desirable to give the piece more forward motion without rushing the tempo. Finally, the percussion in this arrangement are used to provide color to the melodic line, and careful consideration in balancing these instruments will add to the lyrical beauty of the melody.

Unit 6: Musical Elements

Along the Caney Fork has modal tendencies but utilizes the key signatures of B-flat major, E-flat major, and F major. The harmonic rhythm of the piece gradually increases in forward motion over the first two statements of the melody. A permeating rhythm that unifies the entire work is that of the first measure. It consists of two eighths and a half, and is utilized throughout the entire work. In almost every statement of the theme, a different timbre is achieved based on the instrumentation chosen by Hosay. These differences in orchestration provide the melody with a different character with each repetition and express a variety of different emotions.

Unit 7: Form and Structure

SECTION	MEASURE	EVENT AND SCORING
A		
Introduction	1-8	Bassoon and horn
Theme 1x	9-16	Melody in clarinet; accompanied by bass clarinet and bassoon; color added by flutes and bells
Theme 2x	17-23	(same)
Theme 3x	24-31	Melody in flute, oboe, trumpet, and bells; countermelody in saxophone, horn, and euphonium
Theme 4x	32-37	Abbreviated statement of the melody; serves as transition
B	38-51	Melody in flute, oboe, and clarinet; accompaniment in saxophone, horn, and euphonium
A′		
Theme 5x	52-59	Melody in oboe, clarinet, tenor saxophone, trumpet, euphonium, bells
Theme 6x	60-65	Abbreviated statement of melody
Coda	66-end	Introductory material returns in flute and bassoon

Unit 8: Suggested Listening

James Hosay:
> *Cosmic Comrades*
> *First Light on the Chesapeake*
> *Keepers of the Flame*
> *Opening Day!*

Unit 9: Additional References and Resources

Apel, Willi, ed. *Harvard Dictionary of Music*. Second Edition. Cambridge, MA: Belknap Press, 1970.

"The Basic Band Curriculum: Grades I, II, III." *BD Guide*, September/October 1989, 2-6.

Curnow Music Press, Lexington, KY.

Duarte, Leonard P., Daniel S. Hiestand, Carol Ann Prater, and Doy E. Prater. *Band Music That Works*. Volume 1. Burlingame, CA: Contrapuntal Publications, 1988.

Duarte, Leonard P., Daniel S. Hiestand, Carol Ann Prater, and Doy E. Prater. *Band Music That Works*. Volume 2. Burlingame, CA: Contrapuntal Publications, 1988.

Dvorak, Thomas L., Cynthia Crump Taggart, and Peter Schmaltz. *Best Music for Young Band*. Edited by Bob Margolis. Brooklyn, NY: Manhattan Beach Music, 1986.

Kreines, Joseph. *Music for Concert Band*. Tampa, FL: Florida Music Service, 1989.

Rehrig, William H. *The Heritage Encyclopedia of Band Music*. Edited by Paul E. Bierley. Westerville, OH: Integrity Press, 1991.

Contributed by:

Keelan McCamey
Heritage of American Band
Langley Air Force Base
Hampton, Virginia

Teacher Resource Guide

An Irish Interlude
Warren Barker
(b. 1923)

Unit 1: Composer

Born in Oakland, California, Warren Barker attended the University of California at Los Angeles and later studied composition with Mario Castelnuevo-Tedesco and Henri Pensis. Much of his career has focused on composing and arranging for the television and motion picture industry. Various awards and honors have been bestowed upon him in this area. Barker has received commissions from many outstanding music organizations, including the United States Air Force Band, the Royal Australian Navy, and the Northshore Concert Band. He is a noted composer, conductor, and clinician. Barker has written and arranged over 125 works for concert band. Notable works by Barker include *Capriccio for Saxophone and Band; Concertante for Piano and Band; Concerto for Cornet, Flugelhorn and Trumpet; In Praise of Freedom;* and *Jubilaeum.*

Unit 2: Composition

An Irish Interlude, composed in 1986, is an original work for band in one movement. It is dedicated to St. Mary's Concert Band, Derry, North Ireland. A heartfelt letter to the composer from Anthony Carlin, the Director of St. Mary's Concert Band, was the inspiration for this composition. Carlin wrote of the conflict and strife that permeated daily life due to the political situation in Ireland. However, he also wrote of the power of music to heal and create an experience of beauty. Barker has recently composed *An Irish Ayre* for concert band that is similar and worthy of note.

Unit 3: Historical Perspective

The composer expresses the desire to create a uniquely "Irish"-sounding melody. *An Irish Interlude* borrows characteristics of the traditional folk song setting. It has flowing, lyrical lines that are to be played with freedom and expression. In keeping with this style, there are numerous markings to indicate slight variations in tempo.

Unit 4: Technical Considerations

The scales of E-flat major and F major are required for the entire ensemble. It is rhythmically straightforward with eighth notes being the smallest division. A recurring dotted quarter-eighth note motif will require consistent subdivision. Ranges are well within the ability of musicians in their second year of playing, with cornet I reaching G above the staff. Standard concert band instrumentation is utilized, demanding divisi parts in B-flat clarinets I-III, E-flat alto saxophone I-II, B-flat cornets I-III, French horns I-II, and trombones I-III. Percussion is sparsely scored and is utilized in a melodic role and to add color. Rhythmic and melodic independence within each section is necessary. The greatest challenge will be achieving a sustained lyrical line. The phrases are long and may have to be shortened for young performers.

Unit 5: Stylistic Considerations

Careful attention must be given to the melodic line at all times. Dynamic differences are well marked and support the prominence of this line. The tempo is marked *Moderato* and the quarter note should equal 100. Freedom of movement in the lyrical line is achieved by numerous *ritardandos*, *rallentandos*, *meno mosso*, and *piu mosso* markings. This presents a challenge as the ensemble must be sensitive to the conductor at all times. *Legato* playing is necessary throughout the composition.

Unit 6: Musical Elements

The tonality of the work begins in E-flat major and changes to F major halfway through. The harmony is triadic and diatonic with occasional chromaticism. Countermelodies and harmonized accompaniment create a simple polyphonic texture in the second statement of the theme at m. 44. The melody is highly lyrical and utilizes antecedent and consequent phrase structure. Timbrel contrast is achieved by scoring each repetition of the melody with different instrumental families. Triple meter and simple rhythmic structure create a lilting feel.

Unit 7: Form and Structure

Section	Measure	Melodic Voicing
Introduction	1	Cornets, trombones, baritones/ alto clarinets, saxophones, horns
a1	7	Clarinet I, alto saxophone I
a2	15	Clarinet I, alto saxophone I
b	23	Clarinets, saxophones, horns, baritones
a2	31	Flutes, clarinet I, alto saxophone I
Transition	38	Cornets, trombones/flutes, oboes, clarinets
a1	44	Cornets
a2	53	Cornets
b	61	Flutes, oboes, bells/cornets, trombone I
a2	69	Flutes, oboes, clarinet I, alto saxophone I
Coda	77	Cornets/bassoons, alto clarinets, saxophones, horns, trombone I/flutes, bells

Unit 8: Suggested Listening
Stanley Applebaum, *Irish Suite*
Frank Erickson, *Air for Band*
Percy Grainger:
    Australian Up-Country Tune
    Colonial Song
    Irish Tune from County Derry

Unit 9: Additional References and Resources
Barker, Warren. Conversation with the composer, March 1999.

Dvorak, Thomas L., Cynthia Crump Taggart, and Peter Schmaltz. *Best Music for Young Band.* Edited by Bob Margolis. Brooklyn, NY: Manhattan Beach Music, 1986.

Miles, Richard, ed. *Teaching Music through Performance in Band.* Chicago: GIA Publications, Inc., 1997.

Randel, Don M., ed. *Harvard Concise Dictionary of Music.* Cambridge, MA: Belknap Press, 1978.

Contributed by:
Sheryl A. Bowhay
Lambton County Board of Education
Sarnia, Ontario, Canada

Teacher Resource Guide

Balladair

Frank Erickson
(1923–1996)

Unit 1: Composer

Frank Erickson was born in 1923 in Spokane, Washington. His musical studies included piano and trumpet, which he played in high school band. During high school he began to compose music. In World War II he served in the United States Army Air Force and did arranging for army bands. After the war he attended the University of Southern California, where he received a bachelor's degree in 1950 and a master's degree in 1951. There he studied composition with Halsey Stevens and Maria Castel. He taught at the University of California-Los Angeles and at San Jose College. In the early 1950s, Erickson began writing band music. His first published piece was *Little Suite for Band*, published by Bourne Company in 1951. During the next six years, he produced several of his best-known pieces, including *Air for Band*, *Toccata for Band*, and *Balladair*. In the early 1960s, he collaborated with Fred Weber to produce the first division band course. All told, Erickson wrote more than 400 compositions, at least 250 of which are arrangements and compositions for band. He devoted his compositional energies to writing music at the intermediate band level. He is considered by many to be one of the foremost composers of this level of the teaching repertory.

In the April 1987 issue of *The Instrumentalist*, Erickson provided some insights into the development of his style. Erickson cited Host and Vaughan Williams as two composers "who have done the most to influence my own style of composing."

Unit 2: Composition

Erickson includes the following program note about the piece: *Balladair* is written in a modern dance style. This modern dance form (AABA) is probably most common. *Balladair* varies somewhat from the traditional in that there is another section added after B, resulting in the following new form: AABCAA. The harmonies are fairly traditional, with the exception that certain jazz harmonies and progressions have been utilized. *Balladair* was published in 1958 and is approximately two and one-half minutes in length.

Unit 3: Historical Perspective

The period immediately following World War II was a time of tremendous growth in the teaching repertoire. Composers and arrangers coming out of the military experience were looking for opportunities to continue writing music. The teaching repertoire for intermediate young bands had been largely unexplored. As a result of this explosion, a great deal of material was produced by a number of composers, including such well-known writers as Philip Gordon, Clare Grundman, and John Kinyon.

Unit 4: Technical Considerations

Balladair is written for intermediate band and is scored in such a way that it presents very few technical problems. Written in the key of B-flat concert, the scoring is homophonic with some moving interior lines. The parts are idiomatic for each of the instruments. One would want to give consideration to the intonation aspects of the work, particularly the octave leap that occurs in the melody. One would also want to give some additional attention to tuning the chords in the last four-measure phrase of the piece. The rhythmic elements of the piece are straightforward, with a few syncopated rhythms at the very end of the piece which will require some attention from the conductor. There are three parts for percussion: timpani, snare drum, and cymbal. This is very typical of scoring for intermediate band music in the 1950s. With the larger percussion sections present at the turn of the century, one might wish to add a triangle part or fashion a mallet part from the oboe/flute line to involve additional students.

Unit 5: Stylistic Considerations

A successful performance of *Balladair* will hinge on playing with beautiful tone quality in a very *legato* style. Erickson suggests that some of the harmonic movement is very similar to the jazz writing that was prevalent in the mid-century. One of the important jazz compositional devices Erickson employs is the "circle-of-fourths" technique to move through various key centers. By moving through the circle of fourths, he employs secondary dominance primarily to arrive at a momentary tonicization of another key center. With young players, attention is needed to ensure that the accidentals are observed.

Unit 6: Musical Elements

Balladair is in a modified song form, AABCAA. This form is a hybrid of the standard song form, which has a bridge (or B section) that takes one back to the main melody. In this case, an additional phrase is placed between the returns of the melody, making the work longer and more interesting. Melodically and harmonically, Erickson is firmly rooted in the traditional diatonic system and has a gift for writing beautiful melody. The main melodic idea of *Balladair* has a large compass, extending an octave and a third. To create further interest in a relatively simple composition, Erickson uses moving inner lines to give the arrangement a fuller sound. Also, he skillfully uses doublings to make the band sound full and complete in its instrumentation.

In an interview in the April 1986 issue of *Instrumentalist* Magazine, Erickson makes some interesting comments about writing music:

> I am always conscious of several points when writing a piece of music. I always start writing with a sketch, which is basically a three line conductor's score.... I try to make each part as interesting as possible for the players.... I am also conscious of making sure that the piece has a good overall design, that it is not too long or too short and that it reaches the climaxes at the right time. Also important, even in a short piece, is a variety of movement and style.

Unit 7: Form and Structure

MEASURE	KEY	FORM	COMMENTS
Form: Modified song form		AABCAA	
1	B-flat major	A	Main theme presented in upper woodwinds and cornet I; a supportive counterline is presented in mm. 2-3, clarinets, cornets, and alto saxophones
9	B-flat major	A′	Return of the main theme; an exact return until mm. 15-16, when an authentic cadence is used
17	B-flat major	B	Secondary melody in trumpet I; again, interest is created through the use of an interesting counterline; the appearance of e-naturals and f-sharps in m. 24 indicates a modulation to the relative minor

MEASURE	KEY	FORM	COMMENTS
25	c minor	C	A third melodic idea appears at m. 25 in upper woodwinds and cornet I; this phrase begins in g minor and moves through a series of momentary tonicizations in the keys of f major, c major, a minor, g major, and d major, before a momentary repose in f major, the dominant m. 32
33	B-flat major	A	An exact recapitulation of mm. 1-9
41	B-flat	A	The last statement of the A material; first four measures are exactly like mm. 9-12; on beat 4, the woodwinds begin the closing phrase; a four-measure closing phrase has two syncopated chords of interest; the first is a B-flat augmented chord in second invention, which leads to the momentary tonicization of g minor, m. 46; the next syncopation (m. 46 after beat 3) is a c half-diminished chord; the penultimate measure contains two f major chords between which a 4-3 suspension is resolved and leads to the final B-flat chord of the piece

Unit 8: Suggested Listening
Frank Erickson:
Air for Band
Little Suite for Band
Tocatta for Band

Unit 9: Additional References and Resources
Balent, Andrew. *"Frank Erickson-The Composer's Point of View."* The Instrumentalist, Xl, April 1986, 28-34.

Dvorak, Thomas L. *Best Music for Young Band.* Brooklyn, NY: Manhattan Beach Music, 1986.

Miles, Richard, ed. *Teaching Music through Performance in Band*. Volume 1. Chicago: GIA Publications, Inc., 1997.

Rehrig, William H. *The Heritage Encyclopedia of Band Music*. Westerville, OH: Integrity Press, 1991.

Smith, Norman, and Albert Stoutamire. *Band Music Notes*. Lake Charles, LA: Program Note Press, 1989.

Contributed by:
Jay W. Gilbert
Director of Bands and Chair, Music Department
Doane College
Crete, Nebraska

Teacher Resource Guide

Chant Rituals
Elliot Del Borgo
(b. 1938)

Unit 1: Composer

Elliot Del Borgo was born in Port Chester, New York, on October 27, 1938. He holds a B.S. degree from the State University of New York, an Ed.M. degree from Temple University in Philadelphia, and an M.M. degree from the Philadelphia Conservatory, where he studied theory and composition with Vincent Persichetti and trumpet with Gilbert Johnson. Early in his career, Del Borgo taught instrumental music in the Philadelphia public schools. He retired in 1995 from the Crane School of Music at the State University of New York at Potsdam, where he was an Associate Professor of Music. Del Borgo has written over 450 compositions for various ensembles. Over 300 of these pieces have been written for concert band.

Unit 2: Composition

Chant Rituals was written during 1991-92 while the composer was teaching at the State University of New York, Potsdam. It was written on commission for the Grandville, Michigan Band Boosters for the Grandville Junior High School Band. This single-movement piece is in ABA form and takes approximately five minutes and twenty-two seconds to perform. The composer took his inspiration for this piece from his experiences in working with a church choir that performed Gregorian chant and Renaissance motets, as well as from his much earlier, grade six composition, *Chant Variants*. The composer states that *Chant Rituals* is very programmatic and that the title comes from his vision of "primitive peoples going through a chant and an elaborate religious ritual." At the request of the publisher, *Chant Rituals* has recently been arranged by the composer for full orchestra—the first time that Del Borgo has transcribed one of his original band pieces for orchestra. Since initial publication, well over 1,000 copies of this composition have been sold.

Unit 3: Historical Perspective

The extensive use of percussion, the requirement that the band sing a simple Gregorian style of chant, and the modal writing lend both a very contemporary and very ancient flavor to this piece. The piece can be termed "contemporary programmatic." Although programmatic ideas can be found in the works of composers as far back as the fourteenth century, program music first began to rival absolute music in the nineteenth century. Modern composers for band frequently employ program music ideals as the basis for their compositions, evoking certain images or feelings from the listener through compositional techniques such as singing or chanting, playing traditional instruments with non-traditional techniques, or having wind players augment the percussion section by creating percussive sounds.

Unit 4: Technical Considerations

The composition is listed as a grade two piece. Most of the technical demands fall within that grade level, although there are numerous technical and musical challenges in this piece for young players. The 1st trumpet does not go higher than a written F at the top of the staff, but both the 2nd and 3rd clarinet parts do cross the break. The use of some larger intervals in the melodic line in the brass and more commonly in the woodwinds will require rehearsal to maintain facility. The contrapuntal focus of the piece will challenge players to bring out the independent lines and gives all parts significant melodic material. The piece is written using a modified dorian mode. Being somewhat atonal, and with frequent minor seconds and minor thirds in the melodic lines, young players will need rehearsal time to become accustomed to these finger patterns. There are no key signatures in the parts, so players will need to carefully observe and circle the resulting accidentals. A capable alto saxophone soloist is required in the B section. The significant percussion writing requires six players, and two of them will need to play mallet percussion instruments. There is an ad libitum direction for the percussion during the chant, but the initial rhythms are notated and this should pose no problem. The piece begins and ends in common time, with the middle section in 3/4 meter. Some syncopation is utilized, but all rhythms used in the piece are straightforward. Intonation will need to be a focus in rehearsal preparation as there are many unisons, octaves, and open fifths which will need careful tuning.

Unit 5: Stylistic Considerations

Chant Rituals will require the band to perform with convincing *marcato*, *cantabile*, and *sostenuto* styles. The tempo is marked at quarter note = 152, and this marking should be observed in order to generate the excitement needed in the vigorous opening and closing A sections. The extensive percussion parts are a significant contribution to that excitement. The slow (quarter note = 72) B section of the piece is meant to convey an "other-worldly" sound. The chant is consistent with traditional Gregorian-style chants: the simple melodic progression is conjunct and, for half of the band, consists of four notes. The other half of the ensemble is simply required to sustain a concert C on the syllable "Ah." Provision has been made for ensembles that may be unaccustomed to singing. A note to the conductor at the beginning of the chant suggests that the conductor may wish to "mix singing with playing as circumstances dictate." The alto saxophone soloist in this section will need to have good control to achieve a haunting quality to contrast with the voices.

Unit 6: Musical Elements
Because of the use of the dorian mode, there is a high degree of harmonic tension in this piece. The same observation can be made of the melodic writing. The frequent use throughout of half-steps, minor thirds and sixths, and tritones, especially in the woodwind melodies, results in the absence of a tonal center. The approach to harmony in this piece is a very sixteenth century one: the harmony is a result of the interaction of the contrapuntal lines. There are several open fifth harmonies and parallel octaves and double octaves. Most of the chords used come directly from the modal scale. The use of the voices adds another timbre to the band and creates a neutral tone color which contrasts with the dissonant flute line in the B section. The muscular *ostinato* rhythms provide momentum in the opening and closing sections.

Unit 7: Form and Structure
The piece is written in ternary form.

SECTION	MEASURE	EVENT AND SCORING
A	1-4	Introduction; low brass and woodwinds on pedal F; percussion establishes forceful ostinato pattern
	5	First statement of main theme in the trumpets and horns
	8-20	Woodwinds used contrapuntally; expansion of main theme in other parts
	20-24	Transition through descending scale passage in upper woodwinds
	24-33	Expansion of motive from main theme in brass and saxophones

SECTION	MEASURE	EVENT AND SCORING
	33-41	Statement of secondary theme in flutes and clarinets
	41-52	Transition through repetitive thematic fragments in woodwinds
	52-59	Brass chorale statement of secondary theme in horns, trumpets, and trombone I
	59-76	Main theme returns in all brass; further statements of main theme
B	76-84	Ethereal; sustained open fifth; melodic and harmonic tension created at low dynamic level; flute line leads to chant at m. 84
	84-96	Singing; flute melody; percussion begins ad libitum
	96-116	Alto saxophone solo; increasing harmonic tension through minor thirds and half steps; periodic resolution of tension through silences of two and three beats; increased dynamic level and thickness of scoring
	116-119	Climax of B section; reiterated unisonal cluster chords
	120	Flutes establish C concert; chant resumes
A	123	Percussion ostinato resumes at original tempo
	127-143	Manipulation of fragments of main and secondary themes in all parts; increase in dynamic level and thickness of texture
	143-153	Forceful reiteration of main theme in brass, saxophones, and 2nd and 3rd clarinet; use of syncopation
	153-160	Canonic treatment of main theme
	160-165	Repeated woodwind figure over brass chords; harmonic expansion
	165	Last statement of main theme in diminution; ends with unisonal syncopated figure

Unit 8: Suggested Listening
Jay Chattaway, *Mazama*
George Crumb, *Ancient Voices of Children*
Elliot Del Borgo:
    Chant and Jubilee
    Chant Variants
    Distant Voices
Robert W. Smith, *On the Rising Winds*
Michael Sweeney, *Ancient Voices*

Unit 9: Additional References and Resources
Apel, Willi, ed. *Harvard Dictionary of Music*. Second Edition. Cambridge, MA: The Belknap Press of Harvard University Press, 1970.

Del Borgo, Elliot. Toronto, Ontario, Canada. Interview with the composer, January 1999.

Dvorak, Thomas L., Cynthia Crump Taggart, and Peter Schmaltz. Best Music for Young Band. Edited by Bob Margolis. Brooklyn, NY: Manhattan Beach Music, 1986.

Fraedrich, Eileen. *The Art of Elementary Band Teaching*. Fort Lauderdale, FL: Meredith Music Publications, 1997.

Garofalo, Robert J. *Instructional Designs for Middle/Junior High School Band*. Fort Lauderdale, FL: Meredith Music Publications, 1995.

Hoppin, Richard H. *Medieval Music*. New York: W.W. Norton & Company, 1978.

Miles, Richard, ed. *Teaching Music through Performance in Band*, Volume 2. Chicago: GIA Publications, Inc., 1998.

Rehrig, William H. *The Heritage Encyclopedia of Band Music*. Edited by Paul E. Bierley. Westerville, OH: Integrity Press, 1991.

Williamson, John E. *Rehearsing the Band*. Edited by Kenneth L. Neidig. Cloudcroft, NM: Neidig Services, 1998.

Contributed by:
Dennis Beck
Unionville High School
Markham, Ontario, Canada

Teacher Resource Guide

Creed

William Himes
(b. 1949)

Unit 1: Composer
William Himes was born in Flint, Michigan, in 1949. He earned Bachelor and Master of Music Degrees from the University of Michigan. Himes taught public school music in Flint for five years, was an adjunct lecturer in low brass at the University of Michigan-Flint, and also served as the bandmaster of the Flint Citadel Band of the Salvation Army. In 1977, he became Music Director of the Salvation Army's Central Territory, which covers eleven midwestern states. In this capacity, he is also conductor of the Chicago Staff Band, an internationally recognized brass band. Well known for his compositions and arrangements, Himes has more than seventy publications to his credit. He is in demand as conductor, composer, lecturer, clinician, and euphonium soloist, and has appeared throughout the world. In addition to *Creed*, some of Himes other band works include *Caprice*, *Medallion Overture*, *Island Empire March*, and *Voyages on a Rowing Song*. Two of his works have recently been commercially recorded on compact disc, *Jericho* (on the CD *New Horizons*) and *Kenya Contrasts* (on the CD *Constellations*).

Unit 2: Composition
Creed, part of Neil A. Kjos' *Best In Class Performance Selections* series for young bands, was composed in 1988. It is a single-movement work, approximately four minutes and thirty seconds in length, with contrasting tempi and styles. In form it is much like an overture. Kjos designates the difficulty level of the work as grade 2 1/2. It is designed to correlate with page 32 of *Best In Class, Book Two*. Other composers with compositions of similar style and difficulty include Chuck Elledge and Bruce Pearson.

138

Unit 3: Historical Perspective

Singable melodies, contemporary harmonies, and an attempt to include important thematic material in every part characterize the compositions in this Kjos series. Kjos and the composer provide detailed information for the conductor including rehearsal suggestions, a list of terms and definitions, historical references, and ensemble exercises which address rhythm, key and tonal centers, melody and phrasing, and tuning. These exercises are derived from material excerpted form the work.

Unit 4: Technical Considerations

The scales of F major and F dorian are utilized in this work. Articulations include slurred, *staccato*, accented, and *tenuto* passages. While the meter is 4/4 throughout, the tempo and style vary, including sections marked *Solemne e misterioso* (66 beats per minute), *Allegro giocoso* (108-120 beats per minute), *Allegro vivo* (108 beats per minute), and *Piu mosso* (120 beats per minute). Rhythms include eighth notes, dotted-quarter notes, syncopation, and patterns which use one, two, and three pick-up note rhythms. The snare drum part calls for groupings of four sixteenth notes and eighth two sixteenth note patterns. Ranges are easy in all instruments. All clarinet parts include tricky across-the-break passages. There are two horn parts which are almost always doubled in other parts. Percussion parts include timpani, chimes, bells, snare drum, bass drum, suspended cymbal, triangle, and tambourine.

Unit 5: Stylistic Considerations

This work is melodic and romantic in approach. Clearly marked, contrasting styles are required throughout this work including *legato, tenuto*, accents(> ^), *staccato, leggiero, calore*, and *festivo*. There are also ample breath, phrase, and dynamic markings.

Unit 6: Musical Elements

Definitions and suggestions for interpretation are included in the score. Himes states, "While not literally programmatic, this piece seeks to convey a sense of affirmation and trust. The result is music which is descriptive and atmospheric, conjuring a variety of moods ranging from reflection to exultation." Careful attention should be paid to balance so that melodies and melodic fragments can always be heard. Parts with rhythmic *ostinati* should be musically, as well as accurately, executed. Eighth notes with heavy accents (^) should be heard as chords and not percussive pops.

Unit 7: Form and Structure

Section	Form	Measure	Event and Scoring
Section I	a,b	1-15	*Solemne e misterioso;* 4/4; F dorian; introduction of thematic ideas in middle voices and then flute and oboe
Section II	C	16-36	*Allegro giocoso;* F major; melody in canon between alto saxophone/trumpet and upper woodwinds; melody in unison trumpets then upper woodwinds; addition of rhythmic ostinato
	c	37-48	Rhythmic *ostinato* continues with contrasting slurred melody in upper woodwinds
	C	49-60	*Con spirito;* F dorian; development of melody in canon; rhythmic ostinato
Section III	a,b	61-79	*Solemne e misterioso;* to F major; build from p to ff
Coda	c	80-107	*Allegro vivo;* development and manipulation of canonic melody; rhythmic ostinato

Unit 8: Suggested Listening

James Barnes:
> *Riverfest Overture*
> *Sunflower Saga*

James Curnow, *Rejouissance*

Robert Jager, *Pastorale and Country Dance*

Recorded excerpts from many of Himes' compositions may be found at the World Wide Web site of J.W. Pepper: http://www.jwpepper.com

Unit 9: Additional References and Resources

"The Basic Band Curriculum: Grades I, II, III." *BD Guide,* September/October 1989, 2-6.

Dvorak, Thomas L. *Best Music for Young Band.* Brooklyn, NY: Manhattan Beach Music, 1986.

Garofalo, Robert J. *Instructional Designs for Middle/Junior High School Band.* Fort Lauderdale, FL: Meredith Music Publications, 1995.

Lisk, Edward S. *Intangibles of Musical Performance*. Fort Lauderdale, FL: Meredith Music Publications, 1996.

McBeth, W. Francis. *Effective Performance of Band Music*. San Antonio, TX: Southern Music, 1972.

Rehrig, William H. *The Heritage Encyclopedia of Band Music*. Westerville, OH: Integrity Press, 1991.

Strange, Richard E. *Selective Music List for Bands*. Nashville, TN: National Band Association, 1997.

VanderCook, H.A. *Expression in Music*. Miami, FL: Rubank, 1942.

Contributed by:
Wayne F. Dorothy
Visiting Assistant Professor
Morehead State University
Morehead, Kentucky

Teacher Resource Guide

Declaration and Dance
Larry Clark
(b. 1963)

Unit 1: Composer
Larry Clark was born in Clearfield, Florida, in 1963. He holds a bachelor's degree in Music Education from Florida State University and master's degrees in Composition and Conducting from James Madison University in Virginia. Clark taught instrumental music in the public schools of Florida for several years and served as Director of Bands at Syracuse University for four years. In the 1980s, he was active as an arranger and instructor for drum and bugle corps such as the Denver Blue Knights and the Suncoast Sound. Clark served as a staff composer and arranger for Warner Brothers Publications and as editor and producer of their marching band and jazz publications. In 1999, Clark became the Vice President of Instrumental Music for Carl Fischer in New York. His works have been performed internationally and appear on numerous contest and festival performance lists. He regularly serves as a clinician and guest conductor for high school bands throughout the country. In addition to *Declaration and Dance*, other notable works by Clark include *Engines of Resistance* and *Upon a New Horizon*, his most difficult band work to date.

Unit 2: Composition
Declaration and Dance, part of CPP/Belwin's *Beginning Band Series* for young bands, was composed in 1996. Clark states, "This piece is written to be used by beginning bands sometime during the first year of study. The piece is written using the first six notes learned in every band method book—B-flat, C, D, E-flat, F, and G. Within the combination of these notes you will find unique harmonic structure and colorful textures that are not normally found in pieces at this grade level."

Declaration and Dance is a single-movement work with three contrasting musical ideas that alternate throughout its length. The work opens with a bold, declamatory *Declaration*; is followed by a more rhythmic, *marcato-staccato* style *Dance*; and is then coupled with a diatonic melody. Depending on the performance tempo, indicated as *Allegro con brio*, this work is approximately two minutes and forty seconds in length. Other works by Clark, which utilize the same six-note approach, include *Consensus*, *The Clarion Call*, and *Mystic Legacy*.

Unit 3: Historical Perspective

Clark states that the band works of Vincent Persichetti and William Schumann significantly influenced his approach to composition. Clark's original works for band have tended to focus on compositions appropriate for elementary and middle school bands, the area which he believes has the greatest need for more outstanding repertoire. His compositional style is harmonically contemporary, often using major seventh chords, and rhythmically engaging.

Unit 4: Technical Considerations

The scale of B-flat major is utilized in this work (without the A). Articulations include mostly *staccato* and accented passages with only a few slurs. This style can be difficult to attain, especially when beginning band directors are striving to develop continuous, uninterrupted air streams in their young students. The meter (4/4) and tempo (*Allegro con brio*) remain constant throughout the work. Rhythms include quarter notes, half notes, dotted-half notes, paired eighth notes, and simple tied notes. The snare drum part calls for rolls and groupings of four sixteenth notes or eighth-and-two-sixteenth patterns. Flute and oboe parts include a B-flat to C trill. Ranges are easy in all instruments, with clarinets staying below the break and a single bass clef part in octaves. All trumpets are in unison and horns are doubled in other parts. Percussion instruments include bells, xylophone, timpani, snare drum, bass drum, crash cymbals, suspended cymbal, vibraslap, triangle, tambourine, and gong.

Unit 5: Stylistic Considerations

Marcato and *staccato* styles remain consistent throughout the work. Special attention should be afforded the repeated *staccato* eighth notes so that they don't become too "tongue heavy." The composer has indicated accents on the longer melodic notes throughout the work, clearly giving them more weight and rhythmic interest. In the final coda section, this sets up an implied 3/4 feel which is quite unusual in music at this grade level.

Unit 6: Musical Elements

The composer includes descriptive definitions of the work's two main ideas: "declaration—a manifesto/an announcement or affirmation/a solemn statement" and "dance—to move rhythmically in a pattern of steps, especially to music/to leap, skip, etc., as from emotion/a piece of music suited to dancing." The composer also suggests that the tempo be altered to fit the abilities of the ensemble. Along with changing phrase lengths is the use of suspension techniques that add to the uniqueness of this work.

Unit 7: Form and Structure

SECTION	MEASURE	EVENT AND SCORING
Theme A	1-14	*Allegro con brio*, 4/4; B-flat major; declaration idea, based on a minor third, in tutti band; eight measures repeated; authentic cadence begins six measures of transitional material
Theme B	15-27	Dance idea, based on the same minor third, in flute, oboe, bells, and xylophone; repeated with addition of a countermelody and bass clef part the second time
Theme A	28-35	Restatement of Theme A with reduced instrumentation
Theme B,C	35-43	Dance in saxophones, horn, bells, and xylophone with new diatonic melody in upper woodwinds
Theme C	44-56	Transitional material and development of diatonic melody; dialogues between voices; most transparent scoring
Theme B,C	57-64	Theme B in clarinet, saxophones, horn, bells, and xylophone with diatonic melody in flute, oboe, and trumpet
Theme A	65-70	Restatement of Theme A (mm. 28-31); full band added
Theme C	71-79	Implied 3/4; material from Theme C used in a brief coda

Unit 8: Suggested Listening

Bob Margolis:
  Fanfare, Ode and Festival
  Soldiers Procession and Sword Dance
Rex Mitchell, *Introduction and Fantasia*
Vincent Persichetti, *Divertimento, Pageant*
William Schumann, *Chester Overture*
Recorded excerpts from many of Larry Clark's compositions may be found at
  the World Wide Web site of J.W. Pepper: http://www.jwpepper.com

Unit 9: Additional References and Resources

"The Basic Band Curriculum: Grades I, II, III." *BD Guide*,
  September/October 1989, 2-6.

Dvorak, Thomas L. *Best Music for Young Band*. Brooklyn, NY: Manhattan
  Beach Music, 1986.

Garofalo, Robert J. *Instructional Designs for Middle/Junior High School Band*.
  Fort Lauderdale, FL: Meredith Music Publications, 1995.

Lisk, Edward S. *Intangibles of Musical Performance*. Fort Lauderdale, FL:
  Meredith Music Publications, 1996.

McBeth, W. Francis. *Effective Performance of Band Music*. San Antonio, TX:
  Southern Music, 1972.

Rehrig, William H. *The Heritage Encyclopedia of Band Music*. Westerville,
  OH: Integrity Press, 1991.

Strange, Richard E. *Selective Music List for Bands*. Nashville, TN: National
  Band Association, 1997.

VanderCook, H.A. *Expression in Music*. Miami, FL: Rubank, 1942.

Contributed by:

Wayne F. Dorothy
Visiting Assistant Professor
Morehead State University
Morehead, Kentucky

Teacher Resource Guide

Dinosaurs

Daniel Bukvich
(b. 1954)

Unit 1: Composer

Daniel Bukvich received a bachelor's degree in Vocal and Instrumental Music Education from Montana State University. He received a Master of Music from the University of Idaho, where he joined the faculty in 1976. He has taught jazz choir, marching band, jazz ensemble, percussion ensemble, and music theory at the university. Bukvich builds his own percussion instruments and is an active performer throughout the northwestern United States.

Unit 2: Composition

Dinosaurs, composed for the Moscow Junior High School Wind Ensemble, was published in 1991. It is an exciting, yet easily accessible piece that introduces aleatoric techniques to young players. After an extensive introduction, the piece is organized into five sections, each representing a different dinosaur. Each section is relatively short, providing a complete contrast in tempo, meter, scoring, and aleatoric effect. *Dinosaurs* is highly programmatic and presents many rhythmic and timbre concepts which will be new to young players.

Unit 3: Historical Perspective

Program music and aleatoric sounds are key concepts in *Dinosaurs*. Music that attempts to express or depict one or more non-musical ideas, images, or events is said to be programmatic. The composer usually indicates the subject or subjects to be evoked in the title or preface. The suggestive title can be quite vague or it may be specified and detailed (in this case it is quite specified). Programmatic music has flourished at different times, but especially in the nineteenth century. The Romantics were fond of associating music with literature, landscape, or the visual arts. Program music became a way for instrumental music to be understood. Untrained listeners could "understand" a piece by reading the title and letting their imaginations roam.

Dinosaurs uses the depictive approach of program music. The depictive approach is based on the principle of depicting an aspect of non-musical reality by imitating its sounds or motions. Because most things to be imitated or evoked do not have a clear tonal equivalent (such as dinosaurs!), composers have created new sounds and new notation to represent the sounds they wish to imitate. These aleatoric sounds and notations are prevalent in *Dinosaurs*.

Aleatoric music is the use of traditional and non-traditional sounds used in sometimes random and indeterminate ways. This compositional process is mainly a phenomenon of the later twentieth century, but precedents are found throughout Western musical history. Aleatoric effects are created through random key clicking, the blowing of air while changing fingerings, the striking of crystal glasses, singing, body movement, and clapping. Improvisational, high register playing and trilling is also common.

Unit 4: Technical Considerations

The tonal center of *Dinosaurs* is F major/minor, although at times it is highly chromatic and its harmonic structure does not point to any particular key. Students must be able to play in both keys with some facility. While there are few technically challenging sections, there is a somewhat problematic chromatic motive of descending thirds that is repeated many times in the final section. The woodwinds and trumpets must be comfortable in both F major and F minor to successfully master this motive.

Rhythmic ideas are simple but highly repetitive. Students must be careful to keep track of where they are in repeated sections (some are to be repeated as many as eight times), as well as where they are through extended ties and aleatoric passages. The meter is mainly 4/4, with the exception of the final section which is 5/4.

The percussion writing is extensive, and there are six multiple percussion set-ups which can utilize anywhere from six to eighteen players. A detailed percussion set-up chart is included in the score. The percussion is scored for timpani, three suspended cymbals, triangle, sleigh bells, guiro, tam-tam, maracas, tom-toms, claves, bells, vibes, piano, bass drum, two bass maracas, and a stamping tube. Directions for constructing the bass maracas and the stamping tube are also included in the score.

The aleatoric effects are simple to execute, and most involve manipulation of the player's instruments themselves. The players must blow air through their horns while rapidly changing fingerings, click keys, and move valves rapidly while playing very loudly. The flutes are asked to improvise as high and as fast as possible, and the clarinets blow into the mouthpiece and barrel only while opening and closing their hand over the end. The players must also sing a repeated three-note melody, stamp their feet, hand clap, and chant. All woodwinds and trumpets will need crystal glasses (or drinking glasses) of various sizes and a metallic implement with which to strike them.

Unit 5: Stylistic Considerations

Extreme contrasts in dynamics are found throughout the piece. The players must be able to play with a dynamic range from *pp* to *FFF*. There is an extended 23-beat *tutti diminuendo* at the end of the introduction. Players must play ten-beat sustained chords at *forte* dynamic levels and be able to quickly swell from *pp* to *FF*.

Accent, *sforzando*, *staccato*, and *marcato* markings punctuate every section. These markings should be clearly emphasized, if not overdone. Their purpose is for anything but subtlety—rather pure, blatant effect. Each aleatoric effect must be executed purposefully with clear entrances and releases. The success of this piece depends on the drama of each compounding timbre and the intensity of its execution.

Unit 6: Musical Elements

Melodic themes are not used in the piece. Instead the piece uses the combination of rhythmic and harmonic motives and aleatoric effects to depict each scene. The only discernible melody is found in the flute solo in "Swamp of the Iguanadons." But even here, it is really secondary to the musical texture created by the percussion and the singing.

The use of suspended major and minor seconds dominates the harmonic writing. Short, melodic motives are also stepwise, utilizing major and minor seconds. There is much unison writing, both rhythmically and melodically. The texture of each section generally includes a percussive rhythmic foundation on top of which sits thick, dissonant harmonies and aleatoric effects.

Unit 7: Form and Structure

SECTION	REHEARSAL LETTER	EVENT AND SCORING
Introduction	Beginning–C	Six-part rhythmic *ostinato* in percussion; suspended ascending seconds in brass—repeated eight times; woodwinds punctuate last four times with *staccato* eighth notes; climaxes with FF *tutti* rhythm that *diminuendos* for twenty-three beats

SECTION	REHEARSAL LETTER	EVENT AND SCORING
Brontosaurus	C-D	Six-measure stepwise melodic motive in brass—repeated three times; flute/trumpets blow air through horns while rapidly changing fingerings; oboes/saxophones click keys
Triceratops Fanfare	D-E	Triplet fanfare motive in brass; crystals begin and segue to next section
Cave of the Stegosaurus	E-F	Eighth note vibes/bell duet; swelling low brass motive punctuated with *FFF* French horn trills
Swamp of the Iguanadons	F-G	Voices sing three-note motive; flute solo with timpani *ostinato*; ends with frantic tom-tom (ad lib)
Tyrannosaurus Meets the Pterodactyls	G-I	Chanting, clapping, stamping; flutes ad lib high and fast; clarinets make moaning sounds with head joint
	I-K	Sustained brass chords over aleatoric woodwinds; percussion ostinato continues
	K-N	Unison chromatic motive in woodwinds and trumpets; *FF* low brass pedal
Coda	N-End	*ppp* to *FFF crescendo* in percussion; tutti chord climax followed by low brass trill that *crescendos* through the final fermata

Unit 8: Suggested Listening

Daniel Bukvich, *Symphony No.1, In Memoriam, Dresden, Germany, 1945*
Thomas Duffy, *Snakes!*
Donald Erb, *Symphony for Winds*
Ron Nelson, *Morning Alleluias for the Winter Solstice*
John Paulson, *Epinicion*
Russell Peck, *Cave*

Unit 9: Additional References and Resources

Dvorak, Thomas L., Robert Grechesky, and Gary Ciepluch. *Best Music for High School Bands*. New York: Manhattan Beach Music, 1993.

Dvorak, Thomas L. *Best Music for Young Band*. New York: Manhattan Beach Music, 1986.

Contributed by:

Ryan Nelson
University of North Texas
Denton, Texas

Teacher Resource Guide

Ere the World Began to Be

Jack Stamp
(b. 1954)

Unit 1: Composer

Jack Stamp was born in Washington, DC, in 1954 and grew up in the nearby Maryland suburbs. He received a B.S. degree in Music Education from Indiana University of Pennsylvania in 1976, an M.M. degree in Percussion Performance from East Carolina University in 1978, and a D.M.A. degree in Wind Conducting from Michigan State University in 1988, where he studied with Eugene Corporon. His primary composition teachers were Robert Washburn and Fisher Tull. More recently he has worked with Joan Tower, David Diamond, and Richard Danielpour. Stamp is currently Professor of Music at Indiana University of Pennsylvania where he conducts the Wind Ensemble and Symphony Band, and teaches courses in graduate and under-graduate conducting. He is founder and musical director of the Keystone Wind Ensemble, a professional recording group dedicated to the advancement of American concert band music.

Unit 2: Composition

Ere the World Began to Be was commissioned by the Central Middle School Concert Winds and Percussion of Waukesha, Wisconsin, Laura Kautz Sindberg, Conductor, in 1996. The work is based on the thirteenth century plainchant "Divinum Mysterium," better known to many as "Of the Father's Love, Begotten." The title comes from the second line of the hymnal version. The work is based upon an earlier setting of the chant by the composer for brass quintet. However, the wind band version is more expanded and developed.

Unit 3: Historical Perspective

The plainchant of the thirteenth century represents one of the earliest types of notated music. Later, the chant was used as a *cantus firmus* in more elaborate choral and instrumental compositions. In general, hymn tunes, because of their melodic "singability," have always been used through the history of music as a basis for instrumental compositions, including variations technique.

Unit 4: Technical Considerations

The work, commissioned by a middle school band, makes modest demands on the players. It explores the tonal centers of A-flat, E-flat, and B-flat. The range for 1st trumpet extends to A above the staff in one brief section. Due to the non-metric nature of plainchant, the composer has used 5/8 and 7/8 meters to highlight the irregular rhythm of chant. There is a two-measure duet for trumpet and horn.

Unit 5: Stylistic Considerations

Within the scope of the work, every wind player has the opportunity to play the chant. Therefore, the singing quality or plainchant must be explored. There are also powerful chordal statements that require players to play a connected *marcato*.

Unit 6: Musical Elements

This work is filled with a wide variety of compositional techniques that will educate the players to the creative process of the music of their time.

The work opens with a type of "ring off" technique used by twentieth century composers. In the introduction, the first phrase of the chant is stated, with each note of the melody being sustained to also create harmony. At letter A, the first full statement of the chant is presented with a rhythmically irregular bass accompaniment. Halfway through, the chant modulates and is presented as a canon. At letter C, the chant is harmonized in a modal style. At letter E, the winds begin a development section in which the seven different phrases of the chant are presented out of sequence in a contrapuntal setting. As these phrases begin to weave through each other, the low brass present the chant in an augmented form, much as a *cantus firmus* (letter F). At letter G, there is a dramatic shift to G major in which introductory material is used to bridge the contrapuntal statement to the final big chordal statement. The work concludes with a coda based upon the introductory material and a final cadence.

Unit 7: Form and Structure

SECTION   EVENT AND SCORING

I-II   Introduction
Letter A   First half of chant with independent bass in B-flat
Letter B   Second half of chant in canon in E-flat
Letters C-D   Harmonized chant in a chorale style
Letter E   Development section: interweaving lines all based on a
                     phrase of the chant
Letter F   Development continues; chant enters in augmentation
                     in bass voices
Letter G   Transition material
Letter H   Final "hymn" harmonization in augmentation
Letter J   Coda based upon introductory material

Unit 8: Suggested Listening
Timothy Broege, *Sinfonia V*
David Holsinger, *On a Hymnsong of Philip Bliss*
Fisher Tull:
   Introit
   Variants on an Advent Hymn

Unit 9: Additional References and Resources
Dvorak, Thomas L., Robert Grechesky, and Gary M. Ciepluch. *Best Music for High School Band*, edited by Bob Margolis. Brooklyn: Manhattan Beach Music, 1993.

Rehrig, William H. *The Encyclopedia of Band Music*. Edited by Paul E. Bierley. Westerville, OH: Integrity Press, 1991.

Contributed by:
Jack Stamp
Professor of Music
Indiana University of Pennsylvania
Indiana, Pennsylvania

Teacher Resource Guide

Fa Una Canzona

Larry D. Daehn
(b. 1939)

after Orazio Vecchi
(Ca. 1585)

Unit 1: Composer

Larry D. Daehn received his bachelor's degree from the University of Wisconsin at Oshkosh and his master's from the University of Wisconsin at Platteville. His successful teaching career included teaching both vocal and instrumental music at the junior high and high school levels. He is the owner and operator of Daehn Publications, and he has written and arranged numerous works for concert band.

Unit 2: Composition

Fa Una Canzona is an arrangement taken from a collection of four-voice canzonettas published by Vecchi in 1585. Its original title, "Fa una Canzona senza note nere," means *make a song without black notes*. The "black notes" are a reference to dissonance, which was perceived at that time as an obstacle to musical expression. *Fa Una Canzona* is an excellent example of the Renaissance practice of chordal movement in music. It is sectional in structure and employs a variety of textures in its repetitions. Set for concert band in 1990 by Larry D. Daehn, this arrangement preserves all of Vecchi's harmonies and voice leadings. It is seventy-one measures long and is approximately one minute and thirty seconds in duration.

Unit 3: Historical Perspective

Orazio Tiberio Vecchi (1550-1605) was a popular and influential composer in the late sixteenth century. Born and educated in Modena, Italy, his career centered around various positions at cathedrals and courts. The music of *Fa Una Canzona* was published in his third volume of *The Four-Voice Canzonettas* in 1585. The dedication to this volume is inscribed: "queste mie rime, e canto"—"these rhymes and (this) music of mine." (DeFord, p. 3) Vecchi was the first composer to use the term "canzonetta" to define a distinct genre that combined poetry and music. His canzonettas combined traditional features of the rustic Italian folk song called "villanella" with the more complex and refined elements of the madrigal. The style of Vecchi's canzonettas are highly original due to the use of musical imagery and distinctive compositional techniques. The close relationship of poetry to music is witnessed in the strophic form, in which all stanzas of text are sung to the same music. Vecchi's reputation and influence were based on his secular works. His canzonetta books met with instant success and were well known and widely imitated all over Europe.

Text translation: *Fa una Canzona note nere*

> Make a song without black notes, if you ever wished to have my favor. Make it in a mode that invites one to sleep, finishing it softly.
>
> Don't put dissonances into it, because my ears are not used to them. Make it in a mode that invites one to sleep, finishing it softly.
>
> Don't put in proportions or signs against signs; above all, this is my intention. Make it in a mode that invites one to sleep, finishing it softly.
>
> With this style fortunate Orpheus was able to placate Prosperina in the depths. This is the style that sweetly quieted the evil spirit in Saul.

Unit 4: Technical Considerations

The lydian mode starting on B-flat is utilized throughout the work. The instrumentation is suitable for young band and is achievable by a relatively small ensemble. There are parts for flute (and piccolo), B-flat clarinet I-III, E-flat alto clarinet, B-flat bass clarinet, bassoon, E-flat alto saxophone I-II, B-flat tenor saxophone, E-flat baritone saxophone, B-flat cornets I-III, F horn (occasional divisi), trombones I-II, baritone, and tuba. Cross-cueing occurs in low woodwinds and tuba as well as F horn and alto saxophone. Ranges are within the ability of musicians in their second year of playing. Percussion requires one mallet player on bells and/or xylophone and four players covering snare drum triangle, tambourine, tenor drum, and bass drum. Full ensemble and sectional clapping lends a percussive effect to the work. Clarity and precision may prove to be a challenge. Rhythmic demands are very basic, using only quarter and half note combinations. Frequent meter changes provide an excellent teaching tool. The tempo marking is: briskly and rhythmically, half note = 92-100. Daehn suggests that the rehearsal process might begin in a slow four, making a gradual transition to a feeling of two.

Unit 5: Stylistic Considerations
Based on the principle of strict chordal style, ensemble balance is determined by the quality of each chord (major/minor). Percussion is utilized as an independent voice and has several soli passages. Careful balance in its more traditional accompanying role is necessary. Uniform articulation and precise note lengths are vital to the clarity of texture and rhythm. Individual notes are detached, yet the entire ensemble must play with a full tone. Attention should be paid to dynamic contrast, keeping in mind that Renaissance instruments were unable to produce a wide range of dynamics.

Unit 6: Musical Elements
Transcribed from a four-voice vocal setting, *Fa Una Canzona* retains the homorhythmic texture of the original. The tonality of the work is in the lydian mode. Its sectional structure involves repetition of rhythmic and melodic motives. Internal repetition schemes are reinforced by the use of instrumental choirs alone and in combinations. Daehn's scoring demonstrates the Renaissance use of consorts. The melody is stated in five-measure phrases with the exception of the B section, which is structured four measures, seven measures. The frequent use of a repeated single pitch is apparent in each melodic theme and is indicative of the canzona style. Accurate interpretation of the melodic themes are dependent on rhythmic vitality. Daehn emphasizes the important role that rhythm plays by employing ensemble hand clapping as a structural element.

Unit 7: Form and Structure

SECTION	MEASURE	EVENT AND SCORING
A		
(rhythmic motive)	1-5	Full ensemble hand clapping
a1	6-10	Woodwind statement
a1	11-16	Brass statement
(rhythmic motive)	16-20	Sectional hand clapping
a2	21-25	Upper woodwinds and lower brass

SECTION	MEASURE	EVENT AND SCORING
a2	26-30	Upper woodwinds and brass; absence of tuba
(rhythmic motive)	31-35	Percussion only
B		
b1	36-39	Woodwinds and low brass, absence of flute, oboe, cornets
b2	40-41	Flute, oboe, cornets
	42-46	*Tutti*
	36-46	B section repeated
A		
(rhythmic motive)	47-51	Percussion only
a1	52-56	Woodwind statement
a1	57-61	Low woodwinds, cornet 1, low brass
a2	62-66	*Tutti*
B		
b1	36-39	Woodwinds and low brass; absence of flute, oboe, cornets
b2	40-41	Flute, oboe, cornets
	42-46	*Tutti*
A		
(rhythmic motive)	47-51	Percussion only
a1	67-71	Woodwind and brass voices alternate ends with hand clap

Unit 8: Suggested Listening

Thoinot Arbeau/arr. Margolis, *Belle Qui Tiens Ma Vie*
Norman Dello Joio, *Variants on a Medieval Tune*
Claude Gervaise/arr. Margolis, *Fanfare, Ode and Festival*
William Latham, *Court Festival*
Ron Nelson, *Medieval Suite*
Michael Praetorius/arr. Margolis, *Terpsichore*
Tielman Susato/arr. Curnow, *Renaissance Suite*
Tielman Susato/arr. Margolis, *Battle Pavane*

Unit 9: Additional References and Resources

Adkins, Cecil, ed. *Orazio Vecchi L'Amfiparnso: A New Edition of the Music with Historical and Analytical Essays*. Chapel Hill: University of North Carolina Press, 1977.

Daehn Publications, New Glarus, WI.

DeFord, Ruth I., ed. "Orazio Vecchi: The Four-Voice Canzonettas with Original Texts and Contrafacta - Part I Historical Introduction, Critical Apparatus, Texts, Contrafacta." *Recent Researches in the Music of the Renaissance*, Vol. 92, 1993, pp. 1-27, pp. 49-50.

DeFord, Ruth I., ed. "Orazio Vecchi: The Four-voice Canzonettas with Original Texts and Contrafacta - Part II The Music." *Recent Researches in the Music of the Renaissance*, Vol. 93, 1993, pp. 92-93.

Dvorak, Thomas L., Cynthia Crump Taggart, and Peter Schmaltz. *Best Music for Young Band*. Edited by Bob Margolis. Brooklyn, NY: Manhattan Beach Music, 1986.

Garofalo, Robert J. *Instructional Designs for Middle/Junior High School Bands*. Fort Lauderdale, FL: Meredith Music Publications, 1995.

Grout, Donald J. and Claude V. Palisa. *A History of Western Music*. Third Edition. New York: W.W. Norton and Company, 1980.

Miles, Richard, ed. *Teaching Music through Performance in Band*. Chicago: GIA Publications, Inc., 1997.

Randel, Don M., ed. *Harvard Concise Dictionary of Music*. Cambridge, MA: Belknap Press, 1978.

Sadie, Stanley, ed. *New Grove Dictionary of Music and Musicians*. London: MacMillan Publishers Limited, 1980.

Contributed by:
Sheryl A. Bowhay
Lambton County Board of Education
Sarnia, Ontario, Canada

Teacher Resource Guide

Grant County Celebration
Mark H. Williams
(b. 1955)

Unit 1: Composer

Mark Williams was born in Chicago and raised in Spokane, Washington. Williams holds a Bachelor of Arts in Education and Master of Education degrees from Eastern Washington University. He served as Chief Arranger for the 560th Air Force Band and is very active in the Spokane area as a performer on both woodwind and brass instruments. He taught music in the state of Washington for eleven years, specializing in elementary band, and he has served as the director of the Spokane All-City Band Program and the Spokane Elementary Honor Band. He has been a member of the Spokane British Brass Band for the past four years and now serves as the ensemble's conductor. Williams' compositional output includes over 130 works for band, twenty for orchestra, and two for choir. He has earned numerous ASCAP Special Awards, and he is a winner of the Western International Band Clinic's Gralia Competition. Williams is currently a composer for Alfred Publishing Company and is co-author of Alfred's *Accent on Achievement* band method. In addition to *Grant County Celebration*, some of Williams' other band works include *Greenwillow Portrait*, *Bryce County Overture*, *Fanfare for a New Era*, *Metropolis*, numerous arrangements of orchestral standards, and a number of popular Christmas novelty features.

Unit 2: Composition

Grant County Celebration, part of Alfred's *Challenger Band Series* for young bands in the sixth and seventh grades, was composed in the fall of 1991, shortly after Williams left the field of teaching to pursue a career as a full-time composer and arranger. Williams describes Grant County, in eastern Washington near the Big Bend of the Columbia River, as "dry, open, flat, with irrigated farm land, and an occasional tumbleweed, very much the wild west, and beautiful in its own way." It is a single-movement work, approximately three minutes in length, with three distinct sections, the character of which are described by Williams as "a heroic statement of the wild west, a second theme reflecting the strong Spanish culture in the region, and a slow section reflecting the loneliness of the open west." Williams has published a number of other works in the *Challenger Band Series*, as well as works that are both easier and more difficult.

Unit 3: Historical Perspective

Williams describes his arranging and compositional style for young bands as an outgrowth of his study of the John Kinyon *Mini-Score Series*, the Sandy Feldstein and John O'Reilly *Basic Band Series*, both published by Alfred, and the Andrew Balent *Super Sound Series*, published by Warner Brothers. These works include plenty of part doubling and usually a single alto saxophone part and single bass clef part. They often include energetic, rhythmic sections utilizing syncopation, contrasted by smooth, lyrical sections. The *Challenger Band Series* uses two alto saxophone parts and two bass clef parts, making this scoring the next logical step beyond the above-mentioned series. Other composers writing for this level and in this style include David Shaffer, James Swearingen, and Ed Huckeby, as well as those mentioned above. Williams considers one of the main challenges of writing for this level to be "coming up with something that is fun and exciting, with a nice lyric section and interesting content somewhere inside, sort of like vegetables hidden in with the chocolate cake."

Unit 4: Technical Considerations

The scales of B-flat major, E-flat major, and F dorian are utilized in this work. Articulations include *staccato* and accents in the *allegro vivo* sections (138 beats per minute) and slurs and *tenuto* in the *adagio* section (72 beats per minute). Meters include 4/4, 3/4, and two sections of alternating 3/4 and 2/4 measures. Rhythms include eighth notes, dotted quarter note syncopations in 4/4, and the use of two dotted quarter notes per measure in 3/4 with six accompanying eighth notes accented in two groups of three. Rhythmic releases of long notes are indicated throughout. The snare drum part calls for a grouping of four sixteenth notes in several measures. Ranges are easy in all instruments, with flutes in octaves and second clarinets staying below the break. Horns are almost always doubled in other parts. Percussion instruments include snare drum, bass drum, crash cymbals, maracas, claves, tambourine, and wood block.

Unit 5: Stylistic Considerations

An energetic *marcato* style with clean articulation and slight separation is implied in the *allegro vivo* sections, while a smooth *legato* style is required in the *adagio* section. Accented and syncopated figures should be accurate and not rushed, with slight separation. Trumpets, alto saxophones, and horns should use a more detached style of articulation than is indicated in the 3/4 "Mariachi" section. Special attention should be afforded the dotted half note-quarter note rhythms in the bass clef part in mm. 42-49 so that the quarter notes function as pick-up notes to the following measure rather than as ending notes of the measure in which they fall.

Unit 6: Musical Elements

Use of the composer's descriptions mentioned in unit 1 could be useful in establishing appropriate moods for the work's different sections. Depending on instrumentation, the conductor may choose to eliminate certain part doublings for transparency and/or balance. Style and dynamics should match and balance during the woodwind-brass dialogue (mm. 7-13) and flute-clarinet dialogue (mm. 46-51). Definite contrasts in style between the sections will enhance the performance of this work. The F dorian emphasis in the slow section provides for interesting and engaging harmonies, usually not heard in this level of repertoire.

Unit 7: Form and Structure

SECTION	MEASURE	EVENT AND SCORING
Section I: a, A	1-14	*Allegro* vivace 4/4; B-flat major; introduction of main thematic motif in unison trumpets; rhythmic tutti build into a brief percussion transition; "heroic wild west" theme in woodwinds with accompanying dialogue material in brass
Section II: B	15-26	E-flat major emphasis; 3/4; trumpets present "Mariachi" theme in thirds with accompanying material in upper woodwinds and bass voices; partially repeated with alto saxophones and horns added to main theme
b	27-34	Alternating 3/4 and 2/4 measures; transitional material based on mm. 19-22; *decrescendo* without *ritardando*

SECTION	MEASURE	EVENT AND SCORING
Section III:		
a	35-39	*Adagio* 4/4; F dorian emphasis; begins with a one-measure whole note which serves as a "quasi-fermata" transition; expressive "lonely open west" section; restatement of motif a in flutes; most transparent scoring
C	40-51	New melodic material passing from trumpets to flutes; accompanying *ostinato* established in low voices; question-answer dialogue between flutes and clarinets; *ostinato* continues
c	52-57	Transition and build setting up D.C. al Coda; modulation to B-flat major
Section I:		
a, A	1-14	Replayed
Section II:		
B, b	15-30	Replayed
b	58-65	Coda; continuation of alternating 3/4 and 2/4 measures; rhythmic build to close

Unit 8: Suggested Listening

Don Gillis, *Tulsa*

Morton Gould, *Cowboy Rhapsody, Santa Fe Saga*

James Swearingen, *Majestia*

John Williams, *The Cowboys*

Recorded excerpts from many of Mark Williams' compositions may be found at the World Wide Web site of J.W. Pepper: http://www.jwpepper.com

Unit 9: Additional References and Resources

"The Basic Band Curriculum: Grades I, II, III." *BD Guide*, September/October 1989, 2-6.

Dvorak, Thomas L. *Best Music for Young Band*. Brooklyn, NY: Manhattan Beach Music, 1986.

Garofalo, Robert J. *Instructional Designs for Middle/Junior High School Band*. Fort Lauderdale, FL: Meredith Music Publications, 1995.

Lisk, Edward S. *Intangibles of Musical Performance*. Fort Lauderdale, FL: Meredith Music Publications, 1996.

McBeth, W. Francis. *Effective Performance of Band Music*. San Antonio, TX: Southern Music, 1972.

Rehrig, William H. *The Heritage Encyclopedia of Band Music*. Westerville, OH: Integrity Press, 1991.

VanderCook, H.A. Expression in Music. Miami, FL: Rubank, 1942.

Contributed by:
Wayne F. Dorothy
Visiting Assistant Professor
Morehead State University
Morehead, Kentucky

Teacher Resource Guide

Gypsydance
David R. Holsinger
(b. 1945)

Unit 1: Composer

David Holsinger was born on a small farm north of Hardin, Missouri. He earned a Bachelor of Music Education Degree from Central Methodist College, Fayette, Missouri, and a Master of Music in Theory and Composition from Central Missouri State University, Warrensburg, Missouri. He did postgraduate work at the University of Kansas in Lawrence, Kansas, where he served as an arranger for the university bands and the swing choir. Of his many accomplishments, Holsinger is twice the recipient of the ABA-Ostwald Composition Award for *The Armies of the Omnipresent Otserf* and *In the Spring at the Time When Kings Go Off to War*. He has written extensively for all levels of band, from the young band to the professional band, as well as works for band and choir. Included in his list of compositions are *Childhood Hymn*, *Prelude and Rondo*, *HavenDance*, *Liturgical Dances*, *Symphonia Voci*, *Ballet Sacra*, and *To Tame the Perilous Skies*. Holsinger is currently director of the Wind Ensemble at Lee University in Cleveland, Tennessee.

Unit 2: Composition

Being inspired by Bela Bartok and his writing for pedagogical purposes, Holsinger wrote *Gypsydance* to give young musicians an opportunity to experience music written in a modal key (F dorian) as well as a more common major key (E-flat major). It was also written to challenge the young player to focus on playing a variety of styles within one piece.

Unit 3: Historical Perspective

It is very difficult to find young band music which is both challenging yet playable, as well as being quality, artistic music. Very much aware of this problem, Wingert-Jones Music Publishing Company, Kansas City, Missouri, established the *Achievement Series* program and sought respected music educators to contribute appropriate works. *Gypsydance* is one of six pieces written by Holsinger for this series. A companion piece to *Gypsydance* is *The Peasant Village Dance*. Although a little more difficult, it was also inspired by the work of Bela Bartok. While *Gypsydance* provides modal and mixed key experience to the young player, *The Peasant Village Dance* offers the challenge of mixed meter (constantly alternating 3/4 and 2/4 meters). Both works allude to the same European folk song quality.

Unit 4: Technical Considerations

The work is based on the F dorian and E-flat major scales. Scale exercises for these scales are printed on each part. The percussion parts have exercises that stress the need to sense underlying eighth and sixteenth notes. The instrumentation is well suited for the young band: flute, oboe, B-flat clarinet, alto saxophone, tenor saxophone, low woodwind, trumpet/cornet, F horn, trombone, baritone, tuba, and percussion (bells, xylophone, triangle, temple blocks, snare drum, tambourine, and three tom-toms). The rhythm for the winds is mostly whole, half, quarter, and eighth notes and appropriate rests. The snare drum has sixteenth notes as well as some rolls. Both the snare drum part and the tom-tom part require playing "off beats."

Unit 5: Stylistic Considerations

There are three distinctly different styles of playing eighth and quarter notes: 1) unmarked (regular), 2) *staccato*, and 3) accented. The players need to be aware of these different styles, especially that the *staccato* notes need to be played lightly, while the accented notes need a heavier, separated style. Observing these stylistic differences will also strengthen the structural integrity of the piece; the A section needs to be played stylistically different from the B section. It should also be noted that keeping the repeated eighth notes in a consistent *staccato* style for ten measures in the alto and tenor saxophone parts and for fourteen measures in the trombone, baritone, and tuba parts will be a challenge. The use of multiple percussion adds much color throughout the piece.

Unit 6: Musical Elements

The harmonic progressions of the piece are modal, regardless of the fact that the tonality is F dorian or E-flat major. The modulations are generally whole-step progressions rather than the classic dominant-tonic relationships.

Unit 7: Form and Structure

SECTION	MEASURE	EVENT AND SCORING
Introduction	1-2	Fm chord with added ninth
Section A	5-14	The four-measure theme is repeated three times; while some voices are taken away, more voices are added at the interval of a third or a sixth at each repetition of the theme, causing the texture to thicken; a repeated *staccato* eighth note accompaniment pattern is present throughout the section
Section B	15-22	All parts are basically playing unison rhythms, with stylistic contrast evident between the staccato and regular notes of the B theme
Section A	23-31	Has only a one-measure introduction; thematic material is presented only once
Section B	32-39	Thematic material is presented in its entirety, with changes in the assignment of the basic lines
Coda	40-end	Based on thematic material from the A theme

Unit 8: Suggested Listening

Bela Bartok, *Mikrokosmos*, Books 1-4
David Holsinger, *The Peasant Village Dance*
Anne McGinty, *Bartok Folk Trilogy*

Unit 9: Additional References and Resources

Dvorak, Thomas L., Cynthia Crump Taggart, and Peter Schmaltz. *Best Music for Young Band.* Edited by Bob Margolis. Brooklyn, NY: Manhattan Beach Music, 1986.

Garofalo, Robert J. *Instructional Designs for Middle/Junior High School Band.* Fort Lauderdale, FL: Meredith Music Publications, 1995.

TRN Music Publishers, Ruidoso, NM.

Wingert-Jones Music, Inc., Kansas City, MO.

Contributed by:
Winona Holsinger
Graduate Associate
University of North Texas
Denton, Texas

Teacher Resource Guide

A Hymn for Band
Hugh M. Stuart
(b. 1917)

Unit 1: Composer

Active as a school instrumental music teacher and supervisor for thirty-three years in Maryland and New Jersey, Hugh M. Stuart brings a wealth of experience to the field of educational band music. Born in Harrisburg, Pennsylvania, Stuart received degrees from Oberlin Conservatory and Columbia Teachers College. He has also done graduate study at Rutgers, Newark State College, and University of Michigan. In addition to teaching and guest clinician work, he was also an active studio musician, working on radio and television, and in jazz groups before his retirement. His catalog of compositions includes over 100 works for band, orchestra, small ensembles, solos, and instrumental teaching. He now lives in Albuquerque, New Mexico.

Unit 2: Composition

In his notes on the score, Stuart describes *A Hymn for Band* as a piece designed "to help develop a better band sound through the performance of a *legato* style." This quiet work was composed and published in 1985. Directors looking for improvement in tone quality, phrasing, and intonation will find much of value in this piece's simple dignity and flowing melodies leading to a dramatic, full conclusion. The tune is an original one by Stuart, designed to be reminiscent of old church melodies in its phrasal structure and simple, plaintive melody.

Unit 3: Historical Perspective

Since the publication of the *Bay Psalm Book* in 1640, hymns and hymn tunes have formed an important ingredient in the establishment of American music. The first compositions in the young American colony were early efforts at breaking away from the European (mostly British) models of hymn writing. William Billings, the first American composer of any prominence, wrote many hymn tunes and texts in the mid-1700s. In the pedagogical work of Thomas Hastings, Lowell Mason, and Horatio Parker in the mid- and late-1800s, the hymn formed a core element in their efforts to teach music literacy and basic performance techniques. Spirituals, both white and black, are often ascribed as resulting from the cross-breeding of mostly Protestant hymn tunes and texts with the musical traditions of the slaves.

Unit 4: Technical Considerations

A Hymn for Band was composed with the sole intent of focusing on tone and phrasing, so technical considerations are minimal. A key rhythmic element is the quarter note on beat four, tied over the bar to another quarter on beat one. The syncopated eighth tied to a quarter is also used. Ranges are comfortable for the brasses and most woodwinds except clarinet I, which stays above the staff for much of the time. Clarinet II and III stay lower but cross the break frequently. In the dramatic ending, flutes go up to a G above the staff for two beats.

Much of the melody is scored for French horn and alto saxophone, but there is ample cross-cueing for exposed lines. Parts are provided for a full woodwind section, including E-flat contrabass clarinet. There are no percussion parts in the score, but mallet instruments, particularly vibraphone, could easily double other parts and fit well into the ensemble sound.

Unit 5: Stylistic Considerations

A Hymn for Band is all about sustained sound—attention to phrasing and support are critical. The piece has been carefully constructed with many overlapping phrases, aiding the seamless flow of sound. This is an excellent opportunity to focus on the meaning of *phrase in music* and the need for sustained playing and warm tone quality. For the bass line notes which are not slurred, concentrate on a *legato* tonguing with extra length on each quarter note, as if each note had a *tenuto* marking.

The dynamic markings leave much room for interpretation, so shape the melody and experiment with different *crescendo* and *decrescendo* of phrases. Use this music to reinforce your students' ability to follow conducting gesture in expressive playing—change the phrase shaping and contour frequently, and make them play in the manner you conduct.

Unit 6: Musical Elements

A *Hymn for Band* begins in the band favorite key of B-flat and makes one modulation to E-flat. There is prominent use of a countermelody in the horn and alto saxophone part, which Stuart notes should "soar over the melody, if you have the horses." The ending contains several *caesuras*, which require careful cut-off and release from the conductor, along with a dramatic *rallentando* and *crescendo*.

Unit 7: Form and Structure

A *Hymn for Band* is built in three major sections—the first and second in B-flat and the third in E-flat—giving a straightforward A-B-A' form, with an eight-bar coda. The sections are constructed in standard four-bar hymn phrases, four phrases in the A section and three phrases in the answering B section. The second and third phrases of the B section are repeats of the melodic material in the second and fourth phrases of the A section.

KEY	SECTION	MEASURE
B-flat	Section A	1-16
	Section B	17-28
E-flat	Section A	29-44
	Coda (repetition of last A phrase)	45-52

Unit 8: Suggested Listening

J.S. Bach, transcriptions of chorales and chorale preludes by Eric Leidzen, Alfred Reed, Larry Daehn

Frank Erickson:
Air for Band
Balladair

William Latham, *Three Chorale Preludes*

Frank Ticheli, *Amazing Grace*

Ralph Vaughan Williams/arr. Beeler, *Rhosymedre*

Unit 9: Additional References and Resources

Duarte, Leonard P., Daniel S. Hiestand, Carol Ann Prater, and Doy E. Prater. *Band Music That Works*. Volume 1. Burlingame, CA: Contrapuntal Publications, 1987.

Duarte, Leonard P., Daniel S. Hiestand, Carol Ann Prater, and Doy E. Prater. *Band Music That Works*. Volume 2. Burlingame, CA: Contrapuntal Publications, 1988.

Dvorak, Thomas L., Robert Grechesky, and Gary Ciepluch. *Best Music for High School Band*. Bob Margolis, ed. Brooklyn, NY: Manhattan Beach Music, 1993.

Dvorak, Thomas L., Cynthia Crump Taggart, and Peter Schmaltz. *Best Music for Young Band*. Bob Margolis, ed. Brooklyn, NY: Manhattan Beach Music, 1986.

Randel, Don, ed. *New Harvard Dictionary of Music*. Cambridge, MA: Harvard University Press, 1986.

Sadie, Stanley. *Norton/Grove Concise Encyclopedia of Music*. New York: W.W. Norton and Co., 1988.

Contributed by:

Doug Norton
American School in London
London, United Kingdom

Teacher Resource Guide

In the Shining of the Stars
Robert Sheldon
(b. 1954)

Unit 1: Composer

An internationally known composer and clinician, Robert Sheldon began his musical career with a Bachelor of Music Degree from the University of Miami and a Master of Fine Arts Degree from the University of Florida. Sheldon has taught public school instrumental music in Florida and Illinois. He has also taught conducting and music education classes, and directed university bands at Florida State University. He currently maintains a busy composition and teaching schedule in Illinois, while accepting commissions for new works. Awards received by Sheldon include the Volkwein Award for composition and the Stanbury Award for teaching from The American School Band Directors Association, and eight "Standard Awards" from the American Society of Composers, Authors and Publishers. In 1990, he was named Outstanding Bandmaster of the Year by the International Assembly of Phi Beta Mu.

Unit 2: Composition

In the Shining of the Stars is a slow piece designed to produce a mood that is uplifting. Composed in 1996, it utilizes lush melodies and counterlines. The main and secondary themes are placed in different harmonic settings. The work is approximately four minutes in length, with many opportunities for artistic license.

Unit 3: Historical Perspective

Robert Sheldon is well known for producing quality music for bands at all levels. He has received much acclaim specifically for his compositional contributions in the educational repertoire. In the past ten years, there has been a growing need for quality literature for beginning bands. Robert Sheldon has made a significant contribution to this cause. *In the Shining of the Stars* is a well-scored, tuneful piece that can be played by younger bands.

Unit 4: Technical Considerations

The key of E-flat major is used through the first part of the piece, making a transition into A-flat major. Accidentals appear in parts due to the use of passing tones and chromatic chords used for color. The work is written in a slow cut time. Although the piece may seem slow for cut time (half note = 52), it encourages the smooth melodic style which was intended. This piece would be a good introduction to cut time for a young group. Since it would be easy for the conductor to go from cut time back into a four pattern, students can easily learn the concept of cut time. The instrumentation is for standard concert band with very light percussion writing.

Unit 5: Stylistic Considerations

Expression is the key to this work. The flowing lines and counterlines are best played smooth and connected. Phrasing is another important element. Most melodic material can be broken down into four-bar phrases. Dynamic indications help to build these phrases logically. *Crescendos* and *decrescendos* lead one phrase to another. More dynamic inflections can be added through the director's interpretation.

Unit 6: Musical Elements

A rich and sonorous tone quality is required in all voices. Although the melody and harmony are fairly diatonic, Sheldon makes good use of chromatic chords that produce some colorful settings of the melody. Each time the melody is stated, there is a bit more chromaticism involved. One of the piece's climaxes is the transition to the new key of A-flat major. Rising eighth notes are accompanied by a *crescendo* and a suspended cymbal roll. After a build to *ff* in m. 68, the piece fades dynamically to its ending.

Unit 7: Form and Structure

SECTION	MEASURE	VOICING
A	1	Alto saxophone and clarinet melody with middle and low voice accompaniment
A	18	Flute and trumpet melody with full ensemble accompaniment

SECTION	MEASURE	VOICING
B	34	Flute and clarinet 1 melody with woodwind, middle and low brass accompaniment
Transition to A-flat major	42	Begins with half of B statement, followed by a two-bar melodic sequence passed through the ensemble
A	54	Original melodic material in new key is stated in trumpet, clarinet 1, flute, and oboe
Dominant prolongation	68	Dominant chord is sustained with a rising E-flat mixolydian scale in the low brass
Coda	72	Fragmented melody ascends through the ensemble, ending on tonic

Unit 8: Suggested Listening

James Barnes, *Yorkshire Ballad*
Larry D. Daehn, *As Summer Was Just Beginning*
Stephen Foster/Kinyon, *Jeanie*
Percy Grainger, *Irish Tune from County Derry*
Percy Grainger/Bainum, *Australian Up-Country Tune*

Unit 9: Additional References and Resources

Rehrig, William H. *The Heritage Encyclopedia of Band Music.* Edited by Paul E. Bierley. Westerville, OH: Integrity Press, 1991.

Sheldon, Deborah and Robert. *The Complete Woodwind Instructor: A Guidebook for the Music Educator,* Oskaloosa: C.L. Barnhouse Company, 1996.

Contributed by:

Paul Nickolas
Indiana University
Bloomington, Indiana

Teacher Resource Guide

Jeanie

Stephen Foster
(1826–1864)

arranged by John Kinyon
(b. 1918)

Unit 1: Composer

Born on July 4, 1826, in Lawrenceville, Pennsylvania, Stephen Foster became one of the prominent composers of early folk songs in the United States. He was the ninth child of an Irish-American family. Despite little encouragement from his family, Stephen taught himself to compose music. In 1846, when Stephen began working as a bookkeeper for his brother, he began to publish songs. The success of these songs led him to decide upon songwriting as a profession. At the age of twenty-four, Stephen married Jane McDowell, who is believed to be "Jeanie," the subject of this song. During his twenty years of composition, Foster produced over 200 compositions. Some notable songs include *My Old Kentucky Home, Oh! Susanna, Camptown Races, Old Folks at Home*, and *Jeanie with the Light Brown Hair*.

Unit 2: Composition

Jeanie with the Light Brown Hair, the tune for which this composition is based, was originally composed in 1854. From the beginning of their marriage, Stephen and Jane Foster had difficulties. This ballad is believed to be an attempt by Stephen to win his wife back after a temporary separation in 1953. The song itself falls into a category of poetic ballads by Foster. Other songs in this category include *Gentle Annie* and *Beautiful Dreamer*.

Unit 3: Historical Perspective

Foster's place in the forefront of early American songwriters is secure. In the mid-nineteenth century, his style of ballad writing was very popular. Most of these pieces are rooted in Irish traditional songs and British-American airs. It was composed at a time when a need for music was increasing due to a growing middle class who were becoming more involved in music. These nostalgic songs were generally simple and tuneful, which made them approachable by the amateur musician.

Unit 4: Technical Considerations

The piece is almost entirely in E-flat major. Few accidentals are used in transitional areas. Rhythmical elements consist primarily of whole, half, and quarter notes, with few eighth and dotted-half notes. While the meter is mostly common time, Kinyon inserts one measure of 6/4 at the end of the first statement. The only exception to standard concert band instrumentation is the lack of percussion. Instrumental ranges, which may extend beyond a young player's ability, are cornet I (F5) and flute 1 (E6).

Unit 5: Stylistic Considerations

A *rubato*, sustained style is suggested by the arranger for a successful performance. He includes some suggestions throughout the piece for tempo variation. A *legato* style should be used to enhance the tuneful melody. Harmonic material should also be played in a chorale style. Dynamic indications range from *p* to *mf*, suggesting a conservative, understated approach.

Unit 6: Musical Elements

The tonality of the work is based mostly in the key of E-flat major. Kinyon keeps most of Foster's melodic and harmonic concepts, which produces a very consonant sounding piece. The different families of the ensemble are displayed throughout the setting. The brass, woodwinds, and middle voices all receive a chance to play in a smaller ensemble setting.

Unit 7: Form and Structure

SECTION	MEASURE	VOICING
Opening	1	Full ensemble
A1	2	Brass ensemble
A2	10	Brass ensemble
B	18	Woodwinds, French horns, baritones
A3	26	Brass ensemble
B	34	Saxophones, baritone, tuba
A3	42	Full ensemble
Coda	48	Full ensemble, ending with ascending arpeggios

Unit 8: Suggested Listening

James Barnes, *Yorkshire Ballad*
Larry D. Daehn, *As Summer Was Just Beginning*
Percy Grainger, *Irish Tune from County Derry*
Percy Grainger/Bainum, *Australian Up-Country Tune*
Robert Sheldon, *In the Shining of the Stars*

Unit 9: Additional References and Resources

Austin, William W. "Susanna," "Jeanie," and "The Old Folks at Home": *The Songs of Stephen C. Foster from his Time to Ours*. Chicago: University of Illinois Press, 1987.

Rehrig, William H. *The Heritage Encyclopedia of Band Music*. Edited by Paul E. Bierley. Westerville, OH: Integrity Press, 1991.

Sadie, Stanley, ed. *The New Grove Dictionary of Music and Musicians*. 20 Vols. London: Macmillan, 1980. S.v. "Stephen Collins Foster," by H. Wiley Hitchcock.

Contributed by:

Paul Nickolas
Indiana University
Bloomington, Indiana

Teacher Resource Guide

Legend of Knife River
Stephen Bulla
(b. 1953)

Unit 1: Composer

Stephen Bulla holds a degree in Arranging and Composition from Berklee College of Music. Interest in composing for the commercial industry led Bulla to his present schedule of full-time composing. By joining "The President's Own" U.S. Marine Band and White House Orchestra in 1980, his responsibility involves creating musical productions containing many styles and instrumental combinations. Most of his compositions are intended to be performed for Presidential functions and visiting dignitaries. His musical arrangement featured on the PBS television series "In Concert at the White House" features Sarah Vaughan, The Manhattan Transfer, Mel Torme, and Doc Severinsen. A successful career in the commercial industry led Bulla to frequent studio productions involving CD recordings as well as writing music for regional and national advertising campaigns. He also works on numerous commissions in the wind band field which are performed worldwide. These works for band are exclusively published by CMP (North America) and De Haske Music (Europe). Bulla's awards include ADDY Award for best original music/TV spot and ASCAP Performance Award. He manages his busy schedule as a guest conductor, adjudicator, and clinician, and he also serves as music director for The Salvation Army National Capital Brass Band in Washington, DC.

Unit 2: Composition

Legend of Knife River was written when the composer visited near Minot, North Dakota, as a guest conductor at the International Music Camp. The work represents the heart of Sacajawea County, where Sacajawea, a young

Native American interpreter and guide, joined the American explorers Lewis and Clark and helped identify landmarks along their journeys. Sacajawea was also an important mediator for the expedition team when they encountered hostile Indians. A beautiful bronze statue of Sacajawea and her infant son stands by the state capitol in Bismarck.

Unit 3: Historical Perspective
This work represents the early explorers having fear and doubt when traveling into unknown territories. When the explorers would get deeper into the area, they would meet the young Indian interpreter who helped them continue their journey. Thus, the composer's use of folk-like melodies throughout this work varies with the scenes of the explorers' journey. For instance, in order to indicate the fears and doubts of the explorers, the composer uses the dorian mode with a slower tempo. In the section with the faster tempo, the tune "gallops," consisting of many continuous eighth note figures, with *staccato* representing the ease of the journey due to the help of the young Indian.

Unit 4: Technical Considerations
This work does not require an extremely high level of technique. However, an accurate articulation to each note is a must. This includes the continuous quarter notes in the opening, the dotted rhythm throughout the first half of the melodic line, and the eighth notes from the middle to the end of the piece. Instrumentation is basic enough for a youth band to play. The percussion part does not require any special instruments to perform this work. In addition, the writing for the percussion section is not technically complicated. However, accurate articulation and balance in the section is critical.

Unit 5: Stylistic Considerations
In the opening of this work, continuous quarter notes are present; these notes should be steady. To help a youth band perform this section, imagine the explorers being afraid during the unknown journey. In this slow tempo of the first half of this work, maintaining the figure with the dotted rhythm is slightly difficult for a youth group. The *forte* section in the first half should be played in a broad, majestic style. The second half, starting with faster tempo, is in a galloping style. Keeping the consecutive eighth notes light helps to maintain this section. The accompanying flute solo at m. 45 should also be light. Establishing contrast between the slow, ponderous section and the lively gallop section is a key for a successful performance.

Unit 6: Musical Elements
Throughout this work, careful attention should be paid to the accidentals. This suggests that performers be familiar with the keys used in this work: dorian and B-flat major.

Unit 7: Form and Structure

SECTION	MEASURE	KEY	EVENT AND SCORING
A	1-32		
I	1-12	Dorian	Flutes and clarinets alternating solo parts with D pedal tones by alto clarinet, bass clarinet, tuba, and timpani
II	13-32	Dorian	Melodies and pedal tones doubled by other instruments
B	33-end		
I	33-43	Dorian	Melodic instruments in homophonic texture with constant eighth note figure by clarinets
II	44-51	B-flat major	Solo flute briefly featured against flowing contrapuntal lines
I'	52-73	Dorian	Solo flutes featured throughout with homophonic accompaniment
Coda	74-end	B-flat major	Continuation of flute soli against countermelodies in trumpets

Unit 8: Suggested Listening
Stephen Bulla, *Jubiloso*
James Curnow, *Korean Folk Rhapsody*
Howard Hanson, *Chorale and Alleluia*
Bob Margolis: *Fanfare, Ode and Festival* (after Gervaise)
    Soldier Procession and Sword Dance (after Tielman Susato)
W. Francis McBeth, *Chant and Jubilo*
Vincent Persichetti, *Psalm for Band*
William Schuman, *Chester Overture for Band*

Unit 9: Additional References and Resources
Battisti, Frank, and Robert Garofalo. *Guide to Score Study*. Ft. Lauderdale, FL: Meredith Music Publications, 1990.

"Bob Margolis: Fanfare, Ode and Festival (after Gervaise)." *Teaching Music through Performance in Band*. Compiled and edited by Richard Miles. Chicago: GIA Publications, Inc., 1998.

Bulla, Stephen. *Legend of Knife River*. Curnow Records CR97007, 1997. Compact disc.

Jackson, Roland. *Performance Practice Medieval to Contemporary: A Bibliographic Guide*. New York: Garland, 1988.

Kosta, Stefan, and Dorothy Payne. *Tonal Harmony*. New York: McGrawHill, Inc., 1995.

Rehrig, William H. *The Heritage Encyclopedia of Band Music*. Edited by Paul E. Bierley. Westerville, OH: Integrity Press, 1991.

"Sacajawea." *Compton's Interactive Encyclopedia for Windows '95 and Windows 3.1 Version 5.1*. SoftKey Multimedia Inc., 1997.

"Sacajawea." *Microsoft Encarta '96 Encyclopedia for Windows '95*. Microsoft Corporation, 1996.

"William Schuman: Chester Overture for Band." *Teaching Music through Performance in Band*. Compiled and edited by Richard Miles. Chicago: GIA Publications, Inc., 1998.

Contributed by:

Yoshiaki Tanno
Doctoral Associate
Indiana University
Bloomington, Indiana

Teacher Resource Guide

Overture on a Shaker Tune
John Higgins
(b. 1948)

Unit 1: Composer

The writing of John Higgins began to formulate while a student arranger for the University of Michigan bands, under William D. Revelli. Higgins' career has included public school teaching, co-authoring the *Learning Unlimited* string method, and arranging and producing a large catalog of children's musicals. He was President of Jenson Publications until it became part of Hal Leonard Publishing Corporation. He is now Director of Instrumental Publications for Hal Leonard. Higgins is active as a guest-conductor, clinician, and writer. His additional works for band include *Broadway Spectacular*, *Departure One*, *Journey to Bethlehem*, and *Sounds of Hollywood*.

Unit 2: Composition

Overture on a Shaker Tune, published in 1986, uses the popular Shaker tune *Simple Gifts* as the main melodic material. There are two statements of this theme. The first comes after an introduction, and the second finishes the piece after an interlude of material from both the introduction and new development material. The work includes musical elements such as numerous articulations, tempo changes, and modulations to help a young band develop. Performance time is approximately three minutes and twenty seconds.

Unit 3: Historical Perspective

The Shakers were a late eighteenth century division from the Quakers. They believed that God was both father and mother. They practiced a communal life, which included much singing and dancing. Through their beliefs they created music that has lasted to the present. *Simple Gifts* is the most well-known Shaker tune. It has been used as the basis for countless arrangements. Perhaps the most notable setting is in Aaron Copland's *Appalachian Spring* (1943-44).

Unit 4: Technical Considerations

The keys of F major, E-flat major, and A-flat major are used in this piece, requiring both scalar and arpeggiated playing. Accidentals do occur but are infrequent. Rhythmic challenges include extensive syncopation and motion or entrances on weak beats. The meter is 4/4 throughout the work. Minor tempo variations include *ritardandos* and sectional changes such as *maestoso*, *allegro*, and broadly. The scoring is generally doubled, with clarinets being the only section divided into three parts. Range considerations include clarinets crossing the break frequently and first trumpet being comfortable up to top line F. Trumpet has the only solo. Five percussion parts include snare drum, bass drum, suspended cymbal, triangle, xylophone, marimba, bells, and two timpani requiring re-tuning down one step at the key change.

Unit 5: Stylistic Considerations

Understanding and proficiency of articulations, including *staccato*, *legato*, and accents, is required for the entire ensemble. Dynamics range from *p* to *ff* for most instruments and also include *crescendos*, *decrescendos*, and *fp*. Long phrases are preferred as they are marked every eight bars in the *allegro* section.

Unit 6: Musical Elements

Homophonic writing dominates this work. Melody is often harmonized with triadic writing. Accompanimental lines tend to be repeated rhythmic motives following the same harmonies. Some minor seconds are used to create tension but usually resolve quickly. Harmony is generally diatonic, with sporadic use of dominant sevenths and secondary dominant chords.

Unit 7: Form and Structure

SECTION	MEASURE	EVENT AND SCORING
Introduction	1-15	F major; *maestoso*
A	16-33	F major; *allegro*; first half of Shaker tune in trumpet and alto saxophone
	34-40	Second half of Shaker tune harmonized in upper woodwinds
B	41-47	F major; transitional material using fragments from Introduction

SECTION	MEASURE	EVENT AND SCORING
C	48-67	E-flat major; new melodic material in upper woodwinds; trumpet solo; *tutti* playing into second statement of Shaker tune
A'	68-83	A-flat major; broadly; second statement of Shaker tune, upper woodwinds have a repeated accompanimental line
Coda	84-end	A-flat major; *allegro;* uses some material from Introduction

Unit 8: Suggested Listening

Aaron Copland:
Appalachian Spring
Variations on a Shaker Tune
Calvin Custer, *Appalachian Suite*
John Zdechlik, *Chorale and Shaker Dance*

Unit 9: Additional References and Resources

"The Basic Band Curriculum: Grades I, II, III." *BD Guide*, September/October 1989, 2-6.

Duarte, Leonard P., Daniel S. Hiestand, Carol Ann Prater, and Doy E. Prater. *Band Music That Works*. Volume 1. Burlingame, CA: Contrapuntal Publications, 1987.

Duarte, Leonard P., Daniel S. Hiestand, Carol Ann Prater, and Doy E. Prater. *Band Music That Works*. Volume 2. Burlingame, CA: Contrapuntal Publications, 1988.

Dvorak, Thomas L., Cynthia Crump Taggart, and Peter Schmaltz. *Best Music for Young Band*. Edited by Bob Margolis. Brooklyn, NY: Manhattan Beach Music, 1986.

Hal Leonard Corporation, Milwaukee, WI.

Stolba, K Marie. *The Development of Western Music*. Dubuque, IA: William C. Brown Publishers, 1990.

Contributed by:

Mark Duker
Indiana University
Bloomington, Indiana

Teacher Resource Guide

Renaissance Festival & Dances

arranged by Bruce Pearson
(b. 1942)

Unit 1: Composer
Born in 1942, Bruce Pearson's career has included over three decades of classroom teaching. He is best known for writing the *Standard of Excellence* and *Best in Class* band methods. In addition to writing, Pearson has served as a guest conductor and clinician throughout Asia, Europe, and North America, including all fifty states. Other activities include guest lectures at over seventy-five colleges and universities, and keynote addresses for state and national music educators conferences.

Unit 2: Composition
Renaissance Festival & Dances was published in 1995. It is in three movements entitled "Festival," "Pavane," and "Courtly Dance," and may be used in correlation with *Standard of Excellence*, book two (p. 27). Performance time of all three movements is listed as five minutes and twenty-one seconds.

Unit 3: Historical Perspective
Pearson writes in the score:

> The Renaissance period (1450-1600) marked the emergence of new
> ideas and discoveries in art, science, and philosophy. The period
> was influenced by humanism, emphasis on the individual. In this
> conducive environment, creative artists flourished. Some of the
> greatest visual artists of all time, including Boticelli, Leonardo da
> Vinci, Michelangelo, and Titian, created their masterpieces during
> the Renaissance.

While vocal sacred and secular music of the Renaissance reached people of common means in churches in the form of motets, or on the street in the form of expressive madrigals, instrumental music was usually performed for an elite audience. Performances often took place in the homes of the nobility as dance music for balls and social affairs.

Unit 4: Technical Considerations

The keys of A-flat major, C minor, and E-flat major are present in this piece. Accidentals are used very sparingly as passing tones or leading tones to cadence points. The third movement, however, does switch tonality quickly at times, requiring careful observance of accidentals and key signatures. Rhythmic concerns include irregular ties over bar lines and independent motion within sections due to the Renaissance style. Instrumentation is standard with the exception of extensive percussion writing, which has five parts including up to eight simultaneous instruments in some sections.

Unit 5: Stylistic Considerations

Pearson writes in the score:

> *Renaissance Festival & Dances* is a suite of dances based on the music of German composer and publisher, Tielman Susato (1500? - 1561?), and English instrumental music composer, Antony Holborne (? - 1602?). The first movement, "Festival," and the last movement, "Courtly Dance," are rather brisk dances. They should be played with the notes separated and given a "lift." The first beat of each measure should be emphasized. The second movement, "Pavane," is a slow, processional type of dance.

Unit 6: Musical Elements

Understanding of cadences will be important in this work. Phrases in the first two movements generally cadence on the tonic chord. In "Courtly Dance," cadences on the dominant and secondary dominant are more frequent than tonic. Melodic lines are generally homophonic, with occasional independent inner lines. The third movement also alters phrase lengths, often lengthening or obscuring beginnings and ends of phrases. Throughout the work, textures alternate between *tutti* passages, brass and woodwind choirs, and percussion section writing.

Unit 7: Form and Structure

SECTION	MEASURE	EVENT AND SCORING
Movement I: "Festival"		
A	1-8	A-flat major; eight-measure phrase
B-B	9-17	A-flat major; eight-measure phrase repeated
A'-A'	18-33	A-flat major; opening A section twice
C	34-41	A-flat major; eight-measure phrase
B-B'	42-end	A-flat major; B section played twice with three-measure tag at end
Movement II: "Pavane"		
A-A	1-16	C minor; eight-measure phrase twice
B	17-24	C minor; eight-measure phrase, cadences on F minor
C	25-end	C minor; eight-measure phrase
Movement III: "Courtly Dance"		
Introduction	1-8	E-flat major; eight-measure percussion introduction
A	9-17	E-flat major; eight-measure phrase repeated; cadences on B-flat major
B-B	18-33	B-flat major; eight-measure phrase twice; cadences on F major both times
C-C'	34-47	F minor; eight-measure phrase, cadences on A-flat major; related six-measure phrase, then cadences on E-flat major
	48-55	E-flat major; introductory material
A-A-A'	56-end	E-flat major; eight-measure phrase repeated; cadences on B-flat major; final eight-measure phrase is same A material, but cadences on E-flat major

Unit 8: Suggested Listening

Robert Jager, *Colonial Airs and Dances*
William P. Latham, *Court Festival*
Ron Nelson, *Courtly Airs and Dances*
Tielman Susato/Bob Margolis, *The Battle Pavane*

Unit 9: Additional References and Resources

"The Basic Band Curriculum: Grades I, II, III." *BD Guide*,
   September/October 1989, 2-6.

Duarte, Leonard P., Daniel S. Hiestand, Carol Ann Prater, and Doy E.
   Prater. *Band Music That Works*. Volume 1. Burlingame, CA: Contrapuntal
   Publications, 1987.

Duarte, Leonard P., Daniel S. Hiestand, Carol Ann Prater, and Doy E.
   Prater. *Band Music That Works*. Volume 2. Burlingame, CA: Contrapuntal
   Publications, 1988.

Dvorak, Thomas L., Cynthia Crump Taggart, and Peter Schmaltz. *Best Music
   for Young Band*. Edited by Bob Margolis. Brooklyn, NY: Manhattan Beach
   Music, 1986.

Groeling, Charles. "New Music Review." *The Instrumentalist*. June 1996, 54.

Neil A. Kjos Music Company, San Diego, CA.

Stolba, K Marie. *The Development of Western Music*. Dubuque, IA: William
   C. Brown Publishers, 1990.

Contributed by:

Mark Duker
Indiana University
Bloomington, Indiana

Teacher Resource Guide

Sinfonia Six

Timothy Broege
(b. 1947)

Unit 1: Composer

Timothy Broege was born in Belmar, New Jersey, on November 6, 1947. He received a Bachelor of Music Degree with Highest Honors in 1969 from Northwestern University. While at Northwestern, he studied composition and harpsichord. From 1969 to 1971, he taught in the Chicago public schools until accepting a position as an instrumental music teacher at Manasquan Elementary School in Manasquan, New Jersey, where he taught from 1971 to 1980. Many of his works for young band were composed for the Manasquan students. He has written over thirty compositions for band including the Sinfonia series. Broege received the Goldman Award at the 1994 ASBDA Convention for his works for school bands. Currently, he holds a position as faculty member at Monmouth Conservatory of Music, Red Bank, New Jersey, and remains active as a recitalist on harpsichord and organ.

Unit 2: Composition

Sinfonia Six was composed in 1974 for the Concert Band of Manasquan Elementary School, Manasquan, New Jersey, where Timothy Broege taught instrumental music. The work was subsequently revised in 1982. The work is essentially about two kinds of contrast. The first is that of mood or, as the later eighteenth century composers would have it, "effect." The second type of contrast is timbrel. Each movement places a solo instrument or group in opposition to the *tutti* ensemble. The first movement is melancholy, the second playful, the third somber, and the finale boisterous and aggressive.

Unit 3: Historical Perspective

Completed in 1974 and revised in 1982, *Sinfonia Six* was written to provide playable music with merit for young students. *Sinfonia Six* was written in the same style or manner as the seventeenth and eighteenth century instrumental suites. In this manner the work refers to old forms and processes. The publisher added the subtitle "The Four Elements: Earth, Wind, Fire and Water" at the time of the revision in 1982. The composer did not have this concept in mind about the four movements. Instead, his approach was more abstract and was based on the ensemble performing the music with similar emotions and expression. Of particular value to the study and approach to this work are the keyboard suites of Bach, the instrumental concerti grosso of Handel, and the dance suites of Rameau.

Unit 4: Technical Considerations

The work is listed as a grade three, but simplicity of the individual parts could substantiate almost a grade two rating. However, the level of difficulty conductors have found in creating the overall music have led to many describing *Sinfonia Six* as almost grade four. There is a concentration on solo instruments throughout the work. In the first movement, three clarinets form the solo group. In the second, a solo baritone horn is used. This solo is cued *8va alta* for the alto saxophone in a separate "Special Part," which is provided with the complete band set. The third movement uses a duo of trumpet and alto saxophone in a call-and-response pattern, with the full ensemble providing the responses. The finale uses the entire percussion section as a concertante group. The finale movement comes the closest to conventional *tutti* scoring. Much of the vertical sonority of the work is based on stacked thirds, resulting in numerous seventh and ninth chords. Young players often have intonation difficulty with these sonorities.

Unit 5: Stylistic Considerations

Throughout the work, vertical sonorities must be carefully tuned. In the first movement, chordal voicings using sevenths and seconds and ninths are used extensively. The second movement is more melodically driven and is built around the solo line. The third movement is more expressive and melodic, and follows more of a song form approach. The percussion in the fourth movement forms an *ostinato* and provides a firm base for building momentum. As stated earlier, the ensemble must agree on emotional and expressive dimensions. Although the work is not technically difficult, creating the overall ensemble approach can be a challenge.

Unit 6: Musical Elements

Sinfonia Six is essentially about two types of contrast: mood and timbrel. Each movement uses solo instruments in opposition to the *tutti* ensemble. Chordal writing and voicings are important aspects throughout the work. Each movement has its own unique character and should be approached individually. In Movement I there is the use of repeated sections, meter changes, and dynamic contrasts. Movement II also features some meter changes, but features careful scoring behind the solo line. Movement III features the trumpet and alto saxophone duet against the *tutti* ensemble, meter changes, and dynamic contrasts. The percussion *ostinato* highlights the final movement, but overall the full ensemble is more extensively used.

Unit 7: Form and Structure

The overall formal design of *Sinfonia Six* was not a set scheme but more of an overall plan or approach. The work took shape through an individual approach to each movement which was then grouped together, as in the seventeenth and eighteenth century suites. Movement I has a suggested metronome marking of quarter note = 72, and has two repeated sections and a closing section which feature an opposition between a clarinet trio and *tutti* ensemble. Movement II features a solo baritone horn with ensemble accompaniment and has a suggested metronome marking of quarter note = 112. Movement III has a suggested metronome marking of quarter note = 76 and features a duet between alto saxophone and trumpet in a more traditional song form structure. The final movement is faster, with a suggested metronome marking of quarter note = 144. The percussion *ostinato*-like approach features the most extensive use of full ensemble of the four movements. The movement builds from a *piano* marking to *fortissimo* then drops back to *piano* before quickly building back to *fortissimo* in the final measure. Throughout the movement is a feeling of building momentum.

Unit 8: Suggested Listening

Benjamin Brittain, *Suite on Old English Folk Tunes*
Timothy Broege, *Sinfonia* Series
Aaron Copland, *Red Pony Suite*
Gustav Holst, *First Suite in E-flat*
Frank Ticheli, *Fortress*
Any suite-like works of the seventeenth and eighteenth centuries

Unit 9: Additional References and Resources

Grout, Donald J., and Claude V. Palisca. A *History of Western Music*, 4th edition. New York: W.W. Norton & Company, 1988.

Miles, Richard, ed. *Teaching Music through Performance in Band*. Chicago: GIA Publications, Inc., 1997.

Rehrig, William. *The Heritage Encyclopedia of Band Music: Composers and Their Music*. Edited by Paul E. Bierley. Westerville, OH: Integrity Press, 1991.

Contributed By:

Otis French
Associate Conductor
United States Army Field Band
Washington, DC

Teacher Resource Guide

When the Stars Began to Fall
(My Lord, What a Mornin')
Fred J. Allen
(b. 1953)

Unit 1: Composer
Fred J. Allen received a bachelor's degree in Music Education from Abilene Christian University and later a Master of Music Degree from East Texas State University (now Texas A&M at Commerce). Allen began composing and arranging during his eleven years of teaching in the Texas public school system, in the districts of Dimmitt and North Richland Hills. He later became the Director of Bands at Abilene Christian. Fred Allen currently serves as the Director of Bands at Stephen F. Austin State University in Texas.

Unit 2: Composition
Following the success of *They Led My Lord Away*, Allen wanted to write a piece of similar texture with comparable technical aspects. He took an early sketch he wrote in 1978 and began to rework the piece. The resulting piece, *When the Stars Began to Fall*, was completed in 1992, and the first performance was given by the Richland (Texas) High School Band. The work was recorded at the Midwest Band and Orchestra Clinic in December of 1992 by the Duncanville (Texas) High School Band. The piece is dedicated to Doris Allen, the composer's mother.

Unit 3: Historical Perspective
Composers have often used popular hymns as a source of inspiration for their works. *When the Stars Began to Fall* is based on a spiritual/work song from the 1800s entitled *My Lord, What a Mornin'*. Some editions of the song have mistakenly titled it *My Lord, What a Mourning* because of the somber nature of

the work. The text is a loose reference to Matthew 24:29, which speaks of a grand daybreak.

Unit 4: Technical Considerations

The texture of this composition requires students to perform in both *soli* and *tutti* scoring. The trumpet section is featured in many places. While the range is very playable for most younger bands, the support needed to sustain phrases can be taxing for even experienced players. Students should be well versed in E-flat major/c minor as well as have control of a wide dynamic range.

Unit 5: Stylistic Considerations

Directors will want to prepare students for the necessary *legato* articulations found in this composition. The importance of the long phrasal line needs to be carefully explained. The two main exceptions are the repeated eighth note pick-ups (mm. 9, 13, 15, etc.)

and the pattern (low brass at m. 39) which must be played slightly *marcato*.

Unit 6: Musical Elements

The composition centers on the concert key of E-flat major, except for a brief section that moves to the relative key of c minor. Melodic material is very clearly defined with a distinct difference between melody and accompaniment lines. There is one notable area of text painting found in the work: the entrance of the trumpets in m. 9 corresponds with the text "you'll hear the trumpet sound." Conductors may choose to emphasize that line. The optional solo/*soli* section at m. 37 was originally intended as an alto saxophone solo. The cues make it possible to perform the work, even with less-than-ideal instrumentation. According to the composer, the sixteenth note/sextuplet pick-ups to m. 39 need to produce a sweeping effect to the return of the melody.

Unit 7: Form and Structure

MEASURE	EVENT AND SCORING
1-8	Introduction; E-flat major; Theme A in low brass
9-20	Theme B in trumpets; countermelody in French horns
21-30	Theme A in trumpets and flutes
31-38	Theme B (now in c minor) in trumpets and alto saxophone solo

MEASURE	EVENT AND SCORING
39-44	Theme A (trumpets) and Theme B' (low brass and low woodwinds) in E-flat major occurring simultaneously, along with new upper woodwind eighth note idea
45-50	Three closing statements from Theme A

Unit 8: Suggested Listening

Fred J. Allen:
  Fantasy on Barbara Allen
  Moravian Hymn Dance
J.S. Bach/Reed, *Come Sweet Death*
Johannes Brahms/Buehlman, *Blessed Are They*
Adoniram J. Gordon/Allen, *They Led My Lord Away*
Percy Grainger:
  Lincolnshire Posy (second movement)
  Ye Banks and Braes O' Bonnie Doon
David Holsinger, *A Childhood Hymn*
Jack Stamp, *Be Thou My Vision*
Frank Ticheli, *Amazing Grace*
Pavel Tschesnokoff/Houseknecht, *Salvation Is Created*

Unit 9: Additional References and Resources

Johnson, James Weldon, and J. Rosamond Johnson. *The Book of American Negro Spirituals*. New York: The Viking Press, 1969.

Miles, Richard, ed. *Teaching Music through Performance in Band*. Chicago: GIA Publications, Inc., 1997.

Miles, Richard, ed. *Teaching Music through Performance in Band*, Volume Two. Chicago: GIA Publications, Inc., 1998.

TRN Music Publisher, Ruidoso, NM. 1992.

Additional notes by Fred J. Allen.

Contributed by:

Jeff Cranmore
Director of Bands
Dowell Middle School
McKinney, Texas

Grade Three

Teacher Resource Guide

American Riversongs
Pierre La Plante
(b. 1934)

Unit 1: Composer

Pierre La Plante, of French-Canadian descent, was born in Milwaukee in 1934 and grew up in Sturgeon Bay, Wisconsin. He received his bachelor's and master's degrees from the University of Wisconsin at Madison. He has taught at the elementary, secondary, and college levels, which includes classroom, vocal, and instrumental instruction. He currently teaches in the Pecatonica Area School District in Wisconsin, and he is a member of the Wisconsin Music Educator's Conference and the Wisconsin Youth Band Directors Association. Among his compositions are works for band, orchestra, choir, solo literature, and chamber music. La Plante has been a bassoonist with the Dubuque Symphony, the Madison Theatre Guild Orchestra, and the Unitarian Society Orchestra. He currently performs with the Beloit-Janesville Symphony.

Unit 2: Composition

American Riversongs is a setting of folk songs reminiscent of a developing American nation when waterways were central to commerce and expansion of cities. The piece is in ternary form, beginning with a bright, spirited version of "Down the River." The middle section is a lyrical, andante setting of "Shenandoah." The tempo brightens as section three juxtaposes "The Glendy Burk" against a theme based on a Creole bamboula tune. A syncopated ragtime rhythm draws the piece to a fiery conclusion. *American Riversongs* was commissioned by and dedicated to the 1988-89 Oberlin High School Band in Oberlin, Ohio.

Unit 3: Historical Perspective

Since the early decades of the twentieth century, folk song idioms and tunes have been incorporated into wind band compositions. Charles Ives and Aaron Copland are among the most notable composers who have written works based on American folk songs. For his piece, La Plante highlights the region along the Missouri River and, in particular, French-influenced Louisiana. His works are contemporaneous with those of Clare Grundman and Dan Welcher.

Unit 4: Technical Considerations

The scales of B-flat major, E-flat major, and F major are required for the full ensemble. A "brass band" section requires a cornet section duet. Baritone and low reed parts are active. Most parts are doubled with occasional soli and solo voices. The contrapuntal writing becomes intricate, especially in the slow middle section. Balance and precision will be a focus. Clarity and balance are necessary in the *tutti*, loud passages. Section one contains standard rhythms in 6/8 meter. Section two is in 4/4 and 3/4, transitioning to section three, which is in a fast 2/4. This section contains syncopated rhythms and is more challenging than section one.

Unit 5: Stylistic Considerations

Maintaining balance between three and sometimes four moving lines will be a focus as melodies and countermelodies are passed around the ensemble. Attention must be given to pacing lest the piece becomes too loud too soon. *Staccato* playing is necessary over a wide dynamic spectrum and is used in thickly and thinly scored passages. Section one calls for a variety of note lengths simultaneously; a lifted style in the melody will serve to provide clarity. Section two contains lyrical, sustained lines, requiring rich, sonorous timbres. Section three features rapid shifts in dynamic level, style, and orchestration. Attention to clarity and balance will enhance the "layered" effect at the end of the work.

Unit 6: Musical Elements

The melodies and harmonies are essentially diatonic, and the phrase structure is mostly regular. Melodic material often serves a dual role as melody in one phrase and countermelody in another. Section two contains two statements of the melody with phrase extensions. This passage includes the most elaborate polyphonic writing. Section three includes a presentation of two independent themes, which are eventually treated contrapuntally and canonically. Simultaneous statements of these two melodies lead to a *tutti*, *fortissimo* coda.

Unit 7: Form and Structure

SECTION	MEASURE	EVENT AND SCORING
Section 1:		B-flat major, 6/8, bright and spirited
Introduction	1-11	
Theme A	12-55	"Down the River"; antecedent/ consequent repeated individually then stated once together mm. 12-55; melody in upper woodwinds
Bridge	56-63	
Theme A	64-71	Consequent
Section 2:		E-flat major, 4/4, 3/4, moderato
Introduction	72-75	
Theme B	76-99	"Shenandoah"; two statements; melody in brass
Transition	100-107	
Section 3:		F major, 2/4, fast, rhythmic
Introduction	108-119	
Theme C	120-153	"The Glendy Burk"; antecedent (brass band)/consequent
Transition	154-164	
Theme D	165-180	Bamboula tune; antecedent/consequent; melody in flutes; brief tuba solo
Themes C-D	181-195	Canonic C theme; trumpet and baritone/tenor saxophone
Bridge	196-214	*Tutti*
Theme D	215-223	Thinly scored
Theme C	224-231	Canonic
Coda	232-249	"Layered" effect

Unit 8: Suggested Listening

Aaron Copland, *Appalachian Spring*
Louis Moreau Gottschalk, *Bamboula, Op. 2*
Clare Grundman, *Kentucky 1800*
Charles Ives, *New England Triptych*
Pierre La Plante, *Prospect*
Dan Welcher, *Zion*

Unit 9: Additional References and Resources

Nettle, Bruno. *Folk Music in the United States: An introduction*, 3d ed. Detroit: Wayne State University Press, 1976.

Rehrig, William H. *The Heritage Encyclopedia of Band Music*, edited by Paul Bierley. Westerville, OH: Integrity Press, 1991.

Seeger, Charles, et al. "United States of America-Folk Music." Sadie, Stanley, ed., *The New Groves Dictionary of Music and Musicians*.

Contributed by:

Nancy M. Golden
Graduate Conducting Associate
University of North Texas
Denton, Texas

Teacher Resource Guide

Ave Maria
(Angelus Domini)

Franz Biebl
(b. 1906)

transcribed by Robert C. Cameron
(b. 1952)

Unit 1: Composer

Franz Biebl was born in 1906 and presently resides in Hamburg, Germany. He has over 2,000 published works including works for mixed choir, men's chorus, children's operas, and arrangements of American and German folk songs. He became interested in American folk music while being held a German POW during World War II in Battle Creek, Michigan. Biebl worked as a recording technician for Bavarian Radio for most of his life and also served as organist, choirmaster, and teacher at Furstenfeldbruch Kirche in Berlin. His primary teacher was Joseph Haas at the Musiklochschule in Munich.

Unit 2: Composition

Ave Maria was first published in 1964 in Dortmund, Germany, for seven-part men's voices. The version utilized in this transcription, however, is the version for mixed choir selected because it better matches the registration of the wind ensemble or symphonic band. This adaptation is a transcription rather than an arrangement in that every attempt has been made to preserve every possible detail of the original. The only editing which has been made are the addition of limited octave doublings and the addition of bar lines in order to facilitate performance of the freestyle chant sections.

Unit 3: Historical Perspective

As in all settings of *Ave Maria*, the glorification of the Virgin Mary is its spiritual and emotional focal point, thus the use of the Roman Catholic Latin text.

Unit 4: Technical Considerations

Ave Maria is harmonically centered around C major with limited use of chromaticism. Cues are generously provided for oboe 1, bassoon 1 and 2, and horn 1 and 2. There are several range considerations: Both trumpet 1 and bassoon 1 must ascend to written high a, though the latter is cued in alto saxophone 1. In addition, trombone 1 and euphonium are required to reach written high g. The measured free chant at the beginning and at the first ending may be played by any tenor or baritone instrument (preferably euphonium, and at the first ending, euphonium answered by horn), or can be sung in Latin by tenor voices. To facilitate this, the score and all parts contain cues for the Latin text and free chant.

Unit 5: Stylistic Considerations

In observance of late-romantic German choral style, it is essential that the style of playing be a sustained expressive *legato* throughout the composition. Care must be taken not to breathe at bar lines but rather only where marked.

Unit 6: Musical Elements

The harmonic structure is much more in the tradition of Johannes Brahms than that of other post-romantic German composers. Overlapping choirs of sounds utilizing woodwinds and brass are an important element in recreating the effect of overlapping male and female voice parts in the original. For variety and color the instrumentation is intermittently reduced providing contrast between larger sonorities and chamber-like settings.

Unit 7: Form and Structure

MEASURE	EVENT
1-4	Opening chant
5-25	A section
26-34	Second chant
5-25	A section (repeated)
36-52	B section
53-54	Brass Amen
55-56	Woodwind Amen
57-61	Overlapping Amen

Unit 8: Suggested Listening
Johannes Brahms, *A German Requiem*
Richard Strauss, *Allerseelen*

Unit 9: Additional References and Resources
Ayo, Nicholas. *The Hail Mary: A Verbal Icon of Mary*. Notre Dame, IN: University of Notre Dame Press, 1994.

Hancock, Virginia. *Brahm's Choral Compositions and His Library of Early Music*. Books on Demand, 1983.

Sulzer, Johann Georg. *Aesthetics and the Art of Musical Composition in the German Enlightenment*. Cambridge, England: Cambridge University Press, 1992.

Van Waesberghe, Joseph. *Gregorian Chant and Its Place in the Catholic Liturgy*. Reprint Services Corp., 1993.

Contributed by:
Robert Cameron
Director of Bands
Duquesne University
Pittsburgh, Pennsylvania

Teacher Resource Guide

Canterbury Chorale
Jan Van der Roost
(b. 1956)

Unit 1: Composer

Jan Van der Roost was born in Duffel, Belgium, on March 1, 1956. His interest in music was developed at an early age as his father conducted a number of ensembles and his mother sang in the local choir. Listening to music was encouraged and Van der Roost became acquainted with a variety of music, although brass and wind music received particular attention. He soon felt a desire to compose. At the Lemmens Institute in Leuven, Belgium, Van der Roost received a triple laureate diploma in Trombone Performance, Music History, and Music Education. In 1979, he continued studies at the Royal Conservatory at Ghent, graduating with a diploma in Composition.

Van der Roost presently teaches at the Lemmens Institute, where he conducts the choir, brass and wind bands. He is also actively composing, arranging, and working as an adjudicator. A versatile composer, his original compositions for band include *Puszta*, *Four Old Dances*, *Mercury*, *Slavia*, and *Homage*, among others. His works have been performed by such distinguished groups as the Belgian Broadcasting Corporation, the Tokyo Kosei Wind Orchestra, and the Canadian Brass.

Unit 2: Composition

According to the composer, this quiet piece with its broad tones was originally written for brass band at the request of the chairman of Van der Roost's own band, Brass Band Midden Brabant (Belgium). The inspiration for the work was a visit to the magnificent cathedral of the English city of Canterbury where "so many fine compositions sounded throughout the centuries."

Composed in 1993, this single-movement chorale is approximately five and a half minutes in duration.

Unit 3: Historical Perspective

This chorale draws heavily upon the tradition of the Baroque polyphonic organ chorales of J.S. Bach in style and texture. There are several *tutti* passages which use the sonority of the full wind orchestra to emulate a majestic, full organ sound. The Canterbury Cathedral, founded in 597 by St. Augustine, became the mother of British Christianity and held that position for over 1,400 years. Its impressive spires and ancient stained glass work are breathtaking monuments to the incredible history its walls have seen and heard. Originally composed for brass band, Van der Roost rescored this work for symphonic wind band. In the composer's words, this rescoring allowed him to "explore the full richness of colors of this formation." The colors and breadth of the chorale are fitting to the monument which inspired it and the musical tradition it came from.

Unit 4: Technical Considerations

Canterbury Chorale is primarily in D-flat major; however, students should also be familiar with the scales of A-flat major and A-flat harmonic minor. Although not common scales, the chorale style necessitates playing them only as fast as 63 beats per minute in eighth notes. Van der Roost's use of modal mixture requires the flute, bassoon, and low brass parts to be familiar with double flats. The chorale style poses no rhythmic difficulty moving in half, quarter, and eighth notes at a slow pace. There is one short, highly chromaticized section after letter D which utilizes a sixteenth note rhythm. Staggered breathing, as noted by the composer throughout the piece, is necessary for the extended sustained phrases of the chorale. In the "*sonore*" passages after letter C, a *legato* articulation connecting one long note to the next is appropriate. Orchestrated for full wind ensemble, the score includes piccolo, alto oboe, E-flat clarinet, soprano saxophone, contrabass clarinet, and string bass. Cues are included to cover the soprano saxophone and double reed parts. Van der Roost mentions an ad libitum organ part which does not appear in the score but which, in his words, "adds an extra richness, color and power to this piece, making it sound even more broad and grand."

Unit 5: Stylistic Considerations

To fully emulate the majesty of a full "organ style," rich sonorous tones are required. The composer indicates *sonore* in the trombone parts to describe the breadth of note in the now-articulated melody at letter C. It can be assumed this indicator is applicable to the articulated quarter notes which follow the trombone melody. Sustained, centered pitches much cover the full spectrum of dynamics, from *pianissimo* at the opening and conclusion to *fortissimo* at the climax. Balance is essential in chorale style to ensure the melody is not over-whelmed by the chords underneath. Balance is especially crucial in the *tutti*, homophonic section before letter E where all lines move together in block chords as if one organ. Releases must be together and tapered to provide clarity and seamless phrasing.

Unit 6: Musical Considerations

The opening eight measures are repeated, clearly setting the principal chorale melody in D-flat major with a traditional V4-3 suspension cadence. The second motive (as outlined in unit 7) is orchestrated with a thinner texture and centers around the dominant key area of A-flat. The opening interval of a fourth provides melodic material for a sequence which increases the harmonic rhythm at letter D, sounding like a series of V-I progressions. This leads to homophonic, full, organ-like chords from the *tutti* ensemble six measures before letter E. After this grandiose climax, the chorale returns to its serene beginning in D-flat major, winding down through the double reeds and low woodwinds to the low brass, with tubular bells signaling exit from the cathedral.

Unit 7: Form and Structure

Section	Measure	Event and Scoring
A	1-8	Motive 1 (antecedent and consequent) in tonic D-flat major; repeated with flutes and E-flat clarinet second time only; V4-3 cadence
	9-12	Motive 2 (antecedent); double reeds, saxophones, horn 3, and basses; V4-3 cadence in A-flat major
	13-16	Motive 2 (consequent); A-flat minor melody in horn 1 with a countermelody in baritones, over sustained bass
	17-24	Motive 1 now in A-flat major in low brass; V4-3 cadence
	25-28	Motive 2; new antecedent phrase in flute, bassoon, and B-flat clarinets; low brass *crescendo* in the last two measures
	29-32	Motive 2; consequent phrase in A-flat major with clarinet 1 melody and countermelody in alto saxophones; add low brass

SECTION	MEASURE	EVENT AND SCORING
	33-34	Cadential extension; add all woodwinds with suspended cymbal and timpani building to V4-3 cadence in A-flat major
B	35-38	Motive 1; antecedent phrase in A-flat major; sonore; chorale melody now articulated in low brass
	39-42	Motive 1; consequent phrase; melody to trumpets in D-flat major; new quarter note accompaniment in horns, basses, low woodwinds with suspended cymbal; first two measures repeated with all brass added
	43-46	Extension; all brass, low woodwinds, bells, timpani, cymbal
	47-52	*Tutti fortissimo* overall IV-V4-3-I progression returning to tonic of D-flat major at letter D
	53-59	Motive based on opening interval of fourth; sequence begins with low woodwinds and low brass, adding higher instruments progressively, increasing harmonic and rhythmic activity
	60-65	Climax; *tutti*; homophonic chords, *fortissimo*, in dominant key area of A-flat, returning to tonic with *diminuendo* to low woodwinds and brass on D-flat major chord
A	66-78	Motive 1 return in D-flat major in double reeds; hand to horn 1 and trombone, then to baritone, basses, and tubular bells; finish with muted trumpet and trombone D-flat major chord, *morendo*

Unit 8: Suggested Listening

J.S. Bach, *Come Sweet Death*

The Band of the Royal Netherlands Air Force, The Music of Jan Van der Roost, DMH Records 10.001-3

The Band of the Royal Netherlands Air Force, The Music of Jan Van der Roost Volume 2, DHR Records 10.005-3

Larry Daehn, *As Summer Was Just Beginning*

David Holsinger:
A Childhood Hymn
On a Hymnsong of Philip Bliss

William Schuman, *George Washington Bridge. American Dreams.* Cincinnati Wind Symphony, Klavier Records KCD-11048

William Schuman, *When Jesus Wept*

Frank Ticheli, *Amazing Grace*

Paul Tschesnokoff, *Salvation Is Created*

Jan Van der Roost, *Homage. Inspiration.* Band of the Royal Netherlands Air Force, DMH Records 2.016-3

Unit 9: Additional References and Resources

Cummings, David, ed. *International Who's Who in Music and Musicians Directory*, 13th ed. Cambridge: Melrose Press Limited, 1992.

Miles, Richard, ed. *Teaching Music through Performance in Band*, Vol.1. Chicago: GIA Publications, Inc., 1997.

Miles, Richard, ed. *Teaching Music through Performance in Band*, Vol.2. Chicago: GIA Publications, Inc., 1998.

The Online Guide to Canterbury. The Cathedral. [Online] Available: WWWURL:http://www.thycotic.com/canterbury.shtml. Updated:06/20/98.

Van der Roost, Jan. *The Music of Jan Van der Roost* "Composer's Portrait." Holland: De Haske Publications, 1998.

Contributed by:
Jennifer McAllister
Saskatoon, Saskatchewan
Canada

Teacher Resource Guide

Chorale Prelude: Be Thou My Vision

Jack Stamp
(b. 1954)

Unit 1: Composer

Jack Stamp was born in Washington, DC, in 1954 and grew up in the nearby Maryland suburbs. He received a B.S. degree in Music Education from Indiana University of Pennsylvania in 1976, an M.M. degree in Percussion Performance from East Carolina University in 1978, and a D.M.A. degree in Wind Conducting from Michigan State University in 1988, where he studied with Eugene Corporon. His primary composition teachers were Robert Washburn and Fisher Tull. More recently he has worked with Joan Tower, David Diamond, and Richard Danielpour.

Stamp is currently Professor of Music at Indiana University of Pennsylvania, where he conducts the Wind Ensemble and Symphony Band, and teaches courses in graduate and undergraduate conducting. He is founder and musical director of the Keystone Wind Ensemble, a professional recording group dedicated to the advancement of American concert band music.

Unit 2: Composition

Chorale Prelude: Be Thou My Vision was written as a gift to Thomas O'Neal (Director of Bands at Arkansas State University) and Pat Ellison (Director of the Springdale (Arkansas) High School Symphonic Band) for their friendship and wonderful musicianship. The work is based on the hymn tune "Slane," better known to many as "Be Thou My Vision." The work exhibits the composer's love for hymn tunes.

Unit 3: Historical Perspective

The use of hymns or chorales is not a twentieth century idea but dates back to the beginning of polyphony. During the Baroque, Bach perfected chorale preludes and use of hymns or chorales for the basis of compositions. Through the periods of music, hymn tunes have been used as the basis for sets of variations, particularly in English and American music.

Unit 4: Technical Considerations

In the area of instrumentation, though cross-cued in oboe, there is an extended English horn solo in the middle of the work. While the work does not appear difficult, the ability to play individually as well as powerfully in the big chordal section is *essential* in presenting the work. In the final big chordal section, first trumpet does extend to high C and French horn to top line F.

Unit 5: Stylistic Considerations

The interest in this work is in the harmonic language. Therefore, proper balance is essential, including the projection of internal musical lines that create harmonic interest. Particularly in the final chorale at m. 68, careful attention needs to be paid to the French horn line (mm. 68-73, 81) and the low reeds/tuba line (mm. 75-83) as that is where the interest lies.

Unit 6: Musical Elements

This work is filled with a wide variety of compositional techniques that will educate the players to the creative process of the music of their time. The introduction explores two composition techniques: octave displacement and melodic/harmonic stacking. The introduction, primarily in woodwinds, is based on the first six notes of the hymn tune, however, displaced by octaves. In addition, each note is sustained creating a harmony from the notes or the melody. At m. 11, a full, hymnal-style setting is presented in the woodwinds. Again, much of the interest in this harmonization is in the inner parts. At m. 27, introductory material returns in the brass as a transition into the development section. The development section is highly contrapuntal and canonic, and is based on the third phrase of the hymn. Toward the end of this section, the English horn enters with a reflective quality, commenting on the previous section. A transition, still based upon the third phrase, leads into the final "majestic" chorale setting of the hymn. In this section (m. 68), the use of "substitute chords" creates a very interesting and powerful chordal statement. The work ends with the full ensemble restating the introductory material.

Unit 7: Form and Structure

MEASURE	EVENT
1-10	Introduction based upon first phrase of hymn but with octave displacement
11-26	Full statement of hymn tune with traditional harmonization
27-34	Transitional section based upon introductory material
35-67	Development section based upon the third phrase of the hymn tune
68-83	Recapitulation of hymn tune with an elaborate harmonization
84-end	"Coda" based on opening material

Unit 8: Suggested Listening
David Holsinger, On a Hymnsong of Philip Bliss
Vincent Persichetti:
   0 God Unseen
   So Pure the Star,
   Symphony for Band (Movement II)

Unit 9: Additional References and Resources
Dvorak, Thomas L., Robert Grechesky, and Gary M. Ciepluch. Best Music for High School Band, edited by Bob Margolis. Brooklyn: Manhattan Beach Music, 1993.

Rehrig, William H. The Encyclopedia of Band Music. Edited by Paul E. Bierley. Westerville, OH: Integrity Press, 1991.

Contributed by:
Jack Stamp
Professor of Music
Indiana University of Pennsylvania
Indiana, Pennsylvania

Teacher Resource Guide

Courtly Airs and Dances
Ron Nelson
(b. 1929)

Unit 1: Composer

Ron Nelson is a native of Joliet, Illinois. He received his Bachelor of Music degree in 1952, Master of Music degree in 1953, and Doctor of Musical Arts degree in 1956, all from the Eastman School of Music. Dr. Nelson studied in France at the Ecolé Normale de Musique and, in 1955, at the Paris Conservatory on a Fulbright Grant. He joined the Brown University faculty the following year as an Assistant Professor, attaining the rank of Associate Professor in 1960 and Full Professor in 1968. Dr. Nelson served as Chairman of the Department of Music from 1963-73 and, in 1991, was awarded the Acuff Chair of Excellence in the Creative Arts, becoming the first musician to hold that chair. He has gained wide recognition as a composer of choral, band, and orchestral works. His work for band, *Passacaglia (Homage on B-A-C-H)*, won the "triple crown" of wind band composition competitions by winning the National Band Association Prize, the American Bandmasters Association's ABA/Ostwald Band Competition, and the Louis and Virginia Sudler International Wind Band Composition Contest. Some of Nelson's many other works for band include *Aspen Jubilee, Chaconne (In Memoriam…)*, *Epiphanies (Fanfares and Chorales)*, *Lauds, Rocky Point Holiday*, and *Savannah River Holiday*.

Unit 2: Composition

Courtly Airs and Dances is, according to the composer, "a suite of Renaissance Dances characteristic of five European countries during the 1500s. Three of the dances ("Basse Danse," "Pavane," and "Allemande") are meant to emulate the music of Claude Gervaise by drawing on the style of his music as well as the characteristics of other compositions from that period. The work opens with a fanfare-like "Intrada," followed by "Basse Danse" (France), "Pavane" (England), "Saltarello" (Italy), "Sarabande" (Spain), and "Allemande" (Germany). Composed in 1995, *Courtly Airs and Dances* was commissioned by, and is dedicated to, the Hill Country Middle School Band, Austin, Texas, Cheryl Floyd, Director.

Unit 3: Historical Perspective

Social dancing was widespread throughout the Renaissance, both as a social art and in the theater. Dance music, usually written for lute or keyboard in tabulature or for instrumental ensembles in part books, appeared in printed collections by Petrucci, Attaingnant, Susato, and other publishers. These works, with their strong rhythmic patterns so functional in dance music, were often paired in order to contrast their tempi and dance steps (e.g., *Pavane* and *Galliarde, Passamezzo* and *Saltarello, Allemande* and *Courante*). Combinations of dances were significant musically because their pairings gradually lead to larger groupings of pieces, eventually developing into the Baroque forms of the *suite* and *sonata da camera*.

The *Basse Danse*, from both French (basse danse) and Italian (bassadanza) descent, is an elegant, introductory type of dance whose title probably referred to the walking or gliding movements of the feet. A stately dance usually in 3/2 meter, it is often paired in performance with a livelier *pas de Brabant* (Fr.) or *Saltarello* (It).

The *Pavane* is a sixteenth century dance with Italian origins. Named for the region in which it began (Pava or Padua), the dance became quite popular and spread throughout Europe. After a brief loss of popularity in the late sixteenth century, the English virginalists, including William Byrd, Orlando Gibbons, Thomas Morley, and John Dowland, restored and revitalized the *Pavane*, elevating it to its highest point of artistic perfection. A slow, processional dance, it is usually notated in 4/4 or 4/2 meter.

The *Saltarello* (from the Italian verb *saltare* – to jump, skip, leap, spring) is an energetic dance, often in 6/8 meter, with a rolling three-beat feel to each rhythmic unit.

The *Sarabande* has its origins in Latin America and was first known as a wild, sexually suggestive dance whose performance was forbidden. By the early seventeenth century, the dance reached Spain and Italy. Usually notated in 3/2 or 3/4 time, the primary rhythmic unit is typically (in 3/4 time) quarter – dotted quarter – eighth/quarter – half.

The sixteenth century dance version of the *Allemande* (a French term for Germany or German) is a stately processional dance, usually in a duple meter of moderate tempo, in which couples move side by side.

Unit 4: Technical Considerations

Predictably with the Renaissance style, modal harmonies abound throughout the work. The first movement, "Intrada," is based on an F mixolydian scale, the "Basse Danse" in B-flat lydian and g minor, the "Pavane" in F ionian (major), the "Saltarello" in F dorian, the "Sarabande" and "Allemande" in E-flat and F ionian, respectively. Accidentals are used occasionally in most parts. Time signatures featured include 4/4, 3/4, 3/2, and 6/8. Players are expected to sing a unison melodic line (on a "lu" syllable) in the "Sarabande," but it is cued in many parts and features mostly diatonic, stepwise movement in a major key. Rhythms are basic, with combinations of dotted-half, half, dotted-quarter, quarter, and eighth notes. Sixteenth note groupings are mainly in collections of two or four, with occasional dotted-eighth/sixteenth rhythms. The 6/8 rhythms include groupings of three eighths, dotted-quarters, and quarter/eighth motives. Playing ranges are extended for trumpet I (A5) horn I (G5), which also requires a stopped (+) sound, and trombone I (F4). Percussion requirements include parts for five players, plus timpani. The list of instruments required is extensive, including timpani (at least three), marimba, vibraphone, glockenspiel, chimes, snare drum, tenor drum, bass drum with attached cymbal, crash cymbals, suspended cymbal, two triangles, castanets, and sleigh bells.

Unit 5: Stylistic Considerations

Renaissance dance music is a contrast of tempi and musical styles. Typically, the music of the livelier dances ("Intrada," "Saltarello," "Allemande") should feature a lighter, lifted style from the players that highlights and accentuates their lively character. Conversely, the slower dances ("Basse Danse," "Pavane," "Sarabande"), with their smoother, flowing character, require fuller, well-connected phrasing and tone. Although this specific work was not written to accompany dancing, per se, considering the functionality of any dance music, strict tempi and an awareness of physical dance movement are crucial, particularly in the slower dances.

Unit 6: Musical Elements

Renaissance music relies on elements that make it quite different from Romantic and contemporary composition. For example, music in one specific dance or movement usually remains in one key while featuring rhythmic variations or combinations of instrumental colors in order to bring variety to principal musical ideas.

In *Courtly Airs and Dances*, melodies or melodic motives are consistently presented in their entirety, then in typical Renaissance style, variation is created in the shift of instrumental color as the motive returns. In accordance, care needs to be taken to match the articulation, phrasing, and overall style in the performance of all melodies and motives since, at one time or another, they are presented in an assortment of instrumental timbres. In addition, the juxtaposition of Renaissance and twentieth century musical elements help make this an interesting work. For example, a uniquely Nelson progression, featuring polytonal and quartal harmonies ("Allemande," mm. 63-65), help bring finality and brilliance to the close of a dance. In "Saltarello," wonderful colors created by the muted trombones (m. 41) add to the introduction of the harmonic accompaniment.

Unit 7: Form and Structure

SECTION	MEASURE	EVENT AND SCORING
Movement I: "Intrada"		
	1-5	Main rhythmic theme presented in trumpets; features parallel motion in perfect fifths; harmonically rooted in F mixolydian, with F tonic pedal in stopped horns; added color provided by upper winds (mm. 4-5), with percussion accompanying with a variety of motives taken from the theme; primarily homophonic texture
	6-9	Repeat of first phrase, with the added harmonic richness of the slower eighth accompaniment in trombones and baritones
	10-13	Final repeat of initial phrase; fuller instrumental color in both the melodic motive and the tonic pedal; harmonies, featuring parallel triads and fourths, finally present the progressions that were only implied in earlier phrases
	14-16	Brief coda firmly stamping F as the tonic; no third is present in the final chord – only F and C open fifth
Movement II: "Basse Danse"		
A	1-8	Primary theme in oboe, with complimentary countersubjects in horn I, clarinet, and bassoon; harmonically centered between B-flat lydian and g minor; combination of homophonic and polyphonic texture

SECTION	MEASURE	EVENT AND SCORING
A	8-16	Repeat of first phrase; identical in theme and countersubjects, with changes in instrumentation – theme in trumpet I, with countersubjects in trombone I, horn III, and baritone
B	16-24	New idea in flute I and II, shadowed by similar, but less rhythmically elaborate line, in clarinet I and II; centered in g and d minor; melodic and rhythmic elements drawn from primary theme
A′	24-32	Return of primary theme, now with fuller instrumentation (piccolo, flute I, oboe I and II, clarinet I and IV, and trumpet I and II); new harmonic richness with embellishments (including added thirds, passing tones, neighboring tones, and *nota cambiata*)

Movement III: "Pavane"

A	1-8	F major tonality; primary theme in oboe and clarinet (who are instructed by the composer to "blend together as one instrument"), the combination of which is playfully referred to, by Nelson, as a "Cloboe" – a clarinet and oboe playing the melody one octave apart; two similar four-measure phrases, both ending with tonic cadences
	8-16	New descending melodic motive, with rhythmic and stepwise movement drawn from primary theme; new melodic color-oboe and bass clarinet, sounding two octaves apart; two four-measure phrases: first phrase ending with cadence to IV, second phrase ending with cadence in relative key of d minor
B	17-24	Contrasting melody whose rhythmic elements are borrowed from the primary theme; change in texture upper woodwinds and bells; tonal center shifts to d minor

SECTION	MEASURE	EVENT AND SCORING
	25-32	Same music as above, but with change in texture to full brass
A	33-40	Brief return of primary theme in F major; same instrumentation and texture as first presentation

Movement IV: "Saltarello"

	MEASURE	EVENT AND SCORING
	1-8	Introduction – percussion section solo (tambourine, snare drum, tenor drum) sets opening dynamic, color, and tempo
	9-24	Primary theme presented in solo flute, with continued percussion accompaniment; F dorian tonality; divided into two phrases, the first (mm. 9-16) ending on a dominant cadence V, the second (mm. 17-24) ending on a tonic cadence I
	25-40	Repeat of primary theme, with change in color to clarinet I and bassoon; identical in tonal center and cadences to solo flute presentation
	41-56	Transition; pedal F-C tonic presented, with modal progression in trombone I, II, and III – hemiola adds syncopation and interest to the rhythmic underpinning; new colors added to percussion accompaniment (bells, castanets)
	57-72	Primary theme in upper woodwinds, with continued modal accompaniment; tonal center on the dominant (C) of F dorian
	73-88	Identical repeat of mm. 57-72
	89-104	Primary theme with fuller instrumentation in both melodic line and harmonic accompaniment; tonal center remains the dominant; second phrase (mm. 97-104) ends with unusual use of the figure from end of first phrase (m. 96) – phrase ending less conclusive
	105-120	Final presentation of primary theme; full, conclusive cadence on tonic F

Section	Measure	Event and Scoring
Movement V: "Sarabande"		
A	1-14	Two six-measure phrases of primary theme (melodic line sung by portion of the ensemble on "lu")
A´	15-27	Two six-measure phrases of harmonized (in thirds) theme
A	27-34	Return of first half of A
Movement VI: "Allemande"		
	1-8	Two four-measure phrases of main theme; clearly F major; unison trumpet/trombone presentation with F tonic/dominant pedal in woodwinds and mallet percussion
	9-16	Repeat of main theme phrases, but now in trumpets alone, harmonized in perfect fifths, with added harmonic accompaniment in trombones
	17-24	Secondary theme presented in flutes, with harmonic and textural support from clarinet, oboe, and horn
	25-32	Return of main theme, now harmonized with triads; variety includes fuller instrumentation of theme (added clarinets) and rhythmic syncopation in accompaniment voices
	33-41	Return of secondary theme; identical instrumentation
	41-53	Transition – canonic presentation of main theme, first at two-measure, then at one-measure intervals
	54-60	Return to main theme, with fullest instrumentation and harmonic support
	61-71	Coda; contemporary harmonic devices (typical of Nelson's music), including polytonal and quartal harmonies

Unit 8: Suggested Listening

Thoinot Arbeau/Margolis, *Belle Qui Tiens Ma Vie*
Jan Bach, *Praetorius Suite*
Dance Music of the Renaissance [for recorder, dulcian, crumhorn, viola da braccio, viola da gamba, and lute [Sound recording]. RCA Victrola VIC 1328, 1968.

Diversions/Calliope (Musical group): *Dances, Songs and Variations from the 14th-17th centuries*. [Sound recording]. Tempe, AZ: Summit Records, 1990.

Early Music Consort of London; David Munrow, Conductor. *Instruments of the Middle Ages and Renaissance* [Sound recording]. Angel SBZ 3810. 1976.

Gordon Jacob, *William Byrd Suite*

Bob Margolis (after Claude Gervaise), *Royal Coronation Dances*

Bob Margolis (after Michael Praetorius), *Terpsichore*

Ron Nelson:
    Aspen Jubilee
    Lauds
    Medieval Suite
    Rocky Point Holiday
    Sonoran Desert Holiday

New York Pro Musica; Noah Greenberg, conductor. *The Renaissance Band* [Sound recording]. MCA Records MCA 2513, 1973

Peter Warlock, *Capriol Suite*

Unit 9: Additional References and Resources

Apel, Willi. *The New Harvard Dictionary of Music*, Don Michael Randel, ed. Cambridge, MA: Belknap Press, 1986.

Arbeau, Thoinot. *Orchesography; a treatise in the form of a dialogue whereby all may easily learn and practice the honorable exercise of dancing*/Translated by Mary Stewart Evans. New York: Kamin Dance Publishers, 1948.

"Basic Band Curriculum: Grades I, II, III." *BD Guide* (September/October 1989): 2-6.

Corporon, Eugene, and David Wallace. *Wind Ensemble/Band Repertoire*. Greeley, CO.: University of Northern Colorado, 1984.

Duarte, Leonard P., Daniel S. Hiestand, Carol Ann Prater, and Doy E. Prater. *Band Music That Works*. Volume 1. Burlingame, CA: Contrapuntal Publications, 1987.

Duarte, Leonard P., Daniel S. Hiestand, Carol Ann Prater, and Doy E. Prater. *Band Music That Works*. Volume 2. Burlingame, CA: Contrapuntal Publications, 1988.

Dvorak, Thomas L., Cynthia Crump Taggart, and Peter Schmaltz. *Best Music for Young Band*. Edited by Bob Margolis. Brooklyn, NY: Manhattan Beach Music, 1986.

Farkas, Philip. *The Art of Musicianship*. Bloomington, IN: Musical Publications, 1976.

Garofalo, Robert J. *Instructional Designs for Middle/Junior High School Band*. Fort Lauderdale, FL: Meredith Music Publications, 1995.

Grout, Donald J., and Claude V. Palisca. A History of Western Music. Fifth edition. New York: W. W. Norton, 1996.

Konetchy, Ronald. *Renaissance Art and Music* [video recording]. Pleasantville, NY: Clearvue/EAV, 1986.

Kreines, Joseph. *Music for Concert Band*. Tampa, FL: Florida Music Service, 1989.

Ludwig Music Publishing Co., Cleveland, OH.

Munrow, David. *Instruments of the Middle Ages and Renaissance*. London: Oxford University Press, 1976.

Munrow, David. *Bowed Instruments* [video recording]. Princeton, NJ: Films for the Humanities, 1976. 4

Munrow, David. *Brass Instruments* [video recording]. Princeton, NJ: Films for the Humanities, 1976. 6

Munrow, David. *Flutes and Whistles* [video recording]. Princeton, NJ: Films for the Humanities, 1976. 2

Munrow, David. *Keyboard and Percussion* [video recording]. Princeton, NJ: Films for the Humanities, 1976. 5

Munrow, David. *Plucked Instruments* [video recording]. Princeton, NJ: Films for the Humanities, 1976. 3

Munrow, David. *Reed Instruments* [video recording]. Princeton, NJ: Films for the Humanities, 1976. 1

Praetorius, Michael. *The Syntagma Musicum of Michael Praetorius, Volume Two, De organographia: First and Second Parts, plus all forty-two original woodcut illustrations from Theatrum instrumentorum*/English translation by Harold Blumenfeld. New York: Da Capo Press, 1980.

Rehrig, William H. *The Heritage Encyclopedia of Band Music*. Edited by Paul E. Bierley. Westerville, OH: Integrity Press, 1991. S.v. "Ron Nelson."

Sadie, Stanley, ed. *New Grove Dictionary of Music and Musicians*. London: Macmillan Publishers Limited, 1980.

Stolba, K Marie. *The Development of Western Music*. Dubuque, IA: William C. Brown Publishers, 1990.

Sutton, Julia. Il Ballarino: *16th Century Step Vocabulary and Dances* [video recording]. Pennington, NJ: Dance Horizons Video, 1991.

Whitwell, David. *The History and Literature of the Wind Band and Wind Ensemble*. Volume 2, "The Renaissance Wind Band and Wind Ensemble." Northridge, CA: Winds, 1982-1984.

Whitwell, David. *The History and Literature of the Wind Band and Wind Ensemble*. Volume 6, "A Catalog of Multi-part Instrumental Music for Wind Instruments or for Undesignated Instrumentation before 1600." Northridge, CA: Winds, 1982-1984.

Contributed by:

Craig Paré
Director of University Bands
DePauw University
Greencastle, Indiana

Teacher Resource Guide

Deir in De

Warren Barker
(b. 1923)

Unit 1: Composer

Warren Barker attended the University of California at Los Angeles, studied composition privately with Mario Castelnuevo-Tedesco and Henri Pensis, and took a tour of duty in an Air Force band. At the age of twenty-four, he became the chief arranger for "The Railroad Hour," NBC's prime musical radio show. During the following years, he expanded his musical output to include compositions for television and motion pictures, commercial recordings, and the symphonic concert hall. Barker has composed and conducted music for more than thirty-two television series, including the highly rated comedy series, "Bewitched." In 1970, the National Academy of Television Arts and Sciences honored Barker for his original music written for the award winning series, "My World and Welcome to It," based on the life of James Thurber. He was an arranger for the Oscar winning motion picture, "Hello Dolly." His compositions and arrangements have been performed and recorded by a variety of musical artists from Frank Sinatra to the Hollywood Bowl Symphony. Warren Barker now resides on his Northern California ranch and writes exclusively for educational ensembles.[1]

Unit 2: Composition

Deir in De is a Gaelic lullaby from ancient Ireland. The beautiful melody is coupled with simple, descriptive lyrics: "The mother tells her child of ordinary things familiar in the countryside...the cows will be driven to pasture and the child will mind them...the sun will set, the moon will rise, and they will return at the close of day."[2] There are three statements of the melody, with a short interlude between the second and third statements.

Unit 3: Historical Perspective

One can still hear the enchanting Gaelic dialect spoken in the Connemara region of Ireland, the area on the western shores of the island country, around Galway Bay and Donegal. Here, those who continue to speak this beautiful and ancient language live in "Gaeltachts," areas where Gaelic is the primary language. A typical landscape would include many small pastoral fields separated by ancient stone walls, where long-ago laborers cleared the fields of rocks and stones. Small cottages with thatched roofs dot the countryside, with smoke curling from the chimneys. There is no wood here, so the fireplaces burn "peat," the cut-and-dried turf from the boggy soil in areas called "the burren." These are the "ordinary things familiar in the countryside" that so many Irish folk songs describe.

Unit 4: Technical Considerations

This simple and beautiful setting of the traditional lullaby does not require a high level of technical flexibility from an ensemble. Instrument ranges are not extreme, and the piece is very accessible to young bands. There are a few exposed places with sparse scoring where players will need to perform with confidence and presence. The euphonium and cornet soloists should be able to articulate with some clarity during the short interlude section.

Unit 5: Stylistic Considerations

This simple lullaby must be performed with great freedom and flexibility. The *crescendos* and *diminuendos* should be carefully caressed, with the melody always at the fore. At m. 39, during the short interlude before the final statement of the theme, the euphonium and trumpet soli should be played in a light, playful manner, suggesting the images of "leprechauns." During the closing section, from m. 64 to the end, the interplay between the woodwinds and the brass choir depicts the quiet, peaceful ending of day.[3]

Unit 6: Musical Elements

The scoring of this lullaby offers a great deal of variety, and a young band could use this to explore and discuss changing timbres, textures, and tone colors. After a lush, fully orchestrated introduction, the first statement of the melody is begun by unison flutes and clarinets, and a harmonic voice is added after four measures. The last eight measures of the opening melodic statement are scored predominantly for woodwinds, and the second statement begins with the brass choir and saxophones in a new key. The harmonic language is very traditional, although there are some added sevenths, ninths, and chromaticized passing tones as the piece progresses, creating a lush and beautiful harmonic texture. Another interesting harmonic feature of the melody is that it ends on a half cadence each time it is stated. This not only gives harmonic direction to the piece, but it creates an even calmer and peaceful arrival on the final cadence, when the closing section finally leads back to the tonic.

Unit 7: Form and Structure

MEASURE	KEY	EVENT
1-5	F	Introduction
6-21	F	Statement 1
22-38	E-flat	Statement 2
39-46	E-flat, C	Interlude
47-63	F	Statement 3
64-73	F	Closing section

Unit 8: Suggested Listening
Leslie Bassett, *Lullaby for Kirsten*
Percy Aldridge Grainger, *Irish Tune from County Derry*
Brian Hogg, *Llwynn Onn*
Ralph Vaughan Williams, *Folk Song Suite, Movement II*

Unit 9: Additional References and Resources
Barker, Warren. *Deir in De*. Oskaloosa, IA: Chesford Music Publications, 1990.

Kelly, Tom, with Peter Somerville-Large, Seamus Heaney, and Tim Coogan. *Ireland: The Living Landscape*. West Cork, Ireland: Roberts Rinehart Publishers, 1992.

Preston, Patricia Tunison. *Reflections of Ireland*. New York, NY: Smithmark Publishers, Inc., 1991.

Contributed by:
Brian Lamb
Director of Instrumental Studies
Southwest Baptist University
Bolivar, Missouri

---

1   Barker, Warren. *Deir in De*. Oskaloosa, IA: Chesford Music Publications, 1990.
2   Ibid.
3   Ibid.

Teacher Resource Guide

Down Longford Way/Shenandoah

Percy Aldridge Grainger
(1882–1961)

arranged by Leroy Osmon
(b. 1948)

Unit 1: Composer

Percy Aldridge Grainger, a composer and pianist, was born in Australia. His first musical experiences were from his mother, who taught him piano. At age ten, he performed his first recital, and his recognizable talent earned him the opportunity to study in Europe. By age eighteen, he had performed on three continents of the eastern hemisphere and was a recognized authority on the interpretation of Bach. During his travels, he became friends with Edvard Grieg, and the two promoted each other's music until Grieg's death in 1907. Grainger's interpretation of Grieg's *Piano Concerto* earned him great acclaim.

During his years, Grainger became an expert in the collection of folk songs in Australia and the British Isles. He began experiments in random music, electronics, and irregular meter long before Cage, Varèse, and Bartok. After a stint as an army bandsman (where his love for the soprano saxophone and oboe was established), Grainger moved to America, where he became famous in spite of his extremely eccentric behavior and reputation as a (mere) folk song collector and arranger. It has only been after his death (in White Plains, New York) that his foresight as an avant-garde composer has been recognized. It is likely that this troubled genius will be remembered as one of the first "modern" composers. The arranger, Leroy Osmon, is a composer and teacher in Houston, Texas.

Unit 2: Composition

The composition is actually two short folk songs that Grainger "dished up" (his term for *arranged*). *Down Longford Way* is an arrangement in "elastic scoring" (flexible instrumentation) of Katherine Parker's music. Grainger arranged it in 1935. *Shenandoah* was one of Grainger's Sea Chantey Songs for male chorus. Both are arranged by Osmon for standard concert band instrumentation with a few exceptions: there are only two horn parts, and there are parts included for English horn and soprano saxophone. Since Grainger favored the latter two instruments, they should be included, if possible. However, the alto saxophone and the English horn parts are written as a substitute for the soprano saxophone, so it is not completely necessary to have the soprano saxophone. Only three percussion are required. Both *Down Longford Way* and *Shenandoah* last about two minutes each and are very suitable for junior high and high school bands.

Unit 3: Historical Perspective

Grainger arranged these folk songs in the early twentieth century, at a time when he (as well as Bartok and Delius) were doing serious study into native folk songs. Grainger himself traveled many thousands of miles, quite a bit by walking, to hear and record folk songs as they were sung by local singers. He was most interested in the individual interpretation of local singers, which he would then try to incorporate into his own arrangements. Grainger himself made many arrangements of folk songs for a variety of ensembles and orchestrations, as the need and occasion arose.

Unit 4: Technical Considerations

The major challenges in these two folk songs are tuning and balance. The keys of E-flat and F major should be known to the ensemble, and there are a few accidentals. Rhythm is very easy in *Down Longford Way*, and there are no significant challenges. The meter in both songs is 4/4. *Shenandoah* is marked "in eight"; ensembles may need to review counting eight to the bar. There are a few meter changes in *Shenandoah*, but none in *Down Longford Way*. There is one tempo change in *Down Longford Way*. Ranges are overall quite reasonable. Flute I must play f3. Clarinet I and trumpet I must play g2. Euphonium must play high a-flat, and trombone I must play high g. The English horn requires high d3 and e-flat3 written, which is probably impractical. An indication to play the passage an octave lower would be acceptable.

Unit 5: Stylistic Considerations

Articulations are fairly easy and constant throughout. The sixteenth-dotted eighth figure occurs in both songs and should be interpreted with an emphasis on the sixteenth note (called a "Scotch snap"). Grainger indicates in the music the elements of *rubato* needed in regards to tempo. Overall, a sustained, singing line is needed throughout both songs. All instruments having the melody should be encouraged to use vibrato, regardless of brass or woodwind. Note that phrase endings frequently overlap and always occur in the middle of measures.

Unit 6: Musical Elements

The songs stay in the keys of E-flat and F major (respectively) throughout. Grainger's counterpoint is based on the linear style of Bach, so expect equal prominence of secondary lines. Melodic material is passed around through several different instruments, so there is melodic interest through shifting timbres. Harmony is fairly simple, as one might expect in a folk song. A natural rise and fall of the line should be exaggerated and is sometimes indicated already in the music. With the exception of the "Scotch snap" figure, the rhythm is also quite easy throughout.

Unit 7: Form and Structure

SECTION	MEASURE	EVENT AND SCORING
Down Longford Way		
(ABA form)		
A	1-16	
a1 + a2		4+4
b		4
a2		4
B	17-24	4+4
A	25-32	
a1 + a2		4+4
Shenandoah		
(strophic form)		
Introduction	1	
Verse 1	2-12	4+7
Verse 2	13-23	4+7

Unit 8: Suggested Listening

Percy Grainger:
   Country Gardens
   Hill Song #1 and #2
   Irish Tune from County Derry
   The Lads of Wamphray
   Lincolnshire Posy

Unit 9: Additional References and Resources

Bird, John. *Percy Grainger*. Second edition. London: Oxford University Press, 1998.

Lewis, Thomas, ed. *Source Guide to the Music of Percy Grainger*. Pro/Am Music Resources, Inc., 1991.

Mellers, Wilfrid. *Percy Grainger*. London: Oxford University Press, 1992.

Wilson, Brian Scott. "Orchestrational Archetypes in Percy Grainger's Wind Band Music." Diss., The University of Arizona, 1992.

Contributed by:

Jeff Emge
Texas A & M University
Commerce, Texas

Teacher Resource Guide

Highbridge Excursions
Mark Williams
(b. 1955)

Unit 1: Composer

Mark Williams holds a Bachelor of Arts in Education degree and a Master of Education degree from Eastern Washington University. His teaching career includes twelve years at the elementary level, where he served as director of the Spokane All-City Band program. He has toured Europe and the Pacific as a woodwind performer and Chief Arranger for the 560th Air Force Band. He has earned several awards including the Western International Band Clinic's Gralia Competition and numerous ASCAP Special Awards. His extensive experience with young musicians and talent as a composer helped him co-author the popular *Accent on Achievement* band method. Williams served as String Music Editor for Alfred Publishing Company and has over seventy published works for band including *Greenwillow Portrait*, *Fantasy on "Yankee Doodle,"* *The Ash Grove*, *Echoes of the Civil War*, *Northland Saga*, *Kentucky Ballad*, and *March to the Big Top*.

Unit 2: Composition

Highbridge Excursions is a two-movement work that was commissioned by the Fayetteville-Manlius Education Foundation for the Wellwood and Eagle Hill Middle School Bands. The work was first performed on March 14, 1995, with the composer conducting. The first movement, "Song of the Lake," is an original melody in a British folk song style. Driving rhythms characterize the second movement, "Festive Dance." It opens with a Medieval and Renaissance melodic quality and progresses to some contemporary harmonic moments.

Unit 3: Historical Perspective

Like *An Original Suite* by Gordon Jacob and *First Suite in E-flat* by Gustav Holst, the first movement of *Highbridge Excursions* is in a British folk song style without being connected to a specific British folk song. The dotted eighth-sixteenth and sixteenth-dotted eighth pattern create a Scottish snap rhythm, and the lyrical quality of the melody is typical of the British style.

"Festive Dance" begins with the sounds of Medieval and Renaissance music. Several wind works have drawn inspiration from these periods including *Variants on a Medieval Tune* by Norman Dello Joio, *Terpsichore* by Bob Margolis, *Court Festival* by William Latham, and *Sweelink Variations* by Jan Bach.

Unit 4: Technical Considerations

The keys of F major, B-flat major, and C dorian are used in the piece. Instrument ranges are conservative. The first movement requires players to be able to perform the dotted eighth-sixteenth and sixteenth-dotted eighth pattern at a slow tempo. The second movement is in 6/8 time and requires the trombones to perform *glissandos* and grace notes. Players must perform a three against two rhythm with three quarter notes in a measure during a fast 6/8 pulse. The final bar has a septuplet run in the woodwinds.

Unit 5: Stylistic Considerations

The first movement should be in a lyrical, *legato* style. Detached eighth note articulations and accented notes are also called for. The dynamics range from *pp* to *fff*, and the melodies should always stay in a singing style. When the sixteenth-dotted eighth rhythm occurs, an agogic accent should be placed on the sixteenth note on the beat. This will help the sixteenth sound on the beat as opposed to a pick-up to the dotted eighth note.

The second movement is marked *Allegro Vivace*. The melody should have a light character with continuous forward momentum, and the accented notes should be weighted and spaced.

Unit 6: Musical Elements

The first movement is homophonic with brief soli in the trumpet, flute, and oboe (cued in the clarinet). The second movement begins with a unison eight-measure motive that is repeated twice in open fifths. The melody is in the dorian mode. Meanwhile, the harmony gets more dissonant as the music progresses. The three fermatas (m. 135) are polychords with an E-flat major chord in the woodwinds against a D-flat major chord in the brass.

Unit 7: Form and Structure

MEASURE   EVENT AND SCORING

Movement I: "Song of the Lake"

1-8	Theme stated in F major
9-16	Thinner texture; melody in alto saxophone
17-23	Theme in trumpet; countermelody in clarinet; detached eighth notes in the low brass and winds
24-37	Theme fragmented in solo and soli passages
38-46	Final statement of theme in B-flat major

Movement II: "Festive Dance"

47-54	Unison statement of theme
55-62	Theme in open fifths
63-70	Theme in trumpet with rhythmic accompaniment in open fifths
71-77	Theme accompanied by trombone *glissandos* that sound like bagpipes
78-91	Melody is fragmented in the dorian mode over a rhythmic accompaniment
92-99	Melody in trumpet with three quarter notes in a 6/8 pulse
100-111	Powerful trumpet melody ending in a rhythmic *diminuendo*
112-119	Melody in trombone and horn over sustained drone
120-135	Gradual *crescendo* to three polychords in m. 135
136-143	Unison Scotch snap rhythm in m. 142 brings piece to an exciting conclusion

Unit 8: Suggested Listening

Percy Aldridge Grainger, *Lincolnshire Posy*
Gustav Holst, *Second Suite in F for Military Band, Op. 28, No. 2*
Gordon Jacob, *An Original Suite*
Norman Dello Joio, *Variants on a Medieval Tune*
Bob Margolis, *Terpsichore*
Ralph Vaughan Williams, *English Folk Song Suite*

Unit 9: Additional References and Resources

Alfred Publishing Company, Van Nuys, CA.

Apel, Willi, ed. *Harvard Dictionary of Music*. Second edition. Cambridge, MA: Belknap Press, 1970.

Dvorak, Thomas L., Cynthia Crump Taggart, and Peter Schmaltz. *Best Music for Young Band*. Edited by Bob Margolis. Brooklyn, NY: Manhattan Beach Music, 1986.

Miles, Richard, ed. *Teaching Music through Performance in Band*, Vol. 1. Chicago: GIA Publications, Inc., 1997.

Miles, Richard, ed. *Teaching Music through Performance in Band*, Vol. 2. Chicago: GIA Publications, Inc., 1998.

Rehrig, William H. *The Heritage Encyclopedia of Band Music*. Edited by Paul E. Bierley. Westerville, OH: Integrity Press, 1991.

Additional notes provided by Mark Williams.

Contributed by:

Mike Alexander
University of Wisconsin - Milwaukee
Milwaukee, Wisconsin

Teacher Resource Guide

Kenya Contrasts
William Himes
(b. 1949)

Unit 1: Composer
Well known for his compositions and arrangements, William Himes has more than seventy publications to his credit. Himes holds both a bachelor's and master's degree from the University of Michigan. For five years he taught instrumental music in the public schools of Flint, Michigan, where he was also adjunct lecturer in low brass at the University of Michigan-Flint. He continues to be in demand as a conductor, composer, lecturer, clinician, and euphonium soloist, and has made appearances both nationally and internationally.

Unit 2: Composition
This grade three composition features two African melodies from different tribes that are developed in one continuous movement. Originating from two children's counting games, *Wakarathe* comes from the Kikuyu tribe and is sung during a game like "One potato, two potato." *Abot Tangewou* is from the Kipsigis tribe and is sung during a circle game, best described as a mixture of tag and counting to ten. The work is an excellent example by which young bands can develop musical skills alongside developing a respect for the rich cultural heritage of African music. The work is published by Curnow Music Press, Inc. and lasts approximately two minutes and thirty seconds.

Unit 3: Historical Perspective
Published in 1996, the work will contribute to the awareness of a multicultural environment that is vitally important to an ethnically diverse society. The

United States is the point of origin of one of the most influential musical cultures in the world today. Originating from the crossing of two great musical traditions of Europe and Africa, it is nearly 500 years old. A work such as this may instill in the younger musicians of various ethnic backgrounds a sense of their common humanity in making music together. In 1990 at the MENC conference in Washington, DC, Dr. Christopher Small said "that's what seems to me the real nature of what is called music and that's what its function is in human life...."

Unit 4: Technical Considerations

The tonalities fall into the areas of G minor, E-flat major, and F major. The three key areas are delineated by tempo and meter changes, including 3/4 and 4/4. Overall pitch ranges are relatively narrow and comfortable with the exception of the doubled baritone and first trombone part, where pitches extend upward to high D and E-flat. Though much prominence is given to the rhythmic elements of the work, the rhythms themselves are quite simple. Due to considerable doubling of parts, some rehearsal time should be used to establish consistent note lengths and clarity of articulation. Percussion parts include bells, optional timpani (two drums), snare drum, suspended cymbal, plus auxiliaries including shaker, tambourine, and finger cymbals. Bass drum may be used in place of timpani in mm. 1-21.

Unit 5: Stylistic Considerations

The African folk melodies upon which this work is based have a relatively simple melodic structure using as few as three pitches. Contrasting dynamics and styles of articulation are essential to this chant-like work and should be emphasized to maintain interest for performers and listeners alike. The first melody, *Wakarathe*, should be treated simply but also with a strict and stoic rhythmic character. Repetitive *staccato* figures that are treated in a light, separate style juxtaposed with a similar figure and *legato* articulation would possibly be useful as an articulation study. *Abot Tangewou* has a faster tempo and more aggressive style of articulation. To make the chant-like melody more musically effective, all dynamic indications and articulation markings need to be taken quite literally. Again, a variety of articulation gestures will make the work more musically exciting. Much of the expressive musical movement is created in block-like sections.

Unit 6: Musical Elements

The chant-like and repetitive style of these Keynan children's melodies using modal and pentatonic key areas should stimulate the interest of the younger middle school student and provide a change of pace for a concert setting. The primitive qualities of the work can be achieved in the ensemble through a strict attention to a metric pulse, the evenness of dynamic changes, and the

consistency and variety of articulations throughout the ensemble.

Unit 7: Form and Structure

SECTION	MEASURE	SCORING
Introduction	1-12	*Ostinato* bass line supporting layered melodic line; contrasts of *legato* and *staccato* articulations; block scoring used throughout
Wakarathe melody	13-44	Continued use of *ostinato* figure; chant-like melody alternates between instrumental sections; dynamics are understated and range from *mp* to *mf*
Introduction of *Abot Tangewou* melody	45-46	New tempo in 4/4; quarter note = 120; percussive eighth note figures for *tutti* band
Abot Tangewou	47-61	Melody presented by trumpets with fragmented interjections of melody in woodwinds and percussion
Abot Tangewou developed	62-68	A short, three-voice canonic section with *marcato* articulations; key changes to F concert
Coda	69-end	*Listesso* tempo and meter changes to 3/4; a six-measure *diminuendo* in preparation for a one-measure *crescendo* from *p* to *ff* in the percussion section creating a dramatic conclusion

Unit 8: Suggested Listening
Jerry Bilik, *Drums of Africa*
Samuel Coleridge-Taylor, *Rhapsodic Dance-Bamboula*
James Curnow, *African Sketches*
Karl A. Forssmark, *Three African Songs*
Quincy Hilliard, *Variations on an African Hymnsong*
Paul Jennings, *African Road*
Robert Washburn, *Kilimanjaro (An African Portrait)*

Unit 9: Additional References and Resources

Brandel, Rode. *The Music of Central Africa: An Ethnomusicological Study.* The Hague, Netherlands: Nijhoff Publishing, 1973.

May, Elizabeth, ed. *Music of Many Cultures: An Introduction.* Berkeley, CA: University of California Press, 1980.

Rehrig, William H. *The Heritage Encyclopedia of Band Music.* Edited by Paul E. Bierley. Westerville, OH: Integrity Press, 1991.

Contributed by:

Douglas A. Peterson
Director of Instrumental Music
Daytona Beach Community College
Daytona Beach, Florida

Teacher Resource Guide

Lied ohne Worte
(Song without Words)

Rolf Rudin
(b. 1961)

Unit 1: Composer

At the age of ten, composer Rolf Rudin, a native of Frankfurt am Main, won a German national young people's competition with a guitar solo. He then began studies at the Frankfurter Musikhochschule, eventually earning a scholarship from the German National Education Foundation. From 1985 to 1987, he was appointed Lecturer in Music Theory at Frankfurt, resuming that position in 1993 in addition to his work as a freelance composer.

In 1986 Rudin began studies in composition, music theory, and conducting at the Hochschule für Musik in Würzburg, earning a Composition Diploma in 1991 and a Conducting Diploma in 1992. In 1987 he was a scholar at the Richard Wagner Foundation. Two years later, he participated in Edison Denissov's master class in Lucerne, Switzerland. He was later awarded a scholarship by the Bavarian Ministry of Culture for six months' study at the French Cité Internationale des Arts in Paris.

Since 1987 his compositions have won numerous awards and prizes. Those compositions include works for orchestra, women's choir, alto saxophone solo, marimba solo, and chamber music for mixed ensembles, brasses, strings, and clarinets.

Since 1989 Rudin has concentrated his work on compositions for symphonic band or wind orchestra. He has completed the following English titles:

Imperial Prelude, Op. 15; Bacchanalia, Op. 20 (1989)
Symphony No. 1: *Cantus Arborum*, Op. 33 (1990)
Druids: *A Mythical Remembrance*, Part I: Nemeton, Op. 38 (1991-93)

*The Dream of Oenghus: Symphonic Poem after an Irish Legend
   in Two Parts*, Op. 37 (1993, 1994)
Moor of Stars: A Departure, Op. 42 (1994-95)
   (First Prize, Baden-Württemberg Band Association Competition)
Firmament (1995)
Wi(e)derhall: 13 Fragments, Op. 44 (1995-96)
   Submerged City: A Playing of the Waves, Op. 45, and A
   Playing of the Waves, Op. 45a, version for symphonic wind
   orchestra and choir (1997)
   (2d Prize, Corciano, Perugia, Italy International Competition)
The Fading of the Soul: A Lamentation, Op. 48 (1997)
Pale Moon, Op. 50 (1997)
   (First Prize, Baden-Württemberg Band Association Competition)
Song without Words, W.o.o. (1997)
*Night: Pieces and Comments for Solo Alto Saxophone and Symphonic
   Wind Ensemble*, Op. 51
About the End of Time: A Premonition, Op. 52, commissioned for
   the World Association of Symphonic Bands and Ensembles
   1999 International Conference in San Luis Obispo, California

Unit 2: Composition

The State of Rhineland-Palatinate commissioned Rudin to compose a work for the 1997 Eifel Music Days. *The Fading of the Soul: A Lamentation* was the result of this commission. Rudin describes *The Fading of the Soul* as a work that "opens up a new space of spiritual calmness and tonality." A festival band, under the composer's baton, was to perform the new work and others by Rudin. He thought the concert would be very successful, "but I could not conduct an encore by another composer!" *Song without Words* filled this need. Its first performance was on April 5, 1997, with the composer conducting.

Rudin has stated that the work has found many friends, but it is rarely performed as an encore. Often the work appears in church concerts or in other sacred venues. Many conductors use the piece to open concerts or rehearsals.

About five minutes in length, *Song without Words* is published by Edition Flor and distributed in the United States by Shattinger Music Co.

Unit 3: Historical Perspective

Nineteenth century romantic composers tended to break down traditional classical norms, adopting a freer approach. Romantic form often emphasized a lack of sectional definition. Composers often created pieces that were improvisatory in nature or pieces that seemed to begin in the middle of a larger idea. Early nineteenth century critics admired extremes of length or brevity. The Irish composer, John Field (1782-1837), composed short, independent character pieces he called "nocturnes" for solo piano. These earlier short forms were non-programmatic, quasi-improvisatory, and characterized by singing melodies.

In 1830, the first of eight books of short piano pieces by Felix Mendelssohn-Bartholdy (1809-47) was published in London with the title *Melodies for Pianoforte*, Op. 19. For the subsequent seven books, published throughout the rest of his lifetime, Mendelssohn used the title *Lieder ohne Worte*, songs without words. These pieces are characterized by song-like melodies in the right hand. Sometimes they exploited the techniques of the piano, occasionally with virtuosic passages. Except for three of them, the publisher added the programmatic titles by which we know these pieces (e.g., "Spring Song"). Mendelssohn also composed a *Lied ohne Worte*, Op. 109, for cello and piano.

In the last three decades of the twentieth century, composers of classical music have sought to regain their audiences, lost earlier because music was excessively dry and academic. One way to combat this over-intellectualism is composing songs with unabashed romanticism, singable melodies, and recognizable emotional climaxes. Rudin's *Lied ohne Worte* certainly fits within this practice.

Unit 4: Technical Considerations

According to the score, the essential instrumentation for *Song without Words* requires the following instruments: one piccolo and one flute, three clarinets, four saxophones (AATB), three trumpets, two flugelhorns or cornets, two horns, three trombones, two baritones, and two tubas. The required percussion instruments are timpani, orchestral bells, triangle, and suspended cymbal. Three musicians are required to play the percussion parts.

In addition, the score labels the oboe, E-flat clarinet, bass clarinet, and bassoon parts ad libitum (non-essential). The two measures in which the second baritone is different from the first are doubled in the second trombone part. However, the second tuba is not doubled in any other part. Cornets can play the flugelhorn parts, but the darker quality will better bring out the gentle nature of the work.

The baritone parts are challenging. The range extends from F2 below the bass clef staff to A-flat4 in ledger lines. The baritones have a moving contrapuntal line through the piece with the exception of four measures of melodic line doubling horns (mm. 45-48). There is no opportunity for a rest unless two or more baritone players can alternate with each other.

The other brass ranges are reasonable: trumpets and flugelhorns go no higher than A-flat5 above the staff; horns, fifth-line F4; and trombones, F4 above the staff. The tubas' tessitura is low, from F1 in ledger lines to D-flat3 in the staff. The piccolo part is very high and very soft: the last pitch of the work is a concert A-flat7 in ledger lines above the staff. The baritone saxophone part requires a written B-flat3 below the staff to be played softly.

The key of D-flat major sounds good for winds, but clarinetists must be mature enough in their abilities to use comfortably the left-hand C4 fingering on the French/American instrument.

To play the piece, all instruments must be secure in playing both steps and skips with a smooth *legato*. The melody is doubled throughout the piece. However, some individual responsibility is required for the frequent pyramids that characterize the work.

Unit 5: Stylistic Considerations

The first two phrases of *Song without Words* last for eight measures, each without a breath. In each measure, slurs are marked from the first note to the last. If these phrases cannot be taken in one breath, then breathing should be staggered and slurs should be broken at the third beat of the measure to take breaths. In this way the flow of the three eighth-note pick-ups into downbeats is not interrupted.

Three-quarters of the piece's eighty-four measures are marked *piano*. It is important that, while maintaining melodic direction, performers keep the sound soft except for the two climaxes in the piece.

The pyramids are of both types: 1) performers play a fragment of a melody and sustain one of the pitches within the line and 2) performers enter with one of the pitches of a chord and sustain it. In either case, the sustained pitch must come down in volume immediately after it begins.

Unit 6: Musical Elements

Rudin describes *Song without Words* as "a short and simple opus draped in romantic sound." He wanted to compose a piece that was very melodic. Thinking of Mendelssohn's notes on his piano cycle, "he composed the music because he could not say these things with words."

Rudin achieves simplicity in the work by using extended tonal harmonies primarily based on the black-key pentatonic scale: D-flat, E-flat, G-flat, A-flat, B-flat. Occasionally, he introduces an F-natural or a C-natural. In the introduction, which occurs three times, he uses a passing C-flat in the bass line.

Frequent use of a pick-up gesture consisting of three eighth notes leading into beat one or beat three give rhythmic direction to the nearly isorhythmic melodic lines. Most of the phrases are four or eight measures long with the exception of two six-measure phrases.

Unit 7: Form and Structure

Song without Words is through-composed, with some sections beginning with the same material. These returns give the song a strophic feeling while allowing a free development of the musical ideas. Rudin describes his compositional technique this way, "I prefer writing large arcs and wide developments."

MEASURE	MELODY	LABEL
1-4	Baritones	Introduction
5-12	Flute, oboe, 1st clarinet, 1st alto saxophone	A
13-20	Add E-flat clarinet, 2nd alto saxophone	A´
21-24	Add piccolo (8va), flute (8va), E-flat clarinet (8va), 1st trumpet	First digression, *crescendo*
25-28	Add 1st flugelhorn	First digression climax, change of rhythm, *diminuendo*
29-32	Piccolo (8va), flute, oboe, E-flat clarinet	First digression, codetta, return to predominate rhythm, dominant pedal
33-36	Baritones	Introduction
37-44	Flute, oboe, E-flat clarinet, B-flat clarinets (8vb)	A
45-48	Clarinets, horns (8vb), baritones (8vb)	Second digression
49-54	Piccolo (8va), flute, oboe, E-flat clarinet, 1st and 2nd clarinets, 1st alto saxophone (8vb), 1st trumpet (8vb)	Second digression continued, climax and change of rhythm at m. 51
55-58	Add 3rd clarinet, 2nd alto saxophone	Second digression, codetta, *ritardando*
59-62	Piccolo (8va), flute, oboe (8vb), E-flat clarinet, 1st alto saxophone (8vb)	Third digression, new melodic rhythm; harmonic rhythm increases to half notes, 1st clarinet, 1st trumpet countermelody enters at m. 61
63-66	Flute, oboe, E-flat clarinet, B-flat clarinets, alto saxophones, 1st flugelhorn, 3rd clarinet, bass clarinet, bassoon, tenor and baritone saxophones, and baritones continue melody at m. 63	Third digression continues, all eighth notes, *ritardando*
67-70	1st clarinet, 1st alto saxophone, 1st horn	A, first four measures only

MEASURE	MELODY	LABEL
71-74	Clarinets, oboe, piccolo	*Arpeggios* rising through the range
75-80	Baritones; bass clarinets, alto saxophones, clarinets, E-flat clarinet, oboe, flute, piccolo	Introduction, extended with pentatonic scale rising through the band's range
81-84	*Tutti*	Rising pyramid on D-flat with added ninth and sixth (black-key pentatonic chord)

Unit 8: Suggested Listening

Field, John. *Nocturne No. 5 in B Flat*, H. 37. James Galway, flute, and David Measham, conducting the National Philharmonic Orchestra of London. The Classical James Galway. BMG/RCA Victor, 57011.

Field, John. *The Nocturnes of John Field*. John O'Conor, piano. Telarc, 80199.

Mendelssohn-Bartholdy, Felix. *Songs without Words*. Livia Rev, piano. Hyperion, 22020.

Mendelssohn-Bartholdy, Felix. *Songs without Words*, Op. 109. Nathaniel Rosen Plays Brahms, Schumann, and Mendelssohn. Nathaniel Rosen, cello, and Doris Stevenson, piano. John Marks Records, 5.

Rudin, Rolf. *The Dream of Oenghus: Poem after a Legend from Ireland*, Op. 37 (1993/4, 1996). Dream Catchers. Eugene Corporon, North Texas Wind Symphony. Klavier KCD-11089.

Rudin, Rolf. *Lied ohne Worte*. Frank Engelke, Symphoniches Blasorchester Norderstedt. Maestro Musikproduction CD-9711-2.

Rudin, Rolf. *Lied ohne Worte*. Harry D. Bath, Jugendkapelle Kirchheim. BCD 7204.

Unit 9: Additional References and Resources

"About the Works for Symphonic Wind Orchestra by Rolf Rudin." Erlensee, Germany: Edition Flor, 1999.

Randel, Don, ed. *The New Harvard Dictionary of Music*. Cambridge, MA.: The Belknap Press of Harvard University, 1986.

"Biographical Notes-Rolf Rudin." Erlensee, Germany: Edition Flor, n.d.

"Discography: Symphonic Wind Orchestra." Erlensee, Germany: Edition Flor, n.d.

Edition Flor. "Rolf Rudin: Works for Symphonic Wind Orchestra." Saint Louis, MO: Shattinger Music Co., 1998.

Mendelssohn-Bartholdy, Felix. *Lieder ohne Worte*, Books 1-8: Opp. 19, 30, 38, 53, 62, 67, 85, and 102, ed. after autograph by Rudolf Elvers and Ernst Herttrich. Munich: G. Henle, 1981.

Mendelssohn-Bartholdy, Felix. *Songs without Words* (Complete) and Six Children's Pieces, op. 72. New York: Kalmus, 1900.

Rudin, Rolf, facsimile to Ibrook Tower. 3 June 1999.

Rudin, Rolf. *Lied ohne Worte*. Erlensee, Germany: Edition Flor, 1997.

Sadie, Stanley, ed. *The Norton/Grove Concise Encyclopedia of Music*. New York: W. W. Norton and Company, 1988.

Contributed by:

Ibrook Tower
Wind Ensemble Director
Pennsylvania Academy of Music
Lancaster, Pennsylvania

and

Instrumental Music Instructor
Milton Hershey School
Hershey, Pennsylvania

Teacher Resource Guide

A Little Night and Day Music
Samuel Adler
(b. 1928)

Unit 1: Composer

Samuel Adler was born in Mannheim, Germany, in 1928 and emigrated to the United States in 1939. He received his B.M. from Boston University, his M.A. from Harvard, and is the recipient of many honorary doctorates. While serving in Europe with the U.S. Army, he founded and conducted the Seventh Army Symphony Orchestra. This orchestra had a dramatic musical and psychological impact on the cultural scene of Europe, earning the composer the Army's Medal of Honor.

Adler has published over 400 works in many genres including six symphonies, five operas, ten concerti, eight string quartets, orchestral and chamber works, choral music, and songs. His literary works include books on orchestration, choral conducting, and sight-singing, as well as contributions to reference books and magazines throughout the world. He has held positions as professor of composition at North Texas State University and as chairman of the Composition Department at the Eastman School of Music. He has received commissions and grants from the Ford Foundation, National Endowment of the Arts, Rockefeller Foundation, Dallas Symphony Orchestra, Rochester Philharmonic, Mormon Tabernacle Choir, and the city of Jerusalem. He has been awarded a Guggenheim Fellowship, Charles Ives Award, Lillian Fairchild Award, Deems Taylor Award, and Boston University's "Distinguished Alumni Award." He currently teaches composition at the Julliard School.

Unit 2: Composition

A Little Night and Day Music was commissioned by the Carl Fischer publishing company for its 1976 band series. Published in 1977, it was premiered at the Midwest National Band & Orchestra Clinic. It consists of two movements, each of which is supposed to represent the thoughts of an urban dweller about the city that surrounds him. The two movements are to be played without pause. The first movement is an image of night in the city. During the quiet calm some strange noises occur, yet they do not disturb the overall tranquillity of the scene. The second movement seeks to represent the bustling activity of morning in the city. Repetitive rhythmic patterns, traffic noises, and explosive percussion help to create forward motion and excitement.

Unit 3: Historical Perspective

The use of sound to create a picture in the mind of the listener can be traced back to the works of Berlioz and Strauss. Later, Ravel and Debussy created images using a different harmonic and melodic language. Today's composers use an ever-wider palette of tonal colors and timbres.

Unit 4: Technical Considerations

The composer suggests that all parts be played as written but allows for octave displacement if necessary. Certain difficult passages are cued for other instruments. For example, a challenging French horn line could be executed by the alto saxophones. E-flat clarinets and bassoons may be omitted altogether. Oboe parts may be played by flute. In addition to the standard percussion instruments, a cello bow is needed to bow the vibraphone in the opening section.

Unit 5: Stylistic Considerations

Soft, sustained playing is required of all players in the first movement. A buoyant, floating quality is desirable. Alternating breaths will help each section achieve a truly sustained sound. The second movement is very rhythmic, with explosive percussion figures. The winds must play very aggressively with crisp, clear articulation. An effective performance will include great contrast, between both articulated and slurred passages and between movements of the piece.

Unit 6: Musical Elements

In the first movement, Adler uses very soft unisons with some of the instruments trilling to achieve an "atmospheric" quality. Alternating combinations of woodwinds and brasses (muted) playing intervals such as minor seconds, minor ninths, and diminished fifths are also present. These tonal clusters are accompanied by sparse cymbal and mallet instrument sounds. A canonic section written for the woodwinds has each instrument winding through a pattern of all twelve chromatic notes within an octave. This thicker texture then gives way to the underlying brass clusters. Aggressive, rhythmic interplay is a characteristic of the second movement. Use of the percussion instruments is quite different than in the first movement. Drums of several pitches as well as dry metallic and wood sounds are used to create a rhythmic base upon which alternate groups of high- and low-pitched instruments converse.

Unit 7: Form and Structure

MEASURE   MUSICAL EVENT

Movement I: "A Little Night Music"
1-11	Opening; floating texture
12-18	Keyboard percussion glissandos; clarinet patterns
19-29	Brass clusters
30-38	Woodwind canon
38-50	Sustained clusters growing softer

Movement II: "A Little Day Music"
51-59	Rhythmic opening; treble vs. bass groups
60-74	Melodic, sustained woodwinds
75-93	Syncopated, thin woodwind texture, with *ostinato*
94-104	Brass flutter tongue; melodic woodwinds
105-114	Driving rhythms; alternating groups
115-131	Melodic woodwinds
132-143	Highly rhythmic; treble vs. bass groups

Unit 8: Suggested Listening
Samuel Adler:
> *Concerto for Winds, Brass & Percussion*
> *Double Visions*
> *Southwestern Sketches*
> *Symphony No.3 "Diptych"*

Unit 9: Additional References and Resources

Adler, Samuel. *The Study of Orchestration*, 2d ed. New York: W.W. Norton, 1989.

Carl Fischer Music Publishers. New York, NY.

Hitchcock, H. Wiley, and Stanley Sadie, ed. *The New Grove Dictionary of American Music*. London: Macmillan Press Limited, 1986.

Rehrig, William H. *The Heritage Encyclopedia of Band Music*. Westerville, OH: Integrity Press, 1991.

Slonimsky, Nicolas. *Baker's Biographical Dictionary of Musicians*, 8th ed. New York: Schirmer Books, 1992.

Smith, Norman and Albert Stoutamire. *Band Music Notes*. Lake Charles, LA: Program Note Press, 1989.

Vinton, John, ed. *Dictionary of Contemporary Music*. New York: E.P. Dutton & Co., Inc., 1974.

Contributed by:

Sean Flanigan
Instructor of Trombone
Bowling Green State University
Bowling Green, Ohio

Teacher Resource Guide

Lyric Music

Robert Starer
(b. 1924)

Unit 1: Composer

Robert Starer was born in Vienna in 1924 and received his musical education at the State Academy in Vienna, the Jerusalem Conservatoire, and the Julliard School. He became an American citizen in 1957 and has taught at Julliard and at the Graduate Center of C.U.N.Y. where he was named a Distinguished Professor in 1986. Among his honors are two Guggenheim Fellowships, election to the American Academy of Arts and Letters in 1994, the Medal of Honor for Science and Art by the President of Austria in 1995, an Honorary Doctorate by the State University of New York in 1996, and a Presidential Citation by the National Federation of Music Clubs in 1997.

His stage works include three operas as well as several ballets for Martha Graham. His orchestral works have been performed by major orchestras in the United States as well as abroad under such conductors as Mitropoulos, Bernstein, Steinberg, and Mehta. Interpreters of his music include Janos Starker, Jaime Laredo, Paula Robison, and Leontyne Price. The recording of his *Violin Concerto* (Itzhak Perlman with the Boston Symphony under Seiji Ozawa) was nominated for a Grammy. Excerpts from his book *Continuo: A Life in Music* have appeared in the *New Yorker*, *Musical America*, and the *London Times*. In 1997, Overlook Press published *The Music Teacher*, his first work of fiction, and the opening chapter was excerpted in *The Keyboard Companion*. Starer currently resides in Woodstock, New York.

Unit 2: Composition

Lyric Music, written in 1963, is an original composition for band that is approximately four minutes in length. Upon its completion, it was published by Sam Fox under the title *Reverie*. When Sam Fox discontinued publishing, the rights to the piece reverted back to Starer. He then gave permission to Manhattan Beach Music to republish the work in 1988 with a new edition and a new title, *Lyric Music*. This piece, as the title suggests, provides a nice change of pace in any concert program. It features an extended trumpet solo and smooth, melodic lines in the entire band throughout. It is in 6/8 time, unusual for a grade three piece in this style.

Unit 3: Historical Perspective

The composer states that the piece was written "at the suggestion of a friend who said that 'band music does not have to be noisy and bombastic.' It is an essentially gentle piece, although it does rise to a somewhat impassioned climax." There are no qualities to the work that link it historically to an event, yet one cannot dismiss its likeness to pieces such as Frank Erickson's *Air for Band* or James Barnes' *Yorkshire Ballad*.

Unit 4: Technical Considerations

This work may be somewhat deceiving in regard to musical execution. Perhaps the most difficult element facing a younger ensemble will be performing a work in 6/8 time at a slower tempo. The conductor must be sure that the performers are secure with the subdivision of the pulse to ensure musical flow and quarter note and dotted-quarter note entrances that stand alone. Performers must be able to execute musical phrases at a soft dynamic while not allowing tone quality or pitch to suffer. In general, instrumental technique should not be a problem for an ensemble capable of performing grade three literature with a high level of musicianship.

Unit 5: Stylistic Considerations

The piece must be performed in a very gentle manner. As was stated before, the 6/8 meter should be felt by the ensemble so the piece flows. Eighth notes should be played in a *sostenuto* fashion to facilitate lyricism. The composer ends most musical statements by releasing on count one with a tie from the previous bar. Melodic lines should be expressive in nature and some freedom should be given within and at the end of phrases.

Unit 6: Musical Elements

The work has two main themes, the first of which is introduced by the solo trumpet. The second appears in m. 22 in the woodwinds. The composer develops both themes separately and eventually they are woven together in imitative and antiphonal counterpoint. The use of parallel chords, often diatonic seventh chords, suggests an intended feeling of "blues." The composer recommends that in performance "the quality of good sound and beautiful tone be stressed in all instruments." Rhythmically speaking, the piece is not difficult, yet attention must be paid to the length of notes.

Unit 7: Form and Structure

EVENT	MEASURE	SCORING
Theme I	Beginning-22	Solo trumpet states the theme; accompanied by horns, baritones, tuba, clarinets, and alto saxophones
Theme II	22-30	Theme appears in piccolo, oboe, clarinets; it is developed by horns, trombones, baritones, and tuba
Theme I´	30-42	Theme I is developed first by upper woodwinds, then horns and saxophones
Theme II´	42-51	Theme II is developed by low brass, then upper woodwinds
Climax	51-57	Theme I reappears with a different tonality; full band
Thematic	57-67	Both themes are combined in fragments; full band juxtaposition
Theme I´´	67-79	Theme I, in an altered state, reappears in the solo trumpet with chordal accompaniment
Theme II´´	79-82	Theme II reappears in an altered state in the upper woodwinds; full band
Codetta	82-end	Four-bar codetta with developed material from Theme II in upper woodwinds; full band in last two measures

Unit 8: Suggested Listening
James Barnes, *Yorkshire Ballad*
Frank Erickson, *Air for Band*
Robert Starer:
Annapolis Suite
Elegy for a Woman Who Died Too Young
Fantasy On "When Johnny Comes Marching Home"

Unit 9: Additional References and Resources
Manhattan Beach Music, Brooklyn, NY.

Sigma Alpha Iota Philanthropies, Inc.: Robert Starer; available from
http://sai-national.org/phil/composers/rstarer.html;
Internet; accessed 25 February 1999.

Starer, Robert. Basic Rhythmic Training. Hal Leonard Publishing
Corporation, 1987.

Contributed by:
Rodney C. Schueller
Northern Illinois University Bands
DeKalb, Illinois

Teacher Resource Guide

Mazama

Jay Chattaway
(b. 1946)

Unit 1: Composer

Jay Chattaway began composing as a junior high school student in Monongahela, Pennsylvania, which is located near Pittsburgh. His collegiate education was obtained at West Virginia University, the Eastman School of Music, and Catholic University of America.

Professionally, Jay Chattaway served for seven years as Chief Arranger and Composer-in-Residence with the United States Navy Band. After his tour of duty with the Navy, Chattaway joined CBS Records in New York where his many projects included work for Bob James, Maynard Ferguson, Gato Barbieri, and Carly Simon.

After moving to Los Angeles in 1986, he began scoring film projects. To date he has scored twenty-six feature films, including *Missing in Action*, *Red Scorpion,* and Stephen King's *Silver Bullet.*

The composer's television credits include documentaries (e.g., National Geographic, Jacques Cousteau, Space Age, ABC's Shark Chronicles...) and dramatic series such as *Falcon Crest, Star Trek: The Next Generation, Star Trek: Deep Space Nine,* and *Star Trek: Voyager.* Additionally, Chattaway has also composed the music for the virtual reality attraction in Las Vegas, *Star Trek: The Experience.*

Chattaway has written over 200 other compositions for the band medium (all published by William Allen Music). His most recent addition to the repertoire is *Three Rivers,* a grade four composition, commissioned by the Pennsylvania chapter of the Honorary Bandmasters Association, Phi Beta Mu. *Three Rivers* received its premiere at the 1999 Pennsylvania Music

Educators Association Conference by the Duquesne University Wind Symphony, Dr. Robert C. Cameron, Conductor.

Chattaway's honors include four Grammy nominations, four Gold Albums, and various Emmy nominations. His service to the profession includes holding office as Governor of the Music Peer Group of the Television Academy and President of the Society of Composers and Lyricists. He frequently appears as a guest conductor.

Unit 2: Composition

Mazama (Legend of the Pacific Northwest) was written in 1984 as a commission by the Western International Band Clinic whose three-year commissioning project from that time period is outlined under unit 3. The consortia for this project included thirty-seven participating units – schools of various grade levels (grade school through college), two school districts, individuals, and two businesses. Part of the mission of this particular commissioning project is to "create original band music with some significant relationship to the locale of the Pacific Northwest Region." (Jay Chattaway, *Mazama* program notes, 1984.)

Mazama was premiered on November 16, 1984, in Seattle, Washington, by the Oak Harbor Junior High School Concert Band with the composer conducting. The work has become quite successful, although many of the first listeners felt that it would not become popular due to the unusual challenges it offers to the grade three world. *Mazama* is a work that is very accessible to administrators, audience members, and performers alike. Additionally, music educators can appreciate the many well-constructed musical aspects of the composition. The piece has been performed worldwide (including performances in Russia and Japan) and had a mass performance conducted by the composer of approximately 1,400 musicians in Santa Monica, California. Chattaway has also adapted the work for orchestra and choir.

Mazama, like Frank Ticheli's *Cajun Folksongs*, is suitable for good grade three ensembles and honors, high school, and college bands.

It must be stated that the ocarina is an essential instrument in this work. There can be no substitution from the standard band instrumentation for the sound and character of this instrument. An inexpensive ocarina may be purchased through many music stores and catalogs ($5-15). Ocarinas do come in various pitch ranges. The composer does suggest that "two ocarinas of different pitches, could be used with great effect," (Jay Chattaway, *Mazama* program notes, 1984.) and Max McKee, founder of the WIBC, has performed the work with six ocarina-type instruments in Kazakhstan with excellent results. The ocarina part is improvised but does have specific entrances. The part can be found in the flute book.

Unit 3: Historical Perspective

The Western International Band Clinic had its start twenty-one years ago as a professional offering to band directors who could not attend the Midwest National (now International) Band Clinic in Chicago, Illinois. The clinic has grown to become highly attended and includes four 160-piece honor bands plus a director's band. Six guest conductors appear each year.

The commissioning project that included *Mazama* was a three-year project in which two works were commissioned per year (one for young band and one for high school band). The consortium heads approached fifty junior high schools and fifty high schools from the Pacific Northwest (including selected schools in Canada) with a request that each school contribute $50 per work. A variable number of members participated for a given piece. In addition to Jay Chattaway, the commissioned composers were Alfred Reed (*Song of the High Cascades*), Frank Bencriscutto (*Pacific Scene*), Clare Grundman (*Northwest Saga*), John O'Reilly (*Northwest Suite*), and Frank Erickson (*Northwest Passage*). Of the six works, *Mazama* and *Northwest Suite* have experienced the most success.

One of the criteria for the commission was that the piece was to have something to do with the history or heritage of the Pacific Northwest Region. Jay Chattaway chose the subject of the Mazama Indians and incorporated authentic musical and linguistic elements into the work.

The Mazama Indians lived in the area of Mount Mazama, a part of the Cascade Mountain Range in Southern Oregon. The volcanic eruption of Mt. Mazama nearly annihilated the Mazama tribe and created what is now known as Crater Lake. The composer writes: "This piece was first rehearsed on Whitbey Island, Washington, and there were actually some members of the audience of Mazama ancestry. They were very emotional upon hearing the music." (Jay Chattaway, 23 February 1999.)

Unit 4: Technical Considerations

The work is a challenging grade three level composition. The need for the students to be very solid in rhythm and counting is of primary importance. There are two sections in particular that are easily destroyed if the players are unable to maintain a sense of time and rhythm (mm. 86-120; mm. 121-149).

The percussion section must have several members who are very rhythmically solid, with special emphasis on the player assigned to the roto-tom part. Measure 86 begins a repetitious eighth note pattern in 12/8 time in the roto-toms that is grouped 3+3+2+2+2. This section emerges from a clearly standard common time feel. The tambourine and shaker players must also be comfortable with this rhythm, as their parts highlight the note grouping.

There are very active percussion parts throughout the work. A minimum of six solid players is needed, but a section of eight is much better, especially if the group is inexperienced. The following is a listing of parts to be covered/instruments which are needed:

> Flexatone, tubular wind chimes, many animal bells (sleigh bells and the like work well as substitutes), vibra slap, finger cymbals, roto-toms (three different pitches – regular tom-toms work as a substitute), two timpani, snare drum, two tambourines, shakers, suspended cymbal, bass drum (two are preferred), bells, and xylophone (mallet parts can be performed by one player).

The most difficult measures from a mechanical standpoint are mm. 158-159 and mm. 194-195. The conductor must take care not to allow the tempo to become frantic as the fingers and tongue must coordinate for four repetitions of two beats of eighth notes in the interval pattern of up a major second, up a minor third, up a major second, and down a perfect fifth (thus returning to the original note of the group).

The composer challenges the ensemble with a wide dynamic range (*p* to *fff*). The changes in dynamics occur in a variety of ways – *forte piano* attacks, large changes within two or three beats, *subito* changes, and passages that have gradations which occur over the course of several measures. It is very easy for an ensemble of young players to become overly excited at the *fortissimo* sections and overblow so that the sound that is produced is crass. Conversely, it is very easy for an immature group to lose a sense of pulse during the softer entrances due to a lack of proper breath (and embouchure) support and general insecurity.

Unit 5: Stylistic Considerations

The composer presents a variety of styles ranging from the lyrical to the aggressive. Additionally, the ensemble must sing or rather chant in the Mazama language (in octave unison). Chattaway has set the text phonetically to better serve the pronunciation. The chant melody is the main theme or germ of the work and occurs within the range of a perfect fourth.

Chattaway is successful in creating a piece within the means of a good grade three ensemble that also forces individual sections to be independent. Three examples of non-formula style writing follow.

> The flute section is completely exposed on a mostly unison melody at the beginning of the work which is additionally referenced in mm. 38-39 and at the recapitulation (mm. 175-181). The range of the passage is low (c1 to g1) and must be presented in a *legato* fashion with a full, rich sound. The second flutes must be able to hold their own when the parts split to form harmony.

> The clarinet section at m. 27 must have the capability of independent playing between the second and third (and bass) parts. The writing in this section (in the chalumeau register) not only creates

a very flowing and lovely setting upon which the composer places an extensive and lyrical clarinet solo (mm. 31-51) but also serves to establish the new pulse.

The low brass and low woodwind parts have two sequences of rhythmic punctuation (supported by the percussion) (mm. 121-128 and mm. 133-143) that take a great deal of concentration and sense of security. Additionally, m. 121 re-establishes a duple division of the beat coming from the strongly felt triple division of the beat from mm. 86-120. This is a very difficult transition.

Unit 6: Musical Elements

Rhythm (because of the rests between the notes) and dynamics are the two elements that require the most development and concentration. The ability to control the tone within the various dynamic levels is essential. The *tessitura* for each instrument family falls within reasonable ranges for a grade three ensemble. However, there are a few parts whose full range within the work should be highlighted:

The first trumpets must have control of an f#2, the flutes must have a low c, the horn players must have an f2, and the first trombone players must have an f1.

The work possesses no changes to the key signature of one flat and includes very few accidentals.

Unit 7: Form and Structure

The composer writes: "Compositionally speaking, *Mazama* is not constructed as traditional western music. The musical lines are woven together as though on a loom, and the resultant harmonies are the intersection of those lines. Not a melody and chord type of construction at all." (Chattaway, 23 February 1999.)

The shape of the work could be said to be in an overall ABA´ coda format with distinct sections within each division.

SECTION	MEASURE	EVENT AND SCORING
A	1-67	
	1-26	"Dramatically (quarter note = 66)" percussion, ocarina, and flutes; contrasting loud percussion with soft, low flute sounds; flute melody derived from the upcoming chant material
		Chant theme in mm. 7-10 and mm. 17-20 sung by the *tutti*

Section	Measure	Event and Scoring
	27-49	"A little more motion" Clarinets and percussion
		31-49: Clarinet solo based upon the chant theme 37-39: Flute and ocarina interjection
	50-67	*Tutti* texture; new melody (2+2+4); two statements
B	68-161	"Faster, quarter note = 126"
	68-85	Alternation between percussion and *tutti*
	86-120	Compound meter feel (tom-toms written in 12/8); based on groups of eighth notes in 3+3+2+2+2 accent grouping (dotted-quarter + dotted-quarter + quarter + quarter + quarter)
		94-98: New treatment (aggressive) of the chant material 104-120: Varied treatment of the aggressive version of the chant material; pieces of the theme split between choirs of instruments
	121-149	Return to simple meter division of the beat; driving eighth note rhythms in the percussion; four-measure rhythmic punctuation pattern presented by the low brass and low woodwinds highlighted by the percussion; melody presented in mm. 125-128 taken from mm. 52-53
	150-161	"Gradually faster and louder" Transition
	162-178	Percussion cadenza
	171-178	"Slower, gradually"
	171-174	Percussion and ocarina alternate bars
	175-178	Percussion and flute section split each measure
A´	179-186	Tempo I (quarter note = 66) Abbreviated version of mm. 1-26

SECTION	MEASURE	EVENT AND SCORING
Coda	187-198	"Suddenly fast (quarter note = 168)" Transitional material from mm. 150-161

Unit 8: Suggested Listening

Any recording by Carlos Nakai and other Native American performing artists.

Unit 9: Additional References and Resources

Chattaway, Jay. e-mail to Diane Bargiel, 23 February 1999.

McKee, Max. The American Band College. 407 Terrace St., Ashland, OR 97520. website: jeffnet.org/bandworld. 541-482-5030.

Oregon History Center. Research Library, Portland, OR. 503-306-5240.

Contributed by:

Diane M. Bargiel
Director of Instrumental Music and Artist Series
Juniata College
Huntingdon, Pennsylvania

Teacher Resource Guide

Mystery on Mena Mountain
Julie Giroux
(b. 1961)

Unit 1: Composer

Born in Fairhaven, Massachusetts, Julie Giroux was raised in Phoenix, Arizona, and Monroe, Louisiana. She is an accomplished performer on piano and horn; she began playing piano at the age of three. Her first piece was published when she was nine. Giroux attended Louisiana State University and Boston University, and has studied composition with John Williams, Bill Conti, and Jerry Goldsmith. Since 1984, she has been composing, orchestrating, and conducting music for television and films. Giroux has credits for more than eighty films and television programs including *Dynasty*, *The Colbys*, *North and South*, and *North and South Part II - Love and War*. She has arranged for the Academy Awards Show, Dudley Moore, Lisa Minelli, Madonna, Reba McIntyre, Little Richard, Billy Crystal, Michael Jackson, and others. Her efforts have earned her an Emmy Award and several other nominations.

Julie Giroux has written music for concert band since 1983. Her works in the concert band genre include *Mystery on Mena Mountain*, *The Necromancer*, *Space Symphony*, and *Crown of Thorns*.

Unit 2: Composition

As a child, Giroux visited her grandmother at her cabin in the Ozark Mountains in Arkansas. Her experience there led to the inspiration for *Mystery on Mena Mountain*. Written while she was a student at Louisiana State University, *Mystery on Mena Mountain* was the first piece for symphonic band that Giroux published. The piece is programmatic and based on a legend from the Ozark Mountains. The legend grew from the disappearance of two children in the area in 1940. According to the legend, the children climbed Mena Mountain to meet the angels that supposedly lived in the clouds above the mountain and never returned. Approximately five minutes in length, *Mystery on Mena Mountain* is through-composed with distinct sections that depict the legend of the children climbing the mountain. Despite its programmatic nature, creative percussion writing, several tempo changes, and intriguing harmonies make *Mystery on Mena Mountain* an exciting piece of music that would stand on musical merit alone.

Unit 3: Historical Perspective

Franz Liszt (1811-86) is credited with coining the term *program music*, which refers to descriptive music that is inspired by a nonmusical idea. Program music can be traced from at least the fourteenth century. It is often indicated by the title of the work and sometimes contains explanatory remarks or a preface. Ludwig van Beethoven's *Pastoral Symphony*, Hector Berlioz's *Symphonie Fantastique*, Ottorino Respighi's *The Pines of Rome*, Karel Husa's *Music for Prague 1968*, and David Maslanka's *A Child's Garden of Dreams* are all examples of programmatic music with different inspirations. Legends, like the one that inspired *Mystery on Mena Mountain*, also inspired programmatic works such as *Night on Bald Mountain* by Modest Mussorgsky and *The Sorcerer's Apprentice* by Paul Dukas.

Unit 4: Technical Considerations

The piece features the keys of F major, A-flat major, and C major. The opening unison lines can create intonation problems, and chromatic writing is found throughout the piece. The technical demands of the piece are not extreme but do require that the ensemble change tempi and key signatures frequently. Range is only a concern for the first trumpet, with the highest note being a B-flat above the staff. The most difficult writing occurs in the numerous percussion parts. The percussion requirements call for an extensive timpani part, a technically demanding tom-tom and optional xylophone part, and the use of snare drum, bass drum, suspended and crash cymbals, gong, tambourine, chimes, and glockenspiel. The rhythmic challenges include the use of hemiola (mm. 1-27) with the continuous triplets in the timpani, baritone saxophone, bassoon, and tuba parts against the duple rhythms in the rest of the ensemble. Syncopated rhythms are found in both the melodic lines and the accompaniment patterns in the *Allegro* section. The rhythmic *ostinato* in the horns and saxophones (mm. 29-48) has a tricky accent pattern at a quick tempo. Players must also be comfortable with the sixteenth-dotted eighth pattern on the beat as opposed to the dotted eighth-sixteenth, as they both occur several times in the piece.

Unit 5: Stylistic Considerations

Due to the constantly shifting tempi and styles in *Mystery on Mena Mountain*, players must be able to contrast *legato* and accented styles. In the *Allegro* section (mm. 29-73), the woodwinds and trumpets must maintain a singing *legato* style while the rest of the ensemble performs sharply articulated rhythmic passages. In addition to *legato*, *staccato*, and accented markings, the piece also has accented markings with *staccato* and *legato* markings underneath. These should be performed with the appropriate amount of length and weight to the notes. The dynamic range of the piece is extensive, ranging from *pp* to *fff* with carefully marked rapid and extended *crescendos* and *decrescendos*. Several subtle tempo changes must be carefully followed to allow the melodic lines to phrase properly. Stylistic markings should be exaggerated and melodic lines should be played expressively to achieve the maximum amount of drama in the piece.

Unit 6: Musical Elements

Despite the opening key signature of C minor, the opening twenty-eight measures move between C and A-flat major, creating a mysterious, shifting harmony. The piece is primarily homophonic with some intriguing harmonic progressions and melodies. Non-traditional chord sequences and accidentals in the melody are common. A countermelody can be found in the horns and saxophones (mm. 12-26). Compositional devices include the use of an *obligato* rhythm (mm. 29-48) and hemiola (mm. 1-27).

Unit 7: Form and Structure

MEASURE	EVENT AND SCORING
1-28	The sun rises above Mena Mountain. A pedal C in the first 27 measures creates tension as the opening unison theme is repeated three times with increasing density and tempo.
29-72	The children climb the mountain and tire as they reach the top. An *Allegro* tempo with a driving *ostinato* rhythm combines with a bright melody in the woodwinds and trumpets. A fanfare section (mm. 49-59) interrupts the melody. The *ostinato* returns (m. 60) and slows (mm. 68-72) as the children reach the top of the mountain.
73-83	The mist from the clouds clears and 200 white-robed angels appear. An *Adagio* tempo with a mysterious flute and alto saxophone or horn solo leads to a trumpet solo.
84-88	The children are invited to approach the angels, who place a jeweled crown on each child's head. This section

is marked *Religioso* and sounds like a short chorale in the woodwinds.

89-100   The children accompany the angels up to heaven and the clouds return, leaving Mena Mountain as it was before. The *Maestoso* ending is dramatic and triumphant with a final C major chord at a *fff* dynamic.

Unit 8: Suggested Listening

Paul Dukas, *The Sorcerer's Apprentice*
Julie Giroux, *The Necromancer*
David Maslanka, *A Child's Garden of Dreams*
Modest Mussorgsky, *Night on Bald Mountain*
Richard Strauss, *Don Quixote*

Unit 9: Additional References and Resources

Apel, Willi, ed. *Harvard Dictionary of Music*. Second edition. Cambridge, MA: Belknap Press, 1970.

Stolba, K Marie. *The Development of Western Music*. Dubuque, IA: William C. Brown Publishers, 1990.

Additional notes provided by Julie Giroux.

Contributed by:

Mike Alexander
University of Wisconsin - Milwaukee
Milwaukee, Wisconsin

Teacher Resource Guide

The Renaissance Fair
Bob Margolis
(b. 1949)

Unit 1: Composer

Bob Margolis was born in Staten Island, New York, in 1949. He studied music at Brooklyn College before transferring to the University of California at Berkeley to pursue design. He returned to Brooklyn College, completing a Bachelor of Arts in speech and television production in 1974, and a Master of Arts in 1977. Margolis has studied composition with William Schimmel and Robert Starer, and orchestration with Arnold Rosner. In 1981 he founded Manhattan Beach Music, a publishing company with a commitment to high-quality works for band. He has been honored twice by the American Bandmasters Association in composition competitions. His own high-quality works include many arrangements of Renaissance music, an affinity perhaps begun as early as age seven when he began studying the recorder. His works include *Color*; *Fanfare, Ode and Festival*; *Soldiers Procession and Sword Dance*; *Royal Coronation Dances*; *and Terpsichore*.

Unit 2: Composition

The Renaissance Fair was commissioned by the Murchison Middle School Band in Austin, Texas, under the direction of Cheryl Floyd. It was finished in March of 1991 as a sequel to *Fanfare, Ode and Festival*, a work which has become a staple of the junior high repertoire since its publication in 1982. *The Renaissance Fair*, indicates the composer in his preface, is suitable for high school and advanced junior high bands. It is comprised of three movements. *Entry of the Court (Courante CLXXXIII)* from Michael Praetorius' *Terpsichore* begins the work, followed by two movements from Tielman Susato's *Het derde musyck boexken* (called *Danserye*) of 1551. The second movement, "Shepherdesses's Dance," is based on a *basse danse* "Bergerette sans roch," and the third movement, "The Magicians," is from the final folio of *Danserye*, *Galliard (XV)* "Le tout." The work is approximately four minutes long.

Unit 3: Historical Perspective

Michael Praetorius (1571-1621) is a very significant figure when studying the Renaissance. He was composer, theorist, organist, publisher and, perhaps most significantly, author of the three-volume treatise *Syntagma Musicum*, a very important guide to the music of his time. Volume I contained religious music; Volume III, musical theory and notation; and Volume II contained detailed descriptions and woodcuts of musical instruments of the time. Although a majority of his over 1,000 compositions were sacred works, his *Terpsichore* is a collection of Renaissance dances named for the Greek Muse of dancing and published in Germany in 1612. The *Courante* used in the first movement is taken from this set of dances. The *Courante* itself was a French dance which reached its peak popularity in the seventeenth century and is typically in simple triple time at a rapid tempo.

Tielman Susato (ca.1500-ca.1561-4) was a prominent Renaissance musician, composer, and calligrapher who established a music printing shop in 1543 and produced music of the period by such composers as Josquin des Prez, Orlando di Lassus, and Clement Janequin. The second movement is a *basse danse*, a favorite courtly dance of the late fifteenth and early sixteenth centuries which was improvised over a borrowed tenor. In this work the tenor is in the slower-moving line. The third movement is described by Margolis as a "romp of marked vivacity," a description fitting a *galliard*, which was a lively dance in simple triple time. Both the second and third movements are taken from a collection of popular dance pieces, *Danserye*, published in 1551 by Susato.

Other wind works which use Renaissance material include Ron Nelson's *Medieval Suite* and Norman Dello Joio's *Variants on a Medieval Tune*.

Unit 4: Technical Considerations

Students should be comfortable with C and G major scales in sixteenth notes at dotted-quarter note = 90. Some double tonguing for very short segments of these scales is required in the outer two movements of everyone except the low brass. By composer's design, the "winds are arrayed in extreme registers – high in the flutes and low in the contraclarinets." These extremes of register are effective but pose technical and intonation difficulties. The full, ideal instrumentation may also give cause for consideration. There is an important independent string bass part and a contraclarinet part which is doubled in the bass clarinet. In several sections, both the flute parts and the piccolo parts are divisi, requiring two piccolos and four independent flute lines. The dotted rhythm of 6/8 time is prevalent throughout the work and care must be taken for a "lifted" quality. Also rhythmically, syncopations common to Renaissance phrasing must be emphasized. Metric shifts include 6/4, 9/4, 6/8, and 3/8 time. In the third movement there is some ornamentation in the upper parts of the consorts which should be noted.

Unit 5: Stylistic Considerations

Because there was no international pitch standard in the Renaissance, matched sets of instruments were built incorporating graduated sizes. These families of instruments were known as "consorts" and could be defined as *loud* (haut) or *bas* (soft). Renaissance orchestration relied on the alternation of consorts for contrast. Margolis uses the principle of consorts in his arrangements, and care must be taken to balance the groups so the inner lines can be heard. The articulation used must enhance the dance-like character of these pieces and should be "lifted," but with body to each pitch. A variety of articulations are required, and at some places, the composer assists through specific articulation markings, particularly at points of agogic stress. Note that length and articulation styles must be uniform. This is essential to providing the clarity required to distinguish the individual lines which are such an important part of the texture. Tempi may vary, especially in the second movement, as long as clarity and the character of the dance is maintained. Detailed instructions in the percussion parts regarding types of drums and particular mallet choices are important to the authenticity of Margolis' score. In general, close study of the numerous details throughout the score will assist in stylistic interpretation.

Unit 6: Musical Considerations

The polyphonic textures of this work are consistent with the primarily linear dimension of Renaissance music. The bass line serves as a foundation, as in the *basse danse*, where the repeated tenor line establishes form and a sense of tonality but vertically the music is still modal in sound. The inner voices act contrapuntally, not harmonically. Adhering to the Renaissance principle of "consorts," the same musical material is varied by orchestration alone ("Shepherdesses's Dance"), or in the case of m. 25 in "The Magicians," by consort and the twentieth century notion of key. A variety of consorts are used: full band with extremes of register (without trumpets), woodwind consort, horn and low brass consort, and a brass consort which, with the exception of mm. 21-25 of "Entry of the Court," uses either horn or trumpet to the exclusion of the other. Percussion is described in the composer's notes as "color infusers – there for texture and sparkle." This work is Renaissance music through the filter of the twentieth century. Margolis' use of dynamic marks, articulation, mutes, and other details provide important performance indicators, although they would not have appeared in the Renaissance works themselves.

Unit 7: Form and Structure

SECTION	MEASURE	EVENT AND SCORING
Movement I: "Entry of the Court"		
A	1-11	Flute I, both piccolos, full clarinet consort, and parade drum play *courante* in C tonal area
	12-21	*Courante* repeated with addition of full woodwind consort (without saxophones) and string bass, triangle-highlighted entrance m. 12
B	22-25	Beginning with muted trumpet, woodwinds added each measure, low brass and orchestra bells move clearly to cadence in the tonal area of G
	26-28	Piccolos, flutes and double reeds, muted trombones return to C center with *courante* rhythms
C	29-39	Ascending sequence from C to G *tenuto* adds weight to beginning of each sequence, add low woodwinds, low brass, and horns in increments to final cadence
	40-41	Timpani *crescendo* roll to final cadence on C with open chord and one or two per part (no clarinets)
Movement II: "Shepherdesses's Dance"		
A	1-4	Antecedent – melody *p* in flutes, clarinet I and II, alto saxophone I, tenor melody in baritone saxophone, horn, string bass (pizz), and tubular bells
	5-8	Consequent – *mp* piccolos and flutes, oboe, bassoon, and tenor in string bass (arco), low clarinets, bells
B	9-10	*p-mp* clarinet, saxophones, horn, bass (pizz), and high drum begins
	11-12	*f* full clarinet consort alone
	13-14	Woodwind consort (no saxophones), *f* in low clarinets only
	15	9/4 measure, cadence with reduced flutes (two parts), bassoon, and clarinet I

SECTION	MEASURE	EVENT AND SCORING
A	16-23	Horns and low brass repeat A section now *f* and "broadly," fermata with *diminuendo* at the end

Movement III: "The Magicians"

A	1-4	Piccolo through clarinet II with melody, *f*, and celesta accompaniment
	5-8	Repeat first four measures adding the rest of the clarinet family
B	9-16	Change in melody, added ornamentation, alto saxophones and percussion
C	17-20	Change in percussion, woodwinds (without saxophones) begin a descending sequence at *f*
	21-24	*p*, add saxophones, snare drum, and repeat sequence
	24	Elision between cadence of B and brass pick-up flourish into A, 3/8
A´	25-32	Key change to F, trumpets and low brass return to A with added flourishes in flute I and piccolo
B´	32-36	New consort of clarinets, horn, and euphonium
	37-40	Six-part flute, piccolo consort with continuing active percussion
C´	41-44	Woodwind consort (no saxophones) begin descending sequence
	45-47	Piccolo, flute, oboe, bassoon, trumpet, trombone, and percussion; mixed consort; repeat sequence
Cadence	48-49	Frenzied, percussive cadence with rapid articulation, stopped horns, *pp* low brass and a final bass drum hit bring an abrupt, energetic finish

Unit 8: Suggested Listening

Thoinot Arbeau/arr. Margolis, *Belle Qui Tiens Ma Vie*
Pierre Attaignant/arr. Margolis, *Fanfare, Ode and Festival*
Norman Dello Joio, *Variants on a Medieval Tune*
Ron Nelson, *Medieval Suite*
David Noon, *Sweelinck Variations*

Michael Praetorius/arr. Margolis, *Terpsichore*
Tielman Susato/arr. Margolis, *The Battle Pavane*
Tielman Susato/arr. Michael Walters, *Twelve Dances from the "Dansuerye"*

Unit 9: Additional References and Resources

Apel, Willi, ed. *Harvard Dictionary of Music*. Second Edition. Cambridge, MA: Belknap Press, 1970.

Grout, Donald Jay. Ed. Claude V. Palisca. *A History of Western Music*. Fifth Ed. New York: W.W. Norton & Co., 1996.

Sadie, Stanley, ed. *The New Grove Dictionary of Music and Musicians*. 20 Vols. London: Macmillan, 1980.

Whitwell, David. *A Concise History of the Wind Band*. Northridge, CA: WINDS 1.

Contributed by:

Jennifer McAllister
Saskatoon, Saskatchewan
Canada

Teacher Resource Guide

Resting in the Peace of His Hands

John Gibson
(b. 1946)

Unit 1: Composer
John Gibson was born in Texas on February 28, 1946. He holds degrees from Texas Tech and North Texas, and has taught in the Amarillo public schools, at North Texas State, at the University of Arizona, at McMurry University, and at Southern Methodist University. He has completed commissions for the Amarillo Symphony Orchestra, the Tucson Symphony Orchestra, the Lubbock Symphony Orchestra, McMurry University, St. Thomas University (St. Paul), Texas Tech University, high school and junior high school bands, churches, the Texas Music Educators Association, and the Turtle Creek Chorale, and has served as resident composer for the Dallas Wind Symphony. His works have been performed nationally and internationally by a variety of ensembles from the Royal Air Force Band in England, to the Turtle Creek Chorale in Dallas, and from the Texas Music Educators Association All-State Orchestra, to Texas junior high school bands around the state. His catalog of compositions includes works for band, orchestra, chorus, percussion ensemble, and musical theater.

Unit 2: Composition
The work is written for symphonic band. The piece opens with quiet sustained B's in the flute and vibraphone which float high over the opening melodies. This seems to musically portray a state of peaceful rest, effectively expressing the spirit of the title. The work grows from a very gentle opening in the wood-winds through a more active central section followed by a return to the opening state concluded with an instrumental Amen.

Unit 3: Historical Perspective

The piece was written for Dr. Jack Delaney and the Southern Methodist University Meadows School of Arts Wind Ensemble. The genesis of this work can best be told in the words of the composer:

> While visiting the Busch-Reisinger Museum at Harvard University, I encountered a relief sculpture by Kaethe Kollwitz (1867-1945) titled "Resting in the Peace of His Hands." I knew nothing of the artist, nothing of the origin of the work, and nothing of the origin of the title at the time of the encounter.
>
> I discovered that Kollwitz was a significant German artist who was constantly exposed to the suffering of the unfortunate and forgotten people through her husband, a physician assigned to care for the indigent. Her efforts to express that suffering in the midst of her own personal suffering (she lost her son, Peter, to World War I, and her grandson, Peter Jr., to World War II) earned her enormous respect and high position among mainstream German artists, and enemies within the Nazi government. "Resting in the Peace of His Hands" was a very personal work for Ms. Kollwitz, intended to express "the feeling of utter peace," contrary to the major body of her work, intended to express utter torment. She named the work after a quote from Goethe, and intended that it be the central element in the headstone of her family tomb.

Unit 4: Technical Considerations

The writing is of a lyrical, conservative nature. The written dynamics range from *pianissimo* through *forte* with most of the piece restricted to the *mezzo piano* to *mezzo forte* range. The *tessitura* is also conservative, not calling for extremes high or low. Intonation, blend, and balance will be of concern. The orchestration treats the instruments chorally, often with interesting and independent inner parts. The percussion parts are of interest, particularly in the glockenspiel, vibraphone, and chimes.

Unit 5: Stylistic Considerations

The piece requires careful attention to line, articulation, singing tone, and dynamics. Melodic lines are passed from soloist to soloist, frequently overlapping. Care must be taken to have the phrasing of each solo match seamlessly with those preceding. Attention to tone quality at soft and louder dynamics is of the utmost importance for this work.

Unit 6: Musical Elements

Harmonically the work is mildly dissonant, with frequent major seventh chords (omitting the third). The texture is largely polyphonic with much solo writing. Many inner parts have independent melodic lines. Much of the writing is canonic.

Unit 7: Form and Structure

At the broadest level, the work is an ABA form. The opening section is characterized by quiet, *legato* solo entrances accompanied by phrases of choral-type writing. A motif of a rising major or minor seventh is used to build a melody which is passed from instrument to instrument and the harmony. The opening section is subdivided into four smaller sections by a *ritardando* followed by an *a tempo* (mm. 24, 30, 38).

The middle section is contrasted from the outer two by a syncopated *ostinato* in the brass and percussion, and by a quicker tempo. There is a beautiful canonic duet between oboe I and English horn. At m. 63, sixteenth note descending patterns are exchanged between the flutes and single-reed instruments.

The closing section (starting at m. 77) returns to the opening tempo, and the motif based on the rising seventh. At m. 85, motives from the opening section are stated by the full band at a dynamic of *forte*. This is the musical climax of the piece and seems to be a musical answer to the question raised by the preceding sections. The ensemble *diminuendos* to *mezzo forte* at m. 95. The piece remains quiet and (except for a *forte-piano* on beat two in m. 112) becomes "gradually slower and softer." At m. 116, the flutes, oboes, clarinets, and percussion sustain an E major chord (*pianissimo*) while the brass, saxophones, bassoons, and bass clarinets play an extended plagal cadence for five measures, *forte*.

Unit 8: Suggested Listening

Mark Camphouse, *Watchman, Tell Us of the Night*
David Gillingham, *Heroes Lost and Fallen*
David Holsinger, *On a Hymnsong of Philip Bliss*
W. Francis McBeth, *Kaddish*
Thomas Stone, *Shadows of Eternity*
Frank Ticheli, *Amazing Grace*

Unit 9: Additional References and Resources

Battisti, Frank, and Robert Garofalo. *Guide to Score Study for the Wind Band Conductor.* Ft. Lauderdale, FL: Meredith Music Publications, 1990.

Wiesel, Elie. *Night.* New York: Bantam Doubleday Dell Publishing Group, Inc., 1982.

Contributed by:

James L. Klages
Professor of Trumpet
University of Central Oklahoma
Edmond, Oklahoma

Teacher Resource Guide

Rhapsody on American Shaped Note Melodies

James Curnow
(b. 1943)

Unit 1: Composer

James Curnow was born on April 17, 1943, in Port Huron, Michigan, and raised in Royal Oak, Michigan. He received his formal training at Wayne State University in Detroit, Michigan, and at Michigan State University in East Lansing, where he was a euphonium student of Leonard Falcone and a conducting student of Dr. Harry Begian. He has taught in all areas of instrumental music, both at the public school and college and university levels. He is a member of such noted organizations as the ABA, CBDNA, NBA, WASBE, and ASCAP. In 1980, Curnow received the National Band Association's Citation of Excellence. He currently lives in Nicholasville, Kentucky, where he is president, composer, and educational consultant for Curnow Music Press, Inc. He also serves as Composer-in-Residence on the faculty of Asbury College in Wilmore, Kentucky.

Unit 2: Composition

Rhapsody on American Shaped Note Melodies was commissioned by the band directors of Kershaw County, South Carolina, in memory of William Harold (Bill) Basden, Band Director of Camden High School from 1958 to 1976. The piece was written in 1995 and published in 1996. Shaped note singing (or "fasola") emerged in the United States in the early 1800s and was developed by John Conneley. This work is basically a medley of shaped note melodies which were written in this unique manner.

Unit 3: Historical Perspective

Shaped note notation is a system of notation consisting of four different shapes: right triangle (FA), circle (SOL), square (LA), and diamond (MI). This system was designed to aid the singer with sight-singing. The first four degrees of the scale were repeated, forming a scale as follows: FA, SOL, LA, FA, SOL, LA, MI, FA. The singers learned to read music by identifying the shape of each note. Out of this tradition grew several singing schools where people met by the thousands to sing and socialize. Several published collections of shaped note melodies emerged to meet these schools' needs for printed music. In the heyday of this school of singing, Columbia, South Carolina became one of the centers of publication and teaching for shaped note music.

Unit 4: Technical Considerations

Though this work does not present any unusually demanding technical passages, the fact that it is basically a medley of shaped note melodies will present the challenge of smooth transition from one melody to the next. There are many style, tempo, and key changes throughout. As in most works by Curnow, there are many solo passages to feature individual instrumentalists.

Unit 5: Stylistic Considerations

The opening fanfare recurs several times to provide a cohesive link throughout the piece. This brief fanfare must be stylistically the same every time it appears. There are numerous dynamic changes which are important to capture the proper nuance and color contrasts intended by the composer. Above all, the melodies must be allowed to sing.

Unit 6: Musical Elements

There is the use of shaped note melodies which are often based on the pentatonic scale. As stated earlier, there are numerous dynamic changes to help capture the proper nuance and color contrasts. Solo lines are cross-cued for playability. There are meter and tempo changes that correspond to the shifts from melody to melody.

Unit 7: Form and Structure

The overall form and structure is that of a medley of tunes which are connected by a recurring fanfare. The notes of the fanfare were taken from the notes of the tune "Pisgah," the first song introduced in the work. The fanfare should be performed in the same style each time it appears. At rehearsal 65, the fanfare does appear in a slightly different shape or structure (softer, less *marcato*). The work concludes with a recurrence of the fanfare. The basic form of the piece is "Fanfare" (mm. 1-8), first melody "Pisgah" (mm. 9-25), "Fanfare" recurs (mm. 26-32), second melody "Avon, Penitents Prayer" (mm.

33-64), "Fanfare" modified (mm. 65-74), transitional material (mm. 75-85), third melody "Bozrah" (mm. 86-130), fourth melody "Consolation" (mm. 131-164), final "Fanfare" statement (mm. 165-end).

Unit 8: Suggested Listening

Rhapsody on American Shaped Note Melodies, Intrada Festivo, Curnow Music Collection Volume 4, (CD) recorded by James Curnow with Shobi Wind Orchestra, available from Curnow Music.

Duckworth, William. *Southern Harmony* (Collection of Shaped Note Melodies), New York: Lovely Music, 1994.

Unit 9: Additional References and Resources

Rehrig, William. *The Heritage Encyclopedia of Band Music: Composers and Their Music*. Edited by Paul E. Bierley. Westerville, OH: Integrity Press, 1991.

Walker, William. *The Southern Harmony Songbook*. New York: Hastings House, 1939.

Walker, William. *The Southern Harmony, and Musical Companion*. Edited by Glenn C. Wilcox. Lexington: University Press of Kentucky, 1993.

Contributed by:

Otis French
Associate Conductor
United States Army Field Band
Washington, DC

Teacher Resource Guide

Suite Divertimento
Jay W. Gilbert
(b. 1956)

Unit 1: Composer

Jay Gilbert was born in Madison, Wisconsin, in 1956. His musical studies began with piano, then viola, and finally percussion, which he played in high school and college. He attended Madison West Senior High School, where his high school band director, John Rafoth, encouraged him to write arrangements for band and small instrumental ensembles. He then attended the University of Wisconsin-Madison, where he received a Bachelor of Science Degree in Music Education in 1979. After teaching for six years in the public schools of Wisconsin, Gilbert began graduate work at Northwestern University in Evanston, Illinois. At Northwestern, he studied conducting with John P. Paynter and Victor Yampolsky, receiving master's and doctoral degrees in 1986 and 1993, respectively.

Gilbert has not studied composition formally. As a college undergraduate, he was encouraged by several of his teachers to write out short sections of scores by major composers in order to gain insights into the music.

Gilbert is presently Director of Bands and Chair of the Music Department at Doane College in Crete, Nebraska. Prior to his appointment at Doane, Dr. Gilbert was Assistant Director of Bands at Baylor University, Waco, Texas. He has been a frequent guest conductor throughout the United States and Canada.

Unit 2: Composition

Suite Divertimento was commissioned by the Lewisville High School Symphonic Band by Michael T. Brown, assistant director of bands at the school. The composition premiered in the Meyerson Symphony Center in

Dallas, February 7, 1996. It is comprised of three movements: "Prologue," "Pastorale," and "Parade." The main themes for the movements are derived from a four-note motive (B-flat – C – F – G), and reflect the character of the movement's title. The "Prologue" is an eclectic fanfare that combines elements of popular music into a symphonic form. The "Prologue" also serves as a prelude to the more introspective second movement. The "Pastorale" has serene opening and closing sections that surround a stormy middle section. "Parade" opens with a procession of themes and motives that are then used throughout the movement, some of which were presented earlier in the Suite. As the work unfolds, these ideas begin to overlap and build in intensity, as if the parade were passing by the listener. *Suite Divertimento* is approximately nine minutes in length.

Unit 3: Historical Perspective
Numerous suites and divertimenti have been written for instrumental ensembles. A divertimento is an instrumental musical genre dating from the classical style period. It is generally a collection of short, contrasting movements that are light in conception. A suite is an instrumental work comprised of a number of movements as well. *Suite Divertimento* combines elements of popular music with traditional twentieth century compositional practices and forms, with added tone harmonic techniques.

Unit 4: Technical Considerations
The instrumentation for *Suite Divertimento* is for contemporary concert band, with a large percussion section of seven to nine players. The technical demands for this piece are average for its grade level. Conductors will want to give attention to the rhythmic aspect of the piece. The first movement has a driving, underlying pulse for which the horns play syncopated patterns of rhythm that require some attention. *Ostinati* and other rhythmic repetitions have the tendency to be rushed. Additionally, articulations appear throughout the piece that will also require attention. In the second movement, a very lyrical and flowing feeling will be paramount. Generally, the first and third movements are cast brighter than the more introspective second movement. Some care will have to be given to disallow this brightness from becoming edgy. Finally, the players will need to show some sensitivity in the performance of the recapitulation of the theme in the second movement. The second movement requires a high degree of sensitivity to the metrical flow in the parts that accompany the saxophone and clarinet soloists. Attention will also need to be given to the rhythmic detail.

Unit 5: Stylistic Considerations
As mentioned previously, this piece is an eclectic composition reflecting both popular styles of the late twentieth century and traditional forms. Care must

be given to accentuate the stylistic aspects – dynamics, articulations, and rhythms – without sacrificing the rich tone quality of the band. Particular care should be given to accents that occur off the strong beats, and a feeling of drive should be present in both the first and third movements. During the second movement, a more flowing feeling should be generated in the outside sections. The middle section, a stormy interlude, should have as much energy as the band is capable of producing. The third movement is conceived as one long *crescendo*, and younger bands will need to exercise control of dynamic levels. This is particularly true of the percussion writing.

Unit 6: Musical Elements

The melodic ideas for *Suite Divertimento* are derived from the following four-note motive:

This motive also serves to provide some harmonic considerations in the construction of the piece. The main themes for each of the movements are derived from the four-note motive. For example, the first statement of the theme, in m. 9 of the "Prologue" movement, is the interplay of the four notes of the motive.

The second movement theme, presented by the alto saxophone in m. 11, also begins with the construction from the four-note motive.

The main theme of the third movement is actually three of the four notes of the main motive.

The main motive is also orchestrated into the harmonic aspects of the piece. For example, in m. 1 of the first movement, the *ostinato* in the high woodwinds is constructed from the four-note motive scored over two octaves.

In m. 3, the horn fanfare motive is another example of an orchestration for these four notes.

These four notes are subjected to the traditional melodic transformation devices available to composers in the twentieth century. These include inversion, retrograde, rhythmic variation, transposition, augmentation, and diminution. Examples of those can be found throughout the movements of *Suite Divertimento*, and more specific discussion of the use of this motive occurs in the next section.

Unit 7: Form and Structure

Suite Divertimento consists of three movements:
> Movement I: "Prologue" (fast) 1:45
> Movement II: "Pastorale" (slow-fast-slow) 3:30
> Movement III: "Parade" (medium march tempo) 3:35

MEASURE   COMMENTS

Movement I: "Prologue"
(through composed)

Measure	Comments
1	*Ostinato* in high woodwinds and bells; based on four-note motive starting on f concert; under the *ostinato* is the steady pulsing of the hi-hat, which is an important part in this movement
3	Four-note motive is presented as a fanfare in French horns and alto saxophone and vibes transposed to c concert
9	Four-note motive presented as a theme in tonic key by low brass and woodwinds
12	Fanfare motive from m. 3 returns in inversion
16	Return of motive in theme form; builds to m. 24

MEASURE	COMMENTS
24	Motive by trumpets and upper woodwinds in concert key over B-flat major chord with added tone g; horns and alto saxophones play motive transposed to c
29	Upper woodwinds perform an embellished version of the motive from m. 24
30	
31	Horns and cymbals have opening *ostinato* rhythm
32	Mallet percussion perform the four-note motive in a pattern of eighth notes; a foreshadowing of the "Parade" movement
37	Trumpets play another harmonized variant of the motive using only the first three notes until m. 44; in m. 37, the alto saxophone performs a new motive; percussion use brushes
48	Trombones present the four-note motive presented in another form; in m. 51, the material presented in m. 29
57	Last statement of horn fanfare motive from m. 3; flutes play the four-note motive just before final chords

Movement II: "Pastorale"
(ternary form)

1	Clarinet and mallet percussion present four-note motive; trumpets provide third and fifth of chord; this obfuscates tonality until m. 9
9	The accompaniment establishes tonality in A-flat major; after a two-bar introduction, the alto saxophone introduces main melodic idea of the second movement, which is based on the four-note motive; this solo utilizes the palm key register of the instrument
27	Flutes and clarinets present the main melodic idea; countermelody in duple meter is presented by horns and alto saxophones; trumpets join the upper woodwinds in a fully harmonized presentation of the melody; as the statement of the melody ends, the horns (m. 43) play a rhythmic motive derived from the beginning of the movement; this becomes an *ostinato* for the b section
45	The upper woodwinds begin an *ostinato* based on the horn rhythm from the previous two measures; in m. 47, the baritones play a simple scale-wise melody
51	One beat before m. 51, the horns forcefully play the four-note motive which has become two minor second intervals (as opposed to two major second intervals); the orchestration builds to m. 57

MEASURE	COMMENTS
57	Heavy, descending block chords lead to the winding down of the movement; low brass continues the quieting effect until m. 66, where the horn enters to play two notes from the four-note motive; more instruments are added in preparation for a return of the main melody
76	The main melodic idea returns in the solo clarinet with light accompaniment; this is a modified return (not as long as the first)
84	The closing phrase returns to ideas presented in the opening of the movement; the flute presents the four-note motive; the trumpets repeat the opening notes of the movement; the second movement ends with the flute and mallet percussion playing a unison a-flat, the tonic pitch of the movement

Movement III: "Parade"
(free-form march)

1	Playing in unison the band performs the first three notes of the motive starting on b-flat concert; this becomes the basic idea for the movement
2	Timpani begins an *ostinato* that will be used throughout the movement, based on the three-note motive; clarinets play the four-note motive in mm. 5-6, which was first presented by the horns in the first movement; in m. 9, a secondary melodic motive is presented in the alto saxophone, which was also presented before in the first movement at m. 45; a third melodic idea, another little fanfare, is presented in m. 11 by horns; the final melodic motive is presented in m. 14 by the flutes; these ideas return throughout the movement
16	Trombones play the main melodic idea of the piece, which begins with the first three notes presented in the movement; oboes, trumpets, and vibes provide a rhythmic punctuation at the end of the first melodic phrase
25	Trombones continue with the theme; in m. 27, an eighth note *ostinato* figure is performed by the flute, also recapitulated from the first movement; as the presentation of the melody comes to a close, the upper woodwinds and mallet percussion provide another punctuation, this time utilizing the pitches of the four-note motive (m. 36)
39	Alto saxophone presents the secondary theme in its full form; under the melody is inversion of the four-note

MEASURE	COMMENTS
	motive in the horns; timpani continues its *ostinato* based on the first three notes of the motive
54	Trumpet presents the first return of the main theme; this time the punctuations are replaced with motives presented earlier in the movements; horns play the fanfare motive in m. 59, and tenor saxophone and euphonium present a fragment of the second theme; trumpet melody is extended and transitions to the key of D-flat major
76	The low brass play the punctuation motive heard twice before in the movement; in m. 79, the upper woodwinds perform a return of the second theme while the horn continues with an embellished inversion of the four-note motive; the fourth motive is reintroduced in piccolo and xylophone (m. 91); a short bridge phrase, developed from perfect fourth interval in the melodic line, is used to transition back to the tonic key
96	The main melody is recapitulated in the trumpets and clarinets; the horn call returns (m. 101); the secondary theme returns (m. 104); all of these ideas are happening over the timpani *ostinato*, which has been orchestrated into the low brass and woodwind parts; additionally, ascending whole notes in trombones give the work a sense of rising; these ideas converge in m. 110 supporting the main melody; the phrase is extended, leading to the tonalization of c-flat major in m. 117
117	A short presentation of the horn motive passes between instrumental groups; following the horn motive presentation, the movement momentarily settles in orchestration and dynamics
128	A four-bar harmonic transition and *tutti crescendo* lead back to b-flat concert for the final statement of the main theme
132	The main theme is presented first in the trombones (m. 132) and then in trumpets (m. 138). Over the theme, *ostinati* appear in upper woodwind and timpani parts. Fragments of horn motive appear in m. 139. The entire band momentarily takes up the horn motive in mm. 144-146.
147	The main motive is stated for the final time in mm. 147-148; in m. 149, the low brass, woodwinds, and timpani play the motive in retrograde; the piece ends on a B-flat

MEASURE   COMMENTS

major chord with an added sixth; the low brass and woodwinds play the four-note motive as a chord in m. 153; timpani plays its *ostinato* in diminution, and percussion provides a rhythmic punctuation to end the piece

Unit 8: Suggested Listening

John Harbison, *Music for Eighteen Winds*
Vincent Persichetti, *Divertimento for Band*
Ottorino Respighi, *Pines of Rome*

Unit 9: Additional References and Resources

Stolba, K Marie. *The Development of Western Music*. Dubuque, IA. William C. Brown Publishers, 1990.

Contributed by:

Jay W. Gilbert
Director of Bands and Chair, Music Department
Doane College
Crete, Nebraska

Teacher Resource Guide

Sun Dance
Frank Ticheli
(b. 1958)

Unit 1: Composer

Frank Ticheli is currently the Composer-in-Residence of the Pacific Symphony Orchestra and is Associate Professor of Music at the University of Southern California. A native of Louisiana, Ticheli was raised in Texas and received his doctoral and master's degrees in Composition from the University of Michigan, studying with William Albright, George Wilson, and Pulitzer prize winners Leslie Bassett and William Bolcolm. His numerous compositions for winds have brought him many accolades, including the 1989 Walter Beeler Prize (*Music for Winds and Percussion*) and first prize in the 11th Annual Symposium of New Music (*Concertino for Trombone and Band*).

Unit 2: Composition

Sun Dance was commissioned by the Austin (Texas) Independent School District for the Silver Anniversary Celebration of the 25th Annual All-City Band Festival, on March 18, 1997. It is best described by Ticheli in the preface to the score:

> "While composing *Sun Dance*, I was consciously attempting to evoke a feeling: bright joy. After completing the work, I found that the music began to suggest a more concrete image – a town festival on a warm, sun-washed day. I imagined townspeople gathered in the park, some in small groups, some walking hand in hand, others dancing to the music played by a small band under a red gazebo. Throughout the composition process, I carefully balanced the song-like and dance-like components of bright joy. The oboe's gentle

statement of the main melody establishes the work's song-like characteristics, while the work's middle section, a lyrical theme of even greater passion, appears. Several recurring themes are indeed more vocal than instrumental in nature."

The work's dance-like qualities are enhanced by a syncopated rhythmic figure which is not only used in the main melody but is used as the structural building block for virtually everything in the piece, including other melodies, accompaniment figures, and episodes.

Unit 4: Technical Considerations

Sun Dance begins in 4/4 meter with a spirited tempo of quarter note = 132-138. The tempo remains consistent throughout the piece. Meters fluctuate often between 4/4 and 3/4 (6/8), with the eighth note remaining constant. Rhythmic demands are moderate and there is much syncopation. In most cases, 3/4 bars should be done in two, although some of the parts are written in three. A polymetric texture also arises from the metric cross-relation between upper lines (4/4 + 3/4 meter) and the bass line (3/4 meter) in several instances.

The key signature denotes F major, but the tonal center actually begins and ends in C major, developing into the key of F major midway through the piece. A-flat major plays an important role in both development sections. Technical passages are limited to four sixteenth notes and groups of four sixteenth notes, occurring mainly in the introduction and coda.

Both French horn and trumpet ranges are limited to a G above the staff. The French horn writing is basically for two parts. The highest note for the first clarinet part is a high D. Important double reed parts are cued in other parts. There are three percussion parts and one timpani part which can use from five to ten players.

Unit 5: Stylistic Considerations

Ticheli states in the preface, "The interpreter must address the dual relationship between the work's song-like and dance-like qualities. In order to enhance this relationship, he or she must observe carefully the articulations and expressive markings." There are several instances where some instruments have accents and *staccato* marks that are crucial in producing a non-lyrical and dance-like contrast to other instruments playing the lyrical statement. These articulate, dance-like motives must be clear and precise, providing a percussive foil to other more lyrical themes.

In texturally complex sections, the main theme should always sound in the foreground. Strive for a smooth and balanced sound as the theme is transferred from one set of instruments to another.

Unit 6: Musical Elements

The work's main theme (mm. 7-16) establishes the work's lyrical nature and mixolydian modality (C mixolydian). Contained within this theme are two rhythmic motives (one is a syncopated quarter-eighth-quarter figure, and the other is a three eighth note figure) that are used to generate other subsequent themes.

A second theme (mm. 17-25), based on the syncopated rhythm, is a simple and lyrical eight-bar phrase. The third theme (mm. 26-35) is the most rhythmic and dance-like in character. Here a polymetric texture arises from the metric cross-relation between the upper parts (constructed in 4/4 and 3/4 meter) and the bass line (constructed in 3/4 meter). The implied meters occur simultaneously and may be perceived separately, or together as one unit. Later, in mm. 81-85, Ticheli couples this polymetric structure with a polymodal tonal structure (major-minor).

In addition to these themes, all of which are introduced in the work's exposition, a new lyrical theme is introduced in the center of the work, well after the end of the exposition. Although it is derived from part of the main theme, it can be considered entirely new. Ticheli notes that there is quite a long tradition of introducing new themes late in the course of a movement, citing Beethoven's *Eroica* as a notable example.

Unit 7: Form and Structure

SECTION	MEASURE	TONAL CENTER	PHRASE DESCRIPTION
Exposition	1	C major	Introduction
	5		Theme a
	17		Theme b
	26		Theme c
Development 1	36	C major	Theme a
	45	A-flat major	Theme a
	56	F major	Theme a
	67		Theme b
	76		Theme c
	86		Transition
New theme	91	F major	Theme d
	98		Theme d
	105		Theme d
Development 2	113	F major	Theme b
	121	A-flat major	Theme b
	129	C major	Theme b
	138		Codetta

SECTION	MEASURE	TONAL CENTER	PHRASE DESCRIPTION
Recapitulation	143	C major	Theme a
	153		Theme c
	161		Extension
	168		Coda

Unit 8: Suggested Listening

Frank Ticheli:
   Blue Shades
   Cajun Folk Songs
   Fortress
   Postcard
   Vesuvius

Unit 9: Additional References and Resources

Dvorak, Thomas L., Robert Grechesky, and Gary Ciepluch. *Best Music for High School Bands*. New York: Manhattan Beach Music, 1993.

Contributed by:

Ryan Nelson
University of North Texas
Denton, Texas

Teacher Resource Guide

Three Sketches for Winds
Clare Grundman
(1913–1996)

Unit 1: Composer

For almost any musician who has played in a band, Clare Grundman is one of the most recognizable names in band composition. Born in 1913 in Cleveland, Ohio, Grundman is unmistakably one of the leaders in the development of American wind literature for the young student. He has composed over sixty works for band, as well as having arranged many orchestral works for band by such composers as Leonard Bernstein, Aaron Copland, Sir Edward Elgar, and Gustav Holst. His original works for band include *The Blue and the Gray, A Colonial Legend*, four *American Folk Rhapsodies, Fantasy on American Sailing Songs, Northwest Saga, Burlesque for Band*, and *Tuba Rhapsody*.

Unit 2: Composition

Three Sketches for Winds was composed in 1969 and is dedicated to John Paynter and the Northshore Concert Band. The work is in three short movements – "Carousel," "Charade," and "Callithump" (a *callithump* is a noisy, boisterous parade: possibly derived from the French term, *charivari*, that signifies a deliberately distorted and noisy performance) – and is approximately six minutes and fifty-three seconds in length.

Unit 3: Historical Perspective

In the world of band music, particularly for young musicians and ensembles, most of Clare Grundman's music is rich in folk elements and tunes. Rare is the young wind or percussion player who has not studied such American-influenced works as any of the four *American Folk Rhapsodies, The Blue and the*

Gray, *A Colonial Legend*, *Fantasy on American Sailing Songs*, or *Kentucky 1800*, or learned about other countries' folk song heritage by performing his *English Suite*, *Hebrides Suite*, or the *Finnish*, *Japanese*, *Irish*, *Scottish*, or *Welsh Rhapsodies*. In this respect, *Three Sketches for Winds* represents an interesting departure for Grundman in a number of ways. The musical elements, which include the use of quartal harmonies, polytonality, and less reliance on "tunes" than on thematic motives, challenges the musician to understand Grundman's creativity as a composer. His original ideas, combined with contemporary, twentieth century compositional techniques and language, allows the curious and intelligent musician to view/listen to a side of Grundman's work that is not generally familiar to those who know his folk music works for band.

Unit 4: Technical Considerations

For most woodwind and brass instruments, knowledge of their chromatic scales (within their staves for all/above for first chair parts) is necessary since many accidentals are used throughout the entire work. A combination of half, dotted-half, quarter, eighth, dotted-eighth, and sixteenth rhythms are used in the piece. Much of the harmonic structure of the work is based on tonalities and chords that many younger players would not have encountered yet (quartal harmonies, thirteenth chords, polytonality), so it is an important consideration that all wind and brass musicians have a solid sense of personal and ensemble intonation. The unique rhythmic elements of *Three Sketches*, particularly Grundman's employment of syncopation over the bar line (much of the first movement) and irregular phrase lengths (opening of third movement), require an advanced ensemble (and conductor) to have a strong inner sense of pulse and knowledge of the strong and weak beats in measures. Playing ranges are extended for cornet I (A5), trombone I (G4), and baritone (G-flat4). Mutes are needed by all cornet players. Percussion requirements include timpani, bells, xylophone, wood block, three temple blocks, small and large tom-toms, snare drum, bass drum, suspended cymbal, crash cymbals, and triangle.

Unit 5: Stylistic Considerations

Each movement requires great contrasts in tone quality and articulation. "Carousel" features the juxtaposition of full, sustained chords with quick-moving, articulate melodic lines and motives. In order for this combination of disparate musical elements to co-exist effectively, care needs to be taken to not allow one texture or articulation to affect the other. Also, the independence of individual instruments and motivic lines require careful balance.

In "Charade," dynamic balance to the solo instruments (mainly flute, clarinet, and baritone) is the primary goal. In addition, uniform attacks and releases on long-held notes are more difficult than they might seem, so particular attention should be given to how and when players begin and end chordal textures.

The speed and lightness of "Callithump" calls for clear and crisp articulation, quality tone in *staccato* playing, and maintaining the tempo. The latter is difficult since the scoring is independent and sometimes unpredictable.

Unit 6: Musical Elements

A number of non-traditional melodic and harmonic elements are used by Grundman in this work that are clearly a departure from his band pieces that rely on folk tunes for harmonic and thematic ideas. For example, in the "Carousel," quartal melodies and harmonic chord structures in the accompaniment are immediately evident. Irregular phrase lengths and rhythmic structures contradict the meter and bar line in both "Carousel" and "Callithump." In addition, both outer movements' primary themes are centered on dissonant alternation of minor/major second intervals. Harmonies in all three movements feature tonal centers that shift quickly and, at times, to remote and dissonant relationships. In "Charade," for example, major seventh chords are used as harmonic support in the accompaniment. As the development begins, it is supported by chords related at the tritone (A-flat – D), leading to an interesting juxtaposition of polytonal chord (the same D major/A-flat major), first sounded harmonically (m. 160), then melodically (mm. 161-163) in solo clarinet and flute. Harmonies in "Callithump," too, are triadic, but often tritone relationship of chord roots (C – G-flat, A – E-flat) or other unusual relationships are evident.

Another area of interest is in Grundman's scoring for the band. In "Carousel," for example, variety in textures is created through overlapping scoring (where one color or texture begins as another leaves off) or through the use of "pedal chords" that sustain through harmonic/melodic shifts in another voice. In addition, instrumental families are used in typical fashion: upper woodwinds – often lighter, more rhythmic and syncopated lines; brass and lower woodwinds – harmonic support, rhythmic underpinning in longer syncopated passages; percussion – mostly for color and to highlight rhythmic anomalies and cadences.

Unit 7: Form and Structure

Section	Measure
Movement I: "Carousel"	
Section 1	1-36
Section 2	37-62
Section 3	63-81
Section 4	82-94
Coda	95-125

All materials used for the entire movement are presented in the first section (mm. 1-36); rhythmic syncopation is an important feature of all motives, often creating a 3:2 rhythmic feel; quartal harmonic stacks and melodic intervals are abundant (mm. 2-4, 19-24, 31-36, 113-124); polytonal chord clusters, often in contrary motion, are a prominent harmonic device (mm. 95-112); sparse scoring, with typical use of brass vs. woodwind juxtaposition of colors; percussion writing is for color – xylophone and bells highlight woodwind lines, SD/BD/Cym used for creating tension or highlighting rhythmic syncopation; triangle roll begins and ends the movement (and is a bridge to the second movement, as well); development of ideas is primarily through augmentation of an existing motive (i.e., mm. 63-78), or through the transposition of specific motives (i.e., mm. 69-81); coda exploits two important musical ideas: quartal melodic and harmonic structures, and the layered textures created by holding certain chord tones while others change.

SECTION   MEASURE

Movement II: "Charade"
Exposition   126-144
Development   145-160
Recapitulation   161-175

Lyrical, flowing melody presented in solo flute forms the basis for all melodic and motivic development in the movement; rooted in E-flat major, prominent harmonic devices include the use of major seventh chords in the accompaniment, as well as "borrowed" chords and an interesting tritone progression (D to A-flat, mm. 144-148); parallel triadic accompaniment also a distinguishing feature (mm. 149-159); polytonal chords featured again at important cadences (mm. 160 and 174); triangle acts as a bridge from second to third movement.

SECTION   MEASURE

Movement III: "Callithump"
Section 1   176-201
Section 2   202-219
Section 3   220-293
Section 4   294-318
Section 5   319-330 (brief return to section 1 music)
Section 6   331-372 (extended development of section 2 material)
Coda   373-398

Two prominent features of the melodic ideas (initially presented in the cornets – mm. 178-185) include the use of half steps as they relate to the tonic and dominant tonalities in passages (lower and neighboring tones, respectively), and the limited range of a fifth for those melodic motives; development of the ideas generally takes the form of transposed lines in new instrumental colors; return to the primary music is brief and transposed (mm. 319-330); coda begins at m. 373 with a foreshadowing of the final tonic C.

Unit 8: Suggested Listening
Clare Grundman:
    American Folk Rhapsody No. 1
    Burlesque for Band
    Little Suite for Band
    Tuba Rhapsody
Vincent Persichetti, *Divertimento for Band*
Donald H. White, *Miniature Set for Band*

Unit 9: Additional References and Resources

"Basic Band Curriculum: Grades I, II, III." *BD Guide* (September/October 1989): 2-6.

Boosey & Hawkes Music Publishers, NY.

Duarte, Leonard P., Daniel S. Hiestand, Carol Ann Prater, and Doy E. Prater. *Band Music That Works*. Volume 1. Burlingame, CA: Contrapuntal Publications, 1987.

Duarte, Leonard P., Daniel S. Hiestand, Carol Ann Prater, and Doy E. Prater. *Band Music That Works*. Volume 2. Burlingame, CA: Contrapuntal Publications, 1988.

Dvorak, Thomas L., Cynthia Crump Taggart, and Peter Schmaltz. *Best Music for Young Band*. Edited by Bob Margolis. Brooklyn, NY: Manhattan Beach Music, 1986.

Dvorak, Thomas L., Robert Grechesky, and Gary M. Ciepluch. *Best Music for High School Band*. Edited by Bob Margolis. Brooklyn, NY: Manhattan Beach Music, 1993.

Farkas, Philip. *The Art of Musicianship*. Bloomington, IN: Musical Publications, 1976.

Garofalo, Robert J. *Instructional Designs for Middle/Junior High School Band*. Fort Lauderdale, FL: Meredith Music Publications, 1995.

Grout, Donald J., and Claude V. Palisca. *A History of Western Music*. Fifth edition. New York: W. W. Norton, 1996.

Hamm, Charles. *Music in the New World*. New York: W. W. Norton, 1983.

Kostka, Stefan and Dorothy Payne. *Tonal Harmony*. Third edition. New York: McGraw-Hill, 1995.

Kreines, Joseph. *Music for Concert Band*. Tampa, FL: Florida Music Service, 1989.

"Meet the Composer: An Interview with Clare Grundman." *Conductor's Anthology*, Volume 2. Northfield, IL: Instrumentalist Publishing Company, 1989.

Rehrig, William H. *The Heritage Encyclopedia of Band Music*. Edited by Paul E. Bierley. Westerville, OH: Integrity Press, 1991.

Stolba, K Marie. *The Development of Western Music*. Dubuque, IA: William C. Brown Publishers, 1990.

Contributed by:
Craig Paré
Director of University Bands
DePauw University
Greencastle, Indiana

Grade Four

Teacher Resource Guide

Ballad for Band
Morton Gould
(1913–1996)

Unit 1: Composer

Morton Gould was born in Richmond Hill, New York. A child prodigy, he played piano by the age of four and at the age of six published his first composition, a waltz aptly titled *Just Six*. Gould was only eighteen when he was appointed staff pianist at Radio City Music Hall at the time of its opening in 1932. At twenty-one he landed his own radio program on the WOR-Mutual network, conducting a full symphony orchestra for which he composed many of his most notable works. By 1942, Gould's music had been conducted by Leopold Stokowski, Fritz Reiner, Sir John Barbirolli, and Artur Rodzinski. It was also during this time that Arturo Toscanini conducted *Lincoln Legend* with the NBC Symphony. Gould's preeminent stature as a composer of wind music is due not only to the excellence of his works, but also to his early pioneering and promotion of the American band as a legitimate and viable performance medium. Gould was president of the American Society of Composers, Authors and Publishers (ASCAP) for eight years, and he received a wide range of honors during his lifetime, including a Kennedy Center honor, presented by President Clinton in 1994. His other works for band include *West Point Symphony*, *Derivations for Clarinet and Band*, *Saint Lawrence Suite*, *Prisms*, *Mini Suite*, *American Salute*, *Jericho Rhapsody*, *Holiday Music*, and *Santa Fe Saga*.

Unit 2: Composition

Ballad for Band, composed in 1946, was commissioned by the Goldman Band and was premiered by that ensemble on June 21 of the same year. Based on the style and elements of the Negro spiritual, *Ballad* does not contain any direct quotes from existing spiritual melodies. It is, instead, an original expression of what Gould called "the Negro folklore idiom" that intrigued him as a composer: "The spirituals have always been the essence, in many ways, of our musical art, our musical spirit. The spiritual is an emotional, rhythmic expression. The spiritual has a universal feeling; it comes from the soul; from the gut." The work is approximately eight minutes and ten seconds in length.

Unit 3: Historical Perspective

As an active composer in the 1930s, Gould had not written any works for band. In fact, few American composers had taken the medium seriously enough to devote any attention to producing music for band. However, after having heard the University of Michigan Band under William Revelli, Gould "realized what a great music-making machine we had." His first works for winds included transcriptions of two of his own pieces: *Cowboy Rhapsody* and *Jericho*. After *Fanfare for Freedom* (one of eighteen fanfares commissioned by the Cincinnati Symphony), Gould was commissioned by the Goldman Band to write a piece for that group. The resulting work, *Ballad for Band*, is perhaps the earliest example of an original masterwork for band by an American composer. Following *Ballad*, many more American composers began contributing to the band's repertoire, including William Schuman (*George Washington Bridge*), Vincent Persichetti (*Pageant, Symphony for Band, Psalm for Band*), and H. Owen Reed (*La Fiesta Mexicana*).

Unit 4: Technical Considerations

Although the work begins with an initial key signature of four flats, implying A-flat major or f minor, there are many unusual harmonic and melodic factors. For example, the opening figures in the woodwinds and muted brass suggest a pentatonic cluster of tones. In addition, this texture of lines functions both as melodic and harmonic material simultaneously. Other harmonic devices that are not the standard fare in typical band works are also evident, including quartal harmony (chords built on stacks of fourths instead of thirds) and a variety of ninth, eleventh, and thirteenth chords, both in root position and in uncommon inversions. Predictably, accidentals can be found in most instrumental parts. The rhythmic motives are not overly challenging, with whole, half, and quarter notes forming the main rhythmic structure in the two slower sections, while the motive of two sixteenths and an eighth forms the foundation of the middle section's faster, dance-like music. Overall, there are two main challenges for an ensemble: 1) patiently sustaining the slow, expressive character of the two outer sections, with good tone and intonation, and observing the detailed dynamics that create unique colors in the ensemble; and 2) with the independent, mature writing evident in the faster section, creating the illusion of a continuous line. The latter can be quite difficult for any ensemble, especially if they are used to playing music that relies on an abundance of block scoring or frequent cross-cueing. Playing ranges are extended for cornet I (B5), trombone I (G4), baritone (G4), and horn I and III (F5). The cornet and trumpet parts regularly function as separate groups, but cued parts are provided. In addition, two B-flat flugelhorns are required. While their notes are generally doubled, their timbre is an integral component of Gould's sound in this piece. The percussion requirements include timpani, snare drum, bass drum, cymbals, tambourine, wood block, bells, and chimes. The percussion is scored sparsely and primarily in the middle section.

Unit 5: Stylistic Considerations

Slow, expressive playing with full tone, quality intonation (particularly with the shifting tonalities utilized in the work), and the ability to move in unison as an ensemble in slow tempi are required for the true *legato* playing necessary in the outer sections of *Ballad*. Equally challenging is for sections to function independently in dynamic balance and in dynamic gradations (*crescendo, diminuendo*) from each other. This is quite common in Gould's scoring. In fact, it is an essential element of the work. Additionally, a full range of dynamics is required for soloists, independent sections, and families of instruments, as well as for the entire ensemble. For example, fast shifts of dynamics and textures are frequent. In the middle, faster section of *Ballad*, crisp articulation along with clear and precise attacks and *staccato* playing with centered tone and pitch are important skills needed in the woodwinds and brass. The percussion accompaniment is challenging: not in the technical sense but rather in the ability and musical taste of the percussionist to find complimentary sounds for all that they contribute.

Unit 6: Musical Elements

While not literally using any existing spiritual melodies, Gould's concept of the form of the spiritual song and style, with a pentatonic framework in the melody complimented with occasional lowered third scale degree (blues), forms the basis of his original ideas. Integrated into the accompaniment of these melodies are many chords built on stacked fourths (quartal harmony), as opposed to the traditional thirds that are common in most folk and popular music (tertian harmony). This type of accompaniment and harmonic support helps keep the tonal center of any specific section ambiguous – one of the many interesting elements of *Ballad*. Another notable technique in Gould's writing is how he shifts colors so often in his instrumentation. As if viewing a "kaleidoscope of sound," for example, chords shift in color but not in harmonic content (e.g., quartal chord, mm. 41-55). In mm. 6-14, the color change in the brass accompaniment is smooth and subtle. Another interesting aspect of *Ballad's* elements involves melody and harmony at once. At the beginning (mm. 1-5), Gould's melodic and harmonic ideas are one in the same, functioning as melodic elements and as harmonic entities simultaneously. There is also a relation of melodic elements. For the primary motive of the B section (m. 42), Gould recalls the "singing, hymn-like" motive heard earlier in the euphonium (mm. 16-20).

Unit 7: Form and Structure

SECTION	MEASURE	EVENT AND SCORING
A (mm. 1-41)	1-9	Introduction of melodic and harmonic material woodwind and cornet/trombone figures; pentatonic outline of melodic elements obscures true tonic (revealed in m. 29)
	10-15	Primary theme in flutes and oboes, derived from opening woodwind and cornet figures; accompaniment features mellifluous color shifts in brass Clarinets and saxophones reiterate opening material
	16-28	Secondary theme in euphonium (with added horns); continued development of flute/oboe theme, with added English horn color
	29-41	Long-awaited (and first) tonic arrival of E-flat (m. 29); expansion of introductory melodic and harmonic material; cadence – quartal stacking of A,D,G,C,F as the penultimate chord
B (mm. 42-130)	42-47	New, dance-like theme (derived from secondary theme in A section) presented in flute and clarinet I; new tempo is faster, but not necessarily as fast as the next section (m. 48); with two short presentations, each followed by fermatas, this seems to be introductory in character
	48-66	Continuation of dance-like theme, including extension or development of two motives: two sixteenths/eighth rhythmic cell, and quarter/eighth concluding figure from the theme (alternating with rising, then falling interval); crisp rhythms and

SECTION	MEASURE	EVENT AND SCORING
		articulation – texture is opposite to that of A section
	67-85	Two musical devices apparent: 1) development of B section dance-like theme to include longer, song-like elements and phrasing (piccolo, flute, oboe, E-flat clarinet, clarinet I) and 2) continued exploitation of previous accompanying texture
	86-130	New, hybrid theme which combines elements of both A and B primary themes; consistent exploitation and development of this new theme, in intervalic/harmonic content and in instrumentation; occasional references to B theme sixteenth/eighth motive in upper woodwinds (mm. 104-130); climax builds toward arrival at m. 131 through more frequent alternation (antiphonal) between woodwind and brass groupings, leading to iii-ii-I progression chords on B-flat major ninth chord (the iii and ii are chords of the eleventh with the ninths missing)
Transition	131-153	Long anticipated arrival on B-flat major ninth chord; timpani reiterates primary theme of B section; continuation of B section motives throughout the ensemble; introduction of A section flute/oboe theme, anticipating upcoming recapitulation; momentum slowed through new tempo indications (*slackening, slowing down, Slow and freely*); combination of both A and B motives
A	154-182	Return to introductory melodic/harmonic material, with reminiscence of B theme in cornets; tonic arrival in E-flat major (m. 163), with continued tonic pedal apparent through m. 174; interesting color shift on tonic thirteenth chord (mm. 179-182)

Unit 8: Suggested Listening

Afro-American Spirituals, Work Songs, and Ballads [sound recording]. Rounder
  Select, 1998 (Library of Congress Archive of Folk Culture series).

*Been in the Storm So Long: Spirituals, Folk Tales, & Children's Games from
  Johns Island, South Carolina* [sound recording]. Smithsonian Folkways,
  1960.

Morton Gould:
  American Ballads
  Spirituals for String Choir and Orchestra
  Symphony of Spirituals
  West Point Symphony

Morton Gould, *Ballad for Band*:
  Tributes—North Texas Wind Symphony, Eugene Corporon, Conductor,
    Klavier KCD 11070
  American Concert Band Masterpieces—Eastman Wind Ensemble,
    Frederick Fennell, Conductor, Mercury Golden Imports SRI 75086
  American Originals—Air Combat Command Heritage of America Band,
    Langley Air Force Base, Virginia, Col. Lowell E. Graham, Conductor

Negro Folk Music of Alabama, Vol. V [sound recording]: Spirituals. New
  York: Folkways Records, 1950.

Paul Robeson, *Twenty-one Songs and Spirituals* [sound recording]. Memoir
  Classics

Unit 9: Additional References and Resources

Abromeit, Kathleen A., comp. *An Index to African-American Spirituals for the
  Solo Voice*. Westport, CT: Greenwood Press, 1999.

Apel, Willi. *The New Harvard Dictionary of Music*, Don Michael Randel, ed.
  Cambridge, MA: Belknap Press, 1986.

"Basic Band Curriculum: Grades I, II, III." *BD Guide* (September/October
  1989): 2-6.

Corporon, Eugene, and David Wallace. *Wind Ensemble/Band Repertoire*.
  Greeley, CO: University of Northern Colorado, 1984.

Duarte, Leonard P., Daniel S. Hiestand, Carol Ann Prater, and Doy E.
  Prater. *Band Music That Works*. Volume 1. Burlingame, CA: Contrapuntal
  Publications, 1987.

Duarte, Leonard P., Daniel S. Hiestand, Carol Ann Prater, and Doy E.
  Prater. *Band Music That Works*. Volume 2. Burlingame, CA: Contrapuntal
  Publications, 1988.

Dvorak, Thomas L., Cynthia Crump Taggart, and Peter Schmaltz. *Best
  Music for Young Band*. Edited by Bob Margolis. Brooklyn, NY: Manhattan
  Beach Music, 1986.

Farkas, Philip. *The Art of Musicianship*. Bloomington, IN: Musical Publications, 1976.

G. Schirmer, Inc.

Garofalo, Robert J. *Guides to Band Masterworks*. Fort Lauderdale, FL: Meredith Music Publications, 1992.

Garofalo, Robert J. *Instructional Designs for Middle/Junior High School Band*. Fort Lauderdale, FL: Meredith Music Publications, 1995.

Gould, Morton. "The Sound of a Band." *Music Educators Journal* 48 (April/May 1962): 36-47.

Grout, Donald J., and Claude V. Palisca. *A History of Western Music*. Fifth edition. New York: W. W. Norton, 1996.

Kreines, Joseph. *Music for Concert Band*. Tampa, FL: Florida Music Service, 1989.

Oliver, Paul, Max Harrison, and William Bolcom. *The New Grove Gospel, Blues and Jazz: with Spirituals and Ragtime*. New York: Norton, 1986.

Rehrig, William H. *The Heritage Encyclopedia of Band Music*. Edited by Paul E. Bierley. Westerville, OH: Integrity Press, 1991.

Sadie, Stanley, ed. *New Grove Dictionary of Music and Musicians*. London: Macmillan Publishers Limited, 1980. S.v. "Morton Gould" by Ronald Byrnside.

Slonimsky, Nicholas, ed. *Baker's Biographical Dictionary of Musicians*. Fifth Edition. New York: G. Schirmer, 1958. S.v. "Morton Gould."

Stolba, K Marie. *The Development of Western Music*. Dubuque, IA: William C. Brown Publishers, 1990.

Stone, Thomas. "Morton Gould—Champion of the Band." *BD Guide* (January/February 1995): 2-5.

Stone, Thomas. "Morton Gould's *Ballad for Band* (1946): A Musical and Historical Analysis." D.M.A. Lecture-recital, University of Cincinnati, 1994.

Vinton, John, ed. *Dictionary of Contemporary Music*. New York: E.P. Dutton, 1974.

Watkins, Glenn. *Soundings*. New York: Schirmer Books, 1988.

Contributed by:

Craig Paré
Director of University Bands
DePauw University
Greencastle, Indiana

Teacher Resource Guide

Cajun Folk Songs II
Frank Ticheli
(b. 1958)

Unit 1: Composer

Frank Ticheli has become a well-known and often-performed composer of current band literature. He has composed music that is accessible to junior high and middle school bands, and he has made significant contributions to the repertoire of advanced university and professional wind ensembles. In fact, in the first two volumes of *Teaching Music through Performance in Band*, five of Ticheli's band compositions are featured, and four different levels of accessibility are represented. His compositions for band have been awarded several prizes, including the 1989 Walter Beeler Prize, and first prize in the eleventh annual Symposium for New Band Music in Virginia. He has won both the Charles Ives Scholarship and the Goddard Lieberson Fellowship from the American Academy and Institute of Arts and Letters, and he has been awarded the Ross Lee Finney Award and a residency at McDowell Colony.

Currently, Frank Ticheli is the Composer-in-Residence for the Pacific Symphony Orchestra, and he is on the faculty of the College of Music at the University of Southern California. He received his bachelor's degree from Southern Methodist University and his master's and doctoral degrees from the University of Michigan, where he studied with William Albright, Leslie Bassett, William Bolcom, and George Wilson. A native of Louisiana, Ticheli currently resides in California.

Unit 2: Composition

As in his earlier composition of 1991, *Cajun Folk Songs*, Ticheli uses folk melodies as inspiration for this two-movement work. The precise origins of the folk songs are unknown, although the program notes provided in the full score cite the sources that Ticheli used to find the tunes.

The first movement, "Ballad," uses original chorale material combined with two different melodic settings of the same folk song, *Aux Natchitoches*. Natchitoches – pronounced *Nah-kee-TOSH* in French, but *NA-keh-tush* by most present-day Louisianans – is a town in northern Louisiana named after a tribe of Native Americans who once lived in that region. The composer describes the first setting as "a profoundly beautiful aeolian melody dating back to the eighteenth century. The English horn is utilized because of its dark, haunting tone, and its power to evoke the melancholy nature of the original tune." Ticheli richly varies and decorates the melody rhythmically to reflect the natural inflections of the Cajun text. The second setting of the folk song probably dates back to the nineteenth century. The melody is centered in C major, and through an arched melodic line modulates to F major, providing an effective contrast to the first melodic setting.[1]

The opening and closing sections of the second movement, "Country Dance," are based on original music that the composer intended to "evoke the energetic feeling and style of a Cajun two-step, a form commonly used in the dance halls of southern Louisiana. Often, one can hear stylistic similarities to Scottish folk dances, and even the American hoe-down." The contrasting middle section is based on two very old pentatonic folk songs, *Et ous c'est que tu es parti* and *Joe Ferail est un petit négre*. Although neither folk song was originally sung as a canon, the pentatonic nature of the melodies lends itself nicely to the canonic treatment that dominates this middle section of the movement.[2]

Cajun Folk Songs II was commissioned by the Indiana Bandmasters Association and premiered at its annual convention by the Indiana All-State Band in March of 1997. The first movement is dedicated to the memory of the composer's father, and the second movement is a celebration of the birth of the composer's nephew.

Unit 3: Historical Perspective

Many people think that the "Cajuns," or Acadians as they are properly named, are descendants of the French colonists who sailed around the tip of Florida into the Gulf of Mexico and originally settled at the mouth of what is now called the Mississippi River. However, this is not the origin of the Acadians. Throughout the first half of the eighteenth century, the French colonies in Canada and the English colonies in what is now the United States were constantly at war. The Acadians were French by descent, and Acadia, or Nova Scotia, had been French by settlement and possession until 1713 when it was ceded to England at the close of Queen Anne's War. During the ensuing wars between French and English colonies, the Acadians regarded themselves as neutral, being French in sympathy but English in law. The

English to the south looked upon them with suspicion, and the French to the north would have been happy to have their assistance. The New England colonies saw that unless some severe measures were taken, Nova Scotia would not be saved to England, and it was necessary to the safety of New England that Nova Scotia remain English. So it was resolved by England and New England that the Acadians should be dispossessed of their country. So about 6,000 Acadians were taken from their homes and sent to the various English colonies. A large number of the Acadians eventually found their way to Louisiana, which at the time belonged to Spain but was still French in feeling and culture. Here they were well received by those of their own language and religion. They found homes in the fertile country by the river, and today, their descendants are to be found in every parish of lower Louisiana.[3]

Unit 4: Technical Considerations

The opening chorale in the first movement will require players to perform with a nice brass choir approach, utilizing sonorous tone qualities and balanced control at all dynamic levels. As mentioned previously, the first folk song setting calls for an English horn soloist, and although the solo is cued in the alto saxophone, whoever plays the solo must be a mature musician, capable of expressive phrasing. The score denotes parts for oboe 1 and 2 and English horn, but the oboes are tacet during Movement I and the English horn does not play in Movement II, so if an ensemble has a fine double-reed player who can double on oboe and English horn, the piece is accessible from the perspective of personnel.

The second movement is energetic and lively and will require players with some technical facility to perform the rhythmic and melodic lines. Although the syncopations in the accompaniment lines are actually easier to play than they look in notation, the melodic treatments do involve a great deal of syncopation, some of which may be confusing to a younger ensemble. The dance sections call for technically proficient soloists on trumpet, horn, alto saxophone, oboe, bassoon, and euphonium. The soli are carefully cross-cued in other instruments, but the soloists that are used must be technically capable. A brief pastoral section in the middle of the movement requires soloistic playing from oboe, bassoon, horn, and three clarinets. In several places, brass players must be able to articulate very cleanly and clearly, with accents and emphasis on rhythmic energy.

Unit 5: Stylistic Considerations

The "rehearsal notes" provided in the full score to *Cajun Folk Songs II* provide very thorough and useful information for the preparation and performance of this piece. In the first movement, the opening brass chorale is a personal tribute from the composer to his father, and it sets the elegiacal tone of the movement. This section requires mature balance and blend between the trumpet, horns, and trombones. During the outer sections of the movement, the melody should always stay in the aural foreground; however, the composer points out that when other instruments play quarter note triplets in parallel motion with the soloist, they should be equally prominent. The middle section should be played as warm and lush as possible, with natural *crescendos* and *diminuendos* in the ascending and descending lines. The composer warns, however, not to overstate the indicated dynamics.[4]

The second movement, with the exception of the brief pastoral interlude at the close of the middle section, should be played with a lively, energetic feeling. The composer lists several suggestions that will enhance the style of the movement, including exaggeration of accents and *staccato* markings, extra emphasis on *sforzando* articulation to achieve the desired "harmonica effect," and using the percussionists to enhance the festive nature of the movement.[5]

Unit 6: Musical Elements

There are many interesting musical elements present in this piece that would provide excellent teaching opportunities in a rehearsal or classroom setting. The opening movement could be used to teach the aeolian mode and the characteristics of the minor mode as it is contrasted to the second melodic treatment. That second treatment could also be used to teach modulation or tonicization as it moves from C major to F major. The second movement provides an opportunity to teach and discuss the role of the energetic syncopations in the melody and the accompaniment, accents, and even some elements of hemiola.

Unit 7: Form and Structure

Each movement of *Cajun Folk Songs II* consists of an introduction followed by a ternary form (ABA′).

Section	Measure	Event and Scoring
Movement I: "Ballad"		
Introduction	1-15	Brass chorale; E-flat major
A section	16-33	Melody 1; C aeolian
B section	34-60	Melody 2; C major
A′ section	61-73	Melody 1; C aeolian
Movement II: "Country Dance"		
Introduction	1-12	2/4 meter; B-flat major
A section	13-82	2/4 meter; B-flat
B section	83-129	4/4 meter; B-flat, E-flat, F
A′ section	130-220	2/4 meter; B-flat

Unit 8: Suggested Listening

Manhattan Beach Music offers downloadable recordings of almost every piece it has published, including this piece and several others by Frank Ticheli. This innovative resource is available on their World Wide Web page at: http://members.aol.com/mbmband/.

Additional recordings:

Cajun and Zydeco Mardi Gras! (sound recording). Ville Platte, LA: Maison de Soul, 1992. (Maison de Soul: CD-1044).

Strachwitz, Chris, and Maureen Gosling, ed. *J'ai été au bal* (sound recording) = *I went to the dance: the Cajun and Zydeco music of Louisiana.* El Cerrito, CA: Arhoolie, 1990. (Arhoolie CD-331--CD-332).

Ticheli, Frank. *Blue Shades* (1997) on Deja View (sound recording). University of North Texas Wind Symphony. San Juan Capistrano, CA: Klavier, 1998. (KCD-11091).

Ticheli, Frank. Postcard (1991) on *Postcards* (sound recording). Cincinnati College-Conservatory of Music Wind Symphony. San Juan Capistrano, CA: Klavier, 1994. (KCD-11058).

Unit 9: Additional References and Resources

Miles, Richard, ed. *Teaching Music through Performance in Band*, Vol. I. Chicago: GIA Publications, 1997.

Miles, Richard, ed. *Teaching Music through Performance in Band*, Vol. II. Chicago: GIA Publications, 1998.

Nyhan, Patricia. *Let the Good Times Roll: A Guide to Cajun and Zydeco Music.* Portland, ME: Upbeat Books, 1997.

Savoy, Ann Allen. *Cajun Music: A Reflection of a People*, Volume I. Eunice, LA: Bluebird Press, 1984.

Ticheli, Frank. *Cajun Folk Songs II.* Brooklyn, NY: Manhattan Beach Music, 1997.

Contributed by:

Brian Lamb
Director of Instrumental Studies
Southwest Baptist University
Bolivar, Missouri

---

1   Ticheli, Frank. Cajun Folk Songs II (program notes). Brooklyn, NY: Manhattan Beach Music, 1997.

2   Ibid.

3 Hale, Edward Everett, ed. "Introduction and Notes" to Evangeline: A Tale of Acadie, by Henry Wadsworth Longfellow. New York, NY: University Publishing Co., 1897, pp.12-14.

4 Ticheli, Frank. Cajun Folk Songs II (rehearsal notes).

5 Ibid.

Teacher Resource Guide

Colors and Contours
Leslie Bassett
(b. 1923)

Unit 1: Composer

Pulitzer Prize winning composer Leslie Bassett is universally celebrated as one of this century's most important composers and has contributed a wealth of outstanding repertoire for the wind ensemble. In addition to *Colors and Contours*, Bassett has written other works for wind ensemble which include *Designs, Images and Textures* (1964); *Sounds, Shapes and Symbols* (1977); *Concerto Grosso for Brass Quintet and Wind Ensemble* (1982); *Lullaby for Kirsten* (1985); *Fantasy for Clarinet and Wind Ensemble* (1986); and *Wood and Reed Transformed* (1999) for solo bassoon and wind ensemble. He won the Pulitzer Prize for his *Variations for Orchestra* in 1966. Born in Hanford, California, in 1923, Bassett's musical training began on piano and trombone. He began his collegiate studies at Fresno State College and continued them following World War II at the University of Michigan, where he studied composition with Ross Lee Finney. Following his master's degree, he studied at the Ecole Normale de Musique with Arthur Honneger and Nadia Boulanger. Bassett was appointed to the composition faculty at the University of Michigan in 1952 and became department head in 1970 where he held the Albert Stanley Professor of Music chair until his retirement in 1991. He remains active as Professor Emeritus at Michigan.

Unit 2: Composition

Colors and Contours was commissioned by the College Band Directors National Association and was premiered at its twenty-third annual convention in Boulder, Colorado, by the McNeese University Wind Ensemble, David

Waybright, Conductor. The composer states, "The commission was especially intended for bands of modest size (the instrumentation was specified), which are less accomplished in performance skill than are many of our well-known ensembles. Nevertheless, the commission called for an outstanding addition to the band repertory. I have sought to fulfill these requirements and wish performers much joy and pleasure in presenting this music."

The instrumentation is specific but can be performed with a larger ensemble "so long as careful attention is paid to balance; the brass must not overpower the winds." The instrumentation includes:

Flute	3 parts, with third part also on piccolo
Oboe	1 part
Bassoon	1 part
Clarinet	3 parts
Bass clarinet	1 part
E-flat alto saxophone	2 parts
Tenor saxophone	1 part
Baritone saxophone	1 part
French horn	2 parts
B-flat trumpet	3 parts
Trombone	3 parts
Euphonium	1 part
Tuba	1 part
Percussion	3 parts: I) 2 timpani, 3 triangles, suspended cymbal; II) suspended cymbal, glockenspiel, tam-tam, temple blocks, glass wind chimes, snare drum; and III) vibraphone, small bongos, suspended cymbal, bass drum, metal wind chimes
Piano	

It is also noted in the score that there should be a minimum of five flutists (including piccolo), five trumpeters, and six clarinetists, as there are divisi parts for these instruments. Bassett's music is available through C.F. Peters rental division at telephone 212-686-4147; 373 Park Avenue South, New York, New York 10016.

Unit 3: Historical Perspective

Leslie Bassett's music is uniquely well crafted with a rich sense of color, depth, and structure. His harmonic language has been influenced by a variety of compositional techniques developed in this century. While not a strict serialist, Bassett employs some of these techniques within a colorful chromatic idiom. The use of octatonic scales, whole tone harmonies, augmented triads as well as sets created from these triads are used prominently in *Colors and Contours*.

His compositional style demands sensitivity and artistry from an ensemble. As in all his compositions for wind band, the use of color, timbre, and rhythm are unique and have expanded the vocabulary and imagination for wind writing in the last half of the twentieth century.

Unit 4: Technical Considerations

Colors and Contours is designed to be performed by an ensemble of modest abilities, and the sheer technique of the work is accessible to an ensemble of these means. The understanding of the musical derivation and organization will take more time. The orchestration is within a comfortable range for all instruments, and Bassett provides cues for the oboes and bassoons in case it is necessary although not preferred.

There are some sections of unmetered music that will need to be carefully considered and explained as well as a few resonance trills, which require trilling to the same note using a "resonance" or unusual fingering. The percussion has brief episodes of spatial notation in the unmetered sections. The trumpets and trombones must have straight and cup mutes. There is an emphasis on individual responsibility of playing. Bassett writes band music "as if it were an orchestra" and expects soloistic playing which will greatly enhance a student's musical development.

Unit 5: Stylistic Considerations

The "colors" in *Colors and Contours* refers to the way the timbre is affected by the manipulation of essentially four augmented triads and how the orchestration choices continually provide new and interesting colors. These are often treble based. There are lyrical passages in the woodwinds accompanied by muted brass sounds, as well as stinging, short articulations in the percussion which are accentuated by various pitched instruments. This balance and detail is critical to creating the maximum color within the ensemble. There are many and varied coloristic episodes throughout the piece. Bassett utilizes "Klangfarbenmelodie" in one section with the brass. Attention to articulation differences and dynamic nuances are extremely important throughout this composition. The work is rather like an aural watercolor at some points, where sounds and colors blend into others while later sections create very pointed, more oil paint-like episodes.

The "contours" of the work refer (in the composer's own words) to the "sweeping lines moving up and down, such as the quiet, opening mountain range of sounds." The horizontal analysis and phrase architecture provide this "sweeping" contour. Written *accelerandos* and *ritardandos*, both by instruction and augmentation and diminution, create musical lines. The long rhythms are generally reserved for the beginning and ending of major sections. Bassett also makes frequent and selective use of silence and fermatas to create sections. There are unexpected rests and brief silent moments following *crescendos* and *diminuendos* that heighten the sense of tension and repose.

Unit 6: Musical Elements

The musical language employed in this work makes extensive use of the major third. The frequent use of this interval creates augmented triads, which generate whole tone scales and harmonies. This sonority lends itself to a "bright" and "positive" color. Bassett has said that he was very interested in augmented triads during this composition. He began with two augmented triads. The six notes not being used in the first two chords can make two more augmented triads. The juxtaposition and development of these chords or sets result in infinite possibilities.

The introduction begins with a brilliantly scored unveiling of a musical set. While definitely not a strict serialist, Bassett often begins the next phrase with the "missing notes" of the first and further develops the material. The opening pitches of F-sharp, G, C-sharp, A, E-flat, C, B, A are presented in the first bar. The second measure begins with the "missing notes" of A-flat, D, E, B-flat and then continues with the F-sharp, A, C-sharp, C. The missing notes of the second phrase, B, F, E-flat, G, begin the third phrase and are further developed into augmented triads and whole tone material. The constant reworking and development of these ideas in harmonic and melodic contexts creates a unique and masterful variety of colors.

Bassett is quick to mention that he does not compose from a theoretical base but uses his intuition and ear as his musical guide. Balance, scoring, and orchestration are all sounds that he works out and enjoys. It is valuable and interesting to explore the musical language that comprises his intuition.

Unit 7: Form and Structure

This is a single-movement work which is essentially divided into two sections linked by a euphonium cadenza. The first section is characterized by slower music in fluctuating tempi. The second section is faster, set at quarter note = 132.

SECTION	MEASURE	EVENT AND SCORING
Part I:		
Introduction	1-9	(letter B) Unmetered music but calculated timing; fluctuating tempi from quarter note = 48-72-92; creation of augmented triads and whole tone material
Section I-a	10-48	(letters B-F) Continuing tempo variance quarter note = 76-96-112; development from more soloistic textures to homophonic rhythms within a choir; textural variety; choirs of color

SECTION	MEASURE	EVENT AND SCORING
Section I-b	49-88	(letters F-K) Quarter note = 92-112; gradual evolution into E-flat tonal center; introduces octatonic elements; staggered rhythmic entrances; three-voice imitation and rhythmic counterpoint; klangfarben at letter H
Section I-c	89-128	(letters K-P) Quarter note = 120-138 with episodes of unmetered but calculated time; transitional material; long note values at beginning and end of this section
Euphonium cadenza	129	(letters P-Q) Transition into Part II
Part II:		
Section II-a	130-222	(letters Q-AA) Quarter note = 132; unison rhythms turn into choirs; choirs break into motivic activity; returns to mostly unison rhythms; lyrical melodies; harmonic language further developed
Section II-b	123-323	(letters AA-LL) Greatest rhythmic variety; pyramids of note collections; selective use of silence; octatonic sweeps; choirs
Section II-c	324-344	(letters LL-end) Coda of work; long note values in unison rhythm

Unit 8: Suggested Listening

Bela Bartok:
  Concerto for Orchestra
  Lyric Suite
Leslie Bassett:
  Designs, Images and Textures
  Lullaby for Kirsten
  Sounds, Shapes and Symbols
  Variations for Orchestra
Alban Berg, *Kammerkonzert für Klavier und Geige mit 13 Blasern*
Ingolf Dahl, *Sinfonietta*

Unit 9: Additional References and Resources

Davis, Daniel. "Analysis of Three Works for Band by Leslie Bassett." Diss., Cincinnati Conservatory of Music, 1995.

Rachleff, Larry. "An Interview with Leslie Bassett." *College Band Director's National Association Journal* V.2 #1 (winter, 1985): 1-4.

Rachleff, Larry. "Colors and Contours - Leslie Bassett" *College Band Director's National Association Journal* V.2 #2 (winter, 1986): 1-7.

Websites:
http://www.amc.net/member/leslie_bassett/home.html
http:sai-national.org/phil.composers.leslie_bassett

Contributed by:

Sarah McKoin
Director of Bands
University of Buffalo
State University of New York
Buffalo, New York

Teacher Resource Guide

The Dream of Oenghus, Op. 37
Rolf Rudin
(b. 1961)

Unit 1: Composer

Rolf Rudin (b. Germany, 1961) studied music education, music theory, composition, and conducting in Frankfurt and Würzburg. Having completed degrees in composition and conducting by 1992, he has spent most of the past decade as a freelance composer and instructor of theory at the Frankfürter Musikhochschule. Rudin's catalog of compositions – some fifty to date – includes works for several media: solo, choral, orchestral, chamber ensembles, and symphonic winds. Some of his choral, orchestral, and chamber works have won prizes through international competitions. To date, his output for the "symphonic wind orchestra" (the composer's chosen terminology) includes fourteen completed works. His first band work, *Imperial Prelude, Op. 15*, was written in 1989.

Unit 2: Composition

The Dream of Oenghus, Op. 37 is Rolf Rudin's fourth work for band, and it follows his expressed desire to compose in large-scale forms. The duration of the complete work is approximately twenty-one minutes, with Part One (published separately) being approximately seven minutes in length and Part Two consuming the last fourteen minutes. The finely engraved scores provide extensive program notes from the composer. There he explains:

> The musical poem The Dream of Oenghus refers to the Irish legend
> of the same name....In this legend Prince Oenghus has a nightly
> vision when fast asleep: He sees a girl who plays a flute and falls in
> love with her. However, as she keeps disappearing she remains

unattainable for him for the time being. He consequently sets out to search for her until he finally finds the girl. This piece is no musical retelling of this legend; in a way it rather invites reading the story, as there are only single phases and atmospheres of the legend serving as extra-musical sources of imagination....

The composer's notes continue with an explanation that the entire work was originally conceived in a large, two-part form. Part One, however, was crafted first, on a commission by the Confederation of German Band and Folk Music Associations. They requested a test piece for a music festival, with specified guidelines in terms of instrumentation, difficulty, and duration. Part One, published in 1994, has received considerable performance interest by itself. In Part Two (1996), the composer explores and expands upon aspects of the legend and creates formal unity through many musical references to Part One.

Unit 3: Historical Perspective

Dramatic, large-scale forms have been frequent catalysts for creative composition this past century. Most of Rolf Rudin's works exhibit a strong interest in these bold architectures. *The Dream of Oenghus* follows the programmatic tradition of the tone poem, rooted over a century earlier in many symphonic works of composers such as Franz Liszt and Richard Strauss. The piece exceeds twenty minutes in its entirety. It was written shortly after the composer completed his third work for band, *Cantus Arborum, Op. 33* – a full-scale symphony lasting nearly forty minutes. Indeed, of Rudin's completed works for band, all but three of the fourteen are greater than ten minutes in duration.

Unit 4: Technical Considerations

The instrumentation requirements for *The Dream of Oenghus* parallel the standard American band scoring, with notable exceptions in soprano brass – three trumpet parts, two flugelhorn or cornet parts – and in euphonium, where there are two independent parts, the higher one being written as a B-flat baritone part. Vibraphone with motor, gong, and tam-tam join the more commonly used percussion instruments, requiring five percussionists to execute this colorful writing. Expressive solo writing in the winds (beyond an occasional "one only" designation) is limited in Part One to the final flute statement. Part Two affords a bit more solo expression, with brief lyrical passages for piccolo, flute, E-flat clarinet, B-flat clarinet, alto saxophone, trumpet, oboe/flugelhorn (soli), trombone, tuba, and mallet percussion.

There are no key signatures throughout the piece. Naturally, accidentals abound, creating special challenges in early readings. Harmonically, however, the piece is uncomplicated. The work is also very straightforward rhythmically, with the common exception of certain compound meter segments. In general, the individual technical requirements are evenly balanced throughout the scoring, and there is an excellent democracy of melodic opportunities. Part Two is decidedly more difficult than Part One. As example, strong low-register muted trumpet skills are essential. (Free-blowing mutes will help tremendously here.)

Unit 5: Stylistic Considerations

This music requires the performers to express a *cantabile* style through their full range of dynamic levels. The vast majority of melodic material is intended as non-*staccato*; however, the opening of Part Two provides a healthy stretch of more agitated playing. This style is recapitulated towards the final pages of the score before the work rounds out with a consonant pedal point, reminiscent of the piece's opening sounds. As always, balance issues (i.e., relative dynamics within the ensemble) will require careful monitoring from the conductor and players alike. Incidentally, while most of the composer's special indications in the score are printed in German, an English translation of those statements is also provided.

Unit 6: Musical Elements

The melodic and harmonic material of the work is very economical. All sections of the piece can be related back to the original pitch "cell" presented boldly in saxophones and horns, mm. 10-13, and reiterated right away with other instruments joining in echo. This pitch sequence can be observed as a series of downward perfect fourths, each one followed by an upward half step: D, A, B-flat, F, G-flat, D-flat. Stacked in closed position, these tones reveal a very dreamy combination, alternations of the half step with the minor third (for example: D-flat, D, F, G-flat, A, B-flat, etc.). This version of the "cell" is presented first in m. 19, fanning out in both directions from a single concert A. The vibraphone unfolds the complete fan, highlighting the entrance tones of the slurred woodwind material. Part Two of the work opens with the reeds ascending up this "scale" (*fortissimo* and *furioso*), launching a new set of derivative themes from the pitch cell.

Unit 7: Form and Structure

PART ONE (duration = 7 minutes): a three-part form, with the final section recapitulating the first section and connecting to the expansive middle section by way of the closing flute statement.

Section	Subsection	Measure	Event and Scoring
A	Introduction	1-9	Mysterious, dreamy mood established: pedal-point in timpani with soft rolls from gong, tam-tam, and cymbal

SECTION	SUBSECTION	MEASURE	EVENT AND SCORING
	a	10-18	Bold, sustained statements of the pitch cell in horns and saxophones; statement repeated again with lower-pitched instruments added as echo
	b	19-24	Dual ascending and descending statements of the pitch cell (reordered and transposed) ringing trance-like in chimes, vibraphone, and single reeds
	a + b	25-39	A replay of the previous two segments (mm. 10-24) with only slight scoring variations
	a´	40-45	*Tutti* reiteration and extension of the "a" statement, concluding the opening section of the work
B	c	46-53	A sense of folklore proceeds in eight-measure "verses" of a new theme derived again from the cell; piano volume, theme in bassoon, baritone, and euphonium
	c´	54-61	Horns, bass clarinet, and tenor saxophone take up this same theme (now *mezzo piano*); a countermelody develops in vibraphone and B-flat clarinets as the "plot" thickens
	c´	62-69	Oboes, E-flat clarinet, alto and tenor saxophones, and flugelhorns take up the folklore theme; countermelody still present; accompaniment is increasingly active
	c´´	70-77	Ever-strengthening story verse (now *forte* and slightly varied) in trumpets and clarinets; all other sounds also building constantly
	c´	78-85	*Tutti fortissimo* folklore verse marked "faster"; the first segment where the entire wind (and most percussion) coloring is employed together
		86-90	Extension of the verse (*tutti*), softening and then building to the fullest swell of Part One (m. 91)

SECTION	SUBSECTION	MEASURE	EVENT AND SCORING
	c‴	91-99	Massive arrival (*tutti*), including all ringing percussion; music subsides using eight ever-softening statements of the first four notes of the folklore theme
A´	a´	100-105	Subsiding continues, now with the lower instruments slurring downward on the pitch cell as used in the opening segment
	b	106-114	Return of the second theme, this time with a three-measure extension or false start
	c‴ (codetta)	115-118	Solo flute softly resounding the first four notes of the folklore theme

PART TWO (duration = 14 minutes): three large sections; a strong sense of unity is achieved in at least two ways: (1) literal returns to earlier thematic material and (2) the use of new thematic material with the same genesis as the themes of Part One.

Section I: (measures 1-165) very fast tempo – *very boisterous and lively*
From the composer's program notes in the score: "At its beginning already the second part of this composition makes associations – expressed by its ferocity – to the prince's 'aberrations' in his quest for the girl…."

d		1-12	*Tutti forte, furioso*
e		13-30	*Piano, energico*
f		31-36	*Tutti fortissimo, marcato*
d		37-48	Intact return of mm. 1-12
Developmental		49-134	Expands upon all three thematic ideas presented
d		135-141	Last return, *furioso* idea
Transitional		142-165	Reiterating a dream-state

Section II: (measures 166-231) moderate tempo – *calm and flowing*
Again, from the composer's program notes: "…[These associations] appl[y] to the importance of the flute [in the legend] which was alluded to only towards the end of the first part whereas here it is given ample room for development…;"

Section III: (measures 232-395) march tempo – *with excitement and rhythmical*
"…A constantly repeated rhythmical increase of march-like character climaxes in picking up the 'mysterious chant' of the first part [the c theme listed above, beginning here in varied form at m. 301 and growing to a *fortissimo*

intact presentation at m. 337]. In that way it leads to formal unity of the complete work in an evident way...."

Coda: (measures 396-420) slow tempo – *very calm*

c derivative	396-403	Sounded four times in succession, each as a solo between one mallet instrument and a solo wind color
a diminutive	404-408	Curtain call for the Part One opening theme
b referenced	409-411	Final reference for these Part One sounds
Final sustains	412-end	"Relieving" major chords mixed and fading with the same ringing percussion colors as the opening measures of Part One

Unit 8: Suggested Listening

Franz Liszt, Les *Preludes*

Johann de Meij, *Symphony No. 1: The Lord of the Rings*

Rolf Rudin:

Bacchanalia (1990), Deutsche Bläserphilharmonie, Michael Kummer conducting. 98-SS09.

The Dream of Oenghus, North Texas Wind Symphony, Eugene Corporon conducting. Klavier Gold Edition, KCD-11089.

The Dream of Oenghus (Part One only), 1997 Texas All-State Symphonic Band, H. Robert Reynolds conducting. Mark Records, MCD-2374.

Moor of Stars (1994/95), 1997 Texas All-State Symphonic Band, H. Robert Reynolds conducting. Mark Records, MCD-2374.

Richard Strauss:

Ein Heldenleben

Till Eulenspiegel

Unit 9: Additional References and Resources

Edition flor, Erlensee/Germany. Publisher of Rolf Rudin's works.

Shattinger Music Company, St. Louis, MO: exclusive distributor in U.S.A. and Canada for Edition flor publications.

Contributed by:

Patrick F. Casey
Director of Bands
Central Missouri State University
Warrensburg, Missouri

Teacher Resource Guide

Elegy

John Barnes Chance
(1932–1972)

Unit 1: Composer

John Barnes Chance's lyrical, accessible style has earned his works for winds a prominent place in the repertoire. Born in Beaumont, Texas, Chance acquired the nickname "Barney" because his mother objected to people calling him "Jack." He began piano lessons at the age of nine, but when he was twelve he began playing timpani in the Beaumont High School Orchestra and developed a preference for percussion. He began composing in high school. He then went on to the University of Texas to earn bachelor's and master's degrees in Composition, studying with Kent Kennan, Clifton Williams, and Paul Pick. One of his student works won him the Carl Owens Award.

Two years after completing his education, Chance became conductor and arranger of the Fourth United States Army Band. Later, he moved to the Eighth Army Band stationed in Korea. He returned to Texas in 1958 and managed a high fidelity store, also playing timpani with the Austin Symphony Orchestra. With a 1960 Ford Foundation Young Composers Project grant, he left Austin to become Composer-in-Residence for two years at Greensboro Senior High School in North Carolina, where Herbert Hazelman directed bands. At Greensboro, he composed seven works for student ensembles, including his first band composition, which later became *Incantation and Dance*. Chance taught theory and composition at the University of Kentucky from 1966 until his accidental death in 1972 from electrocution while working in his backyard.

Chance's *Variations on a Korean Folk Song* won the American Bandmasters Association Ostwald Award in 1966. His other published works for band include *Blue Lake Overture, Incantation and Dance, Introduction and Capriccio,* and *Symphony No. 2 for Winds and Percussion.*

Unit 2: Composition

Composed in 1970, *Elegy* was one of Chance's last works. The West Genessee High School Band of Camillus, New York, commissioned the work for their performance at the 1970 conference of the New York State School Music Association in Kiamesha Lake, New York. Band director Bruce Burritt decided to commission Chance because the band had recently performed *Incantation and Dance.* He had heard performances of *Blue Lake Overture.* When Chance asked Burritt what kind of piece he wanted, he answered that he imagined something like *Incantation and Dance,* but he thought the composer should be free to write what he wanted. Chance said that he wanted to compose something for band that would challenge his creativity in a style more somber and *legato* than that of his other works. Burritt thought the goal of the commission was to get more good pieces for concert band, so he said a different style would be acceptable.

During the compositional process, Chance kept in frequent contact with Burritt. He called and asked whether the West Genessee Band had an English horn player or good bassoon players, and about appropriate ranges for the musicians. Chance was very concerned about getting the work done on time. Burritt had a photocopy of the score well in advance of the first rehearsal of the piece. And the parts in manuscript were ready for the first rehearsal. Chance spent a week rehearsing with the band. Burritt described Chance as "quiet and genuine, with a dry sense of humor." Chance conducted the first performance of *Elegy* at a pre-convention concert in Camillus and at the performance at the convention. According to Burritt, who has just retired as superintendent of the Avon (NY) school district, the quality of the work met his highest expectations. He is gratified that it has sustained itself and become a part of the standard wind repertoire.

The band was selected to perform two and a half months after the New York convention at the 1971 MENC Eastern Division Conference in Atlantic City. West Genessee Trombonist Bill Palange, now director of bands at Oswego (NY) High School, still has a recording of the performance at the conference. When the band finished playing *Elegy,* Frederick Fennell walked down the aisle applauding the band and the new work.

Chance based *Elegy* on his earlier unpublished work for chorus and strings, "Blessed Are They That Mourn." Fortunately, no one had to die to prompt this commission; the title *Elegy* came from the subject of the choral text. Published by Boosey and Hawkes in 1972, *Elegy* is approximately seven minutes long.

In the 1980s, Chance's widow granted permission to Wilson Ochoa, hornist with the Charleston (SC) Symphony Orchestra, to transcribe the work for orchestra. Boosey and Hawkes later published the transcription. Ochoa's most recent transcription is *Introduction and Capriccio*, which Chance composed originally for piano and strings, and then revised for piano and twenty-four winds. Ochoa's transcription incorporates the piano part into a full orchestral setting.

Unit 3: Historical Perspective

An elegy is a reflective or subjective poem or song, particularly a lament in praise of the dead. The Greeks and Romans composed elegies in a characteristic meter, consisting of distichs or couplets made up of a line of six dactyls and a dactylic line with single accented syllables on the third and sixth feet. A dactyl consists of an accented syllable followed by two unaccented ones.

Unit 4: Technical Considerations

Elegy is a challenging work for a high school band to perform. Its somber, introspective nature makes it difficult for students to warm immediately to the piece. After spending time tackling the unfamiliar smooth, flowing style, students will come to appreciate the work's depth.

The score for *Elegy* shows the following instrumentation: four flutes (1st and 2nd parts divided), two oboes, English horn, six clarinets (1st, 2nd, and 3rd divided), alto clarinet, two bass clarinets (part divided), contrabass clarinet (E-flat and B-flat parts provided), two bassoons, four saxophones (AATB), five trumpets (1st and 2nd divided), four horns (1st and 2nd divided), four trombones (1st divided), two baritones (part divided), and two tubas. The percussion parts require three players to play timpani, gong (tam-tam), chimes, vibraphone, and suspended cymbal.

The English horn part is doubled throughout, except for a solo at m. 111. Chance provided an alto saxophone cue to cover it.

The first trumpet reaches B-flat5 above the staff. The first horn ranges from G3 below the staff to fifth-line F5. The first trombone plays an A-flat4 in ledger lines above the staff, and the third trombone part requires a bass trombone. Its range extends down to A1 in ledger lines below the staff. Performers will need euphoniums with four valves to play the D2 below the bass clef staff in the baritone part. The baritones play an E-flat4 above the staff. The tuba parts have an extremely low *tessitura*, extending down to F1 in ledger lines below the staff. The tubas go up only to fourth-space A-flat2.

Although all lines are doubled, those performing this work should be capable of playing independently because all instruments have important parts. Additionally, performers should be able to maintain support through the dissonances and listen for the resolutions.

After the trill in m. 76, the *nachschlag* grace notes confuse the performers. At a glance, one sees what looks like a turn at the end of the trill, but Chance makes the grace notes a step too high, indicating his intention that the trill have no finishing turn. It is clearer not to have the grace notes at all. If there was still a question, "(no turn)" could have been written over the trill.

The rehearsal numbers are too few and far apart. They do not always represent structural changes in the piece. It is helpful if the conductor's score and all the parts have every measure number penciled in.

Errata Parts:

MEASURE	BEAT	CORRECTION
First Flute:		
39	2	Add *staccato* dot
72	4	Remove second dot from eighth note
76	4	Remove grace note *nachschlag*
79	1-4	Remove *crescendo* mark
80	1-2	Add *crescendo* mark
80	3-4	Add *diminuendo* mark
81	1-4	Remove *diminuendo* mark
91	1	"unis."
120	3	"*ppp*"
Second Flute:		
76	4	Remove grace note *nachschlag*
79	1-4	Remove *crescendo* mark
80	1-2	Add *crescendo* mark
80	3-4	Add *diminuendo* mark
81	1-4	Remove *diminuendo* mark
Oboes:		
12	1	"12" (rehearsal number)
34	4	Add *crescendo* mark under thirty-second notes
35	1	"*f*"
39	2	Add *staccato* dot
72	4	Remove second dot from eighth note
74	2	*Crescendo* mark ends
76	4	Remove grace note *nachschlag*
English Horn:		
17	1	Add dot to half note
39	2	Add *staccato* dot
76	4	Remove grace note *nachschlag*
80	1-2	Add *crescendo* mark
80	3-4	Add *diminuendo* mark

MEASURE	BEAT	CORRECTION

First Clarinet:

19	4	Remove flat from second-space A4
72	4	Remove second dot from eighth note
73	4	Add slur into m. 74
74	4	Add slur across m. 75 into m. 76
76	4	Remove grace note *nachschlag*
80	1-2	Add *crescendo* mark
80	3-4	Add *diminuendo* mark

Second Clarinet:

60	3-4	Don't break slur; continue slur to first beat, m. 62
72	1	Add dot to half notes in both divided parts
75	4	Continue slur into m. 76
76	4	Remove grace note *nachschlag*
80	1-2	Add *crescendo* mark
80	3-4	Add *diminuendo* mark
99	3-4	"8va" (second-space A-flat4, not A-flat3)
100	1	Continue 8va

Third Clarinet:

14	1-4	Remove *diminuendo* mark
16	1-4	Remove *diminuendo* mark
17	1-4	Add *diminuendo* mark
39	2	Add *staccato* dot
42	2	Remove superfluous dot before eighth note
61-62	1-4	Add *crescendo* over both measures
72	4	Remove second dot from eighth note
76	4	Remove grace note *nachschlag*
88	1	Remove dot
93	3	Extend slur into m. 94

Alto Clarinet:

76	4	Remove grace note *nachschlag*

Bass Clarinet:

57	4	Add flat to A-flat3
87	1-4	Add *diminuendo* mark to upper voice

E-flat Contrabass Clarinet:

6	1-4	Add *diminuendo* mark

B-flat Contrabass Clarinet:

6	1-4	Add *diminuendo* mark

MEASURE	BEAT	CORRECTION

Bassoons:

35	3	"unis."
64	1	Change "solo" to "soli"
74	1	"a2"
80	1-2	Add *crescendo* mark
80	3-4	Add *diminuendo* mark

Alto Saxophones:

13	2-4	Add *diminuendo* mark
76	4	Remove grace note *nachschlag*
116	1	Change "*pp*" to "*p*"

Tenor Saxophone:

13	2-4	Add *diminuendo* mark
76	4	Remove grace note *nachschlag*
81	3	Remove ink smudge
89-90	1	Add slur
93	1-4	Add *diminuendo* mark

Baritone Saxophone:

| 80 | 1-2 | Add *crescendo* mark |
| 80 | 3-4 | Add *diminuendo* mark |

Percussion:

| 72 | 4 | Remove second dot from eighth note in vibraphone part |
| 115 | 3 | "(rubber mallets)" in score, "(hard rubber mallets)" in part |

Timpani:

| 44 | 1 | Change five-measure rest to six measures |

First Trumpet:

44	1-3	Add *crescendo* mark
45	1-4	Add *diminuendo* mark
51	3	Add *diminuendo* mark, extend to end of m. 52
117	3	Change "*mf*" to "*mp*"

Second Trumpet:

| 117 | 3 | Change "*mf*" to "*mp*" |

Third Trumpet:

| 117 | 3 | Change "*mf*" to "*mp*" |

MEASURE	BEAT	CORRECTION
First Horn:		
132	2-4	Add *diminuendo* mark
39	2	Add *staccato* dot
46	3-4	Continue slur to end of m. 48
109	1-4	Remove *diminuendo* mark
109	1	Add "*mp*"
110	2	Remove "*mp*"
111	3	Move "*pp*" to beat one
Second Horn:		
9	1-2	Break slur
39	2	Add *staccato* dot
74	4	Add slur to upper voice extending to end of m. 76
93	3	Extend slur into m. 94
First Trombone:		
51	1-4	Add *diminuendo* mark
117	3	Change "*mf*" to "*mp*"
119	1	"*pp*"
Second Trombone:		
80	1-2	Add *crescendo* mark
80	3-4	Add *diminuendo* mark
117	3	Change "*mf*" to "*mp*"
Third Trombone:		
83	3	"^"
84	1	"^"
117	3	Change "*mf*" to "*mp*"
Baritone Treble Clef:		
80	1-2	Add *crescendo* mark
80	3-4	Add *diminuendo* mark
Tuba:		
76	1	Add slur

Score:

MEASURE	BEAT	INSTRUMENTS	CORRECTIONS & DISCREPANCIES
12	1,3	3rd clarinet	Remove accent marks
13	2-4	Alto and tenor saxophones	Add *diminuendo* mark
30	1	Contrabass clarinet	Remove tie from previous measure

Measure	Beat	Instruments	Corrections & Discrepancies
30	1	Baritone	Add tie from previous measure
43	4	1st and 2nd trombones	"*p*"
45	1-4	1st and 2nd trombones	Add *diminuendo* mark
60	1	3rd clarinet	"*pp*"
62	1-2	2nd clarinet	Break slur
62	3-4	2nd clarinet	Add slur
64	1	Bassoons	Change "solo" to "soli"
72	4	1st flute, 1st clarinet, alto clarinet, alto saxophones, vibraphone, 2nd horn	Remove second dot from eighth note
72	4	2nd horn	B-flat in score, A-sharp in part; E-flat in score, D-sharp in part; G-flat in score, f-sharp in part
73	1	2nd horn	C-flat in score, B-natural in part
73	4	2nd horn	D-flat in score, C-sharp in part
74	1	2nd horn	G-flat in score, F-sharp in part
74	4	2nd horn	Upper voice, A-flat in score, G-sharp in part; lower voice, G-flat in score, F-sharp in part
74	4	Timpani	"(Hard sticks)"
76	4	Flutes, oboes, English horn, clarinets, alto saxophones, tenor saxophone	Remove grace note *nachschlag* after trill
83	1,3	Bass and contrabass clarinets	"∧"
83	3	Alto clarinet; bassoons; alto and baritone saxophones	"∧"
84	1	Alto, bass, and contrabass clarinets; alto and baritone saxophones	"∧"
111	3	Alto saxophone (English horn cue)	Add slur into m. 112
116	1	Timpani	"(Soft sticks)"
119	1-4	Alto saxophones	Add *diminuendo* mark

Unit 5: Stylistic Considerations

Take care to keep the tempo (quarter note = 66-72) slow enough that listeners and players can hear the dissonances resolve. The *poco animato* (quarter note = 84-88) lasts only four and a half measures. Here, four quarter notes fill the same time as three quarter notes in the surrounding tempi.

Except for the climax at mm. 77-79 and mm. 84-85, the entire work is *legato*. Performers should imagine playing vocal lines, as *Elegy* was based on a choral work. In the aforementioned *sostenuto* measures, brasses should achieve clarity in the repeated pitches with a sharper quality of articulation, not by introducing spaces after the dotted notes. Performers should be aware of the direction of phrases across bar lines, keeping *crescendos* controlled within dynamic levels. It is helpful for performers to know which instruments double their parts at all times. The doubling changes throughout the work.

At m. 85, flutes, first clarinets, and alto, bass, and contrabass clarinets should be aware that they play *pianissimo* against *fortissimo* in the rest of the band. This allows the fermata to be a very soft sound that remains when the rest of the band cuts off.

Unit 6: Musical Elements

Elegy is characteristic of Chance's neo-romantic style. It demonstrates his preference for low woodwind timbres and long, lyrical, interweaving melodic lines.

Although the text "Blessed Are They That Mourn" begins with a dactyl, the Greco-Roman elegiac meter described above does not seem to have influenced Chance. The work more closely resembles the late Renaissance polyphonic ricercar, a precursor to the fugue. The term "ricercar" means "to seek." Ricercars were instrumental preludes composed to "seek" out the key before liturgical, sacred, or secular songs. *Elegy's* continuous imitation and modulations from G minor at the beginning to C major at the end mark its similarities to the Renaissance form.

Like Howard Hanson, Chance used tonal harmonies with mildly dissonant non-chord tones on nearly every beat. Unlike Hanson, Chance's dissonances do not always resolve with stepwise motion.

Elegy consists of a few motives that combine, elide, and recombine to create a predominantly contrapuntal texture. Chance poured this contrapuntal procedure into a sonatina mold: There is an exposition with two theme areas, no development, and a recapitulation at m. 54. By ending in a different key than the beginning one, the piece departs from the traditional sonatina form. Only for a few phrases does the texture ever become homophonic.

Unit 7: Form and Structure

SECTION	MOTIVE	MEASURE	INSTRUMENTS
I, Period 1, G minor	A	1-3	Bass and contrabass clarinets, bassoons
	A	2-4	Clarinets, 2nd horns
	B	3-5	Flutes, 1st horns
	Gesture U, ascending tetrachord	4-5	Alto and contrabass clarinets, bassoons, baritone saxophone
	B′	5-7	Flutes, 1st horns
	U	5-7	Alto clarinet, bassoons, saxophones
	C	7-9	Flutes, 1st horns
	D	9-11	Flutes, 1st horns
	C	10-12	Clarinets, 2nd horns
	C	11-13	Flutes, alto and tenor saxophones, 1st horns
	C	12-14	2nd and 3rd clarinets, 2nd horns
Period 2	F, descending fourth head motive	12	Alto and bass clarinets, bassoons, baritone
	F′, ascending fourth head motive	13	Contrabass clarinet, timpani, tuba
	F	14	1st flute, oboes, 1st clarinet
	F	15	English horn, 2nd clarinet
	C	13-15	Alto and bass clarinets, bassoons, baritone
	U	14-15	Alto and tenor saxophones, 1st horn
	F	16	Alto and tenor saxophones, 1st horn
	C	16-17	1st flute, oboes, 1st clarinet
	C	16-18	2nd flute, English horn, 2nd clarinet
	C	18-20	Alto and tenor saxophones, 1st horns
	U′	19-20	1st flute, 1st clarinet
	F′	20-21	Bass and contrabass clarinets, baritone saxophone, timpani, 3rd trombone, baritone, tuba
Transition	F″, descending fifth	21	1st flute, oboes, 1st and 3rd clarinets, alto clarinet, alto and tenor saxophones, trumpets, horns, 1st and 2nd trombones
	C	22-24	Trumpets, 1st and 2nd trombones
	D	26-27	Trumpets, 1st and 2nd trombones

SECTION	MOTIVE	MEASURE	INSTRUMENTS
II	G	28-29	1st and 2nd clarinets, alto saxophones, horns
	H	30-31	1st and 2nd clarinets, alto saxophones, horns
	G	32-33	1st and 2nd clarinets, saxophones, 1st and 2nd trombones
Poco animato	J, ascending F minor add flat 6 arpeggio, beginning on the fifth (C)	35-36	English horn, bassoons, saxophones, horns
	J	37-38	Oboes, English horn, alto and tenor saxophones, horns
	J	39-40	Flutes, oboes, clarinets, bassoons
	D	41-42	Flutes, oboes, clarinets, alto and bass clarinets, bassoons
	D	44-45	1st trumpet, harmonized with 2nd and 3rd trumpets, 1st and 2nd trombones
	D´	46-47	1st flute, oboes, 1st clarinets, 2nd horns
	U´´´	46-48	3rd clarinet, alto saxophones
	D	50-51	1st trombone
	D	50-51	Trumpets
	D	52-53	1st flute, 1st clarinet
Recapit. I, Period 1, E-flat minor	A	54-56	2nd flute, alto clarinet, 1st bass clarinet
	A	55-57	2nd clarinet
	B	56-58	1st flute, 1st clarinet
	U	57	Bass and contrabass clarinets
	U´	58-59	2nd flute, 2nd clarinet
	U	58-60	Alto and bass clarinets
	B´	58-60	1st flute, 1st clarinet
	C	60-62	1st flute, 1st clarinet
	D	62-63	1st flute, 1st clarinet
II	G	64-65	Bassoons, horns
	H, 1st half	65-67	Bassoons, horns
	H, 2nd half	67-69	Oboes, vibraphone
	H in sequence	70-72	Oboes, 1st and 2nd clarinets, top voice, vibraphone

SECTION	MOTIVE	MEASURE	INSTRUMENTS
	J	72	Flutes, clarinets, alto saxophones, vibraphone, 2nd horn
Transition		74-77	*Tutti*
Climax	J	78-79	*Tutti*, no bass or contrabass clarinets, or baritone saxophone, or tuba
	C	80-81	*Tutti* woodwinds, no bass or contrabass clarinets, 1st trumpet, horns, 1st trombone
	D	82-86	Flutes, oboes, English horn, 1st clarinet, upper voice, 1st trumpet, 1st trombone
Period 2	F	87	Oboes, 2nd clarinet, 1st horns
	F	88	English horn, 3rd clarinet, 2nd horns
	C	88-90	Oboes, 2nd clarinet, 1st horns
	F	89	Alto and 1st bass clarinets, bassoons, tenor saxophone
	C	90-92	Alto and 1st bass clarinets, bassoons, tenor saxophone
	F	91	1st flute, 1st clarinet
	F	92	2nd flute, alto saxophones
	U	91-93	2nd clarinet, 1st horns
	C	93-95	1st flute, 1st clarinet
	F	93	1st flute, 1st clarinet
	C	93-95	2nd flute, alto saxophones
	U´	97	1st flute, oboes, 1st clarinet, 2nd horns
Transition	F´´	98	1st flute, oboes, clarinets, alto clarinet, tenor saxophone, horns
	C	99-101	English horn, clarinets, alto clarinet, alto and tenor saxophones
	D	101-104	English horn, clarinets, alto clarinet, alto and tenor saxophones
II	G	105-106	1st horns
	H	107-108	1st horns
	G	109-110	Flutes, 1st and 2nd clarinets, 2nd horns
	J	111	English horn (alto saxophone cue)
Coda	Cmaj7#9 chord	112-122	*Tutti*

Unit 8: Suggested Listening

Giovanni Bassano, *Ricercar terza*, Frescobaldi, Bassano, and Gabrieli, Fiati Virtuosi, Analekta/Fleur de Lys, 23013

John Barnes Chance, *Elegy*, Peer Gynt, Frederick Fennell conducting the Tokyo Kosei Wind Orchestra, KOCD-3566

Adrian Willaert, *Ricercar No. 10*, Venetian Music for Double Choir, Erik Van Nevel conducting Concerto Palatius, Accent (Bel), 93101

Unit 9: Additional References and Resources

Anthony, D. A. *The Published Band Works of John Barnes Chance*. Ann Arbor, MI: UMI Company, 1981.

Burritt, Bruce. Telephone interview with Ibrook Tower. 22 June 1999.

Casey, Patrick. "Errata Corner: John Barnes Chance-Elegy." *CBDNA Report*, Spring 1996, 12.

Chance, John Barnes. *Elegy*. New York: Boosey and Hawkes, 1972.

Creasap, Susan, and Rodney C. Schueller. "Incantation and Dance: John Barnes Chance." *Teaching Music through Performance in Band*, Vol. 2. Compiled and edited by Richard Miles. Chicago: GIA Publications, Inc., 1998.

Gudger, William D. "John Barnes Chance (1932-1972), Elegy (arranged for orchestra by Wilson Ochoa)." College of Charleston, 5 January 1998: 2 pars. Online: Internet address http://www.charlestonsymphony.com/chanceochoae.html (10 December 1998).

Kelly, Steven. "John Barnes Chance and His Contribution to Music Education." Diss. Florida State University, after 1990.

Kopetz, Barry E. "An Analysis of Chance's *Incantation and Dance*." *Instrumentalist* (October 1992) 34-46, 107-108.

Ochoa, Wilson. Telephone Interview by Ibrook Tower. 21 June 1999.

The Oxford English Dictionary. Oxford: Oxford University Press, 1971.

Palange, Bill. Telephone Interview by Ibrook Tower. 21 June 1999.

Randel, Don, ed. *The New Harvard Dictionary of Music*. Cambridge, MA.: The Belknap Press of Harvard University, 1986.

Rehrig, William. *The Heritage Encyclopedia of Band Music*. Edited by Paul E. Bierley. Westerville, OH: Integrity Press, 1991.

"Variations on a Korean Folk Song: John Barnes Chance." *Teaching Music through Performance in Band*. Compiled and edited by Richard Miles. Chicago: GIA Publications, Inc., 1997.

Webster's New Universal Unabridged Dictionary, Second Edition. Edited by Jean L. McKechnie. New York: Dorset and Baber (Simon and Schuster), 1983.

Contributed by:
Ibrook Tower
Wind Ensemble Director
Pennsylvania Academy of Music
Lancaster, Pennsylvania

and

Instrumental Music Instructor
Milton Hershey School
Hershey, Pennsylvania

Teacher Resource Guide

Fantasia in G

Timothy Mahr
(b. 1956)

Unit 1: Composer

Timothy Mahr is an Associate Professor of Music at St. Olaf College in Northfield, Minnesota, where he also conducts the St. Olaf College Band. In addition, he teaches courses in composition, conducting, and music education, and supervises instrumental student teaching. Previous to his appointment in 1994 at St. Olaf, Mahr was Director of Bands at the University of Minnesota, Duluth, for ten years and taught instrumental music at Milaca High School (MN) for three years.

Active as a guest conductor and clinician, Mahr is in demand across the nation and in Norway and Canada as a conductor of all-state bands, intercollegiate bands, and honor band festivals. Dr. Mahr is well known as a composer and has over forty works to his credit, twenty-four of which are compositions for band. He received the 1991 ABA/Ostwald Award for his piece *The Soaring Hawk*. He is a recipient of the National Band Association's "Citation of Excellence" and was elected in 1993 to membership in the American Bandmasters Association. Dr. Mahr graduated with two degrees summa cum laude from St. Olaf College in 1977 and 1978 (B.M. in Theory/Composition and B.A. in Music Education). He received his Master of Arts Degree in Trombone Performance from the University of Iowa, where in 1995 he also earned a Doctor of Musical Arts degree in Instrumental Conducting.

Mahr is married to Jill Mahr, musician and educator, and they have two daughters, Jenna and Hannah.

Unit 2: Composition

Fantasia in G was composed in 1982 for the St. Olaf College Band and was premiered by that ensemble under the direction of the composer in January of 1983. The piece was inspired by the first line of Friedrich Schiller's poem *Ode to Joy*: *Freude, Schoner Gotterfunken* (Joy, Bright Spark of Divinity) and the melody from Beethoven's *Ninth Symphony* which provides the basic melodic material for *Fantasia*. The work originated as an organ recessional for his brother's wedding, and Mahr has stated that the work was intended to "get people out of the church."

Unit 3: Historical Perspective

Composed in 1982, *Fantasia in G* draws upon the spirit of both Schiller and Beethoven. While not Romantic in its compositional style, it is a tonal composition that captures the concept of the joyous "bright spark" using the simple yet powerful melody of Beethoven. This work also carries on a long tradition in wind band music of using the percussion as an integral part of the composition, providing not only color and rhythmic vitality, but also motivic material.

Unit 4: Technical Considerations

Fantasia in G moves through a number of key centers, so attention should be paid to accidentals. Be certain that students can hear the moving lines in relation to the shifting centers. Also, the triplet figures in the upper woodwinds (opening 26 measures) and the Alberti bass in the lower woodwinds (mm. 54-88) will present technical challenges. The percussion parts are an integral part of the composition and care should be taken for both rhythmic precision and balance. Some of the solo/soli passage pairings, especially those involving double reeds, piccolo, flute, and soprano saxophone or flugelhorn, will need careful practice for uniformity of style and intonation. Finally, much of the work is based upon fanfares, and balance, rhythmic clarity and, most importantly, uniform attacks and releases must be a primary concern.

Unit 5: Stylistic Considerations

Fantasia in G is an exuberant work which needs to have a constant feel of forward motion. This concept of forward motion (without rushing!) applies not only to the motor figures in the accompaniment but also to the fanfares, chords, and "Ode to Joy" motivic figures, all of which need to feel as though they are constantly expanding. Careful consideration should be given to arrival points and transitions. Conductors should take care in working out their conducting gestures so that players can clearly see and understand the various tempo changes.

Unit 6: Musical Elements

As stated before, the idea of forward motion coupled with exuberance is the most important musical feature to highlight in this work. Also important is the varied use of instrumental color in solo, duo, and fanfare passages. Students will be drawn to this work and can learn a great deal about expressive playing and communicating with an audience from *Fantasia in G*.

Unit 7: Form and Structure

Fanfare 1   (29 measures)   D major (V)
Introduction (4)/ horn fanfare (10)/ trombone fanfare (12)/ *tutti* fanfare (3)

Theme A   (22 measures)   G major (I)
Introduction (4)/ woodwind obligato (8)/ woodwind obligato up M3 (8)/ vamp (2)

Theme B   (28 measures)   Shifting key centers
"Ode" melody (8) G major/ extension (5) F major/ "Ode" melody ornamented (8) G major/ extension (7) E-flat major

Fanfare 2   (21 measures)   Shifting key centers
Transition (4) G major/ trumpet fanfare (4) D major/ horn fanfare (4) B-flat major/ low brass fanfare (5) A-flat major/ horn fanfare (4) E major/ trumpet fanfare (4) G major

Fanfare Development (18 measures)   Shifting key centers
Transition (4) e minor/ trumpet and woodwind quintet (5) A major/ double reed and general (5) D7/ *tutti* fanfare (4) various keys to D major

Ode with Theme A   (32 measures)   G major(16)/ D major(8)/
                                           G major(8)
"Ode" first phrase (8) G major/ "Ode" second phrase (8) G major/ "Ode" third phrase (8) D major/ "Ode" fourth phrase (8) G major

Theme B – Coda   (18 measures)   G major
"Ode" ornamented (8) G major/ "Ode" in augmentation (10) G major

Overview:
Fanfare 1/Theme A/Theme B	Intro and Exposition	(A)
Fanfare 2/Fanfare Development	Fanfare Section	(B)
Ode with Theme A/Theme B-Coda	Truncated Recapitulation	(A)

Unit 8: Suggested Listening

Ludwig von Beethoven, *Symphony #9* (last movement)
Timothy Mahr:
>   *Argentum*
>   *Endurance*
>   *Hymn and Celebration*
>   *The Soaring Hawk*

A CD recording of *Fantasia in G* with Dr. Mahr conducting the St. Olaf Band is available through St. Olaf Records (1-888-232-6523): "Praise the Lord with Drums and Cymbals" WCD 29633.

Unit 9: Additional References and Resources

Ripley, James. "Timothy Mahr's *Fantasia*: An Interpretive Analysis." *The Instrumentalist*, April 1996, 24-32.

Contributed by:

Kenneth Ayoob
Humboldt State University
Arcata, California

Teacher Resource Guide

Festal Scenes

Yasuhide Ito
(b. 1960)

Unit 1: Composer

Yasuhide Ito was born in Hamamatsu City, Shizuoka Prefecture of Tokyo in Japan in 1960. His graduate degree is from Tokyo University of Fine Arts and Music where he studied composition with Teruyuki Noda. He has won awards at the Music Competition of Japan for an orchestral composition and a composition for saxophone. Ito is also a pianist and conductor, serving as principal director of the Tsukuba University Band. He holds teaching posts at Sakuyo Music College, Tokyo Conservatoire Shobi, and Komaba Junior High School. Ito's compositions include *Sinfonia*, *Zweisamkeit*, and *Gradation*.

Unit 2: Composition

Festal Scenes is comprised of four songs from the Aomori Prefecture in Japan. "Jongara-Jamisen" is the first tune used, which explores the interval of a fourth and serves as an introductory fanfare. "Hohai-bushi" is introduced in a soft, *andante*, lyrical setting. A lento section follows with a *forte* statement of "Tsugaru-aiya-bushi." "Nebuta-festival" ends the piece followed by a declarative, rousing coda. The inspiration for *Festal Scenes* came from a friend of the composer who exclaimed, "Everything seems like paradise blooming all together. Life is a festival indeed." This piece was commissioned by the Ominato Band of the Japan Maritime Self-Defense Force and was premiered on October 28, 1986. The American premiere was at the ABA convention in Knoxville, Tennessee, in 1987 by the University of Illinois Concert Band.

Unit 3: Historical Perspective

The use of folk song material is prevalent in twentieth century wind compositions. This piece in some ways continues a tradition that began with Ives and Holst. Among the important Japanese composers of this century are Toru Takemitsu and Michio Mamiya. *Festal Scenes* provides an important contribution to wind literature by exposing listeners to Japanese folk song material being written by a Japanese composer.

Unit 4: Technical Considerations

Eighth notes and sixteenth notes require quick, light articulation. A large variety of articulation styles are used throughout the work, and moderately fast tonguing is required of all performers. Independence is required, as many sections are thinly scored. In the *andante* section, players must sustain pitches in delicate balance at soft, dynamic levels. Quartal harmonies are used throughout. The range in the horn extends to an A above the staff. A slow section contains a lyrical baritone solo. Trumpets play repeated Bs above the staff in a fanfare motive, and strong players are needed overall. The piece calls for a tebiragane and nebuta-deiko, Japanese percussion instruments. The composer suggests using a suspended cymbal in the center for the tebiragane and a bass drum hit by a bamboo stick for the nebuta-deiko.

Unit 5: Stylistic Considerations

Quick, *staccato* playing is required at varying dynamic levels. A variety of articulations from *marcato* to *tenuto* are required. Pedal points are integral in this piece and pitches are sustained in thinly scored passages. *Ostinato* patterns abound, particularly in the percussion section. Woodwinds provide most of the melodic material, with the brass providing a harmonic function. A euphonium, flute duet opens section three, which connects to the thinly scored fourth section. The first theme comes back here, followed by a *fff* coda.

Unit 6: Musical Elements

A variety of pentatonic melodic structures and a mixture of quartal and diatonic harmonies are used throughout. Pedal points and melodic fragments are used to unite the piece. A return of the first theme in the last section further unifies the structure of the work. The first and last movements feature *tutti* passages with *forte* dynamic indications, while the middle movements are more soloistic and gentle. The first melody is in the dorian mode, supported by quartal harmony. The second melody is in F minor. Melody number three is in F major, and the fourth melody is written in the key of G-flat major. The return of the first theme is reworked in F minor, accompanied again by quartal harmony.

Unit 7: Form and Structure

SECTION	MEASURE	EVENT AND SCORING
Theme 1	1-54	*Allegro appassionato*, 2/4 "Jongara-jamisen"; dorian melody stated in winds, D pedal in low brass/reeds, quartal harmony, brass fanfares
Transition	55-74	*Meno mosso*, 3/4, introduces lyricism, fragments of first theme, thin scoring
Theme 2	75-84	*Andante cantabile*, F minor, pentatonic melody in flute solo
Theme 3	85-124	*Lento*; "nebuta-festival"; F major; pentatonic melody; euphonium solo; brief clarinet, oboe, bassoon, and alto saxophone soli
Transition	125-134	*Andante marziale*, B-flat pedal, short bass clarinet solo
Theme 4	135-150	G-flat major, pentatonic melody, motive from bass clarinet solo becomes countermelody
Recapitulation	151-190	*Piu mosso*, F minor return of first theme, melody in upper woodwinds, brass fanfares
Coda	191-201	Timpani solo

Unit 8: Suggested Listening

Jay Gilbert, *Suite Divertimento*
Yasuhide Ito, *Variations from the Northern Sea*
Soichi Konagaya, *Japanese Tune*
Michio Mamiya, *Glory of Catalonia*
Bernard Rogers, *Three Japanese Dances*

Unit 9: Additional References and Resources

Kishibe, Shigeo, et al. "Japan-Folk Song." Sadie, Stanley, ed. *The New Groves Dictionary of Music and Musicians*.

Rehrig, William H. *The Heritage Encyclopedia of Band Music*, edited by Paul Bierley. Westerville, OH: Integrity Press, 1991.

TRN website http://wwwtrn_music.com

Contributed by:
Nancy M. Golden
Graduate Conducting Associate
University of North Texas
Denton, Texas

Teacher Resource Guide

First Suite in F

Thom Ritter George

(b. 1942)

Unit 1: Composer

Thom Ritter George was born on June 23, 1942, in Detroit, Michigan. He exhibited an early interest in music and found his special talents lay in composition and conducting. By the age of ten, he had composed his first musical work, and a mere seven years later he conducted his first concert. He developed his compositional techniques during his high school years under the tutelage of Harold Laudenslager, who had been a pupil of Paul Hindemith.

George attended Eastman School of Music where he earned his bachelor's (1964) and master's (1968) degrees. His primary composition teachers included Thomas Canning, Louis Mennini, Wayne Barlow, John LaMontaine, and Bernard Rogers. George was appointed Composer/Arranger for the United States Navy Band in Washington, DC, in 1966 and remained in this position until 1970. During these years he not only wrote for the Navy Band but often conducted performances of the ensemble.

In 1970, George was awarded his Doctor of Musical Arts from the Catholic University of America. Upon completion of this degree, he accepted the position of Music Director and Conductor of the Quincy Symphony Orchestra (Quincy, Illinois). Then in 1983, he moved to Idaho to become Director of the Idaho State Civic Symphony and Professor of Music at Idaho State University.

During his years of study at the Eastman School of Music, George had been in the conducting class of Dr. Paul White, Associate Conductor of the Rochester Philharmonic. He later continued to develop his conducting skills with advanced studies under Lloyd Geisler, Associate Conductor of the

National Symphony; Boris Goldovsky, opera conducting; and Sir Georg Solti, Conductor Laureate of the Chicago Symphony Orchestra.

His numerous compositional awards include the Edward B. Benjamin Prize, two Howard Hanson Awards, the Seventh Sigvald Thompson Award and, since 1965, a series of annual awards from the American Society of Composers, Authors, and Publishers (ASCAP) for his contributions to American music. In 1973, George received the Quincy College Citation for Meritorious Service. The Pocatello Music Club honored the composer in 1988 with their award "For Community Service Through Musical Excellence." In October 1995, the Idaho State University Alumni Association honored Dr. George by naming him a recipient of the prestigious Idaho State University Achievement Award.

George has composed more than 350 works including several concertos, a series of sonatas written for every instrument of the orchestra, brass quintets, two ballets, *Sextet* for euphonium and woodwind quintet, *Tubamobile*, and *The People, Yes*, a work for soloists, chorus, and orchestra. His works for band include *Hymn and Toccata*, *Proclamations*, *Western Overture*, and *Second Suite in C*. Many of George's compositions have been recorded.

Unit 2: Composition

First Suite in F was composed at the request of Lcdr. Ned E. Muffley for the Navy Band's fiftieth anniversary celebration. Lcdr. Muffley, who was Leader of the Navy Band at the time, conducted the premiere performance of the work at the Kennedy Center for the Performing Arts in the spring of 1975. Of the work, the composer writes that the first movement "is not based on any particular sea chantey," but rather is intended to conjure up the character, energy, and style of sailor's work songs. The second movement, "Song of the Bells," is wistful in character and more symbolic of the grand expanse of water and the ensuing sense of loneliness that may accompany one's musings as he looks out over the empty water. The third movement, "Country Dance," functions as an intermezzo, providing a needed contrast to bridge the moods of the second and fourth movements. The final movement, "Rumba, Rumba," is sheer fun, depicting "Navy men having fun in a South American port." The percussion section provides the characteristic color and flavor for this exciting concluding movement.

The score bears the inscription, "edited by R. Mark Rogers." According to the composer, Rogers, who is the Music Editor for Southern Music Company, conscientiously prepared the score in an effort to make the music technically more accessible to bands of less experience than the Navy Band. The duration of the four-movement work is approximately thirteen minutes.

Unit 3: Historical Perspective

First Suite in F has experienced several transformations since the sixteenth century when pairs of dances, usually one in duple time and the other in triple time, constituted the musical form. By the Baroque era, the suite had evolved into a multi-movement instrumental form consisting of a series of dances, all in the same key. After 1750, the suite generally lost favor, and it was not until the later decades of the nineteenth century that the form regained its popularity. The modern suite is characterized by a grouping of several movements that may or may not be types of traditional dances. It is merely important that each movement represents a separate mood, style, or character. Because the suite is a common orchestral form, it is not surprising that it has found acceptance in the literature for the symphonic band.

The first movement of *First Suite in F* is titled, "Sea Chantey." The chantey (also *shanty* or *chanty*) is an English or American sailor's work song. Designed to help ease the trials of labor at sea, the chantey is rhythmic and tuneful.

The third movement is "Country Dance." The term has been applied to any number of folk dances of English origin. These dances are usually set in eight-measure phrases with a strong rhythmic pulse.

The rumba is an energetic, up-tempo, urban Afro-Cuban dance. According to the *Harvard Dictionary of Music*, it is performed by an instrumental ensemble and a singer who utters nonsensical phrases and syllables. The melodic content is usually an eight-measure theme that is repeated; however, two shorter themes may be employed. The dance itself is characterized by limited foot action and significant movement of the hips and shoulders. The rumba experienced significant popularity with jazz musicians and dancers in the 1930s.

Unit 4: Technical Considerations

The composition is scored for standard full symphonic band instrumentation, and supplemental European parts are available (horns in E-flat, trombones in B-flat treble clef, and tubas in E-flat treble clef). There is an English horn part, but it is cued in the first oboe. The percussion parts are scored for timpani, snare drum, cymbals, bass drum, xylophone, chimes, glockenspiel, triangle, temple blocks, wood block, tambourine, claves, gourd, and maracas, utilizing seven players.

At first glance the work appears to be relatively straightforward and technically accessible by good high school bands and second bands at the university level. However, the lively tempi and the intricate weaving of melodic themes, coupled with the numerous exposed passages and sheer duration of the piece, make this work quite challenging. Consistent and thoughtful cross-cues occur throughout the work and are verbally cited in the score. While the trills, grace notes, frequent stretto entrances, and solo passages for every instrument make this an ideal piece for the advanced band, directors will find a wealth of educational opportunities for the developing high school ensemble.

MOVEMENT I:

The movement begins with a lively six-measure introduction in cut time that establishes a melodic motive and rhythmic energy. There is a perpetual motion feeling that enhances the upbeat, enthusiastic sense of the chantey. Although the rhythmic structure of the movement is essentially imbedded in simple combinations of quarter notes and eighth notes, precise placement of every quarter beat will ensure rhythmic and melodic clarity. Woodwind, trumpet, and euphonium players, in particular, will need to have well-developed articulation skills.

MOVEMENT II:

Open fifths, coupled with a *piano* dynamic level and *largo* tempo in the bassoons and euphonium/tuba parts will require careful attention to phrasing and tuning. These long, quiet, sonorous passages characterize this movement and are best accomplished by mature ensembles with a well-developed approach to breathing and tonal support. Solo lines occur in the oboe, first and second flutes, alto saxophone, English horn, and clarinet.

MOVEMENT III:

This movement is in 6/8 time with a metronome marking of dotted-quarter note = 132. The woodwind parts demand technical facility, particularly in the flutes, oboes, and clarinets. The trumpet parts are often unison but extend to the high C above the staff, with the octave lower indicated as optional. The euphonium range extends from F below the staff to B-flat, four ledger lines above the bass staff. Short but technical soli occur in the bassoon, clarinet, oboe, alto saxophone, and piccolo. Although the 6/8 meter is generally straightforward, there is the use of a hemiola figure, and two and four against three.

MOVEMENT IV:

"Rumba, Rumba" is the most technically demanding movement of the suite. It is set in cut time with a metronome marking of half note = 104. Because of its intricate rhythmic structure (within a relatively straightforward series of rhythm patterns) and its numerous accidentals, less-experienced ensembles will benefit from rehearsing this movement in four. Close attention should be paid to the grace note entrances in the melody. Define both length and placement of the grace note, particularly those that occur after the downbeat. There is a challenging solo for the first trumpet, with a *tessitura* of top space E-flat to high D-flat above the staff; however, the octave lower is indicated as an option. Trills in the French horn part are doubled by the saxophones.

Unit 5: Stylistic Considerations

The composer indicates that the music is clearly marked on the score except for the last movement. Here the composer does not recommend the jazz articulations in the brass parts in mm. 100-106. The intent is to have these passages played as plain notes, with heavy accents at the end of the phrase (mm. 106-107). The second movement demands careful attention to balance and phrasing, consistently striving for a lush, *legato* style until mm. 73-85, when the stylistic indications *Noblimente e molto sostenuto* (noble and very sustained), *eroico* (heroically), and *trattenuto* (delayed, slowed down) offer a deliberate and effective contrast.

Unit 6: Musical Elements

Throughout the suite, primary and secondary eight-measure melodies are introduced, developed, fragmented, and passed from section to section. Although not based on existent tunes, the melodic motives are easily remembered and "feel" as if they were already a part of the listener's musical experience. This sense of familiarity is what makes the work such a joy for the audience since the tunes are easily followed as they wind their way through the piece. The entire work is woven together by the intelligent employment of a variety of compositional devices. The composer works magic by establishing thoroughly memorable, singable tunes, and then proceeds to treat them contrapuntally or use bits and pieces of them to create a musical jigsaw puzzle. This clever development of the delightful melodies and their subsequent melodic motives makes this an engaging composition for performers and conductors.

Because this composition is so very melodic, attention must be given to the phrasing throughout the work. As with any composition, the achievement of balance and tonal blend is of primary concern. In "Rumba, Rumba," work to balance the clusters (e.g., mm. 11-13) so that the second is clearly defined. The contrapuntal techniques employed in the first and fourth movements are especially effective and must be carefully balanced to maintain the integrity of the melodic lines.

Unit 7: Form and Structure

SECTION	MEASURE	EVENT AND SCORING
Movement I: "Sea Chantey"		
F minor		
Introduction	1-6	Woodwinds and trumpets
Motive 1	6-14	Horns/bassoons/euphoniums
	14-22	Piccolo/flute/clarinets
Transition	22-26	Introduction theme

Section	Measure	Event and Scoring
Motive 1	26-34	Trumpets
Motive 2	34-38	Woodwinds
Motive 3	38-42	Trumpet solo
	42-46	Trumpets/euphoniums
	46-54	Woodwinds/full band
Motive 4	54-62	Oboe solo, treated contrapuntally in clarinets
	62-70	Horn/tenor saxophone/euphonium treated contrapuntally in trumpets, fragments in woodwinds, full band
Motive 1	70-78	Horns/bassoons/euphoniums, counterpoint in clarinets
	78-86	Trumpets, counterpoint continues in clarinets
Transition F major	86-90	Introduction theme
Motive 3	90-102	Woodwinds, then trumpets
Transition	102-111	Motive fragments in solo flute, solo oboe, horns, clarinets
	111-115	Introduction theme
F minor – Coda		
Motive 1	115-124	Trumpets/bassoons/euphoniums, counterpoint in woodwinds
Motive 3	124-end	Woodwinds, altered motive

Movement II: "Song of the Bells"
A:

Introduction	1-13	Bassoons/euphoniums/tubas open fifths
Motive 1	13-25	Clarinets/horns
	25-37	Oboe solo, clarinet/alto saxophone solo, horn
Motive 2	37-49	Solo flutes 1 and 2
B, Development:		
Motives 1-2	49-73	Full band
	73-85	Bell tones
A, Recapitulation:		
Introduction	85-91	Bassoons/bass clarinets/euphoniums
Motive 1	91-103	English horn solo
Coda	103-end	Fragments in clarinet, chimes

SECTION	MEASURE	EVENT AND SCORING
Movement III: "Country Dance"		
Motive 1	1-9	Clarinets
	9-16	Oboe solo with clarinets
Transition	16-21	Duples in brass
Motive 1	21-36	Piccolo/flutes/E-flat soprano
Transition	36-47	Quadruples in woodwinds
Motive 2	47-66	Horns/euphoniums, trumpets
Transition	66-73	Woodwind runs
Motive 1	73-88	Trumpets/euphoniums
Coda	88-end	Duples, quadruples, solo entrances in bassoon, oboe, piccolo, tuba
Movement IV: "Rumba, Rumba"		
Introduction	1-3	Trumpets/saxophones
Motive 1	3-11	Piccolo/flutes/clarinets
Transition	11-13	
Motive 1	13-21	Saxophones/euphoniums
Transition	21-24	
Development section:		
Motive 1	24-100	Motive fragments passed around the band, introductory sections, Motive 1 in various instrumentations
Motive 2	100-107	Brass, woodwind sixteenth note runs
Motive 1	107-114	Oboes/clarinets/alto saxophone, trills in horns, bassoons, euphoniums
Motive 2	114-123	Brass, woodwind sixteenth note runs
Motive 1	123-131	Trumpets, woodwinds with stretto entrance
Coda		
Motives 1-2	131-end	Full band, woodwinds – Motive 1, brass – Motive 2

Unit 8: Suggested Listening

Clare Grundman, *Fantasy on American Sailing Songs*
Gustav Holst:
  First Suite in E Flat
  Second Suite in F
Ralph Vaughan Williams, *Sea Songs*

Unit 9: Additional References and Resources

Apel, Willi. *Harvard Dictionary of Music*, 2nd ed. Cambridge, MA: The Belknap Press of Harvard University Press, 1970.

George, Thom Ritter. Correspondence with the composer. 15 March 1999.

Hitchcock, H. Wiley. *Music in the United States: A Historical Introduction*, 3rd ed. Englewood Cliffs, NJ: Prentice Hall, 1988.

Rehrig, William H. The Heritage Encyclopedia of Band Music. Westerville, OH: Integrity Press, 1991.

Southern Music Company, San Antonio, TX.

Tirro, Frank. *Jazz: A History*. New York: W.W. Norton & Company, 1977.

Contributed by:

Susan Creasap
Assistant Director of Bands
Morehead State University
Morehead, Kentucky

Teacher Resource Guide

The Gum-Suckers March
Percy Aldridge Grainger
(1882–1961)

Unit 1: Composer

George Percy Grainger was born on July 8, 1882, in Melbourne, Australia. Percy Grainger's father, John Grainger, was an architect and civil engineer in colonial-era Australia, and several of the official structures (bridges, town halls, and the like) dating from this period were either designed or constructed under his direction. John Grainger's frequent absences from home allowed his wife, the former Rose Aldridge, to exercise without restraint an influence over her only child that shaped his entire world view. Rose Grainger was also her son's first piano teacher, thus shaping not only his attitudes towards life in general but in particular his taste in music. As a result of the lifelong bond between mother and son, when Percy Grainger's professional career as a pianist and composer began, he took his mother's maiden name as his middle name, being thereafter forever known as Percy Aldridge Grainger.

Grainger left Australia in 1895 to study in Frankfurt for a period which lasted until 1901. He began his career as a pianist touring England and the British Commonwealth in the first decade of the twentieth century. At the same time he began to compose and collect the musical folk material which was to provide the raw material for much of his greatest work. He emigrated to the United States at the outset of World War I and enlisted in the United States Army as a musician when the U.S. entered the war. Although he took American citizenship, he never forgot his roots in Australia, and in the 1930s, he oversaw the construction of a museum located on the campus of the University of Melbourne to house manuscripts and artifacts from his life.

Grainger was an iconoclast, forever marching to his own drummer. Many of his odd quirks, while harmless enough viewed from the perspective of the present, tended to alienate him from musicians of his day. His greatest creative work spans a 25-year period beginning in the late 1890s and ending at the time of his mother's death by suicide in 1922. His working habits were such that he often took years to bring a compositional effort to its final form, and the prodigious work of his early years furnished sufficient materials to occupy his efforts from 1922 until his death in 1961. Grainger's interest in the wind band began during the years of his enlistment in the U.S. Army Band stationed at Fort Hamilton. In later years he took a great interest in the public school and university band movement, with appearances on many campuses and an extended period of involvement with the National Music Camp at Interlochen during the 1940s. Although a great deal of Grainger's band music consists of transcriptions for band of earlier orchestral scores, it is generally recognized that the wind band music left by Grainger forms the largest and most significant body of work in the wind repertory.

Unit 2: Composition

The Gum-Suckers March was composed as the fourth movement of Grainger's suite for symphony orchestra entitled "In a Nutshell." This composition illustrates a number of tendencies to be found in much of Grainger's music: 1) he draws upon a variety of musical ideas to construct the composition, quoting material that also appeared in two other compositions, *Colonial Song* and *The Widow's Party,* one of his settings for chorus and orchestra of the poetry of Rudyard Kipling (1906); 2) this score makes great use of the percussion section, in particular calling for a large collection of mallet instruments; and 3) the performance directions throughout feature Grainger's "blue-eyed English," a peculiar language of his own invention in which he sought to purge all terms of non-Nordic derivation.

Unit 3: Historical Perspective

By the time of the composition of *The Gum-Suckers March,* Grainger was an expatriate, a British subject living in America while the British Commonwealth was involved in the greatest war ever fought until that time. The title, *The Gum-Suckers March,* seeks to preserve the composer's connection with his native Australia: the term "gum-sucker" is a name given to natives of the Australian state of Victoria, the composer's home state (much like people from Oklahoma are called "sooners" and residents of Ohio are called "buckeyes"), and refers to the habit of chewing or sucking on the leaves of the Eucalyptus tree, a process that reduces the leaves to a gum-like texture.

Most of the composition of *The Gum-Suckers March* was completed before Grainger left England in late 1914, but it was not scored for orchestra until 1916. The orchestral score was dedicated to Henry and Abbie Finck (Finck was the music critic of the *New York Evening Post,* who wrote very enthusiastically about Grainger's performances as a pianist.) The first sketches of a band version of the march date from the period of Grainger's involvement with the Fort Hamilton Band, and the final band version dates from the years when he was teaching at Interlochen. Although many sketches and parts for both band settings survive, waning interest on the part of band conductors for Grainger's music towards the end of his life so disheartened him that he did not bring the band setting to a final form.

Unit 4: Technical Considerations

The Gum-Suckers March was composed for symphony orchestra and calls for musical skills on a professional level. Consequently, the musical demands of the band version are very high. The scoring calls for a large complement of instruments, including full double-reed and saxophone sections (including English horn, double bassoon, and soprano saxophone), a vast array of mallet percussion instruments, and an important piano part which is not cross-cued to allow for its absence from the performing ensemble. The piece is set in the "band friendly" key of E-flat, but requires great technical flexibility on the part of the woodwinds and great lip flexibility on the part of the brass. Although billed as a "march," the piece has a brief inner section that is rather rhapsodic, which will require skill on the part of the conductor and attention on the part of the ensemble.

Unit 5: Stylistic Considerations

The Gum-Suckers March requires a broad variety of musical styles, including very aggressive playing in the more extroverted moments of the score contrasting with a singing cantabile line when the melody from *Colonial Song* is quoted. Often these elements are superimposed upon each other, requiring independence of musical thought and execution. Conductors who are familiar with Grainger's other original marches, *Children's March* and *Lads of Wamphray*, will see many of the same techniques employed here.

Unit 6: Musical Elements

Among the compositional devices on exhibit in this score is a great deal of musical layering, in which the texture is built by adding successive lines of only occasionally related counterpoint on top of the melody and its accompaniment so that, in the end, the melody and the harmonies attached to it are swamped by the other materials. There are practically no instances of traditional "oom-pah" style accompaniments, high woodwind *obligati*, or tenor line countermelodies. The composer describes the final *tutti* passage as follows: "Toward the end of the piece is heard a many-voiced climax in which clattering rhythms on the percussion instruments and gliding chromatic chords on the brass are pitted against the long notes of the 'Australian' second theme, a melodic counter-theme, and a melodic bass."

Unit 7: Form and Structure

There is no introduction to the march.

MEASURE	SECTION
1-16	First appearance of "The Gum-Suckers" theme, the sixteen bars being organized into subdivisions of nine measures plus seven
17-32	Second statement of "The Gum-Suckers" theme, in *tutti* scoring
33-48	First appearance of the "Australian" second theme (also used in Grainger's *Colonial Song* and *Australian Up-Country Tune*)
49-64	Third statement of "The Gum-Suckers" theme, with melody in tenor line instruments (saxophones, low cornets, horns, trombones, and euphonium)
65-72	First appearance of material drawn from *The Widow's Party* (C minor?)
73-82	Second phrase drawn from The *Widow's Party* (E-flat major?)
83-88	Second appearance of phrase first heard at m. 65
89-99	Rhapsodic section drawn from "dream" music in *The Widow's Party*
100-115	Return to "The Gum-Suckers" theme and original tempo, scored softly for woodwinds and piano
116-139	Material related to both "The Gum-Suckers" theme and *The Widow's Party* is developed (which is the variant and which is the original?)
140-155	Final statement of "The Gum-Suckers" theme, *tutti*, with new accompaniment material, passing with no clear cadence
156-169	Final appearance of second "Australian" theme, above and below which appears increasingly more thickly scored counterpoint which in the end "swamps" the melody entirely
170-175	Cadential extension of the final phrase of the "Australian" second theme
176-185	First set of closing cadential material (Coda I)
186-193	Final closing material (Coda II)

Unit 8: Suggested Listening

Samuel Barber, *Commando March*
William Bergsma, *March with Trumpets*
Emmanuel Chabrier, *Marche Joyeuse*

Percy Grainger:
   Children's March
   Lads of Wamphray
   The Widow's Party

Unit 9: Additional References and Resources

Bird, John. *Percy Grainger.* London, Faber and Faber, 1976.

Lewis, Thomas P. *A Source Guide to the Music of Percy Grainger.* White Plains, NY: Pro/Am Music Resources, 1991.

Mellers, Wilfrid. *Percy Grainger.* New York: Oxford University Press, 1992.

Contributed by:

R. Mark Rogers
Director of Publications
Southern Music Company
San Antonio, Texas

Teacher Resource Guide

Laude

Howard Hanson
(1896–1981)

Unit 1: Composer

Seattle Symphony Orchestra conductor Gerard Schwarz described Howard Hanson as the twentieth century's "first great American composer. ...Before Copland, Diamond, Barber – and in a sense Gershwin – he was Mr. American Music."

Born in Wahoo, Nebraska, on October 28, 1896, the child prodigy began musical study with his Swedish-American mother. He received further training at Lutheran College (Wahoo), University of Nebraska (Lincoln), Institute of Musical Art (New York), and Northwestern University, where he earned a bachelor's degree in 1916.

He then taught at the College of the Pacific in San Jose, California, three years later becoming Dean of its School of Fine Arts. In 1923, he was the first American composer to win the Prix de Rome. While in Rome he completed and conducted the Nordic Symphony, his first. He returned the next year to conduct his symphony in Rochester, New York, home of the Eastman School of Music. George Eastman and President Rush Rhees named him, at the age of twenty-seven, the school's second director. Hanson served in that position for forty years (1924-64).

Called the "Dean of American Music," Hanson received many honors and awards, including thirty-six honorary doctorates, memberships in the Royal Swedish Academy of Music and the National Institute of Arts and Letters, the Alice Ditson and George Peabody Awards, and a Pulitzer Prize for his fourth symphony.

Hanson composed seven works for band or wind ensemble: *Centennial*

March, Chorale and Alleluia, Dies Natalis, Laude, Variations on an Ancient Hymn, March Carillon, and *Young Person's Guide to the Six Tone Scale.*

Unit 2: Composition

Hanson composed *Laude: Chorale, Variations and Metamorphoses* in response to the 1975 commission from the College Band Directors National Association. The title *Laude* reflects the work's intended performance by a collegiate honor band. CBDNA project chairman Frank Bencriscutto asked Hanson to compose a work for a proposed All-American Intercollegiate Band to be conducted by Frederick Fennell. The band would perform the work at the Association's Eighteenth National Conference in Berkeley, California. However, Larry Curtis conducted the California State University Long Beach Band in *Laude*'s first performance at the conference on February 7, 1975.

In his address to the conference, Hanson discussed *Laude*:

> As one comes toward the end of a long life one realizes how many of the influences go back to early childhood. In my musical and religious life the greatest was, undoubtedly, the chorales that I heard as a young boy growing up in Wahoo, Nebraska.

> Much of this influence was subconscious, but it is interesting that my first work for band was…entitled *Chorale and Alleluia.* …The chorale form has also permeated my third, fourth, and fifth symphonies.

> My two most recent compositions for wind ensemble have actually been based on chorale tunes that I remembered from my childhood: the *Dies Natalis,* based on a famous Christmas chorale, and the *Laude,* based on a chorale of praise to the Lord, which is having its first performance today.

> In setting this chorale, which I remember only by the Swedish words that might be translated, "All the world praises the Lord," I took my cue from the 150th Psalm, of which I had made this paraphrase:

>> Praise Him with the sound of the trumpet,
>> with psaltery and harp,

>> with timbrel and dance,
>> with string instruments and organs.

>> Praise Him upon the loud cymbals, the high-sounding cymbals.
>> Let everything that has breath praise the Lord.

Published by Carl Fischer, *Laude* is approximately twelve to fifteen minutes in length.

Unit 3: Historical Perspective

During the early decades of the twentieth century, European music and Old World influences dominated American music. Hanson became an advocate of the music of American composers. In 1925, he founded the American Composers Concerts and in 1930 the annual Festival of American Music. The Festival premiered more than 200 American works during its 41-year existence, with the composers attending both rehearsals and concerts. Hanson's national radio broadcasts in the 1930s and 1940s over NBC helped create an audience for contemporary American music. In 1952, Hanson encouraged Frederick Fennell in creating the Eastman Wind Ensemble, which was to record many original works by American composers for the new medium.

During those early twentieth century decades, American band performances consisted largely of popular music (marches and dances) and arrangements or transcriptions of European orchestral music. These performances were instrumental in creating a demand for European classical works in their original form, necessitating the establishment of American symphony orchestras to perform them. To help fill the void created by the predominance of European music in the wind repertoire, Edwin Franko Goldman's Band began commissioning original works for band in the 1930s and continued that tradition for more than thirty years.

Following the Goldman Band's example, the College Band Directors National Association in 1961 began its commissioning project. In the 1980s and 1990s, CBDNA expanded it, supporting regional commissioning consortiums consisting of as many as a dozen schools and colleges pooling their contributions. Hanson's *Laude* was the sixth of the twenty-five compositions the national CBDNA organization commissioned in the twentieth century.

Unit 4: Technical Considerations

Hanson scored *Laude* for a very large festival band: piccolo and two flutes, two oboes and English horn, E-flat clarinet, five B-flat clarinets (2nd and 3rd parts divided), alto and bass clarinets, two bassoons and contrabassoon, three saxophones (ATB), three trumpets and three cornets, four horns, three trombones, baritone and tuba, and percussion. The score does not specify a string bass part, but the name "Basses (Tuba)" implies that string basses can read that part up an octave. Alternately, string basses can easily play the contrabassoon part.

The percussion parts require nine or ten musicians. For example, in the seventh variation at rehearsal number 24, percussionists play the following instruments simultaneously: timpani, xylophone, tubular bells, temple blocks, tambourine, snare drum, wood block, Chinese cymbals, gong, and bass drum. In addition, the score requires large crash cymbals, a suspended cymbal, a second snare drum, and a second tambourine.

The work includes soli or independent passages for flutes and piccolos, both oboes and both bassoons, clarinet, bass clarinet, and tenor and baritone saxophones. Many of these soli may be doubled, but they are not cross-cued for other instruments. All contrabassoon passages appear an octave higher in the tuba part.

All trumpet and cornet parts require strong, independent players, the 1st cornet and all three trumpets each extending to C-sharp6 above the staff. The 2nd and 3rd cornets and the 3rd trumpet descend to B3 below the staff. The 1st horn extends to top-line F-sharp5, and the 1st trombone and baritone reach G4 above the staff. The 3rd trombone's lowest pitch is first-line g2, which can be played on the tenor trombone. The tuba part extends from C2 below the staff to B3 above the staff, a high *tessitura* spanning a large range. The tuba leaps down a tenth at the climax of variation five.

Although the written key signature is C major, *Laude* is primarily in G. In this key, piccolos, flutes, and clarinets must negotiate thirty-second note passages in variation seven, second and third clarinets crossing the break. In variation five, all woodwinds, trumpets, cornets, and horns must tongue rapidly in sixteenth note sextuplets on repeated pitches.

Variation four is in 6/8 and 4/8 meters in eighth note beats. Musicians who are not used to the eighth note pulse may have difficulty at first playing in these meters, but a little extra rehearsal on this section will help them feel more comfortable.

Two snare drummers and two timpanists (in octaves) play simultaneously to introduce the opening chorale. The players must set up their instruments so as to have full eye contact with the conductor. Variation one also requires two tambourines to be played simultaneously with snare drum sticks.

In variation seven the mallet parts will challenge percussionists technically. Use French-weight cymbals to achieve the sound of "Chinese cymbals" specified in variation seven, depicting "high-sounding cymbals" in the Psalm text. If enough percussionists are not available, the bass drummer may also play the gong at the same time. However, doing so may steal strength from both parts at an important climax in the piece.

The editing of the parts for *Laude* is exceptionally good for such a long work. Although there are a few wrong pitches, most of the errors in the parts are omissions of slurs, other articulations, or tempo markings. There are many discrepancies of pitch notation between the score and the parts that do not affect the performance of the work. However, they can present a barrier to conductor-performer communication in rehearsal.

Errata Parts:

REHEARSAL NUM.	MEASURE	BEAT	CORRECTION
Piccolo:			
17	2	1	Divide eight-measure rest into 6+1+1
17	7	1	Add fermata

REHEARSAL NUM.	MEASURE	BEAT	CORRECTION
1st flute:			
17	2	1	Divide eight-measure rest into 6+1+1
17	7	1	Add fermata
2nd flute:			
11	8	1	Add flat to F6
1st and 2nd oboes:			
4	5	3	"soli"
171	0	1	Divide five-measure rest into 3+1+1
17	7	1	Add fermata
English horn:			
20	11	1	Add fermata
1st clarinet:			
12	5	4	Add natural to final E4
2nd clarinet:			
12	5	4	Add natural to final E4
3rd clarinet:			
5	3	3	"unis."
Alto clarinet:			
26	2	1	Divide seven-measure rest into 6+1
26	8	1	*"poco allargando"*
27	1	1	*"a tempo"*
Bass clarinet:			
8	2	1	Add natural to F4
19	4	3	*"poco rit."*
26	2	1	Divide seven-measure rest into 6+1
26	8	1	*"poco allargando"*
27	1	1	*"a tempo"*
1st and 2nd bassoons:			
4	3	1	"soli"
4	5	3-4	Add *tenuto* lines
4	6	1-2	Add *tenuto* lines
4	6	3-4	Add *staccato* dots
19	4	1	*"poco rit."*
26	2	1	Divide seven-measure rest into 6+1
26	8	1	*"poco allargando"*
27	1	1	*"a tempo"* "mf"
27	4	1	"f"
27	6	1	"ff"
Contrabassoon:			
15	1-2	1	Add slur
26	2	1	Divide seven-measure rest into 6+1

Rehearsal Num.	Measure	Beat	Correction
26	8	1	*"poco allargando"*
27	1	1	*"a tempo"* *"mf"*
27	4	1	*"f"*
Alto saxophone:			
22	5	1	*"mf"*
26	2	1	Divide seven-measure rest into 6+1
26	8	1	*"poco allargando"*
27	1	1	*"a tempo"* *"mf"*
27	4	1	*"f"*
27	6	1	*"ff"*
Tenor saxophone:			
17	9	1	Remove *crescendo* mark
26	8	1	*"poco allargando"*
27	1	1	*"a tempo"* *"mf"*
27	4	1	*"f"*
Baritone saxophone:			
24	7-8	All	Add *tenuto* lines
24	9	1-2	Add slur
26	8	1	*"poco allargando"*
27	1	1	*"a tempo"* *"mf"*
27	4	1	*"f"*
1st trumpet:			
17	3-4	All	Add "3" to each sixteenth note triplet
17	6-8	All	Add "3" to each sixteenth note triplet
2nd 20	1	1	Change to rehearsal number 21
23	2,4	4	Add *tenuto* lines to quarter notes
27	6	1-2	Remove accent marks
26	8	1	*"poco allargando"*
27	1	1	*"a tempo"*
2nd trumpet:			
3	8	1	Change dotted-half note A4 to middle C4
6	8	1	Extend slur into rehearsal number 7
7	3	1	Change whole note A4 to half note first-line E4
7	3	3	Add half note D4 below staff, slur into m. 4
11	3	All	Add accent marks (<) to first note of each sixteenth note triplet
13	1-4	3	Add *tenuto* lines to triplets

Rehearsal Num.	Measure	Beat	Correction
23	2,4	4	Add *tenuto* lines to quarter notes
26	8	1	Remove slur to beat one, second measure, rehearsal number 27
26	8	All	Add *tenuto* lines to quarter notes
26	8	1	"*poco allargando*"
27	1	1	"*a tempo*"

3rd trumpet:

13	1-4	3	Add *tenuto* lines to triplets
11	3	All	Add accent marks (<) to first note of each sixteenth note triplet
23	2,4	4	Add *tenuto* lines to quarter notes
25	8	4	Extend slur into m. 9
25	9	2-4	Add slur into m. 6, beat one
26	8	1	"*poco allargando*"
27	1	1	"*a tempo*"
27	5	2-4	Add *crescendo* mark

1st cornet:

22	6,8	4	Add *tenuto* lines to quarter notes
23	1-2		Break slur between measures
24	4	All	Add *tenuto* lines to all pitches
26	8	1	"*poco allargando*"
27	1	1	"*a tempo*"
27	4	2-4	Add *crescendo* mark

2nd cornet:

3	6	1	Add *tenuto* line
3	9	Double bar	Add fermata
17	1-2	All	Add "3" to each sixteenth note triplet
17	5-8	All	Add "3" to each sixteenth note triplet
21	9	1-2	Add *tenuto* lines
22	6,8	4	Add *tenuto* lines to quarter notes
23	1	4	Change D4 to first-space F4
26	8	1	"*poco allargando*"
27	1	1	"*a tempo*"
27	4	2-4	Add *crescendo* mark

3rd cornet:

6	8	3	Extend slur into rehearsal number 7
7	3	3	Change slur beginning to first beat; extend into m. 5
7	5-6	1	Break slur between measures
17	5-8	All	Add "3" to each sixteenth note triplet

Rehearsal Num.	Measure	Beat	Correction
21	6	All	Add *crescendo* mark
22	6,8	4	Add *tenuto* lines to quarter notes
25	1	1-2	Break slur between beats
26	8	1	"*poco allargando*"
27	1	1	"*a tempo*"
27	4	2-4	Add *crescendo* mark

1st and 2nd F horn:

6	1-4	All	Add slur to second horn extending to fourth beat, m. 4
7	7	1	Add reminder natural to 2nd horn B4
26	8	1	"*poco allargando*"
27	1	1	"*a tempo*"
27	3	2	"*f*"

3rd and 4th F horn:

11	2	All	Add accent marks (<) to first note of each sixteenth note triplet
24	4	All	Remove *crescendo* mark; add *tenuto* marks to each pitch
25	9	2-4	Add slur into m. 10
26	8	1	"*poco allargando*"
27	1	1	"*a tempo*"
27	2	2	"*f*"

1st trombone:

7	5-6		Break slur between measures
26	8	1	"*poco allargando*"
27	1	1	"*a tempo*"
27	2	2	"*mf*"
27	2	2-4	Add *crescendo* mark

2nd trombone:

6	8	1	Remove *crescendo* mark
26	8	1	"*poco allargando*"
27	1	1	"*a tempo*"
27	2	1	"*mf*"

3rd trombone:

7	6-10	1	Add long slur
24	9	1-2	Add slur
26	8	1	"*poco allargando*"
27	1	1	"*a tempo*"
27	2	1	"*mf*"

REHEARSAL NUM.	MEASURE	BEAT	CORRECTION
Baritone bass clef:			
7	9	1	Extend slur into m. 10
26	2	1	Divide seven-measure rest into 6+1
26	8	1	*"poco allargando"*
27	1	1	*"a tempo"*
27	1	2	*"f"*
Baritone treble clef:			
7	9	1	Extend slur into m. 10
21	12	1-3	Add *crescendo* mark
25	1	1-2	Break slur
25	9	2-4	Add slur into m. 10
26	8	1	*"poco allargando"*
27	1	1	*"a tempo"*
27	1	2	*"f"*
Basses (tubas):			
21	6	1	*"mf"*
26	8	1	Remove slur; *"poco allargando"*
27	1	1	*"a tempo"*
27	1	1	*"mf"*
27	4	1	*"f"*
Timpani:			
2	7	All	Add *crescendo* mark to timpano 1
2	8	1	Add *"sfz"* to timpano 1
3	8	1	"II."
4	9	1	"I."
12	10	4	"solo"
26	2	1	Divide seven-measure rest into 6+1
26	8	1	*"poco allargando"*
27	1	1	*"a tempo"*
27	1	1	*"mf"*
27	4	1	*"f"*
Percussion:			
	1-5	1	Add roll slashes to whole notes
	5	2-4	Add roll slashes to second snare drum dotted-half note
	5	2	Remove *"fp"* from second snare drum part; add *"p"*
2	7-8	1	Add roll slashes to whole notes
11	10	1	"One snare drum"
12	10	2	"Snares off"
21	1	1	"Snares on"

REHEARSAL NUM.	MEASURE	BEAT	CORRECTION
23	1	1	Add reminder "*mf*" to tambourine and wood block parts
24	1	1	Add "*f*" to bass drum part; add reminder "*mf*" to snare, tambourine, and wood block parts; add reminder "*f*" to xylophone and temple block parts
26	1	1	Divide eight-measure rest into 7+1
26	8	1	"*poco allargando*"
27	1	1	"*a tempo*"

Score:

REHEARSAL NUMBER	MEASURE	BEAT	INSTRUMENTS	CORRECTION OR DISCREPANCY
3	8	4	Oboes	"a2"
4	5	3-4	Bassoons	Add *tenuto* lines
4	6	1-2	Bassoons	Add *tenuto* lines
4	6	3-4	Bassoons	Add *staccato* dots
4	9	1	Timpani	"I."
6	8	3	3rd trumpet, 3rd cornet	Extend slur into rehearsal number 7
11	1	5	3rd clarinet	F-sharp in score, G-flat in part
11	2	5	3rd clarinet	F-sharp in score, G-flat in part
11	2	5	Alto clarinet	G-sharp in score, A-flat in part
11	2	5	Bass clarinet	F-sharp in score, G-flat in part
11	2	5	Baritone saxophone	C-sharp in score, D-flat in part
11	3	5	3rd clarinet	F-sharp in score, G-flat in part
11	3	6	E-flat clarinet	Add natural to G5
11	4	3	1st trumpet	E-sharp in score, F-natural in part
11	4	4	2nd clarinet	E-flat in score, D-sharp in part
11	4	4	2nd trumpet	E-flat in score, D-sharp in part
11	4	5	2nd trumpet	G-flat in score, F-sharp in part

REHEARSAL NUMBER	MEASURE	BEAT	INSTRUMENTS	CORRECTION OR DISCREPANCY
11	4	4	3rd trumpet	B-flat in score, A-sharp in part
11	5	4	2nd clarinet	E-flat in score, D-sharp in part
11	5	3	1st trumpet	E-sharp in score, F-natural in part
11	5	4	2nd trumpet	E-flat in score, D-sharp in part
11	5	5	2nd trumpet	G-flat in score, F-sharp in part
11	5	4	3rd trumpet	B-flat in score, A-sharp in part
11	6-8	All	2nd trumpet	E-flats in score, D-sharps in part; G-flats in score, F-sharps in part
11	6-8	All	3rd trumpet	B-flats in score, A-sharps in part; D-flats in score, C-sharps in part
11	6	1	Percussion	"2 snare drums"
11	8	1	Baritone saxophone	G-sharp in score, A-flat in part; E-sharp in score, F-natural in part
12	1	1	Piccolo	G-sharp in score, A-flat in part
12	1	4	2nd flute	C-flat in score, B in part
12	1	1	1st clarinet	A-sharp in score, B-flat in part
12	1	2	1st clarinet	G-sharp in score, A-flat in part
12	1	1	3rd clarinet	E-flat in score, D-sharp in part
12	1	2	3rd clarinet	B-sharp in score, C-natural in part; C-sharp in score, D-flat in part
12	1	3	3rd clarinet	A-sharp in score, B-flat in part; C-flat in score, B-natural in part

Rehearsal Number	Measure	Beat	Instruments	Correction or Discrepancy
12	1	4	3rd clarinet	G-sharp in score, A-flat in part
12	1	1	Xylophone	G-sharp in score, A-flat in part
12	1	2	Xylophone	F-sharp in score, G-flat in part
12	2	1	2nd clarinet	C-flat in score, B in part
12	2	1	Xylophone	C-sharp in score, D-flat in part
12	2	4	Xylophone	G-sharp in score, A-flat in part
12	3	2	2nd flute	C-flat in score, B in part
12	3	2	2nd oboe	C-flat in score, B in part
12	3	3	3rd clarinet	A-flat in score, G-sharp in part
12	3	4	3rd clarinet	E-sharp in score, F-natural in part; F-sharp in score, G-flat in part
12	4	1	Piccolo	B-natural in score, C-flat in part
12	4	1	2nd flute	G-flat in score; F-sharp in part
12	4	1	2nd oboe	G-flat in score; F-sharp in part
12	4	2	2nd oboe	A-flat in score, G-sharp in part
12	4	2	E-flat clarinet	A-flat in score, G-sharp in part
12	4	1	2nd clarinet	G-sharp in score, A-flat in part
12	4	1	1st and 2nd clarinet	C-sharp in score, D-flat in part
12	4	1	3rd clarinet	G-sharp in score, A-flat in part
12	4	1	Xylophone	B-natural in score, C-flat in part

REHEARSAL NUMBER	MEASURE	BEAT	INSTRUMENTS	CORRECTION OR DISCREPANCY
12	5	1	1st clarinet	D-sharp in score, E-flat in part; C-sharp in score, D-flat in part
12	5	4	1st and 2nd clarinets	Add reminder natural to first-line E4
12	5	1	Alto clarinet	A-sharp in score, B-flat in part; G-sharp in score, A-flat in part
12	6	1	Alto clarinet	A-sharp in score, B-flat in part
12	6-8	All	1st and 2nd clarinets	C-sharps in score, D-flats in part; B-sharps in score, C-naturals in part
12	6	All	Bass clarinet	A-sharps in score, B-flats in part; G-double-sharps in score, as in part
12	6	All	2nd bassoon	G-sharps in score, A-flats in part; F-double-sharps in score, Gs in part
12	7	1	Bass clarinet	A-sharp in score, B-flat in part
12	7	1	2nd bassoon	G-sharp in score, A-flat in part
12	8	1	Bass clarinet	A-sharp in score, B-flat in part
12	8	1	2nd bassoon	G-sharp in score, A-flat in part
15	1	3	English horn	C-sharp in score, D-flat in part
15	1	3	Alto saxophone	D-sharp in score, E-flat in part
15	1	3	Tenor saxophone	G-sharp in score, A-flat in part
15	2	6	2nd cornet	Add reminder flat to E-flat5
15	4	6	2nd cornet	Add reminder natural to F5

Rehearsal Number	Measure	Beat	Instruments	Correction or Discrepancy
15	5	3	2nd trombone	A-sharp in score, B-flat in part
15	7	2	E-flat clarinet	E-sharps in score, F-naturals in part; C-sharp in score, D-flat in part
15	7	3	E-flat clarinet	G-sharp in score; A-flat in part
16	2	2	E-flat clarinet	F-sharps in score; G-flats in part
16	2	3	E-flat clarinet	A-sharps in score, B-flats in part; D-sharp in score, E-flats in part
16	2	1	Alto clarinet	A-sharp in score, B-flat in part
16	2	2	Alto clarinet	D-sharp in score, E-flat in part; F-sharp in score, G-flat in part
16	2	1,3	Tenor saxophone	G-sharps in score, A-flats in part
16	2	1	Baritone saxophone	A-sharp in score, B-flat in part
16	2	1,3	2nd trombone	F-sharps in score, G-flats in part
16	4	4	Oboes	Reminder flats in both parts
16	4	1	Alto clarinet	G-sharp in score, A-flat in part
16	4	2-3	Alto clarinet	B-sharp in score, C-natural in part; D-sharps in score, E-flats in part
16	4	1	Bass clarinet	G-sharp in score, A-flat in part
16	4	2-3	Bass clarinet	C-sharp in score, D-flat in part; E-sharps in score, F-naturals in part
16	4	1	Baritone saxophone	A-flat in score, G-sharp in part
16	4	1	3rd trombone, bass	C-flat in score, B in part

REHEARSAL NUMBER	MEASURE	BEAT	INSTRUMENTS	CORRECTION OR DISCREPANCY
17	3	1	Alto clarinet	F-double-sharp in score, g-natural in part
17	3	1	Bass clarinet	B-sharp in score, C-natural in part
17	3	1-2	1st horn	E-sharps in score, Fs in part
17	5	2	Bass clarinet	D-sharp in score, E-flat in part
17	5	2	Alto saxophone	A-sharp in score, B-flat in part
17	5	3	Tenor saxophone	B-flat in score, A-sharp in part
17	5	2	1st and 2nd horns	A-sharps in score, B-flats in part
17	5	2	1st trombone	C-sharp in score, D-flat in part
17	5	2	3rd trombone	F-sharp in score, G-flat in part
17	6	1	Tenor saxophone	D-flat in score, C-sharp in part
17	6	1	2nd trombone	C-flat in score, B-natural in part
17	6	1	3rd trombone	G-flat in score, F-sharp in part
17	7	3	Baritone saxophone	D-sharp in score, E-flat in part
17	7	3	3rd trombone	F-sharp in score, G-flat in part
17	7	2	Bass	E-flat in score, D-sharp in part
17	8	2	Bassoons	G-sharp in score, A-flat in part
22	3-4	1	2nd bassoon	Add tie
22	6,8	4	Cornets	Add *tenuto* lines to quarter notes
23	1	1	Percussion	Add reminder "*mf*" to tambourine and wood block parts
23	2,4	4	Trumpets	Add *tenuto* lines to quarter notes

REHEARSAL NUMBER	MEASURE	BEAT	INSTRUMENTS	CORRECTION OR DISCREPANCY
24	1	1	Percussion	Add "*f*" to bass drum part; add reminder "*mf*" to snare drum, tambourine, and wood block parts; add reminder "*f*" to xylophone and temple block parts
24	1-6	All	Timpani	Rolls on sixteenth notes marked "tr" in part
24	7-8	All	Contrabassoon, baritone saxophone	Add *tenuto* lines to each pitch
24	9	1-2	Baritone saxophone	Add slur
24	9	2-3	Timpani	Tied quarter notes are half note in part
26	1-2	All	Piccolo, 1st flute, 1st oboe	Add slur over two measures
26	3-4	1	2nd flute	Add slur over two measures
26	3	2-3	2nd and 3rd trumpets	Exchange parts
26	4	All	2nd and 3rd trumpets	Exchange parts
26	3	2-3	2nd and 3rd cornets	Exchange parts
26	4	All	2nd and 3rd cornets	Exchange parts
26	5	3	2nd clarinet, 2nd trumpet, 2nd cornet	Tied eighth notes are a quarter note in the part
26	6	1	2nd flute, 2nd clarinet, 2nd trumpet, 2nd cornet	Tied eighth notes are a quarter note in the part
26	7	3	2nd flute, 2nd clarinet, 2nd trumpet, 2nd cornet	Tied eighth notes are a quarter note in the part
26	7	1	Horns	Extend slur into rehearsal number 27

REHEARSAL NUMBER	MEASURE	BEAT	INSTRUMENTS	CORRECTION OR DISCREPANCY
26	8	1	1st and 3rd trumpets, 1st and 3rd cornets	Add slur extending to end of second beat, second measure, rehearsal number 27
27	1	1	Bassoons, contrabassoon, saxophones, 2nd and 3rd trombones, timpani	"*mf*"
27	1	2	Bass clarinet, 1st trombone, baritone	"*mf*"
27	2	2	English horn, alto clarinet, 3rd and 4th horns	"*f*"
27	3	1	Contrabassoon, baritone saxophone	"*f*"
27	3	2	3rd clarinet, 1st and 2nd horns	"*f*"
27	4	1	Alto saxophone, tenor saxophone, 2nd bassoon, 2nd and 3rd trombones, bass, timpani	"*f*"
27	4	2	1st clarinet, cornets baritone	"*ff*"
27	6-7	1,3	Horns	Tied eighth notes are quarter notes in part
27	6	1	3rd clarinet, bassoons, saxophones	"*ff*"

Unit 5: Stylistic Considerations

Finding the "*Tempo moderato*" at the beginning of *Laude* is the conductor's biggest challenge. The tempi of the variations derive from the initial one: theme (quarter note = 73); variation one, "*doppio movimento*" (twice as fast); variation two, "*Tempo primo.*" Variation three is in an unrelated tempo: eighth note = 176. Variations four and five are in the same tempo: quarter note = 60.

The tempo in variation five (quarter note = 60) results from the *poco allargando* in the previous section. The *"Tempo primo, giustamente"* (original tempo, strictly) of variation seven must be right to accommodate the thirty-second notes coming in the woodwinds.

THEME:

In the introduction, percussionists must be aware of the absence of a *forte-piano* on the second beat of m. 5. This sets up the *crescendo* into the entrance of the theme at rehearsal number 1.

The slurs with *tenuto* lines over the notes in the chorale theme denote a tongued articulation, like *legato* organ playing. The articulation of the fanfares between chorale phrases must contrast with the accompanying rolls as well as the preceding phrases. Use a light portamento (slurred dots) tongue to achieve this. The two phrases at rehearsal number 2 should be connected almost without a breath. Tubas should be especially careful to stagger their breathing because their first entrance has attracted the listeners' attention. The percussion roll in m. 3 after rehearsal number 3 should extend to the first beat of the next measure to help connect the two phrases. A slight break before the final timpani note of the theme will help to synchronize the release of the whole note in the winds.

VARIATION ONE:

If the two tambourines in this variation tend to cover the bassoons and oboes, the percussionists may, as a last resort, substitute fingers for snare drum sticks. Musicians should take care to interpret the sixteenth notes with precision. At rehearsal number 7, the woodwinds should play the ascending scales with sufficient brightness to be heard through the extended cadence in the brasses.

VARIATION TWO:

Variation two is played in the same style as the theme, with the same attention given to contrast in articulation between the melody and the cadential fanfares. The *senza misura* measure for a minimum of six trumpets and cornets in unison presents intonation problems that the performers should solve together outside of rehearsal.

VARIATION THREE:

The six beats of each measure do not easily divide into 3+3. Use a beat pattern that emphasizes the downbeat but does not emphasize beat four. Percussionists should be aware that, unlike the winds, their parts do not have accents on each beat. Performers should take care to differentiate between the sixteenth note triplets and the dotted rhythms. Clarinets must count carefully in the second ending so they can end together. Timpani have a nine-measure rest before the final solo. Give the players sufficient warning before cueing.

VARIATION FOUR:

The high A5s in the trumpets and cornets can dominate the texture in this variation. It may help to imagine the *mezzo forte* on this pitch as a soft dynamic. The passage for unison trumpets beginning at rehearsal number 14 has no written *crescendo* leading to the high C-sharp6. This is another intonation problem to be solved outside of rehearsal. The trumpeters should imagine a *decrescendo* while increasing breath support as the pitches go higher. All other parts should give dynamic support to the trumpet players in this passage. Determine breathing points in this variation to avoid large breaks at bar lines. The horns' pedal point at rehearsal number 14 changes from the cornets' concert G to B-flat for four measures before returning to G.

VARIATION FIVE:

The theme that carries over from variation four should be quiet enough to hear the triplet fanfares that constitute a new element. Trumpet and cornet articulations should be soft enough to match those of the overlapping horns and woodwinds. At rehearsal number 17, Hanson has written a rhythmic *accelerando*. Because it is already in the music, ignore the "*accel. poco a poco*" until the last two measures before the "*poco allarg.*" Make the brasses and contrabassoon aware of a dynamic target for the end of the *decrescendo* from *fortissimo* to help balance the final chords.

VARIATION SIX:

Make sure the clarinets and horns agree on the level of *pianissimo* as they exchange the *ostinato* chord pattern. The tempo in this variation is somewhat independent of the others. It must be fast enough that the four *ritardandos* can be effective.

VARIATION SEVEN:

As clarinets and horns begin the *ostinato* that dominates this variation, piccolo, flute, and percussion must balance their parts carefully. As each new element enters, all other layers should be balanced so all parts can be heard. At rehearsal numbers 23 and 24, most instruments continue at *mezzo forte* in spite of new instruments' entrances at *forte* or *fortissimo*. Resist the temptation to slow down before rehearsal number 25. Hanson's tempo marking includes the word *giustamente*: keep the tempo strictly. Hanson placed *poco allargando* markings only where he wanted them to occur.

Unit 6: Musical Elements

Hanson, who once introduced Schoenberg to an audience as "the man who made us conscious of the beauty of the major triad," around the time he composed *Laude* correctly predicted the future of neo-romanticism in late twentieth century concert music:

> I recognize, of course, that romanticism is, at the present time, the poor stepchild.... Nevertheless, I embrace her all the more fervently, believing, as I do, that romanticism will find in this country rich soil for a new, young and vigorous youth.

Although his theoretical book *Harmonic Materials of Modern Music* describes a largely mathematical approach to musical composition and analysis, romanticism always dominates *Laude*. This stems from the strong triadic structure of the chorale theme.

Because Hanson intended *Laude* for a large festival band, it has monumental proportions with big climaxes and extended cadences.

The chorale *cantus firmus* is in bar form (AAB), particularly associated with both sacred and secular German strophic songs. The repeated antecedent-consequent period consists of pairs of two-measure phrases. The first phrase ends with an imperfect cadence on a G-major tonic chord, and the second phrase ends with a half cadence on the dominant. The final period reverses the structure, the first two-measure phrase ending with a half cadence, and the final three-measure phrase ending in a full cadence.

Rhythmically, the chorale is straightforward, each period beginning with repeated quarter notes. In the repeated period the marching quarter note movement pauses only for cadences, and in the last period the movement slows to two half notes approaching the final cadence.

Hanson's presentation of the chorale stretches out the ends of each phrase, interpolating fanfares, and making the chorale tune seem more irregular than it was originally. The final cadence stretches out into a four-measure extension.

Beginning with the second period (rehearsal number 2), Hanson harmonizes the chorale with non-chord tones or passing chords on nearly every beat. In the final period, the rhythmic activity increases, with the addition of passing eighth notes.

Variation one is in the form of a chorale prelude, pitting a dotted eighth and sixteenth variation against an augmentation of the theme. Particularly interesting is the ten-measure extension of the final cadence, during which woodwinds play a different ascending scale or mode in each measure. For each new scale the beginning pitch moves down a step. The variation ends with a non-functional cadence.

Variation two mirrors the chorale's opening statement, but the melody appears in inversion, and the percussion do not play. A *senza misura* measure transition to variation three features all trumpets and cornets sustaining the first four pitches of the chorale's inversion: G4, B-flat4, A4, C5. This four-pitch motive becomes the basis for the next four variations.

Variation three is a fantasy on the four-note inversion motive. It begins with a six-pitch *ostinato* that begins with the inversion motive in reiterated triplets. It is repeated once, then transposed up a step. In dotted rhythms, the inversion motive then ascends in sequence. Cornets mimic the end of the sequence with a rising minor third. A xylophone joins the sequence, and the rising minor third becomes a fanfare to descending dotted scales in the woodwinds, fading into nothing. Timpani provide a satisfying final cadence, loudly dropping a fifth.

Variation four is a chaconne characterized by a four-chord *ostinato*: G minor, G half-diminished seventh, C major, and E-flat major. Contained within this chord progression is the inversion motive transposed up a fifth: D, F, E, G.

In variation five, the chaconne chord progression repeats in sequence while fast triplet fanfares emanate from throughout the band. At rehearsal number 7, the harmonic rhythm doubles in tempo. After four more measures, it increases by two thirds again to quarter notes. The climax arrives four measures later, when a G-major chord resolves on a C-major chord in first inversion, root movement of a fourth after so many root movements in thirds. Hanson extends this cadence by five measures.

Variation six provides a respite before the large, extended ending. It continues the chaconne in E minor. After the *ostinato* is heard twice, the solo clarinet enters with a resetting of the chorale in four parallel periods, the final period extended to a cadence on a Picardy third in A minor.

Variation seven is the final praise to the Lord. Returning to the key of G in Lydian mode, it begins with the chorale in ten-beat phrases. The first phrase of the chorale then repeats as an *ostinato* while variations and diminutions enter in layers. The work reaches a *tutti* climax ("Everything that hath breath") at rehearsal number 24, with nine rhythmic patterns going at once.

The passage between rehearsal numbers 25 and 26 introduces a new theme from Hanson's *Third Symphony* that shares an initial descending minor third with the *cantus firmus*. This theme provides a break before the final chorale statement at rehearsal number 26. This contrapuntal statement uses the second species (2 notes vs. 1) and the fourth species (2 notes vs. 1 with ties across the beat). Ending the work is an imitative coda on motives first heard in the final cadence of variation one.

Unit 7: Form and Structure

Section	Event and Scoring
Chorale: *Tempo moderato* (quarter note = 72)	"The composition begins with the chorale theme in unison with the simple accompaniment of percussion and short fanfares." (Hanson, CBDNA Address, 1975)
mm. 1-4	Introduction, two timpani in overlapping octave rolls and two overlapping snare drums, rolling

SECTION	EVENT AND SCORING
Rehearsal number 1	Chorale, period a, brass and saxophone, unison with trumpet, cornet, and woodwind fanfares
Rehearsal number 2	Chorale, period a, harmonized brasses with cornet and woodwind fanfares
Rehearsal number 3	Chorale, period b: *tutti*
mm. 27-30	Final cadence, extended
Variation 1: *Allegro, doppio movimento* (quarter note = 44)	"It is followed by seven variations in varying moods and tempi." Dotted eighths and sixteenths
mm. 1-3	Introduction: two tambourines: *ostinato* throughout variation
mm. 4-8	Period a, Phrase 1 vs. phrase 2: bassoon 1 and 2, oboe 1 and 2, clarinet 1 and 2, tenor saxophone, baritone saxophone soli
mm. 9-11	Fanfares: trumpets, cornets, piccolo, flutes, E-flat clarinet
Rehearsal number 5	Period a, Phrase 1 vs. Phrase 2: bass clarinet and bassoons, oboes, and clarinets
Rehearsal number 6	Period b: brasses in half notes; counterpoint in dotted eighths and sixteenths: piccolo and flutes
Rehearsal number 7	Final cadence, extended; brasses accompanied by dotted eighth and sixteenth note ascending modal scales in each measure; woodwinds, section by section; oboes and bassoons: G major; clarinets and bass clarinets, F lydian; flutes: E phrygian; oboes and bassoons: E-flat lydian; clarinets and bass clarinets, D phrygian; oboes, English horn, and bassoons: C overtone; piccolo, flutes, and 2nd clarinets: 3rd mode of G melodic minor (on B-flat); oboes and 1st clarinets: A locrian; piccolo and flutes: G phrygian
Variation 2: *Tempo primo* (quarter note = 72)	Chorale in inversion, G aeolian
mm. 1-4	Period a: unison soprano, alto and bass clarinets
mm. 5-7	Fanfares in fifths: first clarinets over low brass and timpani C-minor triad in first inversion
Rehearsal number 9	Period a: harmonized in soprano, alto, and bass clarinets, bassoons, tenor and baritone saxophones

Section	Event and Scoring
mm. 12-14	Fanfares in fifths: flutes, oboes, and clarinets over low brass and timpani C-minor triad in first inversion
Rehearsal number 10	Period b: harmonized in horns, low brasses, bassoon, and contrabassoon
mm. 20-22	Fanfares in fifths: flutes, oboes, and clarinets over horn, low brasses, and timpani open fifth on G
m. 23, *senza misura*	Inversion motive (pitches G4, B-flat4, A4, C5): fermatas in trumpets and cornets
Variation 3: *Allegro molto* (eighth note = 176)	Development of inversion motive and fanfare: 6/8 and 4/8 meter: sixteenth note triplets on repeated pitches and dotted sixteenths and thirty-second notes, repeated and *diminuendo*, ending with descending fifth in timpani, *fortissimo*
Variation 4: (quarter note = 60)	Triple meter, chaconne in brasses, bassoons, and saxophones on four chords: G minor, G half-diminished, C major, E-flat major over a G pedal, *diminuendo* to timpani roll *crescendo* leading to variation five
Variation 5: *Stesso* tempo	Chromatic motive from variation four extended in low brasses and with sixteenth note triplet fanfares in all high parts; chaconne chord pattern transposed every four measures
Rehearsal number 17	Inversion motive becomes scale in minor thirds, with written-out *accelerando*, first in dotted-quarter notes, then quarter notes; with repeated sixteenth note triplets in trumpets, cornets, and horns
mm. 21-26	Final cadence in aeolian mode on E with Picardy third
Variation 6: *Lento* (quarter note = 60)	Chorale returns
Rehearsal number 18	*Ostinato* passage continues in half notes: soprano, alto, and bass clarinets alternating with horns
m. 5	Chorale period a modified: solo clarinet, chords continue

SECTION	EVENT AND SCORING
Rehearsal number 19	Chorale period a remodified: solo clarinet continues, chromatic motive from variation four in accompaniment over E pedal in bass clarinet
Rehearsal number 20	Solo clarinet repeats first two periods of variation and finishes with three-measure deceptive cadence on A major
Variation 7: *Tempo primo, giustamente* (quarter note = 72)	"Until variation seven when the chorale melody appears, not in the conventional harmonization, but in the ancient Lydian mode, praising the Lord, as the Psalmist sings," (Hanson, 1975)
Rehearsal number 22	"With loud sounding cymbals, with high sounding cymbals,"
Rehearsal number 24	"With timpani, drums, bells, working up a *crescendo* which becomes, I hope, a veritable avalanche of sound, the percussion inundating the hall with the sound and, literally, 'everything that has breath praising the Lord.'"
Rehearsal number 25	"Suddenly out of this mass of sound appears a simple melody associated with my third symphony and memories of my childhood – and, in some subtle way, which I do not myself understand, with the ancient chorale itself."
Rehearsal number 26	"Above its final cadence is superimposed the serene beauty of the Lutheran chorale, which then moves to its final climax."
Rehearsal number 27	Coda

Unit 8: Suggested Listening

Howard Hanson:

> *Laude*. Rutgers University Ensemble and Chamber Winds. William Berz, Rutgers University Wind Ensemble. Mark, MCD-2002.

> *Laude*. *Laude*. Frederick Fennell, Tokyo Kosei Wind Orchestra. KOCD-three578.

> *Symphony No. 3, Op. 33*. Howard Hanson, Eastman-Rochester Orchestra. New York: Mercury, 1991.

> *Symphony No. 3, Op. 33*. Howard Hanson Symphonies, vol. 2. Gerard Schwarz, Seattle Symphony Orchestra, notes by Steven C. Smith. Hollywood, CA: Delos International, Inc., 1990, DE 3092.

Unit 9: Additional References and Resources

"CBDNA Commissions." *College Band Directors National Association*, 11 November 1998. Online: Internet address http://cbdna.org/cbdna_commissions.html (5 May 1999).

"ELCA Family History Answerer." *National Symphony Orchestra*, September 1996. Online: Internet address http://wwwtest.elca.org/co/timeline/1996.html. (29 May 1999).

Hanson, Howard. *Harmonic Materials of Music: Resources of the Tempered Scale*. New York: Appleton-Century-Crofts, Inc., 1960.

Hanson, Howard. *Laude: Chorale, Variations and Metamorphoses*. New York: Boosey and Hawkes, 1976.

Hanson, Howard. *Symphony No. 3, Op. 33*. New York: Carl Fischer, Inc., 1941.

Holvik, Karl M. CBDNA *President's News-Letter 3* (February, 1974) 1-2.

Johnson, Barry Wayne. *Analytic Study of the Band Compositions of Howard Hanson*. Ann Arbor, MI: UMI Company, 1987.

Perone, James L. *Howard Hanson: A Bio-bibliography*. Westport, CT: Greenwood Press, 1993.

Randel, Don, ed. *The New Harvard Dictionary of Music*. Cambridge, MA.: The Belknap Press of Harvard University, 1986.

Rehrig, William. *The Heritage Encyclopedia of Band Music*. Edited by Paul R. Bierley. Westerville, OH: Integrity Press, 1991.

Sadie, Stanley, ed. *New Grove Dictionary of Music*. London: MacMillan Press, 1986.

Wantanabe, Ruth. "About Howard Hanson." *Institute for American Music History*, 27 September 1998. Online: Internet address http://www.cc.rochester.edu/Eastman/iam/history.html (29 May 1999).

Williams, David Russell. *Conversations with Howard Hanson*. Arkadelphia, AR: Delta Publications, 1988.

Williams, David Russell. "Howard Hanson (1896-1981)," *Perspectives of New Music* 20/1&2 (1981-1982), 12-25.

Contributed by:
Ibrook Tower
Wind Ensemble Director
Pennsylvania Academy of Music
Lancaster, Pennsylvania

and

Instrumental Music Instructor
Milton Hershey School
Hershey, Pennsylvania

Teacher Resource Guide

Medieval Suite
I. Homage to Leonin
II. Homage to Perotin
III. Homage to Machaut

Ron Nelson
(b. 1929)

Unit 1: Composer

Dr. Ron Nelson is a native of Joliet, Illinois. He received bachelor's (1952), master's (1953), and doctorate (1956) degrees from the Eastman School, where he studied with Howard Hanson and Bernard Rogers. He studied in France at the *Ecole Normale de Musique* and at the Paris Conservatory under a Fulbright Grant in 1955. Dr. Nelson joined the Brown University faculty the following year as an Assistant Professor and was promoted to the rank of Associate Professor in 1960 and Full Professor in 1968. He was awarded a Ford Foundation commission for an overture in 1961, a Lima Symphony Orchestra commission in 1962, and a Baptist Foreign Mission Society commission in 1964 for his hour-long oratorio, *What is Man?*. Dr. Nelson has gained wide recognition as a composer of choral, band, and orchestral works. He is the composer of a widely performed cantata, *The Christmas Story*, and an opera, *The Birthday of the Infant*. Other compositions include *Savannah River Holiday*, *Sarabande, For Katherine in April*, *Toccata for Orchestra*, *Rocky Point Holiday*, *Sonoran Desert Holiday*, and choral fanfares and background music for numerous documentary and educational films. In all, Ron Nelson has over fifty published compositions. He is currently living in Thousand Oaks, California.

Unit 2: Composition

Composed in 1981 and arranged for band in 1983, *Medieval Suite* was premiered by the Western Michigan University Symphonic Band. It is scored for full band plus English horn and contrabassoon. The suite is in three movements (times indicated for each):

I. Homage to Leonin (5:00)
II. Homage to Perotin (4:25)
III. Homage to Machaut (6:15)

There are parts for three trumpets and two cornets. The first movement calls for nine different clarinets (3,3,3) in order to cover all of the *divisi* sections. The second and third movements could be performed with as few as six clarinets. Although each movement can be performed separately, it is the composer's wish that all three movements be performed as a suite. A wide array of percussion is needed, including two marimbas, two vibraphones, crotales, and piano. Eight percussionists (plus piano) are therefore required (nine in Movement II) to perform all of the parts. The third movement has two different endings, depending upon whether the movement is performed separately or as part of the suite.

Unit 3: Historical Perspective

At the time this composition was written (1981), many well-known composers were writing for band, both for school groups and for more professional organizations. During the 1970s and 1980s, higher technical demands were being made by composers on the wind ensemble, perhaps spearheaded by Husa's *Music for Prague 1968* and Schwantner's *and the mountains rising nowhere* (1977). The Schwantner composition, in particular, exploited the percussion section's potential for becoming a third choir in the wind ensemble. The amount of percussion writing and performers required in *Medieval Suite* certainly give some credence to this idea. The composition also uses many of the compositional techniques similar to those of Ross Lee Finney. In particular, the use of both traditionally notated sections and aleatoric, celled figures is reminiscent of *Skating on the Cheyenne*. Finally, the 1970s and 1980s were an era of "retro-music," where many serious composers recalled ancient musical traditions.

Unit 4: Technical Considerations

MOVEMENT I (Homage to Leonin):
All members will be expected to perform one or more of the following: singing (range of an octave b-b), aleatoric performance of celled figures, random *accelerandos* and *ritardandos* on repeated pitches, and reading modern graphic notation. In particular, demands of aleatoric performance in the percussion section are considerable. There are no complex rhythms or articulations in the

movement. The tempo is marked at quarter note = 63 throughout most of the movement; there are a few minor tempo changes. The beginning and ending of the movement is aleatoric and (mostly) unmetered. Meters used are simple: 2/4, 3/4, and 4/4. The piano is an integral part of the percussion section and should not be taken lightly. There are no extreme range demands; there is one c-sharp3 for trumpet and one oboe solo.

MOVEMENT II (Homage to Perotin):
With the exception of a short passage by bass clarinet and marimba 1, the entire movement is written in conventional notation. Throughout, the meter is 6/8 at 132 beats per minute. All clarinets and trumpet 1 must play d3, and there is a tricky pattern at letter G involving repeated octave leaps in the flutes. There are no overly difficult rhythms; the tempo is the main technical factor.

MOVEMENT III (Homage to Machaut):
This movement is by far the most soloistic of the suite. Soli are required for flute, oboe, English horn, clarinet, alto clarinet (cued), a bass clarinet/string bass duet (cued), trumpet 1 and 2, horn, and trombone 1 and 2. Horn 1 and 3 must play a2, and clarinet 1 must play f-sharp3. Rhythm, meter, and tempo are quite simple. The last twelve measures are quite similar to the first movement and use many of the same compositional techniques.

Unit 5: Stylistic Considerations

In the most general sense, the suite is an ABA form, whereas the outer two movements are mostly *legato* and slurred while the second movement has many passages that are separated. In regards to the singing in the first and third movements, recording of chant might be helpful in order to understand the slight flexibilities of tempo used in the (current) performance practice of chant. Note that, in both movements where singing occurs, tempo indications are approximate. Nelson specifically indicates parts to be sung "...in a blended *sotto voce*" style. This would seem to indicate both equal blending of men's and women's voices, as well as a singing technique free of unnecessary vibrato. Aleatoric cells in the outer movements have some freedom of tempo, too; use the given rhythms as a guide. Instrument parts in the outer movements give excellent opportunities for playing longer lines with expressive phrasing (e.g., *crescendo* and *diminuendo*). The conductor has quite a bit of interpretive freedom. In the second movement, articulations and phrasing must be more standardized, as a constant tempo is used nearly throughout the movement. In particular, the concept of hemiola gives excellent opportunities for the teaching of duple versus triple meter. The second movement is more similar in style to many of Nelson's better-known works for band. Throughout, extreme care must be taken not to let the percussion section dominate the group timbre; careful consideration of mallet instrument placement in the ensemble will help with this challenge.

Unit 6: Musical Elements

As would be expected, the harmony used throughout is modal, certainly not tonal in the traditional sense. Even in the second movement, tone clusters and the use of pedal define much of the harmony. Some discussion or examples of modal harmony might be helpful. The medieval motet defined tonal centers through many of the same devices Nelson uses, such as repetition of pitches, prevalence of fifths and fourths, and rhythmic *ostinato*. Melody in the outer movements is largely based on the e dorian scale (singing) and stepwise motion (instrumental). The second movement is more closely aligned with motet practice of the fourteenth and fifteenth centuries. The texture in most of the suite is quite thick, but some wonderfully chamber-like passages are written in the outer movements. In regards to rhythm, Nelson has used everything from improvisatory passages and unmetered pitches to highly contrapuntal hemiola figures in 6/8 meter.

Unit 7: Form and Structure

MEASURE	TONAL CENTER	SECTION
Movement I: "Homage to Leonin"		
ABA arch form		
1-21		A (beginning to C)
1-2	e dorian	Introduction
3-21	e dorian	A
22-78		B and Development (C to F)
22-39	Varies	Minimalist development of chant; euphonium f diminished scale over e pedal
40-47		Continued layering in of instruments
48-68		a-flat diminished chant material over increasing parallel harmony
69-78		Climax and transition: b minor material over e pedal
79-89	e dorian	A (F to end) Similar to beginning, but shortened and used as coda
Movement II: "Homage to Perotin"		
Arch form		
1-6	C pedal with modal harmony	Introduction (Beginning-A)
7-39		Fanfare (letter A-B)
40-73		A (letter B-D)
40-56		a1

MEASURE	TONAL CENTER	SECTION
51-73		a2 (elaborated)
74-117	c minor over b-flat pedal	B (letter D-F)
74-92		b1
93-117	Transition to F	Fanfare 2
118-152	f pedal quasi "V"	Development (letter F-H)
153-186	c minor over b-flat pedal	B (letter H-J); shortened with transition
187-194	c pedal	Introduction repeat (letter J-K)
195-228		A (includes a1 and a2) (letter K-M)
229-267		Fanfare, used as coda (M-end)

Movement III: "Homage to Machaut"
Strophic – three verses with coda

1-12	d minor	Verse 1 (beginning-B); 5+4+3 phrases
13-24	d minor	Verse 2 (letter B-D); 5+4+3 phrases
25-43	d minor then transition	Verse 3 (D-1 after F); 5+4+5+4+2 phrases
44-47	e dorian	Coda (if performed separately)
48-59	e dorian	Coda (if performed as a suite)

Coda material comes from first movement for cyclical effect.

Unit 8: Suggested Listening

Bob Margolis:
  Color
  Terpsichore
Ron Nelson:
  Epiphanies
  Passacaglia
  Rocky Point Holiday
Fisher Tull, *Sketches on a Tudor Psalm*

Unit 9: Additional References and Resources

Huggins, Dom, ed. *The New Oxford History of Music*: vol. 2: Early Medieval Music up to 1300. London: Oxford University Press, 1969.

Parrish, Carl, ed. *A Treasury of Early Music*. New York: W.W. Norton and Co., 1958.

Patterson, Stephen. "Profile of Composer Ron Nelson." *The Instrumentalist*, Vol. XLVIII, June 1994, 49.

Slonimsky, Nicolas, ed. *Baker's Biographical Dictionary of Music and Musicians*. Eighth edition. New York: Macmillan, Inc., 1992.

Contributed by:
Jeff Emge
Texas A & M University
Commerce, Texas

Teacher Resource Guide

Molly on the Shore
Percy Aldridge Grainger
(1882–1961)

Unit 1: Composer

George Percy Grainger was born on July 8, 1882, in Melbourne, Australia. He had no formal education of any kind as a child, but was instructed in all academic subjects by his mother, the former Rose Aldridge. She was also his first piano teacher, thus shaping not only his attitudes towards life in general but in particular his taste in music. As a result of the lifelong bond between mother and son, when Percy Grainger's professional career as a pianist and composer began, he took his mother's maiden name as his middle name, being thereafter forever known as Percy Aldridge Grainger.

Percy Grainger left Australia in 1895 to study in Frankfurt for a period which lasted until 1901. He began his career as a pianist touring England and the British Commonwealth in the first decade of the twentieth century. At the same time, he began to compose and collect the musical folk material which was to provide the raw material for much of his greatest work. He emigrated to the United States at the outset of World War I and enlisted in the United States Army as a musician when the U.S. entered the war. Although he took American citizenship, he never forgot his roots in Australia, and in the 1930s, he oversaw the construction of a museum located on the campus of the University of Melbourne to house manuscripts and artifacts from his life. He died in White Plains, New York, in 1961.

Percy Grainger was a fierce nationalist and a fervent believer in the superiority of the art created by members of the Northern European races, including the Icelanders, the Danes, the Norwegians, and the various inhabitants of the British Isles. It was his desire to become to English music what

Grieg was to Norwegian music or Smetana was to the music of Bohemia: he sought ways to introduce the folk idioms of English music into the concert hall. In an effort to find the broadest possible audience, many of his folk music settings exist in various versions for many different ensembles. His settings of folk music were always distinctive, unmistakably his own from the harmonies chosen to the elimination of all terms of Italian derivation in his scores (thus the term "piccolo" disappears, to be replaced with "small flute").

Grainger's interest in the wind band began during the years of his enlistment in the U.S. Army Band stationed at Fort Hamilton. In later years he took a great interest in the public school and university band movement, with appearances on many campuses and an extended period of involvement with the National Music Camp at Interlochen during the 1940s. Although a great deal of Grainger's band music consists of transcriptions for band of earlier orchestral scores, it is generally recognized that the wind band music left by Grainger forms the largest and most significant body of work in the wind repertory.

Unit 2: Composition

Molly on the Shore is a setting of two reel tunes, the first being entitled "Molly on the Shore" and the second being "Temple Reel." Neither tune was collected by Grainger; his source for both melodies was *The Complete Petrie Collection of Ancient Irish Music*, collected by Sir Charles Villiers Stanford. All in all, there are no less than 1,582 melodies in the collection. In the setting Grainger "strove to imbue the accompanying parts that make up the harmonic texture with a melodic character not too unlike that of the underlying reel tune."

Unit 3: Historical Perspective

The first version of *Molly on the Shore* dates from 1907 and is set for string quartet; it is number one of the series that Grainger grouped under the heading "British Folk-Music Settings." It is not an understatement to say that this was Grainger's first "hit." With adaptation for performance by full string orchestra and later for full symphony orchestra, *Molly on the Shore* soon appeared in the repertory of conductors throughout Europe and the United States (Richard Strauss performed it in Berlin). Other adaptations for various chamber ensembles were to appear prior to the composer's version for wind band. All of the various versions are essentially identical in musical content, length, and form.

Unit 4: Technical Considerations

Molly on the Shore was conceived for professional musicians and requires technical skills on a near professional level. The musical demands of the band version are perhaps higher than for any of the orchestral versions for the simple reason that the Cork reel tunes which Grainger chose for his setting are "fiddle" pieces and, as such, are idiomatic for performance by string instruments, taking advantage of open strings, various characteristic bowing techniques, and a sort of "perpetual motion" playing that is relatively simple for strings but very difficult for wind instruments to achieve. The key of the original (G, with modulations to major and minor keys as far away as F major) is admirable, suited for string performance, but the band version is pitched a half step higher in A-flat, with modulations as far as G-flat, requiring prodigious technical skill from the members of the ensemble. The woodwind parts are considerably more challenging than the brass parts, although the trumpets and euphoniums have a number of challenging passages. The scoring calls for standard band instrumentation, with the addition of double bassoon (Grainger originally wrote for contrabass sarrusophone) and soprano saxophone, and a substantial array of mallet percussion instruments (including bells, steel marimba or vibraphone, hammerwood [Grainger's term for "xylophone"], wooden marimba, and celesta).

Unit 5: Stylistic Considerations

Molly on the Shore requires fewer musical styles than any of Grainger's other works, as it is set in one tempo throughout with one or the other of the two Cork reels present from the third measure of the piece until the very end. The dynamic range extends from *pppp* to *ffff* and includes all manner of articulations from the most brittle *staccato* to the most toneful *legato*. As the reel tunes are rather monochromatic in their nature, all of the contrast is to be found in the accompanying material with which Grainger surrounds the tunes.

Unit 6: Musical Elements

The technique employed by Grainger in all of his settings of folk music is something of a variation technique – one in which the melodic materials themselves are seldom subject to change and development, but rather the surrounding accompaniment is constantly varied and developed. Grainger takes special advantage of the tonal ambiguity of the melody "Temple Hill," as it is set in the dorian mode. Among the accompanimental devices on exhibit in this score is musical layering, in which the texture is built by adding successive lines of related counterpoint on top of the melody and its accompaniment so that in the end the melody and the harmonies attached to it are sometimes somewhat overshadowed by the other materials. *Ostinato* figures and long-held, double-pedal points occur in a number of passages. The melody occurs in the bass line only once (in a sort of reversible counterpoint, wherein the melody descends to the lower voices with accompanying material above). *Stretto* in imitation similarly occurs only once. Alto and tenor line counter-melodies abound. There are practically no instances of traditional "oom-pah" style accompaniments, though in one passage a "pah-oom" pattern occurs (the lower instruments are off the beat with the upper voices on). The high woodwind have descending chromatic scale *obligati* in a few passages. The setting begins and ends very softly, albeit with a "stinger" marked *ffff*, but within the structure of the piece, the pattern of climax and relaxation offers needed contrast.

Unit 7: Form and Structure
There are three separate eight-measure fragments which constitute the reel "Molly on the Shore," and two separate eight-measure fragments drawn from "Temple Hill."

MEASURE	SECTION
1-10	Two-bar introduction and Molly segment no. 1 is heard above a low woodwind *ostinato*; A-flat major
11-18	Molly no. 2 is stated above *ostinato* continuation
19-26	Molly no. 3 is stated in low woodwinds and string bass with clarinet accompaniment
27-36	Molly no. 1 recurs amid thickening orchestration
35-42	Molly no. 2 in first full band *tutti*
43-50	Temple Hill no. 1 appears (still A-flat major)
51-58	Temple Hill no. 2 appears, *tutti*, first appearance of *ff*
59-65	Molly no. 1, "pah-oom" accompaniment
67-75	Molly no. 2 appears in *stretto*
75-82	Molly no. 3 appears *legato* in altered form
83-90	Molly no. 1 recurs, altered Molly no. from previous phrase metamorphoses into countermelody
91-98	Molly no. 2, mallet percussion enter for first time, accompaniment begins to overshadow reel tunes
99-106	Temple Hill no. 1 recurs, a whole tone lower than first appearance, over double pedal tone which implies A-flat minor
107-114	Temple no. 2 over continuation of pedal
115-122	Temple no. 1, at same pitch level as m. 99 recurs, but tonality has settled in to G-flat major; countermelody in alto voices
123-130	Temple no. 2 at same pitch level as m. 107; *tutti* scoring; in G-flat; stepwise quarter note countermelody in accented brass voices
131-138	Molly no. 1 with direct modulation back to A-flat; thickening orchestration
139-146	Molly no. 2 harmonized; *tutti ff* scoring; first appearance of descending chromatic scales
147-154	Molly no. 1, new countermelody and accompaniment figures

MEASURE	SECTION
155-162	Molly no. 3 recurs (weakly scored with near certainty of being covered by accompaniment); mallet percussion re-enters; woodwind chromatics
163-170	Temple no. 1, a third lower than at m. 99 recurs, over double pedal suggesting f minor; *ostinato* in mallet percussion
171-178	Temple no. 2, a third lower than at m. 107 over increasingly thinning texture
179-186	Molly no. 1; A-flat major; very sparse accompaniment; same countermelody as at m. 147
187-195	Molly no. 2 harmonized; *pp* accompaniment, diminishing to *pppp*, with stinger marked *ffff*

Unit 8: Suggested Listening
Leroy Anderson, *Irish Suite*
Percy Grainger:
   Molly on the Shore (other settings for string and full orchestra, string quartet)
   Scotch Strathspey and Reel
   Spoon River
Various composers, *Riverdance*, soundtrack

Unit 9: Additional References and Resources
Bird, John. *Percy Grainger*. London, Faber and Faber, 1976.

Fennell, Frederick. *Molly on the Shore, An Interpretive Analysis*, Evanston, IL, The Instrumentalist, October 1983.

Lewis, Thomas P. *A Source Guide to the Music of Percy Grainger*. White Plains, NY: Pro/Am Music Resources, 1991.

Mellers, Wilfrid. *Percy Grainger*. New York: Oxford University Press, 1992.

Contributed by:
R. Mark Rogers
Director of Publications
Southern Music Company
San Antonio, Texas

Teacher Resource Guide

Of Sailors and Whales
W. Francis McBeth
(b. 1933)

Unit 1: Composer

William Francis McBeth was born on March 9, 1933, near Lubbock, Texas. He is Professor Emeritus of Theory and Composition at Ouachita University in Arkadelphia, Arkansas. In addition, he is Conductor Emeritus of the Arkansas Symphony Orchestra where he served as Artistic Director. Residing in Arkansas for over forty years, he was appointed Composer Laureate by Governor Bob C. Riley in 1975. A composer for various musical genres, his interest in wind music has been a driving force in the development of its literature, and his compositional style is reflected in younger composers. Dr. McBeth earned his degrees from Hardin-Simmons University, University of Texas, and Eastman School of Music. Among his influential teachers are Clifton Williams, Wayne Barlow, Kent Kennan, and Howard Hanson. His numerous works for winds include *Beowulf, Kaddish, Through Countless Halls of Air, Masque, and Wine from These Grapes.*

Unit 2: Composition

"*Of Sailors and Whales* is a multi-movement work based on five scenes from Herman Melville's *Moby Dick*. It was commissioned by and is dedicated to the California Band Directors Association, Inc., and was premiered in February 1990 by the California All-State Band, conducted by the composer. The work is sub-dedicated to Robert Lanon White, Commander USN (ret.), who went to sea as a simple sailor." (composer's notes)

Each movement portrays a different character from the Melville novel. In "Ishmael," the tonal center is C, McBeth's way of referring to Melville, "I go to sea (C) as a simple sailor." "Queequeg" combines the exotic nature of solo double reeds with the barbaric presence of the percussion to depict the mystical nature of this character. "Father Mapple" is unique in that it requires the ensemble to sing a simple chorale. The relentless rhythmic pulse of "Ahab" suggests the Captain's obsession with hunting his nemesis. "The White Whale" incorporates contemporary aleatoric notation along with extensive percussion scoring to create a musical illustration of the great beast.

The composition is fifteen minutes in length, and the composer suggests that short statements from Melville's novel (which are provided in the score) be shared with the audience in order to understand the concept of each movement.

Unit 3: Historical Perspective

Programmatic music was conceived in the early nineteenth century as part of the Romantic period. Composers during this era associated their instrumental music with poetic, descriptive, or narrative subject matter. This music absorbed the subject matter and transformed it into purely musical concepts. Composers such as Berlioz, Liszt, Debussy, and Strauss would often base their compositions on existing literary works or concepts.

Of Sailors and Whales is an excellent twentieth century example of this mode of expression. Each movement portrays in musical terms the composer's impression of a character in the novel. An earlier McBeth work, *Beowulf*, was conceived with a similar concept in mind. Other twentieth century composers of wind music, such as Karel Husa, Morton Gould, and Mark Camphouse, have written compositions within a programmatic frame of reference. McBeth takes this romantic notion of program music and fuses it with contemporary techniques to produce a unique and interesting composition.

Unit 4: Technical Considerations

This work demands a thorough understanding of McBeth's concepts regarding balance and blend within the ensemble as well as each individual section. Extremes in dynamic range will pose problems in balancing *tutti* passages. The colors, especially in low brass and low reeds, can be masked if attention is not paid to this area.

In order to perform the second movement successfully, winds and brass must be able to single tongue sixteenth notes evenly at 96 to the quarter note. Low woodwinds and brass are asked to perform a tricky dotted-sixteenth and thirty-second note passage which is difficult from both a technical and a stylistic standpoint. The third movement requires students to sing octaves, two-part, and occasional four-part harmony with clear diction and balanced ensemble.

The last movement requires a first trumpet with a solid high D in the player's range. This is particularly problematic occurring at the end of a fifteen-minute composition where endurance is likely a factor. In addition, there are several passages of aleatoric notation which will need to be explained and rehearsed separately to ensure success. Demands on the woodwinds, trumpets, and mallets revolve around familiarity with diminished, chromatic, and modal scales in C, D, F, E-flat, and A.

Unit 5: Stylistic Considerations

McBeth's music is by nature very dramatic and should be presented in this fashion. Care should be taken that the full spectrum of dynamic range is achieved as printed. His usage of percussion reinforces these effects and should be carefully followed. However, the differences in instrumental color are dependent on precise balancing of sonorities within each family and each section. The ensemble can easily become very treble-oriented in sound if allowed to play without regard to balance while emphasizing this wide dynamic range.

Articulation style is crucial to the success of this composition. Performers should be able to differentiate between a light *staccato*, a separated *marcato*, and a connected *legato* style. McBeth is very precise with his articulation markings in regard to phrasing and spacing. These markings must be followed faithfully.

Unit 6: Musical Elements

McBeth's melody evolves around short motives that grow in complexity throughout the movements. The interval of a minor third is important in both melodic development and tonal center relationships. McBeth often modulates the key center a minor third in either direction to change the mood of the piece (e.g., "Ishmael" in C, "Queequeg" in E-flat). His usage of the minor third in the development of motives in "The White Whale" is also characteristic of his compositional style.

The composer uses triadic harmony as the basis of his harmonic structure. However, he often stacks these chords to achieve polytonal sonorities. Rhythmically, a driving sense of pulse and sub-division provides forward momentum for the *allegro* movements.

Unit 7: Form and Structure

SECTION	MEASURE	KEY	EVENT AND SCORING
Movement I: "Ishmael"			
Theme A	1-27	C major	Clarinet, flute, horn, trumpet
Theme B	28-35	A major	Brass
	36-49	C major	Woodwinds, horn
Theme B´	50-58		Flute, glockenspiel, low brass
	58-80	b minor	Upper brass and woodwind
Theme A	81-94	C major	Clarinet, flute, horn

SECTION	MEASURE	KEY	EVENT AND SCORING
Movement II: "Queequeg"			
Introduction	1-5	E-flat major	Upper brass and woodwind
Motive A	6-22		Clarinet
Motive B	23-38	c minor	Oboe, bassoon
Motive B′	39-54		Brass
Motive B	55-61	d minor	Low brass and woodwind
B augm	62-71	a-flat minor	Trumpet, flute
Introduction	72-76	E-flat major	Upper brass and woodwind
Motive A	77-91		Clarinet
Motive B	92-97	d minor	Low brass and woodwind
Coda	98-107	E-flat major	Horn, trumpet, flute
Movement III: "Father Mapple"			
Phrase A	1-16	d minor	Unison-octaves
Phrase B	17-26		Two- to four-part
Phrase A	27-37		Unison to four-part
Movement IV: "Ahab"			
Introduction	1-8	f minor	Low brass and woodwind
Motive A	9-22		Clarinet, flute
Motive B	23-42	c minor/f	Horn, euphonium, saxophone
Motive B	43-57	f minor	*Tutti*
Motive A/B	58-77	d minor/g	Clarinet, flute, trumpet
Motive A	78-91	D pedal	*Tutti*
Coda	92-106	A-flat to F major	*Tutti*
Movement V: "The White Whale"			
Introduction	1-20	D pedal	Brass, percussion
Motive A	21-38	C pedal	Fugue
Motive B	39-60	f minor	Low brass
Introduction	61-69	B-flat pedal	Woodwinds
Motive C	70-103	Sequences	Horn, clarinet
Motive A	104-119	E pedal	Trumpet
Motive B	120-131	d minor	Low brass
Coda	132-144	C major	*Tutti*

Unit 8: Suggested Listening

Morton Gould, *Jericho Rhapsody*
Howard Hanson:
  Dies Natalis
  Merry Mount Suite

W. Francis McBeth:
  Lauds and Tropes - In Praise
  The Sea Treaders
  They Hung Their Harps in the Willows
Claude T. Smith, *Eternal Father, Strong to Save*
Clifton Williams:
  Fanfare and Allegro
  Symphonic Suite

Unit 9: Additional References and Resources

Kopetz, Barry. "Of Sailors and Whales: An Interpretive Analysis." *The Instrumentalist*, February 1996, Vol. 50, No. 7.

McBeth, W. Francis. *Effective Performance of Band Music*. San Antonio, TX: Southern Music Company, 1972.

McBeth, W. Francis. "The Score: Mechanics of Preparation." *The Instrumentalist*, May 1990, Vol. 44, No. 10.

Smith, Norman, and Albert Stoutamire. *Band Music Notes*. Lake Charles, LA: Program Note Press, 1989.

Contributed by:

Leslie W. Hicken
Director of Bands
Furman University
Greenville, South Carolina

Teacher Resource Guide

An Original Suite
Gordon Jacob
(1895–1984)

Unit 1: Composer

Gordon Jacob was a rather prolific and versatile composer, arranger, peda-gogue, conductor, and author. His oeuvre includes approximately 400 original compositions ranging from a solo work lasting thirty seconds, to a wide variety of chamber works, to large-scale choral, orchestral, and band compo-sitions (for both military and brass bands). Born in London as the youngest of ten children, Gordon Percival Septimus (he was the seventh son) had ample examples of talented amateur musicians and composers within his family. His fascination with music began when Jacob was a young child. By the age of nine, he was composing his first songs. By the age of thirteen, he was writing full orchestral scores, and at the age of fourteen, as a student at Dulwich College, he was given his first opportunity to conduct an orchestra.

Jacob's difficulties in the early part of his life included the loss of his father when young Jacob was only three, the loss during World War I of his brother Anstey (the sibling to whom he was closest), and his own participa-tion in and survival of World War I. Jacob wrote, "I believe that there were only about 60 survivors...out of about 800 in our battalion.... No wonder I felt as I did, that I should have to try in some way to justify my miraculous preser-vation." (Wetherell, Eric. *Gordon Jacob—A Centenary Biography*, London: Thames, 1995, 22.)

Jacob's teaching career was spent in large part as a faculty member at his alma mater, the Royal Academy of Music. As a reflection of this man of good humor and good character, Eric Wetherell states, "Aware that I was in danger of painting a rosy picture of a man entirely without faults, I tried hard to find someone who could point to a flaw in his character. I could find no one to say a harsh word about him." (Eric Wetherell, *Gordon Jacob – A Centenary Biography*. London: Thames Publishing, 1995, 5.)

"Music is not a branch of higher mathematics and it is the pursuit of the abstruse and problematical for its own sake that is the besetting sin of much contemporary music...but the impulse behind all artistic endeavour should surely be to produce a thing of satisfying and unique beauty." (Gordon Jacob, *The Composer and His Art*, Westport, CT: Greenwood Press, 1986, 26-27.)

Unit 2: Composition

An Original Suite was written in 1923 under the name of *Suite for Military Band* while Jacob was a student at the Royal Academy of Music. Published in 1928, it was the publishing company, Boosey & Hawkes, that gave the suite its present title. Jacob did not like the title and unsuccessfully tried to have it changed. The reason for the designation of *An Original Suite* is explained by Gordon Jacob as follows:

> At that time very little original music was being written for what was then "military" band, so the title was a way of distinguishing that it was an original work rather than an arrangement – not that the music was very original in itself.... The slow movement is Irish rather than English "folky," the reason being that the *Londonderry Air* was extremely popular and much admired during the '20's. (Thompson, Kevin. "Gordon Jacob in Conversation," *Journal of the British Association of Symphonic Bands and Wind Ensembles*, Volume 1, Spring 1982, 3-5.)

The work is in three movements, "March" (*Allegro di marcia*), "Intermezzo" (*Andante, ma non troppo*), and "Finale" (*Allegro con brio*). Total performance time is approximately nine minutes and fifteen seconds. Only a condensed score is available through the publisher, Boosey & Hawkes. An errata sheet by Barry Kopetz is available in the June 1990 edition of *The Instrumentalist*, which is cited in this guide under Unit 9.

Unit 3: Historical Perspective

By the turn of the twentieth century, Great Britain's empire stretched into India, South Africa, Egypt (in reality, if not legally), Australia, Canada, and portions of the East Indies. Although many of the colonies were self-governing by the onset of World War I in 1914, Great Britain continued to maintain a stronghold on its territories. Gordon Jacob's eldest brother was in the Indian Army as was his paternal grandfather, while his father was a member of the India Civil Service.

World War I (1914-18) left a battered Europe in its wake. England and France had suffered immense losses in lives, the Austro-Hungarian Empire had been dissolved, the Bolsheviks seized power in Russia in 1917, and the Facists in Italy in 1922. Isolationism fueled nationalistic tendencies in both Europe and the United States in the aftermath of the war.

Musically speaking, the first quarter of the twentieth century was filled with experimentation and individuality. The contradictive elements of exploration of non-Western music and its elements (whole tone and additional pentatonic scales, complex meters, modal melodies, static harmonies...) versus the isolationist and nationalistic movements carried over from the nineteenth century and intensified as a result of World War I contributed to the diversity of style that unfolded during the period prior to World War II. Significant composers (Bartok, Kodaly, Janacek, Vaughan Williams, Holst, and Grainger, to name a few) involved themselves in the documentation of and compositional use of national folk songs. The new success of documentation and ethnomusicological advances were in part due to the invention of recording devices.

The early part of the twentieth century was unlike any other period in the history of philosophical thought and of subsequent movements in the arts. Debussy, Mahler, Schoenberg, and Stravinsky were essentially writing their landmark masterpieces in the same time period. Simultaneously, Holst, Elgar, Vaughan Williams, Ravel, and Gershwin were also composing their great works. Never before had so many extremely different styles and philosophies of composition, and of music itself, existed at the same time.

Composers whose music had a notable influence on Gordon Jacob included Vaughan Williams, Holst, and Stravinsky. Additionally, Jacob himself declared that Russian music had a greater impact on his style than the music of his native land.

A sample of works written by the time Gordon Jacob composed *An Original Suite for Military Band* follows:

Debussy	*Nocturnes*, 1899; *La Mer*, 1905; *Jeux*, 1913
Mahler	*Das Lied von der Erde*, 1911
Schoenberg	*Pierrot lunaire*, 1912
Stravinsky	*Petrushka*, 1911; *Le Sacre du Printemps*, 1913; *Symphonies of Wind Instruments*, 1920; *Octet for Wind Instruments*, 1922-23
Holst	*First Suite in E-flat*, 1909; *Second Suite in F*, 1911; *The Planets*, 1916
Vaughan Williams	*Fantasia on a Theme of Thomas Tallis*, 1909; *Pastoral Symphony*, 1922
Ravel	*Daphnis et Chloe*, 1909-11; *Le Tombeau de Couperin*, 1917
Walton	*Facade*, 1921-22
Gershwin	*Rhapsody in Blue*, 1924

Unit 4: Technical Considerations

MOVEMENT I:

The most mechanically difficult passages lie in the upper woodwind lines. Proficiency is needed within the keys of g minor, B-flat major, and F major, in particular. The woodwind sixteenth note passage in mm. 17-18 utilizes the arpeggios of g minor ninth, E-flat major, and d minor, while mm. 46-49 assign the flutes and E-flat clarinet sixteenth note triplets on beats three and four. The first cornet solo part does have a three-measure excerpt that is reminiscent of a solo cornet part in a brass band work. This rather conjunct sixteenth note passage in mm. 88-90 falls almost completely within the key of concert F major and is simply a repetition (with octave displacement) of the upper woodwind line from mm. 84-86. Two of the most difficult measures in the work appear at mm. 96-97 (taken from m. 33) where the technique is rather easy and the activity level rather low. However, the sudden dynamic change to *pianissimo* coming from *fortissimo* coupled with one group that enters either with "two-three" or "four-one" versus another group that enters "and-three" or "and-one" give cause for timid behavior resulting in unclear attacks that interrupt the pulse and create tone and intonation difficulties from lack of support and loss of time. The high B natural (b2) in the final chord of the first trombone part is notable with regard to range.

MOVEMENT II:

The technical difficulty in this movement lies in the chromaticism that appears in the development section. Students will need to become accustomed to reading accidentals and hearing the changes in harmony. Letter C does pit eighth note triplets against duple eighth notes, which certainly presents certain dangers to the sense of time and style throughout the nine-measure *legato* passage.

MOVEMENT III:

The "Finale" has several areas of technical concern. Measures 1-24 include a running eighth note line in compound duple meter at quarter note = 132 against the remaining parts, which are in simple duple meter, including the theme. The second clarinet, alto and tenor saxophone parts have the entire passage, while solo and first clarinet parts, for example, participate only in mm. 1-9. Bass clarinet, bassoon, and euphonium have the triplets for eight bars at letter A. The cornet I and II parts from mm. 52-58 (letter E) alternate beats for a sixteenth note articulated passage, which is juxtaposed with the slurred triplets of the woodwinds.

Unit 5: Stylistic Considerations

MOVEMENT I:

A marked consideration in a quality performance of this work is reflected in the many skillful dynamic changes that are required. The well-written transitions of the first movement require a mature handling of dynamic changes while maintaining a sense of forward motion so as to make the contrast without hindering the tone and intonation.

The stylistic changes between the themes of Movement I also require careful attention. *Legato, staccato,* majestic, bold, and lyrical characteristics are all displayed in the music.

MOVEMENT II:

As with most slow movements of this genre, a player and ensemble must be sensitive to the lyricism and passion of the melody. All parts must support the forward motion and nuances as dictated by the melody. The entire ensemble (the solo alto saxophonist in particular) needs to have a warm, centered, and resonant tone with a solid sense of pitch.

The section beginning at letter C (mm. 48-56) is perhaps a bit Debussy-like in its juxtaposition of the gently rocking triplets against the lyrical, broad, *pianissimo* melody.

MOVEMENT III:

This movement contains a great deal of contrast between the melody and the accompaniment. The very disjunct and *marcato* first theme contrasts with the fast-paced, flowing *legato* of the accompaniment. The first part of the second theme opens as a rather lyrical melodic line in sixteenth notes, which contrasts with the descending *staccato* eighth note line in the brass. The second portion of that theme finally unites styles of melody and accompaniment; however, it contrasts with the style of the previous four measures. The contrast can also be witnessed in the polytonality that exists at the opening of the movement between the melody and accompaniment – g minor and B-flat major, respectively.

Immature players will most likely struggle with the harmonic changes and the contrasting nature of the parts. This movement is not as well crafted as its predecessors, which may account for a dirth of recordings of this otherwise worthy composition.

Unit 6: Musical Elements

The rhythms are very basic throughout the work with the exception of the polyrhythms that occur as stated above in Units 4 and 5. The harmonic structure of the third movement can be very taxing on the ears of younger players. There are a number of overlapping chords and very brief moments of open fifths in addition to the chromaticism of letter C.

Primary keys within the piece include g minor, B-flat major, c minor, a minor, b-flat minor, and F major.

Unit 7: Form and Structure

Movement I:

MEASURE	EVENT	SCORING
1-2	Introduction	Solo snare drum (*forte diminuendo*)
3-11	Theme 1	In g minor with pentatonic inflections; phrase structure is 2+6

Rehearsal A

11-21	A´	Theme is presented up an octave and includes a variation (mm. 17-18) and extension (mm. 19-20)

Rehearsal B

21-29	Theme 2	Change to a detached style, lighter character; phrase structure is 4+4 (a+a´)
29-35	"A" inference	2+2+3; chromatic descent in accompaniment; references from mm. 3, 10, 19, and 24

Rehearsal C

36-37		Introduction (transition) to new theme
38-45	Theme 3	2 (Introduction)+2+2+2+2; imitation in cornets and trombones in mm. 44-45
46-49		Reference to B theme; motive from m. 21; 2+2

Rehearsal D

50-53		Interlude, modulatory in character reference to A (mm. 3-4); 2+2 (extension of m. 55) descending pattern, octave displacement

Rehearsal E

58-64	Theme 4	*Legato* in character; 3.5+3.5 (a+a´)
54-71		
72-75		Measure 75 is an extension

Rehearsal F

76-83	A´	

Rehearsal G

84-91	B´	

Rehearsal H

92-95	A´	Includes chromatic descending line from m. 29 in accompaniment
96-97	Coda	Material from m. 33
98-99		Material from the end of m. 10
100-102		Material from mm. 1-2

Movement II:

Although the movement begins as if it were in C major, the majority of the work is in a minor. There are some references to harmonic and melodic forms of the a minor scale; however, a large portion is in natural minor.

MEASURE	EVENT	SCORING
1-17	Theme	The theme is stated from the first notes of the movement via an alto saxophone solo beginning on an anacrusis (pick-up eighth notes) into the first full measure
Rehearsal A 18-34	A′	Restatement of the theme with an altered accompaniment
Rehearsal B-D 35-67		Development section
Rehearsal E 68-75	A″	Final statement of the theme in a truncated form
Rehearsal F 76-90	Coda	

Movement III:

MEASURE	EVENT	SCORING
1-2	Introduction	Clarinets and saxophones
3-24	Theme 1	7+8+7 (a+b+a′)
25-40	Theme 2	(4+4) + (4+4) (a+b+a′+b′)
41-44		Transition or bridge
45-66	A′	Altered accompaniment
67-78	Coda	Which references the second theme

Unit 8: Suggested Listening

Percy Aldridge Grainger:
   Colonial Song
   Irish Tune from County Derry
   Lincolnshire Posy
Gustav Holst:
   First Suite in E-flat
   Moorside Suite
   Second Suite in F
Gordon Jacob:
   The Battell
   Fantasia on an English Folk Song
   Flag of Stars

Music for a Festival
Tribute to Canterbury
William Byrd Suite
Ralph Vaughan Williams:
  English Folk Song Suite
  Fantasia on a Theme of Thomas Tallis
  Fantasia on Greensleeves
  Toccata Marziale

Unit 9: Additional References and Resources

Battisti, Frank. *The Twentieth Century American Wind Band/Ensemble*, Fort Lauderdale, FL: Meredith Music Publications, 1995.

Dvorak, Thomas L., Robert Grechesky, and Gary M. Ciepluch. *Best Music for High School Band*, edited by Bob Margolis, Brooklyn: Manhattan Beach Music, 1993.

Jacob, Gordon. *The Composer and His Art*. Westport, CT: Greenwood Press, 1986. Originally published: London: Oxford University Press, 1955.

Kopetz, Barry, "Gordon Jacob's An Original Suite," *The Instrumentalist*, XLIV June 1990, 22-30, 53-56.

Kreines, Joseph. *Music for Concert Band*. Tampa: Florida Music Service, 1989.

Rehrig, William H. *The Heritage Encyclopedia of Band Music*. Edited by Paul E. Bierley. Westerville, OH: Integrity Press, 1991.

Stycos, Roland. *Listening Guides for Band Musicians*. Portland, ME: J. Weston Walch, 1991.

Tarwater, William Harmon, Jr. "Analyses of Seven Major Band Compositions of the Twentieth Century" (Ph.D. diss., George Peabody College for Teachers, 1958).

Thompson, Kevin. "Gordon Jacob—I Aim at Greater Simplicity Nowadays," *The Instrumentalist*, XXXVIII September 1983, 38-39.

Thompson, Kevin. "Gordon Jacob in Conversation." *Journal of the British Association of Symphonic Bands and Wind Ensembles*, Volume 1, Spring 1982, 3-4.

Wetherell, Eric. *Gordon Jacob—A Centenary Biography*. London: Thames Publishing, 1995.

Whiston, J. Alan. "Gordon Jacob: A Biographical Sketch and Analysis of Four Selected Works for Band" (Ph.D. diss., The University of Oklahoma, 1987).

Additional Acknowledgements:

Jon C. Mitchell, Chair, Department of Music, University of Massachusetts at Boston.

Timothy Reynish, Head, Wind & Percussion School, Royal Northern College of Music, Manchester, UK, England.

Contributed by:

Diane M. Bargiel
Director of Instrumental Music and Artist Series
Juniata College
Huntingdon, Pennsylvania

Teacher Resource Guide

Psalm for Band

Vincent Persichetti

(b. 1915)

Unit 1: Composer

Vincent Persichetti was born on June 6, 1915, in Philadelphia, Pennsylvania. He received his formal music education at Combs College of Music, Curtis Institute, and Philadelphia Conservatory. He studied composition with Paul Nordoff and Roy Harris, conducting with Fritz Reiner, and piano with Alberto Jonas and Olga Samaroff. In 1942, he was appointed head of the Composition Department at the Philadelphia Conservatory. He became a faculty member of the Juliard School of Music in 1948. Persichetti was appointed Editorial Director of the Music Publishing firm of Elkan-Vogel, Inc. in 1952.

Unit 2: Composition

Psalm for Band was Persichetti's second composition for wind band. It was commissioned by the Alpha Chapter of the Pi Kappa Omicron National Band Fraternity at the University of Louisville. *Psalm* was first performed by the University of Louisville Symphonic Band on May 2, 1952, with the composer conducting. Dr. Persichetti gives us the following program notes:

> *Psalm for Band* is a piece constructed from a single germinating harmonic idea. There are three distinct sections, a sustained chordal mood, a forward moving chorale, followed by a Paean culmination of the materials. Extensive use is made of separate choirs of instruments supported by thematic rhythms in the tenor and bass drums.

This work was selected by the Committee on Original Band Music of the College Band Directors National Association as one of eight most outstanding band compositions written in several years prior to that date.

Unit 3: Historical Perspective

The 1950s was a decade of great development of wind literature. Some of the most respected composers in the world were writing for the wind band medium. Other composers turning out compositions for wind bands besides Persichetti were Virgil Thompson, Robert Russell Bennett, Paul Hindemith, William Schuman, and Roy Harris. Persichetti wrote fourteen wind band pieces and 166 compositions in all. He had been composing for nearly twenty years before composing his first piece for wind band. That piece was *Divertimento for Band* written in 1950. *Psalm* was his second composition for the same medium.

Unit 4: Technical Considerations

Psalm is written in standard wind band orchestration. The piece only requires two percussionists. A third player can be added to play the "on the rim" sections of the piece. It begins with a clarinet choir playing, which makes it important to have a full clarinet section, as well as all the color clarinets. There are five separate trumpet and cornet parts. The first section requires the first and second cornet players to play C and A-flat above the staff. Due to the harmony used by the composer, it is also important to have full French horn and trombone sections to cover all the voices in the chords.

Unit 5: Stylistic Considerations

Psalm is a single-movement work divided into three distinctly different sections. The first is very *legato*, with the phrases overlapped to give it a flowing, non-stop motion. The second section is marked *Piu Mosso* with the piece staying in a *legato* style but with more of a driving feel. The tempo increases in this section from quarter note = 104 to the second = 126. Persichetti uses the tempo to create a driving feel without having to change the overall style. The third section is in great contrast to the first two sections. The third is marked *Allegro Vivace*, and the quarter note = 152. This section is more articulate. He sets the brass playing sustained against the woodwind lines being very articulate.

Persichetti's music has been described by some as "Grace and Grit." This piece has "grace" written in the first two sections and "grit" coming into play in the third. He brings back both in the end of the third section, which plays the piece out.

Unit 6: Musical Elements

Persichetti has this piece divided into three distinct sections. The first, "Moderato," has all of the thematic materials being motivic. He is able to overlap all the changes in orchestration by dovetailing each entrance of a new phrase with the exit of the previous phrase. This gives the first section a very sustained sound. Most of the chords used in this first section are predominately major and minor. Most dissonances are created by suspensions and passing tones. There are a few dissonances that are created by B major and b minor triads occurring simultaneously.

The second section, "Piu Mosso," uses a chorale theme from m. 10. The chorale theme is broken into 3-2-3-2 measure patterns. His scoring in this section changes from an open scoring in the clarinets to a closed scoring in the other woodwinds. This section begins with a call and response between the clarinets and the other woodwinds. He then uses the brass in much the same way, finishing out that particular section.

The third section, which is quarter note = 152, uses many short motifs. Persichetti then uses variations of the themes and motives he has used in the piece. During this section the harmonic structure uses polychords, polytonality, and polymodality. An example of this is major against minor keys through parts of this section. He again uses call-and-response techniques between the brass and woodwinds.

Unit 7 : Form and Structure

SECTION	MEASURE	MUSICAL TEXTURE
Section I:		
Theme A	1-9	Clarinets
Theme A1	9-12	Horns, low brass
Theme B1		2nd clarinet melody
Theme B2	12-17	1st and 3rd clarinet (countermelody)
Episode	16-20	Trombone
	19-23	Woodwinds
Theme C	23-27	Trombone, low brass
	27-34	Woodwinds
Theme B1, B2	34-38	Woodwinds
Theme C	38-42	Brass
Theme D	42-45	Clarinets
	45-48	Horns
Theme E	48-52	Cornet, flute
Theme C	52-57	Woodwinds
Theme C altered	57-61	Full band
Theme D altered	61-63	Clarinet, saxophone
Theme C	63-65	Cornet
	65-67	Trombone
Theme D altered	67-73	Instrument families
Theme D complete	73-76	Clarinets
Bridge C material	76-83	Tuba, saxophone

SECTION	MEASURE	MUSICAL TEXTURE
Section II:		
Theme F1	83-85	Clarinets
Theme F2	85-87	Woodwinds
Theme F3	87-90	Clarinets
Theme F4	90-92	Woodwinds
Episode	93-97	Woodwinds, low brass
Theme F1	97-99	Clarinets
Theme F2	99-101	Woodwinds
Episode	101-104	Woodwinds (brass interjections)
Theme G	104-106	Horn, low brass
Episode F material	105-110	Woodwinds
Episode	110-117	Brass
Transition F material	117-119	Woodwinds
Theme A1	119-121	Brass-woodwind-brass
Theme B1, B2 coda	122-126	Woodwind
Section III:		
Theme A variations	127-131	Brass (woodwind interjections)
Theme F altered	131-138	Brass (woodwind rhythmic variations)
Episode Theme F (canonic)	138-143	Brass
Theme H	144-147	Full band
Recapitulation (variations of m. 127)	147-151	Full band
Episode Theme F (imitative)	152-159	Brass
Theme H	160-164	Full band
Theme H1	165-174	Full band
Theme C (3 variations)	175-181	Brass
Theme D	181-183	Full band
Theme H	184-188	Woodwind (trumpets) Trumpets (augmentation of H)
Episode	188-191	Full band
Theme H altered (imitative)	192-199	Full band
Polychordal	199-202	Full band
Theme H (variation)	203-208	Woodwinds
Theme H1	209-211	Woodwinds
Theme D	211-213	Trumpets
Theme F1	213-215	Woodwinds
Theme F2	215-217	Brass

SECTION	MEASURE	MUSICAL TEXTURE
Theme F3	217-220	Woodwinds
Theme F4	220-223	Brass
Theme F1	223-225	Woodwinds/brass
Theme F2	225-226	Trumpets/trombones
Theme F4	226-232	Woodwinds/brass
Theme H1 coda	233-242	Woodwinds/low brass
Theme F1	242-243	French horn
Theme H (material)	244-end	Full band

Unit 8: Suggested Listening

Vincent Persichetti:
   Divertimento
   Pageant
   Symphony for Band No. 6
William Schuman, *George Washington Bridge*

Unit 9: Additional References and Resources

Morris, Donald Alan. "The Life of Vincent Persichetti, with Emphasis on his Works for Band." Ph.D. Diss., The Florida State University, 1991.

Morris, Donald Alan. "Vincent Persichetti Remembered: Music from Gracious to Gritty." *The Instrumentalist*, XLVII/4 November 1992, 30-38.

Rehrig, William H. *The Heritage Encyclopedia of Band Music*. Westerville, OH: Integrity Press, 1991.

Smith, Norman, and Albert Stoutamire. *Band Music Notes*. Lake Charles, LA: Program Notes Press, 1989.

Workinger, William Colvin. "Some Aspects of Scoring in the Band Works of Vincent Persichetti." diss., New York University, 1970.

Contributed by:

Brad Genevro
Assistant Director of Wind Studies
University of North Texas
Denton, Texas

Teacher Resource Guide

Secular Litanies, Op. 90

Martin Mailman
(b. 1932)

Unit 1: Composer

Dr. Martin Mailman is currently Regents Professor of Music and Composer in Residence at the University of North Texas, Denton. A composition student of Louis Mennini, Wayne Barlow, Bernard Rogers, and Howard Hanson, he received his B.M., M.M., and Ph.D. degrees from the Eastman School of Music, Rochester, New York. Dr. Mailman has received numerous awards, among which include two American Bandmasters Association/Ostwald prizes for composition (*Exaltations* in 1983 and *For Precious Friends Hid in Death's Dateless Night* in 1989), the National Band Association/Band Mans Company prize for composition (*For Precious Friends Hid in Death's Dateless Night* in 1989), the Edward Benjamin Award, a National Endowment for the Arts Composers Grant (1982), and the 1982 Queen Marie-Jose Prize for composition (*Concerto for Violin and Orchestra* in 1982). His works include chamber music, band, choral, and orchestral music, film scores, television music, an opera, and a requiem for chorus, orchestra, and soloist. A frequently sought-after clinician and teacher, Dr. Mailman has served as guest conductor-composer at more than ninety colleges and universities across the United States and Europe.

Some of his other works for band include *Geometrics 1 for Band, Op. 22; Concertino for Trumpet and Band, Op. 31; Liturgical Music for Band, Op. 33; Geometrics 3 for Band, Op. 37; Geometrics 4 for Band, Op. 43; Association No. 1 for Band, Op. 45; Shouts, Hymns, and Praises, Op. 52; A Simple Ceremony: In Memoriam John Barnes Chance, Op. 53; Decorations for Band, Op. 54; Let Us Now Praise Famous Men, Op. 56; Geometrics 5 for Band, Op. 58; Night*

Vigil, Op. 66; *Exaltations*, Op. 67; *The Jewel in the Crown*, Op. 78; *Toward the Second Century*, Op. 82; *Concertino for Clarinet and Band*, Op. 83; *Bouquets*, Op. 87; *Concerto for Wind Orchestra (Variations)*, Op. 89; *Secular Litanies*, Op. 90; and *Pledges*, Op. 98.

Unit 2: Composition

Secular Litanies is a single-movement work for symphonic winds commissioned by the University of North Texas Bands to honor Robert A. Winslow, Director of Bands Emeritus. It was completed in November 1993 and first performed in 1994 by the University of North Texas Symphonic Wind Ensemble, conducted by Dennis Fisher. The piece is a grade four difficulty, lasts about seven minutes, and is published by Southern Music Company (S633).

Unit 3: Historical Perspective

Mailman belongs to a generation of late twentieth century composers that includes Ron Nelson, John Barnes Chance, and Fisher Tull. He was one of the composers selected to participate in the Ford Foundation Project, which was an important vehicle for several aspiring musicians. He is currently in demand as composer, conductor, and clinician, and his works are already highly respected, as is evidenced by his *For Precious Friends Hid in Death's Dateless Night* being the first composition to be awarded both the National Band Association/Band Mans Company prize for composition in December 1988 and the American Bandmasters Association/Ostwald prize for composition in January 1989.

Unit 4: Technical Considerations

The piece is challenging for all players. All instruments are required to play independently, and specific sections are frequently featured and exposed. The piece has no key signatures, so accidentals abound. There are a few changes of meter, but only on the quarter note level. The tempo remains consistent except for a couple of *ritardandos*. There are articulations of every kind. Contrasts and repetitions are vitally important, and the conductor must make them happen. Instruments frequently have exposed sections or soli, and the percussion section is featured prominently (especially xylophone), as are the piccolo and tuba. The work is scored for standard symphonic band instrumentation, plus an extensive percussion list. The conductor and ensemble must have a clear conceptualization of the piece and its presentation to successfully perform the work.

Unit 5: Stylistic Considerations

Articulations should be as accurate as possible. All markings in the score support this. Each movement (and, most of the time, section) has its own style. There are gradual *diminuendos* and *crescendos*, steady dynamics, and tremelos. The intensity and movement of the music should be equal to the phrasing, articulation, rhythms, and principles of the line. This is a twentieth century work with twentieth century sounds that should be approached with an open-minded, omniscient, aesthetic interpretation.

Unit 6: Musical Elements

A "litany" is a prayer consisting of a series of invocations and petitions, each sung or recited by a deacon or other person, to which the congregation responds with a phrase, such as "Kyrie eleison." In this case, however, a rhythmic figure acts as the invocation. It is stated during the first few measures. This figure is then used throughout the piece as points of entrances, points of imitation, and rhythms that rise out of dense textures. The piece is composed in ABA form. The B section features several different instrumental litanies that enter and repeat to create different sound and motivic combinations. One such litany features solo piccolo, solo tuba, and xylophone. The "secular" part of the title simply means this is a non-liturgical work.

Unit 7: Form and Structure

SECTION	MEASURE	EVENT AND SCORING
Section 1	1-23	Theme A (brass, saxophones)
	24-39	Theme A (upper woodwinds), hemiola introduced in brass
	40-51	Hemiola (upper woodwinds), Theme A in low instruments
	52-53	Theme A
	54-65	Theme B (flutes, clarinets) above percussion "atmosphere"
	66-74	Theme B (trombones, tubas) above percussion and upper woodwind "atmosphere"
	75-81	Closing based on Theme A
Section 2	82-99	Fugato subject (piccolo, tuba, xylophone) with interruptions
	100-117	Fugato continued with Theme B fragments
	118-130	Theme B with fugato subject interruptions
	131-135	Closing
Section 3	136-151	Theme A
	152-156	Hemiola (woodwinds)
	157-171	Theme A with atmosphere elements (see m. 54)
	172-183	Closing

Errata:

m. 36   Add "*cresc. poco a poco*" to all parts other than trumpets
             and horns
m. 68   Trombones should be marked "open"
m. 98   Piccolo should have same triplet rhythm as tuba and xylo-
             phone on beat 2
m. 99   Alto and tenor saxophones should have "*f*" on beat 4
m. 103   Alto and tenor saxophones should have "*f*" on beat 3
m. 108   Alto and tenor saxophones should have "*f*" on beat 1
m. 129   Trombone I is C-natural on beat 1
mm. 131-134 All entrances should have "*fp cresc.*"
m. 133   The third note in the clarinets should be E-natural, not F
m. 133   The last note in the alto saxophone should be D-natural,
             not E
m. 134   Beat 2 in clarinets should be B-natural (it is missing a
             natural sign)
m. 135   The first nine notes (beats 1-3) in the alto saxophone part
             are a minor third too high

Unit 8: Suggested Listening

Martin Mailman:
  A Simple Ceremony: In Memoriam John Barnes Chance, Op. 53
  Alarums for Band, Op. 27
  Association No. 1 for Band, Op. 45
  Bouquets, Op. 87
  Concertino for Clarinet and Band, Op. 83
  Concertino for Trumpet and Band, Op. 31
  Concerto for Wind Orchestra (Variations), Op. 89
  Decorations for Band, Op. 54
  Exaltations, Op. 67
  Geometrics 1 for Band, Op. 22
  Geometrics 3 for Band, Op. 37
  Geometrics 4 for Band, Op. 43
  Geometrics 5 for Band, Op. 58
  Let Us Now Praise Famous Men, Op. 56
  Liturgical Music for Band, Op. 33
  Night Vigil, Op. 66
  Pledges, Op. 98
  Secular Litanies, Op. 90
  Shouts, Hymns, and Praises, Op. 52
  The Jewel in the Crown, Op. 78
  Toward the Second Century, Op. 82

Unit 9: Additional References and Resources

Baker, Theodore. "Mailman, Martin," *Baker's Biographical Dictionary of Musicians*. 6th ed., revised by Nicolas Slonimsky. New York: Schirmer Books, 1984.

Ewen, David. *A Comprehensive Biographical Dictionary of American Composers*. New York: G.P. Putnam & Sons, 1982.

Mailman, Martin. *Bouquets, Op. 87*. Dick Clardy and the Colony High School Wind Symphony. Compact disc "1994 Midwest Band and Orchestra Clinic Concert" Mark Custom Recordings MW94MCD-10, 1994.

Mailman, Martin. *Bouquets, Op. 87*. Joseph W. Herman and the Tennessee Technological University Symphony Band. Compact disc "1998 Carl Fischer Concert Band Sampler" CN-98085, 1998.

Mailman, Martin. *Concertino for Clarinet and Band, Op. 83*. Matthew Mailman and the Oklahoma City University Symphonic Band, Patricia Card, clarinet. Compact disc "Martin Mailman - *Concertino for Clarinet and Band, Op. 83*" (available through Carl Fischer), 1997.

Mailman, Martin. *For Precious Friends Hid in Death's Dateless Night, Op. 80*. Eugene Corporon and the University of North Texas Wind Symphony. Compact disc "Dialogues and Entertainments" KCD-11083, 1997.

Mailman, Martin. *For Precious Friends Hid in Death's Dateless Night, Op. 80*. Cleveland, OH: Ludwig Music (SBS-270), 1990.

Mailman, Martin. *Geometrics No. 4, Op. 43*. Compact disc "Warner Brothers Music for Concert Band Symphonic Band Series" CATCD95-4, 1998.

Mailman, Martin. Interview by Matthew Mailman, 18 January 1999.

Mailman, Martin. *Liturgical Music, Op. 33*. Jack Stamp and the Indiana University of Pennsylvania Symphony Band. Compact disc "IUP Concert Bands of 1998," 1998.

Mailman, Martin. *Secular Litanies, Op. 90*. Jack Stamp and the Indiana University of Pennsylvania Wind Ensemble. Compact disc "IUP Concert Bands – 1996," 1996.

Mailman, Matthew. Unpublished personal files. Oklahoma City, OK.

Miles, Richard, ed. "Martin Mailman - Exaltations, Op. 67." *Teaching Music through Performance in Band*, Volume 2. Chicago: GIA Publications, Inc., 1997, pp. 442-446.

Miles, Richard, ed. "Martin Mailman - *Liturgical Music, Op. 33.*" *Teaching Music through Performance in Band*, Volume 1. Chicago: GIA Publications, Inc., 1997, pp. 259-262.

National Band Association Selective Music List for Bands

Rehrig, William H. *The Heritage Encyclopedia of Band Music*. Westerville, OH: Integrity Press, 1991.

Speck, Frederick. "Analysis: Martin Mailman's *For Precious Friends Hid in Death's Dateless Night.*" *Journal of Band Research*. Vol. 26/I/Fall 1990, pp. 14-29.

Contributed by:

Matthew Mailman
Director of Bands and Associate Professor of Music
Oklahoma City University

Teacher Resource Guide

Suite Provençale

Jan Van der Roost
(b. 1956)

Unit 1: Composer

Born in Duffel, Belgium, in 1956, Jan Van der Roost was introduced to wind band music at a very young age. This music had a profound influence on him, and he soon decided to begin composing. At the Lemmons Institute in Belgium, he received a triple-laureate diploma in trombone performance, music history, and music education. He continued his studies at the Royal Conservatories in Ghent and Antwerp beginning in 1979, and graduated with a diploma in composition. Presently, Van der Roost teaches at the Lemmons Institute, where he conducts and teaches composing and arranging. Van der Roost has been very active as a composer for wind band in the last fifteen years and has written a number of outstanding works, including *Canterbury Chorale*, *Flashing Winds*, *Four Old Dances*, *Mercury*, *Puszta*, and *Rikudim*. A Unit Study of his composition *Homage* can be found in Volume 2 of *Teaching Music through Performance in Band*. His band works have been performed all over the world by many of the world's leading wind organizations.

Unit 2: Composition

Suite Provençale was composed for symphonic band in 1989. It is a four-movement suite based on authentic folk tunes from the southern region of France named Provence. Each of the movement titles is in an old French/Latin language called *Catalan*. Each movement reflects the character of the particular folk song. "Un ange a fa la crido" (the plea, or appeal, of the angel) is like a *bourrée*, an old French dance. "Adam e sa Coumpagnou" (Adam and his companion) is an old love song, "Lou Fustie" (the carpenter) is a fast dance, and finally, "Lis Escoubo" (a whistle tune/popular ballad) is a *farandole*, another old dance form. In the latter, the old folk music tradition in which musicians play a whistle with one hand and a drum with the other hand is represented in the musical setting.

Unit 3: Historical Perspective

Suite Provençale is based on folk songs from an area in France known as Provence. This area is located between the French Alps and the Rhone River on the Mediterranean Sea. At one time it was a powerful political entity, but it was incorporated into the country of France just after the French Revolution. Provence has kept a degree of economic and social unity based on its traditional industries: sheep raising and olive growing. Additionally, tourism has an important economic impact on the region. Recently, there has been a revival of interest in provincial language and literature. *Suite Provençale* is a testament to that interest. The titles of the movements are in old French and may even be in Catalan, which is an old French/Latin romance language.

Folk music has long been an important part of cultures all over the world. A very strong relationship has developed between Western folk music and art music over the last 125 years. Near the end of the nineteenth century, Western intellectuals began to take an interest in and show appreciation for folk and peasant life. Further, the advent of recorded sound made it possible to study and preserve the traditions. Before recorded sound, folk music was carried forward by what we call the oral tradition. The oral tradition means it was passed by word of mouth, from one generation to the next. Folk tunes would be modified or transformed in some way as they were passed through the generations, unlike art music where a composer writes the music down so that it can be faithfully reproduced. One of the most important collectors of folk tunes at the turn of the century was Percy Grainger. Grainger was not only an important collector of this music, he also arranged many folk songs for wind band. Others followed suit, including Holst and Vaughan Williams, and the French composer, Darius Milhaud. To this day, composers use folk tunes as the basis of new works for wind band. Such is the case with Van der Roost's *Suite Provençale*.

Unit 4: Technical Considerations

Suite Provençale is written to be accessible for the average high school band. Each part is roughly equivalent in the technical demands of rhythm and syncopation. There are some syncopated rhythms that will present challenges for less-experienced players, and there are moments in the piece that will require some attention to balance and blend. The tonality of each of the movements is generally conservative and tends to stay in closely related major and minor keys. There are a few key instruments necessary to make the performance of the piece successful. A fine piccolo, 1st clarinet, 1st trumpet, and 1st baritone player are essential for making a quality performance. Additionally, a balanced instrumentation would ensure proper effect from the harmonic and compositional effects employed by Van der Roost. Overall the writing is very idiomatic and should present few technical problems.

Unit 5: Stylistic Considerations

Like Grainger's *Lincolnshire Posy*, each movement is a setting of a folk tune. Subsequent repetitions of the folk theme are subjected variations in orchestration, rhythm, and dynamics. The variation of the underlying new material keeps the folk melodies fresh and interesting for both players and listeners. Van der Roost says of the piece that he has scored some "spicy" notes. By this he means that there are pitches, harmonic progressions, and compositional devices (such as trills) that fall out of traditional folk music structures. It is the addition of these elements that make this piece such a charming addition to the repertoire.

Unit 6: Musical Elements

The first three movements of *Suite Provençale* are built on folk song themes that are in binary form (meaning that there are two parts to the theme: an A phrase and a B phrase). The fourth movement is a particular kind of dance called a *farandole*. This is a French dance from the French Provence region, performed by men and women who together form a long chain holding hands and follow a leader through a series of patterns to music played on a pipe or flute, and a drum. It is still danced today. The first movement is like a *bourrée*, which is a quick dance popular in the seventeenth century.

Because these are traditional folk melodies, the general harmonic and rhythmic structure is very straightforward. All movements are in duple meter. Van der Roost's "spicy" notes take several forms. Some are interesting chord progressions; some are dissonance. Van der Roost also uses parallelism and, in some cases, "modal blurring" in which he changes a few of the accompaniment notes to obfuscate a clear sense of modality. At the very end of the last movement of the piece, Van der Roost offers some chords that defy analysis because they are cluster chords of pitches that are orchestrated out in the band. Most of the time, the settings are homophonic, meaning that the melody is heard over some kind of accompaniment. There are a couple of instances where Van der Roost uses a countermelody to create additional interest in a particular passage of the piece. Van der Roost also makes use of the Picardy third at the end of the interior movements of the work. (A Picardy third is the sounding of a major chord at the end of a composition which has been in a minor key. The practice of using a Picardy third has existed for some 400 years.)

Unit 7: Form and Structure

Movement I: "*Un ange a fa la Crido*"
(the plea, or appeal, of the angels)
This movement is in three verses, which are varied in each repetition. Each verse consists of a theme in two-part form (AB). The movement is harmonically centered in the key of B-flat major.

MEASURE	EVENT AND SCORING
1	Verse 1 of the folk song in brass; woodwinds join in m. 4
9	Woodwinds, horn, and baritone present the first four bars of the B section; brass present the last four measures
17	Horns have melodic line in the presentation of verse 2; clarinets play an ascending syncopated accompaniment line
25	Horns continue with the first four bars of the B material; trumpets and piccolo complete B phrase
32	A two-bar extension of spicy chromatic chords in brass and low woodwinds
35	Third verse of folk song theme, scored for full band; theme begins in canonic imitation
43	B section scored again for woodwinds with baritones for the first four measures; brass section completes the B phrase
51	A one-measure extension of a *fortissimo* b-flat major chord occurring after the completion of the B phrase

Movement II: "*Adam e sa Coumpagno*"
(Adam and his companion)
This slow movement consists of a folk song whose theme is two repeated phrases (AABB). The theme is presented twice and is scored differently each time. The movement is composed in g minor with momentary forays to natural and melodic minor scale forms.

MEASURE	EVENT AND SCORING
1	Theme in first clarinet and oboe, accompaniment in woodwinds and low brass
5	Repeat of A phrase; horns provide a short, countermelodic idea
9	Trumpet starts B phrase with accompaniment in brass
13	Trumpets continue repetition of B phrase for two bars; woodwinds complete last phrase
18	Baritones begin second verse of folk song and play both statements of the A phrase; this time upper woodwinds present a new countermelody in which accidentals give it a modal quality
26	Trumpets begin to phrase with brass accompaniment
30	Baritones present second statement of B phrase, at first as a solo, then joined by trombones, horns and, finally, tuba; movement ends quickly on a Picardy third

Movement III: *"Lou Fustie"*
(a proper name pronounced Foo-stē-ā)
Like the second movement, the folk song is a binary-structured melody consisting of two repeated phrases (AABB). The tempo is fast. The theme is presented four times in the key of g minor, with some verses in dorian mode.

MEASURE	EVENT AND SCORING
1	First verse begins with melody in baritones accompanied by an open fifth drone in low brass and woodwinds
8	Trumpets and horns present first B phrase; clarinets play repetition of B phrase
17	Woodwinds perform a phrase with chordal accompaniment, which occurs regularly on the weak beat

MEASURE	EVENT AND SCORING
25	Woodwinds continue with B phrase; muted brasses play the second repetition of phrase
32	Low brass and woodwinds play A phrases in parallel fifths; over the melody, high brasses play chords constituted of fourths, giving this section a feeling of bi-tonality
41	Trumpets present B phrases over syncopated chords; rhythmic activity diminishes during repetition of the B phrase in preparation for fourth verse
49	The fourth and last statement of folk song melody in piccolo, bass clarinet, and tuba; drone, reminiscent of the beginning of the movement, returns along with a linear chromatic voice in clarinets
57	B phrase presented in woodwinds
61	Full brass enter at the second statement of the B phrase; woodwinds join and build to m. 65
65	Full band score *forte* plays one final four-bar statement of the B phrase; combination of trills and rhythmic activity make this a very exciting closing statement, which ends with a Picardy third in g major

Movement IV: "*Lis Escobo*" (a *farandole*)
(a proper name: the first sounds like "lease";
the surname is accented on the first syllable)
This movement is a provencal dance tune with the phrase structure AABC. The overall form of the movement is four statements of the *farandole* theme, with a sixteen-measure setting of A phrase material into the relative minor. It is composed in the concert key of b-flat major.

MEASURE	EVENT AND SCORING
1	After four-measure introduction by side drum, piccolo, oboe, and bassoon present a complete statement of the *farandole* theme in unison, to drum accompaniment

MEASURE	EVENT AND SCORING
36	Percussion color change for side drum to tambourine; a drone is added in muted brass; second complete statement of the *farandole* theme is scored in flute, clarinet, and muted trumpet
71	Another four-bar introduction to the third statement of the theme; a rhythmic figure using the tonic and dominant pitches is performed in low voices; theme is presented at first by the horns, with subtle trills and rhythm patterns in woodwinds and upper brass
91	Upper woodwinds are briefly given the melody; horns pick up the melody again at m. 99; sparse accompaniment figures in the orchestration
107	Transposed and slightly varied A phrase material set in the relative minor; on the repeat, the woodwinds provide a harmonized countermelody
116	Brass take up the fourth and final statement of the *farandole* theme; brass choir alternates phrases with the woodwind choir during this rendition; full band joins together for the last phrase
156	A four-bar extension based on the last phrase material is accompanied by a circle of fourths progression
159	A nine-measure closing phrase begins in tonic key with scale patterns and scoring building to a *tutti fortissimo*; in mm. 164-165, the band performs two cluster chords which momentarily blur the tonality; this short extension comes to an abrupt halt, with the final two chords sounding clearly the dominant and finally the tonic

Unit 8: Suggested Listening

Percy Grainger, *Lincolnshire Posy*
Gustav Holst, *Second Suite in F*
Darius Milhaud, *Suite Française*
Jan Van der Roost:
    Four Old Dances
    Puszta
    Rikudim
Ralph Vaughan Williams, *English Folk Song Suite*

Unit 9: Additional References and Resources

Apel, Willi. *Harvard Dictionary of Music*. Cambridge, MA: Harvard University Press, 1972.

Encyclopedia Britannica. 1983 edition.

Miles, Richard. ed. *Teaching Music through Performance in Band,* Volume 2. Chicago, IL: GIA Publications, Inc., 1998.

Murphy, Howard. *Form in Music for the Listener.* Camden, NJ: Radio Corporation of America. 1948.

Rehrig, William H. *The Heritage Encyclopedia of Band Music.* Edited by Paul E. Bierley. Westerville, OH: Integrity Press, 1991, 1996.

Sadie, Stanley, ed. *New Grove Dictionary of Music and Musicians.* London: Macmillan, 1980.

Van der Roost, Jan. Correspondence with Jay Gilbert dated 27 December 1995.

Contributed by:

Jay W. Gilbert
Director of Bands and Chair, Music Department
Doane College
Crete, Nebraska

Teacher Resource Guide

Symphonic Songs for Band
Robert Russell Bennett
(1894–1981)

Unit 1: Composer

Robert Russell Bennett was born in Kansas City, Missouri. He grew up on a farm, where he learned to play a variety of musical instruments (including violin and trombone) from his father, a bandmaster, and piano from his mother. In Kansas City from 1909 to 1913, he studied harmony and counterpoint with Carl Busch. In 1926, he began a six-year period of study in Europe, which included four years of study in Paris with Nadia Boulanger, considered by many Americans as this century's most influential music teacher.

Bennett was one of America's most important and influential musicians from 1930 through 1980. He had an unparalleled career as a brilliant arranger of music for the American musical theatre, and he is credited for establishing what is often called the "Broadway Sound." For over three decades, the majority of America's best-known Broadway hits were arranged for pit orchestra by Bennett. He did the orchestrations for over 300 musicals, including shows by Irving Berlin, Jerome Kern, Cole Porter, George Gershwin, Vincent Youmans, Frederick Loewe, and Richard Rodgers. Widely imitated and admired throughout the world, Bennett more than any other person can be credited for making music arranging an art.

Bennett was very successful as a composer, writing in a wide variety of forms including opera, operetta, concerti, symphonies, tone poems, suites, chamber music, vocal music, keyboard music, movie and television scores. His musical successes include many highly deserved commissions and awards, including the Oscar, the Christopher, and the Emmy awards. He received an honorary doctorate and the highest musical citation the city of New York can offer, the Handel Medallion. In 1975, he published a book on orchestration, *Instrumentally Speaking*. Other works for band by Bennett include *Suite of Old American Dances*, *Four Preludes for Band*, *Down to the Sea in Ships*, and *Autobiography for Band*.

Unit 2: Composition

Symphonic Songs for Band is a three-movement suite of dances or scenes as much as they are songs. According to the composer, the name comes from the tendency of the principal part to sing out a fairly diatonic tune against whatever rhythm develops against the middle instruments. This work represents an originality and imagination that embodies many of the elements that made America and American music unique during the mid-1900s.

The suite opens with the "Serenade" that becomes quite tuneful with an energy and exuberance unlike the serenades of Mozart, Schubert, or Brahms.

"Spiritual," the middle movement in A-B-A form, first presents a tune that sounds as if its roots came from an African American folk tune with blues-like harmonies. The opening melody has a simplistic beauty that is followed by a middle section that has an irreverent innocence created through the use of syncopated jazz/ragtime rhythms and colorful harmonies.

The final movement, "Celebration," recalls an old-time country fair with cheering crowds of spectators, an old-time calliope, whistling of birds, a circus act or two, and the inevitable mule race. *Symphonic Songs for Band* was a commission by the Kappa Kappa Psi Band Fraternity, and the first performance of the work was given at the 1957 national convention in Salt Lake City by the National Intercollegiate Band.

Unit 3: Historical Perspective

Symphonic Songs for Band was written during a time when there were a large number of great composers that were being encouraged to write masterworks for bands. A selected list of these composers and works they wrote for band during this time period include: *The West Point Symphony* and *Ballad for Band* by Morton Gould; *Suite Francaise* by Darius Milhaud; *La Fiesta Mexicana* by H. Owen Reed; *Tunbridge Fair* by Walter Pistion; *Canzona* by Peter Mennin; *Divertimento for Band* and *Symphony No. 6* by Vincent Persichetti; *Symphony in B-flat* by Paul Hindemith; *Chorale and Alleluia* by Howard Hanson; *Fanfare and Allegro* by Clifton Williams; *Symphony No. 3* by Vittorio Giannini; *American Overture for Band* by Joseph Jenkins; and *Celebration Overture* by Paul Creston. Prior to this period (1940-60), there were only a handful of major composers, such as Holst, Vaughan Williams, Jacobs, Schmitt, and Grainger, who were writing original masterworks for band. From his early association with the town band, the jazz bands of the early 1920s, the military bands of World War I and World War II, to the musicals he orchestrated, Bennett had little trouble finding his own language and style of writing for wind band.

Unit 4: Technical Considerations

The primary technical challenge in the first movement is rhythmical. The first movement is in 3/8 meter and should be performed in a bright enough tempo so that it can be conducted with one beat to a bar. In the first twenty-one measures and briefly near the end of the movement, there is a hemiola that gives the music a 3/4 feel over every two measures. The first statement of the primary song is by woodwinds in a duple figure over the 3/8 measure in one (two against three), further use of the hemiola. Underneath the melodic material there is continuous use of a syncopated sixteenth-eighth-sixteenth note figure, or a hemiola, that gives the accompaniment a feeling of 3/4 every two measures. There are brief soli for cornet, trombone, and oboe.

The technical challenges in the second movement fall in the fragmented solo statements of the primary song. Instruments with solo passages are euphonium, cornet, horn choir, English horn, flute, and piccolo.

The final movement is technically demanding because of the facility needed to play chromatic and other sixteenth note passages in the woodwind parts. At times the xylophone doubles the woodwind parts and presents some of the same technical challenges. Brass and other percussion parts are not as active as the woodwind parts, but they do go by quickly and require clean and precise articulations with the syncopated rhythmic figures. There is a short euphonium solo near the end of the movement. There are several other passages that are not marked soli but are exposed for the tenor saxophone, bassoon, oboe, flute, euphonium, and timpani.

Unit 5: Stylistic Considerations

There are a number of stylistic and musical challenges that must be considered to give a credible performance of this work. Throughout this piece the styles of European classical music and jazz are presented together. Informed decisions are needed to be made about when to play in one style or the other. In particular, attention needs to be given to articulations, the styles of attacks, and types of releases. In some passages one may choose to use an articulated "T" release for short *staccato* notes. In other passages, care needs to be taken not to allow this articulation to be used on releases (for example, the sixteenth note releases in the euphonium solo in Movement III should not be played with articulated releases). Throughout this piece careful attention needs to be given to the style of the syncopated figure written, eighth-quarter eighth or sixteenth eighth-sixteenth. There are times when this figure works well when played *staccato* and other times when playing with a more *legato* tongue and longer note lengths gives the music a more characteristic relaxed jazz feel.

Unit 6: Musical Elements

MOVEMENT I:

The use of hemiola throughout the movement is a primary musical element of the movement that requires good rhythmic security for an ensemble to successfully perform this movement.

MOVEMENT II:

In this movement care should be taken to keep relatively similar volumes from one solo statement to the next to give continuity to the complete statement of the primary song. In the middle section of the movement, there is the strong influence of ragtime and American dance music from the 1920s and 1930s in the rhythmic figures and harmonies used. Care should be given in the performance in this section to capture a light dance feel, almost soft-shoe in character.

Movement III:

Musically, the last movement is a festive celebration that is boisterous, carefree, and humorous, with interludes of calm, imaginative musical wit. Some of the close harmonies and dissonance used in juxtaposition to familiar melodies that should be sung out reminds one of passages in the music of Ives. This movement is an excellent example of how descriptive a language music can be in the hands of a fine composer.

Unit 7: Form and Structure

SECTION	MEASURE	EVENT AND SCORING
Movement I: "Serenade"		
Introduction	1-23	Hemiola; basses, horn, euphonium
	9-21	Motive I; used as transition; melodic and accompaniment material cornet, trombone
	17-20	Motive II; trumpet, high woodwinds
A	23-61	Main theme; high woodwinds with brass and percussion
Interlude	57-73	Accompaniment
	57-60	Motive I from introduction, brass
	61-64	Motive I from introduction, woodwinds, horns
	65-72	Hemiola; trumpet, oboe; Motive I, cornets, saxophones
	73-76	Motive I, solo cornet
	77-80	Motive I, solo trombone
	81-87	Motives I and II, trumpet, saxophone

SECTION	MEASURE	EVENT AND SCORING
A	89-118	Main theme, high woodwinds; Motive I, used as accompaniment, trumpet, cornet
Interlude	115-151	
	115-118	Motive I, brass and percussion
	119-122	Motive I, woodwinds and horn
	123-130	Motive I, cornet
	131-142	Transitional material based on Motive I; clarinets, tambourine, snare drum
		Transitional material based on Motive I; euphonium, saxophone
B	151-225	Second theme with Motive I used for accompaniment; full ensemble
	191-204	Second theme, solo oboe
	205-224	Transitional material based on Motive I; clarinets, xylophone
	225-230	Hemiola; opening material in introduction
A1	231-262	Main theme, woodwinds; Motive I accompaniment, trumpet
	261-268	Motive I, cornets
Closing	269-285	Second theme fragment, brass; Motive I, high woodwinds, low brass
Coda	285-300	Full ensemble

Movement II: "Spiritual"

Introduction	1-11	
	3-4	Motive I, euphonium solo
	5-6	Motive II, flute, oboe
A	11-18	First theme, solo cornet, flute, and oboe
	19-25	Second theme, English horn, horn choir; octave/dominant pedal point, timpani, piccolo, flute, bells
	26-35	Interlude using motives from the first theme; cornet, oboe
	36-44	Second theme restatement
B	45-56	First theme, *tutti* woodwinds and brass
	57-64	Second theme, English horn, clarinet
	65-70	Second theme restatement, euphonium; countermelody, piccolo, flute, clarinet

SECTION	MEASURE	EVENT AND SCORING
	71-74	Interlude using accompaniment Motive III from B section (m. 46)
	75-78	Motive III used as transition, trumpets; *obligato*, high woodwinds
A	79-86	First theme, cornet, euphonium; Motive III, timpani, tuba
	85-86	Motive III, upper woodwinds
	87-89	Second theme, horn choir, flute, oboe, clarinet, saxophone
Coda	95-102	
	95-99	Motive III, horn, snare drum with brushes, tuba
	100-101	Fragment from Motive II, piccolo solo

Movement III: "Celebration"

A	1-26	First theme, cornets, euphonium; Motive I, (*obligato*) high woodwinds
	26-36	Motive II, transition material
	26-29	Motive II, trombone
	30-33	Motive II, woodwind soli
	30-34	Motive II altered, cornet, trumpet, horn, euphonium, trombone
	38-53	Second theme (Old Grey Mule song), trumpet, trombone
	54-57	Motive III, (*staccato* eighth note figure) high woodwinds, trumpet
	58-61	Motive IV, (*legato arpeggio*) cornet, trombone, high woodwinds
	62-65	Motive III, (*staccato* eighth note figure) high woodwinds, trumpet
	66-69	Motive V, (*legato* line) cornets
	70-73	Motive III altered, trumpets, trombone
	74-77	Motive V, trumpet, trombone, with woodwind *obligato*
	78-85	Transition, full ensemble
	86-99	Second theme (Old Grey Mule), low brass
	86-99	Motive III used as accompaniment figure, full ensemble
	100-104	Transition material to waltz/calliope section

SECTION	MEASURE	EVENT AND SCORING
B (interlude)	105-119	Calliope/waltz, flute, E-flat clarinet melodic material; accompaniment, trumpet, horn, tuba
	119-127	First theme, partial statement, cornets; Motive I, high woodwinds
	128-137	Transition to bird section, low woodwinds, saxophones, bird whistle
	137-157	Motive VI (bird section)
	137-146	Bassoon, tenor saxophone, bird whistle
	147-157	Motive VII (bird section), oboe, flute, low brass, horn, euphonium
	158-174	Motive VIII, transition to closing upper woodwinds, trumpet, euphonium
	170-173	Motive VIII, euphonium solo
C (closing)	174-185	Percussion interlude, wood block, snare drum, timpani, tom-tom
	186-193	Motive IX, saxophone, trombone
	187-193	Chromatic woodwinds without oboe
	194-205	Motive X, woodwinds
	206-213	Motive XI, marcato brass, *legato* clarinet
	214-218	Wind whistle
	218-238	Motive XI and wind whistle without *legato* clarinet
	238-259	Second theme final statement, full ensemble

Unit 8: Suggested Listening

Robert Russell Bennett:
  Suite of Old American Dances
  Symphonic Songs for Band
Morton Gould, *Ballad for Band*
Clare Grundman, *Three Sketches for Band*
Charles Ives, *Old Home Days*

Unit 9: Additional References and Resources

Battisti, Frank. *The Twentieth Century American Wind Band/Ensemble*. Fort Lauderdale, FL: Meredith Music, 1995.

Bennett, Robert Russell. *Instrumentally Speaking*. Melville, NY: Belwin Mills, 1975.

Claghorn, Charles Eugene. *Biographical Dictionary of American Music*. West Nyack, NY: Parker Publishing, 1973.

Smith, Norman E. *March Music Notes*. Lake Charles, LA: Program Note Press, 1986.

Contributed by:
Marcellus Brown
Boise State University
Boise, Idaho

Teacher Resource Guide

Three London Miniatures

Mark Camphouse
(b. 1954)

Unit 1: Composer

Mark Camphouse is currently Associate Professor of Music and Director of Bands at Radford University in Virginia. At Radford, he has served as conductor of two Virginia-based professional ensembles: The New River Chamber Winds and Skyline Brass. In 1998-99, Professor Camphouse served a one-year appointment as Acting Dean of Music at New World School of the Arts in Miami, Florida.

Camphouse received his formal training at Northwestern University, where his principal private teachers included John P. Paynter (conducting), Alan Stout (composition), and Vincent Cichowicz (trumpet). He is active as a guest conductor, clinician, and lecturer, traveling to over thirty states, Canada, and Europe. His music has been performed by distinguished ensembles such as the U.S. Marine Band, U.S. Army Band, Her Majesty's Royal Marine Band, Dallas Wind Symphony, and Northshore Concert Band. Camphouse was named winner of the 1991 National Band Association Composition Contest with his work *To Build a Fire*, runner-up in both the 1986 and 1988 American Bandmasters Association Ostwald Competition, Regional Finalist in the 1992 White House Fellowship Competition, and recipient of the Radford University Dedmon Award for Professorial Excellence.

Other works for winds include *Tribute; A Movement for Rosa; Watchman, Tell Us of the Night;* and *Symphony from Ivy Green for Soprano and Wind Orchestra*, with text from the writing of Helen Keller.

Unit 2: Composition

Three London Miniatures was commissioned for the Woodward Academy Bands in College Park, Georgia. Camphouse writes of *Three London Miniatures:*

> I have had the pleasure of visiting Great Britain on three occasions; twice for professional-related work in 1975 and 1995, and most recently while on a vacation during the Holiday Season, December-January 1996-97. If I had to select a "favorite" foreign city, London —with its warm people, unique urban charm, and rich historic and cultural traditions—would certainly rank at the very top. While all of the musical arts thrive in that fascinating city, the majestic and dignified traditions associated with English choral singing in particular are especially impressive and memorable to experience. Movement I of *Three London Miniatures* (Westminster Hymn) centers around a sturdy, and originally composed hymn tune having a decidedly Anglican flavor. Intermittent brass fanfares represent the regal and ceremonial traditions of Westminster Abbey. Movement II (For England's Rose) is an expressive, lyrical tribute to the late Princess Diana (1961-1997). Movement III (Kensington March) is a spirited, petite march in the English style.

Unit 3: Historical Perspective

Camphouse identifies Movement I, "Westminster Hymn," as an originally composed hymn tune of "a decidedly Anglican flavor." Writing in this style of English hymn, historical tradition of a choral setting, primarily syllabic and homophonic in texture, provides a well-chosen glimpse back to this practice in this setting for band. Movement II, "For England's Rose," is a very beautiful and flattering tribute to the late Princess Diana and all of her benevolence and charm. Movement III, "Kensington March," provides an accessible channel to another traditional custom of English musical history, the march.

Unit 4: Technical Considerations

Three London Miniatures is orchestrated for standard band instrumentation, with much of the scoring in sections or groups of instruments. There are opportunities for flute and alto saxophone soloists to be highlighted on very beautiful, lyrical lines. Ranges for all instruments are moderate, and technical demands are accessible to less-experienced or developing bands. Double-reed parts are generally also doubled with other instruments within the score.

Rhythms are not complex yet considerably varied utilizing many meter changes: 2/4, 3/4, 4/4, and 5/4. These changes, combined with many tempo changes throughout the suite, provide rewarding challenges for players and conductor.

Unit 5: Stylistic Considerations

The first movement, "Westminster Hymn," requires sustained *legato* playing throughout the hymn with *marcato* passages in the brass fanfares. The second movement, "For England's Rose," will challenge players to play very expressively with excellent tone quality to bring out the beauty in this movement. The third movement, "Kensington March," requires a light march-quality approach throughout with uniform articulations throughout. Precise rhythm, combined with a crisp *staccato* to contrast the *sostenuto* section, will assist in increasing the intensity and providing drive to the end of the march.

Unit 6: Musical Elements

Three London Miniatures includes an original hymn, a ballad, and a short march. These three movements provide a tremendous opportunity for contrasting styles and materials within the same work. The harmony is tonal, and the melodies are clearly scored throughout, usually in regular phrases. Interesting changes in color, textures, and dynamics occur within each of the three movements. Effective transitions and occasional phrasal changes are often assisted through the use of different meters.

Unit 7: Form and Structure

SECTION	MEASURE	EVENT AND SCORING
Movement I: "Westminster Hymn"		
Introduction	1-10	*Lento Mistico*
A	11-26	*Con Moto*
B	27-34	*Festivamente* (brass fanfare)
A	35-50	*A tempo*
A material (varied)	51-62	*Piu mosso*
A material (varied)	63-67	*Tranquillo*
transition into return of B section		
B	68-77	*Festivamente*
A (key change)	78-94	*Maestoso*
Movement II: "For England's Rose"		
Introduction	1-4	*Adagio Lamentoso*
Theme I	5-12	*Dolente*
Theme II	13-20	*Con Moto*
Variation on Theme II	21-28	*Tempo I*
Closing	29-31	*Rallentando*
Movement III: "Kensington March"		
Introduction	1-8	*Spirited*
A	9-16	*Lightly*
B	17-24	(mm. 25-27 extension)

Section	Measure	Event and Scoring
A	28-47	(round-type material)
		(mm. 44-47 extension)
Trio	48-63	*Nobilmente*
Variation on	64-80	*Lightly and brilliantly!*
trio material		
Closing	80-86	*Largamente*

Unit 8: Suggested Listening

Mark Camphouse, *A Movement for Rosa*
Gustav Holst, *Second Suite in F*
Joaquin Rodrigo, *Adagio Para Orquestra De Instrumentos De Viento*
Hugh Stuart, *Three Ayres from Gloucester*
Ralph Vaughan Williams, *Symphony No. 2, "London"*

Unit 9: Additional References and Resources

Grout, Donald J., *A History of Western Music*, revised edition. New York: W.W. Norton & Co., 1973.

Sadie, Stanley, ed. *Norton Grove Concise Encyclopedia of Music*, New York and London: WW Norton & Company, Macmillan Press, London, 1988.

Contributed by:

Cheryl Fryer
University of North Texas
Denton, Texas

Teacher Resource Guide

Variations on a Bach Chorale
Jack Stamp
(b. 1954)

Unit 1: Composer

Jack Stamp was born in Washington, DC, in 1954 and grew up in the nearby Maryland suburbs. He received a B.S. degree in Music Education from Indiana University of Pennsylvania in 1976, an M.M. degree in Percussion Performance from East Carolina University in 1978, and a D.M.A. degree in Wind Conducting from Michigan State University in 1988, where he studied with Eugene Corporon. His primary composition teachers were Robert Washburn and Fisher Tull. More recently, he has worked with Joan Tower, David Diamond, and Richard Danielpour. Stamp is currently Professor of Music at Indiana University of Pennsylvania, where he conducts the Wind Ensemble and Symphony Band, and teaches courses in graduate and under-graduate conducting. He is founder and musical director of the Keystone Wind Ensemble, a professional recording group dedicated to the advancement of American concert band music.

Unit 2: Composition

Variations on a Bach Chorale was commissioned by the Maine Chapter of the National Band Association and premiered by the Maine All-State Band in 1996, with Lewis Buckley conducting. The work is based on the Bach chorale "Nimm von uns, Herr, du treuer Gott" (Have mercy, Lord, and hear our prayer) and is in four movements: "Fanfare-Chorale," "Cantus Firmus," "Recitative," "Fugue-Final Chorale." The work is dedicated to American com-poser David Diamond. During the summer of 1974, Stamp studied with Diamond. One of his assignments was to harmonize a Bach chorale using "modal harmony." The eventual result was this four-movement work.

Unit 3: Historical Perspective

Variation technique has been employed by composers since the beginning of instrumental music. Bach was a master of the form, as exhibited in his *Goldberg Variations*. Since Bach's "revival" by Felix Mendelssohn, composers have been fascinated by his compositions, composing pieces based upon his earlier works or even compositions based on the musical "pitches" of his name: B-A-C-H. Likewise, many of his works, particularly those for organ, have been transcribed for the wind band. The variation technique itself has appeared prominently in band music, most notably in John Barnes Chance's *Variations on a Korean Folk Song* and Norman Dello Joio's *Variants on a Medieval Tune*.

Unit 4: Technical Considerations

Each variation (movement) poses a different technical challenge. "Fanfare-Chorale" puts demands on the brass and requires the ensemble to play in the keys of F minor and B-flat minor. "Cantus Firmus" is a "percussion feature" which requires seven percussionists, including four timpani, xylophone, temple blocks, tom-toms, snare drum, bass drum, and cymbals. Rhythmic and metric complexities in the percussion parts coupled with hemiola-type *ostinati* in the winds make this movement a challenge for both player and conductor. "Recitative," though not difficult, demands intonation awareness. There are brief soli for flute, oboe, English horn, bassoon, alto saxophone, clarinet, French horn, and trombone. "Fugue-Final Chorale" presents two problems. Though the movement is not difficult, the complexities of the fugue require careful attention to the linear movement of each contrapuntal line. The final chorale, though tonal, is quite dense chordally and requires attention to balance, intonation, and the ability to sustain.

Unit 5: Stylistic Considerations

Again, each variation demands a contrasting stylistic consideration. "Fanfare-Chorale" requires independent playing from all members so that Bach's original harmonization is heard complete and full. "Cantus Firmus" requires contrasts between a highly rhythmic accompaniment with a slower, sustained *cantus firmus*. "Recitative" is the most transparent movement, requiring sensitivity in all performers, particularly those with the brief soli. Due to the highly contrapuntal nature of the final movement, "Fugue-Finale Chorale," emphasis on clarity of individual lines is of the utmost importance.

Unit 6: Musical Elements

Each movement (variation) allows the teaching of formal design and/or a twentieth century compositional technique.

MOVEMENT I: "FANFARE-CHORALE"
The "fanfare" is based upon the first phrase of the original chorale and is har-

monized in a polychordal setting. The chorale is then stated twice in its original form as harmonized by Bach.

MOVEMENT II: "CANTUS FIRMUS"
The title suggests the technique used in this movement. The opening percussion statement is based on the opening phrase of the chorale. Subsequently, different *ostinato* "layerings" accompany augmented statements of the chorale.

MOVEMENT III: "RECITATIVE"
This movement is based entirely on a motive derived from the third measure (second phrase) of the chorale.

MOVEMENT IV: "FUGUE-FINAL CHORALE"
This movement features a three-voice fugue based on a motive from the first measure of the chorale. Coupled with the fugue is the original chorale in augmentation in the bass voices. The final chorale is an example of a "modal harmonization."

Unit 7: Form and Structure

Movement I: "Fanfare-Chorale"

MEASURE	EVENT AND SCORING
1-14	Fanfare based on motives from the first two phrases of the chorale
15-26	Original chorale in f minor stated in the woodwinds
27-29	Transition/modulation
30-42	Original chorale in B-flat minor stated in the brasses
43-end	"Unresolved" type of ending which leads to the second movement

Movement II: "Cantus Firmus"

MEASURE	EVENT AND SCORING
1-12	Percussion introduction based on first phrase of chorale
13-21	Brass *ostinato*, with the first phrase of the chorale stated as a "cantus" in the upper winds in A minor
22-30	The *ostinato* appears in the upper winds as low brass and low reeds present the "cantus" in B-flat minor based on the second phrase of the chorale
21-42	*Ostinato* shifts to trumpets and trombones, with the "cantus" based on the third phrase of the chorale appearing in double octaves in the upper winds and lower voices

MEASURE	EVENT AND SCORING
43-49	The percussion "cadenza" returns in a modified form, still based on the first phrase of the chorale, but somewhat inverted
50-58	The final *ostinato* is an example of pandiatonicism and hemiola, as the seven notes of the opening phrase of the chorale accompany a final chordal statement in the brass

Movement III: "Recitative"

This movement is in a free form. The first thirteen measures are simple "reflections" on the second phrase of the chorale via solo instruments. At m. 14, a brief development section leads to a full ensemble statement of the short motive (mm. 20-28). At m. 28, a "modal harmonization" of the chorale is presented (mm. 29-39). This was one of the exercises presented to Mr. Diamond at Stamp's lesson. The movement concludes quietly with continued solo "reflections" on the motive.

Movement IV: "Fugue-Final Chorale"

MEASURE	EVENT AND SCORING
1-4	Statement of the initial fugue subject in clarinets
5-8	Second statement in alto saxophone and English horn
9-12	Third statement in bassoon, tenor saxophone, and euphonium
13-16	Further development of the three-voice fugue
17-28	As the three voices continue their "interplay," the original chorale tune appears in low reeds and low brass in augmentation
29-34	Transition material based on fugue subject
35-46	Full band modal harmonization of chorale
47-50	Coda ending based on chorale motive

Unit 8: Suggested Listening

J.S. Bach:
> Prelude and Fugue in B-flat
> Toccata and Fugue in D Minor

John Barnes Chance, *Variations on a Korean Folk Song*
Norman Dello Joio, *Variants on a Medieval Tune*

Unit 9: Additional References and Resources

Dvorak, Thomas L., Robert Grechesky, and Gary M. Ciepluch. *Best Music for High School Band*, edited by Bob Margolis. Brooklyn: Manhattan Beach Music, 1993.

Rehrig, William H. *The Encyclopedia of Band Music*. Edited by Paul E. Bierley. Westerville, OH: Integrity Press, 1991.

Contributed by:
Jack Stamp
Professor of Music
Indiana University of Pennsylvania
Indiana, Pennsylvania

Grade Five

Teacher Resource Guide

Circuits

Cindy McTee
(b. 1953)

Unit 1: Composer

Cindy McTee is Professor of Music Composition at the University of North Texas. She is from a family of amateur musicians who encouraged her interest in music and the arts. In the course of her undergraduate studies at Pacific Lutheran University, she spent a year in Poland studying with Krzysztof Penderecki. She credits Penderecki as both a musical and a professional influence. She continued her studies, earning a master's degree from Yale University and a Doctor of Philosophy in Music Composition from the University of Iowa. Professionally, she has developed an excellent reputation with performances by major American and international orchestras. She has also received several prestigious commissions, including a Fellowship from the National Endowment for the Arts. In 1992, her work was recognized by the American Academy of Arts and Letters with the Goddard Lieberson Award.

Unit 2: Composition

The original version of *Circuits* was an orchestral work completed in 1990. It is orchestrated so that it can be played by either a small chamber orchestra or a full orchestra. The expanded instrumentation calls for an additional player for the doubled woodwinds and trumpets, two additional horns to the original pair, and two additional trombones from the chamber version's single player. A tuba is also added. The percussion remain at three in both versions. On hearing the premiere, McTee's colleague Martin Mailman, well known for his own compositions for band, suggested that a version for wind ensemble would be well received. McTee quickly completed the wind ensemble version, which also dates from 1990, and it was introduced as her first mature work for winds. A final revision was completed in 1992. The orchestration of the new version is close to the full orchestra setting. The third oboe became an English horn and the third bassoon a contrabassoon. A saxophone quartet (SATB), bass and contrabass clarinets, and euphonium parts were added. A string bass part and the percussion are retained. McTee suggests that the title reflects several aspects of the work. The use of *ostinato*, short recurring ideas, and unrelenting kinetic energy all are circuitous connections. McTee views *Circuits* as a critical development in her style that has continued in her later works.

Unit 3: Historical Perspective

McTee's music is part of an eclectic trend of the late twentieth century. Her works use materials associated with many different movements. The influence of minimalists can be seen in *ostinato*. Jazz and jazz-like elements infuse both the harmony and the orchestration. The driving rhythms, led by the percussion, further connect the work to twentieth century popular idioms. Philosophically, McTee seeks to write music that connects to the audience on multiple levels. She interacts with the intellect in using organized structures and humor, and engages the body with rhythmic motion.

Unit 4: Technical Considerations

Circuits is a technically demanding work. Although only six minutes long, the tempo of quarter note = 152 demands intense concentration and unrelenting technique. The woodwind parts are the most demanding. Based largely on octatonic scales, the woodwinds must articulate rapid passages that do not fall into traditional patterns. *Arpeggios* are most commonly either diminished or augmented. The brass parts are significantly less demanding than the woodwinds. The brass are required to provide effects such as punch chord interjections, trombone *glissandi*, and bell tones. McTee also calls for rapid multiple tonguing. The percussion parts require intricate accuracy but are not technically demanding. Because *Circuits* is constructed in complex motives, described by McTee as "sound objects," parts often must work together to create composite ideas. This requires significant ensemble skills and technical accuracy.

Unit 5: Stylistic Considerations

Circuits is predominantly a dance-like movement. In a very crisp and articulate style, the dance is propelled by *ostinati* that establish the character and structure of the work. A familiarity with jazz articulation and inflection is especially important in the middle section of the work. McTee's style depends on juxtaposing musical ideas and requires the performers to clearly present contrasts and connections.

Unit 6: Musical Elements

The harmonic language of *Circuits* is predominantly octatonic. This provides a palette of tertian harmony without the implications of traditional tonality. *Ostinati* are used to provide the kinetic energy that is the signature of the work and to help define the formal structure. Small, recurring motives combine to form recognizable ideas that McTee calls "sound objects." Using these sound objects, she creates expectations in the listener. Humor is introduced by the way she satisfies and fails to satisfy the created expectation.

Unit 7: Form and Structure

Circuits is in three large sections. It can be described as ABA with a short introduction and coda; however, the return is not a recapitulation of the first A section. Musically, in the A section, the sixteenth note is the predominate pulse; in the B section, it is the eighth note. This analysis will identify the various motives and sound objects in order to indicate their juxtaposition and layering.

SECTION	MEASURE	EVENT AND SCORING
Introduction	1-9	Percussion
A	10-108	
a	10-29	*Ostinato* that creates the first "sound object," first heard in its complete form in m. 14
b	30-36	Octatonic runs with brass interjections
c	37-54	New *ostinato* pattern
	52-54	First appearance of cadential formula related to "walking bass line" from the B section
d	55-70	Octatonic runs for soloists; accompaniment anticipates B material
b	71-74	
a	75-80	
	75-77	First appearance of a sound object scored in flute, glockenspiel, and vibraphone
b	81-100	Expanded contrapuntally
	98-100	Second appearance of B cadential formula
a	101-107	
	101-102	Percussion, derived from introduction
	106-107	Second appearance of a sound object scored in flute, glockenspiel, and vibraphone

SECTION	MEASURE	EVENT AND SCORING
B	109-172	Delineated by "walking bass line" in eighth note pulse. This line is layered with a *legato* motive (e) and a brass interjection based on a trombone *glissando* and a "punch" chord (f)
e		Occurs four times, beginning in mm. 117, 127, 141, and 150
f		Occurs five times, beginning in mm. 118, 129, 136-137 (two statements), 147, and 151-155 (expanded, with the "punch" chords becoming two sets of a pair of sixteenth notes and an eighth note)
A	172-260	Measure 172 is layered and functions in both the last measure of the B section and the first measure of the return
b	174-177	
g	178-179	First appearance of brass multiple tonguing motive
a	180-181	
g	182-183	
a	184-186	
b	187	
g	188	
b	189	
g	190-191	
d	192-217	
e	218-225	Expanded to a *legato* melody
b	226-229	
a	230-234	
	230	Percussion, derived from the introduction
g	235-236	
a	237-239	
e	240-248	
c	249-257	
Coda	258-260	Third appearance of material based on B cadential formula

Unit 8: Suggested Listening

John Adams:
  A Short Ride in a Fast Machine
  Grand Pianola Music
Cindy McTee:
  California Counterpoint: The Twittering Machine
  Circuits

Unit 7: Additional References and Resources

McTee, Cindy. *Circuits*. Eugene Corporon and the University of Cincinnati College-Conservatory of Music Wind Symphony. Compact disc KCD-11042, 1992.

McTee, Cindy. *California Counterpoint: The Twittering Machine*. Eugene Corporon and the University of North Texas Wind Symphony. Compact disc KCD-11070, 1995.

McTee, Cindy. *Soundings*. Eugene Corporon and the University of North Texas Wind Symphony. Compact disc KCD-11084, 1997.

This study guide was prepared with material from an unpublished DMA Thesis (in progress) by Matthew McInturf, entitled *The Wind Music of Cindy McTee: Circuits, California Counterpoint: The Twittering Machine, and Soundings*, including an interview and materials from Cindy McTee. Both are used by permission.

Contributed by:

Matthew McInturf
Sam Houston State University
Huntsville, Texas

Teacher Resource Guide

Country Band March

Charles E. Ives
(1874–1954)

transcribed by James Sinclair
(b. 1947)

Unit 1: Composer

Charles Ives was born in Danbury, Connecticut, in 1874. His father, a band-master, also taught music theory, piano, and violin. George Ives fostered in his son not only a love of music but also a fierce unconventionality in his approach to it. Charles attended Yale University, where he studied composition with Horatio Parker and organ with Dudley Buck. After his graduation in 1898, Ives devoted his regular working hours to the insurance business and composed in his spare time. With Julian Myrick he founded what became one of the largest and most successful life insurance agencies in the country. Ives' music, largely inspired by American subjects, was distinguished by an extraordinary originality. He experimented with polytonality, polyrhythms, quartertones, and other modernistic devices long before they appeared in the works of European composers. Very little of his music was played in public until 1939 – when Ives was 65. Ives won the Pulitzer Prize for music in 1947, and he died in 1954.

Unit 2: Composition

Throughout his life, Ives was fascinated by bands and band music. Although he wrote ten pieces for band, only two youthful marches survive intact. *Country Band March* was not written for band; it was sketched out for chamber orchestra in 1905. Ives later returned to the sketches and incorporated the raw materials into three of his most important works: the "Hawthorne" movement of the *Concord Sonata*, "Putnam's Camp" from *Three Places in New England*, and the second movement of the *Fourth Symphony*. Ives scholar James Sinclair, who deciphered Ives' *Country Band March* sketches and conducted the orchestral premiere in 1974, also made the band transcription, which was first performed in 1973 by the Yale University Band, conducted by Keith Wilson.

Unit 3: Historical Perspective
Unlike most early twentieth century American composers, who wrote "respectable" music patterned after European models, Ives was more interested in music as it related to real life. For his musical inspiration he turned to hymn and folk tunes, popular and patriotic songs, and even ragtime. He was also fascinated by the way this music was sung and played by everyday people. *Country Band March* is one of Ives' most successful early efforts in this vein. With just a little imagination, we can visualize – as Ives certainly did – a motley collection of former musicians, fortified by frequent visits to the hard cider barrel, finally mustering the nerve to begin the rehearsal. The introduction is horribly out of tune and the players have difficulty maintaining the beat (mm. 3, 5-7). No sooner does the band finally get together than the percussion turns the beat over (mm. 15-19). Throughout the march, players get into trouble (mm. 30-35), then find their way back (m. 36). If players get totally lost, they just make up something – perhaps a tune from a different piece (mm. 53-59, cornet). As the players' lips get tired, the errors become even more disastrous, culminating in a section where no one can find the beat (mm. 126-129). After a miraculous unison eighth rest (m. 130), the group finally gets back together – at least for a while. Everything finally falls totally apart (mm. 174-180), only to be saved by trombone *glissandi* (m. 180) leading to the final tag ending. Unfortunately, the alto saxophones aren't watching and miss the cut-off (m. 183), and the group responds with a "normal" stinger (m. 184). All this – and much more – takes place in a little more than four minutes!

Unit 4: Technical Considerations
Rhythmic security is absolutely essential in the performance of *Country Band March*. The music must be played accurately for the audience to get the jokes. The triplets in mm. 30-35 and mm. 105-108 must be accurate, but not exaggerated. The non-measured triplets in mm. 76-79 provide three options for the melody (E-flat clarinet, alto clarinet, or cornet). The soloist must line up the beginning of each triplet with the appropriate part of the 2/4 meter. The horns are advised to listen only to the tune (not bothering to watch the conductor!) and line up their offbeats accordingly. All three parts must be seated within hearing distance of each other and should be rehearsed a few times by themselves. When played accurately, this is a most effective moment. The rhythmic meltdown in mm. 126-129 must be played correctly – even more important

are the unison eighth rests in mm. 130 and 174. It is advisable to add a caesura after m. 180, except for 1st and 2nd trombones, who hold on to their notes and begin a loud, slow *glissando* which ends at the conductor's cue for m. 181.

Unit 5: Stylistic Considerations

Country Band March should be played in a lightly detached march style, especially the bass line. Slurred passages should be played smoothly, but not dragged. Ives uses two kinds of accents: the normal horizontal accent and the vertical accent, which does not imply a short, explosive attack (as in jazz) but rather asks that the note be treated as a downbeat, a note that is stressed but not treated as syncopation. For example, the upper woodwind part in mm. 87-93 should not sound syncopated, just "off." This is exciting and difficult music, but it is also durable and forgiving – especially when players recover quickly from their mistakes and always play with conviction.

Unit 6: Musical Elements

The most important elements in *Country Band March* are the borrowed and original tunes, which must be heard by the listener whenever possible. This is best achieved by playing the tunes accurately and articulately rather than depending on constantly increasing volume. The location of these tunes is as follows (largely derived from James Sinclair's Preface to the Orchestral Score):

MEASURE	INSTRUMENT(S)	BORROWED AND ORIGINAL TUNES
8	Upper voices	*Country Band March* theme (Ives)
20	Flutes, clarinet 1	Fragment, possibly a quotation
20	Clarinets 2 and 3, alto clarinet, saxophones	Unidentified tune
24	Oboes, trumpets	*London Bridge*
26	Piccolo, flutes	*The Girl I Left Behind Me*
30	(triplets)	Unidentified tune
44	Oboes, clarinets, saxophones, cornets 2 and 3	*Country Band March* theme (Ives)
44	Cornet 1, trumpets	*Arkansas Traveler*
44	Piccolo, flutes, E-flat clarinet	*Massa's in de Cold Ground* (Stephen Foster)
44	Percussion	Traditional roll-off
50	Piccolo, flutes	*Marching through Georgia* (Henry Clay Work)
51	Trumpets	*Massa's in de Cold Ground* (Foster)
52	Upper woodwinds	*Marching through Georgia* (Work)

MEASURE	INSTRUMENT(S)	BORROWED AND ORIGINAL TUNES
53	Cornet 1	*Sempre Fidelis* (John Philip Sousa)
55	Alto saxophones, horns	*Battle Cry of Freedom* (G.F. Root)
59-60	Trumpets, piccolo	*Yankee Doodle*
61	*Tutti*	*Yankee Doodle*
62	Cornets 1 and 2, trumpets	*Massa's in de Cold Ground* (Foster)
64	Oboe	Unidentified tune
76	E-flat clarinet or alto clarinet or cornet 1	*Violets* (Ellen Wright)
77	Flutes	*London Bridge*
80	Alto saxophone	Fragment, possibly a quotation
82	Piccolo, flute, E-flat clarinet	*Marching through Georgia* (Work)
82	B-flat clarinets	*Marching through Georgia* (Work)
87	Piccolo, flutes, oboes, E-flat and B-flat clarinets	*London Bridge*
94-104	Cornets, clarinets 1 and 2, oboes	*London Bridge*
103	Alto saxophone	Fragment, possibly a quotation
105	(triplets)	*My Old Kentucky Home* (Stephen Foster)
109	Upper woodwinds, trumpets	*London Bridge*
111	Trombone	*Yankee Doodle*
131	Oboes, clarinets, cornets, trumpets	*Country Band March* theme (Ives)
131	Piccolo, flutes, E-flat clarinet	*London Bridge*
131	Trombones 1 and 2	*Country Band March* countermelody (Ives)
141	Cornets 1 and 2	*British Grenadiers*
142	Clarinets	Unidentified tune
160	Piccolo, flutes	*Country Band March* countermelody (Ives)
160	Oboes, E-flat clarinet, alto saxophones	*British Grenadiers*

MEASURE	INSTRUMENT(S)	BORROWED AND ORIGINAL TUNES
160	B-flat clarinets, cornets, trumpets	*Country Band March* theme (Ives)
166	Piccolo, flutes	*Marching through Georgia* (Work)
181	Piccolo, flutes	*London Bridge*
181	Oboes, clarinets, alto saxophones, cornets 2 and 3, trumpets	*Country Band March* theme (Ives)

The sketches of *Country Band March* do not contain the tune "British Grenadiers" in mm. 141-149 (cornets 1 and 2). Ives added this tune when he recycled the earlier material for use in "Putnam's Camp." Sinclair did not include it in the orchestral score to the march, but he did add it to the band transcription. It therefore may be omitted at the conductor's discretion. Also, the sketches for *Country Band March* show the final stinger with a "?" in Ives' hand. We cannot know the composer's final feelings about this particular passage, but the "lost saxophone" joke is heightened when the stinger is omitted. Again, this is up to the conductor.

Unit 7: Form and Structure

MEASURE	SECTION	DESCRIPTION
1	Introduction	Out-of-tune opening, rhythmic misalignment
8	Main section	*Country Band March* theme
30		Transitional material
44		*Country Band March* theme
59		Transitional material
64	"Trio"	Alternation of more relaxed material (mm. 64-68, 94-108) with rhythmically agitated and texturally complex sections (mm. 82-93, 109-112) [*Da Capo* after m. 112]
1	Introduction	Out-of-tune opening, rhythmic misalignment
8	Main section	*Country Band March* theme
30		Transitional material
44		*Country Band March* theme
59		Transitional material
64-68	"Trio"	Play first five measures then take the coda

MEASURE	SECTION	DESCRIPTION
113	Coda	Continues "Trio" material
117		Transitional "build-up" in clarinets and cornets
126		Rhythmic breakdown (where's the beat?)
131		*Tutti* (key abruptly modulates from B-flat to A-flat)
	Main section	*Country Band March* theme and countermelody
142		Transitional material
160		*Country Band March* theme and countermelody
168	Coda	Melodic and rhythmic fragmentation
180		Final breakdown
181-184		Tag ending (*Country Band March* theme)

Unit 8: Suggested Listening

Charles Ives:
  Country Band March (orchestral version)
  Country Band March (band transcription)
  Fourth Symphony
  Second Piano Sonata "Concord"
  Three Places in New England

Unit 9: Additional References and Resources

Ives, Charles E. *Country Band March*, orchestra score edited by James Sinclair. Bryn Mawr, PA: Merion Music, 1976.

Perlis, Vivian. *Charles Ives Remembered - An Oral History*. New Haven: Yale University Press, 1974.

Sinclair, James. A *Descriptive Catalogue of the Music of Charles Ives*. New Haven: Yale University Press, 1999.

Swafford, Jan. *Charles Ives, A Life with Music*. New York: W.W. Norton & Company, 1996.

Contributed by:

Kenneth Singleton
Director of Bands
University of Northern Colorado
Greeley, Colorado

Teacher Resource Guide

Danza de los Duendes

Nancy Galbraith
(b. 1951)

Unit 1: Composer

Nancy Galbraith was born in Pittsburgh, Pennsylvania, on January 27, 1951, where she began piano studies at the age of four with her mother, Alverta Hoffman Riddle. She later studied with pianist Fredrick Schiefelbein, then with Father Ignatius Purda at St. Vincent's College. She also studied music theory and piano at the Carnegie Mellon Preparatory School of Music. Besides piano, Galbraith also studied clarinet with the Pittsburgh Symphony's Jerome Levine. Her bachelor's degree in Composition is from Ohio University (1973), and her master's degree in Composition is from West Virginia University (1978). She has continued her education at Carnegie Mellon University, studying composition with Leonardo Balada. Galbraith currently resides in Pittsburgh, where she is Associate Professor of Composition and Theory at Carnegie Mellon University and organist/music director of Christ Lutheran Church.

Her creative output consists of a sizable volume of sacred music as well as music for orchestra, chamber music, and winds. In 1988, the Pittsburgh Symphony premiered Galbraith's *Second Symphony, Morning Litany*. In the fall of 1996, Ocean Records released "New Energy of the Americas," which includes Galbraith's *Piano Concerto No. 1* performed by Ralph Zitterbart with the Cincinnati Chamber Orchestra, conducted by Keith Lockhart. *Rhythms and Rituals* was premiered by The Renaissance City Winds with pianist Patricia Prattis Jennings. Another work for winds, *With Brightness Round About It*, was recorded by the Carnegie Mellon Wind Ensemble.

Galbraith has received numerous honors and awards, including a 1989

Creative Advancement Award to attend the Warsaw Autumn 32nd International Festival of Contemporary Music in Poland, the 1991 Ohio University Achievement in Music Award for outstanding alumni, a grant to study at the Juan Antxieta Center for Musical Studies in Bilbao (Spain), and a 1994 ASCAP award.

Unit 2: Composition

Program note for *Danza de los Duendes*:

> *Danza de los Duendes* (Dance of the Goblins) refers to elfin beings, who are mischievous and mean spirited, victimizing children at play during siesta when their parents are asleep or inattentive. Hiding in trees and bushes, los duendes are often blamed for minor and sometimes major recreational accidents and are thought to be the spirits of dead children now dwelling in a state of "ghostly purgatory." The work was arranged for winds by the composer after acclaimed orchestral performances by the Argentinean Orquesta Sinfónica de Tucumán and the Pittsburgh Symphony.

Composed in 1991 and premiered by the Orquesta Sinfónica de Tucumán and the Pittsburgh Symphony in 1992, Galbraith transcribed the work for wind symphony in 1996. The Carnegie Mellon University Wind Ensemble gave its premiere that year.

On the topic of programmatic music, Galbraith writes:

> This is not really a piece about goblins! Most of my music is non-programmatic, and this is no exception. I compose with purely musical intentions, and I begin to think about titles only after I have finished writing. My titles are only intended to vaguely allude to the mood or general content of the music.

Unit 3: Historical Perspective

Galbraith's quintessential American style employs a wide array of post-modern elements, including lyricism, polyrhythm, diatonic harmony, and minimalistic color. Her work has been praised for its "energetic combination of melody and rhythm, its bright orchestral palette, and its lyrical finesse." This work combines the unique post-modern elements of an American composer, who happens to be a woman and a subject associated with Latin America.

Unit 4: Technical Considerations

Because of the minimalist nature of this work, control in the upper woodwinds and brass is an important consideration. Syncopated rhythms throughout the piece are not complex but may need careful rehearsal in order to layer the polyrhythms and balance the instrumentation. The constant undulating rhythm must support the structure, not dominate it. Maintaining a constant momentum with the multitude of layers will enhance the performance.

Unit 5: Stylistic Considerations

Though minimalist in some regards, the overall intent is dynamic. The main theme and counter-themes must be recognized and brought out above the underlying texture. Though carrying a Latin American subject, the style is essentially contemporary American, with syncopation suggesting a nod to jazz influences.

Unit 6: Musical Elements

The polyrhythmic foundation of this work is its greatest element. Layering of melodies and harmonies can be enhanced by precision in the syncopated rhythmic motives. Covering a wide range of dynamics, balance should be particularly focused upon.

Unit 7: Form and Structure

SECTION	MEASURE	EVENT AND SCORING
Introduction	1-46	(C major) Brilliant, leading to syncopated motives
Exposition	47-142	(C major/A minor/F major)
A theme	51-56	Motive presented by trumpets, followed by various instruments
Climax statement	127-142	*Fortissimo* statement of motive with counter-theme (m. 129)
Transition	143-152	
Development	153-259	(A-flat major) Smaller instrumentation
Transition	260-286	(E major) Pulsating quarter notes, single pitch
Extended transition	287-321	Slower tempo, brass chords
Coda	322-374	*A tempo*, building layers
Final statement of A theme	360-374	

Program note for the wind symphony version:

> *Danza de los Duendes* begins with an introductory section that makes use of high woodwind textures and percussion. The introduction closes with falling runs into a quiet pulse in the clarinets. The main theme is then stated in the four trumpets. It is answered by various instruments and eventually is stated by the whole ensemble in an explosive climax which evolves into a repeated quarter note octave in the upper winds and large *fortissimo* chords

in the brass. The development section then follows, making use of the percussion and piano as background texture over which lyrical melodies are stated in the woodwinds. The section closes once again with the loud repeated quarter note octave, which *decrescendos* into a single quarter note pulse in the bass clarinet. The piano enters very quietly as accompaniment for soft and lush brass chords. The bass clarinet again enters with a pulsating rhythm. Ideas are gradually layered on top leading to a rousing, dramatic restatement of the main theme, which closes the piece.

Unit 8: Suggested Listening

John Adams, *Short Ride in a Fast Machine*
Nancy Galbraith:
   Danza de los Duendes (1991, orchestral version)
   Rhythms and Rituals (1995/97)
   With Brightness Round About It (1990/93)
   If Rachael in a Yellow Rose (1996)
   Elfin Thunderbolt (1998)
Frank Ticheli, *Blue Shades*

Unit 9: Additional References and Resources

Nancy Galbraith's website:
   http://www.andrew.cmu.edu/user/ngal/

Subito Music Publishing, Inc.

Contributed by:

Tony Spano, Jr.
Culver City High School
Academy of Visual and Performing Arts
Culver City, California

Teacher Resource Guide

Daughter of the Stars
(A reminiscence on Shenandoah)
Warren Benson
(b. 1924)

Unit 1: Composer

Warren Benson is one of the most talented and comprehensive artists on the modern stage. Best known as a composer with more than eighty major commissions, and with performances and recordings throughout the world, he has at the same time been quietly traveling as a conductor, teacher, and lecturer speaking in three languages, whose literary work has been translated into Spanish and Japanese. His teaching activity has been centered at Ithaca College and at the Eastman School of Music. "His wind band compositions have been among the most important of this century" (United States Marine Band 200th Anniversary Compact Discs Album, Booklet notes, p. 42). The American Symphony stated that "his two symphonies are landmarks in band music.... These two substantial symphonies – in their different ways – demonstrate the high potential that is offered by the concert band of today...."

Unit 2: Composition

Daughter of the Stars, based on the folk tune *Shenandoah*, was commissioned by the Bishop Ireton Symphonic Wind Ensemble and conducted by Dr. Garwood Whaley for the opening of their new concert hall. In his preface, the composer writes:

> This one-movement work introduces the tune into a rather abstract setting before proceeding to other material found on the work *Shenandoah* –

musical pitches for each letter:

S	H	E	N	A	N	D	O	A	H
E-flat	B	E	G	A	F	D	C	A	B

as composers have done before, since and including J.S. Bach. A seldom-used rhythm, the barcarole, rocks back and forth until the evenly repeated chords lay groundwork for a rather more surreal set of three-note chordal melodic fragments. The work hints at its beginning and ends quietly with respect for the history of the region, the tune ascending toward its place of rest as daughters of the stars are wont to do.

The pitches are used in no particular series order but rather as generalized scalar orders subject to the usual manipulation.

Unit 3: Historical Perspective

Benson has contributed many significant works to the wind ensemble repertoire, including *The Solitary Dancer, Symphony for Drum and Wind Orchestra, Symphony No. II - Lost Songs, The Drums of Summer,* and *The Leaves Are Falling.* Each of these expressive and challenging works has established a new direction and standard for wind repertoire.

The following comments in this resource guide are a summation of the author's conversations with composer Warren Benson and Colonel Timothy Foley, conductor of the United States Marine Band.

Unit 4: Technical Considerations

Although the rhythmic texture is primarily long notes, the level of difficulty is at least a grade six. Telling an ensemble that any work is difficult prior to the initial reading may lead to a negative environment. Rather, demonstrating and explaining how each part emerges from, leads to, and blends with another part will assist each player in knowing and communicating his or her own part in the whole. The challenge lies in maintaining and directing inner energy within long note values and a slow tempo.

It is essential for all players to develop meaningful, long tones that grow, decay, and change intensity and pitch. In addition, establishing appropriate energy and feel of the silence which emerges from or leads to sound is important in shaping the lines. Try to breathe sound into the tone and develop tones which are fat with pitch. Control of long tones and creating six different dynamics – *pp, p, mp, mf, pf,* and *ff* – is fundamental for the interpretation of this work.

Trombones should strive for a solid, rich tone beginning at m. 8, very *legato* and articulated with direction to m. 17. The sixteenth note in m. 13 must be emphasized and played with rhythmic integrity. The horn entrance at m. 14

must immediately create a presence as the low f in the tubas establishes the tonal area. The mallet sticking in mm. 52-58 should be as the chord is written, with two doubles rather than four singles.

Skilled conducting at m. 58 will anchor confident entrances with warm, expressive tone color while establishing the return to the *a tempo* at m. 59. The clarinets should rise out of silence at m. 72 by beginning the tone without the tongue and increasing the airstream until pitch emerges while maintaining section balance and a suitably rich sound. The marimba should be played as triplets (a standard abbreviation is indicated) rather than rolls. The percussion at m. 79, as always, are extremely important in establishing rhythm and color. Leave the damper off the vibraphone at m. 80, allowing it to ring as long as possible; the cymbal, tam-tam, and bass drum answer this in turn, all in a reflective style. The bass drum at m. 82 needs a harder beat but should be played without rushing. The trumpets at m. 83 must blow hard through the mandatory whisper mutes to create the feeling of being far away. The timpani at m. 84 must not sound like a roll as it leads to the downbeat at m. 85. The challenge is to *crescendo* while accelerating slowly, with the majority of the *crescendo* emerging at the end of the bar. One must wait after striking the drum at m. 85 before continuing with a *piano* roll to allow the head to resonate.

Unit 5: Stylistic Considerations

Balance is critical throughout the work. The winds and percussion must balance each other, while the harmonic structure demands that the chords be rich on the bottom. A synthesizer can be used instead of a contrabass clarinet. All must sound very *legato* and avoid bumpy or percussive effects. In addition, the clarinets should not *diminuendo* too quickly, but should sustain the sound in mm. 6-8 so the saxophone sound prevails but does not dominate.

Short note values need a feeling of emphasis and weight, while long note values should have direction. The sixteenth note entrances by the woodwinds should be played with length and emphasis in mm. 17-19, followed by great rhythmic accuracy of the tenor saxophone and euphonium line in m. 20.

Notes should be played with a rich, full sound, particularly at the ends of phrases such as in m. 16. The two-note pick-up into m. 32 actually establishes the barcarole section. It may need to be subdivided to establish the feeling of the 6/8 section (which should be conducted in six). Balance of the chord at m. 36 combined with the "*legato*, leaning" style which continues in m. 37 establishes the barcarole style.

The oboe's impassioned, free solo line moves the tempo ahead to its repose in m. 43. Elongating the last eighth note of m. 42 will set up the *calmando* in m. 43, while the percussion should let the ends of the notes ring in mm. 40-44. Measure 46 should be a full, rich sound with unhurried thirty-seconds in m. 48. The flutes at m. 85 should observe the phrasing while maintaining pitches and *crescendo* as they descend. The low b in the flute chord at m. 88 may need doubling to create a full sound. At m. 89, a roll is indicated in the marimba, with a very expressive rise and fall of dynamics – almost "solo-like," with the last note of the sixteenth figure being allowed to ring. Soft mallets are needed to accomplish this.

Unit 6: Musical Elements

Benson often uses an accent which, Foley suggests, should be interpreted as an important rhythmic entrance rather than a hard, tongued accent. He also encourages that the sixteenth notes and shorter-valued notes be played "rich with pitch and with emphasis" as the composer says. Benson reinforced this concept by suggesting that the flutes in m. 4 should be "connected with a *legato* tongue."

A three-note motive is introduced at m. 25, beat 2; this motive should be performed with the lower note receiving the emphasis so that it is heard and creates the feeling of a continuous *crescendo* within the motive.

Try to gauge the *rallentando* of m. 49 by incrementally increasing the distance between the pulses throughout the bar rather than slowing abruptly. Monitor the quarter note decay in m. 49 until it is almost silent, then use the last eighth note to assist the transition to the next section.

Allow the flutist to have ownership of the solo while establishing a beautiful backdrop of clarinets and saxophones for the solo. Encourage a free, improvisatory rhythm for the flute in mm. 53-54. The flute at m. 56 should remain on the b for a significant amount of time while having the courage to stretch m. 57, deliberately unfolding one section to the next.

Full sound and good intonation in the saxophones at m. 58 (conducted in six), including the baritone saxophone line at m. 59 together with a full sound in the mallet percussion through m. 60, will lead to the transition at m. 62. Return to a three pattern at m. 62 to lead the clarinet line to m. 66 while stretching the last beat of m. 65 to establish the new tempo at m. 66.

The initial four notes of m. 66 are critical in that they unfold the sequence which follows. Subdivision of the beat may be of assistance at m. 66, with a return to the three pattern at m. 67 for the quintuplet sweep which pushes to the third beat. At m. 71, a more somber style is created. The *legato*, pulsating, tolling figure established in the trombones confirms the tempo. The balance of the B-flat minor chord against the C and G in the bassoons, euphonium, and tubas is critical. The clarinets at m. 72 should "rise out of silence" rather than merely "come in."

An impassioned ending is critical beginning at m. 92 as the percussion swell and recede when the earlier three-note motive returns, with the emphasis on the lower pitch of the motive to give it the feeling of a continuous *crescendo*. Measures 99 and 100 create an echo as the crotales emerge underneath it. The crotales lead to m. 103, which might be subdivided to create a calm, flowing feeling over the C major chord in the lows at the *pp* level – the clarinet subtone, which must be unbelievably soft. Measure 111 is a momentary return to the original tempo followed by an immediate return to the molto *rallentando*, concluding with the final crotale pitch that should be allowed to ring as long as possible.

Truly invest in this work, as it is musically, emotionally, and intellectually challenging and fulfilling. Capture the passion and direction of Benson's extraordinary musical lines by guiding them to create and release tension. Deliver the musical strength and energy, which emerges not only through melodic lines and motives, but through rhythm as well. Carefully place the subdivisions found between parts without accent, as these rhythms propel the lines, colors, and textures while conceiving the larger picture of musical line and rhythm. For instance, the eighth note pulse at the beginning moves into the barcarole style, which transcends via the *rubato* flute solo to the repeated quarter note chords. The rhythmic intensity between the glockenspiel and marimba underpins the transition to the coda. The "interjections" can be surprising (as in the timpani at m. 84) or move to a climax (as in mm. 65-67). Use the energy of each measure to create a rainbow of sound.

The ethereal, precious colors and textures of this work are to be cherished. If each timbre is the result of or leads to another color while the melodic line and motives are masterfully woven into the texture, one will immediately be absorbed into this exquisite mosaic of sound.

Errata:

m. 17	Add *diminuendo* in trombones
m. 19	Percussion III should be *mp* rather than *mf*
m. 21	Tenor saxophone should be G-sharp rather than G-natural
m. 21	Flute ties over to m. 22
m. 24	Flute III should be C-sharp rather than C-natural
m. 25	Clarinet III *crescendos* on beat 1 and again on beat 2 to the and of 3, followed by a *diminuendo* at m. 26
m. 35	No I in the flutes or piccolo
m. 37	Add dotted quarter rest on beats 7-9
m. 41	Add a slur in the oboe from the *f* to the and of beat 2 in m. 42
m. 43	Piccolo should be b rather than a
m. 54	Baritone saxophone should be a rather than g
mm. 69-70	No alto saxophone I
m. 78	Percussion IV beat 2 should be B-natural and beat 4 should be B-flat
mm. 94-96	Baritone saxophone should be F-sharp
m. 102	Tuba, last quarter note should be a half note
m. 110	Eighth note = 36 or 40
m. 112	Eighth note = 40 rather than quarter note = 40

Unit 7: Form and Structure

The work, which is eleven and one-half minutes long, is comprised of three sections, beginning with the "Shenandoah" theme and continuing to a barcarole. Evenly repeated chords follow, establishing the groundwork for the three-note chordal melodic fragments. A coda closes the work. The form follows:

SECTION	MEASURE	DESCRIPTION
Part I	1-17	"Shenandoah" theme in mosaic
"Shenandoah" theme	17-32	Motive extends and leads to barcarole
Part II barcarole theme	32-50	Bacarole variation
	50-71	Flute solo transition on the theme
Part III	71-93	Evenly repeated chords
	94	Return of three-note motive/theme
Coda	103	Coda

The work opens with percussion and woodwinds establishing an eighth note foundation, with each note having the same articulation and quality so that the "Shenandoah" theme can be integrated into the texture. Since the opening four measures incorporate a note on each eighth note pulse, rhythmic integrity is critical; however, one should not conduct the subdivision. Benson suggests a tempo of eighth note = 72. Foley suggested that one should be in almost a "Zen-like" mindset to establish the appropriate style. The feeling to m. 17 is one sweeping gesture while moving under duress as if a hand were in the middle of one's back. Measures 17-31 have a sense of compulsion as the sixteenth notes in mm. 20, 24, 25, and 27 propel the music. The lushness of m. 26 changes moods as one is eased into the second section at m. 32.

The second section at m. 32 has a lifting, swaying feeling as if lilting to a barcarole, with an impassioned oboe solo leading to a rich, full textural climax. A relative calming at m. 43 prepares for the next swell to m. 48, followed by a quiet blanket of sound in m. 50 as the flute solo at m. 50 begins the transition to m. 71. The clarinet at m. 57 keeps the transition going as the rhythmic barcarole re-emerges. The clarinet lines move to the second beat of m. 66 where the tempo is re-established as the thirty-second note sequence unfolds followed by silence at m. 67, which prepares the quintuplet sweep. The B-flat minor chords against the C and G at m. 71 changing to f minor in m. 74 begin the move to closure. Eighth note subdivisions in mm. 80-82 propel the texture ahead, while the bass at mm. 85-87 provides the foundation for the flutes that must really *crescendo* rather than *diminuendo* at m. 88 so that the C chord grinds against the F pedal point. Measure 92 to the end demands being impassioned as the alto saxophone answered by the tenor saxophone, bassoon, and euphonium in mm. 93-94 are resolved in their response to the woodwind motive.

A coda at m. 103 is a "whispering reminder from whence we came." The C and G in the lows carefully support the clarinet subtone. The final sound becomes a rich, satisfied silence.

Unit 8: Suggested Listening
Warren Benson:
The Leaves Are Falling
Solitary Dancer
Symphony No. II - Lost Songs
Claude Debussy, *Nocturnes*
Joseph Schwantner, *and the mountains rising nowhere*

Unit 9: Additional References and Resources
Baker's Biographical Dictionary of Musicians. 8th Edition to Present. Indianapolis, IN: Also Century Edition, 2001.

Benson, Warren. Personal communication, January and August 1999.

Butterworth, Neil. *The American Symphony*. London: Scholar Press, 1998, Ashgate Press, Vt., 1998.

Foley, Tim. Personal communication, February and August 1999.

George, Roby Granville, Jr. "An Analysis of the Compositional Techniques Used in Selected Wind Works of Warren Benson." DMA thesis, University of Cincinnati, 1995.

Harbison, William G. "Analysis: The Passing Bell of Warren Benson." *Journal of Band Research* XXI/2 (Spring 1986): 1-8.

Hunsberger, Donald. "Discussions with Warren Benson: The Leaves Are Falling." *College Band Directors National Association Journal* I/1 (Spring 1984): 7-17.

Nagaer, Alan. *The Complete Music of Warren Benson*. Ph.D. Thesis, Florida State University, Tallahassee, FL, 1999-2000.

Norcross, Brian. "Spotlight on American Band Education." *Music Educators Journal*, 78:5 (January 1992): 53-58.

The President's Own United States Marine Band. The Bicentennial Collection Booklet notes on this 200th Anniversary 10 CD set of The President's Own United States Marine Band, p. 42.

Contributed by:
Paula Holcomb
Director of Bands
State University of New York—Fredonia
Fredonia, New York

Teacher Resource Guide

Divertimento for Winds and Percussion

Roger Cichy
(b. 1956)

Unit 1: Composer

Roger Cichy has a diverse background as both a composer/arranger and a music educator. He holds degrees from Ohio State University. His composition teachers include Edward Montgomery, Marshall Barnes, and Joseph Levey.

As a music educator, Cichy was a successful band director for grades five through twelve in Mars, Pennsylvania. Following the completion of his Master of Arts in Music Education at Ohio State University, he served as Associate Director of Bands at the University of Rhode Island and Iowa State University, where he directed the marching band, concert band, and basketball pep band. He left the faculty at Iowa State to devote his full time to composing and arranging.

As a freelance composer and arranger, Cichy writes for high school and college bands, professional orchestras, and the commercial music industry. He has over 250 compositions and arrangements accredited to his name. Cichy has received numerous composition awards from The American Society of Composers, Authors, and Publishers (ASCAP) for serious music. His works range from small ensemble literature to compositions and arrangements for marching band, concert band, and symphony orchestra. He is widely sought as a composer for commissions and frequently appears as a composer-in-residence.

Cichy's other works include *Galilean Moons*, a four-movement work written for wind orchestra and premiered by the University of Georgia Wind Symphony at the College Band Directors National Association (CBDNA) national convention in February 1997; *Colours*, a six-movement work commissioned by the Kansas State University Symphony Band; ...*Make a Joyous*

Sound, commissioned by the Des Moines Symphony; and *BBC Forever!*, commissioned by the Brass Band of Columbus. Cichy has just completed a new commission to honor the 150th anniversary of Wisconsin statehood. The work, *Wisconsin Soundscapes*, was premiered in May 1998 by the University of Wisconsin-Superior Symphonic Band.

Unit 2: Composition
Divertimento for Winds and Percussion was written as a tribute to three American composers who shared a common interest: Aaron Copland, Leonard Bernstein, and George Gershwin were each intrigued with jazz and each incorporated elements of the idiom into his own music. Cichy became interested in Bernstein's writings on the influence of African-American music and the effects of jazz on the works of Copland and Gershwin. He has used the musical notes C (Copland), B (Bernstein), and G (Gershwin) to form the nucleus for much of the thematic and harmonic material in *Divertimento*. These three notes are dominant in three of the work's four movements.

Unit 3: Historical Perspective
In 1993, Cichy was commissioned by the Des Moines Symphony to compose an orchestral work. The resulting composition, *Divertimento for Strings, Winds and Percussion*, was performed as an encore piece in 1994 and transcribed for wind band within about six months of its composition. It has received numerous performances from premiere college and professional wind bands in the country. It was premiered by the Iowa State University Band at the College Band Directors North Central Convention in Omaha, Nebraska, in February 1994.

Unit 4: Technical Considerations

MOVEMENT I: "EXALTATION"
This forceful fanfare is keyed in concert C but diverts in several chromatic directions. The opening motive (C-B-G) and its echo recur throughout the movement in various guises. The meter changes frequently, primarily in simple meters of three, four, five, and six. Woodwind parts are mainly decorative in the outer sections but dominant in the airy middle portion of the movement. The percussion section, led by the timpani, participates in its own transitions.

MOVEMENT II: "FOLLIES"
The composer indicates quarter note = 144 and "animated." Metrical and rhythmic challenges abound for player and conductor alike, as meters change at the measure level (the A theme is 5/4, 4/4, 2/4, 4/4, 3/4, 3/8). However, the melodies and accompaniment do not create a jarring sound to the ear. The middle section is an alternating 3/4 - 3/8 time signature. The composer plays with the major/minor third relationship in the main theme (ascending major

triad followed by descending minor third), and makes use of the minor second harmony. The bass line, replete with tritones, adds a humorous, warped effect. The flute actually plays the tonic-dominant line in the opening! Scoring is sparse at times, with many interesting instrumental combinations creating colorful timbres.

MOVEMENT III: "REMEMBRANCE"
This contemplative blues ballad-like movement is in the key of G. The C-B-G is sounded (in a varied order: G-C-B) in the supporting bass line (bass clarinet) in the opening, but does not play an important part in the melodic material. Metrically, 3/4 dominates most of "Remembrance," although each phrase of the main melody finishes off in 4/4. Scoring is for woodwinds, horns, and percussion (including harp and celesta), and is often highly transparent. A harpist is needed, although the composer allows for a piano or synthesizer substitution. Celesta is required as well.

MOVEMENT IV: "SALUTATION"
This final dance returns to the key of C in a quick quarter note = 132 tempo, with a 4/4 time signature throughout. Compared to the other three movements, there is a greater amount of scoring by instrument families and sections, and more doubling. The form is rondo-like and features two sections in which thematic material is superimposed. Some material from earlier movements (I and II) returns at the end of the movement to help unify the four parts. The eighth note groupings vary, sometimes unpredictably, in their irregularity.

Unit 5: Musical Considerations
Divertimento for Winds and Percussion is a challenging work for all sections of the ensemble, requiring mature technique, range, and endurance.

MOVEMENT I: "EXALTATION"
The trumpet section must be well-rehearsed and flexible for the quick, large interval leaps which comprise the fanfare figure. Articulation in the brass, low woodwinds, and percussion should be crisp and spaced. The central section should be lush and connected, with special attention given to the drag triplet rhythmic accuracy. The first statement of the middle section is thinly scored, but the second, fuller section should be as dark as possible, with careful tuning considerations given to the parallel fifths. Some special effects (trumpet flutter tongues, horn *glissandi*) also create rehearsal opportunities.

MOVEMENT II: "FOLLIES"
This charming movement is full of deceivingly difficult rhythmic and stylistic figures. Woodwinds especially are faced with nimble passagework and a necessary sense of "easygoing" style. Even when the scoring becomes multi-layered, it is important to maintain lightness of articulation in all

voicings. Balance must be continually checked as the layering stratification alters. The jazz elements incorporated require uniformity in accents, syncopated styles, grace note usage, and *staccato*.

MOVEMENT III: "REMEMBRANCE"
Intonation and tonal balance create significant difficulties in this movement. Accompaniment figures must maintain a homogeneous sound while playing under solo voices. Harp intonation is critical and is particularly difficult in the face of not having been playing for the first two movements. The horn counterline at m. 17 must emerge strongly, and weight should be added to emphasize the dissonant entries.

MOVEMENT IV: "SALUTATION"
More jazz figures are brought into this movement, including syncopation and stylistic accents. The conductor must carefully balance the varying accompaniment patterns (which should be most energetic at m. 8) under the solo instruments. Measures 52 and 69 must not be overplayed, and attention should be given to making the combined themes distinguishable.

Unit 6: Musical Elements
All of the following musical elements are incorporated: fanfare, motivic unity, blue notes, ABA, major/minor third, superimposition, rondo, canon, jazz ballad, and thematic unity/allusion.

Unit 7: Form and Structure

SECTION	MEASURE	EVENT AND SCORING
Movement I: "Exaltation"		
The opening movement is A-B-A.		
1	1	Trumpet *tutti* and brass fanfare (all C, B, and G), sixteenth punctuation, and descending minor third motive (chromatic mediant relationship), with major/minor chord prominent
	4	Percussion (timpani, snare drum, tam-tam, crash cymbal, tom-toms) *tutti* with fanfare rhythms
	6	Variation on fanfare in imitation, descending thirds and major/minor chords
	9	Percussion *tutti* transition
	11	Trumpet fanfare, sixteenth punctuation (ascending M2)

SECTION	MEASURE	EVENT AND SCORING
2	15	Clarinet section lyrical *tutti* (drag triplet, two quarter theme), oboe and flute *obligato* rhythms – the C-B-G is stacked vertically
	22	Full woodwind, horn, tuba with lyrical theme
	26	Transition in upper woodwinds (major thirds emphasis); flute duet, oboe/bassoon trio; *ritardando*
3	29	Fanfare material returns (in different meters), functioning as layered *ostinati* (vamps?); sixteenth punctuation (M2), descending minor thirds and major/minor chords; rhythms are slightly time-shifted, and there is a compression of presentation of familiar materials
	31	Trumpet fanfare in imitation with horns, layering of trombones and low woodwinds; this sets up the "big moment" at m. 33, in which C-B-G appears in the bass line and *ostinati*, and 3+3+2 eighth note groupings abound
	36	Fanfare motive (joined by woodwinds), horn *glissandi*, minor thirds, major seventh leaps, clashes Last measure is a powerful *tutti* descending m3/clash chord

Movement II: "Follies"

A	1	First theme in clarinets (based on the major triad followed by minor descending minor third), accompanied by bass clarinet and flute *staccato* notes (flute plays V-I tuba line!)
	7	Repeat of theme with alto saxophones and all clarinets, adding baritone saxophone bass notes

SECTION	MEASURE	EVENT AND SCORING
	13	Third presentation of theme with flutes added, oboe and piccolo add short notes, bass clarinet/bassoon/tenor saxophone; add bass, snare with brushes accompanies
B	19	Melodic material functions as accompaniment now: *staccato* eighth notes in clarinet/alto saxophone/muted trumpet/xylophone, accompanied by short notes in 3+3+2 groupings (based on triad theme) and then added syncopation, low brass provide a quasi-string bass improvisational solo
A	27	First theme returns in flute/trumpet/ xylophone, bass notes in low woodwinds and low brass
	35	Transition/key change
C	37	3/4 - 3/8 alternating section, melody in flute/oboe, light scoring with punchy afterbeats in saxophones and muted trumpets, bassoons/bass clarinets provide downbeats
	55	Second presentation of C theme in trumpets and flutes, accompaniment in low brass and horns
	73	Transition
A	80	Return of A theme in clarinets
	86	A theme (*tutti* texture)
B	92	B theme returns in clarinets, with added emphasis in muted trumpets (see m. 19)
	100	Transition (contrary motion)
A	103	A theme returns with a two-count canonic imitation in low woodwinds and low brass (m. 109 is one of the first measures with all "downbeats"!)
	111	Dovetailing of main theme motive to upper *tessitura* instruments Final "surprise" chord (m2)

SECTION	MEASURE	EVENT AND SCORING
Movement III: "Remembrance"		
A	1	Duet (flute and E-flat clarinet), accompanied by clarinet family
A	9	English horn/clarinet theme, accompanied by saxophones and harp
B	17	Clarinets accompany different solo figures in flute and celesta, horn has countermelody which enters on dissonance and then resolves
B´	25	Flute/E-flat clarinet/alto saxophone/ celesta, melody over counterline in tenor saxophone/horn
A	33	Theme returns in flutes and horns, all woodwinds accompany
A	41	Solo English horn and clarinet over clarinet family and harp Ends delicately with flutes, clarinets, celesta, and harp

Movement IV: "Salutation"

Two main ideas dominate this movement: the A idea (syncopated rhythm at m. 2) and the B idea (melody at m. 13). The sixteenth ragtime-like figure (C) also plays a significant role.

Introduction	2	Overlapping fragments in disjointed, syncopated rhythm (A) in low brass and low woodwinds, echoed and extended by upper woodwinds, minor third and major/minor heard in trombones and trumpets
	9	Accompaniment (3+3+2 and 2+3+3 groupings) presented, *diminuendo*
A	13	Flute and alto saxophone jazz-like melody over clarinet/bassoon/percussion light accompaniment (3+3+2)
	23	Two-layer density transition (with alternating A and B snippets)
A	30	*Tutti* ensemble – B melody in woodwinds, accompaniment in brass
	38	New idea (sixteenth figure) passed around to introduce new upcoming section

SECTION	MEASURE	EVENT AND SCORING
B	43	Xylophone and trumpet solo with ragtime sixteenth melody, alternating (2+2+2+2 vs. 3+3+2) accompaniment passed around from clarinets to saxophones, horns and clarinets with afterbeats
	47	Flute/oboe/English horn (and mallets add) with melody
A/B	52	*Tutti* section – piccolo/clarinet/trumpet/xylophone B melody, flute/English horn/clarinet/trumpet A melody superimposed, trombone/euphonium with second movement A fragments, and others with (3+3+2 and 2+2+2+2) accompaniment
B	60	Return of B material in flute and clarinet solo, light accompaniment
	64	Alto saxophone/xylophone solo material, added piccolo in m. 66
A/B	69	Return of *tutti* section (see m. 52)
Coda	77	Continued layered section, fanfare triplet figures from Movement I appear in trumpets and flourish in woodwinds, time shifts in mm. 79-80 in brass
	83	Pyramidal stacking of Movement II theme snippet, followed by unison sixteenth figures (also derived from Theme 2) with half-step relationships from the "correct note" Last four measures are all C's, G's, and B's; concludes with major/minor chord and unison concert C stinger

Unit 8: Suggested Listening

Divertimento for Winds and Percussion has been released on a 1995 recording by the University of North Texas Wind Symphony conducted by Eugene Corporon on the Klavier label (KCD-11070). A recording of the orchestral (original) version is available from the composer.

Other divertimenti:
Bela Bartok, *Divertimento for Strings*
Leonard Bernstein, *Divertimento for Orchestra*

Karel Husa, *Divertimento for Brass Ensemble and Percussion*
Anthony Iannaccone, *Divertimento for Orchestra*
Vincent Persichetti, *Divertimento for Band*
Gunther Schuller, *On Winged Flight: A Divertimento for Band*
Germaine Tailleferre, *Suite Divertimento pour grand orchestra d'harmonie*

Also divertimenti of Haydn, Mozart, and others

Leonard Bernstein:
   Prelude, Fugue, and Riffs
   Slava!
   Dance music from *On the Town, West Side Story, On the Waterfront,*
   and *Fancy Free*
Aaron Copland:
   Appalachian Spring
   Down a Country Lane
   El Salon Mexico
   Emblems
   Latin American Sketches
   An Outdoor Overture
   Quiet City
   The Red Pony
   Rodeo
George Gershwin:
   An American in Paris
   Cuban Overture
   I Got Rhythm Variations
   Rhapsody in Blue

Unit 9: Additional References and Resources

Bernstein, Leonard. *Findings*. New York: Simon and Schuster, 1982.

Greenberg, Rodney. *George Gershwin*. London: Phaidon, 1998.

Peyster, Joan. *Bernstein: a Biography*. New York: Billboard Books, 1998.

Pollack, Howard. *Aaron Copland: The Life and Work of an Uncommon Man*. New York: Henry Holt, 1999.

Contributed by:

Scott A. Stewart
Director of Instrumental Music
Emory University
Atlanta, Georgia

Teacher Resource Guide

Early Light

Carolyn Bremer
(b. 1957)

Unit 1: Composer

Dubbed a composer "driven by hobgoblins of post modernist cant" and an "unpredictable extension of Brahms," Carolyn Bremer indites a catalog of diverse, entertaining, sardonic, and provocative works. She came to composition somewhat late – at the age of 24 – on the heels of intensive training as an orchestral bassist. As of late, she has come to regard the questions raised in issue-oriented, experimental and political music, and multimedia settings as central to her work as a composer, conductor, and educator.

Her catalog contains works based on the Clarence Thomas Confirmation Hearings (*I Have a Nightmare*), an AIDS-related death of a childhood friend (*Not a Witness*), feminism (*She Who*), the close proximity of madness with the creative mind (*Sciamachy*), and a *Concerto for Woodblock and Politically Correct Tape*. Stockholm's Kammarensemblen, San Francisco-based Earplay!, the Oklahoma City Philharmonic, Synchrony, Anacapa String Quartet, and Trio Contraste have performed her works.

She is under exclusive contract with Carl Fischer, Inc. for all works but the *Sonata for Clarinet and Piano*, which is published by Arsis Press of Washington, DC. CRS has released a recording of the sonata, and her arrangement of *Early Light* for wind ensemble has been recorded for Klavier Records by the University of North Texas Symphonic Winds and will be released in late 1997. Her works have been featured at major festivals, including the 1995 UN Conference on Women's Rights in Beijing, Edinburgh Fringe Festival, Bloomingdale House of Music Mostly Women Composers Concerts in New York City, Bowling Green New Music and Art Festival, the

International Congress on Women in Music in Vienna, The International Interdisciplinary Conference on Women in Adelaide, and Music Alaska Women Festival.

Bremer has received grants from Meet the Composer, the Regents of the University of California, and University of California Intercampus Arts Council, and she has been named an AAUW Recognition Awardee for Emerging Scholars. She holds the Sandra and Brian O'Brien Presidential Professor in Music at the University of Oklahoma. Bremer studied at the Eastman School of Music, CalArts, and received her Ph.D. in Composition from the University of California, Santa Barbara. Her teachers include Edward Applebaum, Mel Powell, Joseph Schwantner, Emma Lou Diemer, and Buell Neidlinger. Currently she is head of the composition program at the University of Oklahoma, where she directs the New Century Ensembles.

Note: Composer information is taken from Carolyn Bremer's website [www.ou.edu/music/CRB], which is copyrighted.

Unit 2: Composition

Early Light, originally composed for orchestra in 1995, was arranged for wind ensemble by the composer in 1996. The title is derived from words from *The Star-Spangled Banner*, which provides much of the motivic material of the work.

Unit 3: Historical Perspective

The musical language of Bremer in this work is rooted in the aesthetics of post-serialist and post-minimalist composition. Extensive percussion writing, including marimba, places it clearly in a late twentieth century idiom. The writing is clearly tonal, but there is free use of unresolved seconds. The music is a complex web of shifting meters and themes, yet it appeals to the casual listener as well as the musician. This is Dr. Bremer's second work for wind ensemble.

Unit 4: Technical Considerations

While virtuoso runs are few, this work requires a mature level of articulation skills, including delicate double-tonguing in the brass and flutes. Some ranges are large, including C6 for the trumpet and B-flat5 for horn (A5 slurred and *mezzo-piano*). The work requires a mature percussion section, including a very solid timpanist and a marimbist who can read bass clef.

Unit 5: Stylistic Considerations

The predominant style of *Early Light* is a sprightly, sparkling 6/8, requiring a clear tone and facile articulation skills. Lyrical passages are presented in the middle section of the work. The rhythmic feel shifts between duple meter and triple meter frequently, and the work closes with bold, fanfare-like figures.

Unit 6: Musical Elements

The work is almost entirely diatonic within the key of B-flat major. Rhythmic elements include many typical 6/8 rhythms, including the siciliano figure. The tension between duple and triple meter is a motivic element in the piece. Fragments of *The Star-Spangled Banner* are introduced near the middle of the work and provide the motivic elements that bring the piece to a close.

Unit 7: Form and Structure

Early Light is constructed in a loose arch form. The reversal of Transition 1 and Theme 1 in the final A section creates a palindromic effect.

SECTION	MEASURE	EVENT AND SCORING
A	19	Theme 1
Introduction	40	Transition 1 – 6/8 vs. 3/4 meter
	63	Return of introductory material
	71	Return of Theme 1
	91	Transition 1a – duple/triple/quadruple meter conflict; foreshadowing of Theme 2
B	109	Theme 2 (derived from *The Star-Spangled Banner* fragment)
	130	Transition 2 – duple/triple meter conflict; harmonic elements from introduction
	146	Return of introductory material
C	153	*The Star-Spangled Banner* fragments throughout ensemble
B	184	Theme 2
A	195	Return to Transition 1
	216	Theme 1
	234	Coda – *The Star-Spangled Banner* fragments treated as cadential figures; Theme 1 reprise

Unit 8: Suggested Listening

Ludwig van Beethoven, *Symphony No. 7*, Movement I, *Vivace*
Leonard Bernstein, "America" from *West Side Story*
Charles Ives, "The Fourth of July" from *Holidays Symphony*
Michael Torke, *Green*

Unit 9: Additional References and Resources

Carolyn Bremer: *Early Light*. Performed by the North Texas Wind Symphony, Eugene Corporon, Conductor. Klavier Records no. KCD-11083, *Dialogues and Entertainments*.

The Klavier website:
www.klavier-records.com.

Bremer's personal website:
www.ou.edu/music/CRB.

Contributed by:

Darin Schmidt
Indiana University
Bloomington, Indiana

Teacher Resource Guide

Festive Overture

Dmitri Shostakovich
(1906–1973)

arranged by Donald Hunsberger
(b. 1932)

Unit 1: Composer

Dmitri (Dmitriyevich) Shostakovich is widely regarded as the leading Soviet composer. With Serge Prokofiev and Aram Khachaturian, he completes the "Big Three" composers of the Soviet era. Alternately hailed and reviled by the ruling communist party, he consistently answered his critics with his music. New Grove states that his work is based on "...his view of the Soviet composer as, first and foremost, a citizen with a moral duty to his fellow citizens."

Born in St. Petersburg (September 25, 1906), his early childhood displayed no great talent for music. Adolescence, however, brought with it the blossoming of his creative skills. His first works, based upon events in World War I and the revolution in Russia, brought his talents to the attention of his parents, who enrolled him in the Petrograd Conservatory, where he gained the support of the director, noted composer Alexander Glazounov. The Petrograd Conservatory, previously known as the St. Petersburg Conservatory, had already produced the notable alumni Serge Prokofiev and Igor Stravinsky. Besides his work in composition, Shostakovich made great strides as a pianist and graduated in 1923 from both the composition and piano courses.

As a composer, Shostakovich gained fame with his *First Symphony* (1923). Written in his senior year at the Petrograd Conservatory, immediately following its premiere in 1926 it was acclaimed throughout the world as a masterwork, and indeed remains often played today. Also noted as a pianist, Shostakovich won the Chopin contest in Warsaw in 1927.

The year 1936 saw a dramatic reversal, with Pravda, the official paper of the communist party, attacking his heretofore successful opera *Lady Macbeth*: "...the music quacks, grunts and growls, and suffocates itself..." Seen by Soviet composers of the time as an official denial of contemporary techniques (such as those pioneered by Berg and Schoenberg), Shostakovich's reply was the huge *Fifth Symphony*, a work that quickly restored him to favor with the party.

During World War II, Shostakovich became a symbol of Soviet resistance to the Nazis. His image, which appeared on the cover of *Time* magazine wearing a fireman's helmet, and his *Symphony No. 7*, The Lenningrad, premiered on air in the United States by Toscanini, and the NBC Symphony Orchestra represented to the west the might of the Soviet Union and their struggle. Shostakovich's other war Symphony (*Symphony No. 8*) is regarded more highly by critics; however, official approbation followed his victory symphony (*Symphony No. 9 (1946)*) which did not contain the right note of triumph for the party. In a decree issued in February 1948, Shostakovich again found himself in trouble with officialdom for "...anti-democratic tendencies in music...."

In response, Shostakovich withheld his music from the public, and when his reply came with his *Tenth Symphony* (1953, following the death of Stalin), it was received with ambivalence. In time the work has come to be seen as a masterwork, and it contains an autobiographical motive DSCH (represented in music by D – E-flat – C – B). The work eventually restored Shostakovich to favor, and he embraced the Soviet system, disavowing serialism and other avant-garde techniques and becoming a symbol of the state composer. Interestingly, 1962 saw the successful revival of *Lady Macbeth*, retitled *Katerina Izmaylova*, the opera that had created the first official uproar in 1936.

Shostakovich visited the United States a number of times, often as an official representative of the Soviet government, the last being in the year of his death, 1973.

Donald Hunsberger is a faculty member of the Eastman School of Music in Rochester, New York, where he conducts the world-renowned Eastman Wind Ensemble. Dr. Hunsberger holds bachelor's, master's, and doctoral degrees from the Eastman School of Music, where he studied trombone with Emory Remington and Frederick Stoll, and conducting with Frederick Fennell and Howard Mitchell. He is the author of numerous articles and books, and has released many recordings, including the landmark "Carnival" recording with Wynton Marsalis on cornet.

Unit 2: Composition

The term "overture" is derived from the French "oeverture," denoting a "piece in two or more sections that formed a solemn introduction to a ballet, opera or oratorio." (*New Grove Dictionary of Music*) More recently the dramatic overture, attached to a large work such as a ballet or opera, gave rise to the concert overture. The dramatic overture was often detached from the original works and performed as a concert piece in its own right. This practice continues today—witness the great popularity of Mozart's overture to *The Magic Flute* or *Don Giovanni*. The late classical and early romantic composers in the late eighteenth and early nineteenth centuries began labeling works as overtures despite their not being attached to a larger work. One of the earliest examples for the wind band world is Mendelssohn's *Overture for Winds* (Op. 24), written as *Nocturo* in 1924 and renamed *Overture* by the composer in 1838.

Shostakovich released the *Festive Overture* (Op. 96) in 1954, following the premiere of his *Symphony No. 10*. Like many works of this period, its gestation is uncertain. Scholars are uncertain as to whether the composer did not write any works in the few years following the 1948 decree or merely held back works he had written.

Festive Overture is a bright, bravura work for band that requires a great deal of control from all sections. Its interjections and long lines seek mature responses across the ensemble. In his introduction, Hunsberger states that the piece:

> ...contains one of Shostakovich's greatest attributes—the ability to write a long, sustained melodic line combined with a pulsating rhythmic drive. In addition to the flowing melodic passages, there are also examples of *staccato* rhythmic sections which set off the flowing lines and the variant fanfares. It is truly a "festive" overture.

Unit 3: Historical Perspective

Festive Overture (Op. 96) is among the most-performed transcriptions for band. The work, written in 1954, follows the release of his *Tenth Symphony* in 1953 and the restoration of Shostakovich in official circles as a "composer of the people." The 1948 decree, aimed at many composers but singling out Shostakovich, condemned his music as too German and the preferred listening of "...nobody but foreign bandits and imperialists." A hiatus followed the decree, and the next major work following it (the *Tenth Symphony*) was dark, ambivalent but undeniably Russian. The *Festive Overture*, while far from dark, retains that distinctive Russian flavor.

The overture received its first performance on the thirty-seventh anniversary of the October revolution.

Unit 4: Technical Considerations

The overture has much to challenge the entire ensemble. From the brass lines that open the work calling for secure and confident players, to the solo clarinet that introduces the *Presto* theme, Hunsberger asks the entire ensemble to maintain control in difficult technical passages. At various times, the entire woodwind section has the *Presto* theme, or part of it, and even eights are the key to passing this around the ensemble.

The brass also have difficult eighths and face the task of trying to play the accompaniment parts well below the volume of the woodwinds. The offbeats that often accompany the melody, particularly later in the work, can be extremely difficult to place depending on the tempo of the performance. Hunsberger, who played euphonium in the Eastman Wind Ensemble, has written a euphonium part that requires good performers. Besides the flying eighth notes when the euphonium has the theme, the part moves readily into the upper register, sometimes in soft passages.

Unit 5: Stylistic Considerations

Considerable attention will need to be taken in the balance of this work. The orchestral version has the transparency of the strings to balance against the light woodwind sounds, while in the band transcription it is very easy to overpower the melody. The *Presto* theme offers the performer challenges, too; care must be taken to give the line forward motion, even through the long notes. However, it should remain light and never labored.

At rehearsal number 17, the ensemble is imitation strings *pizzicato*. The delicacy of sound is difficult for the ensemble to match, and it is rarely performed with the required lightness.

A note about tempi: Orchestral recordings of this work tend to be faster than those generally chosen in performance of this transcript. Care must be taken to choose a tempo that strikes the right balance between excitement and playability.

Unit 6: Musical Elements

The output of Shostakovich has a distinctive Russian flavor, which is evident in this work. While it remains formally very cogent, the work is strongly suggestive of Russian folk music. It is not programmatic but is evocative of the (real or imagined) spirit of Soviet peasant workers that would have been strongly approved by the government of the period. Like works of Grainger and Bartok, *Festive Overture* does not quote folk song but rather uses folk idioms to suggest a pre-existing folk melody.

Unit 7: Form and Structure

Form Summary:
Fanfare
Sonata form
Fanfare
Coda

MEASURE	REHEARSAL	THEME	KEY	
1		Introduction	A-flat	Fanfare
27	4	P1	A-flat	Primary theme (P1) – solo clarinet with low brass
63	7	Transition		Transition
103	11			(P1 varied) low brass melody
127	13	S1	E-flat	Secondary theme (S1) Cor anglais (English horn), trumpet, and horn
175	17	Development		Develops S1 first (E-flat theme)
191	18			Develops P1 (clarinets) (C-flat)
219	20	Transition		Uses transition theme
225	21	Recapitulation	A-flat	(P1) A-flat inverted in bass; dominant prolongation all the way to rehearsal number 23
249	23	S1	A-flat	With P1 varied in upper woodwinds
299	26	Transition		Uses transition theme as coda to the sonata form
345	30	Introduction		Fanfare recapitulation
362	33	Coda	A-flat	Based on secondary theme

Note: A triplet figure in orchestral score (mm. 357-358-359 – starting five bars before rehearsal number 33) that appears in the trumpet part has been omitted by the arranger.

Unit 8: Suggested Listening

Felix Mendelssohn, ed. Boyd, *Overture for Band*
W.A. Mozart, *Overture to The Magic Flute*

Dmitri Shostakovich:
  Symphonies 1, 5, 8, and 10
  Folk Dances (arr. R. Reynolds)
  Hamlet Suite (arr. Suchoff)

Unit 9: Additional References and Resources

Martynov, Ivan Dmitri Shostakovich. *The Man and His Work*. Translated by T. Guralsky. New York: Greenwood Press, 1969.

Norris, Christopher, editor. *Shostakovich: The Man and His Music*. London: Lawrence and Wishart, 1982.

Schwarz, Boris. "Shostakovich, Dmitri," *The New Grove Dictionary of Music and Musicians*. 3rd ed. Edited by Stanley Sadie. London and New York: MacMillan and Grove Dictionaries of Music, 1980.

Temperley, Nicholas. "Overture," *The New Grove Dictionary of Music and Musicians*. 3rd ed. Edited by Stanley Sadie. London and New York: MacMillan and Grove Dictionaries of Music, 1980.

Volkov, Soloman, editor. Testimony: *The Memoirs of Dmitri Shostakovich*. Translated by Antonina Bouis. London: Hamish Hamilton, 1979.

Contributed by:

Alan Lourens
Lecturer in Music
Conductor, Wind Ensemble
Western Australian Conservatorium of Music

Teacher Resource Guide

Galactic Empires
Battlestar of the Andromeda Nebula, Evenstar of the Magellanic Cloud, Earthstar of the Milky Way

David Gillingham
(b. 1947)

Unit 1: Composer

David Gillingham, a native of Waukesha, Wisconsin, is currently Professor of Music and Interim Director of the School of Music at Central Michigan University. He has received numerous honors at Central Michigan University, including the Excellence in Teaching Award, a Research Professorship award, a summer Fellowship award, and the 1998 President's Award for Scholarship and Creativity.

Dr. Gillingham is a prolific composer for winds and percussion. His most popular works include *Stained Glass* for percussion; *Heroes, Lost and Fallen* for band; *Apocalyptic Dreams* for band; *Waking Angels* for chamber winds and percussion; and *Concertino for Percussion and Wind Ensemble.* His compositions for winds and percussion have been performed at the New Music for Winds Symposium, the DeMoulin Band Composition, the National Band Association Convention, the Percussive Arts Society, the Music Educators National Convention, and the College Band Directors National Association Convention, to name a few. Roger Dennis, Jere Hutcheson, James Niblock, and H. Owen Reed were his composition teachers.

Unit 2: Composition

Galactic Empires is written for large symphonic band, including piano and extended percussion. It was commissioned by the Revelli Foundation's Paynter Project for the 1998 Honor Band of America. Mr. Gary Green conducted the premiere on March 14, 1998, at the Bands of America National Concert Band Festival in Indianapolis, Indiana.

The composer favors programmatic titles as a point of inspiration. *Galactic Empires* is the result of a fascination with the endless boundaries for the universe. It is a musical journey through three galaxies. Each of the three connected movements represents a "star" (named in the title) in a particular universe. The dedication reads, "To my son, Garrett, who shares my curiosity for the unknown."

Unit 3: Historical Perspective

Galactic Empires is part of a trend in music for winds and percussion in the late twentieth century that incorporates jazz elements, is highly programmatic, emphasizes colors and events, expands the use of percussion, and explores a great range of dynamics.

Unit 4: Technical Considerations

Galactic Empires is intricate rhythmically. Performers are asked to differentiate between duple and triple figures often within a single measure. Several tempo and meter changes occur that are logical. Ranges are not overly extensive, excluding the French horn writing. Due to the chromatic nature and rate of tempo, finger dexterity could be a clarity problem for French horns and trumpets. Experienced bass clarinet, piano, bassoon, and piccolo soloists are required. Much of the music is written in *ff* to *fff* dynamic range, sometimes creating articulation, tone, and balance issues beyond the usual. The percussion writing is idiomatic and, typical of Gillingham's music, vital to the work. Brake drums, crotales, and hi-hat are required in addition to an array of brass mutes. Both singing and flutter tonguing are used as timbrel effects. The score is written in C, and the duration of the piece is approximately ten and a half minutes.

Unit 5: Stylistic Considerations

Galactic Empires includes a broad range of expressive markings. The dynamic range explores all areas from *ppp* to *fff*. Subtle uses of articulation expand the element of "weighted" sound including light *staccato*, heavy *staccato*, dramatic accents, melodic accents, and *tenuto*. The "dreamy" section emphasizes romantic, *legato* lines, while the "somewhat jazzy" section is more of a "funk" feel.

Unit 6: Musical Elements

Dr. Gillingham writes about his melodic, harmonic, and rhythmic elements:

Melodic traits: The tritone is favored in sinister melodic passages, while the lydian mode is used frequently.

Harmonic traits: In use are modal progressions, chromatic mediant relationships, tone cluster, extended sonorities, and jazz-type sonorities.

Rhythmic traits: There is an affinity toward asymmetrical meters and asymmetrical divisions of the beat. Lines are often held across the bar. Syncopated and jazz rhythms are also prevalent.

Form: The work is in three connected movements.

Unit 7: Form and Structure

MEASURE	MUSICAL ELEMENTS

Section I: "Battlestar of the Andromeda Nebula"
(*ferociously*, quarter note = 160)

1-13	Low brass, low reed, bass drum *ostinato*
3-13	Theme I, French horns, trumpets
14-21	Woodwind, percussion *ostinato*
15-22	Low brass, low reed, derivative of Theme I
23-30	Low brass, low reed, bass drum *ostinato*
	Theme I, French horns, trumpets
31-34	Extension

Section II:
(*dark and mysterious*, quarter note = 80)

35-42	Piano, bass clarinet, piccolo motifs of Theme II
38	New idea in French horn based on m3
43-47	Saxophone *ostinato*
	Theme II in piccolo and bass clarinet
48	Trumpet and French horn fanfare
50-54	Oboe duet based on m3
56-58	Low brass idea based on Theme I, trumpet fanfare
60-66	Low brass and English horn chorale, trumpet fanfare

Section III:
(quarter note = 160)

67-94	Low brass, low reed *ostinato*; battle between low brass, French horns, trumpets, timpani using ideas related to Theme I; low brass, French horn, trumpet interplay of augmented motifs from Theme I

MEASURE	MUSICAL ELEMENTS
87-94	Woodwind *ostinato*
95-98	Extension
99-101	Transition with piano

Section IV: "Evening Star of the Magellanic Cloud"
(*dreamily*, quarter note = 60)

102-114	Theme III heard in piano, flute, soprano saxophone, and euphonium; tone clusters
115-119	Low brass chorale; dotted-quarter note = 60
120-130	Theme III in trumpet then in saxophones
125-130	Clarinet *ostinato*
131-138	Tone cluster effects; quarter note = 60
139-141	Piano and piccolo interlude
142-145	Brass expanding harmonies; flute clusters
146-148	All sing part of Theme III
149-154	Theme III in soprano saxophone
160-167	Hints of Theme III from English horn, piano, flute, and piccolo
168-179	Transition using motifs from Theme IV

Section V: "Earthstar of the Milky Way"
(half note = 120)

180-213	Woodwind, low brass *ostinato*
182-190	French horns; Theme V
191-197	Brass extension and fanfare
198-203	Euphonium, French horn, contrabass clarinet soli; Theme V
204-212	Trumpets, French horns; Theme V

Section VI:
(quarter note = 60)

213-223	Chorale, oboe, French horn soli related to Theme III

Section VII:
(quarter note = 120)

223-228	Woodwind motifs from Theme VI; French horn motif from Theme V
229-236	"Somewhat jazzy" Theme VI in tenor saxophone, baritone saxophone, bass clarinet, bassoon
231-249	Motifs and interruptions from Theme V heard in trumpet, trombone, French horn
237-249	Low brass, low reed *ostinato*
250-257	Brass fanfare

MEASURE	MUSICAL ELEMENTS

Section VIII:
(half note = 120)

250-257	Brass fanfare
257-278	War-like march in timpani
259-269	Brass fanfare from Theme V
270-294	Woodwind and low brass *ostinato*
281-294	Trumpet and French horn augmentation of Theme V

Section IX: "Coda"
(*ferociously*, quarter note = 160)

295-314	Coda; includes rhythmic *ostinato* from Section I, motifs from Theme V all ending in a C major triad

Unit 8: Suggested Listening

Warren Benson, *The Passing Bell*
David Gillingham:
    Concertino for Percussion and Wind Ensemble
    Heroes, Lost and Fallen

Unit 9: Additional References and Resources

Bachelor, James. *A Crescent Still Abides: The Elegiac Music of David Gillingham*. Dissertation in progress, University of Oklahoma, 1999.

Gillingham, David. *Heroes, Lost and Fallen*. Eugene Corporon and the University of Cincinnati College-Conservatory of Music Wind Symphony. Compact disc KCD-11042, 1992.

McRoy, Jim, "David Gillingham, Composer and Educator: Analysis of Three Works for Band." Dissertation in Progress: Ball State University, 1999.

Miles, Richard, ed. *Teaching Music through Performance in Band*. Vol. II. Chicago: GIA Publications, Inc., 1998.

Contributed by:

Richard A. Greenwood
Director of Bands
University of Central Florida
Orlando, Florida

Teacher Resource Guide

Grand Symphonie Funèbre et Triomphale

Hector Berlioz
(1803–1869)

Unit 1: Composer

Louis Hector Berlioz is among the most enigmatic musical figures of the nineteenth century. Disdained by his critics and rivals, exalted by supporters, Berlioz's music was often misunderstood, as it defied convention while extending the boundaries of romantic music. Berlioz's early musical experiences include the cursory study of the flageolet and flute. Prior to his first compositions, written at the age of thirteen or fourteen, Berlioz studied the treatises on harmony by Rameau and Catel. These provided him with the basis of his early musical language. The son of a prominent doctor in La Côte-St-André, Berlioz, succumbing to the wishes of his father, seemed headed for the medical profession by age seventeen. He entered medical school in Paris in 1821 and received his *baccalauréat de sciences physiques* in early 1824. During that time, his passion for music intensified. He frequented Paris opera houses and was particularly interested in the work of Gluck. In 1822, he managed to be admitted to Le Sueur's composition class at the Paris Conservatoire who admonished him in 1824 to be "no doctor or apothecary but a great composer."

In 1826, Berlioz was formally admitted to the Conservatoire, where he continued his studies with Le Sueur and studied counterpoint and fugue with Antonin Reicha. Between 1827 and 1830, he entered the Prix de Rome competition four times, receiving second prize in 1828 for *Herminie* and the grand prize in 1830 for his cantata, *La mort de Sardanapale*. To win the prize, Berlioz reportedly restrained his individuality in order to present a conventionally acceptable style to the judges. During that time period, Berlioz also found two great sources of inspiration in the works of William Shakespeare and the music of Beethoven, particularly the *Third* and *Fifth Symphonies*. These served to ignite the emotional and dramatic elements within the composer that are hallmarks of his style. The Shakespearean influence supplied the basis for works including *Roméo et Juliette* (1839), *Béatrice et Bénédict* (1860-62), and *Les Troyens* (1856), while scholars credit Berlioz's symphonic output to the power of Beethoven. The *Symphonie fantastique* (1830) brought the emotional elements of these influences, in combination with those of the composer, to grandiose proportions. In 1831, Berlioz reluctantly took up residence in Italy as a condition of the Prix de Rome. His fifteen months there provided important influences as he drew inspiration from the countryside and its people rather than its art and music which, according to his memoirs, he disdained. In general, the 1830s saw a lack of acceptance for Berlioz's music by the Paris establishment. His compositions were considered eccentric, forcing him to begin a second career as a critic in order to make a living.

In 1834, *Harold en Italie* was composed at the request of Paganini, and when in 1835 a performance of the work was bungled by its conductor, Berlioz resolved to conduct his own music. This led to yet another outgrowth of his career, that as one of the first specialist orchestra conductors, for which he would be in great demand outside of France for his skills and musical insights. That same year, 1835, also saw the beginnings of a work of huge proportions entitled *Fête musicale funèbre á la memoire des hommes illustres de la France*, which was to be in seven movements. Only two movements were completed; however, numerous scholars suggest that these became the outer movements of the *Grande Symphonie Funèbre et Triomphale* (1840). Berlioz's compositional output includes symphonies, overtures, orchestral music, operas, cantatas, and songs. Additional notable works include *Requiem* (1837), *Te Deum* (1849), *L'enfance du Christ* (1850-54), and *Le carnaval romain* (1844).

Along with his prodigious compositional output, Berlioz is responsible for the *idée fixe*, the reoccurring theme associated with the image of the beloved, a treatise on orchestration entitled *Grande traité d'instrumentation et d'orchestration modernes* (1843), and numerous critical essays about the music of his age. In general, Berlioz defied the musical conventions of his time. His music and ideas were concerned with inspiration, expression, and emotionalism rather than the rigidity of form. His sense of flexible phrase lengths, melody, counterpoint, rhythm, and orchestration made his a unique voice of the nineteenth century.

Unit 2: Composition

The *Grande Symphonie Funèbre et Triomphale* was commissioned by Minister of the Interior, Charles de Rémusat, for the *fête de juillet*, which commemorated the tenth anniversary of the July (1830) Revolution. Originally titled *Symphonie militaire* and referred to by Berlioz in letters simply as the "July Symphony," the work was performed for the inauguration of the Bastille column on July 28, 1840. The commission of 10,000 francs, as reported by the *Revue et Gazette musicale*, was for a funeral march and solemn music to be performed as the bodies of the dead were lowered into the ground. To this Berlioz added an Apotheosis as the third movement of the symphony.

The original titles of the three movements were "Marche funèbre," "Hymn d'adieu," and "Apothéose," with the second and third movements grouped together. Berlioz reworked the piece twice: the first time in early 1842 (adding strings largely in support of the winds) and again later that year (adding choral text written by Anthony Deschamps to "Apothéose"). It was for the September 26, 1842 performance that the "Hymn d'adieu" was renamed "Oraison funèbre" and the work renamed *Symphonie Funèbre et Triomphale*. In a letter to his father, dated July 30, 1840, Berlioz reported that the composition of the *Symphonie* took less than forty hours. Scholarly examination of the work by A.E.F. Dickinson revealed that the trombone solo of the "Oraison funèbre" was derived from a vocal solo in the abandoned opera *Les francs juges* that predates the *Symphonie*, and the melodic ideas for the opening *sostenuto* of the first movement were also extant in the opera. Other scholars conjecture that the outer movements of the *Symphonie* were preexisting as the two finished movements of the proposed seven-movement *Fête musicale funèbre á la memoire des hommes illustres de la France*. This has not been proven, as the music of *Fête musicale funèbre* was lost; however, these factors in combination with a brief commission period led to the rapid work by Berlioz.

The circumstances surrounding the premiere of the *Symphonie* are well documented. Knowing that the music would be lost in the outdoors, Berlioz attempted to procure the Panthéon for his final rehearsal that was to also serve as the premiere. His request was rejected; however, he was able to procure the *Salle Vivienne*, and the premiere took place with Berlioz conducting on July 26 for an audience of friends, critics, and musicians that reportedly included Chopin. The performance was so successful that Berlioz was engaged for four more concerts of the work by the impresario, two of which actually occurred. The outdoor performance on July 28 included six performances of the "Marche funèbre" and "Apothéose" during the procession that wound from the church *St-Germain-l'Auxerrois* to the *Place de la Bastille*, with Berlioz, dressed in his national guard uniform and walking backwards, conducting a band of 207 musicians. The "Hymn d'adieu" was performed at the *Place de la Bastille* immediately following the burial ceremony. A final performance of the "Apothéose" was drowned out by the premature maneuvers of the attending National Guard, complete with the cadence of some fifty side drums. Reporting on the *Symphonie*, Richard Wagner wrote in the Dresden *Abendzeitung* on May 5, 1841:

I am inclined to rank this composition above all Berlioz'[s] other ones: it is noble and great from the first note to the last. Free from sickly excitement, it sustains a noble patriotic emotion which rises from lament to the topmost heights of apotheosis. When I further take into account the service rendered by Berlioz in his altogether noble treatment of the military wind band – the only instruments at his disposal here,...I must say with delight that I am convinced this Symphony will last and exalt the hearts of men as long as there lives a nation called France.

Unit 3: Historical Perspective

The beginning of the nineteenth century witnessed a marked change in the perspectives of art, music, literature, and society. The classical ideals of order, control, equilibrium, and restraint prevalent in the last half of the eighteenth century gave way to new models. This so-called romantic century cherished originality, freedom, passion, self-expression, and the pursuit of absolute perfection. The works of Goethe and Beethoven inspired new streams of expression, giving rise to new generations of artists. The societal changes brought about by the industrial revolution moved the population from the countryside into the cities. In reaction, the arts became enamored with nature. Nationalist pride flourished, as did the struggles for equality among the classes. These, coupled with the rise and fall of Napoleon, shaped European culture throughout the course of the century.

Unit 4: Technical Considerations

The key centers of the movements are f minor, G major, and B-flat major, respectively. These should not present great difficulties; however, the frequent tonicizations of new key centers coupled with the use of neapolitan motions will dictate careful attention to harmonic direction, balance, and intonation. Prudent observance of the differences between dotted eighth-sixteenth, quarter-eighth triplet and dotted eighth-sixteenth-eighth triplet rhythms is essential. Certain passages within both the "Marche funèbre" *and* "Apothéose" require clear tonguing of repeated notes by the woodwinds. The majority of the bassoon and trombone parts utilize tenor clef, necessitating competence with this by the performers. The "Oraison funèbre" requires the trombone soloist to possess strength, clarity, and musical depth in order to effectively perform the movement. In addition, the range demands include high b-naturals for the soloist.

Unit 5: Stylistic Considerations

The overriding factor when considering the style of each movement is its respective function within the original ceremony. "Marche funèbre" was used for the transfer of the remains of the dead heroes of the July Revolution to the

Place de la Bastille, literally, a march to the tomb. Therefore, its character must be duly somber. The tempo marking, *Moderato un poco lento*, allows for some latitude; however, the tempo needs to be such that the weight of the underlying structure and the lamenting nature of the melodic ideas remains intact. The "Oraison funèbre," used for lowering the remains into the tomb, has three distinct sections: mm. 1-38, marked *Adagio non tanto*; mm. 39-52, *Andantino*; and mm. 58-108, *Andantino poco lento e sostenuto*. The trombone recitative of the first section requires ample freedom and should not be rushed. The relationship between sections two and three should give the effect of slowing down for the final section. In addition, the *sostenuto* marking should be applied to the lengths of all notes, giving the quarter and eighth notes full value and direction.

The "Apothéose" was intended to uplift the crowd and ignite their sense of nationalistic fervor. Marked *Allegro non troppo e pomposo*, care should be taken not to associate this with a march tempo of quarter note = 120, as was done by Goldman in his edition of the work. The intended effect of the previous movements and the grandiose nature of the "Apothéose" may easily be destroyed by too fast a tempo. Additionally, this movement was performed six times during the funeral procession. It is unlikely that the tempo preferred by Goldman was used by Berlioz during the original occasion. Other Berlioz works using *Allegro non troppo e pomposo* vary in speed from quarter note = 100 to quarter note = 138, depending greatly on the character of the individual piece. The underlying rhythmic structure of the "Apothéose" and the nature of the music itself easily support tempi to the slower side of this metronomic range.

Unit 6: Musical Elements

Each movement of the work necessitates attention to a variety of musical elements. The nature of "Marche funèbre" is somber yet complete with numerous emotional outbursts. Careful attention to sudden dynamic changes from *fortissimo* to *pianissimo*, extended *crescendi*, sequential figures, and tension and resolution in the harmonic structure is essential. Central concerns within "Oraison funèbre" include suitable balance between the trombone soloist and the *tutti*, a singing quality within the trombone recitative, and appropriate proportions between the tempi of the various sections. Likewise, the tempo of "Apothéose" will determine the character of the movement and should be carefully addressed. In addition, attention to balance, dynamics, and the major thematic statements in "Apothéose" is needed, as much of the movement is marked at a *fortissimo* level.

Unit 7: Form and Structure

SECTION	MEASURE	EVENT AND SCORING
Movement I:		
Exposition	1-47	Theme 1 with various permutations; f minor
Introduction	1-3	Tenor drums, horns, trumpets, and cornets
Theme 1	4-7	A+B phrase structure; flute, E-flat clarinet, clarinet I
Transition	8-13	Transition using thematic material
Transition	14-24	Harmonic digression and return; development of Theme 1
Theme 1A	25-28	B phrase pitches altered, rhythm intact; upper woodwinds, cornets; f minor
Cadential	29-32	*Tutti*
Transition	33-47	Harmonic digression and return; development of Theme 1
Development	48-155	Episodic development of Theme 1; introduction of Theme 2
Episode 1	48-70	Development using melodic sequences; climax mm. 65-70
Episode 2	70-95	Use of pedal point; horn/trumpet calls climax mm. 88-92
Theme 2	95-99	Oboe, clarinet I in A-flat major
Episode 3	95-124	Theme 2 plus development
Episode 4	125-137	Bassoon, trombone III, ophicléide soli followed by partial statement of Theme 1 in F major
Episode 4A	138-155	Episode 4 repeated with reharmonization and cadential extension
Recapitulation	156-239	Themes 1 and 2 presented in tonic
Exposition	156-174	Exact repetition of mm. 4-42 with new transition to C pedal
Episode 2A	175-197	Repeat of Episode 2 with newly composed trombone/bass clarinet soli
Cadential	198-199	Reworked cadence borrowed from mm. 93-94
Transition	200-206	Trombone/bass clarinet soli; cadential transition to Theme 2
Episode 3A		Presentation of Theme 2 plus development in f minor

SECTION	MEASURE	EVENT AND SCORING
Coda	240-280	Use of pedal point, transition to F major

Movement II:

Introduction	1-8	*Tutti*
A Section	9-38	Trombone recitative with woodwind/horn accompaniment; ensemble *tutti* mm. 32-38
B Section	39-57	Trombone/bassoon duet (mm. 40-45) followed by continuation of trombone solo
C Section	58-108	Trombone solo continues with woodwind doubling (mm. 88-95)

Movement III:

Introduction	1-17	Brass and percussion
Exposition	18-48	AABA march
Theme 1	18-26	*Tutti*/repeated
Theme 2	27-40	*Tutti*
Theme 1	41-48	*Tutti*
Development	49-190	Episodic development of thematic material
Episode 1	49-56	Development based on B phrase of Theme 1
Episode 2	57-80	Low brass/low reed melody with woodwind material based on Theme 2
Episode 3	81-97	Development based on A phrase of Theme 1 with canonic treatment
Episode 4	98-190	Extended development with transition to tonic
Recapitulation	191-228	Restatement of Themes 1 and 2
Coda	229-241	Unexpected motion to A major followed by a return to B-flat major

Unit 8: Suggested Listening

Hector Berlioz:
   Requiem
   Symphonie Fantastique
   Te Deum
Charles-Simon Catel, *Overture in C*
Anton Reicha, *Commemoration Symphony*
Richard Wagner, *Trauersinfonie*

Unit 9: Additional References and Resources

Barzun, Jacques. *Berlioz and the Romantic Century*, Vol. 1. Columbia University Press, 1969.

Berlioz, Hector. *Memoirs of Hector Berlioz*, ed. David Cairns. Alfred A. Knoff, 1969.

Berlioz, Hector. *Selected Letters of Hector Berlioz*, ed. Hugh MacDonald, trans. Roger Nichols. W.W. Norton & Company, 1971.

Cooper, Donald A. *An Historical Account, Criticism, and Modern Performance Edition of the Grand Symphony for Band by Hector Berlioz*. University of Montana, 1967.

Dickinson, A.E.F. *The Music of Berlioz*. Faber & Faber, 1972.

Holoman, D. Kern. *Berlioz*. Harvard University Press, 1989.

MacDonald, Hugh. *Symphonie Funèbre et Triomphale*, preface. Bärenreiter-Verlag: Kassel. 1966.

Sadie, Stanley ed. *The New Grove Dictionary of Music and Musicians*, Vol. 2. Macmillan Publishers Limited, 1980.

Contributed by:

Robert Meunier
Director of Bands
Drake University
Des Moines, Iowa

Teacher Resource Guide

The Hound of Heaven
James Syler
(b. 1961)

Unit 1: Composer

James Syler, raised in New York and Florida, was educated at Northern Illinois University (B.M.), University of Miami (M.M.), and University of Texas at Austin. He has studied composition privately with Alfred Reed, Karl Korte, Anthony Vazzana, and Michael Colgrass. In 1992, Syler was awarded an artist-residency at the Hambidge Center for the Arts in Georgia. He has expressed his interest in the wind band medium through the writing and publishing of five works: *The Hound of Heaven* (1988/rev. 1992), *Fields* (1994), *Minton's Playhouse* (1994), *Storyville* (1996), and *O Magnum Mysterium* (1996). Syler is currently an adjunct faculty member at Flagler College in St. Augustine, Florida. His music is available directly from the composer at Syler Music, 166 Marine Street, St. Augustine, Florida, 32084.

Unit 2: Composition

The Hound of Heaven is a twenty-minute programmatic composition in six sections for large wind symphony. The work is based on an 1893 poem of the same name written by British poet Francis Thompson (1859-1907). *The Hound of Heaven* received the Seventeenth Annual National Band Association Composition Contest Award (1993) and the First Colonel Arnold D. Gabriel Composition Award (1993) sponsored by the United States Air Force Band.

The allegorical title describes God as the loving hound who is in pursuit of the lost hare, the individual soul. Section I depicts the fearful attempt by the hare to flee from God knowing all the while that he is being pursued.

Section II tells of how the fugitive hare tries to escape, in his imagination, to the beauty of the heavens. He finds it pointless and, in Section III, decides to turn to the little children. He believes he can find happiness there, but just as the children begin to respond, they are suddenly taken away by death. He is now a desperate soul who, in Section IV and in one last attempt, turns to nature for repose. But nature, as beautiful as it is, is unable to fill the void in his heart, and he again hears the footfall of his pursuer. There is nothing left now – he has tried everything – and in Section V he is smitten to his knees. In a dream, he sees his past life wasted on foolish pursuits, none of which has given him love and happiness. The chase is over. In Section VI, the loving Hound of Heaven stands over him and the gloom which he thought would follow surrender is only the shade of God's hand coming down to embrace him. He realizes his foolishness and now knows he has true love and happiness as his pursuer speaks to him with the words, "I am He Whom thou seekest!"

Unit 3: Historical Perspective

The concept of program music is one with which many contemporary composers are well versed. In a desire to represent or symbolize nonmusical events, concepts, or images, music has for decades turned to song, dance, the arts, and the literary community as sources of inspiration. A number of notable works have expounded their creative foundation from a diverse source of origin: painting (*Scenes from the Louvre*); war songs (*Music for Prague 1968*); dance (*Suite of Old American Dances*); places and structures (*Suite Francaise; George Washington Bridge*); hymns and spirituals (*Chorale and Shaker Dance, Amazing Grace*); folk songs (*Cajun Folk Songs, Folk Song Suite, Lincolnshire Posy*). Band works with a distinct poetic inspiration include *The Leaves Are Falling; and the mountains rising nowhere; For Precious Friends Hid in Death's Dateless Night; Heroes, Lost and Fallen; Shadows of Eternity; The Hound of Heaven*. Literary volumes have also served as a launching pad for such noted compositions as *Symphony No. 1: The Lord of the Rings; Winds of Nagual; Illyrian Dances; A Child's Garden of Dreams*.

Syler's programmatic depiction of Thompson's poem is skillful in its attempt to embrace an intermingling of musical styles while highlighting the poem's distinct story. *The Hound of Heaven* is surely Syler's musical attempt to "depict the truth and depth of the poem's universal message."

Unit 4: Technical Considerations

The antiphonal trumpet speaks between each section and serves as the musical voice of the Hound of Heaven. As such, the solo trumpet part does not place virtuosic technical demands on the performer but necessitates a soloist with a bold spirit and impeccable tone. The percussion requirements are reasonable. Increasing the number of wind chimes (doubling or tripling the part) will remarkably emphasize the overall ethereal effect. The piano is important to the musical score; its role in m. 244 and in mm. 279 through 286 are imperative and are not doubled in any other voice. Contrabass clarinet, contrabassoon, and string bass add tremendously to the harmonic coloring of the work and should be included whenever possible. Confident soloists are needed for the thematic motif statements in mm. 275 through 286; bringing the soloists to the front of the stage will allow each thematic element to be heard with heightened distinctness.

Unit 5: Stylistic Considerations

The Hound of Heaven extends to both listener and performer an expressive, dramatic, and imaginative musical work evoking a spectrum of images and events. The music is challenging yet enriching. Those dedicated to the work will quickly become immersed in its alluring ability to communicate its programmatic ideas through both sheer power and a reflective musical aura. Syler's concept of orchestration, texture, and craft is impressive. What emerges is a work worthy of a powerfully dramatic style skillfully contrasted with a lyrically haunting radiance.

Unit 6: Musical Elements

The musical elements encountered in *The Hound of Heaven* are numerous: *ostinato*, *rubato*, thematic fragmentation, consonance and dissonance, canon, extreme contrasts of dynamic and tempo, remarkable themes, and soloistic episodes are recognizable characteristics of the work. Identifying and labeling each of these areas and, in turn, presenting a formal framework to the ensemble during the rehearsal process can be especially enlightening. The solo antiphonal trumpet should be located off-stage, preferably elevated and placed near the back of the performance site for greatest effect. Strict adherence to tempi (most especially those over quarter note = 152) is remarkably consequential to the desired musical message. The score is transposed.

Unit 7: Form and Structure

MEASURE	TEMPO	EVENT AND SCORING
I: "I Fled Him, Down the Nights"		
1-13	quarter note = 152	Brass surges and timpani punctuation m. 11; Theme A; horn and cornet
14-21		Random woodwind figures; brass and timpani dialogue m. 17; Theme A; trombone m. 20; Theme A; trombone and horn
22		Timpani bridge

MEASURE	TEMPO	EVENT AND SCORING
23-31	quarter note = 160	Tuba, bassoon, bass *ostinato*; woodwind and percussion punctuation
32-46		Increasing texture and dynamic m. 32; Theme A; clarinet and piccolo m. 35; Theme A; saxophone m. 37; Theme A; piccolo, oboe, English horn m. 39; Theme A augmented; trombone and euphonium m. 40; Theme A; saxophone
47-66	quarter note = 184	Theme B; antiphonal trumpet; full ensemble rhythmic punctuations; canonic treatment of Theme B, fragmentation
67		Point of arrival, sustained tonic
68-75	quarter note = 76	Antiphonal trumpet bridge based on Theme A

II: "The Gold Gateways of the Stars:

76-86	quarter note = 60	Motif 1 "chant"; woodwinds in thirds; horn and trombone response in thirds
87-98	quarter note = 160	Additive woodwind ostinati, drone A
99-112		Theme C; trombone and euphonium; increasing texture through additive *ostinati*
113-119		Theme C; canons/*ostinati*, drone A-flat
120-131		*Ostinati*, syncopated brass chords, drone G
132-137		Point of arrival; legato woodwind *ostinati*
138-160		Increasing intensity, density, and dynamic; m. 156, discrepant antiphonal trumpet
161		Point of arrival, percussive strike
162-168	quarter note = 60	Brass chords; Motif 1 "chant" in woodwinds
169-173		Antiphonal trumpet cadenza based on Theme A

MEASURE	TEMPO	EVENT AND SCORING

III: "Within the Little Children's Eyes"

174-183	quarter note = 160	Motif 2; solo trumpet transition
184-223	dotted-quarter note = 88	Theme D; canonic treatment piccolo, oboe, flute, bassoon, baritone saxophone, English horn; m. 204, Theme E, cornet and euphonium; diminishing texture
224-226	quarter note = 60	Percussive accentuation
227-230		Antiphonal trumpet bridge based on Theme A

IV: "Nature's – Share With Me"

231-240	quarter note = 60	Theme F1; oboe and trumpet
241-248		Theme F2; horn and trumpet; fragmented motifs
249-262		Theme F3; flute, English horn, tenor saxophone; intensified antiphonal trumpet

V: "And Smitten Me to My Knee"

263-267	quarter note = 60	Fierce accents; sustained antiphonal trumpet
268-274	quarter note = 63	Increasing intensity, texture, dissonance; continued harmonic density; fragments of themes presented randomly m. 275, Theme B, trumpet m. 276, Theme A, horn m. 277, Movement II *ostinati*, piano m. 278, Theme C, trombone m. 279, Theme D, piccolo m. 280, Theme E, euphonium m. 281, Theme F, oboe
287-292		Brass chords; twelve-note ensemble chord; percussive accentuation
293-300		Antiphonal trumpet bridge based on Theme F

VI: "I Am He Whom Thou Seekest"

301-312	quarter note = 56	Theme F; bass clarinet, bassoon, euphonium, oboe, horn, tuba
313-330		Theme F; lush harmonic texture, *rubato*

MEASURE	TEMPO	EVENT AND SCORING
331-346		Point of arrival, gradually diminishing texture and thematic material
347-375		Solo trumpet and antiphonal trumpet dialogue based on Theme F; chime resolution

Unit 8: Suggested Listening

Warren Benson, *The Leaves Are Falling*
Michael Colgrass, *Winds of Nagual*
David Gillingham:
    A Light Unto the Darkness
    Heroes, Lost and Fallen
Martin Mailman, *For Precious Friends Hid in Death's Dateless Night*
Tom Stone, *Shadows of Eternity*
James Syler, *Fields*

Unit 9: Additional References and Resources

The Hound of Heaven is recorded on:
    Music for Winds & Percussion. Northern Illinois University Wind
        Ensemble, Stephen Squires, Conductor.
    The Wall. The United States Air Force Band, Washington, DC, Alan L.
        Bonner, Conductor.

Thompson, Francis. *The Collected Poetry of Francis Thompson.* London:
    Hodder and Stoughton, 1913.

Thompson, Francis. *The Hound of Heaven and Other Poems.* Boston:
    International Pocket Library, 1936.

Contributed by:

Glen J. Hemberger
Director of Bands
Southeastern Louisiana University
Hammond, Louisiana

Teacher Resource Guide

In Evening's Stillness
Joseph Schwantner
(b. 1943)

Unit 1: Composer

Joseph Schwantner was born in Chicago on March 22, 1943, and is currently Professor of Composition at the Eastman School of Music, University of Rochester, where he has taught since 1970. He has also served on the faculty of the Julliard School and was the 1987-88 Karel Husa Visiting Professor of Composition at Ithaca College, Ithaca, New York. Schwantner received his musical and academic training at the Chicago Conservatory and at Northwestern University, where he completed a doctorate in 1968. From 1982 to 1985, Schwantner served as Composer-in-Residence with the Saint Louis Symphony Orchestra as part of the MEET THE COMPOSER/Orchestra Residencies Program funded by Exxon Corporation, Rockefeller Foundation, and National Endowment for the Arts. He has been the subject of a television documentary entitled, *Soundings*, produced by WGBH in Boston for national broadcast. His work, *Magabunda*, "four poems of Agueda Pizarro," recorded by the Saint Louis Symphony, was nominated for a 1985 Grammy Award in the category of "Best New Classical Composition," and his *A Sudden Rainbow*, also recorded by the Saint Louis Symphony, was nominated for "Best Classical Composition."

Unit 2: Composition

In Evening's Stillness was commissioned by the Illinois Band Directors Association in 1996. It is published by Helicon Music Corporation and distributed by European American Music Distributors.

 In Evening's Stillness is a single, continuous movement based loosely on an austere poem by the composer. This poem, which is not included in the score, is as follows:

> In evening's stillness.
>   a gentle breeze,
> distant thunder
>   encircles the silence.

The work is scored for woodwinds, brass, amplified piano, and an expanded percussion section. Emphasis is placed on the equality of timbre between these four elements.

The fifteen-minute work calls for piccolo, three flutes, three oboes, English horn, three B-flat clarinets, bass clarinet, three bassoons, contrabassoon, three trumpets in C, four horns in F, three trombones, one tuba, piano (amplified, *sostenuto* pedal required), five percussion, including Percussion I: tam-tam, vibraphone (bowed), xylophone, timbales, bongos, marimba (shared with Percussion II); Percussion II: bass drum, crotales, two triangles, marimba, vibraphone (shared with Percussion I); Percussion III: tam-tam, vibraphone (bowed), chimes, four tom-toms, marimba (shared with Percussion IV); Percussion IV: bass drum, two triangles, glockenspiel, marimba, vibraphone (from Percussion III); Percussion V: timpani.

Unit 3: Historical Perspective

Schwantner's first work for wind band, *and the mountains rising nowhere*, became a landmark composition in the wind band repertoire. His second work for wind band, *From a Dark Millennium*, has found a similar place in the repertoire without the extreme technical demands of the previous work. *In Evening's Stillness* completes the "trilogy" of works and is, by most opinions, the middle movement.

Unit 4: Technical Considerations

In Evening's Stillness incorporates a number of contemporary notational concepts. Almost all of Schwantner's works are composed in Mirco notation. Time signatures of 2/8, 3/8, 4/8, 5/8, 7/8, 5/16, 6/16, and 4/dotted-eighth note are used with subdivisions as small as a sixty-fourth note. *In Evening's Stillness* departs from this practice, avoiding notational fractions smaller than an eighth note. The piano part is integral to the entire work. Percussion set-up is extremely important in regard to dynamic balances within the entire ensemble and shared equipment among the percussionists. Many sections include intricate episodes of "shared monody."

Although the work does contain some specific challenges to performers and conductor, it has been successfully performed by both college and high school ensembles. The challenges for the performer include rhythmic notation, complexity of rhythm, changing meters, singing and whistling and, especially for the less-experienced performer, extremes of range and volume. For the conductor, the challenges also include ensemble balance and maintaining a melodic flow throughout a sectional work.

Unit 5: Stylistic Considerations

Schwantner states that some of his intentions in composing the work included creating a work for winds and percussion that did not sound "like a band piece." He was further interested in writing a work: (1) where the percussion section would be on an equal footing with the woodwinds and brass, (2) to further exploit the process of synthesis between tonal and non-tonal musical materials, and (3) to expand the sonorous timbrel and articulative resources of a large ensemble by having performers engage in "extra performance activities" – such as singing, whistling, and playing glass crystals. Some of the key stylistic elements relate to the way in which he utilizes the elements of rhythm, timbre, and texture in a number of contemporary and traditional techniques.

Music as complex as Schwantner's must be interpreted with the same careful attention to basic elements as earlier music. Often the language of contemporary music is not familiar to the players; they must often play in techniques or styles with which they are not conversant. As an example, the clarinetist's role in a Beethoven symphony is quickly obvious to him through his training and background. The player knows how the motion of the music is generated and how he/she contributes to the various textures and progress of the work. The player is readily aware of when he/she is an ensemble player and when he/she is a soloist, and adjusts intonation and volume to fit the changing circumstances.

Schwantner also uses a timbre and textural technique he refers to as "shared monody." This is a melodic idea that is shared by partial doublings among several instrumental voices. According to Schwantner, this technique is a single, linear event that is melodically shared by many players, with each single player entering and sustaining a different pitch of the theme in order. These notes become a single line in which many participate, as differentiated from a single player on a solo line.

Unit 6: Musical Elements

MELODY:
In many cases, the familiar "singable" themes of tonal music are replaced in much twentieth century music with shorter motives that take on a more angular, instrumental character and are often layered upon one another to produce new sonorities. These shorter elements are not necessarily treated with the theme, harmony, bass line, and *obligato*-like settings players are accustomed to hearing.

One of the characteristic features of *In Evening's Stillness, From a Dark*

Millennium, and *and the mountains rising nowhere* is what Schwantner terms "shared monody," as described above.

A traditional performance problem lies in the player's perception of his part as only a component of a larger melodic unfolding. In a contemporary setting, it becomes more difficult. The performer must understand that with an entrance that is only the third part of a triplet, he/she is participating in a solo-like melodic line that may even be one component of four lines. Equally often, these lines in *In Evening's Stillness* are presented as an aggregate in the percussion and piano/celesta. The participating players have a strong reference both rhythmically and melodically.

Schwantner frequently initiates these melodic fragment lines in percussion because of the sharp attacks created by the instruments. This percussion sound creates ensemble concerns when mixed with winds. While two clarinets playing together may have a slight difference at the moment of attack without being discernible, two percussion instruments attacking together, especially melodic percussion with hard mallets, may only be a nano-second apart, but the difference is heard. When winds are mixed with percussion, the differences are sometimes very difficult to solve.

HARMONY:

Schwantner uses "static pillars" of harmonies – much like the music of Varèse – in which single sonorities or "blocks of sound" are unchanged for a period of time. Often, angular motives themselves become the harmony as they are held or suspended. While traditional melodies move above a harmonic base, the effects of suspending their sound would be the same as playing a Mozart sonata with the pedal always down.

When a chord spanning three octaves is played, it is very difficult to hear inner voices unless there is a great deal of registral space between notes. When eight or nine notes of a chord are articulated one at a time, the ear perceives each note and they are then allowed to sustain. "Successive articulation" of each note of a chord helps clarify the harmonic entity. These "stable pillars" of harmony develop their own tonal centers which are more static than in progressions in a traditional triadic sense.

FORM:

In *In Evening's Stillness*, instrumental color, tempo, dynamics, accumulation of textured density, and changing of density outline the form of the piece and create moments of tension and release, propelling the work in time.

Schwantner provides additional development through changes in color as the musical lines change shape – thick and thin – rather than manipulations of musical materials and ideas. The composer is always concerned with how the sound changes in time from point A to point B. In many instances, his music tries to maximize coloristic and timbrel possibilities of the wind ensemble.

It is also important to bring out the violent contrasts in the work. Very soft (*ppp*) sections may explode into very loud (*fff*) sections without preparation. The music may take unexpected twists and turns from one part of the texture to another. Young musicians may not be sufficiently exposed to such dramatic changes to perform them successfully, and the conductor must be insistent on achieving these effects. Subtleties of dynamics are also integral, as often the *pianissimo* becomes *mezzo-piano* and the *fortissimo* becomes *mezzo-forte*.

Frequent meter changes and asymmetrical patterns are another unfamiliar area for the young musician. If these are treated in a melodic sense, they are often more readily mastered.

Unit 7: Form and Structure

Form:

The fundamental outline is ABBABB. Each ABB section contains similar material and manipulations.

The first A section begins with the piano, low winds, and percussion introducing the first pitch class set. The piano (m. 10) starts an *arpeggio* pattern that is used throughout the work. Finally, the first full pitch class set is introduced at m. 28. This is followed by a "fanfare" figure in low winds and percussion. The B^1 section is a long, orchestrated *crescendo* with two chorales (1/2). This concludes with a shared monody fanfare using the same material. Section B^2 is the same form as B^1 using altered chorales (3/4) and ending with the full pitch class set from the A section. (See figure 1.)

The second half of the work is an approximate mirror of the first half. The fanfare is followed by the "introduction" material to form A^2. B^3 is similar to B^1 using expanded chorales (5/6). B^4 begins with chorales 7/8, then places the chorale *ostinato* over the fanfare figure (B-flat only). The work ends with piano, triangle, and timbales. (See figure 2.)

Compositional Materials:

The introduction is built on an accumulated pitch class of:

F-flat – A-flat – E-flat – B-flat – C-flat – D-flat

The first complete pitch class set occurs at m. 28 (fanfare). The entire set is a diatonic collection with no particular pitch class as a tonic. The diatonic collection is expressed by the first seven notes of the series without any pitch class duplications. The first five notes and the last eight notes are a pentatonic subset of the diatonic collection. This pentachord is a familiar Japanese scale (kumoi-joshi) which, in its traditional arrangement, would be spelled E-flat, F-flat, B-flat, C-flat (with E-flat as the lowest note). As with the overall diatonic collection, there doesn't seem to be any effort to make one pitch a focal pitch class within the scale.

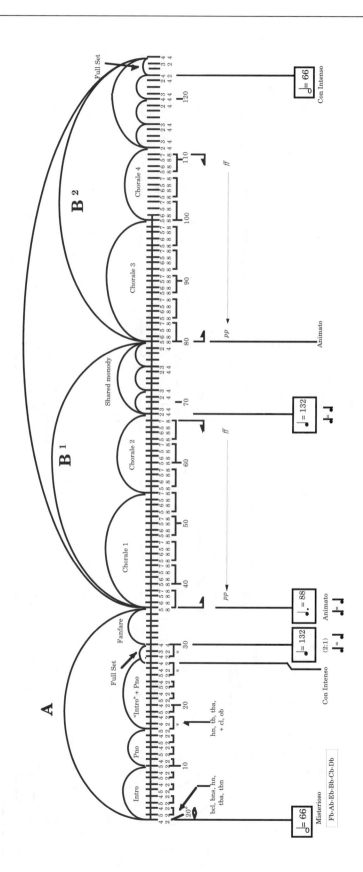

Figure 1

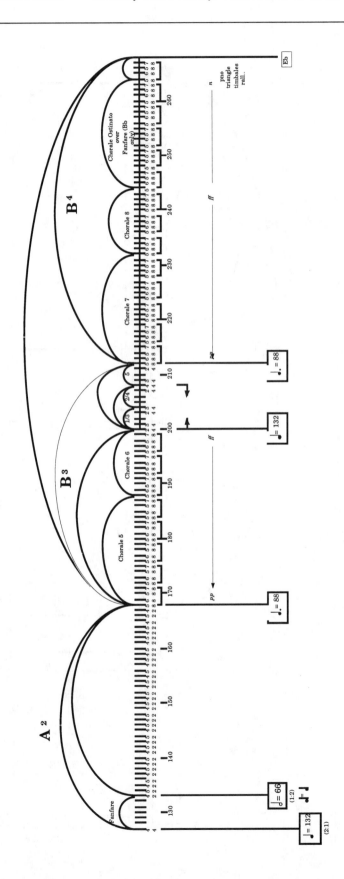

Figure 2

The G-flat and the D-flat are the two pivotal pitch classes, which belong to the diatonic collection but not the Japanese scale. They appear together in the series and, unlike the other pitch classes, they appear only once.

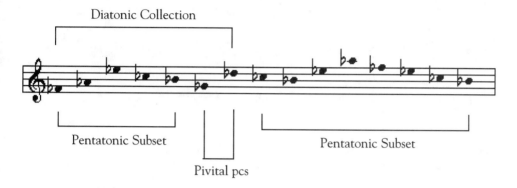

The ordering of the collection is given with possible relationships.

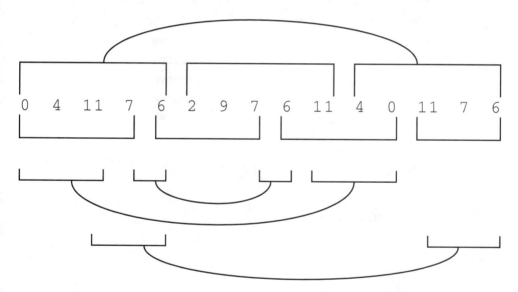

The chorale *ostinato* of 5/5, 6/8, 5/8, 7/8 is based on the "tonic" of the chorale and is highlighted by the placement of accents within the motive. (See the following page.)

INSTRUMENTATION:
Schwantner scores this work for woodwinds and horns in fours, trumpets and trombones in threes with tuba, piano, and five percussionists. This is typical of the expanded, or double, wind orchestra section. As in his other wind works, Schwantner's treatment of the amplified piano places it on an equal sonic value as the winds and percussion. This is the first work for winds in

Chorale No. 1 (mm. 40-67)

which Schwantner has scored three B-flat clarinets. His other works are scored for only two.

The composer has indicated a specified seating arrangement.

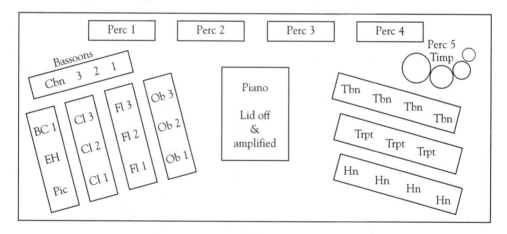

This unusual seating places like woodwinds (flutes, oboes, and clarinets) in stacked rows, with the second and third parts projecting through the principal parts. Bassoons, brass, and percussion are in a more traditional seating arrangement within each section. Bass clarinet, English horn, and piccolo are stacked like the upper woodwinds. The piano is placed in the center, lid off and amplified, to visually and acoustically ratify the equality of the four instrumental sections: woodwinds, brass, piano, and percussion. The bass clarinet is near the bassoons, which share line often.

Unit 8: Suggested Listening

Joseph Schwantner:
A Sudden Rainbow
Aftertones of Infinity
and the mountains rising nowhere
Elixir
From a Dark Millennium
Music of Amber
New Morning for the World
Sparrows

Unit 9: Additional References and Resources

Renshaw, Jeffrey. "Conducting Analysis: Joseph Schwantner's and the mountains rising nowhere." *The Instrumentalist*, IVV January 1991.

Renshaw, Jeffrey. "Conducting Analysis: Joseph Schwantner's From a Dark Millennium." *The Instrumentalist*, IVIV September 1989.

Renshaw, Jeffrey. "Interview with Joseph Schwantner." *The Instrumentalist*, IVV May 1991.

Contributed by:

Jeffrey H. Renshaw
Director of Bands
University of Connecticut
Storrs, Connecticut

Teacher Resource Guide

Morning Music
Richard Rodney Bennett
(b. 1936)

Unit 1: Composer

Richard Rodney Bennett was born on March 29, 1936, at Broadstairs in Kent, England. His family was musical. His mother, a student of Gustav Holst, had been a composer in her younger days and had written lyrical chamber music that showed the influence of Debussy. She was also a notable performer and counted the composers John Ireland and Constant Lambert among her friends. While still a child, Bennett was acquainted with the music of Britten, Lambert, and Walton, and began composing during World War II. Several works written during his adolescence are still well thought of today.

Bennett entered the Royal Academy of Music in London in 1953, where he studied composition with Lennox Berkeley and Howard Ferguson. He quickly found academic circles restrictive and never completed his diploma. Part of the reason for this estrangement was his interest in twelve-tone serialism, which began around age sixteen, at a time when it was still largely discounted by British music schools. He began attending the Darmstadt Summer School in 1955 and met many prominent proponents of the avant-garde, including Stockhausen, Boulez, Maderna, Nono, and Berio. In 1957, he won a French government scholarship to study for two years with Boulez in Paris. He returned to London in 1959 and quickly established himself as a versatile and innovative young composer. Between 1963 and 1965, he taught at the Royal Academy of Music, and during the 1970-71 academic year, he was a visiting professor of composition at Peabody Conservatory in Baltimore. In 1979, he moved to New York City, where he resides today.

Bennett maintains a strong interest in film music, TV, and jazz. His first film score, *Blind Date* (1955), was written while still a student and employed by a jazz band. In the subsequent three decades, he composed no fewer than fifty film scores. He also writes extensively for TV. Jazz, which he considers "his hobby and his passion," has been a consistent influence. An accomplished jazz pianist, he wrote two works specifically for jazz ensembles, *Jazz Calendar* (1964) and *Jazz Pastorale* (1969), and jazz inflections can be detected in many other compositions.

In addition to *Morning Music*, Bennett has written three works for wind band: *Flowers of the Forest: Reflections on a Scottish Folk Song for Brass Band* (1989), *The Four Seasons* (1991), and *Concerto for Trumpet and Wind Orchestra* (1993).

Unit 2: Composition

Morning Music was commissioned by the British Association of Symphonic Bands and Wind Ensembles, and was written in New York between July 19 and August 17, 1986. It was premiered in Boston on July 25, 1987, at the third International Conference of the World Association for Symphonic Bands and Ensembles (WASBE), performed by the Northshore Concert Band conducted by Timothy Reynish. The British premiere occurred in Manchester a few months later, on October 31, 1987, performed by the Royal Northern College of Music Wind Orchestra conducted by Timothy Reynish. The score is prefaced with a quotation from William Wordsworth:

> This city now doth a garment wear
> The beauty of the morning, silent, bare.
> Ships, towers, domes, theatres, and temples lie
> Open unto the fields and to the sky,
> All bright and glitt'ring in the smokeless air....

This quotation provides *Morning Music* with its form and, to a large extent, its style. The work consists of seven movements – "Prelude," "Ships," "Towers," "Domes," "Theatres," "Temples," "Finale" – all of which are played without pause. While not specifically programmatic, each movement does contain elements suggested by the titles. "Ships" is in 6/8 time, like a sea chanty; "Towers" is permeated with bell sounds; "Domes" has the character of a chorale; "Theatres" is full of brief fanfares and changes style several times, like the characters in a play; and "Temples" presents a unison melody that evokes plainchant through the use of repeated notes (like reciting tones) and mixed meter.

Scored for a large wind ensemble that includes a wide array of percussion instruments, piano, harp, and double bass, *Morning Music* is approximately seventeen minutes long.

Unit 3: Historical Perspective

Since adolescence, Bennett has been committed to twelve-tone serialism, but his application of serial principles has never been dogmatic. His tone rows are often imbued with tonal implications, and strict adherence to serial techniques has always been subservient to his interest in lyricism, rhythm, and texture.

This approach is immediately apparent in *Morning Music*. The tone row on which this work is based is gradually revealed during the "Prelude," but appears as a distinctive lyrical theme that will be the primary integrating element of the entire work. Repeated several times at the beginning of the work to establish its recognizability, it then recurs in various permutations throughout all movements. Virtually all of the harmony and counterpoint can also be easily related to the row, but Bennett's interest in texture and timbre leads him to employ row segments in highly creative ways. His usage often approaches pitch set theory, with an obvious concern for intervallic content rather than the precise ordering of row fragments.

During the 1970s, Bennett and his friend, Thea Musgrave, became very interested in the introduction of dramatic elements into abstract music. This preoccupation is best observed in the series of works entitled *Commedia*, in which characters from the *Commedia dell' arte* are assigned to particular instruments. Considering his interest in dramatic principles and in film music, it seems hardly surprising that he would have selected a visual image as the inspiration for *Morning Music*.

Unit 4: Technical Considerations

The "Prelude" is in 2/2 meter, *Molto moderato*, half note = 58. Lyrical in style, it initially places substantial emphasis on the high register of the wind ensemble. The primary theme is presented a total of four times in different scorings and in a gradually accumulating texture. Each of these appearances is identified by an expression marking such as *dolce* or *cantabile* and must be highlighted by the performers. The movement reaches a climax at m. 46, which ushers in a brief transition at a faster tempo (*Con moto*, half note = 63), leading to the next movement.

"Ships" is in 6/8, *Allegro giocoso*, dotted-quarter note = 126. Initially, the primary theme is presented in disjunct rhythm in the high register accompanied by trumpet fanfares and bass figures incorporating melodic fourths. A more lyrical segment follows that presents the theme in horns and trumpets over a simple accompaniment. Both of these sections are restated, leading to a change of tempo and meter (2/4, *Molto vivo*, quarter note = 132). A brief segment for brass alone presents the theme or derivatives of it simultaneously in several voices, then the beginning of the movement is recalled texturally but in the new meter. High register control, fluency with rapid, non-tonal melodic fragments, and careful attention to balance are the technical requirements necessary for an effective performance. This movement ends on a unison low C under a fermata.

"Towers" is in 3/4, *Molto mosso*, dotted-half note = 72. Throughout this movement Bennett employs the instruments of the wind ensemble, percussion, and others in the creation of bell sounds. The non-percussion sounds are presented as closed-position harmonies in the middle register and require careful attention to balance in order to generate the impression of both the impact of the striker within the bell and the ringing that follows. The initial material is revisited several times, and at m. 252 a transitional passage appears that involves a *Klangfarbenmelodie* descending through the woodwinds. Concern for rhythm and intonation are essential in accomplishing a convincing linking of the melodic fragments, most of which transfer on unison pitches. While much of this movement is centered in the middle register, the upper woodwinds again ascend into their high register during the concluding segment. "Towers" concludes with a fermata over a chord that sounds like a peal of bells ringing into silence. The *diminuendo* at the end of this chord is a crucial part of this programmatic idea.

"Domes" is in common time, *Andante tranquillo*, quarter note = 72. This movement contrasts with the preceding one in virtually every aspect. The slow tempo and extremely restrained dynamics gives it a sacred character – like a chorale. The technical demands are also opposed to earlier music. Here the performers must sustain long phrases at very soft volumes and also be sensitive to balance during dense, contrapuntal textures in the woodwinds that always involve at least four independent lines. Conductors need to be aware that in the initial measures the primary theme appears in parallel major thirds in flute and clarinet. Balance is again important later in the movement, beginning at m. 355, when this same theme reappears in the flutes. Like the previous movements, the final chord of "Domes" is extended by a fermata.

"Theatres" is in 2/4 meter, *Vivo*, quarter note = 126. As if to illustrate a variety of characters or theatrical events, this movement changes style several times. It opens with a swift, rising melodic line constructed of wide intervals and accompanied by trumpet fanfares. The style is very delicate, demanding crisp articulations. A brief saxophone solo ushers in a new subsection that recalls big-band jazz. The saxophones are featured throughout this subsection and should always be in the forefront of the texture. Considerable dynamic control is required in the robust timpani solo that appears next and leads to yet another style change. Two successive harmonic pyramids are built up from the lowest register, are crowned by a reference (in piccolo and flute) to the big-band music from earlier in the movement, and are concluded with a bass clarinet solo consisting of a rapid descending scalar passage. Since each of the entries making up the pyramids is marked *dolce*, the conductor must ensure that no entry is accented and that the ensuing chord does not cover the flute/piccolo motive. The final sound of the movement is a unison low D under a fermata.

"Temples" is marked *Molto moderato*, quarter note = 66. Although it starts in 3/4, this movement changes meter almost every measure, requiring careful counting by all performers. In the initial measures, unison clarinets and bassoons present a low register melody that necessitates precise tuning. In addition to the rhythmic and intonation challenges, this movement, like "Domes," demands that the performers sustain long lines at very soft dynamics. At m. 497, Bennett makes the obvious connection between "temples" and "domes" by recalling music from the earlier movement with its dense woodwind counterpoint. Conductors need to ensure that this relationship is audible. In this instance, these woodwind passages are opposed to brass chorale phrases like the antiphonal choruses of church music, creating both coordination and balance challenges. In the final subsection of the movement, the brass phrases are combined with the chant-like melody. The movement concludes with several octaves of the single pitch C.

The "Finale" has three sections but essentially presents no new material. The first section is in 6/8 meter, *Presto con brio*, dotted-quarter note = 140, and recalls the music of "Ships." The second section is in 3/4, dotted-half note = 74, and revisits the material presented in "Towers." The final measures are marked *Maestoso*, quarter note = 74, and are an altered restatement of the "Prelude," since they present the primary theme at its original pitch, played by the high voices of the ensemble. A rapidly accumulating texture leads to a climactic ending.

At first glance, this score appears to present limited technical challenges. However, closer inspection reveals considerable use of quartal intervals, both melodically and harmonically, that will require careful preparation by performers. Also, many of the textures are highly transparent, with instruments often in extreme ranges and extensive use of dynamic shadings and accents. These elements demand competent, sensitive players with highly developed listening skills. Several movements, notably "Ships," "Towers," "Theatres," and the "Finale," employ fast tempi.

Unit 5: Stylistic Considerations

This work is an excellent example of the twentieth century fascination with timbre and texture. Many passages are set in very delicate textures and colored by imaginative timbrel mixes. Since all of the melodic content is drawn from a single tone row and derived from one primary theme, much of the contrast is generated through alterations of timbre and texture rather than of pitch and rhythm. There is substantial variety of style among the movements, and these distinctions need to be systematically prepared and presented so that the pictorial images underlying each section are comprehensible by audiences.

Another important aspect of this work's soundscape is the simultaneous presentation of unison melodic ideas in contrasted articulations. These textures might be termed "accent-plus-resonance" since the beginnings of sustained pitches are pointed up by short, accented notes in another voice. Such heterophonic textures can be found in many works by other twentieth century composers, such as Stravinsky, Hindemith, and Gunther Schuller. When they appear, they need to be carefully balanced to ensure that the contrast in articulation is clearly heard.

Unit 6: Musical Elements

MOVEMENT I: "PRELUDE"
As with most serialized compositions, the initial section is given over to the introduction of the tone row that is the basis of this work: F, C, D, C, A, E, G, F, B, B, A, D. Bennett, however, does more than simply present a pitch set. The notes of his row are set out in a distinctive primary melody with a number of recognizable motives that can be used for melodic, harmonic, and contrapuntal constructions. The row appears to be divided into the unusual segments of seven notes and five notes since the motives using these pitches are both repeated in the initial presentation of the complete primary theme, and this procedure recurs frequently throughout the work. It is also interesting that the final chord of the work uses the first notes of each of these segments. The first sounds are all in the high register. These bright, fragile tones have the character of string harmonics and are probably a depiction of the "glitter" that is mentioned in the text. With each repetition of the melody, the texture accumulates and becomes more animated. The faster transitional passage beginning at m. 46 introduces a harmonic motive consisting of on-the-beat dissonance quickly resolving to a consonant chord that will be a primary element of "Towers" and other parts of the score.

MOVEMENT II: "SHIPS"
The primary theme set in disjunct rhythm in the highest register of the ensemble is a rather traditional means of depicting the sparkle of bright sunlight on water. This picture is enhanced by the accompanying trumpet fanfares and bass lines rising in fourths that generate a breezy, energetic character. A few measures later, a lyrical countermelody is added to the texture, and with it the important "accent-plus-resonance" idea appears for the first time. Lyricism dominates the contrasting B section that arrives at m. 71. The primary theme is presented by the horns, doubled in heterophony by the trumpets, and accompanied very simply. These two ideas alternate throughout the movement.

MOVEMENT III: "TOWERS"
A jubilant cacophony of morning bells forms most of this movement. An inversion of the tone row provides the melodic material, but strict serial principles are not as important as the timbrel/textural idea. As the movement progresses, the compass is expanded beyond the middle register, but the musical concept remains unchanged. The first genuine contrast appears at the

previously mentioned transitional passage identified as a *Klangfarbenmelodie*. Each of the fragments of this "tone color melody" is drawn from the last part of the row and, since each is but a measure long, go by very quickly. A brief section follows that presents subdued bell sounds, perhaps a depiction of distant towers or an allusion to the muffled bells of funeral rites. While this section is brief, it does generate substantial contrast and might be considered a B section. The conclusion of the movement is an enhanced version of A section material.

MOVEMENT IV: "DOMES"
Solemn and restrained, this movement recalls the lyricism of the "Prelude." Initially, the texture is homophonic like a chorale, but the primary theme appears in parallel major thirds in the upper voices. The quiet dynamics create the impression of distance, perhaps as one might hear monastics celebrating morning rites behind a cathedral alter screen. The contrasting music in this movement is comprised of an oboe solo based on the primary theme, accompanied by multiple strands of woodwind counterpoint, all of which are built from row segments. As with "Ships," these two ideas alternate throughout the movement. The final subsection (C) presents another textural contrast. The flutes play the primary theme over a brass chorale and a rhythmically active woodwind accompaniment in a style that is reminiscent of a chorale prelude. The final two chords are constructed from row fragments but present a striking *plagal* effect.

MOVEMENT V: "THEATRES"
After the solemnity and restraint of the previous movement, the brisk, ascending melody that opens the A section of this movement is a considerable surprise. Although not immediately obvious, this melody is another derivative of the primary theme with a radically altered profile. Its angular nature and the accompaniment of light trumpet fanfares gives this music a humorous quality, suggesting comedy or perhaps farce. This melody evolves throughout this subsection and ultimately arrives in the high register, presenting motives that recall the final part of "Ships." The subsequent jazzy subsection B that follows is perhaps intended to suggest musical comedy or dance and is based on row fragments, although the precise ordering of pitches has been forsaken in favor of the overall effect. This music has the feeling of "swung" rhythms despite being precisely notated. The ensuing timpani solo might be intended to evoke the actions of a clown, which are often associated with percussion effects. Two repetitions of a unique texture, previously identified as harmonic pyramids, conclude the movement. These pyramids are verticalizations of the first hexachord of the row in different transpositions, and it is unclear how they might relate to the pictorial image underlying this movement.

MOVEMENT VI: "TEMPLES"
The A section of this movement introduces monophony, a texture new to this piece. The melody, presented in unison by low-register clarinets and bassoons, is a variant on the inversion of the primary theme. Rhythmic flexibility and the presence of repeated notes give this melody the character of plainsong, and the texture recalls other aspects of sacred music as well. The chant-like tune is presented in brief phrases that are answered by brass chorale motives in a style reminiscent of the *versicle/response* technique of a church cantor and congregation. The B section begins as a quotation from "Domes"; however, the brass chorale phrase from A is interpolated between the two statements of the earlier music, creating the impression of antiphonal choirs on opposing balconies. The opposing choruses and the cantor are drawn together into a single, unified statement in the concluding section of the movement.

MOVEMENT VII: "FINALE"
No new musical elements are presented, but this movement creates the overall form of the work by recalling earlier material. The first two sections function as a recapitulation since they restate, in order, much of the first two contrasting sections of the work. The final *Maestoso* brings a hint of arch form by returning to the very beginning of the composition, albeit in a substantially altered textural context.

Unit 7: Form and Structure

SECTION	MEASURE	EVENT AND SCORING
Movement I: "Prelude"		
A	1-17	Initial presentation of the primary theme in piccolo, later doubled by flute; spare high-register accompaniment
A^1	18-29	Second statement of primary theme in oboe, accompanied by horns, bassoons, and tuba
A^2	30-45	Third statement of theme in horns, later doubled by flutes and oboe; animated accompaniment in an accumulating texture; *accelerando* in final measure
A^3	46-50	Transitional section, faster tempo; truncated theme in piccolo, flutes, oboes and, later, clarinet; harmonic motive in brass

SECTION	MEASURE	EVENT AND SCORING
Movement II: "Ships"		
A	51-70	Primary theme in disjunct rhythm in high voices; accompanied by trumpet fanfares and brief rising bass figures; later lyrical countermelody (near row form) in bass trombone supported by "accent-plus-resonance" in bassoon
B	71-86	Lyrical statement of primary theme in horns with accent-plus-resonance in trumpets; angular accompanying figures in bassoons
A	87-99	Abbreviated version of earlier music
B	100-109	As above, flutes and oboes double the horn melody in the final bars
Transition	110-115	Faster tempo; change of meter; rhythmically altered version of the primary theme at its original pitch in the high voices; harmonic motive from the transition at the end of the "Prelude" in the brass
C	116-129	Trumpets and trombones present simultaneous row forms; accent-plus-resonance in double bass; saxophones present accompanimental figures based on row fragments
A^1	130-146	Like original material, but in the new meter
B^1	147-156	Melody in horns, accent-plus-resonance in trombones; cadence on unison low C
Movement III: "Towers"		
A	157-188	Bell sounds in brass and percussion
A^1	189-216	Same material rescored into woodwinds and percussion, later full ensemble
A	217-228	Abbreviated version of previous material
A^1	229-251	As above but with fuller scoring
Transition	252-267	Descending *Klangfarbenmelodie* in woodwinds
B	268-288	Distant bell sounds initially in woodwinds and percussion, later in brass and percussion

SECTION	MEASURE	EVENT AND SCORING
A²	289-325	Repeat of earlier material but with fuller scoring leading to climax and cadence

Movement IV: "Domes"

A	326-335	Primary theme in parallel major thirds in flute and clarinet; homophonic accompaniment in the style of a chorale
B	336-341	New melody derived from the primary theme in oboe; contrapuntal accompaniment in solo woodwinds and horn
A¹	342-347	Brass chorale
B	348-354	Repeat of earlier material transposed and extended
C	355-367	Chorale prelude; primary theme in flutes, brass chorale, and animated woodwind accompaniment; plagal effect in last three measures

Movement V: "Theatres"

A	368-405	New variant of the primary theme with altered rhythm and profile initially in bassoons and horns, later the high voices; light trumpet fanfares and accent-plus-resonance in trombones as accompaniment
B	406-443	Jazz-influenced section featuring the saxophones, and a brief E-flat clarinet solo
C	443-455	Timpani solo
D	456-476	Two harmonic pyramids constructed as a verticalization of the first hexachord of the tone row; melodic motive from B in piccolo and flute; rapid, descending bass clarinet solo

SECTION	MEASURE	EVENT AND SCORING
Movement VI: "Temples"		
A	477-496	Chant-like, unison melody derived from the inversion of the primary theme played by low clarinets and bassoons, and presented in short phrases separated by chorale motives in brass
B	497-509	Recall of the woodwind contrapuntal writing from "Domes"; two repetitions are separated by a phrase of the brass chorale
A¹	510-518	Chant-like melody played by clarinets, bassoons, and horns, accompanied by the brass chorale
Movement VII: "Finale"		
A	519-609	Recapitulation of much of "Ships"
B	610-628	Recapitulation of part of "Temples"
C	629-646	*Maestoso*; recall of the "Prelude"; primary melody in high voices; accumulating texture leading to ultimate climax and final cadence

Unit 8: Suggested Listening

Richard Rodney Bennett:
    Concerto for Trumpet and Wind Orchestra
    The Four Seasons
Edward Grieg, *Morning from Peer Gynt*
Franz Joseph Haydn, *Symphony No. 6 (Le Matin)*, Hob. I:6
Maurice Ravel, *Levée du jour from Daphnis and Chloé*
Recording: *Morning Music: Midnight Music*; The Royal Northern College Wind Orchestra, conducted by Timothy Reynish; Doyen CD, DOY CD 037.
Gunther Schuller:
    Divertimento: On Wingéd Flight
    Meditation
    Study in Textures

Unit 9: Additional References and Resources

Craggs, Stewart R. *Richard Rodney Bennett: A Bio-Bibliography*. Westport, CT: Greenwood Press, 1990.

Cummings, David M., ed. *International Who's Who in Music and Musician's Directory*. 14th ed., 1994/5. Cambridge, England: Melrose Press Ltd., 73.

Sadie, Stanley, ed. *New Grove Dictionary of Music and Musicians*. 20 vols. London: Macmillan Publishers Ltd., II (1980): 496-99

Slonimsky, Nicholas, ed. *Baker's Biographical Dictionary of Musicians*. 8th ed. New York: Schirmer Books (1992): 154-5.

Contributed by:

Keith Kinder
Associate Professor of Music
McMaster University
Hamilton, Ontario, Canada

Teacher Resource Guide

Sea Drift

Anthony Iannaccone
(b. 1943)

Unit 1: Composer

Anthony Iannaccone studied at the Manhattan School of Music and the Eastman School of Music. His principal teachers were Vittorio Giannini, Aaron Copland, and David Diamond. During the 1960s, he supported himself as a part-time teacher (Manhattan School) and orchestral violinist. His catalog of approximately fifty published works include three symphonies, as well as smaller works for orchestra, several large works for chorus and orchestra, numerous chamber pieces, a variety of works for wind ensemble, and several extended *a cappella* choral compositions. His music is performed by major orchestras and professional chamber ensembles in the U.S. and abroad.

Iannaccone has received awards, commissions, and grants from many organizations, including the 1988 National Band Association's Annual Composition Contest in 1988 and the 1995 American Bandmasters Association/Ostwald Composition Competition. He is a frequent guest conductor of both instrumental and choral ensembles, particularly at college and university campuses throughout the country. He has been a member of the faculty at Eastern Michigan University since 1971, where he directs the Collegium Musicum and teaches composition, orchestration, and arranging.

Unit 2: Composition

Sea Drift was written in 1992 on a commission by the Delta Iota Chapter of Phi Mu Alpha Sinfonia and the Sinfonia Foundation, in celebration of Western Michigan University's 25th Annual Spring Conference of Wind and Percussion Music, April 2, 1993. The work was awarded first prize in the 38th

Biennial American Bandmasters Association/Ostwald Composition Competition in 1995. Approximately eighteen minutes in length, the piece is written in three movements whose titles derive their inspiration from three poems in the Walt Whitman collection entitled *Sea Drift*: I) "Out of the Cradle, Endlessly Rocking" (9:20); II) "On the Beach at Night" (5:00); and III) "Song for All Seas" (3:40). The composer provides the following notes about the piece in the score:

> "Out of the Cradle, Endlessly Rocking" is a poem that blends extended metaphor with a variety of techniques to deal with a tri-partition core: birth, life (love), and death (rebirth). The poem is in the form of a childhood reminiscence, told by the poet about an experience involving a mockingbird that loses his mate, the sea, and the poet's self-discovery of his poetic voice.
>
> Much of this poem and the first movement of *Sea Drift* implies an undulating, rocking quality with music that rises and falls or swells and ebbs. Peaks of happiness plunge to troughs of despair, all against background of the endlessly rocking cradle of life and death – the sea. The music of the first movement is filled with both the longing and the wave-like qualities suggested by Whitman's poem. The sad song of the mockingbird is fused with the song of the poet and the whispers of the sea to form a unity and a reconciliation out of diversity and conflict. The poetic trio of bird-boy-sea is symbolized in the music by the timbres of flute/clarinet (oboe)/horn. The complete cycle of birth-life-death is suggested by an overall trajectory of cumulative and disintegrating textures, unfolding in music which is, by turn, lyrical/static, angular/dynamic/conflicting, and finally, song-like and static again.
>
> The second movement, "On the Beach at Night," evokes a reflective scene in which a father and child are contemplating a sky of shimmering stars, some of which appear to be devoured by ravenous dark cloud masses. Out of this symbolic celestial conflict, several stars, some delicate, some radiant, emerge victoriously, intimating the poet's mystical intuition of the immortality of cosmic spirit. The music, marked *sognando* (dreaming), is built on an interplay of resonant, ringing sonorities. These sonorities range from delicate and gentle treble sounds to lustrous richer full ensemble chords with sharp attacks and overlapping decays. The top notes of these chords outline song-like material heard earlier in the first movement.
>
> The third movement, "Song for All Seas," is marked *Like wind over waves*. This music, like that of movements one and two, is largely

derived from the pitch materials first heard in the clarinet solo at the beginning of movement one. Here, however, these pitches are transformed into rhythmic and textural shapes that suggest the mercurial energy of the sea. Tranquil waves are quickly altered into aggressive surges of water and energy. The movement ends in climactic swells of colliding rhythmic figures which culminate in a final burst on B-flat.

Unit 3: Historical Perspective

Anthony Iannaccone has received many awards, including the National Band Association's annual composition contest in 1988 with his *Apparitions* (1986), and the 1995 American Bandmasters Association/Ostwald Composition Competition for *Sea Drift* (1992). In addition to these two works, his compositions for band include *Of Fire and Ice* (1977); *After a Gentle Rain* (1979); *Images of Song and Dance, No. 2: Terpsichore* (1980); and *Plymouth Trilogy* (1981).

In *Sea Drift*, the inspiration of Walt Whitman's poetry sets the stage for the programmatic elements of the music to be explored throughout this work. The external influences of program music provide an excellent opportunity to engage musicians in exploring the creative process of musical composition. The vivid pictures captured by Iannaccone in this work are enhanced and referenced by earlier compositions, such as Claude Debussy's *La Mer*, that use water and the sea as inspiration. Iannaccone presents the wind literature with a very rare and unique piece for our repertoire.

Unit 4: Technical Considerations

While tempi in this piece range from quarter note = 40 to quarter note = 184, the first movement is mostly written in a medium tempo, with the second movement being very slow and the third movement using the brighter tempi. Due to the programmatic nature of the piece, the tempi fluctuate throughout, and the use of tempo *rubato* is quite prevalent. Extreme dynamic contrasts are the rule, and rhythmic variety is an important component. Musicians should be comfortable with the use of multi-layered polyrhythms and notation that includes thirty-second notes as well as sixteenth, eighth, and quarter note triplets.

The scoring for this work is for standard band instrumentation along with separate parts for celesta and piano that will require two players. The percussion section requires four performers, three of whom must have fluent mallet percussion skills. There are important, intricate parts for bells, xylophone, vibraphone, and two marimbas. These percussion parts, along with the celesta and piano parts, provide crucial timbres for the work. There are extended solo passages for flute, oboe, clarinet, and horn, especially in the first movement.

Unit 5: Stylistic Considerations

The highly programmatic nature of this work suggests a need for the performers to be familiar with the repertoire of symphonic tone poems as well as other Romantic-styled works with references to the sea. Mature, sensitive, and subtle performance techniques are crucial to the performance of this work.

The work is through-composed, with alternating contrasts of floating, connected, dream-like sounds vs. rhythmic and harmonic bursts of sound that demand exacting precision and crisp, clear articulation.

Unit 6: Musical Elements

In his article, "Anthony Iannaccone, An Introduction to His Work," Max Plank states that Iannaccone's "music has evolved from an early neoclassicism through more or less strict serialism to become a highly distinctive and personal language, assessable in his large audience music, esoteric in his music for small audiences." Plank continues, "Important musical elements in his compositions include the assertion or dissolution of tonality as a structural device, the manipulation of timbrel elements to evidence musical motion or progression, distinctive composite sounds, and a textural layering influenced, in part, by his interest in medieval music."

Sea Drift encompasses diatonic, chromatic, and twelve-tone elements found in the music of Debussy, Barber, and Copland. There is an absence of key signatures throughout the work, with all accidentals notated by the composer. Chromaticism is the rule, with polytonal colors present throughout. In spite of this, the piece has a distinctive, diatonic quality to its melodies, which are passed around to various soloists and sections throughout the work.

Unit 7: Form and Structure

MEASURE	EVENT AND SCORING
Movement I:	
1-19	A long introduction (quarter note = 100) establishes the "dreamy, wave-like" quality of the piece; includes soli for flute, oboe, clarinet, and horn accompanied by upper woodwinds and mallet percussion
20-29	Half tempo (quarter note = 50); melody interspersed between flute and oboe soloists
30-39	Return to tempo one; saxophones and the full brass section are added to the music; rhythmic *fp* bursts of sound (crashing of waves effect)
40-48	Contrasting transition section, reminiscent of the introduction; fluctuating tempo; short soli for oboe, clarinet, and horn

MEASURE	EVENT AND SCORING
49-59	Strict tempo; ascending and descending sixteenth notes in the upper woodwinds, celesta, piano, and mallet percussion; light, punctuated rhythmic passages in the saxophone and brass sections; tempo *ritardandos* to next section
60-87	*Meno mosso* (quarter note = 60); melodic material interspersed between flute and oboe soloists, accompanied by horn choir; in m. 73, solo music is transferred to clarinet, with accompaniment provided by low woodwinds, celesta, piano, and mallet percussion
88-115	Transition section; tempo (quarter note = 100) accelerates at m. 93 (quarter note = 108); rhythmic and dynamic bursts of sound are presented from the entire ensemble; there is chromaticism for all parts, with sixteenth note passages at very loud dynamics passed around the ensemble; a long-tone, dolce melody in the upper woodwinds and horns in m. 103 is presented on top of the rhythmic bursts of sound
116-126	Sparse scoring and soft dynamics; upper woodwinds play triplets against eighth and sixteenth note accompaniment in the ensemble; this leads to the full ensemble playing *fortissimo* rhythmic bursts
127-132	Meter changes from 4/4 to 3/4; hemiola effect is set up between various sections, culminating in a unison, sixteenth note rhythmic burst in m.132
133-144	This transition section features heavy, sixteenth note rhythmic activity, along with a short, three-measure *tenuto* long-tone melody in the saxophones and brasses; this section serves as a transition to m. 145, with an *accelerando* beginning in m. 143
145-154	Fastest section of the movement (quarter note = 126); short, rhythmic bursts of sound against an undulating sixteenth note background, ending with a rhythmic statement in the percussion section
155-177	This coda section is marked *Adagio subito* (quarter note = 50), as the meter changes back to 4/4; there is a return to the very thin-sounding accompaniment of the woodwinds beneath the melodic material shared between the flute, oboe, and clarinet soloists; this section also presents a return to the opening style, eventually fading to *ppp* chords in the woodwinds, celesta, and piano; timpani has the final statement of the rhythmic motive

MEASURE	EVENT AND SCORING

Movement II:

1-6	Introduction has a 2/4 meter signature with a tempo marking of (quarter note = 50); the movement is marked *Sognando* (dreaming); soft, bell-like chords are played on the downbeat of each measure, punctuated by thirty-second notes in the solo flute and celesta
7-12	A horn duet, with a reflective quarter note melody, serves as a short interlude
13-22	Extended return to the material presented in m. 1; however, this section is *forte* and with the thirty-second notes moved to the clarinet with celesta
23-30	Repeat of m. 1 material, with more voices added; syncopated horn notes help to set up the next section
31-48	Strict tempo (quarter note = 50); melody in flutes and piano; passed to clarinet, celesta, and vibraphone; then back to flutes and piano
49-55	This transition section presents a horn solo in 3/4 with harmon-muted trumpet accompaniment
56-72	Music returns to 2/4 meter, with the tempo accelerating (quarter note = 60); return to opening, bell-like chords, with full ensemble playing *forte*
73-77	Short flute, oboe, and clarinet soli in 3/4
78-91	*Meno mosso* (quarter note = 50), with fluctuating tempi; solo for horn, with material answered in flutes and clarinets; false climax at m. 85, followed by a similar build-up to m. 91
92-97	Eventually slowing (quarter note = 40), this coda section moves to long-held chords by the upper woodwinds, with the last rhythmic statement made by celesta, piano, bells, and vibraphone

Movement III:

1-18	Marked "Like wind over waves," this movement begins in 4/4 at a medium-fast tempo (quarter note = 120); continuous sixteenth note pattern begins in the clarinets and two marimba parts that continues through to m. 24; opening with melodic material in the horns, the tension builds until the entire ensemble is contributing to the rhythmic build-up
19-24	A harmon-muted trumpet solo is the main focus of this section, over the moving sixteenth notes in the clarinets and marimbas; horns provide short, fanfare-like rhythmic punctuations

MEASURE	EVENT AND SCORING
25-29	Ascending sixteenth note triplets build tension, eventually ending with trumpets playing a sixteenth note *diminuendo*
30-37	This section presents a triplet, march-like figure that begins in the trombones and is passed around the ensemble, often against sixteenth notes in the accompaniment
38-44	Moving to 3/4 meter, this section begins with syncopated triplet figures underscoring an ascending quarter note line in the trumpets, horns, and piano, eventually adding upper woodwinds to the timbre
45-58	This transitional section, marked *ritenuto,* leads to a fermata in m. 48; this is followed by ascending sixteenth notes in the upper woodwinds, celesta, piano, and vibraphone; m .52, marked *Meno mosso* (quarter note = 108), continues toward a concluding fade-away
59-74	Marked *Tempo primo* (quarter note = 120), this section contains a return to the opening horn material from the beginning of the movement; eventually leads to a *cantabile* melodic line heard in the piccolo, flute, oboe, horn, celesta, and vibraphone
75-92	Beginning with a change to 2/2, this section accelerates to the fastest tempo in the piece (half note = 92), with punctuating chords in the brass, eventually ascending to the full ensemble
93-119	The climax of the entire work is in the last twenty-six measures of the piece, as the ensemble trades rhythmic, fanfare-like figures between the upper and lower winds; all punctuated by strong drum activity in the percussion section, with the entire ensemble playing at a *fff* level to the end

Unit 8: Suggested Listening

Claude Debussy, *La Mer*

Anthony Iannaccone:

   After A Gentle Rain

   Apparitions

   Of Fire and Ice

Anthony Iannaccone. *Band Compositions by Anthony Iannaccone*. Anthony Iannaccone, Cornell University Wind Ensemble. C.U.W.E.-34, 1983.

Anthony Iannaccone. *The Compositions of Anthony Iannaccone*. Max Plank, Eastern Michigan University Symphonic Band. Golden Crest ATH-5072, 1980.

Anthony Iannaccone. *Sea Drift: Wind Music of Anthony Iannaccone*. Max Plank, Clarion Wind Symphony. Albany Records, 1998.

Unit 9: Additional References and Resources

Plank, Max. "Anthony Iannaccone, An Introduction to His Work." *Journal of Band Research*, Vol. 25, No.1, Fall 1989, 65-67.

Rasmussen, Richard Michael. *Recorded Concert Band Music, 1950-1987*. Jefferson, NC: McFarland Press, 1988.

Rehrig, William H. *The Encyclopedia of Band Music*. Edited by Paul E. Bierley. Westerville, OH: Integrity Press, 1977.

Contributed by:

James Popejoy
Doctoral Conducting Associate
University of North Texas
Denton, Texas

Teacher Resource Guide

Short Ride in a Fast Machine

John Adams
(b. 1947)

transcribed for band by Lawrence T. Odom
(b. 1936)

Unit 1: Composer

Composer, clarinetist, and conductor, John Adams' initial instruction in clarinet began with his father and then with Felix Viscuglia of the Boston Symphony Orchestra. During the summer of 1965, he also studied conducting under Mario di Bonaventura at Dartmouth College. Adams subsequently earned both a B.A. (1969) and an M.A. (1971) at Harvard University, where he studied composition with Leon Kirchner, David Del Tredici, and Roger Sessions. A freelance clarinetist since 1967, Adams occasionally substituted with the Boston Symphony Orchestra and is noted for giving the first performances of Piston's *Clarinet Concerto* in Boston, New York, and Washington. He also served as composer-in-residence at the Marlboro Festival (1970) in addition to teaching at the San Francisco Conservatory (1972-82), where he directed the New Music Ensemble. During this time, Adams was instrumental in commissioning and performing several works by leading and emerging experimental composers. However, perhaps the most significant circumstance in his development as a composer was his relationship with the San Francisco Symphony and its conductor, Edo de Waart, whom he served as new-music advisor and composer-in-residence from 1978-85. The enviable opportunity of working with a fine orchestra in the early stages of his career had a profound impact on Adams' future as a composer.

During this formative period, Adams became interested in electronics, jazz, and other experimental American composers such as John Cage,

Christian Wolff, Morton Feldman, and Robert Ashley. These interests, complemented by a move to California in 1971, drew him away from the academic structuralism on which he was nurtured. Distinctive in his style, Adams differs from many of his contemporary minimalists in that he writes detailed, through-composed, formalized music that is also quite accessible.

A recipient of several honors, Adams has received such diverse awards as a Guggenheim Fellowship in 1982, a "Grammy" Award for Best Contemporary Composition (*Nixon in China*) in 1989, and the 1995 Grawemeyer Award for his violin concerto.

Unit 2: Composition

Commissioned for the opening concert of the Great Woods Festival in Mansfield, Massachusetts, *Short Ride in a Fast Machine* is an invigorating work of unrelenting rhythmic energy and complexity. In reference to the title, Adams stated, "You know how it is when someone asks you to ride in a terrific sports car, and then you wish you hadn't?"

Short Ride was premiered on June 13, 1986, by the Pittsburgh Symphony, Michael Tilson Thomas, Conductor. This wind transcription was rendered by Lawrence T. Odom, former arranger/transcriber and harpist for the United States Air Force Band and Orchestra in Washington, DC.

Unit 3: Historical Perspective

Adams has been hailed as one of the most acclaimed composers of the second generation of minimalists and one of minimalism's most distinctively individualistic proponents. Conversely, Adams has described himself as a minimalist who has become bored with minimalism. The principal features of minimalist technique include repetition in conjunction with a simple harmonic palette, usually involving tertian voicings and some form of tonality. Thus, the minimalist technique often produces long periods of harmonic stasis, characterized by consonance and built from repeated patterns and pulses. However, in most of his works, Adams employs the characteristic features of minimalist technique to explore minimalism's expressive potential.

Composers who have engaged in minimalist techniques, including Adams, have generally sought to communicate with a wide audience. They are deliberately trying to nurture a broader base of patrons. This revived interest in attracting a wide following, perhaps unprecedented since before the time of Wagner, has alienated many composers and scholars. It begs the question, can truly well-crafted serious music be accessible to a wide spectrum of consumers? Adams is inclined to believe that it can and probably should. Establishing an immediate connection with his audience through the feelings his music generates is a prime concern for Adams. He claims that important art can reach your inner spirit, touch you in the center of your soul, and affect you. He contends that his harmonic style is a basic human necessity and maintains that our response to tonal music is not so much cultural as genetic. Adams' aesthetics – his desire to communicate to a broader audience, his assimilation of other musical styles, his reliance on intuition, and his adoption of diatonicism – have contributed to his striking harmonies and harmonic successions.

The preponderance of research on Adams consists almost entirely of program notes, liner notes, interviews, short articles, performance and record reviews, and biographical sketches. Adams considers Michael Steinberg to have been the most successful commentator on his music. Steinberg has written program notes for many of the San Francisco Symphony's concerts of Adams' works and has recently been appointed program annotator for the New York Philharmonic. Timothy Johnson has also begun some important research of Adams' music and, in particular, his harmonic practices.

Unit 4: Technical Considerations

The obvious technical demands are underscored by an expanded wind ensemble instrumentation, which includes solo clarinets in A, two synthesizers, and celesta. Relentless metric modulation, diverse voice exchanges, tempo, and hemiola create a work of overriding rhythmic complexity which requires a keen sense of subdivision and attention to detail. The majority of technical challenges are relegated to the upper woodwinds and keyboard instruments. However, all the brass and remaining woodwind voices will encounter extreme ranges and matters of endurance, especially trumpet I, cornet I, and horns.

Unit 5: Stylistic Considerations

Except for the eighth note *ostinato* in the solo clarinets and the broad statement in the brass beginning in m. 138, the articulations are predominantly very detached and accented. Adams's subtle manipulation of rhythmic and metric variance will require strict adherence in order to reproduce the seamless quality of the work. However, all of these factors will be lost if the overall characteristics of high energy and assertiveness are not observed.

Unit 6: Musical Elements

Following the minimalist tradition, much of Adams's music consists of long passages employing a single set of pitch classes, usually encased within a single diatonic set. In many of these passages, the pitch classes form complete diatonic triads or seventh chords corresponding to chords of traditional tonal music, with no additional pitch classes. In other passages, textural and registral formations imply traditional triads or seventh chords, but additional pitch classes obscure these chords to some degree.

Adams's sudden key shifts after long periods of static harmony constitute perhaps the most distinguishing feature of his music. Employing unabashed consonances and diatonic orientation, Adams has juxtaposed harmonic areas in new ways that simultaneously recall aspects of traditional tonal music.

According to Johnson, Adams employs triads or seventh chords in two basic operations. The first operation shifts one or two pitch classes chromatically either up or down in a specific sequence. Beginning with a minor triad or seventh chord, either the third and/or seventh is raised, or the fifth and/or root is lowered. This operation can be applied in four different variations: (1) shifting only the third up by a minor second produces a major triad or major-minor seventh chord with the same root as the original chord; (2) shifting the third and seventh up by a minor second produces a major seventh chord with the same root (this shift does not apply to triads since the seventh is omitted); (3) shifting the fifth down by a minor second produces a diminished triad or half-diminished seventh chord with the same root; and (4) shifting the root and fifth down by a minor second creates a major triad or major seventh chord with a root a minor second below that of the original chord. As a result, beginning with a minor triad, the operation produces both of the other two triad types, and with seventh chords, the operation produces all three of the other diatonic seventh chords.

The second operation begins with a major triad or seventh chord and replaces the lowest pitch class of the original chord (root) with a new pitch class a third above the highest pitch class of that chord. This operation produces only one triad or seventh chord: a minor triad or minor seventh chord whose root now lies a major third above that of the original chord.

Furthermore, by combining these two operations, a whole new set of chord types emerge and can be employed. Accordingly, the two operations and their two ordered combinations produce seven chord succession types; the first operation produces four types, and the second operation and the two combinations produce one type each. Johnson has labeled the individual chord successions according to the operation producing their association: *shift* (for operation one involving pitch classes shifting by a minor second), *cycle* (for operation two involving the cycle of thirds), and *shift-cycle* or *cycle-shift* (for the two combinations).

These methods are almost never employed in strict fashion, as one might expect in the process music of Arvo Pärt, but are deliberately integrated in Adams's own eclectic style. *Short Ride in a Fast Machine* begins with the wood block reinforcing the metric pulse and a three-note motive (D, E, and A) first stated melodically by the solo clarinets and keyboard instruments. By m. 3, the cornets initiate a vertical arrangement of the motivic material as harmonic punctuations. Both the wood block and undulating eighth note *ostinato* function as "connective tissue" for the entire work. The primary key centers are D and E-flat.

Unit 7: Form and Structure

SECTION	MEASURE	EVENT AND SCORING
1	1-28	Entrance of wood block quarter notes and eighth note *ostinato* in solo clarinet and keyboard instruments; integration of vertical arrangement of same pitch cell (D, E, and A) by brass voices and sextuplet statements in upper woodwinds
2	29-51	Resumption of brass quarter note figures and introduction of glockenspiel and crotale colors; subsequent voice exchange in upper woodwinds becomes increasingly complex
3	52-79	Initial entrance of low woodwind voices supported by horns and bass drum
4	79-81	Transition juxtaposes sudden thinning of texture
5	82-121	E-flat centricity, 4 vs. 3 hemiola pattern introduced in bass line coupled with textural layering increases dynamic energy and momentum
6	122-132	Broader statements of C and A pedal in bass voices; restatement of eighth note *ostinato* in keyboard
7	133-137	Transitional (return of original material from Section 1 but in altered form)
8	138-180	Cornets and trumpets begin expansive statement of new augmented material supported by canon-like supplementary material in the horns, euphonium, and cello; cessation of wood block voice
9	181-188	Codetta (D major)

Unit 8: Suggested Listening

John Adams:
  Fearful Symmetries
  Grand Pianola Music
  Harmonielehre
  Harmonium
  Nixon in China

Steve Reich:
Sextet,
Six Marimbas
Terry Riley, *In C*

Unit 9: Additional References and Resources

Hitchcock, H. Wiley, and Stanley Sadie, eds. *The New Grove Dictionary of American Music*, I. New York: MacMillan Press, 1986.

Johnson, Timothy A. *Harmony in the Music of John Adams: From Phrygian Gates to Nixon in China*. Ph.D. Dissertation, State University of New York at Buffalo, May 1991.

Morton, Brian, and Pamela Collins, eds. *Contemporary Composers*. Chicago: St. James Press, 1992.

Porter, Andrew. "Nixon in China: John Adams in Conversation," *Tempo*, no. 167 (December 1988), 25-30.

Randel, Don Michael, ed. *The New Harvard Dictionary of Music*. Cambridge, MA: Harvard University Press, 1996.

Rimer, J. Thomas. "John Adams, Nixon in China; Leonard Bernstein, A Quiet Place," *American Music*, XII, no. 3 (Fall 1994), 338.

Slonimsky, Nicolas, ed. *Baker's Biographical Dictionary of Musicians*, 7 ed. New York: Schirmer, 1984.

Steinberg, Michael. Jacket notes for John Adams. *Nixon in China*. Performed by the Orchestra of St. Luke's. Electra Nonesuch, 9 79193-1, 1987.

Steinberg, Michael. Notes taken from conversations during February of 1997.

Stone, Thomas. Jacket notes for John Adams. *Short Ride in a Fast Machine*. Performed by the Cincinnati Wind Symphony, Eugene Corporon, Conductor. (Klavier, KCD-11058), 1993.

Contributed by:

Gordon R. Brock
Director of Bands
University of North Dakota
Grand Forks, North Dakota

Teacher Resource Guide

Sounds, Shapes, and Symbols
Leslie Bassett
(b. 1923)

Unit 1: Composer

Leslie Raymond Bassett was born January 22, 1923, in Hanford, California. After graduating from high school, he studied for several semesters at Fresno State University. World War II and wartime service interrupted his education while he served for thirty-eight months as a trombonist in the 13th Armored Division Band of the U.S. Army in California, Texas, France, and Germany.

Bassett's early training on piano and trombone led to his arranging music for various concert and jazz bands. When the war ended, he returned to Fresno State University to study composition with Arthur Bedahl and Mirriam Withrow. He received a Bachelor of Arts Degree in 1947 with an emphasis on instrumental and choral music education.

Bassett received his master's degree in Music Composition from the University of Michigan in 1949 and his doctorate in 1956. While at Michigan, he studied with Homer Keller and Ross Lee Finney.

Bassett's compositions extend over a wide range of performance ideas. Some of his works for band/wind ensemble include:

Colors and Contours (Peters, 1984)
Concerto Grosso (Peters, 1982) Ann Arbor, MI, 2/4/83
Designs, Images and Textures (Peters, 1966) Ithaca, NY, 4/28/65
Sounds, Drums, and Trumpets (1974)
Sounds, Shapes, and Symbols (Peters, 1978) Ann Arbor, MI, 3/17/78
Symphonic Sketch (Composer's facsimile edition)
Fantasy for Clarinet and Wind Ensemble (1988)
Lullaby (for Kristen) (Peters, 1985)

Bassett has been the recipient of many honors and awards, including the coveted Prix de Rom (1961-63), Pulitzer Prize in Music in 1966 for *Variations* for orchestra, named chairman of the University of Michigan Composition Department in 1970, won the National Institute of Arts and Letters award in 1964, the Albert A. Stanley Distinguished Music Award (University of Michigan), and in 1984 the Henry Russel Lecturer Award, the highest faculty honor at University of Michigan.

Unit 2: Composition

Sounds, Shapes, and Symbols was written in 1977 and published in 1978. The piece was commissioned by the University of Michigan Symphony Band, H. Robert Reynolds, Conductor, and was premiered in Ann Arbor, Michigan, on March 17, 1978.

This four-movement work provides a study in colors and textures, brilliant sonorities, and an extended range. The work opens with a series of quasi-like fanfares as well as ascending and descending cascading lines. The second movement is dark, with mellow sonorities overlapped by shrill woodwind pyramids. The third movement employs non-traditional wind techniques, including improvisatory sections in all instruments as well as repetitive rhythms. The fourth movement is the most incisive and rhythmically varied of the four movements. The entire work is approximately twelve minutes in length.

Unit 3: Historical Perspective

Sounds, Shapes, and Symbols is one of many pieces commissioned by the University of Michigan Symphony Band. Bassett has been influenced by the music of Bartok. His compositions for band are extremely imaginative, especially in light of his dislike for the "standard" orchestrational elements and techniques employed in music of the band repertoire. Bassett is a serialist and uses schemes to help reshape and reuse his musical vocabulary.

The musical structure of the piece combined with interesting sound and woven techniques makes it a rather unique and different wind band piece.

Unit 4: Technical Considerations

The work demands musical and technical maturity from all players. Harmonies used employ the likes of tritones and perfect fourth sonorities, augmented triads, and the octatonic scale. There is a wide variety of meter, tempo, and style changes, and demanding, yet subtle adjustments on the part of the players and conductor. The rhythmic diversity includes accelerations, *ritards*, grand pause, and specific sound durations. Unison sixteenth notes and fast eighth notes unfold whole tone or octatonic collections in sweeping, virtuosic gestures, and the occasional 3/8 measures affect the steady flow of the musical line. Players must be capable of great control.

Unit 5: Stylistic Considerations

In Russell Mikkelson's dissertation of "Sounds, Shapes, and Symbols," the following summary of elements of musical styles is offered:

> *Sounds, Shapes, and Symbols* displays four distinctive elements of musical style. First, formal areas in this piece often are generated from the continuous reworking and reshaping of pitch materials. For example, several important intervallic gestures are identified relatively early in the work. These basic materials return in a reshaped and recast form, which help to define many of the key structural areas. Second, chords are constructed from available pitches which are limited invariably by antecedent pitch choices. Five-note chords are common, and are a favorite of Bassett. Third, the manipulation of time would appear to be an important parameter to this composer. Implied meters, unusual metric placement, and syncopated rhythms serve to generate a feeling of rhythmic elasticity rather than "clock" time. Fourth, the orchestration provides contrasts between perceived brilliance and instrumental warmth through the use of extreme dynamics and ranges, and the composer's characteristic instrumental doublings.

Unit 6: Musical Elements

Musically and technically, *Sounds, Shapes, and Symbols* is a demanding piece of music. There are numerous range challenges as well as rhythmic and tonal diversity to keep the best player interested and motivated.

The piece offers a variety of tempi, tonal centers, solo vs. soli passages, and rhythmic challenges throughout. There is frequent manipulation of thematic material to maintain a high level of concentration and interest as well as unpredictability for the performer and audience alike. Dynamics, articulations, and tempo markings are clearly stated, offering variety and challenge.

Percussion parts are interesting, challenging, and quite busy in their individual parts and array of instruments used.

Unit 7: Form and Structure

Movement I (quarter note = 138) exhibits four main structural characteristics: (1) the use of fermatas to divide formal areas, (2) the use of antecedent-consequent phrases to achieve a unifying relationship among ideas, (3) the use of isolated ensemble entrances which contribute to the movement's sectionalization, and (4) the use of elided phrases within each formal area to propel the music forward.

Movement II (quarter note = 52) is comprised of formal areas containing two or four structural divisions. These phrases are all elided in pairs. This movement uses the fermata at the end of the movement, unlike Movement I which relies on the fermata for structural divisions.

Movement III (quarter note = 148) uses three main elements as structural devices: (1) unmetered music, (2) isolated ensemble entrances, and (3) fermatas.

Movement IV (quarter note = 144) employs antecedent-consequent phrases, sweeping phrases, counterpoint, fermatas, and a coda. Isolated ensemble entrances, changing meters, and tempo changes create an exciting and energetic finish.

Unit 8: Suggested Listening
University of Illinois Symphonic Band, James F. Keene, Conductor
  (recording #128)
Educational Record Performance-Library, #11, Designs, Images, Textures

Unit 9: Additional References and Resources
Bassett, Leslie. Home Page
  http://www.amc.net/member/Leslie_Bassett/home.html.

Educational Record Reference Library #54, Liner Notes.

Johnson, Ellen S. *Leslie Bassett: A Bio-Bibliography*, Bio-Bibliographies in Music Ser. Series #52. Greenwood Publishing Group, Inc., 1994.

Mikkelson, Russel. A study of *Sounds, Shapes, and Symbols* by Leslie Bassett: A contemporary composition for band. Dissertation, DMA, 1993, University of Wisconsin.

Mikkelson, Russel. Interpreting Leslie Bassett's *Sounds, Shapes, and Symbols*, Journal of the Conductors Guild.

Peters, C.F. Home Page
  http://www.editions-peters.com.

Rehrig, William H. *The Heritage Encyclopedia of Band Music*. Edited by Paul E. Bierley. Westerville, OH: Integrity Press, 1977.

Sadie, Stanley, ed. *The New Grove Dictionary of Music and Musicians*. 20 vols. London: Macmillan Publishers Ltd., 1980.

Sigma Alpha Iota International Home Page
  http://www.sainational.org/phil/composers/lbasset.html.

Slonimsky, Nicolas. *Baker's Biographical Dictionary of Musicians*, 7th ed. New York: G. Shirmer, 1984.

University of Illinois Band Recording #128, Liner Notes.

Contributed by:
Frank C. Tracz
Director of Bands
Kansas State University
Manhattan, Kansas

Teacher Resource Guide

Symphony in B-Flat (Symphonie Pour Musique d'Harmonie)

Paul Robert Marcel Fauchet
(1881–1937)

edited by James R. Gillette (1886–1963)

and F. Campbell-Watson

Unit 1: Composer

Limited information is available on the composer of the *Symphony in B-Flat*. Further clouding the issue is the fact that the first American edition and early program notes on the composition attributed the work to the wrong composer. Dr. Jon Mitchell has written that the unfortunate confusion of the names "Fauchey" and "Fauchet" led to decades of false information concerning the composer of the *Symphony*:

> The American publication of the work, following the American premiere in 1933 by James Gillette and the Carleton College Band, gives credit to another French composer with a phonetically similar name – Paul Fauchey (1858-1936) – who was a composer of light operas. The true composer of the work, Paul Robert Fauchet [1881-1937], was a professor of theory at the Paris Conservatoire. He composed little, having written two masses, some motets, a bass vocalise, and some theory lessons. *The Symphonie Pour Musique d'Harmonie*, then, may be his chief opus.[1]

Unit 2: Composition

Symphonie Pour Musique d'Harmonie, known in the United States as *Symphony in B-Flat*, is a large, four-movement symphony written in a post-romantic style. The work is nearly thirty minutes in length, obviously influenced by and nearly the scope of Hector Berlioz's monumental *Symphonie Funèbre et Triomphale*. Fauchet composed the work for, and was premiered by, France's famed *Batterie et Musique de la Garde Republicain*. The original score was first published in Paris by Evette & Schaeffer in 1926, ostensibly the year of its composition.

The original 1926 publication of the *Symphony* called for a European band instrumentation, including E-flat alto horns as well as trombones and euphoniums in B-flat. To make the piece more accessible for American bands, James Gillette (1886-1963) undertook the task of preparing a new edition in 1933. He completed the first and last movements of the piece, while F. Campbell-Watson made a new performing edition of the two inside movements. Gillette was a prominent arranger and composer in the 1920s, having composed at least one symphony for winds, and brought wide recognition to the band at Carleton College, which he conducted from 1923. Gillette performed the American premiere of Fauchet's *Symphony in B-Flat* in 1933 at Carleton College in the new edition.

Although Gillette has done the profession a great service in providing the American edition, it is unfortunate that the score and parts are plagued by so many pitch errors. A modern edition of the first and last movements would prove a highly attractive proposition for an enterprising publisher or doctoral candidate. The two inside movements contain fewer errors.

The movements follow the traditional symphonic form set down by composers more than a century earlier:

I. Overture:	*Maestoso-Allegro deciso*	
	Maestoso solemne-Animato (11:00)	
II. Nocturne:	*Lento* (5:30)	
III. Scherzo:	*Vivo, giocoso, molto leggiero* (6:30)	
IV. Finale:	*Allegro vivace* (5:45)	
	Total Time: (28:45)	

Although the movements may be performed separately, the symphonic proportions and variance of mood and tempo would be lost. Those willing to devote one-half of a concert to this artful and unique music will be justly rewarded.

Unit 3: Historical Perspective

Composed early in the century, the *Symphony* is free from the clichés that have crept into much twentieth century wind band music. It is an eclectic work that draws strongly from several traditions while maintaining an impressive and unique synthesis. Relying heavily upon classical forms and infusing romantic ideals of expressive melody and lush harmony, the *Symphony* provides an opportunity for the modern wind band to engage in music-making on a most artistic level. Fauchet often uses the delicate textures and harmonies of French Impressionism, but is capable of the sweeping form and vibrant lyricism of German Romanticism as well. His mastery of and devotion to this wide range of musical styles (as one would expect from a professor of theory) is evident throughout.

The notes in the American edition of the *Symphony in B-Flat* state that the composition has the distinction of being "the first Symphony for Band." Of course, it is now known that this is not the case. One need only recall Berlioz's *Symphonie* written in 1840, Anton Reicha's *Commemoration Symphony* of 1815, and Françoise Gossec's *Symphonie Militaire* written in 1793. Nevertheless, it must be considered one of the first symphonies written for the medium and one of the most substantial, serious wind band compositions in history.

In his writing on the *Symphony*, Jon Mitchell sums up the historic place of the music:

> The composer chose to follow in the footsteps of the French symphonists Saint-Saëns and d'Indy rather than take up the newer styles being developed by Schmitt, Ibert, and "Les Six." In an era when composers—particularly those stationed in France—were discarding the forms and methods of the past, Fauchet's symphony, while not appearing to be entirely anachronistic in character, has its roots deeply entrenched in the past. A masterpiece of counterpoint and instrumentation, the work is clearly from the pen of a learned music theoretician.[2]

Unit 4: Technical Considerations

The *Symphony* calls for standard large band instrumentation with oboe II doubling on English horn, one B-flat bass saxophone, four cornets, two trumpets, and four trombones. Soprano saxophone is called for in the "Finale." While four percussionists are sufficient for three of the movements, the "Scherzo" calls for five percussionists playing parts for timpani, snare drum, bass drum, cymbals, triangle, and bells. Fauchet's part for string bass – preferably doubled with several players – gives needed reinforcement to the lower octave, resulting in a resonant and deep harmonic underpinning.

There are some modest technical difficulties in the work. Triple tonguing for trumpets is a must. Several exposed passages for horn solo, horn duet, and horn quartet require depth in that section. Additional soli for English horn and trumpet give principal players opportunities to demonstrate an expressive and confident tone. The difficult dotted-eighth/sixteenth-eighth rhythm in

6/8 meter in the first movement, as well as other woodwind passages in the third movement, call for a quick and light articulation many younger players may find challenging.

As one might expect from such a work in the Romantic vein, numerous *ritardandos* and *accelerandos* give the music an expressive ebb and flow that will challenge even the most advanced bands. In addition, the music frequently calls out for an unwritten *rubato* that will provide unending possibilities for advanced musicianship. Passages that introduce chromaticism in a tonal context and movement through rarely heard keys also provide interest and challenge for mature players.

The conductor must make decisions about how to treat the rather confusing *tremolo* markings found at the beginning of the "Overture," and the flutter-tonguing asked of the clarinets and saxophones in the "Finale." It is recommended that the breathmarks found in percussion parts at the end of the first movement be removed in favor of one long, sustained roll.

Unit 5: Stylistic Considerations

Befitting its musical content, the stylistic approach to the piece must be one of full-bodied, Romantic expression and flexibility combined with Impressionistic subtlety and lightness of tone. Opportunities abound in each phrase to give shape and direction to the melodic material. Long, flowing phrases are the hallmark of this music, and attention to the *grande ligne* as the music moves from one arrival point to another gives the performance an expression that is rarely heard in wind music. A constant lyricism runs through the piece and should be first and foremost in the minds of players and conductor alike for a convincing performance.

The "Nocturne" provides the wind band an opportunity to pursue this lyricism to the fullest extent. The words appearing under the horn solo in the first measure of the movement extol us not to forget: *molto sostenuto ed espressivo*. As the theme repeats, building in tension and texture, the inexorable motion toward and arrival at the climax certainly qualifies this movement as one of the most beautiful in the repertoire. Campbell-Watson's edition describes the movement as follows:

> As in the other movements of the Fauchet *Symphony*, the "Nocturne" possesses individual distinction and charm. The mood and color seem rather unusual for a Frenchman, in that an almost Nordic mysticism permeates the canvas, with a trace of the tonal system employed by his better-known contemporaries. There is true poetry here, coupled with musical artistry of the highest order.[3]

The "Scherzo" offers a unique challenge in its demand for a quick and light articulation from all instruments, delivering a mercurial, dance-like character. Executing the grace notes as a part of the musical line and adding a natural accent to each of them brings a vibrancy to the music. The character of the "Trio" can be effectively captured through eschewing all temptation to treat the hemiola pattern as a syncopation and maintaining a fluid *sostenuto*. Perhaps rehearsing the passage while conducting in three beats for every two bars will help to instill the proper metric feeling in the ensemble.

Unit 6: Musical Elements

Fauchet has constructed an extremely tight-knit structure built upon a minimum of musical material within each movement. The distribution of important melodic lines throughout the instrumentation requires that each section contribute equally and accurately to the flow and momentum of the piece. Frequent interplay of motives between solo instruments or sections (*Durchbrochenearbeit*) creates a colorful and varied scheme of orchestration that is a delight to the ear when performed well.

Homophonic passages that allow the lyrical melodies to come forth are skillfully alternated with passages of counterpoint that demand the interpreter to carefully balance the various voices.

Fauchet employs a nineteenth century harmonic palette throughout much of the work. Periodic forays into various modes, especially in the interior movements, lend a somewhat exotic feel to the work. Whole-tone scales, particularly in the "Trio" (Pastorale) of the "Scherzo" movement, provide an impressionistic sound to several passages.

The melancholy, brooding melody of the "Nocturne," accompanied by a wide array of surprising and sophisticated harmonic changes, make this slow movement one of the treasured gems of the repertoire. Jon Mitchell writes:

> The gentle dorian second movement ("Nocturne") is in sharp contrast to the extroverted first. In this movement Fauchet shows us that he is equally adept at handling the band's timbrel resources in a slow, tranquil setting as he is in a complex *tutti* structure. Although the movement begins with a horn call in G dorian, all types of major and minor triadic harmonies are employed.[4]

Rhythmic *ostinati* are periodically used, most notably accompanying the principal themes of both the "Overture" and "Nocturne," and in the "Trio" of the "Scherzo." In addition, the latter *ostinato* passage employs a hemiola pattern in the timpani, underpinning the melodic horn-fifths above.

Unit 7: Form and Structure

Movement I: "Overture"
Maestoso-Allegro deciso
Maestoso solemne-Animato
Form: *Sonata Allegro* with Introduction and Coda

Section	Measure	Event and Scoring
Introduction	1-36	*Maestoso* introduction (B-flat major)
Exposition	37-94	Principal theme (B-flat major)
	95-120	Transition theme (B-flat major)
	121-153	Secondary theme (F major)
	153-166, 167-177	Transition
Development	178-302	Development
Recapitulation	303-316	Recapitulation of principal theme (B-flat major)
	317-341	Recapitulation of secondary theme (B-flat major)
	342-356	Recapitulation of *Maestoso* introduction (B-flat major)
Coda	357-373	Based on principal theme (B-flat major)

Movement II: "Nocturne"
Lento

This movement consists of eight statements of an eight-bar theme in various melodic and harmonic guises, each statement comprised of a pair of four-bar phrases. Snippets of the introductory horn theme are woven into the texture throughout the movement as a counterpoint to the principal theme. Although the "Nocturne" is not an example of the typical ABA pattern, the departure from the tonic-dominant axis at m. 37 can be construed as a B section, with a return to the tonal center and original mood at m. 53.

Section		Measure	Event and Scoring
Introduction		1-12	Solo horn introduction (G dorian)
A	A	13-20	Principal theme (G dorian)
	A^1	21-28	Restatement of theme (D dorian)
	A^2	29-36	Varied statement of theme (D major)
B	A^3	37-44	Varied statement of theme (B-flat major)
	A^4	45-52	Climactic statement (varied) of theme (B-flat dorian)
A	A	53-60	Recapitulation of principal theme (G dorian)
	A^1	61-68	Varied statement of theme (D dorian)
	A^5	69-76	Varied statement of theme (G dorian)
Coda		77-82	Extended cadence of principal theme

Movement III: "Scherzo"
Vivo, giocoso, molto leggiero
The "Scherzo/Trio" movement takes on the traditional minuet/trio (ABA) form, accomplished with a *da capo* of the opening material. The "Scherzo" proper consists of seven sections alternately presenting a principal and secondary theme. The contrasting "Trio" section is limited to seven statements of a single sixteen-bar theme based on the minor third found in the principal theme.

Section		Measure	Event and Scoring
Scherzo			
	A	1-20	Principal theme (B-flat major)
	B	21-44	Secondary theme (D dorian)
	A^1	45-62	(D major)
A	B	63-78	(G major)
	A^2	79-96	(G major)
	B	97-109	(G major)
	A	110-133	(B-flat major)
Trio (Pastorale)			
	A	134-149	"Trio" principal theme (E-flat major)
	A	150-165	Restatement of "Trio" theme
B	A	166-181	Restatement of "Trio" theme
	A	182-197	Restatement of "Trio" theme
	A	198-213	Restatement of "Trio" theme
	A	214-235	Restatement of "Trio" theme (with extension)
	A	236-251	Restatement of "Trio" theme
A	*Da Capo* of "Scherzo"		

Movement IV: "Finale"
Allegro vivace
Form: Sonatina

Section		Measure	Event and Scoring
A		1-106	Principal theme (B-flat major)
	a	1-36	Part 1
	b	37-74	Part 2
	a	75-94	Return of principal theme
		95-106	Codetta
B		107-206	Secondary theme (E-flat major)
	a	107-122	Part 1
	a	123-138	Theme with imitation
	b	139-166	Part 2

a	167-182	Restatement of theme
a	183-206	Restatement of theme
	207-230	Retransition
A	231-276	Recapitulation of principal theme (B-flat major)
	277-295	Codetta (reference to secondary theme)
	296-303	Transition (augmentation of secondary theme)
B	304-331	Recapitulation of secondary theme in augmentation with reference to principal theme in clarinet (B-flat major)
	332-341	Coda

Unit 8: Suggested Listening

Hector Berlioz, *Symphonie Funèbre et Triomphale*
Paul Fauchet, *Symphony in B-Flat*. University of Illinois Concert Band; Mark Hindsley, Conductor. Record #31.
Gabriel Fauré, *Chant Funeraire*
Françoise-Joseph Gossec, *Symphonie Militaire*
Jacques Ibert, *July 14th Overture*
Anton Reicha, *Commemoration Symphony*
Florent Schmitt, *Dionysiaques*, Op. 62, No. 1

Unit 9: Additional References and Resources

Fauchet, Paul. *Symphony in B-Flat—Nocturne*. New York: Witmark & Sons, 1949.

Fauchet, Paul. *Symphony in B-Flat—Scherzo*. New York: Witmark & Sons, 1948.

Goldman, Richard Franko. *The Band's Music*. New York: Pitman, 1938.

Goldman, Richard Franko. *The Wind Band*. Boston: Allyn and Bacon, 1961.

Mitchell, Jon C. "Paul Robert Marcel Fauchet: *Symphonie Pour Musique d'Harmonie (Symphony in B-Flat)*." *Journal of Band Research*, XX (1985), 8-26.

"Romantic Sensibilities." The Wisconsin Wind Orchestra; Lawrence Dale Harper, Conductor. Mark Records Compact disc, 1998.

Slonimsky, Nicholas, ed. *Baker's Biographical Dictionary of Music and Musicians*. 7th ed. New York: G. Schirmer, 1984.

Swanzy, David. "The Wind Ensemble and Its Music During the French Revolution." Unpublished Ph.D. dissertation, Michigan State University, 1966.

Wright, Al, and Stanley Newcomb. *Bands of the World*. Evanston, IL: The Instrumentalist Co., 1970.

Contributed by:

Lawrence Dale Harper
Director of Bands
Carroll College
Waukesha, Wisconsin

---

1   Mitchell, Jon C., Compact Disc Liner Notes, "Romantic Sensibilities," The Wisconsin Wind Orchestra; Lawrence Dale Harper, Conductor (1998), Mark Records.
2   Mitchell, Jon C., "Paul Robert Marcel Fauchet: Symphonie Pour Musique d'Harmonie (Symphony in B-Flat)," *Journal of Band Research*, XX (1985), 11-12.
3   Fauchet, Paul, *Symphony in B-Flat – Nocturne* (New York: Witmark & Sons, 1949).
4   Mitchell, Jon C., Compact Disc Liner Notes, "Romantic Sensibilities," The Wisconsin Wind Orchestra; Lawrence Dale Harper, Conductor (1998), Mark Records.

Teacher Resource Guide

Symphony No. 19
Nikolai Yakovlevich Miaskovsky
(1881–1950)

edited by Paul Hinman
(b. 1954)

Unit 1: Composer

Nikolai Miaskovsky was one of the most renowned Russian composers of the early twentieth century. He was born in Novo-Georgievsk, which is near Warsaw, on April 20, 1881. Because his father served as an officer in the Russian Army Engineering Corps, Miaskovsky spent much of his early child-hood moving between Oreburg, Kazan, and Nizhny Novgorod. In 1895, the family moved to St. Petersburg where Nikolai, like his father, enrolled in the Military Engineering College. He graduated in 1902.

Miaskovsky was like many Russian composers in that he received his earliest musical instruction and training from within his immediate family, studying both piano and violin. His interest in composition developed later, with his first attempts taking place between 1896 and 1898.

In 1903, he moved to Moscow and began to study harmony with Reinhold Gliere. From about that time until 1906, Nikolai also studied music theory with Kryzhanovsky. By the middle of 1906, he had enrolled in the St. Petersburg Conservatory, where he had the opportunity to study with Rimsky-Korsakov and Lyadov. He graduated in 1911.

In 1914, Miaskovsky enlisted in the Russian Army, where he served until as late as 1921. Although he served as the commander of a brigade during World War I, Miaskovsky considered war to be "a manifestation of animal instincts and a contemptible animal act." (Yakubov, 1994). Following his military tenure, he moved to Moscow where he devoted himself to music. The

Moscow Conservatory appointed Nikolai as Professor of Composition in 1926, a position he held for the remainder of his career. At the Conservatory, he taught and influenced several noted composers, including Khachaturian, Kabalevsky, and Muradeli.

Unit 2: Composition

Nikolai Miaskovsky wrote 27 symphonies, several concertos and sonatas, 13 string quartets, 118 songs, and other compositions, including five works for military band. Although his primary interest was in orchestral writing, *Symphony No. 19* is unique in that it was composed for winds and percussion. *Symphony No. 19* fulfilled a promise by Miaskovsky to Russian Military Bandmaster, Ivan Vassillivitch Petrov, that he would write a work for military band. The original plan was for this work to have been a simple one-movement overture, but due to a surge of creative energy, Miaskovsky was able to expand the work to a full, four-movement symphony. Miaskovsky used very traditional and formal compositional techniques in the creation of this very dynamic, nationalistic work. Completed in January 1939, this work is one of the first symphonies written for band.

Unit 3: Historical Perspective

Miaskovsky enjoyed his most significant attention beginning in the early 1920s. At that time many European conductors, such as Koussevitzky, Stokowski, and Coates, were performing his symphonies with the most prestigious orchestras. His close friend and colleague, Prokofiev, also promoted his work. Frederick Stock, conductor of the Chicago Symphony, was also a very enthusiastic promoter, and both *Symphony No. 13* and *Symphony No. 21* were dedicated to him. As a result of the regular performances, Miaskovsky's music became a popular addition to the American orchestral repertoire. Many ranked him among the top ten composers of his time, and like Rachmaninov, Strauss, Sibelius, Stravinsky, Shostakovich, and Prokofiev, he was expected to be considered one of the world's greatest composers of his era.

Miaskovsky was much less a promoter of his own work, suggesting that he had no need to hear his music performed. His interest was in composition as a means to improving his orchestrational technique. Furthermore, he felt that his music was not understood:

> Can it be that the psychological world is so foreign to these people? Is my world indeed more complex than that of Shostakovich? I am not comparing his music, I consider his *Fifth Symphony* a truly great masterpiece, but when Gauk conducts this work, everyone seems to think that they understand it completely...but when Gauk puffs over my *Seventeenth Symphony*...I feel that neither he nor the listeners understand or feel anything. (Asafiev, 1940)

He was a quiet and intelligent man who was able to blend charm and aristocratic dignity with a keen sense of humor.

The outbreak of World War I forced Miaskovsky back into military service and a position on the front line of several campaigns. He became a victim of shell shock and was ultimately transferred away from the battlegrounds. During this period, his political views developed a somewhat democratic slant. The abdication of Nicholas in the days of the February Revolution and the consequent attempted coup by Lenin reinforced his movement toward a radical position. These events, and the political and ideological unrest of the Revolution, had a profound impact on his writing style, and his music began to take on a folk song quality. Miaskovsky began to compose works reflecting the artistic and social outlook of the genuine Soviet citizen. This was considered by many to be a radical view, and this view often placed him in an unpopular position. It is suggested that his radical political position may have, in part, caused the governmental leaders to systematically remove much of his music from the performance mainstream.

During the 1930s and 1940s, many of Miaskovsky's contemporaries fled Russia and became internationally recognized. Miaskovsky, on the other hand, remained in Moscow and continued to write his uniquely nationalistic works. Throughout this period, he received numerous individual and national awards yet continued to be considered a subversive.

In 1948, he was given an opportunity to retract his political views and to resume his position as one of the musical leaders of his time. Being of the older generation, Miaskovsky refused to renounce his nationalistic ideals or to accept the efforts of the young Socialist society. As a result, many of his musical compositions were removed from circulation.

Unit 4: Technical Considerations
The first movement is predominantly in E-flat major. The second movement begins and ends in G minor, with the middle segment in B-flat major. The third movement begins and ends in B-flat major, with short segments in A minor and A-flat major in the middle of the movement. The "Finale" begins in E-flat major, modulates to B-flat minor, and then returns to E-flat for the ending of the work.

The technical demands are advanced for all sections. The clarinets have especially exposed rapid articulation passages. All voicings are called upon to play exposed soloistic passages. Trumpet 1 is written to high C, and the part tends to linger in the top of the staff for long periods of time. The upper woodwind demands are substantial for flute, E-flat clarinet, and 1st B-flat clarinet. Second clarinets will play up to written high E, and the 3rd clarinets play to written high E-flat. Solo clarinet, trumpet, and euphonium are exploited throughout. Percussion requirements and demands are minimal. Varied ensemble voicings are used antiphonally and in counterpoint. As a result, the balance of contrasting instrument choirs and voicings will be a constant concern throughout all movements.

Unit 5: Stylistic Considerations

Each of the four movements is unique unto itself and would stand alone. The first movement takes on somewhat of a martial quality; the articulation is generally very detached with a rhythmic pulse that moves in a somewhat strict 2/4 time. The second movement presents the characteristics of a European waltz. The third movement is a beautifully sensitive, ballad-style folk song with long lyric phrases that expose each voicing of the ensemble. There is liberal use of rubato movement, especially in the transitional passages. The "Finale" opens with a brilliant trumpet fanfare and is written as a somewhat heroic, march-style movement that alternates between segments in 6/8 and 2/4. The march-style passages are interrupted by a passionate lyric segment that, although representing new material, resembles the folk songs from the third movement.

Unit 6: Musical Elements

This work is one of the first – if not the first – symphonies written for band. It is written in the style of many of the early twentieth century Russian symphony composers. The orchestrational techniques are typical of the wind and percussion writing found in music written for symphony orchestra; however, the instrumentation has been expanded. The variations in texture and the assorted harmonic devices assist in maintaining some of the intrigue achieved throughout the work. The melodic lines are often long and lyric, requiring virtuoso technical and musical skill. The varied styles require a demonstration of tremendous emotional range. Tempo variations within each movement provide contrast and character to the music, while the meter for each movement remains consistent. A wide variety of compositional resources are displayed, and the unique orchestrational colors of the wind symphony are explored.

Unit 7: Form and Structure

MEASURE	KEY	EVENT
Movement I: *Allegro Giocoso*		
1-10	E-flat major	Introduction (*maestoso*)
11-25		Theme 1 presented by cornets
26-30		Transitional material based on introduction material
31-45		Development of Theme 1
46-53		Transitional material augmented by an *allargando*
54-64	B-flat major	Theme 2 presented by cornets

Measure	Key	Event
65-72		Theme 3 presented by cornets and euphonium
73-98	E-flat minor	Development of Theme 2
99-130	B-flat major	Theme 4 presented simultaneously in two forms
131-141		Transitional material
142-147		Motives from Theme 3 presented in the woodwinds in counterpoint with the introductory material
148-152	G-flat major	Restatement of introduction in rhythmic diminution
153-161		Restatement of Theme 1 in the clarinets
162-168	C major	Statement of Theme 1 in the tubas and low winds
169-182	D-flat major	Development of motives taken from Theme 2
183-191		Theme 1 restated in the cornets
192-198	B-flat major	Theme 2 restated in saxophones, low brass, and low winds
199-205	C-flat major	Fugal presentation, at one-measure time intervals, of first motive from Theme 2
206-211		Presentation of first motive from Theme 2
212-217		Fugal presentation, at one-beat time intervals, of first motive from Theme 2
218-228	A minor	Statement of Theme 4 in euphonium and tenor saxophone
229-236	B-flat major	Restatement of the introduction in the tubas and low winds
237-251	E-flat major	Recapitulation: Theme 1 reintroduced in the upper winds
252-258		Transitional material
259-287	C minor	Theme 2 reintroduced
288-292	B-flat major	Theme 3 reintroduced
293-302		Transitional material derived from Theme 2
303-333	E-flat major	Theme 4 presented simultaneously in two forms
334-344		Transitional material: same as m. 131

MEASURE	KEY	EVENT
345-360		Coda based on the material from the introduction

Movement II: *Moderato*

MEASURE	KEY	EVENT
1-4	G minor	Introduction
5-26		Theme 1 presented in the solo and 1st clarinet part
27-49		Theme 1 repeated with additional voicings and added complexity in the accompaniment
45-54		Transitional material predominantly in solo clarinet
55-72	B-flat major	Theme 2 presented in upper woodwinds and solo clarinet
55-72		Exact repeat of previous material
73-84		Theme 3 presented in solo clarinet part
85-86		Transitional material
87-94		Theme 2 presented in original form
95-103		Harmonic augmentation of a two-measure motive from Theme 2
103-107		Transitional material
108-123		Theme 1 reintroduced with an *obligato* woodwind accompaniment
124-135		Transitional material augmented with an *accelerando*
136-138	E-flat minor	Rhythmic diminution of motive taken from Theme 1 includes a tempo change
139-146	B minor	Continuation of Theme 1 development
147-149	F minor	Change of key frame for motive taken from Theme 1
150-157	C minor	Continuation of Theme 1 in new key frame
158-185		Harmonic progression against an A-flat pedal point presented as a two-beat hemiola
186-199		Similar progression against an E pedal point presented as a two-beat hemiola
200-210		Transitional material to set up a repeat of above material
150-210		Exact repeat of material
211-225	E-flat major	Theme 2 reintroduced by oboe and 1st clarinet

MEASURE	KEY	EVENT
226-233		Transitional material leading to the recapitulation
234-271	G minor	Recapitulation of Theme 1
272-end		Coda using fragments from all three themes

Movement III: *Andante Serioso*

1-19	F mixolydian	Theme 1 presented in the low winds and tuba
20-25	D minor	Brass section chordal interlude
26-35	F mixolydian	Theme 1 restated in trumpet and euphonium
37-49	D-flat major	Woodwind section chordal interlude
50-74	A minor	Theme 2 presented in the upper winds and augmented by a tempo change
75-89	A-flat major	Theme 3 presented by the oboe, with a clarinet triplet *obligato* accompaniment
90-101		Theme 2 restated in flute and trumpet
102-113	D-flat mixolydian	Theme 1 reintroduced with a full ensemble chordal accompaniment
114-124	F mixolydian	Theme 1 presented by horn, with upper woodwind accompaniment
125-130	D minor	Brass chordal interlude reintroduced
131-140	F mixolydian	Theme 1 restated in the trumpet and euphonium
141-147	B-flat major	Woodwind chordal interlude reintroduced
148-end	B-flat mixolydian	Concluding section, primarily chordal, but with short, arpeggiated passages in the euphonium

Movement IV: *Vivo*

1-4	E-flat major	Trumpet fanfare introduction
5-36		Theme 1 introduced in the cornets and upper woodwinds
37-46		Transitional material based on fragments from Theme 1 and played in sequence
47-62	C minor	Theme 2 introduced in the low winds and continued in the cornets and horns
63-84	B minor	Theme 2 restated in a new key
85-124	B-flat minor	Theme 3 presented by cornets, horns, and then upper woodwinds

MEASURE	KEY	EVENT
125-136	G-flat major	Theme 4 presented in the cornets
137-148	A-flat minor	Theme 4 continued in a new key
149-154	E-flat major	Restatement and extension of the introductory fanfare
155-176		Theme 1 reintroduced in the original form
171-180		Transitional material using fragments of motives played in sequence
181-196	G minor	Theme 2 reintroduced
197-218	F-sharp minor	Theme 2 restated in a new key
219-234	F minor	Theme 3 presented by the horns
235-250	A-flat major	Theme 3 presented by the low brass and low winds
251-258	F minor	Motive from Theme 3 restated by upper woodwinds and brass
259-270	D-flat major	Theme 4 reintroduced in the horns
271-284	E-flat major	Theme 4 repeated in the horns and cornets
285-290	B-flat major	Restatement of the extended introductory fanfare
291-317	E-flat major	Recapitulation
318-326		Transitional material setting up the coda
327-end		Coda: restatement of the introduction to Movement I

Unit 8: Suggested Listening

Vittorio Giannini, *Symphony No. 3 for Band*
Morton Gould, *Symphony for Band*
Paul Hindemith, *Symphony in B-flat for Band*
Nikolai Miaskovsky:
   Symphony No. 13
   Symphony No. 21
Vincent Persichetti, *Symphony No. 6 for Band*

Unit 9: Additional References and Resources

Abelyan, L., ed. *Symphonies No. 24, 25.* Evgeni Svetlanov, Conductor. The State Symphony Orchestra. Compact disc jacket notes. Russia: Melodiya Record Company, 1992.

Austin, William. *Music in the 20th Century: from Debussy through Stravinsky.* New York: W.W. Norton & Co.

Chobanova, Ani. *Miaskovsky: Symphony No. 5; Kabalevsky: Symphony No. 2*. Dimiter Manolov, Conductor, The Plovdiv Philharmonic. Compact disc jacket notes. Russia: Meodiya Record Company, 1990.

Ikonnikov, Alexei. *Miaskovsky: His Life and Work*. New York: Philosophical Library, Inc., 1946.

Rehrig, William. *The Heritage Encyclopedia of Band Music*. Bierley, Paul, ed. Vol. 1, Westerville, OH: Integrity Press, 1991.

Ter-Mikaelian, Marina, translator. *Symphony No. 6 in Eb Minor. Op. 23.* Kirill Kondrashin, Conductor, USSR Symphony Orchestra and Yurlov Russian Choir. Compact disc jacket notes. Russia: Russian Disc. 1959, remastered 1994.

Yakubov, Manashir. *Nicolai Y. Miaskovsky*. Misha Rachelevsky, Conductor, Chamber Orchestra Kremlin. Compact disc jacket notes. Moscow: Claves Records. 1994.

Contributed by:
Paul R. Hinman
Director of University Bands
East Tennessee State University
Johnson City, Tennessee

Teacher Resource Guide

Symphony No. 3 ("Shaker Life")

Dan Welcher
(b. 1948)

Unit 1: Composer

Dan Welcher, born in Rochester, New York, in 1948, is a contemporary American composer of growing prominence. His compositions, three of which were nominated for the Pulitzer Prize, cover nearly every genre. Welcher studied piano and bassoon, earning degrees from the Eastman School of Music and the Manhattan School of Music. He was the principal bassoonist in the Louisville Orchestra from 1972-78, concurrently teaching theory and composition at the University of Louisville. He served as the Assistant Conductor of the Austin Symphony Orchestra (1980-90) and also as Composer-in-Residence for the Honolulu Symphony Orchestra from 1990-93. He created the New Music Ensemble at the University of Texas at Austin, where he currently is Professor of Composition.

Unit 2: Composition

Welcher's *Symphony No. 3* ("Shaker Life") comprises two separate movements: "Laboring Songs" and "Circular Marches." "Laboring Songs" was commissioned in 1997 by three Texas band programs: L.D. Bell High School, Colony High School, and Duncanville High School. "Circular Marches" was also commissioned in 1997 by the American Bandmasters' Association. Though each movement may be performed individually, both were created to form a two-movement symphony.

"Laboring Songs" consists of six Shaker hymn tunes and melodies. It opens with a wordless melody attributed to "Mother" Anne Lee, the founder of the Quaker religion. It progresses to the second melody, later fully presented in the composition to be "Sad Days." As the tempo increases, "Shaker Life" breaks forth. When this dies down, an angelic flute choir plays another wordless song, "supposedly given in dictation by an angel to its unknown transcriber." The piece continues with "Turn to the Right," while interrupted by the shuffle tune "Followers of the Lamb." This movement concludes with the wordless "Mother Anne" melody, while fractions of the other melodies echo between phrases.

"Circular Marches" opens with the famous "Shaker Shout" representing the "call to worship." The piece then progresses through various types of marching music, shuffles, and additional appearances of the "Shaker Shout." Music in these sections is a combination of original music and quoted Shaker melodies. Both the *ostinato* and quickstep melody are twelve-tone. Midway through the movement the part song, "Come Contentment, Lovely Guest," enters and eventually returns later in the piece. The movement concludes by bringing back the "Shaker Shout."

Unit 3: Historical Perspective

It is quite common in music for composers to use hymnody and folk tunes as melodic material for instrumental compositions. Welcher states:

> I have been interested for several years in certain spiritual practices outside the mainstream of American religion and have put this interest to work in a number of musical idioms…. For *Symphony No. 3*, I have mined the deep spiritual and musical lode of the Shakers, a Protestant sect (originally called the "Shaking Quakers") that emigrated from Great Britain to New England in the mid-eighteenth century. This group, founded by "Mother" Anne Lee and two of her brothers, is now nearly extinct – chiefly because its practice of celibacy has kept its members from reproducing. As the number of converts has waned, the surviving Shakers have diminished in number to such a degree that fewer than a dozen living practitioners of the religion remained when I began to write the piece in 1997. In researching the Shakers' other music, I looked at well over 300 spiritual songs, hymns, wordless melodies, and laboring songs.
>
> The piece does not tell a story; it is not a "picture" of Shaker life in the nineteenth century. But it does attempt to express a sense of spiritual journeying, moving within its ten minutes from pure solo song to mystic angelic choirs, and finally to communal ecstasy and religious joy.

"LABORING SONGS"

"Laboring Songs" refers to the use of vocal music in Shaker worship: the "band" of singers would stand in the middle of the meeting house, while the other worshippers would "labor," executing marches, shuffles, and various other dance-steps as a means of worshipping God. The "shaking" that often overtook them in their zeal was mentioned in the music as well, and references to "shaking" in such songs as "Come Life, Shaker Life" would infer that the physical movement was an outward manifestation of a desire to rid the body of unclean thoughts and desires:

> Come life, Shaker life,
> Come life eternal;
> Shake, shake out of me
> All that is carnal.

The opening melody, "Mother Anne," is one of the earlier Shaker melodies. There are no words to this melody because early Shaker music had no words; words were considered to be too worldly. As this melody progresses, it "draws more adherents to it, as the Shakers themselves were able to do, through its simple strength and purity." The melody, "Turn to the Right," refers to the dance movement that usually accompanies this hymn and the personal action of turning and "getting right with God."

"CIRCULAR MARCHES"

A "circular march" is a specific march, but choreographed almost like a square dance. "The vocal band would stay in place, singing a certain kind of marching song, while the other worshippers executed wheels-within-wheels, counter-marches, and other elaborate patterns; often so detailed and difficult that outsiders were amazed at the memory required." The opening "Shaker Shout" is an instrumental representation of what the Shakers did with their voices in the beginning of their worship services. It is a building up of triads that end in a sort of yodel. The sections where two or three different marches appear loosely represents the Shaker worship event itself. The remainder of the movement progresses toward "spiritual contentment," which finally occurs in the end of the composition.

Unit 4: Technical Considerations

In both movements, Welcher incorporates asymmetric meter, changing meter, polymeter, polytempi, and free meter. Players must be able to play in tempi independent to the rest of the ensemble and the conductor. The woodwinds must be able to play rapid, slurred passages. All players must play rapid, articulated passages and must be able to differentiate the various articulation markings to perform them accurately. Welcher gives specific directions to the percussion as to what mallets and beaters to use. Students must bow the vibraphone, tam-tam, and crotales, and also the play on the strings of the piano. Welcher also gives specific directions to wind players and the conductor regarding certain sections of the music.

"LABORING SONGS"
The hymn, "Followers of the Lamb," is in 12/16 but overlaps the harmony in 6/4. Welcher gives the conductor directions to conduct in two different meters (one in each hand). If this is not possible, the conductor should continue in 6/4 and allow the players in 12/16 to align their melody accordingly. When the ensemble resumes together in 6/4, the "shuffle" melody returns, although rewritten in 6/4. Though it retains the same rhythmic structure, style, and tempo, the phrasing does not line up with the new meter and becomes more difficult to perform with the same style. Lyrical solo playing is required of trumpets, flutes, saxophones, and euphoniums.

"CIRCULAR MARCHES"
Trumpet, horn, trombone, and saxophone sections must be able to perform breath accents accurately. Trumpets and clarinets are required to play *glissandi* with only their tuning slides or by use of "lipping" down and up. Trombones must also perform *glissandi*. The timpanist must *glissando* as well by rolling on an inverted cymbal placed on the timpani head while adjusting the pitch with the pedal. In one section, Welcher scores the ensemble into two separate bands (Band 1 and Band 2). Both bands play in 4/4, but at two different tempi. Band 1 plays at quarter note = 138 and Band 2 plays at quarter note = 92, which works out to be two against three. He gives instructions for the conductor to beat both meters, one in each hand, or continue conducting Band 1 at quarter.

Unit 5: Stylistic Considerations

Research and discussion of the hymn tunes and melodies used in *Symphony No. 3* ("Shaker Life") will facilitate an understanding of their style and function in the Shaker religion and, consequently, how they relate to the overall growth of the composition and each individual movement. It is also beneficial to discuss the development and practice of twelve-tone music so as to better understand the *ostinato* line and quickstep melody in "Circular Marches." Players must be able to play in the style of one meter while reading and being conducted in another. Many players, either individually or in sections, must be able to perform independently from the other sections of the ensemble. Trumpets and clarinets must be able to manipulate the pitch of their instruments to perform the *glissandi* in a "nasty" style. It is important that the clarinets can be heard in this section. Players must also give special attention to the specific articulation markings. These markings are essential to the atmosphere of the music.

Unit 6: Musical Elements

Melody: Folk/hymn melodies, modality, twelve-tone organization
Harmony: Polytonality, atonality, tonal centers, chord clusters, *ostinato*
Rhythm: Motives, free-rhythm/meter, polytempi, polymeter, canon
Form: Rounded, "ABA"
Sound: Middle *tessitura* of instrument range, off-stage performance, texture ranging from solo to small group to full ensemble, use of "lipping" and tuning slide to change pitch, breath accents

Unit 7: Form and Structure

Form	Measure	Event and Scoring

Movement I: "Laboring Songs"
Overall structure: ABA

Form	Measure	Event and Scoring
A	1-20	F mixolydian; "Mother Anne"
	21-30	Transition
	31-43	c minor; "Sad Days," partial statement
	44-57	F mixolydian; "Mother Anne"
	58-74	a minor; "Shaker Life"
	75-93	Transition through circle of fifths; "Shaker Life"
	94-140	Modulatory, c-sharp minor; "Shaker Life" continues, "Sad Days" overlaps
B	141-145	No key, percussion; "Introduction" to new section; rhythmic foreshadowing of new melodic material in percussion
	146	D major; "Angelic Choir"; percussion continues underneath choir
	147-162	B-flat major; "Turn to the Right"
	163-166	g minor; "Followers of the Lamb"; polymeter 12/16 vs. 6/4
	167-172	G major/g minor; "Turn to the Right" with "Followers of the Lamb"
	173-190	Transition; "Turn to the Right" followed by "Followers of the Lamb"
	191-196	C major; "Turn to the Right" with transition into A
A	197-215	F mixolydian; "Mother Anne"; previous melodic and harmonic material presented in background

FORM	MEASURE	EVENT AND SCORING

Movement II: "Circular Marches"
Overall structure: ABA

FORM	MEASURE	EVENT AND SCORING
A	1-20	G major; introduction, "Shaker Shout"; rhythmic motives presented
	21-50	Atonal, B-flat center; twelve-tone *ostinato* joined by "The Sealed Promise"
	51-82	G major; compound meter melody; chord cluster harmony
	83-96	G tonal center; transposed *ostinato* simultaneously with "The Sealed Promise" and compound meter melody
B	97-109	d minor; "Come Contentment, Lovely Guest"
	110-132	Atonal; transposed and inverted *ostinato*; chord cluster harmony
	133-170	Atonal; quickstep melody with *ostinato* in different *tempi* (*ostinato* fades out leaving quickstep melody)
A	171-179	B-flat major; "Shaker Shout"
	180-195	D major; compound meter melody
	196-228	E-flat/c minor; compound meter melody simultaneously with "Come Contentment, Lovely Guest"
	229-end	D-flat vs. E-flat; transposed *ostinato* with "The Sealed Promise" (melody in canon) with "Shaker Shout"

Unit 8: Suggested Listening

Dan Welcher:

Walls and Fences: Five Tactile Experiences (1970)
"Three Places in the West:"
    Arches: An Impression for Concert Band (1985)
    The Yellowstone Fires for Wind Ensemble (1988)
    Zion for Wind Ensemble (1996)
Symphony No. 1 for Orchestra (1991)
Symphony No. 2 for Large Orchestra: "Night Watchers" (1994)
Castle Creek: Fanfare/Overture for Large Orchestra (1989)

Unit 9: Additional References and Resources

Historical information for this study guide is taken from the composer's program notes. Other information is from correspondence with the composer. Both are used with permission.

Theodore Presser Company: *Dan Welcher* [WWW page]; available at <http://www.presser.com/welcher.html>; accessed 1 February 1999.

Tiedman, Richard. "A Distinctive Voice," *American Record Guide*, 58, July 1995, 30.

Contributed by:
Courtney Snyder
Graduate Conducting Assistant
Baylor University
Waco, Texas

Teacher Resource Guide

Symphony No. 3 ("Slavyanskaya")

Boris Kozhevnikov
(1906–1985)

scored for American bands

by John R. Bourgeois
(b. 1934)

Unit 1: Composer

Kozhevnikov was born in Kharkov in 1906. He graduated from the Kharkov Music and Dance Institute in 1933, after which he served as the conductor of various musical theaters until his appointment to the Moscow Conservatory in 1940. Kozhevnikov died in 1985 in Novogorod.

He composed over seventy works for Russian military bands, including five symphonies which were written between 1943 and 1977. His other compositions included marches, overtures, rhapsodies, suites, and tone poems. His orchestra works included *Dance Suite on Ukrainian Themes* (1935), *Sinfonietta* (1936), *Joyful Overture* (1937), *Trumpet Concerto* (1938), *Intermezzo* (for four trombones), songs, and dance pieces.

Unit 2: Composition

The new edition scored for American bands of *Symphony No. 3*, was recorded and edited by John R. Bourgeois. Bourgeois provides the following insights:

> I first came to know of the *Symphony* through my Norwegian friend and band buff, Jan Ericksen, of Norwegian Radio, Oslo. At that time our knowledge of wind music in the USSR was very scant and

obtaining information or performance materials was practically nil. However, Jan was and continues to be the master of musical protocol and he circuitously obtained a score and set of parts for me. Later Jan was the person who was singularly responsible for achieving a state of "musical détente" between the US and USSR through his Norwegian Radio broadcasts of the Marine Band and the great "First Independent Performing Orchestra of USSR Ministry of Defense" under the direction of General Mikailov. The response to these broadcasts by the Marine Band in the Soviet Union was enormous and were to lead to the historic exchange tour by both groups in 1989 and 1990. The Kozhevnikov Symphony was originally scored in typical Russian wind band instrumentation, i.e., piccolo, two flutes, E-flat clarinets, three B-flat clarinets, two bassoons, four horns, two cornets, two trumpets, four tenor horns, baritone, three trombones, tuba, and percussion. Note the absence of saxophones (Stalin had banned the use of saxophone in 1937 as being a "Bourgeois" instrument). My records show that the first US performance (using the Russian parts and transferring them into our instrumentation) was on March 15, 1987, on the Marine Band Showcase Series in John Philip Sousa Band Hall in Washington, DC. The audience's enthusiastic response led me to feature the *Symphony* on the band's annual concert tour in the fall of that year.

The *Symphony* is in four movements:

> Movement I: "Allegro" (3:30)
> Movement II: "Valse" (4:30)
> Movement III: "Vivo" (2:10)
> Movement IV: "Moderato" (4:09)

Unit 3: Historical Perspective

The unexpected thaw after almost fifty years of Cold War and the political collapse of the Soviet Union has resulted in a national artistic renaissance and the disclosure of much Russian art and music which was heretofore unknown to the West. Among all of this new music to be discovered is a large body of original works composed for Soviet military bands. Some of these works, including *Symphony No. 3 ("Slavyanskaya")*, truly have lasting musical significance.

Unit 4: Technical Considerations

Symphony No. 3 requires a high level of technical skill throughout the ensemble. All parts contain melodic material and are of interest to the individual performer. This four-movement work is of major symphonic proportion, with a total performance time of nearly fifteen minutes. Endurance will be a major factor in programming this work. Kozhevnikov frequently uses the *tutti* trumpet section as the primary melodic vehicle, requiring long periods of playing without rests. The composer has written a *divisi* euphonium part and has scored the euphoniums in a very high *tessitura* throughout the work. The opening movement utilizes solo oboe passages and some exposed technical passages for the bassoon. The second movement is a slow, lyrical waltz featuring two solo clarinets; it is the least technically demanding movement. The third *scherzo* movement places high technical demands on the upper woodwinds. The opening solo piccolo and e-flat clarinet passage will require the most proficient players. Maintaining a light, rapid, *staccato* style without allowing the tempo to slow will be a challenge in the upper woodwinds. The final movement utilizes the unison trumpets, trombones, and euphoniums as the prime melodic carrier. The movement contains solo passages for the cornet and clarinet.

Unit 5: Stylistic Considerations

Kozhevnikov's style is simple and direct, utilizing strong Russian folk-like melodies throughout the *Symphony*. His writing contrasts sections of homophonic material with sections of skillful contrapuntal writing. Balance will pose a concern for conductors, particularly during contrapuntal sections where melodies are voiced closely together. A strong sense of musical independence is needed from players who are frequently required to perform independent material in extreme ranges or against a more dominant, coloristic partner. Careful shaping of the melodic lines will give maximum interest and direction to the musical content. Although the composer has organized his musical ideas into specific blocks or cells, he utilizes abrupt dynamic and stylistic shifts throughout each section for contrast and punctuation. The conductor must ensure such contrasts are executed faithfully.

Unit 6: Musical Elements

The *Symphony* is set in a traditional neo-classic format, with four movements. Unlike the classic symphony, however, the composer has eliminated the slow movement. The opening movement in f minor is set in sonata form. The opening A theme, introduced by the trumpets in m. 5, has a bold *marcato* character. Later repetitions of the A theme are presented against a countermelody set in the low brass and low woodwinds. In contrast, the lyric B theme in A-flat major is introduced by the euphonium and woodwinds in m. 38. A second statement of the B theme is accompanied by a sweeping, lyrical countermelody in the bassoon and euphonium. The development section, mm. 75-105, is highly contrapuntal, with much melodic material placed only in the bassoons. After a brief transition, the recapitulation returns to f minor at m. 110. Unlike the exposition, Kozhevnikov presents both statements of the B theme with countermelodies. A brief transition, mm. 157-164, leads to a false redevelopment reminiscent of Beethoven's symphonic music. A brief, four-measure coda energetically concludes the movement.

The second movement is a slow, lyric waltz. Set in D-flat major, the movement could be considered a rounded binary or incipient ternary form. The movement presents the A material between mm. 1 and 33, with two solo clarinets introducing the theme followed by statements in the flutes and upper woodwinds. Kozhevnikov sets the B theme for *divisi* euphoniums reinforced by two horns in m. 34. This section moves into a quasi-development of the A and B themes between m. 50 and m. 66. A repeat to m. 34 restates the B theme and AB development section. A three-measure transition starting in m. 67 (the second ending) introduces the closing section over a dominant pedal in mm. 70-77. The movement concludes with a spirited eight-measure coda marked "fast (in one)."

The third movement, marked *Vivace*, has a scherzo-like character with virtuoso demands placed upon the woodwinds. The form roughly follows a rondo pattern of ABACA. The movement is set in F major, with the A theme introduced immediately in the piccolo and E-flat clarinet. A second statement of the theme is presented in the *tutti* clarinets and is followed by a third in the upper woodwinds and cornets. The B theme in c minor is hocketed between the solo oboe and solo clarinet, with each instrument alternating one-measure statements. After a single F major statement of the A material in m. 43, a heavy, *marcato* C theme in d minor is introduced at m. 51 in the low brass and low woodwinds. A lyric woodwind treatment of the C material moves the tonal center to a minor and a return of the *marcato* C theme in m. 67. A brief restatement of the A theme in m. 73 leads to a technically sparkling coda in m. 85.

The final movement, marked *Moderato* (joyously), returns to the bold Slavic style of the opening movement, with the brass as the dominant melodic color. The form in the final movement is sonata-allegro, although the composer freely shifts modality through much of the thematic material. An eight-measure, fanfare-like introduction leads to the A theme stated by the unison trumpets in m. 10, with the tonal center shifting between f minor and F major. The theme is interrupted by a contrasting four-measure lyric interjection only to return to a *marcato* conclusion. An eight-measure modulatory transition, mm. 25-32, leads to the B theme in m. 33. The second theme is a broad, lyric line presented in the euphonium and tenor saxophone, and later in the flutes and upper woodwinds. Kozhevnikov puts this theme in the relative minor but freely shifts modality from d minor to D major. A highly modulatory development section begins in m. 56. Sixteen measures into the development, however, the composer introduces a short, new melody (Theme C), which gives this movement a momentary sonata-rondo character. In m. 101, the recapitulation returns to the tonality of f minor, with the thematic material again in the trumpets. The composer places the return of the B material in the subdominant, with the modality shifting between B-flat major and b-flat minor. A 23-measure closing section, mm. 148-170, leads to the coda in m. 171. During the opening measures of the coda, the composer reintroduces an augmentation of the C theme in the low brass and low woodwinds. The *Symphony* triumphantly concludes with eight measures of *tutti* F major chords.

Unit 7: Form and Structure

SECTION	MEASURE	TONAL CENTER	MUSICAL EVENT
Movement I:			
Introduction	1-4	f minor	
A¹	5-12		*Marcato* trumpet
A²	13-19		A with countermelody
Bridge	20-27		
A³	28-35		A with countermelody
Transition	35-37		
B¹	38-53	A-flat major	Lyric euphonium and woodwinds
B²	54-68		B with countermelody
Transition	68-74		
Development	75-105		Highly contrapuntal
Transition	106-109		
Recapitulation A¹	110-117	f minor	A in trumpets
A²	118-127		A with countermelody
B¹	128-143	A-flat major	B with countermelody
B²	144-157		B with countermelody
Transition	157-164		
False Development	164-171	f minor	
Coda	171-179		
Movement II:			
A¹	1-16	D-flat major	A in clarinets, flutes
A²	17-33		A with countermelody
B	34-49	c minor	
Development AB	50-66	D-flat major	A and B with countermelody
Transition	67-69		
Closing	70-77		Dominant pedal
Coda	78-85		Faster tempo shift

SECTION	MEASURE	TONAL CENTER	MUSICAL EVENT
Movement III:			
A¹	1-8	f minor	A in piccolo/e-flat clarinet
A²	9-16		A in clarinets
A³	17-22		*Tutti* statement
Transition	23-24		
B¹	25-32	c minor	Hocketed theme
B²	33-40		*Tutti* statement
Transition	41-42		
A	43-50	F major	
C¹	51-58	d minor	*Marcato* low brass
C²	59-66	a minor	Lyric statement
C³	67-72	d minor	*Marcato* low brass
A	73-84		
Coda	85-97	F major	Sequential development
Movement IV:			
Introduction	1-4	F major/minor	
A	9-24		A in trumpet
Transition	25-32		
B¹	33-48	d minor	Lyric euphonium/woodwinds
B²	48-55		
Development	56-100	Modulatory	*Tutti*
C	71-78		Low brass
Recapitulation A	101-116	F major/minor	A in trumpet
Transition	117-124	Modulatory	
B¹	125-140	B-flat	Cornet/clarinet
B²	141-147		*Tutti* statement
Closing	148-170	Modulatory	
Coda-C aug.	171-182	F major	

Unit 8: Suggested Listening

Anatol Liadov, arr. Goldman, *Eight Russian Folk Songs*
Nikolai Miaskovsky, *Symphony No. 19 in E, Op. 46*
Serge Prokofiev:
    Athletic Festival March, Op. 69, No. 1
    March, Op. 99

Unit 9: Additional References and Resources

Biographical Dictionary of Russian/Soviet Composers. New York and Connecticut: Ho & Dimitry Feofanov - Greenwood Press, 1989.

Muzykal'naya Entsiklopediya (Soviet Encyclopedia of Music). Yu, Keldysh, ed., 1973.

Sovetskiye Kompozitory: Kratkiy Biograficheskiy Sparvochnik (Soviet Composers: A Short Biographical Dictionary). G. Bernandt & A. Dol'zhansky, eds., Moscow, 1957 rev. 1978.

Vsesoyaznoye Agentstvo Po Okhrane Avtorskikh (VAAP). Soviet Licensing Agency.

Ocherki Sovetskogo Muzkal'nogo Tvorchestra. Vol. 1. B Asafyer, et al., eds. Moscow-Leningrad. 1947.

Contributed by:
Edward Harris
Director of Bands
California State University/Stanislaus
Turlock, California

Teacher Resource Guide

Variations for Wind Band

Ralph Vaughan Williams
(1872–1958)

transcribed by Donald Hunsberger
(b. 1932)

Unit 1: Composer

Ralph Vaughan Williams was born in Down Ampney, England, on October 12, 1872, and died in London, England, on August 26, 1958. He is one of England's most respected composers. While Vaughan Williams is known primarily as a composer, he was also active as a conductor, researcher, editor, writer, and organist.

His formal music study was at the Royal Conservatory of Music (R.C.M.) in London and at Cambridge University. His composition teachers included Hubert Parry and Charles Villiers Stanford at the R.C.M (1890-92), and Charles Wood at Cambridge University (1892-95). In 1896, he studied composition with Max Bruch in Berlin, Germany. He received a Mus.D. degree in 1901 from Cambridge University. In 1904, he joined the Folk Song Society, whose members included Gustav Holst and eventually Percy Grainger. In 1919, Vaughan Williams began teaching at the R.C.M. He lived the majority of his life in London. However, for a brief time he studied orchestration with Maurice Ravel in Paris. He also made three brief visits (1922, 1932, 1954) to the United States, where he engaged, lectured, and conducted.

Vaughan Williams' compositional output includes nine orchestral symphonies, other works for orchestra (such as *Variations on a Theme by Thomas Tallis*), operas (including *The Pilgrim's Progress*), choral works, solo works, and his band works, including *English Folk Song Suite*, *Toccata Marziale*, *Flourish for Wind Band*, and *Sea Songs*.

Unit 2: Composition

Variations was originally written by Vaughan Williams for brass band. Historically, concert bands and brass bands had their beginnings, in part, with the fifes, drums, and trumpets associated with European courts and armies. Early military music generally fell into one of two categories: cavalry music or infantry music. Trumpets and kettledrums were associated with the cavalry music, while bagpipes and fifes were associated with the infantry. The brass band is considered a descendant of the cavalry band.

Brass bands began to appear in England around 1833. British brass bands flourished as organizations which provided wholesome recreation for factory and mine workers. The popularity of those early British brass bands continues today in Britain, as witnessed by the large number of amateur British brass bands associated with industrial enterprises and collieries (i.e., coal mines). In Britain, a sizable body of brass band repertoire has been developed, including original compositions by leading British composers such as Sir Edward Elgar, John Ireland, Gustav Holst, and Ralph Vaughan Williams.

Brass band festivals and contests are regular events in Britain. It was for the 1957 National Brass Band Championship of Great Britain that Vaughan Williams was commissioned to write his *Variations for Brass Band*. The work was transcribed for orchestra by Gordon Jacob and titled *Variations for Orchestra*. The transcription for large wind ensemble was done by Donald Hunsberger and titled *Variations for Wind Band*.

Unit 3: Historical Perspective

Vaughan Williams composed his *Variations* concurrently with his *Symphony No. 9*, in E minor. The opening four-bar theme of *Variations* is used throughout his *Ninth Symphony* as well. Both *Variations* and the *Ninth Symphony* were completed shortly before Vaughan Williams's death.

As members of the Folk Song Society, Vaughan Williams, Holst, and Grainger are considered three of the most important and influential composers for band of the twentieth century. At a time when few composers were writing for band, they established the traditions of British band literature through composition of original works. Vaughan Williams, like Holst and Grainger, had a lifelong interest in British folk songs. Vaughan Williams's fascination of English folk songs resulted in his research throughout England for melodies, texts, and historical information. Collecting hundreds of English traditional tunes, he set many of them for voice and used them as thematic materials in his compositions. So pervasive was the use of English folk song in his compositional style that many of his original melodies have been mistaken for authentic folk songs. Although *Variations* is set to an original theme by Vaughan Williams, the influence of folk song on the compositional style of *Variations* is evident. Sweeping, lyrical lines; bold, choral-like statements; florid figures; delicate, intertwining solo lines; use of modal writing and harmonies; and counterpoint are among the traits of *Variations* that are unique to Vaughan Williams's folk song style of composition.

Unit 4: Technical Considerations

Variations for Wind Band is scored for a mature ensemble with an *extended* compliment of woodwind, brass, and percussion instruments. The extended instrumentation is essential in achieving the sonority and timbrel qualities of the score. Choirs of instruments are used throughout the work alone and in combination, producing an array of rich tonal colors. Exclusion of any of the extended instrumentation will limit the effectiveness of the scoring. The extended scoring includes flute I-II-III (third flute doubling alto flute), piccolo, E-flat soprano clarinet, B-flat soprano clarinet I-II-III, B-flat bass clarinet, BB-flat contrabass clarinet, bassoon I-II, contrabassoon, B-flat soprano saxophone, E-flat alto saxophone, tenor saxophone, E-flat baritone saxophone, B-flat trumpet I-II, B-flat piccolo trumpet I-II, B-flat flugelhorn I-II, F horn I-II-III-IV, trombone I-II-III-IV, euphonium (divisi), tuba (divisi), string bass, timpani, harp, snare drum, bass drum, cymbals, triangle, bells, xylophone, and celesta.

The wind parts require technically proficient players who are comfortable playing the full range of their instruments. The ensemble must be "flexible" to achieve nuance of *rubato* essential to the aesthetics of the work. Chorale-like sections of the work require maturity of tone, tonal blend and balance, and subtlety of phrasing. Articulated contrapuntal passages require precision and balance in order to achieve transparency and clarity of intertwining lines. The theme and variations require the ensemble to play a vast array of articulations, tempi, and dynamics.

Unit 5: Stylistic Considerations

Variations for Wind Band is a collection of a theme and eleven variations. As a contest piece for the 1957 National Brass Band Championship of Great Britain, Vaughan Williams challenged each band with its ability to perform various styles, tempi, articulations, and dynamics. The opening theme is majestic and sustained. Each subsequent contrasting variation of the theme requires an ensemble which has a thorough understanding of and training in numerous musical styles and forms. Since all of the variations are relatively brief in length, the ensemble must perform each stylistic variation accurately and convincingly in order to achieve an overall integrated aesthetically rewarding musical performance.

Theme-*Andante maestoso*
Variation 1-*Poco tranquillo* (a bit quiet, peaceful)
> The style requires *legato* and *quasi portamento* (gliding from note to note) articulations.

Variation 2-*Tranquillo cantable* (quiet, singing, lyrical)

   The style requires a *legato* articulation.

Variation 3-*Allegro* (lively, in a quick tempo)

   The style requires full note values yet separated (not *marcato*).

Variation 4-*Allegro* (canon) (lively, in a quick tempo)

   A canon may be defined as a contrapuntal device (counterpoint, "point against point," note against note, melody against melody) whereby a melody stated in one part is imitated strictly and in its entirety in one or more other parts. The style requires broad and sustained articulations as well as *legato* articulation.

Variation 5-*Molto sostenuto* (very sustained)

   The style requires *legato*, *quasi portamento*, and *quasi pizzacato* (plucked) articulations.

Variation 6-*Tempo di valse* (in the tempo of a waltz)

   A waltz may be defined as a dance in moderate triple meter. The style requires a three pulse of "strong-weak-weaker," giving a feeling of "one" to a bar.

Variation 7-*Arabesque: Andante sostenuto*

   The term "arabesque" ("of the Arab, moorish ornament, one of the basic poses in ballet") is used in this variation in the sense of figuration and "moorish" ornamentation of the theme. The character of the "arabesque" is that of a "casual" nature in a moderately slow tempo. The style requires a sustained manner of performance.

Variation 8-*Alla Polacca*

   "Alla Polacca" translates as "in a Polish style." It is used also as the generic name for Polish dances, usually the "polonaise." As is the case with this variation, the polonaise is typically a dance of a festive character in moderate triple meter consisting of phrases without an upbeat, and frequently utilizes a repeated rhythmic motif. The style requires a light *staccato* articulation that is separated and lifted, but not clipped.

Variation 9-*Adagio* (a slow tempo, slower than *andante* but not as slow as *lento*)

   The style requires a sustained *legato*, chorale-like quality.

Variation 10-*Allegro Molto* (*Fugato*) (very fast, lively tempo)

   The term "fugato" may be defined as a passage in fugal (fugue) style that is part of a primarily non-fugal composition. The main characteristics of a fugue are (1) they are written in contrapuntal style with a texture of a number of individual voices (usually three or four); (2) they are based on a melody called a subject, which is stated at the beginning of the fugue by one lone voice; and (3) the lone voice is imitated in other voices in close succession. The elements essential to every fugue are as follows:

   - Subject: a theme
   - Answer: the transposition and imitation of the subject

- Countersubject: the continuation of the subject creating counterpoint to the answer (if this occurs more than once, it is called the countersubject; if it occurs only once, it is called free counterpoint)
- Stretto: imitation of the subject in close succession (the answer enters before the subject is completed)
- Episode: a section of the fugue that does not include a statement of the subject

The style requires light *staccato* and *portamento* articulations.

Variation 11-*Chorale*

A chorale is defined as a hymn tune of the German Protestant Church, or one similar in style. The style requires a *legato*, "chorus-like" (singing) performance.

Unit 6: Musical Elements

Irregular phrase structures and modal tonalities are pervasive musical elements of the work. Throughout the work there is not one dominant-to-tonic (V-I) cadence. The entire work is built on the opening theme, which consists of three main phrases (ABA') with a two-measure extension as follows:

A MOTIVE	B MOTIVE	A' MOTIVE + EXTENSION
1st phrase	2nd phrase	3rd phrase
4 measures	3 measures	5 + 2 measures
C major to A dorian	A major to A dorian	A dorian to C major

Each of the three phrases of the theme oscillates between scale degree one (C major) and scale degree six (A minor/A major). Because of the "modulation" to VI in the third measure, and the long pedal point on A for the second phrase, and the strong A dorian effect in the first five measures of the third phrase, ten measures of the theme are centered on A (VI in C). Only the opening two measures and the closing two measures are clearly in C major. The work, however, clearly ends in C major (Lydian cadence). The fourth scale degree of C (and the sixth scale degree of A) is used in the theme only once, in m. 10, then it is F-sharp. This note (F-sharp) is what gives the dorian effect in A minor and the Lydian effect in C major.

Unit 7: Form and Structure

"Theme and Variations" may be defined as a musical form resulting from the consistent application of "variation techniques" (changes, alterations) so that a musical "theme" (melody) is followed by a varying number of modified restatements ("variations").

FORM	MEASURE	SCORING
Theme:		
A	1-4	C major (pentatonic) to A dorian (m. 4)
B	5-7	A major to A dorian (m. 6)
A´	8-12	A dorian to A major (picardy 3rd) (m. 12)
A´ extension	13-14	C major (C lydian cadence II-I, II with raised fourth scale degree)
Variation 1:		
A	1-4	C major
B	5-7	E major (with lowered sixth and seventh scale degree)
A´	8-12	E aeolian and A aeolian (mm. 9-10)
A´ extension	13-14	Modulation to F major
Variation 2:		
	1	Arrival of F major
A	2-6	Oboe/bassoon; F major to A aeolian (m. 7)
B	4-7	Flute; F major to A aeolian (m. 7)
A´	8-10	Flute; D aeolian (VI of F major)
A´ extension	10-13	D aeolian
Variation 3:		
A	1-6	D aeolian to D lydian (raised fourth scale degree)
A´	7-10	D lydian (mm. 8-10 D aeolian in upper woodwinds and D dorian in bass)
Variation 4:		
A/A´ motive idea	1-5	C mixolydian (C major with lowered seventh scale degree); low brass/reeds at m. 1 with upper brass/reeds in canon at m. 2 a perfect fifth above
B motive idea	6-11	A mixolydian; at m. 6 low brass/reeds in canon at the octave
A´ motive idea	11-20	A melodic minor to A dorian (m. 13) to A aeolian (m. 14); low brass/reeds at m. 11 with upper brass/reeds in canon at m. 12 at the octave
A´ extension	21-23	A aeolian

FORM	MEASURE	SCORING
Variation 5:		
A motive idea	1-15	A dorian and A aeolian mixed to D dorian (m. 9); A motive in horn and English horn with free inversion in trumpet and clarinet
B motive idea	16-25	D dorian to A aeolian (m. 22); B motive in bassoon, bass clarinet, contrabassoon, contraclarinet, and baritone
A´ extension motive idea	26-27	Modulating to C minor
Variation 6:		
A motive idea	1-13	C minor, beginning at m. 16
B motive idea	13-25	G phrygian in upper voices with G 3 dorian in lower voices
A´ motive idea	24-30	C aeolian; A´ motive in piccolo and flugelhorn
A´ extension idea	31-32	C aeolian; A´ motive in oboe and celesta
Variation 7:		
A motive idea	1-8	F major; A motive expanded in bassoon
B motive idea	9-12	A major (lowered sixth and seventh scale degrees in woodwind runs); B motive in horn and trombone (mm. 9-12) and bassoon, soprano/alto/ tenor saxophone, piccolo, trumpet, flugelhorn, baritone (mm. 13-16)
A´ extension idea	16	Modulating to A major
Variation 8:		
B motive idea	1-7	A major (with lowered sixth scale degree) to C major (m. 6)
B motive last four notes in stretto	8-22	C major
A motive idea with rhythmic transformation (flute, oboe, bassoon); B motive idea as the accompaniment (horns, flugelhorn, baritone)	22-32	C major with brief shift to A mixolydian (m. 26) then to Cm over an A pedal (m. 29) moving to E major (m. 32)

FORM	MEASURE	SCORING
B motive idea	32-37	E major to E aeolian (m. 36)
A idea (low brass/reeds)	38-44	E aeolian with shift to quasi C lydian (m. 39)
B motive last three notes	45	Moving to C major
B motive idea in canon	46-51	C major; canon at the octave (flute, oboe, clarinet, soprano saxophone; and alto-tenor-baritone saxophone, horns)
B motive idea in stretto	52-59	C major
A´ extension idea	60-61	Modulation to A-flat major

Variation 9:

A motive idea	1-21	A-flat major with emphasis on F major chord (mm. 4, 8, etc.)
B motive idea	22-30	F phrygian with picardy third on tonic
B motive cadence idea	31-32	F phrygian
B motive last four notes	33-34	Phrygian cadence to C major

Variation 10:

A´ idea extension	1-2	C major
A motive idea (subject)	3-8	C major; fugue subject derived from diminution of A motive
A motive idea (answer)	5-14	C major; fugue answer at the dominant (clarinet, alto-tenor saxophone)
B motive idea	6-10	C major; countersubject derived from B motive; countersubject entrance on dominant
A motive idea	8-15	C major; stretto (English horn, soprano saxophone, flugelhorn; and flute, oboe, piccolo, piccolo trumpet)
A motive idea	11-13	C major; subject in variation in A minor (low reeds and brass)
A motive idea	14-16	C major; incomplete entrance on D dorian (baritone, low reeds; and flute, oboe)
A motive idea	17-22	C major; stretto (low reeds/brass; and English horn, clarinet, trumpet); augmentation (flute, oboe)

FORM	MEASURE	SCORING
A motive idea	23	Moving to C major with phrygian cadence over the bar line of mm. 22-23
Variation 11: A motive idea with very transformation of motive	1-34	C major (oscillates between C major and A minor in m. 1); C major lydian (m. 8); E major (m. 15); C major/A aeolian (mm. 17-18); A dorian (m. 28); A mixolydian (mm. 33-34)
A motive variant (harp, string bass, baritone, low reeds)	21-24	C major moving to A aeolian
A´ motive variant	25-34	A aeolian to D dorian (m. 28)
A motive idea from fugato (Variation 10)	34-41	C major to A dorian (m. 40)
A´ motive extension idea	42-43	A dorian
A´ motive extension (last three notes of second measure)	44-46	A major with lydian cadence to C major

Unit 8: Suggested Listening

Ralph Vaughan Williams:
> *English Folk Song Suite*, Movement. II (Intermezzo-"My Bonny Boy")
> *Symphony No. 9, in E minor*
> *Toccata Marziale*
> *Variations for Orchestra*, transcribed by Gordon Jacob

Unit 9: Additional References and Resources

Apel, Willi. *Harvard Dictionary of Music*. Second ed. Cambridge, MA: The Balkan Press of Harvard University Press, 1970.

Goldman, Richard Franko. *The Concert Band*. New York: Rinehart and Company, Inc., 1946.

Rehrig, William H. *The Heritage Encyclopedia of Band Music*. Edited by Paul Bierley, Westerville, OH: Integrity Press, 1991.

Contributed by:
Victor A. Markovich
Professor of Music
Director of Bands and Winds/Percussion Studies
Wichita State University
Wichita, Kansas

Grade Six

Teacher Resource Guide

A Child's Garden of Dreams
David Maslanka
(b. 1943)

Unit 1: Composer

David Maslanka was born in New Bedford, Massachusetts, in 1943. As a high school student, he was a member of the Greater Boston Youth Symphony Orchestra, and he studied clarinet with Robert Stewart at the New England Conservatory. He later attended the Oberlin Conservatory (B.M. 1965), studying clarinet with George Waln and composition with Joseph Wood. In 1963 and 1964, he attended the Mozarteum in Salzburg, Austria, working in composition with Cesar Bresgen and conducting with Gerhardt Wimberger. He did graduate studies at Michigan State University (M.M. 1968, Ph.D. 1971), with H. Owen Reed in composition, Paul Harder in theory, and Elsa Ludwig in clarinet.

Maslanka's compositions have been performed throughout the United States and in numerous foreign countries. His works for winds and percussion have become especially well known. They include, among others, *A Child's Garden of Dreams; Concerto for Piano, Winds, and Percussion*; the 2nd, 3rd, and 4th *Symphonies; In Memoriam; Tears*; and *Mass*. Percussion works include *Variations on Lost Love* (for marimba solo), *Arcadia II: Concerto for Marimba and Percussion Ensemble, Crown of Thorns* (for keyboard percussion), *Montana Music: Three Dances for Percussion*, and *In Lonely Fields* (for percussion and orchestra). In addition, he has written a wide variety of chamber, orchestral, and choral pieces.

Maslanka's works are published primarily by Carl Fischer, Inc. of New York and have been recorded on CRI, Novisse, Klavier, Cambria, Mark, Summit, and Albany labels. Between 1970 and 1990, he served on the faculties of SUNY Geneseo, Sarah Lawrence College, New York University, and CUNY Kingsborough. He is now a freelance composer and lives in Missoula, Montana. Maslanka is an ASCAP composer.

Unit 2: Composition

A Child's Garden of Dreams (1981) is a large-scale grade six composition of five movements, with an approximate duration of thirty-two minutes. Available through the rental library of Carl Fischer, Inc., this challenging composition requires highly competent, fearless, and well-focused players on every part. The conductor must possess these same qualities and work towards a solution to what the composer (Maslanka, 1999b) sees as the central issue of successfully performing *A Child's Garden of Dreams*: "How do you get *past the notes* to the *music?*"

The titles of the movements were drawn from a collection of twelve extraordinary dreams that a young girl of eight had had that were reported in *Man and His Symbols* by Carl Jung, et al. The composer became aware of this book through a psychologist friend. While reading the book as he waited for his wife at a doctor's office, Maslanka came across the discussion of these dreams and was instantly struck by the possibility of using them musically. Shortly thereafter, he made the connection to the wind piece commissioned by John and Marietta Paynter.

The title, *A Child's Garden of Dreams*, is a variation on the title of a collection of poetry by Robert Louis Stevenson, "A Child's Garden of Verses." Maslanka had said that he wanted a title that would give a whimsical tone to the questions of death and transformation that were touched upon by the young girl. The rather formal reserve of the title *A Child's Garden of Dreams* gives no clue as to the actual nature of the piece, a notion that appeals to Maslanka (Wubbenhorst, 1994).

The titles of the five movements are as follows:

I. There is a desert on the moon where the dreamer sinks so deeply into the ground that she reaches hell.

II. A drunken woman falls into the water and comes out renewed and sober.

III. A horde of small animals frightens the dreamer. The animals increase to a tremendous size, and one of them devours the little girl.

IV. A drop of water is seen, as it appears when looked at through a microscope. The girl sees that the drop is full of tree branches. This portrays the origin of the world.

V. An ascent into heaven, where pagan dances are being celebrated; and a descent into hell, where angels are doing good deeds.

It is important to have some knowledge of how Maslanka went about composing *A Child's Garden of Dreams*. When asked how he had finally chosen the five dreams from the original twelve, Maslanka had this to say (Wubbenhorst, 1994):

> I typed all twelve dreams on a single sheet of paper, put the paper on the piano in front of me, and started finding musical ideas in bits and pieces as I read each dream. It was a process of letting them "light up" one at a time. The ones that came forward the strongest got used in the piece....This process involved meditation. With each dream, I tried to imagine a real picture, to put myself in that picture and to allow the emotions and insights of that experience to come through my own system. The starting point was always a particular dream. The music is representative of the dream, though it does not describe it in a literal sense. I tried to create a parallel musical universe by sinking as deeply as possible into my unconscious to unite the dream and the musical imagery. I believe that there is a connection in one's unconscious where the music and the dream become one.

Unit 3: Historical Perspective

A Child's Garden of Dreams was commissioned by John and Marietta Paynter in 1981 and is dedicated to them and to the Northwestern University Symphonic Wind Ensemble. The actual composition of the work occurred during June, July, and August of 1981, with the premiere performance on February 26, 1982, at the North Central Division meeting of the College Band Directors National Association held that year in Columbus, Ohio.

At the time of the commission, John Paynter asked for a *major* work for wind ensemble. Maslanka had no restrictions placed upon him regarding length and was able to write freely. Instrumentation of the basic wind ensemble was assumed along with additional things such as electric organ, piano, harp, and whatever percussion one might imagine. Paynter made only one request: he wanted the wind equivalent of the Bartok *Concerto for Orchestra*. The composer has acknowledged his awe of this particular work of Bartok's, and so this particular commission became a high challenge.

Maslanka cites many composers as influential, but he has a special affinity for J.S. Bach. He plays and sings two to three of the Bach chorales every day before beginning to compose as a means of becoming centered. Stravinsky's *Rite of Spring* is identified as a strong influence upon *A Child's Garden of Dreams*, while other composers (e.g., Milhaud, Varese, Bartok, Brahms, Debussy, Schoenberg, Berg, and Webern) remain in the background of his thinking. American composers who are admired include Gershwin,

Ives, Carter, Partch, and Cage, as well as the serialists, Babbitt, Sessions, and Wourinen.

Unit 4: Technical Considerations

There can be no doubt that *A Child's Garden of Dreams* is difficult, but every technical challenge that must be managed provides a musical reward — individually and collectively — for the performers, conductor and, perhaps most importantly, the listeners. The composer believes that music contains within itself a power to communicate its essence despite some deficiencies in performance level. Mind you, Maslanka is *very* keen that all performance be of the highest level possible; he also understands that this "power" is embodied in an energy that pulls the performers along, literally forcing all to reach a higher level than they might have expected. A point is inevitably reached when the music embraces and lifts its performers, time flows as it can only in peak experiences, and the performance is over before one knows it (Wubbenhorst, 1994).

Conductors and performers both experience this alternate flow of time. Conductors experience a particular paradox because they know they must release the music to performance so that it can happen and yet they are trained to be "in charge" at every instant. The issue is one of trusting the musicians with the music, of not being afraid or overly cautious. This trust is built up over time in rehearsal. When the music making happens properly, the performance space "heats up." The music becomes larger than the conductor and the ensemble. Each individual is making a maximum contribution; the whole is bigger than the sum of the parts (Maslanka, 1999a).

When you get past all of the typical "technical" concerns that exist in this composition, one is left with the hardest to define — what Maslanka calls a "passionate imagination for sound." It remains with the conductor to hear in his/her imagination what is indicated by the notation (c.f., Unit 5) and then work to achieve that image in real sound among the players. Patient work must be committed to find the *true values* of instrumental color combinations and to develop various textures. Once players experience this true value and have confidence in it, they then begin to have ownership of the piece. Often this aspect of music making is passed over because "there isn't time" to dwell on each issue. However, in Maslanka's mind, the central issue of rehearsal is to transfer ownership of the music to the ensemble. This is done most efficiently by doing the patient, detailed work of finding true values. You may not be able to cover *every* detail, but this kind of work has a generalizing effect, and the musical rewards that come forward are astonishing (Maslanka, 1999c).

Unit 5: Stylistic Considerations

It may be said of any music that one must begin with a literal reading of the given notation (i.e., correct tempi, notes, durations, dynamics, phrasing, etc.). Every musical element in the composer's chosen notation must be the entrance point into the learning process. In the case of Maslanka's A *Child's Garden of Dreams*, in fact in all of his music, this should be heard as a composer's imperative. Not all composers take the care that Maslanka does when he commits notes to manuscript paper. What appears on *his* page is as close to his pure intent as he can convey through conventional means, so be as literal as possible. If this seems like too many elements to keep track of at first, choose just one – for instance, tempo. Maslanka states that a strict adherence to tempo allows the whole musical shape to emerge. He has characterized the conductor as a channel for the music; to accomplish this, the conductor must be open and willing to trust the music completely. Once this step is taken, the music enters into the performance space in a powerful way.

> [Please refer to M-*Notes*, i.e., "Maslanka-Notes" that appear within Unit 7 for more specific concerns. These are comments shared with the author of observations he has made during countless rehearsals and performances of A *Child's Garden of Dreams* (Maslanka, 1999a).]

Unit 6: Musical Elements

As you look at the musical examples that appear in Unit 7, you should be particularly mindful of two gestures that appear throughout the entire length of this work. They appear so often that it would be difficult to identify each instance. These musical examples are drawn from Wubbenhorst's 1991 *Thematic Compendium*, an unpublished analysis of melodic material from A *Child's Garden of Dreams*. The examples are all notated at concert pitch, identify the measure in which the gesture begins, and are intentionally non-rhythmic in notation. Open note heads represent principal material; closed note heads are secondary and/or passing in function. When it appears, beaming serves to unify a melodic gesture visually. It is possible, indeed useful, to play or sing through these examples from beginning to end in whatever rhythmic flow you feel appropriate at that moment. What you will be left with is the over-arching melodic flow of all five movements compressed into an easily digestible five-minute interval.

The first gesture, referred to as the "Here I Am" motive, appears for the first time in m. 9 of Movement I. It represents an announcement to the dreamer from the "other side," which draws her fearlessly onward. According to Maslanka, it symbolizes "an unidentified something calling to the little girl from the other side of death while she skims across the surface of the moon. It is a bright and hopeful image in that it expresses a promise of life beyond death and of an ultimately superior existence in the beyond."

The second gesture appears for the first time in m. 47 of Movement I, and is actually labeled "...epiphany..." at m. 118 of Movement IV. Maslanka has described this motive as the ultimate metaphoric representation of the dreamer's emergence to fully transformed consciousness (Booth, 1994). The composer sees this musical moment as the opening of human awareness to the power of transformation represented by Christ. Maslanka is quick to point out that Christian imagery has great force for him personally but that *A Child's Garden of Dreams* is not "Christian" music. His feeling is that all religious traditions have their own imagery for the forces of transformation and that these could just as easily be substituted.

The second movement, "A drunken woman...," uses a literal quote of *Black Is the Color* (c.f., m. 8 of Movement 2). Maslanka composed this movement first, followed by I, III, IV, and V, and as the first composed, perhaps one should consider entering into the study of *A Child's Garden of Dreams* here as well. Once familiar with the *Here I Am* and *Epiphany* motives, you will discover elements of each embodied within *Black Is the Color*, in essence the central musical impulse of the entire five-movement work. Maslanka has said that his use of this tune was intuitive, but he felt it to be correct. The *drunken woman* represents a powerful involvement with life in the flesh on earth. As she falls in the water and is transformed, she passes from physical to spiritual awareness (Wubbenhorst, 1994).

With each of the dream images, Maslanka imagined a real picture into which he placed himself. This process, what is often called "lucid dreaming," allows the emotions and insights of the experience to come through the composer's own system. Through this, Maslanka has the sense of a connection in his unconscious where the dream imagery and music become one. As with the melodic exercise referred to at the start of this unit, it would be useful for conductor and performer alike to try lucid dreaming as a possible means of understanding the deeper impulses that run through this music. To really perform *A Child's Garden of Dreams*, you must get past the notes to the music. In the privacy of study, try opening your mind to enter the space of each dream image. Make the literal picture as clear as you can. Watch and follow as the dream image moves and changes. It feels like focused daydreaming. It may seem odd to you at first, but this exercise presents a direct means of affecting the transfer of musical ownership that this composer speaks so often and so passionately about.

Unit 7: Form and Structure

Maslanka does not think in terms of form as a preconception, but acknowledges that classical forms tend to emerge as an end result. The following form analysis is adapted from David Booth's wonderful DMA document, "An Analytical Study of David Maslanka's *A Child's Garden of Dreams*" (Booth, 1994). [This is a terrific treatise and one that is highly recommended to anyone interested in *A Child's Garden of Dreams*.] The musical examples are drawn from Wubbenhorst's 1991 *Thematic Compendium*, an unpublished analysis of melodic material from *A Child's Garden of Dreams*. M-Notes, i.e., "Maslanka-Notes," are comments shared with the author by David Maslanka regarding common interpretive errors.

M-Notes: Fast tempi in the whole piece must be truly at the marked speeds. Ensembles CAN play sixteenth at quarter 176, CAN do quarter at 192 in the last movement. It is always the conductor who is afraid to try. Tempi (fast and otherwise) require at least the minimum that is marked. It is important to study out the tempi with a metronome rather than guessing what the music seems to feel like. In the first and last movements, my tendency is to go slightly faster than marked. With regard to the organ, real organs have for the most part been unavailable. Substitute a synthesizer and work to make an agreeable sound. Harp can be synthesized, but the real thing is much preferred.

Movement I: There is a desert on the moon where the dreamer sinks so deeply into the ground that she reaches hell.

M-Notes: Demand true *f* and *ff* - true *p* and *pp*. Dynamic contrast is of real significance in this entire composition. Make dramatic differences. For example, in m. 5 of this movement the marimba is marked *mp*, but to give the effect, the player will have to play louder. At m. 57, sustained tones need accent, then back off so that sixteenth triplets can be heard. Horns at m. 67 can be open. The tam-tam at m. 74 must be heard without being overdone. I have never used the optional oboe/E-flat clarinet in place of trumpet at m. 86. From m. 107 to end, there IS a *diminuendo*, there is NOT a *ritardando*.

Section A: "Submergence below consciousness" (mm. 1-56)

m. 9: "Here I am"   m. 18: "Ascent" (partial)

m. 28: "Ascent"

m. 39: "Ascent" (full line)

m. 47: "Epiphany" motive

Section B: "Immersion into hell's inferno" (mm. 57-68)

m. 57: "Black is the color" (segment in retrograde)

m. 60: "Epiphany"

m. 64: "Black is the color" quote

Section C: "Transformation and reemergence" (mm. 69-111)

m. 75: "Epiphany"

m. 85

m. 97: "Harmonics—like insects on a summer night"

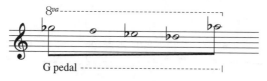

m. 100: "Epiphany"

m. 107

Movement II: A drunken woman falls into the water and comes out renewed and sober.

> *M-Notes:* Dynamics must be such that harp, piano, percussion, and slide whistle all come through. The absolutely steady and clear after-beat pulse is the key to the movement. "Imagination for sound" is important to consider as you create the melded timbre of alto flute (preferred to flute if available), whisper-muted trumpet, and bass clarinet. Marked dynamics for this trio provide a clue for timbrel balance.

Introduction: (mm. 1-6)
First Refrain:
 A1   (mm. 7-25) *Black Is the Color*

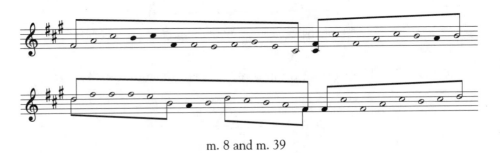

m. 8 and m. 39

 B1   (mm. 26-37) "Reflections" solo oboe

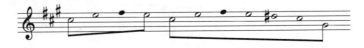

m. 26: "Reflections"

Second Refrain:
 A2   (mm. 38-56) *Black Is the Color*
 B2   (mm. 57-73) "Reflections" solo oboe

m. 57: "Epiphany" materials

Closing Resolution: (mm. 74-78)

Movement III: A horde of small animals frightens the dreamer. The animals increase to a tremendous size, and one of them devours the little girl.

M-Notes: Tempo at quarter note = 176! The damped piano in m. 1 doesn't work well. I have taken to having the cluster played staccato, *sffz*, without damping or pedal. Percussion dynamics should be carefully worked out throughout the movement. Most often people get excited and play too loud at the beginning and the end. When properly played, this movement should cause the nape hairs to rise. In mm. 108-113, more oboe and not too much alto saxophone. Note that in mm. 152 and 156 the crash cymbal and tam-tam are NOT in the scoring of these chords. Winds and brass must play the chords at mm. 152 and 156 with exactly the same intensity as those at mm. 140, 144, and 148.

Section A: Introduction and growth of the animals
  mm. 1-10   Drum groups
  mm. 11-28   Clusters and frantic "swirling"
  mm. 29-49   Entrance of the "Monster" [E-flat ascending to D-flat]
  mm. 50-93   "Monster" grows to tremendous size
  mm. 94-108   "Monster" achieves full size
Section B: "Cruel Joke," teasing and devouring of prey
  mm. 109-134 Devouring the dreamer (*A kiss is just a kiss*)

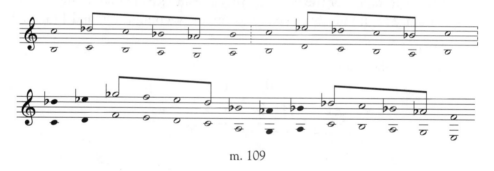

m. 109

  mm. 135-159 Drum groups as transition material
Section C: Voice of death triumphant
  mm. 140-159 "Terrible cry of the beast"

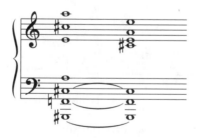

m. 140: "Terrible Cry of the Beast" (repeated 5 times)

  mm. 160-178 Drum groups in diminishing volume

Movement IV: A drop of water is seen, as it appears when looked at through a microscope. The girl sees that the drop is full of tree branches. This portrays the origin of the world.

> *M-Notes:* The formal organization of this movement is largely delineated by shifts in tempo as marked by double bars. This movement is the heart of the piece and presents the greatest challenges. The first task is to conceive the tempo structure. Many conductors simply ignore the marked tempi and go with what they think the music feels like. DON'T DO THIS! The whole structure of the movement depends on an accurate rendering of tempo structure. Of course there is some leeway and room for interpretation, but the foundation work is with a metronome. Measures 57-60 will require as much patient work as it takes to make the passage work. Take the time to do this. The tempo at m. 61 MUST be at least quarter note = 82. The oboe solo almost always wants to slow down. Be sure clarinets are heard in mm. 69-70 and mm. 95-96. At m. 71, the quarter MUST be a minimum 164 (twice 82). In m. 90, the quarter must be a minimum 82. Bass rhythms must be distinct in mm. 116 and 117. Measure 123 must be in the 74-78 range for the quarter. After the alto saxophone begins its solo in m. 132, it must become passionate between mm. 139 and 143.

Section A:

    a1   subsection

        mm. 1-20   Introduction

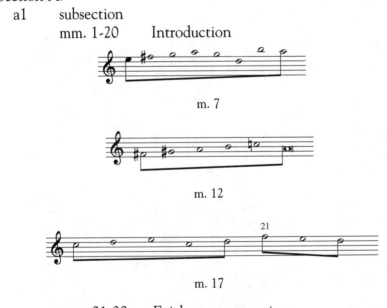

m. 7

m. 12

m. 17

        mm. 21-32   *Epiphany* permutations

m. 23

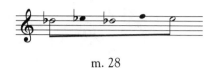

m. 28

mm. 33-44   Closing dissolves into a "fuzzy mist"

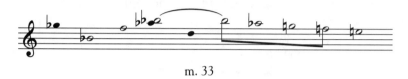

m. 33

b1   subsection
        mm. 45-47   Rising *Epiphany*-like contours
        mm. 48-56   Expressions of *Epiphany* and "Sunlight…"

"Epiphany"

m. 45

m. 51

m. 54

Section B:
c1   subsection
        mm. 57-60   Non-metered "Quiet Forest"
        mm. 61-70   *Epiphany* derivations and M2nd motive

m. 61 and 91

m. 62   m. 64

d subsection (double-time)
      mm. 71-89   Quotes from Movements I and III

m. 74

c2   subsection (*a tempo*)
      mm. 90-111   *Epiphany* derivations and M2nd motive

m. 99

m. 100

m. 105

m. 106

Section A':
    b2   subsection
      mm. 112-118 Build to climactic "…epiphany…"

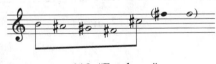

m. 118: "Epiphany"

mm. 119-127 *Epiphany* resolved and "Terrible cry" echo

m. 123

a2   subsection

    mm. 128-138 Recapitulation of opening material with solo oboe and alto saxophone *obligato*

    mm. 139-145 Saxophone emerges as solo voice

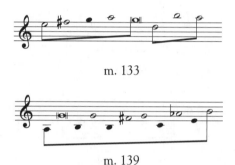

m. 133

m. 139

mm. 146-158 *Epiphany* voice development

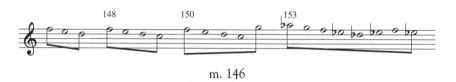

m. 146

    mm. 159-170 Last "Cry" from solo oboe and closing dissolve into the "fuzzy mist"

Movement V: An ascent into heaven, where pagan dances are being celebrated; and a descent into hell, where angels are doing good deeds.

M-Notes: The formal organization of this movement is marked by modulations between tonal centers of C and D-flat. I prefer the tempo a touch on the bright side. This movement is a study in keeping a steady tempo. Between mm. 33 and 39, the flutes should play 8va, and as written at m. 40. From mm. 49-78, the marimba, horns, tenor and baritone saxophones keep the pulse in this passage. Liven the pulse by adding accent to each beat. At m. 186, begin the *accelerando* early in this passage and get to quarter note =

192 by m. 193. Do not let the energy collapse at m. 209. The tempo must be minimum quarter note = 96. Tempo must stay absolutely steady in the last measures. I do mean "NO SLOWING."

Section A1   (mm. 1-32)

Wavy motion "water" motive and *Here I Am*

m. 1   m. 3

m. 16: "Epiphany"

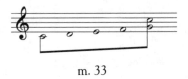

m. 20: "Here I am"

Section A2   (mm. 33-48)

Ensemble *ostinato* (Alison's motive) and *Here I Am* in 5/4

m. 33

Section A3   (mm. 49-78)

a1   subsection

mm. 49-64   "Memory of Poulenc" *wavy motion, Here I Am,* and *Epiphany*

m. 49: "Memory of Poulenc"   m. 50

m. 58: "Epiphany"

a2　　subsection

　　　　mm. 65-78　　Oboe solo then to clarinet – *Black Is the Color*

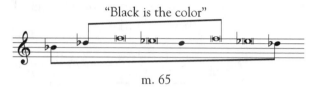

m. 65

Section B1　　(mm. 79-107)

b1　　subsection

　　　　mm. 79-95　　Four-note "Bubble" *ostinato* begins and builds with addition of "fancy march cadence" that plays against the established pulse until the climax at m. 96

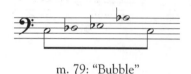

m. 79: "Bubble"

b2　　subsection

　　　　mm. 96-107　　*Ostinati* continue with displaced *Epiphany* sixteenths

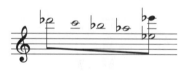

m. 96: "Epiphany"

Section C1　　(mm. 108-116)

　　　　　　Interlude based upon a fusion of *Here I Am* with *The Real Thing* 1960s Coca-Cola motive

m. 108: "Fusion Section"

Section D　　(mm. 117-137)

　　　　　　"Spiky, machine-like" derivations of elements from B1 and C1 with a rhythmically displaced trumpet *obligato* (mm. 119-137)

Section B2   (mm. 138-184)
   b3   subsection
       mm. 138-166 *Elevator chimes* gesture [A-flat, E-flat, C, A-flat]
              with b1 material

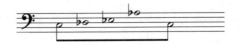

m. 138: "Bubble" motive returns

C pedal

m. 138

   b4   subsection
       mm. 167-184 Extended b2 material

m. 167

Section C2   (mm. 185-208)
          Stringendo version of C1 (fusion interlude)

Section A4   (mm. 209-242)
          Wavy motion, elevator chimes, and *Here I Am*

m. 210

"Here I am"

mm. 220, 227, and 232

Unit 8: Suggested Listening

David Maslanka:

A Child's Garden of Dreams
    (Cincinnati College-Conservatory of Music, Eugene Corporon,
      Conductor, KCD-11030)
    (University of Massachusetts-Amherst, Malcolm W. Rowell, Jr.,
      Conductor, HPD-233)

A Tuning Piece: Songs of Fall and Winter for Symphonic Band or Wind
    Ensemble

Concerto for Marimba and Band

Concerto for Piano, Winds, and Percussion

Four Pieces for Band

Golden Light - A Celebration Piece for Wind Ensemble

Heart Songs for Band or Wind Ensemble

Hell's Gate for Symphonic Band or Wind Ensemble
    (University of Arizona, Gregg I. Hanson, Conductor, Albany
      Records TROY 309)

In Memoriam for Wind Ensemble
    (Cincinnati Wind Symphony, Mallory Thompson, Conductor,
      Summit Records DCD 192)
    (University of Texas at Arlington, Ray Lichtenwalter, Conductor,
      TMEA 90-MC-2)

Laudamus Te for Symphonic Band or Wind Ensemble
    (University of Arizona, Gregg I. Hanson, Conductor, Albany
      Records TROY 309)

Mass for Wind Ensemble, SATB Chorus, Boy Choir, and soloists
    (University of Arizona, Gregg I. Hanson, Conductor, Albany
      Records TROY 221-22)
    (Illinois State University, Stephen K. Steele, Conductor, TD14701)

Montana Music: Chorale Variations for Symphonic Wind Ensemble

Morning Star - A New Song for Wind Band

Prelude on a Gregorian Tune for Band

Rollo Takes a Walk for Band

Sea Dreams Concerto for Two Horns and Wind Orchestra

Symphony No. 2 for Concert Band
    (University of Massachusetts-Amherst, Malcolm W. Rowell, Jr.,
       Conductor, HPD-233)
    (University of Arizona, Gregg I. Hanson, Conductor, Albany
       Records TROY 309)
Symphony No. 3 for Symphonic Wind Ensemble
    (University of Connecticut, Gary D. Green, Conductor)
Symphony No. 4 for Symphonic Wind Ensemble
    (University of Texas at Austin, Jerry Junkin, Conductor, TMEA
       1994-MCD-2)
Tears for Symphonic Band or Wind Ensemble
    (University of Massachusetts-Amherst, Malcolm W. Rowell, Jr.,
       Conductor, Albany Records TROY 206)
UFO Dreams - Concerto for Euphonium and Wind Ensemble
Variants on a Hymn Tune for Euphonium Solo and Young Wind Ensemble

Unit 9: Additional References and Resources

Booth, David Martin. "An Analytical Study of David Maslanka's *A Child's Garden of Dreams*." DMA document, The University of Oklahoma, 1994.

Maslanka, David. Telephone interviews with and letters to Thomas Wubbenhorst, 10 October 1989 - 14 February 1991.

Maslanka, David. Letter to Thomas Wubbenhorst, 17 June 1999a.

Maslanka, David. Telephone interview with Thomas Wubbenhorst, 29 June 1999b, Kennesaw, GA - Missoula, MT.

Maslanka, David. Telephone interview with Thomas Wubbenhorst, 5 July 1999c, Kennesaw, GA - Missoula, MT.

Wubbenhorst, Thomas Martin. "David Maslanka's *A Child's Garden of Dreams*: A Perspective of the Musical Economy of Means." Transcript of a lecture-recital, University of Missouri - Columbia, 1991.

Wubbenhorst, Thomas Martin. "Thematic Compendium: An Analysis of Melodic Material from *A Child's Garden of Dreams*." Unpublished document, University of Missouri - Columbia, 1991.

Wubbenhorst, Thomas Martin. "A Child's Garden of Dreams: Conversations with David Maslanka," *CBDNA Journal*, Number 10 Spring/Summer 1994, 2-8.

Author Notes:

Special thanks to Dr. Susan Tepping — School of Music, Georgia State University — for the preparation of the musical examples included in this *Teacher Resource Guide*.

Contributed by:

Thomas Martin Wubbenhorst
Associate Professor of Music
Georgia State University
Atlanta, Georgia

Teacher Resource Guide

Apotheosis of This Earth

Karel Husa
(b. 1921)

Unit 1: Composer

Karel Husa was born on August 7, 1921, in Prague, Czechoslovakia. He studied violin and piano, but his family had hopes that he would pursue a career in engineering. He began his engineering study, but the school was soon closed due to the Nazi occupation of Czechoslovakia. He enrolled at the Prague Conservatory and began his studies in composition. After World War II, Husa completed his studies at the Conservatory and moved to Paris, where he enrolled in the Ecole Normale. There he studied composition with Arthur Honegger and Nadia Boulanger, and conducting with Andre Cluytens. The Academy of Musical Arts in Prague accepted his studies in Paris and awarded him the Doctorate of Music in 1947. Husa remained in Paris, composing and conducting throughout Europe. In 1959, he accepted a faculty position at Cornell University in Ithaca, New York, and he and his family became American citizens. In 1969, Husa won the Pulitzer Prize in Music for his *String Quartet No. 3*. He has composed works for orchestra, chorus, band, voice, piano, and chamber ensembles. Husa's compositional style is uncompromisingly modern, often employing massive structures and extended techniques for the instrumentalists. He often takes his inspiration from issues and events of our own time.

Unit 2: Composition

Apotheosis of This Earth was commissioned by the Michigan School Band and Orchestra Association and dedicated to Dr. William D. Revelli, Conductor of Bands at the University of Michigan, upon his retirement. It was premiered by

Dr. Revelli and the University of Michigan Symphony Band in 1971. The work depicts mankind's degradation of the earth and its possible destruction if these trends are not reversed. The work is approximately twenty-five minutes in length and is in three movements: "Apotheosis," "Tragedy of Destruction," and "Postscript." It is a remarkable work – intense, violent, and finally introspective – presenting innumerable challenges to the ensemble. In 1990, Professor Husa scored a version of *Apotheosis of This Earth* for wind ensemble and chorus.

Unit 3: Historical Perspective

Professor Husa has provided the following remarks:

> The composition of *Apotheosis of This Earth* was motivated by the present desperate stage of mankind and its immense problems with everyday killings, war, hunger, extermination of fauna, huge forest fires, and critical contamination of the whole environment.
>
> Man's brutal possession and misuse of nature's beauty – if continued at today's reckless speed – can only lead to catastrophe. The composer hopes that the destruction of this beautiful earth can be stopped so that the tragedy of destruction – musically projected here in the second movement – and the desolation of its aftermath (the "postscript" of the third movement) can exist only as fantasy, never to become reality.

Husa's particular concern for the plight of whales is manifested in the "whale sounds" of the second movement, represented by ascending *glissandi* in the winds. Husa gained insight into these sounds in Ithaca from Dr. Roger Payne and his wife, Katie Boynton, who study whale communication.

Unit 4: Technical Considerations

Apotheosis of This Earth is a difficult work that places great technical demands on the performers. Extremes of register and demanding technical passages are among the many challenges. The work makes use of contemporary notation as well as a variety of extended instrumental techniques, including quarter-tones, pitch bending, *glissandi*, flutter tongue, indefinite high and low pitches, indefinite change of speed, and a variety of mute effects for the brasses. As in many of Husa's works, a large percussion section is employed.

Unit 5: Stylistic Considerations

Apotheosis of This Earth uses massive textures and highly dissonant sonorities in its construction. The work also makes use of aleatoric elements. In the first movement (mm. 134-141), the xylophone presents a cadenza-like passage with durations in seconds. In the second movement, motivic fragments are again stated in an unmetered environment (m. 121), creating a highly chaotic effect. The work is highly evocative: the "whale sounds" of the second movement (particularly the horn *glissandi* of mm. 132-140) represent an anguished and moving cry for help. In the third movement, the use of vocal recitation produces a striking stylistic effect. Here, the syllabic repetition provides a haunting counterpoint to the accompanying wind activity, and finally coalesces into a complete statement of "This Beautiful Earth."

Unit 6: Musical Elements

MOVEMENT I: "APOTHEOSIS"
With a single A in the glockenspiel, "the earth first appears as a point of light in the universe." This begins the methodical unfolding of a twelve-note pitch series and a textural expansion that continues as a "descending *crescendo*," or wedge, through the first section of the work. The work's harmonic and melodic material is derived from the twelve-note pitch collection, manifested as four trichordal pitch sets:

Example 1: Trichordal Pitch Sets

A highly dissonant, increasingly dense texture is built from the trichordal interval set, particularly major and minor seconds. The texture expands downward through the ensemble, with an accompanying *crescendo*. A number of important melodic and rhythmic motives begin to appear based on trichordal pitch material. These first occur in the percussion and continue in the low woodwinds (mm. 21-39).

The texture continues to expand with the entrance of the brasses, and trumpet *glissandi* appear in mm. 41-45. The low brass complete the textural expansion with a statement based on the initial trichord (mm. 49-52). An extended melodic line begins in m. 53 in the horns. The horn melody is accompanied by a quarter note quintuplet rhythmic motive in the timpani. This motive increases in frequency as the *crescendo* builds. These melodic and rhythmic elements are developed and expanded, reaching a massive climax in m. 133. A new section begins in m. 134, featuring a frenetic cadenza-like statement in the xylophone based on the opening trichord:

Example 2: Xylophone Statement (m. 134)

The dissonant texture again expands downward through the winds as the xylophone becomes more agitated. The xylophone statement finally gives way to imitative statements in the upper woodwinds, which eventually diminish in number as the section closes (mm. 141-142). The woodwind figures occur in free time, creating a frenzied, almost chaotic effect.

The final section (mm. 143-167) recalls motives and sustained pitch clusters from the opening sections. This final series of statements begins violently in the percussion and brasses, then quickly diminishes in intensity as final statements in the upper woodwinds recall motives from the xylophone cadenza. The movement concludes as quietly as it began.

MOVEMENT II: "TRAGEDY OF DESTRUCTION"

The second movement begins with an introduction in the melodic percussion, which continues as an *ostinato* in the opening section. In m. 5, the trumpets, horns, and saxophones begin to introduce the movement's principal pitch-motto. This motto begins with a single sixteenth note, in octaves, and is subsequently built as a pitch succession based on trichordal material. Each phrase begins the building process anew, extending the pitch succession. The isorhythmic texture also thickens with each phrasal statement, building increasingly dissonant sonorities based on the intervals of the opening trichord:

Example 3: Vertical Structures in Pitch-Motto Statements

In m. 38, the pitch succession gives way to a highly agitated line in the upper woodwinds, followed by a quarter note triplet figure (m. 40) in the lowest voices, again derived from the trichordal interval set. In m. 50, the pitch-motto reappears, now fragmented with staggered entrances, creating a more chaotic effect. This fragmentation continues, alternating with trilled pitch clusters in the upper woodwinds and *glissandi* in the trombones.

Example 4: Pitch-Motto Statements (mm. 55-56)

This chaotic activity finally yields in m. 62 to a highly dissonant cluster of minor seconds in the upper woodwinds. This rhythmic *ostinato* begins a new section and is derived from the motto's sextuplet figure. These figures alternate with more sustained rhythms in the brasses and low woodwinds. In m. 82, the upper woodwind *ostinato* gains a melodic element, beginning with a unison statement in the clarinets:

Example 5: Clarinet *Ostinato* (mm. 82-83)

The texture then expands as voices join in rhythmic unison. The result is a relentless rhythmic drive that culminates in a series of brass *glissandi* and sustained pitch clusters (beginning in m. 97), as the percussion continue the *ostinato*. Rhythmic fragments begin to return (mm. 104-114) and finally give way to a chaotic, highly fragmented series of statements based on trichordal pitch material in free time (m. 121).

The intensity increases further with a frenetic xylophone cadenza with upper woodwinds flutter tonguing in the extreme upper register (m. 129-131). This frenzied activity is soon joined by horn *glissandi* and flutter-tongued pitch clusters in the low brass. In m. 140, the texture widens further as the trumpets and saxophones are asked to play the highest possible pitches, and the low brass and low woodwinds the lowest possible pitches. In m. 166, the pitch-motto returns, undergoes a final aleatoric treatment in m. 175, then yields to a sustained pedal in the extreme low register, which dies away amid progressively elongated rhythmic figures in the percussion.

MOVEMENT III: "POSTSCRIPT"

The third movement asks the question, "Why have we let it happen?" Its desolate quiet is presented in stark contrast to the violent, destructive elements of the first two movements. The solemn opening section in the clarinets and flutes gives way in m. 12 to a haunting, fragmented recitation of "This Beautiful Earth." The texture begins to expand, and various rhythmic and melodic motives are recalled from the first two movements. A second syllabic recitation (mm. 23-25) is followed by a series of staggered rhythmic figures drawn from motives of the second movement. The textural expansion and rhythmic activity, however, create a very different effect here. Instead of producing the chaotic violence of the second movement, the hushed activity of the "Postscript" carries a haunting feeling of resignation and regret.

The clarinets again begin a unison melodic statement in m. 28. A recitation soon follows amid hushed, sustained chords in the winds. The texture begins to thin, and a unison statement of "This Beautiful Earth" finally appears in m. 47. The voices fade and the texture thins further with a series of solo woodwind pitches and a statement of repeated pitches in the horn. Another unison vocal recitation fades underneath a final statement in the piccolo recalling the xylophone motives of the first and second movements. The final measures die away in the upper woodwinds and melodic percussion as a single voice is heard: "Beautiful."

Unit 7: Form and Structure

SECTION	MEASURE	EVENT AND SCORING
Movement I: "Apotheosis"		
Section I	1-52	Texture expands from a single pitch in the glockenspiel; dissonances arise based on trichordal intervals
	53-70	Extended melodic line in horns; texture thickens, intensity builds
	71-119	Melodic line with dotted rhythm appears in woodwinds with dissonant voicing; moves to saxophones, horns, trumpets; flutter tongue in brasses, pitch bending in woodwinds
	120-133	Massive texture continues to build in intensity; trumpets, woodwinds move to upper register
Section II	134-142	Xylophone cadenza in free time against dissonant web in upper woodwinds and trumpets; aleatoric fragmentation of pitch material in upper woodwinds
	143-167	Pitch clusters in brass, woodwinds; texture thins as final statements appear in flute, E-flat clarinet, oboe
Movement II: "Tragedy of Destruction"		
Section I	1-4	Introductory figures in melodic percussion over low brass/low woodwind pedal
	5-36	Pitch-motto based on trichordal material built in five successive statements with increasing level of dissonance
	37-62	Melodic activity becomes increasingly chaotic; *glissandi* in low brass; pitch-motto becomes fragmented

Section	Measure	Event and Scoring
Section II	63-81	Rhythmic *ostinato* in woodwinds (minor second pitch cluster)
	82-99	Clarinets begin melodic *ostinato*; winds join *ostinato* as texture and intensity build
	100-118	*Ostinato* continues in percussion amid sustained dissonances; winds rejoin *ostinato*, building intensity
Section III	119-128	Pitch-motto presented in aleatoric environment; fragmented and chaotic
	129-131	Xylophone cadenza based on trichordal pitch set; flutter-tongued octaves in upper woodwinds
	132-141	Xylophone continues (unmetered) with sustained dissonances in winds; violent horn *glissandi*; massive textures
	142-145	Pitch-motto reappears in upper woodwinds in approximate retrograde
	146-165	Sustained pitch clusters in winds over rapid figures in melodic percussion
Coda	166-175	Pitch-motto returns in trumpets, horns, woodwinds; aleatoric (m. 175)
	176-183	Extreme low brass/low woodwind pedal; gradually diminishes in intensity as percussion motives become augmented
Movement III: "Postscript"		
Section I	1-11	Clarinets build unison (echo tones); dissonance builds in upper woodwinds
	12-24	Syllabic recitation in voices; dissonant pulsation in trumpets with Harmon mutes followed by echo tones in clarinets, trichordal statements in percussion; restatement in voices
	25-27	Agitated rhythmic motive staggered in woodwinds based on first trichord; sextuplet *ostinato* in tom-toms
Section II	28-46	Unison clarinet statement now in upper register; vocal statements staggered amid sustained dissonance
	47-56	Unison statement: "Beautiful Earth"; solo woodwind statements appear with trichordal motives in percussion

SECTION	MEASURE	EVENT AND SCORING
	57-68	Final unison vocal statement: "This Beautiful Earth"; piccolo recalls xylophone motive; final statements in solo voice, flute, and xylophone as movement dies away

Unit 8: Suggested Listening

Band/Wind ensemble works by Karel Husa:

Al Fresco for Concert Band
An American Te Deum (with Chorus and Baritone Solo)
Apotheosis of This Earth
Concertino for Piano and Winds
Concerto for Alto Saxophone and Concert Band
Concerto for Percussion and Wind Ensemble
Concerto for Trumpet and Wind Ensemble
Concerto for Wind Ensemble
Divertimento for Brass and Percussion
Elegy for Wind Ensemble
Fanfare for Brass Ensemble
Festive Ode (Highgate) [with chorus]
Music for Prague 1968
Smetana Fanfare

Unit 9: Additional References and Resources

Haithcock, Michael. "Karel Husa Talks About Composing." *The Instrumentalist*, April 1982, Vol. 36, no. 9, 22-25.

Husa, Karel. "Apotheosis of This Earth: Some Thoughts." *The ABA Journal of Band Research*, 1973, Vol. 9, no. 2, 6-9.

Husa, Karel. "Meet the Composer: Karel Husa—Apotheosis of This Earth." *The Instrumentalist*, August 1973, Vol. 28, no. 1, 35-36.

Paynter, John. "New Music Review—Apotheosis of This Earth." *The Instrumentalist*, May 1972, Vol. 26, no. 10, 76.

Scatterday, Mark. "Karel Husa: Apotheosis of This Earth." *BD Guide*, September/October 1993, 10-20.

Contributed by:

Bradley P. Ethington
Associate Director of Bands
Syracuse University
Syracuse, New York

Teacher Resource Guide

Arctic Dreams
(for symphonic wind ensemble)
Michael Colgrass
(b. 1932)

Unit 1: Composer

Michael Colgrass was born on April 22, 1932, in Chicago and was raised in the small town of Brookfield, Illinois. His first musical experiences were as a jazz drummer in the Chicago area from 1944-49, and in 1956, he graduated from the University of Illinois, where he studied percussion with Paul Price and composition with Eugene Weigel. Colgrass also studied composition with Lukas Foss at the Berkshire Music Center and Tanglewood Summer Festival in 1952, and with Darius Milhaud at the Aspen Music Festival in 1953. He continued his studies in composition several years later with Wallingford Riegger (1958-59) and Ben Weber (1959-62). After serving twenty-one months as a timpanist in the Seventh Army Symphony Orchestra in Germany, Colgrass moved to New York City in 1956. While in New York City, Colgrass freelanced as a percussionist with such diverse groups as Dizzy Gillespie, the original *West Side Story* production on Broadway, Stravinsky's Columbia Recording Orchestra, the Modern Jazz Quartet, and the New York Philharmonic.

Colgrass has received widespread recognition and numerous awards for his compositions. He has received commissions from many prominent organizations, including the New York Philharmonic, the Boston Symphony Orchestra, the Detroit Symphony Orchestra, and the Toronto Symphony Orchestra. His works have been performed by all of the major American and Canadian symphony orchestras, and they continue to be performed by major ensembles throughout the world. Colgrass won the Pulitzer Prize in Music in 1978 for *Déjà vu* (for four percussionists and orchestra), a work commissioned and premiered by the New York Philharmonic. He also won an Emmy Award from the National Association of Television Arts and Sciences in 1982 for the documentary film *Soundings: The Music of Michael Colgrass*. Other prizes include two Guggenheim Fellowships, grants from the Rockefeller Foundation and the Ford Foundation, first prizes in the Barlow International, the Sudler International, and the National Band Association Composition Competitions (*Winds of Nagual*), and the 1988 Jules Leger Prize for New Chamber Music. He has composed over fifty works for stage, soloists, chamber ensembles, orchestras, and wind ensembles. Colgrass' original scores for wind ensemble include *Winds of Nagual* (1985), *Arctic Dreams* (1991), and *Urban Requiem* (1995). Colgrass transcribed *Déjà vu* for wind ensemble in 1986.

Although he makes his living as a composer, Colgrass devotes much of his time to presenting workshops in the psychology and technique of performance, where he teaches his own blend of Grotowski physical training, mime, dance, neuro-linguistic programming, and self-hypnosis. He also enjoys giving workshops for children in the creative process.

Unit 2: Composition

Arctic Dreams is a tone poem for symphonic wind ensemble, inspired by the Arctic and by the lives and legends of the Inuit (the "eskimos") who live there. Colgrass lived for a short time with an Inuit family in Pangnirtung, Baffin Island, just north of the Arctic Circle. He was fascinated by their way of life, their humor, and their sense of mystery and wonder at the awesome nature around them. To Colgrass, the Arctic represents a great unconscious, and it is from Barry Lopez's modern classic, "Arctic Dreams," that the composer draws the title for this massive and fascinating work.

Arctic Dreams is a large-scale work set in seven movements. The first movement, "Inuit Landscape," begins with a solo trombone representing a lone human being calling out over a vast space amidst the sounds of wind and storm. The second movement is titled "Throat Singing with Laughter," in which Colgrass presents the indomitable spirit of the Inuits through their sense of humor. Throat singing is a unique form of Inuit music, created by the rapid in- and out-takes of breath on fast rhythms, which incites an almost continual laughter in the singers and onlookers alike. The third movement, "The Whispering Voices of the Spirits Who Ride with the Lights in the Sky," presents mysterious mutterings that make a gradual transformation into the dancing and undulating lights of the aurora borealis. The fourth movement, "Polar Night," is a montage of Arctic sounds (ghosts, wind, and wolves), through which the listener hears the voices of Norwegian sailors whose boat is frozen in the ice for the winter.

The fifth movement is titled "Spring Light: Ice Floating in the Sun." This movement depicts the end of winter and the beginning of the spring thaw. The intensification of the musical sounds represents the constant increase of arctic sunlight to an almost unbearable brightness. This movement leads directly into the sixth movement, "The Hunt," which portrays the resurrection of life during the spring and the rituals and activities surrounding the start of the long-awaited caribou hunting season. The final movement is titled "Drum Dancer," a joyous and brilliantly rhythmic celebration inspired by the sculptures of Karoo Ashevik.

Unit 3: Historical Perspective

Arctic Dreams was commissioned by James Keene for the 100th Anniversary of the University of Illinois Symphonic and Concert Bands, and to honor the retirement of Jack McKenzie, Dean of the College of Fine and Applied Arts. The composer acknowledges The Canada Council for the Senior Arts Grant that enabled him to travel to the Arctic for research and development for *Arctic Dreams*. The work is respectfully dedicated to Rosie Okpik and Enukie Akulukjuk of Pangnirtung.

    Arctic Dreams was premiered by James Keene, conducting the University of Illinois Symphonic Band in the Foellinger Great Hall of the Krannert Center for the Performing Arts on January 26, 1991.

Unit 4: Technical Considerations

Virtuosic part writing along with technical demands of the highest order for woodwinds, brass, and percussion typify the music of Colgrass, and such is certainly the case in *Arctic Dreams*. In the preparation and performance of this work, the composer inherently places the responsibilities of contemporary professionalism and excellence in training, preparation, and musicianship in the hands of the conductor and ensemble members alike. The rhythmic elements throughout *Arctic Dreams* are complex and diverse, with substantial metrical demands and frequently changing tempi and meter. The tonal language is very powerful, imaginative, and expressive, and Colgrass is continually juxtaposing a tonal sense of melodic lyricism with a more complex presence of harmonic atonality.

    The composer indicates that the scoring of *Arctic Dreams* is for symphonic wind ensemble and specifically calls for the following wind instruments: six flutes (six double piccolos and three double alto flutes), three oboes, three bassoons, contrabassoon, E-flat clarinet, six B-flat clarinets, bass clarinet, B-flat contrabass clarinet, soprano saxophone, alto saxophone, baritone saxophone, six trumpets, six horns, six trombones (two bass trombones), two euphoniums, and two tubas. The score also calls for one player on celesta and piano, one harp, an accordion, two contrabasses, and an optional fife.

    The extensive percussion score calls for six players and includes the following instruments: timpani, bongos, two conga drums, two piccolo snares, two concert snares, two field drums, two bass drums, three large cymbals, medium gong, large gong, two water gongs, two triangles, a string of free-hanging bells, two sets of sleigh bells, medium alarm bell, reco-reco, sandpaper blocks, lion's roar, crotales, glockenspiel, Parsifal bells, vibraphone, two sets of chimes, and xylophone. Although it is possible to use members of the wind ensemble for the necessary vocal parts in "Throat Singing with Laughter" and "Polar Night," it is recommended that the conductor utilize experienced singers. All of the above-mentioned parts are essential for performance, and outstanding soloists are required on trombone, oboe, flute, soprano saxophone, bassoon, piccolo (optional E-flat clarinet), baritone saxophone, trumpet, and all percussion.

Unit 5: Stylistic Considerations

Arctic Dreams is a tone poem of great sweep and expressive power that combines Colgrass' own experiences of living above the Arctic Circle with an Inuit family with images from Barry Lopez's book. The work is in large part defined by the presence of a unifying theme in each of the seven movements. The dominant thematic element, while enhancing the unification of the work, promotes a strong sense of uniqueness and identity in each of the movements through a brilliant progression of thematic transformations. The effect of the lone Inuit singing out over the tundra in "Inuit Landscape" is to be heroic and lyrical in character. The soloist is surrounded by the wind and flurries of blowing Arctic snow, effectively presented by the *portamenti*, flurries of scales, trills, and flutter-tongued passages in the upper woodwinds and brass. Other effects include the shifting and cracking of ice deep beneath the surface (a common sound in the Arctic), presented by the bass drum and powerful chord clusters, and a sense of cold and isolation in the wide-open spaces that is portrayed through the sounds of open chords and the dark, foreboding harmonies.

"Throat Singing with Laughter" is a high-spirited and imaginative movement inspired by the spirit of the Inuit, who are great practical jokers and have a wonderful sense of humor. The Inuit laugh easily and frequently, which is perhaps due to the conditions in which they live. Their daily existence in the life-threatening conditions of the Arctic reminds them that they are not in control of their environment and that some higher power is. This relieves them from the pressures of life that those in a more modernized society feel in a technological culture – a culture in which many humans presuppose control over the elements of life. Humans can't control nature, and the conflict between what humans feel they should be able to and what they are actually able to do creates stress, which is endemic to technological living.

In "Whispering Voices," the idea is for the ensemble to be as light, gossamer, and ethereal as possible. A series of solo passages are intended to be *quasi-rubato* while being accompanied by quietly sustained chords in the winds, celesta, and harp. Brief interludes and ad-lib measures reveal ethereal "mutterings," and it is through these "mutterings" that impressions of the aurora borealis are ultimately revealed.

"Polar Night" is a mysterious-sounding movement that utilizes a series of "non-traditional sound effects" from members of the wind section. The flutes and clarinets (and occasionally low brass) provide the ominous sounds of the blowing Arctic wind (specific performance instructions provided by the composer) along with the distant cries of the wolves (trombone) that reaffirms the spirit of this movement. The wind effects are open to free improvisation, and the intent of these effects should make the listeners want to "put up their collars to stay warm." Other factors unique to this movement include spine-tingling "ghost voices" (that should sound like an eerie kind of spirit or wind) and the Norwegian sailor band. The stranded band of sailors sing from afar (off stage), with rough, low, uncultivated voices, and seem to slur the words as if drunk. The sailors fade in and out for an effect similar to that of a radio phasing in and out of clarity through the wind.

The intent of "Spring Light: Ice Floating in the Sun" is to make the band shimmer with color. This movement begins with the faintest glimpse of light and gradually intensifies through the effects of a slowly sustained ensemble *crescendo*. The ensemble ultimately achieves a powerful climax, increasing in brilliance to the maximum levels of a blinding radiance. This leads directly into "The Hunt," the penultimate movement that reveals an exotic ritualistic episode (seemingly paganistic), with a dialogue between solo piccolo, baritone saxophone, and timpani. A powerfully dissonant chorus interrupts a short interlude, and this leads directly into the start of "the hunt." Thundering sounds of thousands of approaching caribou (muffled drums), solo snare drums depicting rifle shots, and painful animal outcries (low brass) bring the movement to a staggering conclusion.

As the title suggests in the final movement ("Drum Dancer"), the spirit of the music reveals the basic impressions of tribal dancing and celebrations reminiscent of Inuit life. The first portion of the movement brings forth an extensive series of dialogues between the highly rhythmic and dance-like percussion and tunefully brilliant passages in the ensemble winds. The middle section combines a series of imaginative scenes that portray images of Inuit life with elements of reprise from earlier movements. The work concludes with a sequence of intensification for the entire ensemble that builds in sound, energy, and mass – all directed toward the powerful and triumphal climax of the final measure.

Unit 6: Musical Elements

Much of the musical language presented in *Arctic Dreams* defies classification and is perhaps easier to listen to than to describe. The unifying theme and melodic style are lyrical and passionate (the composer spent a good amount of time developing the theme prior to starting the actual work). Each movement presents the unifying thematic materials in such a manner that the entire work can be conceptualized as developmental variations on a theme. The harmonic content at times seems strictly tonal (e.g., in a definite key and consequently subject to traditional tonal relationships).

Unit 7: Form and Structure

MEASURE   EVENT AND SCORING

Movement I: "Inuit Landscape"

1   Free recitative, open bar, trombone soloist (amplified if possible) represents lone Inuit heroically singing out over the vast Arctic tundra; F-sharp minor tonal center

2-45   Winds and percussion provide extensive accompaniment for the soloist; sounds of the ensemble portray the chilling effects and sounds of the Arctic extreme; scales, trills, *portamenti*, and flutter tongues in upper brass and woodwinds allude to the effects of wind, snow, and flurries; percussion and chord cluster effects represent shifting and cracking of ice deep beneath the surface; dark and foreboding harmonies promote a sense of cold, isolation, and wilderness, while the open chords are characteristic of the harmonic style, depicting wide-open space

Movement II: "Throat-Singing with Laughter"

46-55   Segue into movement from "Inuit Landscape"; introduction of "throat-singing"; distant sounds from throat-singers, interludes of woodwind *portamenti*, dark and open harmonic colors continue mysterious nature of materials presented in first movement

56-65   Sequence of male and female throat-singers accompanied by C major thematic materials in upper woodwinds; the organized rhythmic sounds of the throat-singing are interrupted by the laughter of the throat-singers themselves (usually women – essentially a "laugh session" at times) and by others standing nearby

66-69   Interlude of rhythmically disjunct passages; voices of onlooking Inuit men responding to the throat-singers with guttural voices, similar to masculine Inuit mutterings; use of "lion's roar" and "sandpaper blocks" as primary percussive instruments can represent "gruff male outcries" and "sniffling," respectively

70-88   Continued sequence of throat-singing and laughter; an initial spirit of ease and comfort, in which a sense of melody begins to evolve out of the laughter; elements

MEASURE	EVENT AND SCORING
	of surprise follow, characterized by frequent interruptions of the throat-singing patterns by abrupt laughter
89-96	Interlude of rhythmically disjunct passages; extended laughter with supporting orchestration that promotes sensations of randomness and improvisation; effects of free laughing make this sound unmeasured and some what spontaneous
97-end	Celebratory, high-spirited conclusion that combines free laughter with rhythmic laughter; the wind ensemble scoring provides for the alignment of selected voices with the "laughter" while other voices create a bright and joyful concluding statement of the thematic materials

Movement III: "The Whispering Voices..."

112-119	Oboe solo passage, first of several subsequent thematic statements; unifying theme surrounded by subtle and mysterious presence of celesta and softly sustained flutes
120-121	Interlude #1; movement of lights or other spiritual figures in the Arctic skies can be related to brief passages in clarinets and muted trumpets
122-126	Continuation of theme in soprano saxophone, supported by accompaniment of harp and softly muted trumpets
127-130	Interlude #2; slightly longer and enhanced instrumentation than in Interlude #1
131	First of four ad-lib measures that are essentially extensions of the interludes; three-way dialogue in flutes and low woodwinds, and water gong effect (as noted in score) of a "mumbling weird creature"; each ad-lib measure is different, which enhances a sense of changing perspective and increasing mystery in the nature of the music
132-136	Continuation of thematic material in solo flute, accompanied by celesta and a supporting harmonic and timbrel cast of flutes, oboes, and clarinets
137-140	Interlude #3; similar to before, but again longer and more inclusive
141	Ad-lib measure #2, emphasizing four-way dialogue in trumpets, trombones, and French horns
142-151	Continuation of theme in soprano saxophone

MEASURE	EVENT AND SCORING
	accompanied by harp and muted brass; general texture becomes more complex, enhanced by the inclusion of "mutterings" or "whispering voices" from the previous interludes
152-157	Bridge of melodic line scored for piccolo soli (*senza vibrato*) with an accompaniment of "mutterings" in harp, celesta, and assorted woodwinds
158	Ad-lib measure #3, dialogue of murmuring and mutterings of several in flutes, saxophones, bassoons, and trumpets
159-163	Continuation of thematic "bridge" in soli piccolo amidst more chattering in the ghost voices; glockenspiel support for the piccolo line enhances the thematic presence and creates a more "ethereal" presence
164-167	Interlude and transitional passage; intensification of sounds can allude to winds blowing curtains of lights and more activity in the ghostly spirits
168	Ad-lib measure #4, "like blinking lights," with more involvement of percussion instruments; *pizzicato* harp and contrabass enhance percussive sonorities in general
169-199	Concluding thematic section, utilizing parallelism in the flutes and clarinets; continual presence of the mallet percussion, celesta, and harp enhance the ethereal effect, while the brighter tempo indicates increased celestial activity
200	Final ad-lib measure; overall effect is of "gossamer curtains undulating in the sky" (aurora borealis), effectively provided in an extended *diminuendo* with detailed, yet seemingly randomized, assignments for percussion, celesta, piano, harp, and contrabass

Movement IV: "Polar Night"

201-202	Introduction of "polar wind" effects in piccolo, flutes, and clarinets
203-204	Distant and mysterious wolf cry effect in trombone (bucket mute), supported by ominous sonority of low bassoon, French horn, and contrabass amidst the "polar wind"
205-209	Bassoon solo; introduction of thematic material
209-214	Interlude; sequence of ghost voices, polar wind, and three distant wolf cries

MEASURE	EVENT AND SCORING
215-219	Brief continuation of thematic material (bassoon), concluding with lone wolf cry
220-233	Interlude; polar wind, distant sounds of gruff and drunken Norwegian sailors singing (phasing in and out); mystical sonority enhanced by soft chordal presence in trumpets (Harmon mutes)
233-237	Continuation of theme, with parallel presence in ghost voices; continued sound effects of Arctic wind
238-244	Brief interlude for Norwegian sailors
245-251	Continuation of theme in bassoon and ghost voices amidst dark harmonic sonorities and polar wind
252-262	Final sailor chorus sequence
263-277	Final thematic statement (bassoon solo), supporting sounds in ghost voices, polar wind effects, distant wolf cry, and dark harmonic sonority of low woodwinds, French horns, and contrabass

Movement V: "Spring Light: Ice Floating in the Sun"

278-286	Light emerging into the sun. Quasi "niente" beginning, gradual intensification of ensemble volume and brightness as dynamic levels and instrumentation are increased
286-303	Introduction of thematic material; thematic ambiguity due to the parallelism of densely structured harmonies that seem to absorb a clearer presence of a true melodic line; the basic effect is enhanced rhythmically through a sense of melodic augmentation and hemiola, and by a frequency of colorful dynamic swells
304-313	Continuation of thematic material with effects of intensifying brightness provided through increasing dynamic levels and a sonority of brass and enhanced percussion (glockenspiel, chimes, vibraphone)
314-329	Final sequence of thematic and ensemble sonority intensification, increasing to levels of unbearable brightness and blinding radiance in the final four measures

Movement VI: "The Hunt"

330-364	Thematic elements introduced through melodic dialogue between solo piccolo (optional E-flat clarinet) and baritone saxophone; ritualistic and violent paganistic atmosphere enhanced through character of solo melodic lines, accompaniment in bass voices, and timpani solo

MEASURE	EVENT AND SCORING
365-372	Thematic interlude, mysterious and spiritual character portrayed through slow *glissandi* and scalar passages in alto flute, clarinets, muted trombones, celesta, harp, and contrabass; theme initially provided in solo E-flat clarinet and followed in close imitation by soprano saxophone and oboe
373-382	Final presentation of thematic materials through powerful and violent ensemble chorus; final phase of the ritualistic episode leading into the start of the hunt
383-389	Hunt sequence featuring the approaching sounds of thousands of stampeding caribou; the initial open measure provides the effects of a gradual ensemble *crescendo* with assorted cues and entrances at the discretion of the conductor; subsequent entrances in snare drums and low brass portray the sounds of rifle shots and violent cries of animal pain

Movement VII: "Drum Dancer"

390-449	Opening sequence providing images of an Inuit tribal dance and celebration; primary thematic statements appear in statements by the oboes, clarinets, trumpets, French horns, trombones, and euphoniums; strong rhythmic elements highlight percussion ensemble sonorities with frequent soli passages; final episode evolves through a sequence of rhythmic transformation (metric modulation) that lead into the second phase of the movement
450-500	Savage dancing sequence initially dominated by percussion, low brass, and woodwinds, with subsequent thematic entrances in soprano brass voices; the steadiness of rhythm is ultimately interrupted in the final sequence by a series of rhythmically disjunct passages
501-513	High-spirited and celebratory thematic interlude, concluding with a percussion bridge that serves as a transition into the following sequence
514-562	Thematic sequence of impressionistic scenes and episodes portraying different aspects of Inuit life in the Arctic; effects revealed in various sections are subjective, and each of the sections represents some form of reprise in that they provide samples of each movement from the whole piece; this can perhaps be

MEASURE   EVENT AND SCORING

                 understood to represent a final unification of the
                 composition
563-621   Trumpet call initiates the final intensifying sequence
                 for the ensemble; an extended passage that is highly
                 percussive and rhythmic in nature; further development
                 of thematic motives is continued, and the power and
                 energy of the final musical statement of the
                 composition is directed toward a powerful and climactic
                 conclusion

Unit 8: Suggested Listening
Michael Colgrass:
  Déjà Vu
  Winds of Nagual

Unit 9: Additional References and Resources

Bohle, Bruce, ed. *The International Encyclopedia of Music and Musicians*. New York: Dodd, Mead, and Company, 1985.

Colgrass, Michael. *Arctic Dreams*. New York: Carl Fischer, 1991.

Cummings, David, ed. *International Who's Who in Music and Musicians Directory*. Cambridge, England: Bath Press, 1992.

Hanna, Frederick. "An Interpretive Analysis of *Arctic Dreams* by Michael Colgrass." Dissertation, The New England Conservatory of Music, 1997.

Lopez, Barry. *Arctic Dreams: Imagination and Desire in a Northern Landscape*. New York: Bantam Books, 1996.

www.michaelcolgrass.com

Contributed by:
John Cody Birdwell
Director of Bands
Texas Tech University
Lubbock, Texas

Teacher Resource Guide

Awayday

Adam Gorb
(b. 1958)

Unit 1: Composer
Adam Gorb was born in 1958 in Cardiff, the capital of Wales. In 1963, he moved to London. Gorb completed his undergraduate degree at Cambridge University, where he studied with Hugh Wood and Robin Holloway. He directed several musicals on Broadway before returning to the Royal Academy of Music in London and earning his master's degree in Composition. In 1995, he won the Match Composition Prize. Gorb is now a member of the music faculty at the London College of Music and Media at Thames Valley University in London. He has written numerous works for various instrumental and vocal combinations. In addition to *Awayday*, his other most notable work for winds is entitled *Metropolis* (1992).

Unit 2: Composition
Awayday is a lively, upbeat composition that is described as a good "curtain raiser" by the composer. Gorb's experience as a Broadway musical director asserts itself as jazz rhythmic elements, dazzling sonorities, and humorous motives jump to the foreground. The composer makes no effort to hide his tributes to *West Side Story* and *Candide*, but puts them to effective use in this highly energetic work for winds. The composition is cast in an extended sonata form.

Unit 3: Historical Perspective
Awayday was commissioned by Timothy Reynish, who conducted the first performance with the Royal Northern College of Music Wind Ensemble at

Bridgewater Hall, Manchester, England, on November 27, 1996. Composed to fill the need for a "seven-minute curtain raiser," *Awayday* suggests a holiday – something carefree and fun. Gorb writes, "Imagine Bernstein, Gershwin, and Stravinsky in a convertible speeding down the highway," to describe his work which captures the spirit of Broadway overture.

Unit 4: Technical Considerations

Awayday is scored for standard band instrumentation with the addition of integral parts for E-flat clarinet, contrabassoon, string bass, and piano. An extensive battery of percussion instruments is also included. With a tempo marking of *presto*, half note = 144, the first six measures present a problematic rhythmic pattern of silent downbeats and paired eighth note upbeats. This rhythmic motive recurs again in the development and recapitulation. Jazz-inspired rhythms and hemiola appear throughout the piece in shifting meters of 3/2, 2/2, 3/4, 5/4, and 7/8. Primary key centers are a minor, E major, and A-flat major. There is also a strong lydian scalar influence in the upper woodwind writing. Horns are required to play using "stopped" technique, and trombones must read tenor clef. Double-tonguing passages exist for both trumpets and trombones. Ranges are extended for both B-flat clarinet (b3) and alto saxophone (f-sharp3).

Unit 5: Stylistic Considerations

Awayday must be approached with a familiarity of articulations characteristic of "Broadway" show music – particularly those inherent in the music of Bernstein, Gershwin, and Sondheim. In addition, subtle articulations reflecting the jazz idiom are required throughout the work. Percussionists may wish to vary the ride cymbal rhythms to reflect patterns more relevant to swing and jazz as opposed to the notated quarter notes.

Unit 6: Musical Elements

Although *Awayday* is unified by a main tonal center of A minor (lydian mode), many of the vertical harmonies utilized are quite exotic and jazz-influenced. Gorb scores the piece using the key signature of A minor (with transposing instruments utilizing their appropriate relative key signatures), but with the amount of chromaticism found in the piece, it may have been just as appropriate to follow the lead of many modern composers and use no key signature at all, deferring instead to the use of an abundance of accidentals.

The piece opens with an energetic rhythmic motive which lays the foundation for the entire piece. Harmonically, the chords used would best be described as clusters grouped over traditional bass sonorities, producing a jazz-like sound reminiscent of bebop piano voicings. Minor and major seconds are important harmonic intervals in these chords, although the second chord is composed entirely of whole steps (Fig. 1).

Figure 1

Minor and major seconds become important melodic intervals as well after the introduction. The first theme appears at rehearsal number 2, first in the trombones and echoed by the horns. Major and minor triads are alternated in an energized rhythmic motive which is used throughout the composition (Fig. 2).

Figure 2

At rehearsal number 3, the main theme is contrasted by a countermelody in the bass voices, which serves to fill the silent beats of the main melody in a hocket-like style (Fig. 3).

Figure 3

The two melodic ideas are freely developed in the following measures, producing a rich sonority and complex rhythmic pattern at the same time. A walking bass line adds forward rhythmic motion and reinforces the jazz style of the piece. At rehearsal number 4, the upper woodwinds add a scalar line reminiscent of the flourishes heard in the introduction. Development continues until rehearsal number 8, when a new, contrasting *legato* theme is introduced in the saxophones (Fig. 4). As in classical sonata-allegro form, this melody is stated in the dominant key of E major, with some added extensions (major sevenths, ninths, and thirteenths) retaining the modern jazz harmonies. Although this theme is more *legato* in character, the syncopated rhythms help retain the energy of the previous sections.

Figure 4

The second theme is developed until a brief return of the initial theme at rehearsal number 11. Both themes are then juxtaposed in free development until a return of the opening chords of the introduction at rehearsal number 14 – this time only in the upper voices over sustained octaves in the bass voices. More development of the first rhythmic theme ensues, including breaking up the rhythmic motive in a bell tone-like fashion among the brass. The rhythmic motion eventually settles into sustained chords in the brasses by rehearsal number 19 – first with stacked perfect fourths, then thirds. At rehearsal number 20, the first theme is broken up between piano/double bass and bass clarinet/bassoons, this time in A-flat. A new third theme, again in a contrasting *legato* style, is presented first in the tenor saxophone five measures later, and becomes the basis for the next developmental section (Fig. 5).

Figure 5

This new theme is passed freely among the upper woodwinds for the next main section, while the brasses and low woodwinds continue with the energetic first theme, reinforced again by a walking bass line. A brief 3/4 section appears at rehearsal number 23, which features a new melodic idea in the upper woodwinds. This new theme contains rhythmic elements of the first theme and also melodic elements derived from the third theme (Fig. 6). Development of this theme is limited, but it provides a nice contrast to the surrounding duple-time sections.

Figure 6

Development continues to a climax at rehearsal number 29, when the percussion section is featured, preparing for a recapitulation of the original material at rehearsal number 30. Again following sonata-allegro form, the second theme is recapitulated at rehearsal number 34 in the saxophones (as before). An *allargando* at rehearsal number 36 leads into another statement of the first theme in E-flat clarinet and solo B-flat clarinet, followed by chords in the low brass which leads to a restatement of the first theme in the dominant key center of E. A very chromatic section follows, leading back to the original key of A minor at rehearsal number 39. Again, the first theme is presented over a walking bass line. The chord clusters of the introduction are restated at rehearsal number 40, adding rhythmic energy to the ending bars until the woodwinds add a flourish of scale patterns to bring the piece to a conclusion.

Unit 7: Form and Structure

An overall diagram of *Awayday* reveals the sonata-allegro structure, with an emphasis on primary themes and their development.

SECTION	EVENT AND SCORING
Opening	Introduction (13 measures, *tutti*)
Theme 1	Rehearsal number 2 (rhythmic motive in A minor): stated first in the trombones and then horns; a hocket-like countermelody appears in the low instruments; instrumentation later enlarged to include saxophones (rehearsal number 3) and trumpets (rehearsal number 7)
Theme 2	Rehearsal number 8 (contrasting *legato* melody in E): stated first in saxophones, then upper woodwinds (rehearsal number 9)
Development	Rehearsal number 10 to rehearsal number 20: Themes 1 and 2
Theme 3	Five after rehearsal number 20 (lyrical melody in A-flat mixolydian): stated first in tenor saxophone, then expanded to other saxophones, flute, oboe, and 1st clarinet
Theme 4	Six after rehearsal number 23 (3/4 melody, contains elements of Theme 1 and Theme 3 in E-flat): stated first in flutes, oboes, E-flat clarinet, and 1st/2nd B-flat clarinets – later developed in 1st/2nd trumpets and all upper woodwinds
Development	Rehearsal number 25 to rehearsal number 29: Themes 1 and 3
Interlude	Rehearsal number 29: mambo-like percussion break

SECTION	EVENT AND SCORING
Theme 1 (repeated)	Rehearsal number 30 (original key of A minor): stated first in saxophones, then horns, then trumpets/trombones
Theme 2 (repeated)	Rehearsal number 34 (again in E): stated first in saxophones, then upper woodwinds and trumpets (rehearsal number 35)
Theme 1 (repeated)	Eight after rehearsal number 37 (dominant key center of E): stated first in tuba/bassoons, then horns (three after rehearsal number 38), then trumpets/trombones (rehearsal number 39)
Coda	Rehearsal number 40: return of chord clusters from introduction; final flourish of scale patterns in woodwinds

Unit 8: Suggested Listening

Leonard Bernstein:
   Overture to Candide
   West Side Story (Soundtrack)
Adam Gorb, *Metropolis*
John Kander and Fred Ebb, *Cabaret* (Soundtrack)
Stephen Sondheim, *Side by Side* (Soundtrack)

Unit 9: Additional References and Resources

Cannava, Edward S. "Band Classics Revisited: Leonard Bernstein 'Selections from West Side Story'." *The Instrumentalist*, 45:7, February 1991: 66.

Drabkin, William. "Sondheim, Stephen (Joshua)." Stanley Sadie, ed., *The New Grove Dictionary of Music and Musicians*. London: Macmillan, 1980. XVII, 509.

Ganzel, Kurt, ed. *The Encyclopedia of The Musical Theater*. New York: Schirmer Publishing Co., 1994. S.v. "Cabaret," I, 205-07.

Ganzel, Kurt, ed. *The Encyclopedia of The Musical Theater*. New York: Schirmer Publishing Co., 1994. S.v. "Candide," I, 218-19.

Ganzel, Kurt, ed. *The Encyclopedia of The Musical Theater*. New York: Schirmer Publishing Co., 1994. S.v. "West Side Story," II, 1543-44.

Gorb, Adam. "Awayday." *Deja View*. Corporon/North Texas Wind Symphony. KLAVIER 11091, 1998.

Gorb, Adam. "Metropolis." *Metropolis*. RNCM Wind Orchestra. SERCD2400.

Jackson, Richard. "Bernstein, Leonard." Stanley Sadie, ed., *The New Grove Dictionary of Music and Musicians*. London: Macmillan, 1980. II, 629-31.

Mathieson, Kenny. "Bernstein, Leonard." Brian Morton and Pamela Collins, eds., *Contemporary Composers*. Chicago and London: St. James Press, 1992. 95-98.

Mathieson, Kenny. "Sondheim, Stephen (Joshua)." Brian Morton and Pamela Collins, eds., *Contemporary Composers*. Chicago and London: St. James Press, 1992. 879-80.

Rozen, Brian D. "Leonard Bernstein's Educational Legacy." *Music Educators Journal*, 78:1, September 1991, 43.

Slonimsky, Nicolas, ed. *Baker's Biographical Dictionary of Musicians*. New York: Schirmer Publishing Co., 1992. S.v. "Bernstein, Leonard," 173-75.

Slonimsky, Nicolas, ed. *Baker's Biographical Dictionary of Musicians*. New York: Schirmer Publishing Co., 1992. S.v. "Sondheim, Stephen (Joshua)," 1744.

Contributed by:

Joseph P. Missal
Director of Bands
Oklahoma State University
Stillwater, Oklahoma

Research assistance provided by Lane Davis, Todd Malicoate, Jerry West, and Michael Westbrook.

Teacher Resource Guide

Caricatures

Jere T. Hutcheson
(b. 1938)

Unit 1: Composer

Jere T. Hutcheson has written for a variety of media, including opera, orchestra, chorus, wind symphony, and chamber ensemble. A native of Marietta, Georgia, Hutcheson studied composition with Helen Gunderson, Ernst Krenek, Gunther Schuller, and H. Owen Reed. He has been a member of the theory and composition faculty at Michigan State University since 1965 and was appointed Chairperson of Composition in 1975. Hutcheson has been awarded composition fellowships from the Guggenheim Foundation and the Berkshire Music Center at Tanglewood, and accorded grants from the National Endowment for the Arts and the Martha Baird Rockefeller Fund for Music. In 1976, he was cited as "Distinguished Composer of the Year" by the National Music Teacher's Association. His works for winds include *Sensations for Symphonic Band and Audience* (1972), *Passacaglia Profundus* (1973), *Colossus* (1975), *Earth Gods Symphony* (1977), *Chromophonic Images* (1978), *Concerto for Piano and Wind Orchestra* (1981), *Five French Portraits* (1988), *Caricatures* (1997), and *More Caricatures* (1999). Hutcheson is co-author of the book *Musical Form and Analysis*.

Unit 2: Composition

Caricatures was written for, and dedicated to, the Michigan State University Wind Symphony and its conductor, John L. Whitwell, as part of a commissioning project celebrating the 125th anniversary of the Michigan State Bands. *Caricatures* presents nine different impressions as described by the composer:

I. Marcel Marceau - "Stealth." Marcel Marceau is trapped in a mysterious box. The escape route is laden with traps, but the spider-like mime finds his way.

II. Edgar Allan Poe - "The Pit and the Pendulum." Edgar Allan Poe skillfully created haunting atmospheres of terror. His manipulation of phrasing and rhythm intensified mood through sound.

III. Emma Thompson - "Exercise in Deep Breathing." I once happened upon a TV show entitled "Emma," a one-woman *tour de force* written, directed, acted, and danced by Emma Thompson. There was a scene in which Emma, lying on her back, created a symphony of arched, high-pitched, speech-like sounds, playful and expressive. I will never forget it.

IV. Camille Saint-Saëns - "Scales." Can you recall that moment in the third movement of the *Organ Symphony* when the two pianos enter with a barrage of scales and arpeggios? The idea seems to me to be an intrusion on the natural form of the composition, an idea which should not have been allowed entry; but at the same time, I find the idea itself appealing.

V. Vincent Van Gogh - "Canticle." The great Dutch painter Vincent Van Gogh suffered great pain. He also filled his canvasses with strength and beauty.

VI. Erik Satie - "A Day in the Life of Erik Satie." Erik Satie rebelled, not only against the weight of the German tradition and academia in general, but against French impressionism, which he felt could go no further. His aesthetic was Dadaist, even before the term *Dadaism* was coined.

VII. Dorothy Parker - "Love and the Opposite." Armed with a caustic wit and an elegant, often dry style, Dorothy Parker expressed the bright and the bitter sides of love as no one else.

VIII. Andy Warhol - "The Giant Soup Can Machine." Andy Warhol stunned the art world with his series of reproductions of everyday items.

IX. Jackson Pollock - "Driplets in Triplets." My caricature of Jackson Pollock is more a caricature of one of his canvasses than of the artist himself.

Unit 3: Historical Perspective

According to Webster, a *caricature* is defined as *an exaggeration by means of often-ludicrous distortion of parts or characteristics.* In writing *Caricatures,*

Hutcheson has created a highly distinctive setting. Through ingenious exploration, the composer presents a landmark musical portrayal of nine remarkable artists and their distinct peculiarities, attributes, and spirits. The language of *Caricatures* is familiar: the versatile forces of the large wind symphony. It is the message which creates the intrigue through a remarkable similarity to the artists themselves and to their own indisputable craft.

Perhaps not as popular as extolling historical events, locations, or traditions (i.e., *Zion*; *Music for Prague 1968*; *Urban Requiem*; *A Movement for Rosa*; *A Light Unto the Darkness*; *Symphony No. 3: Shaker Life*; *La Fiesta Mexicana*; *George Washington Bridge*), the idea of musically depicting an individual, artist, or works of art has been a part of wind music for many years. Florent Schmitt chose the title *Dionysiaques* in 1913 to commemorate the gods of drama and wine. Michael Colgrass' "musical fable" *Winds of Nagual* depicts Carlos Castaneda's apprenticeship with Indian sorcerer don Juan Matis. *Scenes from "The Louvre"* by Norman Dello Joio renders *Ancient Airs* in a celebration of the museum's famous collections. *Aldo Forte* was inspired by five paintings of a Dutch master in writing his *Van Gogh Portraits*. In *Caricatures*, however, Hutcheson has merged history with artistic vision, resulting in a work of unique distinction in a highly engaging framework.

Unit 4: Technical Considerations

Caricatures is forged in nine distinct movements of between one minute, forty seconds and three minutes, twenty seconds in duration. If performed in its entirety, the work spans twenty-two minutes. The ensemble demands are formidable, with extensive percussion instrumentation and movements of wide-ranging technical difficulty. Ensembles with limited resources may consider performing select movements of the work to target musical strengths.

The instrumentation includes a minimum of six flutes, sixteen clarinets (one E-flat, twelve B-flat, two bass, one contrabass), three bassoons (including contra), five saxophones (including soprano and bass), piano, and six percussionists. Bass saxophone is doubled in higher registers throughout, although the ensuing foundation of contrabass clarinet, contrabassoon, and bass saxophone is extraordinary. The use of piano is essential to several movements, notably "Scales."

Percussion requirements include two xylophones, crotales, amplified log drum, slapstick, Jew's harp, pistol, prize fight bell (or metallic bell sound), and a siren (or siren whistle). All are vital to the musical score. A phone number for securing a genuine prize fight bell (used in "A Day in the Life of Erik Satie") is found in the full score. The idea of the prize fight bell is entirely Hutcheson's, perhaps inspired by a typewriter and other "novel" instruments necessary for Satie's *Parade*. Directions in amplifying four percussion instruments (log drum, claves, metal plate, congas) are also found in the score; four microphones are needed in select situations.

Each movement provides its own varying degree of technical demand. Movement I requires surreptitious flute, soprano and alto saxophone soloists. Movement II necessitates resolute and unfailing percussion. Movement III features short solo segments for clarinet and tuba. Movement IV provides the greatest technical demand for the entire ensemble. Steadfast attention must be paid to articulation while exploring scales in numerous keys (b, c, d-flat, d, e-flat, g) presented in rapidly cascading sixteenth and thirty-second notes. The masterfully crafted ending demands less technical proficiency but heightened attention to balance and style. Movement V focuses on a nine-measure trombone solo in tenor clef and a short e-flat clarinet solo in the altissimo register. Movement VI presents issues of rhythmic timing in its widely varying metric patterns. Movement VII stipulates tantamount rhythmic precision. Movement VIII contains a demanding hemiola requiring percussion to maintain its pulse seemingly removed from the woodwinds and brass. Movement IX contains delicate rhythmic figures and challenging meter issues. Confident entrances and the conscientious observation of silences are a necessity.

Unit 5: Stylistic Considerations

The essence of each caricature is vital to the overall effectiveness of the music and its representation of each artist. The challenge facing conductors and ensembles is faithfulness to the unique quality of each movement: mystery, terror, lilt, steadfastness and brightness, strength and beauty, rebellion, biting and pointed, urgently mechanical, lightly pointillistic. In every case, choosing the suitable style for each artist's caricature and preserving the integrity of that approach throughout the movement is an undeniable key in realizing the composer's intent.

Unit 6: Musical Elements

The musical elements contained in *Caricatures* are numerous: rhythmic challenge, wide-ranging dynamics and tempi, extreme textural contrasts and solo and *tutti* sections, a prolific application of scales, rich harmonic vocabulary, smooth lyricism to rugged prominence, issues of balance and blend, melodies of rich musical shape and color. Sharing the formal framework with an ensemble during the rehearsal process will assist in achieving the necessary contrasts in style which are unique to each artist and to each caricature. The score is in C.

Unit 7: Form and Structure

MEASURE	TEMPO	EVENT AND SCORING
Movement I: Marcel Marceau—"Stealth"		
1-9	quarter note = 60	Solo flute
10-12		Bridge
13-20		Soprano and alto saxophone duet

MEASURE	TEMPO	EVENT AND SCORING
21-34		Muted brass in minor seconds

Movement II: Edgar Allan Poe—"The Pit and the Pendulum"

1-35	quarter note = 132	Rapidly cascading figures building in texture and descending in *tessitura* m. 8: high oboe "screaming" descending line mm. 13-21: trumpet, bassoon, English horn added to "screaming" line mm. 22-35: trombone and saxophone "screaming"
36-51	quarter note = c.60	Percussive attacks, shifting claves and metal plate; additive harmonic clusters

Movement III: Emma Thompson—"Exercise in Deep Breathing"

1-22	dotted-quarter = 63	Woodwind, horn, euphonium exchange "Emma Thompson" motif; muted trombone "wa-wa"
23-43	dotted-quarter = 84	Dissonance, syncopation; use of slapstick and Jew's harp
44-64	dotted-quarter = 63	Woodwind, horn, trumpet exchange based on motif rhythm mm. 57-60: solo tuba mm. 61-64: English horn, bassoon, saxophone, and clarinet motif

Movement IV: Camille Saint-Saëns—"Scales"

1-4	quarter note = 100	Piano scale in B
5-13		Ascending scales based in C
14-19		Cascading scales based in D-flat
20-26	quarter note = 80	Oboe and bassoon duet; scales based in D
27-34	quarter note = 100	Cascading scales based in E-flat; cantabile countermelody
35-37		Piano and vibraphone based in C
38-42		Bitonal scales based in A-flat and D
43-47		Transition based in B
48-52		Piano 6s in G against sixteenth note scales
53-56		G major transition
57-64		Thematic material based on Offenbach *Orphée aux enfers* "can-can" in piano mm. 61-64: theme in clarinet and trumpet

MEASURE	TEMPO	EVENT AND SCORING
65-70	quarter note = 200	Double-time transition based in F
71-78		Clarinet and trumpet theme in G
79-84		Bridge in F
85-92		Clarinet theme in G; countermelody in piccolo
93-98		Oboe, clarinet, trumpet theme
99-110		Four-note motifs based on theme; simultaneous ascending and descending G scales
111-114		In one; *l'istesso* tempo; ascending and descending triplet figures
115-131		In two; *l'istesso* tempo; converging ascending and descending patterns
132-138		G major material; descending scale; *pianissimo* punctuation

Movement V: Vincent Van Gogh—"Canticle"

1-7	quarter note = 80	Introduction; descending pattern
8-16		Trombone and oboe solos
17-23		Euphonium solo
24-36		Ascending melodic figures; euphonium and alto saxophone duet; tuba and horn duet
37-50		*Glissandi*, E-flat clarinet and trumpet soli
51-54		Coda; rich harmonic fabric with gradually fading *ostinato* figure

Movement VI: Erik Satie—"A Day in the Life of Erik Satie"

1-18	quarter note = 80	Segment 1, Theme A; solo trombone and saxophone three-note motif alternating with woodwinds and xylophone
19-23	quarter note = 120	Segment 2, Theme B; bassoon
24-61		Segment 3, Theme C; clarinet and woodwinds
62-66		Segment 4, Theme B; flute, soprano saxophone
67-98		Segment 5, Theme D; contrabassoon material based on Theme C inversion; euphonium solo; final notes based on inverted Theme A motif

Movement VII: Dorothy Parker—"Love and the Opposite"

1-10	dotted-quarter = 56	Baritone saxophone and timpani soli

MEASURE	TEMPO	EVENT AND SCORING
11-17	dotted-quarter = 72	Full ensemble biting rhythmic figures in alternation with timpani
18-35	dotted-quarter = 56	Tenor saxophone, trumpet, oboe, clarinet, baritone saxophone, and timpani soli
36-42	dotted-quarter = 72	Full ensemble biting rhythmic figures in alternation with timpani
43-47	dotted-quarter = 56	Alto saxophone, baritone saxophone, vibraphone

Movement VIII: Andy Warhol—"The Giant Soup Can Machine"

1-16	quarter note = 152	Alto saxophone, oboe, and clarinet motif based on B, D, E, F
17-35	quarter note = 120	Low brass motif based on B-flat, D-flat, E-flat, E, F, G-flat
36-52		Lyrical trumpet theme over driving rhythm
53-58		Solo clarinet theme
59-71		Transition based on B, D, E, F motif
72-83		In one; winds with motif in hemiola with percussion
84-111		In two; thinning motif pulse texture from brass to woodwind to piano

Movement IX: Jackson Pollock—"Driplets in Triplets"

1-3	quarter note = 60	Trumpet and vibraphone
4-34	eighth note = 152	Ascending and descending patterns
35-37	quarter note = 76	Horn and trombone lyrical figure
38-52		Durchbrochene arbeit figures
53-58		Bridge material based on broken figures
59-66	quarter note = 116	Vivo; driving woodwind and xylophone figures with piercing piccolo and E-flat clarinet
67-71		Bridge; quarter note = 116 to m. 76
72-121	eighth note = 152	Ascending and descending patterns
122-127	quarter note = 76	Bridge material based on broken figures
128-134	quarter note = 116	Vivo; driving woodwind and xylophone figures with piercing piccolo and E-flat clarinet
135-148	quarter note = 76	Coda; descending woodwind and xylophone figure derived from mm. 4-8

Unit 8: Suggested Listening
Michael Colgrass, *Winds of Nagual*
Norman Dello Joio, *Scenes from "The Louvre"*
Aldo Forte, *Van Gogh Portraits*
Camille Saint-Saëns, *Symphony No. 3 "Organ"*
Florent Schmitt, *Dionysiaques*

Unit 9: Additional References and Resources
Caricatures is recorded on: *Deja View*. The North Texas Wind Symphony, Eugene Corporon, Conductor. Klavier KCD-11091.

Contributed by:
Glen J. Hemberger
Director of Bands
Southeastern Louisiana University
Hammond, Louisiana

Teacher Resource Guide

Dialogues and Entertainments
William Kraft
(b. 1923)

Unit 1: Composer

William Kraft was awarded two Anton Seidl Fellowships at Columbia University, graduating with a bachelor's degree, cum laude, in 1951 and a master's degree in 1954. His principle instructors were Jack Beeson, Seth Bingham, Henry Brant, Henry Cowell, and Eric Hertzman, among others. He received his training in percussion from Morris Goldenberg and in timpani from Saul Goodman. Kraft has had a distinguished career as a composer, conductor, timpanist, and percussionist. In his long association with the Los Angeles Philharmonic, he functioned as percussionist (1955-62), timpanist (1962-81), and frequent conductor of contemporary and children's concerts. From 1981 to 1985, he served as Composer-in-Residence and Founding Director of the Los Angeles Philharmonic New Music Group. Among his numerous awards are the American Academy of Arts and Letters, two Guggenheim Fellowships, and two Kennedy Center Friedheim Awards. His commissions and grants include the Library of Congress, Ford and Rockefeller Foundations, Los Angeles Philharmonic, and many others. He is currently chairman of the Composition Department and holds the Corwin Chair at the University of California, Santa Barbara.

Unit 2: Composition

Dialogues and Entertainments was composed on a commission of the University of Michigan Wind Ensemble and dedicated to their conductor, H. Robert Reynolds. The piece was completed in Los Angeles in September 1980 and received its premiere performance in Ann Arbor during the twenty-first national conference of the College Band Directors National Association on February 13, 1981. The piece uses two texts that appear in the final movement. The first is by the composer himself and the second by Robert Frost.

> Let not the black sun deceive you.
> Let not the son of the black night deceive you.
> Let not the sun of the black night deceive you.
> —Kraft

> The leaves, tree at my window, window tree,
> My sash is lowered when night comes on;
> But let there never be curtain drawn between you and me.
> The leaves shall bare their truths.....
> —Frost

Unit 3: Historical Perspective

In composing this piece, Kraft used very diverse compositional techniques. The diversity can be noticed in the melodic and harmonic language covering periods from twelve-tone to late Renaissance. William Harbinson, in his analysis of the piece, best describes this as "passages demanding the precision of Boulez alongside passages allowing the freedom of Cage." Kraft is able to draw on many compositional techniques, such as indeterminacy, sound-mass, improvisation, staging, and quotation. Be aware that this piece is not a collection of musical effects but a well-crafted piece of art. Again, quoting William Harbinson, "with a refined sense of timbrel shading, of textural growth, and of dramatic pace, the composer manipulates the manifold components of his musical language to create the personal idiom revealed in *Dialogues and Entertainments.*"

Unit 4: Technical Considerations

This piece is not orchestrated in the traditional wind band setting. It requires four flutes, three doubling on piccolo and one on alto flute. It also requires four oboes, clarinets, bassoons, saxophones, trumpets, trombones, eight horns, two tubas, and one string bass. The orchestration for the percussion section is very detailed. It requires six percussionists plus a timpanist. Other considerations include the equipment needed to perform the piece. A set of Swiss hand bells is needed as well as two sets of octave crotales. Staging is also a very vital facet to the composition. There are five different stations needed in the performance hall to perform the work. A soprano soloist is needed to perform the last movement. Most of the instrumentalists are required to play a percussion instrument, being the hand bells and crotales. The composer is very specific in his explanations in the score and gives a table of explanations of his graphic signs. The third and fourth movements require the woodwinds to have strong technical facility through many fast passages.

Unit 5: Stylistic Considerations

Dialogues and Entertainments, in many ways, is a study of textures. Clarity will need to be achieved by a combination of balance and articulation. Style can be attained by the proper use of articulation. Although *legato* in many sections, the ensemble might need to articulate out of a *legato* style in order to be heard. The thick chords and clusters written will require proper balancing to hear all the notes in their respective chords. The third movement, entitled "Homage St. Marks," is written to emulate Gabrieli's music as performed in St. Mark's Cathedral. Proper staging will assist the performance a great deal. The composer has gone to extreme measures in marking the score with appropriate articulations, dynamics, and phrase markings. The conductor will need to follow all of the road maps to ensure the piece is represented as the composer intended.

Unit 6: Musical Elements

Movement I uses several compositional techniques to accomplish the goals the composer set forth. Indeterminate events are established right away in the percussion dialogue between the timpani and tom-toms. Octatonic harmonies find their way throughout the piece, as do many multi-tone clusters. Kraft uses a series of dots and dashes to create a Morse code section with the brass where he spells out several names of the music faculty at the University of Michigan. Finally, the first movement ends with an ascending minor third statement in the low brass. Movement II is an interlude orchestrated solely for percussion. This interlude is created by "random" *glissandi* performed by metal rods on various sizes of tam-tams. This gives way to Movement III. In this movement, Kraft uses quotes from three different sources for material. Pietro Lappi's *Canzon 26*, Gabrieli's *Sonata Pian e Forte a 8*, and Hassler's *Laudate Dominum*. These three pieces are quoted with the use of off-stage and antiphonal groups reminiscent of the days of St. Mark's Cathedral. These quotations are happening simultaneously with several contemporary-based band interjections from stage. Movement IV uses the text of Kraft and Frost. The first line of the text is used to explore the darker, more expressive colors of the ensemble. The B section of this movement uses a piccolo quartet and lyric woodwinds, expressing the hope-inspiring lines of the text. Several progressive techniques are used in the A section of the movement, producing a vast array of imaginative timbres. The soprano soloist is required to use vocal techniques developed by Ligeti, Cage, et al., in works of the 1960s. These techniques included elongating pronunciation of the initial word of the text, accentuating "T" and gradually changing the timbre from the consonant "L" through the vowel "E." The chaotic, improvised climax is reminiscent of several dramatic passages in the works of Penderecki.

Unit 7: Form and Structure

SECTION	MEASURE	EVENT AND SCORING
Movement I:		
Introduction	1-7	Timpani and tom-tom dialogue with sustained chord
A Section	8-15	Motif handed down through the woodwinds with the trumpets playing names in Morse code
B Section	16-25	Clarinet solo begins the section with flourishes of woodwinds and keyboard percussion
Coda	26-30	Euphonium solo with sustained woodwinds
Movement II (Interlude):		
A Section	1-20	Metallic sounds and with drastic volume contrast (only percussion scored)
B Section	21-30	Keyboard percussion playing melodic fragment of first movement (only percussion scored)
Movement III:		
A Section	1-16	Rapid flourishes by woodwinds open this section, accompanied by slowly shifting clusters, which ends with *fortissimo* brass and chime interjections
B Section	17-42	Using the special staging, music from the Renaissance quoted from all off-stage groups
C Section	43-76	Woodwind flourishes give way to bowed crotales clusters, which give way to the return of the Renaissance quotes
Movement IV:		
A Section	1-44	Using his own text, the composer uses dark scoring of registers to augment to text; off-stage players return to stage during the performance while speaking the text
B Section	45-77	Composer now uses the Frost text for the second section of the movement; using rhythmic statements over sustained clusters

SECTION	MEASURE	EVENT AND SCORING
Coda I	78-92	Brings back a variation of the woodwind flourishes from the third movement while rhythmic pulses take over the percussion scoring
Coda II	93-103	Variations on the motif that was introduced in the first movement is set in a call-and-response setting; Morse code returns at the end in percussion spelling "Love," "Truth," and "Peace"

Unit 8: Suggested Listening

Giovanni Gabrieli, *Sonata Pian e Forte a 8*
William Kraft:
    Concerto for Four Percussion Soloists and Orchestra
    Nonet for Brass and Percussion
    Suite for Brass
    Triangles: Concerto for Percussion and Ten Instruments
Pietro Lappi, *Canzon 26*

Unit 9: Additional References and Resources

Cope, David H. "Timbre modulation-the compositional technique of moving sound continuously and evenly from one timbre to another." *New Directions in Music*, 3rd ed. Dubuque, IA: Wm. C. Brown Company Publishers, 1981.

Kraft, William. *Dialogues and Entertainments*. "Dialogues and Entertainments," University of North Texas Wind Symphony. Klavier Label. Compact disc KCD-11083.

Contributed by:

Brad Genevro
Assistant Director of Wind Studies
University of North Texas
Denton, Texas

Teacher Resource Guide

Dionysiaques, Op. 62
Florent Schmitt
(1870–1958)

modern adaptation by Guy M. Duker
(1916–1998)

Unit 1: Composer

Florent Schmitt was born in 1870 in Blâmont, located in the former province of Lorraine in northeastern France. He died in the Paris suburb of Neuilly-sur-Seine in 1958. During his life, Schmitt studied composition with Massenet and Fauré at the Paris Conservatory, and received numerous musical honors, including the Prix de Rôme in 1900, for his cantata *Sémiramis*. Schmitt composed for virtually every genre except opera, drawing inspiration from such diverse sources as the Bible, oriental lore, Edgar Allan Poe, and Hans Christian Andersen. His large body of work includes orchestral, choral, and chamber compositions, as well as ballets and film scores. *Dionysiaques* is his major work for band, though he also wrote a Turkish divertissement called *Sélamlik* (Op. 48, No. 1), and two unpublished compositions, the *Marche du 163e R.I.* (Op. 48, No. 2) and *Hymne funèbre* (Op. 46, No. 2), the latter using men's chorus. His best-known wind chamber work is *Lied et Scherzo*, Op. 54, dedicated to Paul Dukas and written for solo horn and nine winds. Schmitt's style reflects an eclecticism typical of his era, interweaving Romantic grandeur and drama with an Impressionistic harmonic influence. Compositional clarity and order of thought are effectively counterbalanced by masterful, original orchestration and pronounced rhythmic vigor.

Unit 2: Composition

Dionysiaques was written in 1913, although World War I delayed publication and the premiere until 1925. This first performance was given by the ensemble for which Schmitt wrote the piece – the Garde Républicaine Band, one of the finest bands in the world. The noun "dionysiaques" refers to the games and revels of ancient Greek festivals held to honor Dionysus, the god of wine. The Dionysian cult rituals every spring involved storytelling, wine-drinking, frenzied dancing, and animal mutilation, and though Schmitt left no explanation of his title, the character of the music leads the listener to believe that he may have intended a generalized musical depiction of these rites. Certainly, the rhythmic vitality and exploration of color in the work make it exciting for performer and audience alike. At the same time, the form of this single-movement, ten-minute composition is firmly rooted in traditional motivic organization, and students wishing to explore their individual parts as they fit into the totality would find this work both interesting and rewarding. Indeed, this composition will demand much work from the performers due to writing that requires excellent technical facility and a strong, independent rhythmic sense from each player. *Dionysiaques* is a musically accessible and ultimately satisfying work that provides a multi-layered learning experience for the mature ensemble.

Unit 3: Historical Perspective

Schmitt was stylistically influenced by the boisterous use of color found in the works of Rimsky-Korsakov and also those of his own countryman, Chabrier. In the latter composer, he also admired a piquant exoticism that pervaded no fewer than eighteen of his own compositions. From Fauré, his teacher, he assimilated a clarity of texture, lyricism, freedom of harmonic succession, and a good sense of proportion, though in temperament he was closer to the bold audacity of Berlioz. Schmitt was more sympathetic toward German Romanticism than his French contemporaries, and his ties to Impressionism were largely limited to the choice of harmonic vocabulary. Though Schmitt was deemed a conservative due to his disdain of extremism and his Romantic grandeur of conception, *Dionysiaques* was far ahead of its time in the context of the band world, as the composition displayed an exploitation of color differences and an attention to the details of orchestration that were virtually unprecedented. These marks of distinction unfortunately propelled the piece into oblivion at a time when school and community bands, under the grip of the Sousa/Gilmore influence, were playing transcriptions, popular music, novelty numbers, and marches. Even as this programming standard was evolving to become more inclusive, there still remained the formidable obstacle of the scoring of *Dionysiaques* for a uniquely French instrumentation that was unlike the American standard imposed by organizations such as the American Bandmasters Association (the American adaptation was constructed by Guy

M. Duker in 1975). Finally, this composition required excellent players throughout the ensemble – a challenge for the conductor and group used to liberal cross-cueing and doubling. In addition to all of these traits, *Dionysiaques* was distinctive and important historically as one of very few significant original band works from France.

Unit 4: Technical Considerations

In *Dionysiaques*, there are keys that take root only to be obliterated; in fact, there are no substantial stretches of music that remain in a single key area. The underlying harmonies are largely nonfunctional, and the music demands performers who are flexible enough to handle rapid changes in scale patterns (including major and minor), modality, exotic scales using augmented and diminished intervals, some rapidly executed whole-tone scales and, of course, those French "part diatonic, part chromatic" structures so familiar to anyone who has performed solo works from the Paris Conservatory school. The whole of the piece is motive-based, and every motive departs from the interval of the half step, so chromaticism is certainly the rule rather than the exception. Just as Schmitt establishes tonality only to thwart it, he treats rhythm in similar fashion, indicating regularity of meter while constantly going against it through syncopation, use of ties, shifting accents, and odd beat groupings. Instrumental entrances fit together intricately, for example, as players must enter on various notes of a sixteenth note sextuplet figure. This requires excellent internal subdivision, and the aural effect is rewardingly fresh and vital. Individual leadership is called for in many ways, as there is a large percentage of sparse, exposed textures, there is much divisi writing throughout, and even those on third part have to be soloists. In the same vein, instruments that usually do not play rapidly articulated passages must do exactly that in *Dionysiaques*, for example in the tongued sixteenth note sextuplet patterns (quarter note = 100) given to the low reed section. This testing of technique is extended to the use of extreme registers, particularly the high end used to achieve very bright ensemble timbres. In a composition that is all about huge contrasts and quick changes, the player is often asked to cover the entire instrument range within one measure, in the context of a fast technical passage. Regarding the myriad issues of technique in *Dionysiaques*, it can only be said that original and varied scoring is a trademark of the composer and a driving force in this work, and that conquering these considerable challenges will reap equally great rewards.

Unit 5: Stylistic Considerations

At a basic level, *Dionysiaques* may be called a tone poem that contrasts two diverse styles: spontaneous musical wanderings versus rhythmic, deliberate power gestures. Whether exotic, impish, passionate, or savage, the music requires an expressive and extroverted conductor who has the technique and the ideas to successfully pace the transitions between the earthy and the ethereal. Schmitt provides very few verbal descriptions in the score to help the conductor with interpretation; rather, the style clues are in the extremely careful marking of the music itself, from the differentiation of accent types to the written-in subtleties of ebb and flow in the slower passages. Even balance is addressed quite specifically, as the composer often requests one or two on a part or, conversely, asks a section to "bring out" a line that should dominate. Articulation marks often reinforce thematic contrasts in traditional ways, amplifying the difference between slurred, smooth chromatic melodies and tongued, disjunct lines. Less conventionally, Schmitt requires much soft *staccato*, fast articulation even in the low voices, and double tonguing in all brass instruments, all of which demand a lightness of touch from the performers. While this poses formidable technical obstacles, it also greatly contributes to the uniquely French sound of *Dionysiaques*.

Unit 6: Musical Elements

Schmitt's harmonic procedures reflect a creative adaptation of traditional vocabulary. At times, tonal centers are established only to dissipate quickly through devices such as parallelism; more often, triads and seventh chords are used without forward-moving progression, for example with root movement a tritone apart. Still, relative consonance and dissonance create repose and momentum, and help delineate form by grouping thematic ideas according to their character. The unrest of dissonant passages is traditionally reinforced with greater rhythmic activity, increased dynamic level, and rises in pitch. Specifically, rises by half steps often signify an infusion of energy (unfolding gradually or suddenly wrenching upward), while chromatic descents foster a winding down effect. The linear half step is, in fact, the generating idea of each of the four principal motives that comprise the thematic material in *Dionysiaques*. There are no long melodies, and musical interest is created through motivic development in the form of transposition, extension, truncation, and inversion. Of course, the element of rhythm, so essential in the identity of Schmitt's robust style, figures prominently in the manipulation of motives and even serves a programmatic function in the music, as extension of the forceful/disjunct motives triumphs over the shortened calmer/conjunct motives late in the piece. Truncation – that is, the premature cutting off of a rhythmic event – can also create a feeling of tumult, as if things are happening "too soon" as the music bombards the listener. Schmitt is a master of rhythm manipulation, and he successfully balances standard momentum-creating devices such as *ostinato* with effects that blur the written meter: use of rests on downbeats, offbeat entrances, ties, syncopation, and shifted accents. There is also a blurring technique in orchestration – a cumulative scoring where the composer continually adds colors, often in rhythmically de-emphasized spots, so that the composite timbre is constantly changing. Though this procedure

creates greater difficulty for the players who must deal with the rhythmic intricacies, it does make possible some interesting effects of "scored *crescendos*," and
it makes color as important as rhythm and dynamics in creating motion. For
contrast, Schmitt also scores some passages with an ideal of clarity in mind,
assigning various instrumental families separate lines of a texture. Color is actually an important aural marker as *Dionysiaques* begins, as the four main motives
are grouped by timbre: the two rhythmic and disjunct motives are scored for low
brass and woodwinds, while the other two, rhythmically flexible and conjunct,
are played by high woodwinds. The color contrast serves to underline the differences in motivic character early in the piece. Later on, timbre contrast takes
on cataclysmic proportions, as bright woodwind and brass flourishes come to a
sudden halt, leaving a dark (and comparatively sparse) low note. Extreme
ranges, coupled with agile technique demanded of all players, allow Schmitt to
explore a maximized color potential.

Unit 7: Form and Structure

Large Form	Measure	Internal Form
Introduction	1-16	Motives introduced – musical wanderings
A	17-20	Theme A1 – meandering clarinet solo
	21-24	Theme A2 – fluid flute/alto saxophone duet
	25-29	Theme A3 – louder, more impassioned
	30-31	Transition
	32-39	Theme B – energy burst
	40-41	Transition
	41-50	Introduction, varied, with Theme A1 fragment
	50-59	Theme C – energy burst
	59-61	Transition
B	62-65	Theme D1 – fast, rhythmic *tutti*
	66-71	Theme D2 – clarinet soli, building
	72-73	Theme D3 – big afterbeats
	74-77	Theme D1, varied
	78-83	Theme D2, varied
	84-85	Theme D3, varied
	86-93	Theme B, varied
	94-97	Transition
	98-103	Theme D2, varied
	104-105	Theme D3, varied
	106-111	Theme D2, varied
	112-113	Theme D3, varied

LARGE FORM	MEASURE	INTERNAL FORM
	114-117	Theme E – chordal *tutti*
	118-121	Transition
	122-131	Theme F – fast, *legato* reed section
	132-135	Theme E, transposed
	136-139	Transition
	140-153	Theme F, subsiding
A′	154-162	Theme A3, varied
	162-165	Transition
	166-183	Theme C, building in three stages
	184-194	Introduction, varied
B′	195-200	Introductory passage to D2
	201-206	Theme D2, varied
	207-215	Theme D2, varied
	216-223	Transition
	224-231	Theme B, varied
	232-237	Transition
	238-241	Theme E, transposed
	242-247	Theme D2, varied
	248-251	Theme D3, varied
	252-266	Theme E and D fragments compete
	267-270	Theme D3, varied
Coda	271-274	Melody of Theme E, rhythm of Theme D2
	275-285	Theme D2, varied
	286-289	Themes D2 and D3 combined
	290-291	Theme D3, varied
	292-299	Theme D2, varied

Unit 8: Suggested Listening

Emmanuel Chabrier, *España*
Ingolf Dahl, *Sinfonietta*
Paul Dukas, *The Sorcerers Apprentice*
William H. Hill, *Danses Sacred and Profane*
Roger Nixon:
    Fiesta del Pacifico
    Reflections
H. Owen Reed, *La Fiesta Mexicana*
Ottorino Respighi:
    Huntingtower
    The Pines of Rome
Nicolai Rimsky-Korsakov, *Sheherazade*
Bernard Rogers, *Three Japanese Dances*

Florent Schmitt, *La Tragédie de Salome*
Joaquin Turina, *La Procesión du Rocío*

Unit 9: Additional References and Resources

Brody, Elaine. *Paris: The Musical Kaleidoscope 1870-1925*. New York: George Braziller, 1987.

Brun, Francois-Julien. "The Band and Orchestra of the Republican Guard of Paris." *Journal of Band Research* 3 (Spring 1967): 15-18.

Carse, Adam. *Musical Wind Instruments*. Introduction by Himie Voxman. London: Macmillan & Co., 1939; reprinted, New York: Da Capo Press, 1965.

Cooper, Martin. *French Music from the Death of Berlioz to the Death of Fauré*. London: Oxford University Press, 1951; reprinted, 1969.

Durant, Will. *The Story of Civilization*. Vol. 2: *The Life of Greece*. New York: Simon & Schuster, 1939.

Janda, Diane C. "Dionysiaques, Op. 62: An Original Composition for Band by Florent Schmitt." D.M.A. thesis, University of Cincinnati, 1993.

Myers, Rollo. *Modern French Music from Fauré to Boulez*. New York: Praeger Publishers, 1971.

Paynter, John. "Can Your Band Read French?" *The Instrumentalist*, 11, March 1957, 40, 55, 80.

Pieters, Francis. "Music from the Garde Républicaine of Paris." *Winds* 5 (Summer 1990): 30-33.

Rehrig, William H. *The Heritage Encyclopedia of Band Music*. 2 vols. Edited by Paul E. Bierley. Westerville, OH: Integrity Press, 1991.

Ringo, James. "The Lure of the Orient." *American Composers Alliance Bulletin* 7 (1958): 8-12.

Rousseau, Eugene. "Comments on Orchestral Winds in Paris." *The Instrumentalist*, 15, May 1961, 44-45.

Note: The principal biographical sources for Florent Schmitt are in French and are included in the bibliography of the thesis by Diane Janda listed above.

Contributed by:
Diane Janda
Conductor of the Concert Band
Lycoming College
Williamsport, Pennsylvania

Teacher Resource Guide

El Salon Mexico

Aaron Copland
(1900–1990)

transcribed by Mark Hindsley
(1905–1999)

Unit 1: Composer

Aaron Copland was born on November 14, 1900, in Brooklyn, New York. His musical works ranged from ballet and orchestral music to choral music and movie scores. His music from the ballets *Billy the Kid, Rodeo,* and *Appalachian Spring* has inspired the instantly familiar "American Landscape" sound of movies, television, and radio.

Copland began composing in his teens. He studied harmony with Rubin Goldmark, who taught him conventional, fundamental harmony. In June of 1921, Copland traveled to France to attend the newly founded music school for Americans at Fontainebleau. Here he became the first American student of the brilliant teacher, Nadia Boulanger. After three years in Paris, he returned to New York with his first major commission: writing an organ concerto for the American appearances of Madame Boulanger. His *Symphony for Organ and Orchestra* premiered at Carnegie Hall in 1925.

Copland's growth as a composer mirrored important trends of his time. After his return from Paris, he worked with jazz rhythms in his *Piano Concerto* (1926). His *Piano Variations* (1930) established an advanced personal style. In the 1930s, he changed his orientation toward a simpler style, creating such works as *El Salon Mexico* (1933-36). In his later years, Copland's work reflected the serial techniques of the so-called twelve-tone school of Arnold Schoenberg.

In addition to composing, Copland was active as a conductor, speaker, pianist, teacher, and author. He died on December 2, 1990, at the Phelps Memorial Hospital in Tarrytown (Westchester County), New York.

Unit 2: Composition

El Salon Mexico was inspired following a trip to Mexico in 1932. Carlos Chavez, enamored with the music of Copland, invited him to visit Mexico as his guest. Copland provides this explanation of the work:

> No doubt I realised [sic] even then that it would be foolish to attempt to translate into musical sounds the more profound side of Mexico: the Mexico of the ancient civilizations or the revolutionary Mexico of to-day [sic]. In order to be able to do that, one must really know the country. All that I could hope to do was to reflect the Mexico of the tourists; because in that "hot spot" one felt, in a very natural and unaffected way, a close contact with the Mexican people. It wasn't the music that I heard, but the spirit that I felt there, which attracted me. Something of that spirit is what I hope to have put into my music.

El Salon Mexico was written for orchestra (piano arrangements preceded the orchestration) and later transcribed for band in 1972 by Mark Hindsley.

Unit 3: Historical Perspective

El Salon Mexico was the first work of Copland's to enjoy widespread popularity. Both critics and audiences received the work with great praise. Performances in London and Paris in 1938-39 and the recording made by Koussevitzky and the Boston Symphony Orchestra brought international recognition to Copland. Within one year following its publication in 1938, *El Salon Mexico* had been performed by fourteen American orchestras, five foreign ensembles, and two radio orchestras. This widespread exposure led Boosey & Hawkes to offer the composer a contract to publish all of his works.

Known earlier in his career as a "modernist," Copland experimented with *El Salon Mexico* in an effort to try a different (simpler) style of writing. A two-piano version, made for the composer by a young Leonard Bernstein, was premiered on October 11, 1935, by Copland and John Kirkpatrick. The orchestral version received its premiere on August 27, 1937, in Mexico City by the Orquerta Sinfonica de Mexico, with Carlos Chavez conducting.

Unit 4: Technical Considerations

Rhythmic intricacies permeate *El Salon Mexico*, creating many challenges for players and conductor. Throughout the work there are great numbers of mixed meters, metrical changes, asymmetrical rhythms, and tempo changes. Many solo passages assist in tying together sections and elements of the work, and require artistic and skillful players to complete this aspect of the work.

Accents are a prominent feature and must be brought out to aid in the syncopation and nationalistic character of the melodies. This is a complex piece that requires mature players/ensemble to achieve the desired effect.

Unit 5: Stylistic Considerations

El Salon Mexico was written in admiration of the Mexican people and culture. Copland was intent that *El Salon Mexico* reflect the experiences he enjoyed so much in Mexico and requested it be played as much in the style and flavor of the culture as possible. The folk tunes are simple melodies used to create a wonderful score of intermingling variations on the melodies and rhythms of the tunes optimized by Copland's ingenuity. It is necessary to try to capture the simpleness of the original tunes and the flavor of the people who created them in performing this work. In his book, *Copland, 1900-1942*, the composer speaks of a 1938 performance in London with Sir Adrian Boult conducting, where he requests "that the traditional orchestral E-flat clarinet play with the flavor of a native Mexican instrument." Though intrigued with the native percussion instruments of Mexico, this score calls only for a gourd to be used in addition to traditional percussion instruments.

Unit 6: Musical Elements

Musical material gathered for *El Salon Mexico* was from existing Mexican folk songs taken from a collection by Frances Toor, *Cancionero Mexicano* and *El Folklore y la Musica Mexicana*, by Ruben M. Campos. Copland modifies and combines melodies and fragments of the melodies from these folk tunes to fill the content of this work.

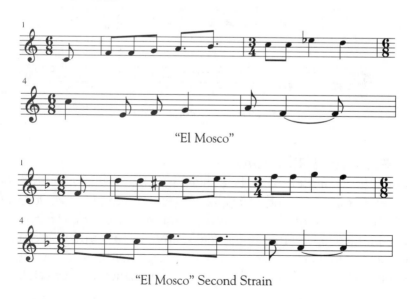

"El Mosco"

"El Mosco" Second Strain

"El Palo Verde"

"El Palo Verde" Second Strain

"La Jesusita"

"La Jesusita" Second Strain

Unit 7: Form and Structure

The form of *El Salon Mexico* can be divided into four primary sections enclosed between an introduction and coda/closing section. An effective description of much of the structure of this work is one of a sentence form – fairly complete melodic content shaped often in musical sentences rather than distinct periods or other larger, more defined forms. Sophisticated rhythmic content combined with simple melodic material make this form and structure successful.

References to folk tunes on the next page indicate most closely related material.

Section	Measure	Event and Scoring
Introduction	11-18	*Allegro Vivace*; introduction of arpeggiated figure based on *El Palo Verde* that recurs throughout the piece
Section I	19-33	*Moderato (rubato)*; trumpet solo with clarinet cadenza using material from *La Jesusita*
	34-60	*Piu mosso*; bassoon and tenor saxophone (originally bass clarinet) duet introduce material from second strain of *El Mosco*
	61-72	Further variations on *El Palo Verde* begin with an alternating 6/8, 3/4 rhythm
	69-72	*A tempo*; slight transition into an area based on *El Mosco*
	73-102	Gradually a trifle slower; material from *El Mosco* presented in cornets, flutes, and clarinets, combined with duple and triple eighth note patterns underneath
Section II	103-123	*Allegro Vivace*; arpeggiated motive returns in material related to introduction (*El Palo Verde*)
	124-133	Variation
	134-144	Fuller ensemble scoring, still variations on *El Palo Verde*
	145-155	Return to ideas introduced at m. 61 using more harmonized voices
	156-172	*A tempo*; introductory arpeggio appears in horns and new rhythmic fiber 5/8, 6/8, 7/8
	173-182	Back to arpeggio/introduction material
Section III	183-198	*Moderato molto (rubato)*; introduces clarinet solo with material from *El Mosco*
	199-210	*A tempo*
	211-226	*Piu mosso*; based on *La Jesusita*
	227-256	Tempo as before, *moderato molto*; oboe solo; piccolo and E-flat clarinet solo lead into m. 257
	257-287	English horn solo; later E-flat clarinet solo comes with increasing rhythmic intensity

SECTION	MEASURE	EVENT AND SCORING
	288-304	E-flat clarinet solo (m. 292); rhythmic momentum is growing, propelling the melody into m. 305
	305-323	$\frac{6+2}{8}$ motor rhythm creates greater intensity, leading the music into the final section at m. 324
Section IV		(*Material from sections of Allegro Vivace – Section II*)
	324-332	Relates to section at m. 133
	333-352	Relates to section at m. 113
	353-363	A *tempo*; relates to section at m. 145
	364-394	Relates to section at m. 156
Coda (closing)	395-406	Relates to introduction material

Unit 8: Suggested Listening

Aaron Copland:

El Salon Mexico
> Klavier KCD-11048: Cincinnati Wind Symphony, Eugene Corporon, Conductor.
> Deutsche Grammophon 431 672-2: New York Philharmonic, Leonard Bernstein, Conductor.

Emblems
Rodeo
Three Latin American Sketches

Joaquin Rodrigo, *Concierto de Aranjuez*
Igor Stravinsky, *Symphony d'Instruments a vent*

Unit 9: Additional References and Resources

Butterworth, Neil. *The Music of Aaron Copland*. New York: Toccata Press, 1985.

Campos, Ruben M. El Folklore y la Musica Mexicana.

Cole, Hugo. "Aaron Copland," *Tempo*. No. 76, 1966, pp. 2-4; No. 77, 1966, pp. 9-12.

Cole, Hugo. "Popular Elements in Copland's Music," *Tempo*. No. 95, 1971, pp. 4-8.

Copland, Aaron, and Vivien Perlis. *Copland*. Volume 1: 1900-1942, New York: St. Martin's/Marek, 1984.

Sadie, Stanley, ed. *Norton Grove Concise Encyclopedia of Music*. New York and London: WW Norton & Company, 1988.

Toor, Frank. *Cancionero Mexico*. Mexico: Frances Toor, 1931.

Contributed by:
Cheryl Fryer
University of North Texas
Denton, Texas

Teacher Resource Guide

Fantasy Variations on George Gershwin's "Prelude II for Piano"

Donald Grantham
(b. 1947)

Unit 1: Composer

Donald Grantham earned his Bachelor of Music degree from the University of Oklahoma and his D.M.A. in Composition from the University of Southern California. Grantham's composition teachers have included Halsey Stevens, Robert Linn, and Nadia Boulanger. He is the recipient of numerous awards and prizes in composition, including the Prix Lili Boulanger, the Nissim/ASCAP Orchestral Composition Prize, First Prize in the Concordia Chamber Symphony's Awards to American Composers, the NBA/William Revelli Composition Award (two First Prizes), First Prize in the ABA/Ostwald Composition Competition, First Prize in the National Opera Association's Biennial Composition Competition, three awards from the National Endowment for the Arts, and a Guggenheim Fellowship. His music has been praised for its "elegance, sensitivity, lucidity of thought, clarity of expression and fine lyricism" in a citation awarded by the American Academy and Institute of Arts and Letters. In recent years, his works have been performed by the orchestras of Cleveland, Dallas, Atlanta, and the American Composers Orchestra, among many others. He has also fulfilled commissions in media, from solo instruments to opera. The composer resides in Austin, Texas, and is Professor of Composition at the University of Texas at Austin. His music is published by Peer-Southers, E.C. Schirmer, and Mark Foster, and a number of his works have been commercially recorded. He is co-author with Kent Kennan of *The Technique of Orchestration*, Fourth Edition, published by Prentice-Hall.

Unit 2: Composition

Grantham writes of his *Fantasy Variations*:

> George Gershwin's (1898-1937) *Second Prelude for Piano* is the
> second in a set of three preludes composed in 1926 – his only work
> for solo piano. The set has been popular with performers and
> audiences since its first appearance, and even as severe a composer
> as Arnold Schoenberg found it intriguing enough to orchestrate.
> My attraction to the work is personal, as it was the first piece by an
> American composer I learned as a piano student. In *Fantasy
> Variations*, both of the "big tunes" in the piece are fully exploited,
> but they do not appear in recognizable form until near the end.
> The work begins with much more obscure fragments drawn from
> the introduction, accompanimental figures, transitions, cadences,
> and so forth. These eventually give way to more familiar motives
> derived from the themes themselves. All of these elements are
> gradually assembled over the last half of the piece until the themes
> finally appear in more or less their original form.

Unit 3: Historical Perspective

George Gershwin, one of the most beloved American composers, wove his
way into the fabric of American life through his music. As an essentially self-
taught musician, Gershwin worked his way from a song plugger in Tin Pan
Alley to a world-renowned composer. Grantham's *Fantasy Variations* is a
remarkable tribute to the ingenuity and creativity of Gershwin.

Unit 4: Technical Considerations

Fantasy Variations is a work of significant stature. It requires great artistry and
skill from all performers. Rhythmic content is decisive and very challenging.
Woodwind players will find technical demands extensive, yet rewarding. One
of the primary performance considerations is rhythmic accuracy and drive.
Frequent use of mixed meter requires the conductor and performers to remain
aware of rhythmic groupings and subdivisions between triple, duple, and compound meters, providing a solid rhythmic feeling. Articulation and accent
placement are critical to a good performance. Accents are a prominent feature and must be brought out. Another challenge will be the key centers used
throughout.

Unit 5: Stylistic Considerations

A strength of this work is that it requires both very expressive playing and
great attention to technical and rhythmical detail. Careful attention to
dynamics, clarity of attack, and phrasing based on proper tempi is required.
Markings in the score support and assist in this area. Experience with jazz style
is helpful for the performers of this piece. Insistent jazz rhythms and

punctuations are exuberant and vibrant. Dissonance created befitting this style must be played confidently, and parts should be balanced accordingly.

Unit 6: Musical Elements

As stated earlier by the composer, material for *Fantasy Variations* comes from Gershwin's *Second Prelude for Piano*. Initial variations do not give away the origin of the material, while gradually the themes of the Gershwin *Prelude* unfold more readily to the ears. The following elements serve as primary ingredients in the twenty variations included in *Fantasy Variations*. These musical elements are provided by Donald Grantham; they are from the version for two pianos, which is one-half step higher than the band version:

Unit 7: Form and Structure

Information below provided by Donald Grantham:

	Intro.	A Variation 1	2	3	4	5	6	7	8
Form:		a ____ b ____ a						Fugue (63 mm.)	
Key:	E	c# _____			c#(unstable)	Ab _____			c#
Basis:	3,2,1	3,2	2,1	3,2	4,1,2	1,2	4,5	5	3

	B 9	10	11	12
Form:	a ____ b ____ a			codetta
Key:	bb,Db	Eb	bb,Db	
Basis:	6	7	6	6,2,8

	A′ 13	14	15	16	17	18	19	20	Coda
Form:	Intro' a ____		b __	a _____		Th.1	Th.2	Canon	
Key:	Db _____		bb __	Db _____		c# ___	F# __	a/A ___	f#/F#
Basis:	8,3	8,3,9	9,3,2	9	9			5	1,2,3

Unit 8: Suggested Listening

Johannes Brahms, *Variations on a Theme by Handel*, Op. 56A

George Gershwin:
Second Prelude for Piano
Second Prelude from Three Preludes (Arr. Krance)

Donald Grantham, *J'ai ete au bal*

Unit 9: Additional References and Resources

Grantham, Donald. *Fantasy Variations*. Eugene Corporon and the North Texas Wind Symphony, 1999.

Grantham, Donald. *Fantasy Variations*. Jerry Junkin and the University of Texas Wind Ensemble, 1998. Compact disc 2697-MCD.

Grantham, Donald. *Southern Harmony*. Eugene Corporon and the North Texas Wind Symphony, 1999.

Sadie, Stanley, ed. *Norton Grove Concise Encyclopedia of Music*, New York and London: WW Norton & Company, Macmillan Press, London, 1988.

Contributed by:

Cheryl Fryer
University of North Texas
Denton, Texas

Teacher Resource Guide

For Precious Friends Hid in Death's Dateless Night, Op. 80

Martin Mailman
(b. 1932)

Unit 1: Composer

Dr. Martin Mailman is currently Regents Professor of Music and Composer-in-Residence at the University of North Texas, Denton. A composition student of Louis Mennini, Wayne Barlow, Bernard Rogers, and Howard Hanson, he received his B.M., M.M., and Ph.D. degrees from the Eastman School of Music, Rochester, New York. Dr. Mailman has received numerous awards, among which include two American Bandmasters Association/Ostwald prizes for composition (*Exaltations* in 1983 and *For Precious Friends Hid in Death's Dateless Night* in 1989), the National Band Association/Band Mans Company Prize for Composition (*For Precious Friends Hid in Death's Dateless Night* in 1989), the Edward Benjamin Award (*Autumn Landscape* in 1955), a National Endowment for the Arts Composers Grant (1982), Composer of the Year (named by the Texas Music Educators Association in 1989), and the 1982 Queen Marie-Jose Prize for Composition (*Concerto for Violin and Orchestra* in 1982). His works include chamber music, band, choral, and orchestral music, film scores, television music, an opera, and a requiem for chorus, orchestra, and soloist. A frequently sought-after clinician and teacher, Dr. Mailman has served as guest conductor-composer at more than ninety colleges and universities across the United States and Europe. Some of his other works for band include *Geometrics 1 for Band, Op. 22; Concertino for Trumpet and Band, Op. 31; Liturgical Music for Band, Op. 33; Geometrics 3 for Band, Op. 37; Geometrics 4 for Band, Op. 43; Association No. 1 for Band, Op. 45; Shouts, Hymns, and Praises, Op. 52; A Simple Ceremony: In Memoriam John Barnes Chance, Op. 53; Decorations for Band, Op. 54; Let Us Now Praise Famous Men, Op. 56; Geometrics 5 for Band,*

Op. 58; *Night Vigil*, Op. 66; *Exaltations*, Op. 67; *The Jewel in the Crown*, Op. 78; *Toward the Second Century*, Op. 82; *Concertino for Clarinet and Band*, Op. 83; *Bouquets*, Op. 87; *Concerto for Wind Orchestra (Variations)*, Op. 89; *Secular Litanies*, Op. 90; and *Pledges*, Op. 98.

Unit 2: Composition

For Precious Friends Hid in Death's Dateless Night, Op. 80, is a three-movement work for symphonic winds inspired by the sonnets of William Shakespeare (1564-1616). It was first performed on November 10, 1988, by the University of North Texas Symphonic Wind Ensemble, conducted by Dr. Robert A. Winslow. With the exception of the title of the second movement, written by the composer, the titles of the remaining movements are taken directly from the lines of Shakespeare's sonnets (which follow). The piece is a grade six difficulty, lasts about twenty minutes (each movement is roughly of equal length), and is published by Ludwig Music.

About his piece, the composer writes:

> The dilemma of, on the one hand, my long-standing aversion to writing program notes for my music, and on the other, a request from a valued colleague for written comments about my work, *For Precious Friends Hid in Death's Dateless Night*, may very well remain unresolved. While I do not mind making appropriate verbal remarks to performers during a rehearsal of my music, I do find myself loathe [sic] to write or speak comments under other circumstances. I feel that if I have done my work as a composer properly, the music will not benefit from my words.
>
> I am reminded of the time when I was being interviewed by a reporter after the premiere of my *Concerto for Violin and Orchestra* in Geneva. She began the interview by telling me a wonderful story of her impression of my piece, then asking me if this was indeed my creative motivation for the work. It was not, but had I written whatever my thoughts about the work may have been, she would have never had the freedom to create her own rich imagery.
>
> I can say that very few of my works had the same birth as this one. I was sitting reading the Sonnets of Shakespeare when I came across the title line. I was stunned by it and within an hour or so had composed the opening of the work. The remainder of the work came about as much of my music has, through very hard work and long hours of private labor. The titles of the first and third movements were not difficult to settle on, and as a matter of fact, may have been selected before the music. Search as I may, Shakespeare presented no appropriate title for the second movement and finally I had to settle

for words less eloquent than his but descriptive nonetheless.

In the end, I hope the magnificent words that inspired me will offer each listener an opportunity to share the experience I had when I read them and attempted to express in sound and time the incredible sense of humanity and spirit of Shakespeare.

SONNET 30
When to the sessions of sweet silent thought
I summon up remembrance of things past,
I sigh the lack of many a thing I sought,
And with old woes new wail my dear time's waste.
Then can I drown an eye, unus'd to flow,
For precious friends hid in death's dateless night,
And weep afresh love's long since cancell'd woe,
And moan th' expense of many a vanish'd sight.
Then can I grieve at grievances foregone,
And heavily from woe to woe tell o'er
The sad account of fore-bemoaned moan,
Which I new pay as if not paid before.
    But if the while I think on thee, dear friend,
    All losses are restor'd, and sorrows end.

Movement I: "Mournful hymns did hush the night"
    SONNET 102
    My love is strength'ned, though more weak in seeming;
    I love not less, though less the show appear;
    That love is merchandiz'd whose rich esteeming
    The owner's tongue doth publish everywhere.
    Our love was new, and then but in the spring,
    When I was wont to greet it with my lays;
    As Philomel in summer's front doth sing,
    And stops her pipe in growth of riper days.
    Not that the summer is less pleasant now
    Than when her mournful hymns did hush the night,
    But that wild music burthens every bough,
    And sweets grown common lose their dear delight.
        Therefore, like her, I sometime hold my tongue,
        Because I would not dull you with my song.

Movement III: "Which by and by black night doth take away"
    SONNET 73
    That time of year thou mayst in me behold
    When yellow leaves, or none, or few, do hang

Upon those boughs which shake against the cold,
Bare ruin'd choirs where late the sweet birds sang.
In me thou seest the twilight of such day
As after sunset fadeth in the west,
Which by and by black night doth take away,
Death's second self, that seals up all in rest.
In me thou seest the glowing of such fire
That on the ashes of his youth doth lie,
As the death-bed whereon it must expire,
Consum'd with that which it was nourish'd by.
    This thou perceiv'st which makes thy love more strong,
    To love that well which thou must leave ere long.

Unit 3: Historical Perspective

Mailman belongs to a generation of late twentieth century composers that includes Ron Nelson, John Barnes Chance, and Fisher Tull. He was one of the composers selected to participate in the Ford Foundation Contemporary Music Project, which was an important vehicle for several aspiring musicians. He is currently in demand as composer, conductor, and clinician, and his works are already highly respected, as is evidenced by his *For Precious Friends Hid in Death's Dateless Night* being the first composition to be awarded both the National Band Association/Band Mans Company Prize for Composition in December 1988 and the American Bandmasters Association/Ostwald Prize for Composition in January 1989.

Unit 4: Technical Considerations

The piece is very technically challenging for all players. All instruments are required to play independently, and specific sections are frequently featured and exposed. The piece has no key signatures, so accidentals abound. There are changes of meter within movements, but only on the quarter note level. The tempi remain consistent within the movements. There are articulations of every kind. Contrasts and repetitions are vitally important, and the conductor must make them happen. Instruments frequently have exposed sections or solos, but the percussion section is featured prominently, especially in the second movement. All instruments are essential; the work is scored for standard symphonic band instrumentation, plus double bass, harp, piano, English horn, contrabassoon, celesta, soprano voice, and an extensive percussion list (including a bass marimba). The soprano voice appears only in the third movement; the singer should be sitting unobtrusively with the flutes for the entire work. The singer is required to taper a high C and may sing an optional E on the last note of the piece. The conductor and ensemble must have a clear conceptualization of the piece and its presentation to successfully perform the work; the piece does not "play itself." For that reason, only advanced ensembles and conductors should attempt its performance.

Unit 5: Stylistic Considerations

Articulations should be as accurate as possible. All markings in the score support this. Each movement (and, most of the time, section) has its own style. There are non-standard notations to indicate waves of sound, unmetered measures, unequal quarter notes (on cue), gradual *diminuendos* and *crescendos*, steady dynamics, and uneven tremolos. While a drive should propel the work throughout, the open atmosphere of moments in the first and third movements require great patience and understanding by the conductor and ensemble. The intensity and movement of the music should be equal to the phrasing, articulation, rhythms, and principles of the line. This is a twentieth century work with twentieth century sounds and also Romantic impressions; it should be approached with an open-minded, omniscient, aesthetic interpretation.

Unit 6: Musical Elements

The work is not programmatic; rather, it is inspired from a literary source. *For Precious Friends* sets a mood and deals with emotions and feelings that leave the power and impact in the *music* – not the referential external. Other examples of works for band of this ilk would include *Emblems* by Aaron Copland, *Hammersmith* by Gustav Holst, and *From a Dark Millennium* by Joseph Schwantner. As with Shakespeare's sonnets, the flow and relationship of one movement to another, the imagery, the subtlety, the use of medium, the economy, and the passion are all components in this work.

The first movement, "Mournful hymns did hush the night," begins with a statement from the horns of the primary theme found in all of the movements. It utilizes powerful scoring of brass and percussion sharply contrasted with delicate sounds of celesta, harp, glockenspiel, and woodwinds that state the "chorale" melody. Several motives are established which recur throughout the other movements, such as descending scales with bell sounds. These descending scales are heard in several different settings, including unmetered sections, within waves of sound, and as a brass chorale. Additionally, both alto saxophone and euphonium have poignant soli.

The second movement, "Broken loops of buried memories," is composed of rapid and rhythmic motivic fragments over a bass marimba *ostinato*. The "broken loops," played by such instruments as percussion, muted trombones, tuba, basses, low reeds, and upper woodwinds, coalesce throughout the movement until the end when all instruments play a unison final rhythm. The "broken loops" often serve as quasi-*ostinati* for more lyrical events that represent the "buried memories." Throughout the movement, motives and snippets are used, reused, and changed. The movement is perpetual; the sixteenth notes in the bass marimba give the impression of a piece that has always been sounding and will continue to sound forever, and what one hears is only a brief segment of that timelessness. Within that segment, there are several points of arrival, each larger than the previous, but from the movement's first statement of the snare drum, the ultimate goal and climax is the last three notes played by the percussion. The fact that the first and last thing heard is virtually the same lends itself to the idea of eternity. Every single note in the movement contributes; there is not a single note to spare with an astonishing economy of material and purpose.

The third movement, "Which by and by black night doth take away," moves from the ethereal sounds of English horn, muted trumpets, celesta, harp, piccolo, and soprano voice through an extended *crescendo* to a stunning climax utilizing the solo soprano soaring above the full texture of the band. The soprano vocalizes on the syllable "ah." During the movement, statements from previous movements are heard as remembrances of things past, thereby cyclically unifying the entire work.

Unit 7: Form and Structure

SECTION	MEASURE	EVENT AND SCORING

Movement I: "Mournful hymns did hush the night"

	MEASURE	EVENT AND SCORING
	1-4	Opening motive
	5	Chorale melody (phrase 1) – waves of sound; unmetered measure
	6-9	Opening motive
	10	Chorale melody (phrase 2) – waves of sound; unmetered measure
	11-20	Opening motive (chorale melody and waves of sound interpolated, mm. 15-17)
	21-29	Opening motive – waves of sound accompaniment; euphonium solo melodic version of chords in waves of sound
	30-35	Descending scalar motive
	36-47	Alto saxophone solo (minor third theme)
	48-60	Opening motive (somewhat developed)
	61-65	Transition (upper woodwinds, piano, glockenspiel)
	66-70	Woodwind waves of sound with chorale melody
	71-85	Opening motive
	85-100	Brass chorale
	101-114	Climax
	115-122	Descending scalar motive

SECTION	MEASURE	EVENT AND SCORING

Movement II: "Broken loops of buried memories"

Section I	1-5	Loop 1 (percussion) – based on three-note rhythm
	6-13	Loop 1 (percussion, woodwinds, and harp)
	14-24	Loop 1 (percussion, low brass, low winds)
	25-30	Loop 2 (basses, low brass)
	30-33	Loop 3 (upper winds, harp, percussion)
	33-36	Loop 1 (percussion)
	37-45	Loop 2 (basses, low brass)
	45-49	Loop 3 (upper winds, harp, percussion)
Section II	49-56	"Buried memory" (upper brass, basses, low brass)
	56-57	Loop 3 (upper winds, harp, percussion)
	58-67	"Buried memory" – somewhat developed (upper brass, basses, low brass)
	68-73	Loop 3 (upper winds, harp) and descending clusters
	74-80	Loop 2 (basses, low brass)
Section III	81-87	"Buried memory" with long-note theme (clarinet) – references Movement I
	88-94	"Buried memory" in canon with long-note theme (oboe, English horn, euphonium)
	95-101	"Buried memory" long-note theme (woodwinds)
	102-108	Transition material
	109-120	Minor third theme (horns) – originates from m. 36, Movement I, alto saxophone solo
	121-126	Transition (woodwinds, harp, piano)
	127-129	Loop 3
Section IV	130-146	*Fugato* (piccolo, xylophone, flutes, clarinet 1, oboe, E-flat clarinet) based on a spreading out of notes from m. 6 into melodic form
	147-149	"Buried memory" and loop fragments
	150-152	Descending clusters (see m. 73)
	153-154	False Loop 1

Section	Measure	Event and Scoring
Section V	154-160	Loop (basses, low brass)
	161-169	"Buried memory" (upper winds) (see trumpets m. 50)
	170-177	Rhythmic augmentation of *fugato* subject
	178-185	Augmentation of canon with loops
	186-190	Minor third theme (horns) with "chorale" melody from Movement I with flutes (see m. 109)
	191-212	Development of "buried memory" (woodwind atmosphere, quasi-chorale in brass)
	213-217	Loop 1 (woodwind tremolo, trumpets) and descending clusters
	218-222	Extension of clusters
	223-226	Transition and *crescendo*
	227-229	Loop 1
	229-230	Interruption of Loop 1 (percussion)
	231-234	Chord stacking
	235	Loop 1 finished
	236	Final use of three-note rhythm to end the loops (percussion)

Movement III: "Which by and by black night doth take away"

	Measure	Event and Scoring
	1-7	Descending scalar motive (piano, double bass, harp, mallets) – from Movement I
	8-15	English horn solo based on long-note theme from Movement II, m. 81
	16-22	Descending scalar motive (piano, double bass, harp, mallets) – from Movement I
	23-28	English horn solo based on long-note theme from Movement II, m. 81
	23-34	Descending scalar motive (piano, double bass, harp, mallets) – from Movement I
	35-51	Soprano vocalise with upper woodwind accompaniment
	52-63	Soprano vocalise solo based on Movement I, minor third theme
	64-77	Descending scalar motive from Movement I, with Movement I opening theme

SECTION	MEASURE	EVENT AND SCORING
	78-82	Soprano vocalise solo based on Movement II, long-note theme
	83-94	Movement I chorale melody in horn and euphonium
	95-101	Soprano vocalise solo based on chorale melody, with *tutti* waves of sound
	101-103	Rhythmic motive from Movement II, m. 50 (trumpet)
	104-106	Final three chords

Unit 8: Suggested Listening

Martin Mailman:

A Simple Ceremony: In Memoriam John Barnes Chance, Op. 53
Alarums for Band, Op. 27
Association No. 1 for Band, Op. 45
Bouquets, Op. 87
Concertino for Clarinet and Band, Op. 83
Concertino for Trumpet and Band, Op. 31
Concerto for Wind Orchestra (Variations), Op. 89
Decorations for Band, Op. 54
Exaltations, Op. 67
Geometrics 1 for Band, Op. 22
Geometrics 3 for Band, Op. 37
Geometrics 4 for Band, Op. 43
Geometrics 5 for Band, Op. 58
Let Us Now Praise Famous Men, Op. 56
Liturgical Music for Band, Op. 33
Night Vigil, Op. 66
Pledges, Op. 98
Secular Litanies, Op. 90
Shouts, Hymns, and Praises, Op. 52
The Jewel in the Crown, Op. 78
Toward the Second Century, Op. 82

Unit 9: Additional References and Resources

Baker, Theodore. "Mailman, Martin," *Baker's Biographical Dictionary of Musicians*. 6th ed., revised by Nicolas Slonimsky. New York: Schirmer Books, 1984.

Ewen, David. *A Comprehensive Biographical Dictionary of American Composers*. New York: G.P. Putnam & Sons, 1982.

Mailman, Martin. *Bouquets, Op. 87*. Dick Clardy and the Colony High School Wind Symphony. Compact disc "1994 Midwest Band and Orchestra Clinic Concert" Mark Custom Recordings MW94MCD-10, 1994.

Mailman, Martin. *Bouquets, Op. 87*. Joseph W. Herman and the Tennessee Technological University Symphony Band. Compact disc "1998 Carl Fischer Concert Band Sampler" CN-98085, 1998.

Mailman, Martin. *Concertino for Clarinet and Band, Op. 83*. Matthew Mailman and the Oklahoma City University Symphonic Band, Patricia Card, clarinet. Compact disc "Martin Mailman - *Concertino for Clarinet and Band, Op. 83*" (available through Carl Fischer), 1997.

Mailman, Martin. *For Precious Friends Hid in Death's Dateless Night, Op. 80*. Eugene Corporon and the University of North Texas Wind Symphony. Compact disc "Dialogues and Entertainments" KCD-11083, 1997.

Mailman, Martin. *For Precious Friends Hid in Death's Dateless Night, Op. 80*. Cleveland, OH: Ludwig Music (SBS-270), 1990.

Mailman, Martin. *Geometrics No. 4, Op. 43*. Compact disc "Warner Brothers Music for Concert Band Symphonic Band Series" CATCD95-4, 1998.

Mailman, Martin. Interview by Matthew Mailman, 18 January 1999.

Mailman, Martin. *Liturgical Music, Op. 33*. Jack Stamp and the Indiana University of Pennsylvania Symphony Band. Compact disc "IUP Concert Bands of 1998," 1998.

Mailman, Martin. *Secular Litanies, Op. 90*. Jack Stamp and the Indiana University of Pennsylvania Wind Ensemble. Compact disc "IUP Concert Bands - 1996," 1996.

Mailman, Matthew. Unpublished personal files. Oklahoma City, OK.

Miles, Richard, ed. "Martin Mailman - *Exaltations, Op. 67*," *Teaching Music through Performance in Band, Volume 2*. Chicago: GIA Publications, Inc., 1997, pp. 442-446.

Miles, Richard, ed. "Martin Mailman - *Liturgical Music, Op. 33*," *Teaching Music through Performance in Band, Volume 1*. Chicago: GIA Publications, Inc., 1997, pp. 259-262.

National Band Association Selective Music List for Bands.

Rehrig, William H. *The Heritage Encyclopedia of Band Music*. Westerville, OH: Integrity Press, 1991.

Speck, Frederick. "Analysis: Martin Mailman's *For Precious Friends Hid in Death's Dateless Night*." *Journal of Band Research*. Vol 26/I/Fall 1990, pp. 14-29.

Contributed by:
Matthew Mailman
Director of Bands and Associate Professor of Music
Oklahoma City University

Teacher Resource Guide

From a Dark Millennium
Joseph Schwantner
(b. 1943)

Unit 1: Composer

Joseph Schwantner was born in Chicago on March 22, 1943. He is currently Professor of Composition at the Eastman School of Music at the University of Rochester, were he has taught since 1970. He has also served on the faculty of the Julliard School and was the 1987-88 Karel Husa Visiting Professor of Composition at Ithaca College, Ithaca, New York. Schwantner received his musical and academic training at the Chicago Conservatory and at Northwestern University, where he completed a doctorate in 1968. From 1982 to 1985, Schwantner served as Composer-in-Residence with the Saint Louis Symphony Orchestra as part of the MEET THE COMPOSER/Orchestra Residencies Program funded by Exxon Corporation, the Rockefeller Foundation, and the National Endowment for the Arts. He has been the subject of a television documentary entitled, *Soundings*, produced by WGBH in Boston for national broadcast. His work, *Magabunda*, "four poems of Agueda Pizarro," recorded by the Saint Louis Symphony, was nominated for a 1985 Grammy Award in the category of "Best New Classical Composition," and his *A Sudden Rainbow*, also recorded by the Saint Louis Symphony, was nominated for "Best Classical Composition."

Unit 2: Composition

From a Dark Millennium was commissioned by the Mid-America Band Directors Association in 1980. It is published by Helicon Music Corporation and distributed by European American Music Distributors.

From a Dark Millennium is a single continuous movement based loosely on an austere poem by the composer. This poem, which is not included in the score, is as follows:

SANCTUARY........
deep forests
a play of Shadows,
    Most ancient murmurings
from a dark millennium
    the trembling fragrance
of the music of amber.

The work is scored for woodwinds, brass, piano and celesta, and an expanded percussion section. Emphasis is placed on the equality of timbre between these four elements. Schwantner continues to explore the vocal resources within the ensemble he integrated into his first wind work, *and the mountains rising nowhere*, by requiring the instrumentalists to sing – "celestial choir" – and whistle.

The eleven-minute work calls for three flutes (2nd and 3rd double on piccolo), three B-flat clarinets (1st doubles on E-flat clarinet; 2nd and 3rd double on bass clarinet), two oboes, English horn, three bassoons, three trumpets in B-flat, four horns in F, four trombones (4th is bass trombone), one tuba, two contrabass, piano (amplified, *sostenuto* pedal required), celesta, five percussion playing marimba, six roto-toms, two vibraphones (four contrabass bows for "arco" playing), glockenspiel, crotales (mounted octave set), xylophone, chimes, four timbales, three tom-toms, four suspended cymbals, two tam-tams, large triangle, two bass drums, and timpani.

Unit 3: Historical Perspective

Schwantner's first work for wind band, *and the mountains rising nowhere*, became a landmark composition in the wind band repertoire. *From a Dark Millennium* has found a similar place in the repertoire without the extreme technical demands of the previous work. *From a Dark Millennium* is a "re-orchestration" by the composer of the second movement, "Sanctuary," from *Music of Amber*, which was commissioned to commemorate the tenth anniversary of the Da Capo Chamber Players.

Unit 4: Technical Considerations

From a Dark Millennium incorporates a number of contemporary notational concepts. Almost all of Schwantner's works are composed in Mirco notation. Time signatures of 2/8, 3/8, 4/8, 5/8, 7/8, 5/16, 6/16, and 4/dotted eighth note are used with subdivisions as small as a sixty-fourth note. Spatial notation, senza mazura, and time line notation is also used. Instrumental ranges are in the highest tessitura for most instruments. The piano part is integral to the entire work. All wind players and double bass are required to either sing or whistle. Percussion set-up is extremely important in regard to dynamic balances within the entire ensemble and shared equipment among the percussionists. Many sections include intricate episodes of "shared monody."

Although the work does contain some specific challenges to performers and conductor, both college and high school ensembles have successfully performed it. The challenges for the performer include rhythmic notation, complexity of rhythm, changing meters, singing and whistling and, especially for the less-experienced performer, extremes of range and volume. For the conductor, the challenges also include ensemble balance and keeping a melodic flow in a sectional work.

Unit 5: Stylistic Considerations

Schwantner states that some of his intentions in composing the work included creating a work for winds and percussion that did not sound "like a band piece." He was further interested in writing a work: (1) where the percussion section would be on an equal footing with the woodwinds and brass, (2) to further exploit the process of synthesis between tonal and non-tonal musical materials, and (3) to expand the sonorous timbrel and articulative resources of a large ensemble by having performers engage in "extra performance activities," such as singing, whistling, and playing glass crystals. Through the use of some key stylistic elements, he utilizes the elements of rhythm, timbre, and texture in a number of contemporary and traditional techniques.

Music as complex as Schwantner's must be interpreted with the same careful attention to basic elements as earlier music. Often the language of contemporary music is not familiar to the players; they must often play in techniques or styles with which they are not conversant. As an example, the clarinetist's role in a Beethoven symphony is quickly obvious to him or her through training and background. The player knows how the motion of the music is generated and how he or she contributes to the various textures and progress of the work. The player is readily aware of when to be an ensemble player and when to be a soloist, and adjusts his or her intonation and volume to fit the changing circumstances. In *From a Dark Millennium*, these responsibilities are not as clearly identifiable, and the conductor must assist as the translator of motives, harmony, form, development, and meter as broader understandings are reached.

Schwantner also uses a timbre and textural technique he refers to as "shared monody." This is a melodic idea that is shared by partial doublings among several instrumental voices. According to Schwantner, this technique is a single, linear event that is melodically shared by many players, with each single player entering and sustaining a different pitch of the theme in order. These notes become a single line in which many participate as differentiated from a single player on a solo line.

Unit 6: Musical Elements

MELODY:

In many cases the familiar, "singable" themes of tonal music are replaced in much twentieth century music with shorter motives that take on a more angular instrumental character and are often layered upon one another to produce new sonorities. These shorter elements are not necessarily treated with the theme, harmony, bass line, and *obligato*-like settings players are accustomed to hearing.

One of the characteristic features of both *From a Dark Millennium* and *and the mountains rising nowhere* is what Schwantner terms "shared monody," as addressed above.

A traditional performance problem lies in the player's perception of his or her part as only a component of a larger melodic unfolding. In a contemporary setting, it becomes more difficult. For an entrance that is only the third part of a triplet, the performer must understand that he/she is participating in a "solo"-like melodic line that may even be one component of four lines. Equally often these lines in *From a Dark Millennium* are presented as an aggregate in the percussion and piano/celesta. The participating players have a strong reference both rhythmically and melodically.

Schwantner frequently initiates these melodic fragment lines in percussion because of the sharp attacks created by the instruments. This percussion sound creates ensemble concerns when mixed with winds. While two clarinets playing together may have a slight difference at the moment of attack without being discernable, two percussion instruments attacking together, especially melodic percussion with hard mallets, may only be a nano-second apart and the difference is heard. When winds are mixed with percussion, the differences are sometimes very difficult to solve.

HARMONY:

Schwantner uses "static pillars" of harmonies – much like the music of Varèse – in which single sonorities or "blocks of sound" are unchanged for a period of time. Often, angular motives themselves become the harmony as they are held or suspended. While traditional melodies move above a harmonic base, the effects of suspending their sound would be the same as playing a Mozart sonata with the pedal always down.

When a chord spanning three octaves is played, it is very difficult to hear inner voices unless there is a great deal of registral space between notes. When eight or nine notes of a chord are articulated one at a time, the ear perceives each note and they are then allowed to sustain. "Successive articulation" of each note of a chord helps clarify the harmonic entity. These "stable pillars" of harmony develop their own tonal centers that are more static than in progressions in a traditional triadic sense.

FORM:

In *From a Dark Millennium*, instrumental color, tempo, dynamics, accumulation of textured density, and changing of density outline the form of the piece and create moments of tension and release, propelling the work in time.

Schwantner provides additional development through changes in color as the musical lines change shape – thick and thin – rather than manipulations of musical materials and ideas. The composer is always concerned with how the sound changes in time from point A to point B. In many instances, his music tries to maximize coloristic and timbrel possibilities of the wind ensemble.

It is also important to bring out the violent contrasts in the work. Very soft (*ppp*) sections may explode into very loud (*fff*) sections without preparation. The music may take unexpected twists and turns from one part of the texture to another. Young musicians may not be sufficiently exposed to such dramatic changes to perform them successfully, and the conductor must be insistent on achieving these effects. Subtleties of dynamics are also integral, as often the *pianissimo* becomes *mezzo-piano* and the *fortissimo* becomes *mezzo-forte*.

Frequent meter changes and asymmetrical patterns are another unfamiliar area for the young musician. If these are treated in a melodic sense, they are often more readily mastered.

Unit 7: Form and Structure

SECTION 1: (mm. 1-16)

The work begins with an *ostinato* first presented in the piano and vibraphone, and gradually expanded to include a second vibraphone, glockenspiel, and celesta. The opening pitch (F) is echoed by stopped horns and a choir of "chanters" and percussion (chimes and triangle). The chant requires the woodwinds to sing the pitch F at the unison with recurring accents. Men may need to sing falsetto so all of the singing is consistently in unison, not in octaves, and without vibrato. The *ostinato* itself is created from an octatonic scale (F-sharp, G-sharp, A, B, C, D, E-flat, F) that is "syncopated" by alternately reversing the F and F-sharp in each measure, with the F-sharp always accented.

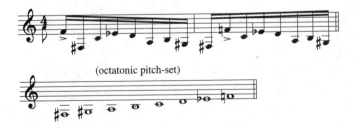

(octatonic pitch-set)

This figure is repeated and played a total of eight times. It is important that the *sostenuto* pedal of the piano, celesta, and vibraphone be held throughout this section, creating an overlapping of the individual note sounds.

The tempo of eighth note = 56 in 4/8 requires a steady pulse. A *crescendo* starting in m. 10 is reinforced by the entry of the remainder of the brass section in m. 11. The surges of sound created by the brass and singers are easily controlled by conducting a *crescendo* and *diminuendo*, reaching its peak on beat three of each bar – symmetrical dynamics. The half-beat rest that separates each entrance can be interpreted uniformly by having the ensemble breathe directly on the rest and interpret the accent starting each segment more as a well-defined beginning than as a burst of sound. The chant can be performed with the same rest separation as the wind parts, being careful that the quality of sound does not become forced. The difficulty lies in not letting the surge of sound become too loud too early or not grow enough into its climax at mm. 17-18. The accent that occurs in the stopped 1st horn, marked "*lantano*" or distant (later in trumpet 1), must be exaggerated in order for the stopped sound to penetrate the texture.

A word about "micro-rhythmic-notation" would be appropriate at this time. The basic pulse division of the bar is the eighth note, with sixteenth notes receiving a half beat, thirty-second notes a quarter beat, etc. These rhythms can be translated into more easily recognizable forms by mentally "doubling" the value of each note until the notational system is more familiar. The addition of beat bars into the parts is also a help at first and in some of the more complex sections later in the work.

SECTIONS 2 AND 3: (mm. 17-34 / 35-50)
The climax of the *first* section is reached in mm. 17-18, with a pair of double accents first in a rhythmic unison of brass, keyboard, and percussion followed by piano, celesta, and percussion. The sound of the second entrance should not be dampened and must ring as long as possible. The ending accent in the brass connecting the two measures must be performed with a surge of air stopped immediately on the downbeat of m. 18.

Here, too, the "celestial choir" (flutes, oboes, clarinets, and bassoons) changes the sung syllable from the attacked "tah " to an "oo" and with a slight *crescendo* into an "ah." In m. 20, the "choir" begins its own motive.

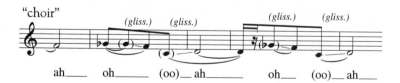

This four-measure motive is repeated four times and continues the on-the-beat/off-the-beat syncopated rhythm with which the opening *ostinato* began.

Measure 20 introduces two new ideas into the work. The first is a series of vertical chords in the percussion based upon the pitches of the octatonic set introduced at the start of the piece. These chords are performed by four percussionists on two vibraphones drawing contrabass bows across the end of the key plates to produce the pitches. The bow articulations should be coordinated, but no attempt should be made to coordinate these chords with the rest of the ensemble. Since four players are performing on two instruments, it works well to have players one and three stand on the correct side of the instrument while players two and four stand on the back side. Player one becomes the leader, and the others bow their notes watching player one for the pulse. The leader should be facing the conductor and wait for the others to find their notes before starting the next entrance. It also helps to number the key plates in order of performance for players two and four because pitches are difficult to read upside down. The eight pitches are then repeated again in order until the ensemble reaches m. 35.

The second event that starts at m. 21 is a flute solo highlighted at the beginning of each phrase by the piano and celesta. Some freedom of expression should be allowed in the rhythmic interpretation as long as the flow and dynamics are not hindered. This continues until m. 27, when the ending pitches of the flute solo are taken over by a "choir of whistlers" (horns, trumpets, trombones, tuba, and contrabasses). Intonation is a challenge, which can be helped by having the whistlers begin the first two pitches (A – A-flat) at a very low dynamic, allowing them to accurately match the flute pitch. As is the case with the sung *glissandi*, the whistle *glissando* should be slow and somewhat even, with a slight *crescendo* on the descending second *glissando*, providing an ethereal effect. Careful attention should be given the sung B-flat in m. 34 that is the transition into Section 3.

At this point the pianist is directed to silently depress the lowest possible octave B-flats and D-flats and then release the keys with the *sostenuto* pedal depressed. This will cause these notes to ring sympathetically when other notes are played. Caution is needed here to ensure that the pedal remains down at all times, or the process of "ringing" will be lost.

Section 3 is marked "dark and foreboding" at the metronome marking of eighth note-dotted eighth note = 56. The time signature indicated is:

A third rhythmic *ostinato* is introduced in m. 35, which develops harmonically as well as gradually increases in density as additional instruments are added. The *ostinato* becomes a two-part texture at the fourth measure (m. 38) with the addition of the piano (right hand), while at the same time the singing and whistling choirs *diminuendo* to *niente*. The rhythmic stress of this line gives the illusion that the beginning of the syncopated triplet is the downbeat.

As various instruments are added to the density, care should be taken to hold the tempo back until the *stringendo* at m. 46. The brass fanfare-like climax at mm. 48-50 must be given careful attention to articulation of long and short duplets, which creates a strong drive to the end.

The *fermata* at the end of m. 50 should be just short enough to allow the ringing sound in the hall to nearly die away and long enough for the pianist to silently depress all of the keys (full chromatic) at the bottom of the keyboard with the left forearm. The *sostenuto* pedal must be added while the keys are still depressed, as it was in m. 34.

SECTION 4: (mm. 51-64)

There is a fermata on each of the first three beats of m. 51. The woodwinds sustain a *pianissimo* chord, without vibrato, while the brass create a *fortissimo* surge of sound ending in a *marcato* accent in the piano. The fermatas should be long enough so as to allow the woodwind/piano sound to ring and start to decay before the next surge begins.

This same brass effect is presented again in m. 52 but with a triplet figure in the percussion replacing the fermatas. Beats two, three, and four of m. 53 must be carefully worked out. One effective solution is to have the entire ensemble sing the rhythm together. This helps establish both the tempo and the connection of the three beats. Care should be taken to ensure that the fives are of equal length and that the tempo of the two sets of fours (4:3 / 4:2) are not performed at the same speed. The change of articulation from "*sostenuto* accent" to "*sostenuto*" and back to "*sostenuto* accent" is important to the momentum of the line.

This next section is marked "exuberantly" in 4/8 at the tempo of eighth note = 96. The three-measure motive in mm. 54-56, and repeated in mm. 62-64, is presented in the piano, celesta, vibraphones, glockenspiel, and crotales at the dynamic of *fff* and is "colored" by Schwantner's "shared monody" in the treble woodwinds.

The percussion sounds should be allowed to ring freely at all times. The sustaining effect of the woodwinds helps create a harmonic atmosphere while the woodwind rhythms are outlined with the help of the constant reference in the percussion.

The five bars that separate these two phrases are marked 6/8 *misterioso*. The double-octave unison duet of solo flute and bassoon should appear to float out of and back to the *sospeso* (floating) – *senza vibrato* double-octave A played by the piccolos and clarinets. This phrase starts at a *subito ppp*, and the previous sounds should be allowed to ring into this measure. The *ppp* is abruptly interrupted by a brass chord that explodes then immediately disappears, only to surge again into the next measure. Care should be taken not to allow the percussion (cymbals and triangle) to cover the woodwind sounds.

Measure 65 echoes the *misterioso* bars with a *subito pp*. The thirty-second note articulations in the 4th trombone and piano should be barely discernable. This section is marked *con elevazone ed elegante*.

The arpeggiated chord presented in the celesta and piano (m. 66) is repeated in the next measure (m. 67) by the trombones and woodwinds. As this is repeated, stopped horn and muted trumpet answer each other in a "horn call" similar to the opening measures of the work. It is important that the brass calls cut through the sustained sounds of the ensemble. The 3rd horn adds the final accent to the horn's call, while the trumpet ends its call without the accent.

Attention should be given to the swells in the woodwind/trombone sounds. Notice that the 1st clarinet grows to *ff*, while the others are only at *mp*.

SECTION 6: (mm. 75-91)
This section is an expansion of melodic material from Section 4 with the *ostinato* from Section 1. Schwantner writes a wonderful quartet which starts with a G-flat drone in unison B-flat clarinets, stopped horn, and flute (two octaves higher). A quartet of flute, English horn, E-flat clarinet, and bassoon enter two measures later with a rhythmically challenging melody which, according to Schwantner, is rarely performed light enough. A two-octave G-flat (E-flat clarinet should have an E-flat written, not E-natural) joins the drone, and the melody emerges. This accompaniment must be kept at the *pp* level, with the exception of the sudden *ff* accents that mark the syncopation. The texture does not change until m. 88 when the brass voices enter from *niente* with their chord.

The brass *glissando* at the end of m. 90 is answered by a dramatic swell in the full woodwinds into the next section.

SECTIONS 7, 8, AND 9: (mm. 92-94 / 95-100 / 101-108)
Suddenly the brass explodes with an *ostinato* of "shared monody" based on the celestial choir motive in Section 1. This is played by four unison horns.

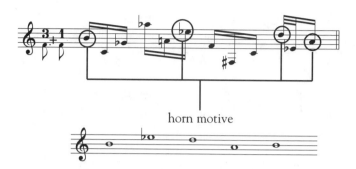

horn motive

At m. 95, the woodwinds, keyboards, and percussion emerge from the brass *ff* with a *ppp ostinato* labeled "*sub. delicatamente*" in 6/8 at eighth note = 96. The sixteenth note pulse remains the same as the previous section. The brass then return whistling the original motive. Pitches for the whistlers are heard in the flutes, with the starting note given at the end of the previous measure by the 1st flute.

The texture explodes dramatically again as the woodwinds and keyboards sustain the chord first heard in m. 18. The brass then repeat the *ostinato* from m. 92 in the meter of 3/8 + 1/dotted-eighth. This effect can be emphasized by having the brass play a slight *f–mf* on each accent. After the woodwind/keyboard chord returns, the *ostinato* from m. 95 is presented, this time re-scored for *tutti* winds and keyboards.

The battery percussion starts a rhythmic *ostinato* at the beginning of this section. It appears first in a "shared monody" that grows dynamically to a unison rhythm in mm. 107 and 108 and eventually elides with the winds. The percussion sound should not grow too soon, as it will cover the winds prematurely.

SECTION 10: (mm. 109-120)
Two rhythmic elements are layered at the beginning of this section to create a dense texture. The rhythmic counterpoint is divided by register: flutes, oboes, English horn, clarinets, trumpets, horns, and celesta have one texture while bassoons, trombones, tuba, and contrabasses have another. The piano combines the rhythms of both layers in the one part.

The height of this energy is reached at the end of the fourth bar through the downbeat of the sixth bar. A combination of the *poco diminuendo* and the descending figure of the bass clef instruments brings the tension to rest in m. 117.

The next four bars gradually grow in successively stronger swells. The percussion *ostinato* from Section 9 is reintroduced one instrument at a time and builds to the beginning of the next section. The depth of the *crescendo* grows and returns to *pp* each time until the end of the fourth bar, which ranges from *p* to *ff*.

SECTION 11: (mm. 121-132)
This section is played four times (A,B,C,D) building into a complex four-part texture. The first presentation (A) is performed by percussion alone. The rhythm develops from the *ostinato* in Section 9. The twelve-bar rhythm is modified in the fourth and seventh bars.

The next three presentations are based on a four-bar framework. When the bass instruments begin the second statement (B), the percussion change from *f-ff* to *mf-mp* so as not to cover the entering instruments, although the intensity of the percussion figure should not change. This is a place were a second tuba may be needed to help the lower octave density come through.

The third repeat of the twelve measures (C) adds the treble instruments (trumpets and 1st trombone). Percussion are brought up to a dynamic of *f*. The final repeat (D) adds the high treble instruments, including celesta. The piano changes to a part D at the same time.

Like many of the seemingly complex elements in this work, each of these lines will benefit from being isolated and rehearsed at a slower, subdivided tempo.

Ensemble balance throughout this section must be handled with great care. The problems can vary drastically depending upon the physical set-up of the ensemble.

An overall dynamic of *ff* must be modified with two concerns. The first is the ability of each line to be accurately understood when it enters and becomes an equal part of the thickening texture. The second concern is the dynamic intensity of the following section, which must grow even stronger.

SECTION 12: (mm. 133-138)
Here is the final climax of the work. The brass section presents chords in a unison rhythm that, along with a duet with the percussion, first *crescendos* for two bars then sustains *fff* for two bars. This elides into a continuance of per-cussion sound (rolled tam-tams and suspended cymbals) that prolong the *crescendo* to the final moment of tension.

The brass chords are the harmonic progression from Section 4, m. 51.

The problems here involve not allowing either the brass or percussion sounds to distort their volume or quality of articulation. The percussion entrance in m. 136 should start at a lower dynamic level than the last note in the brass so that the following *crescendo* has room to grow. All of this must be kept in per-spective by both conductor and players. The *intensity* should be at the extreme, with the volume within reasonable range.

SECTION 13: (mm. 139-159)
This is a coda based on the "whistle motive" from Section 2 and the *ostinato* from Section 3. The sudden change of dynamics and mood should appear to

emerge from the preceding climax. The *l.v. al niente* in the percussion should be allowed to ring undampened through its natural decay. Most of the first measure of the low *ostinato* (previously marked "dark and foreboding") may not be heard from the audience. The players should not try to play above their indicated dynamic.

The "choir of whistlers" entering in m. 144 now includes twenty-eight players as opposed to the eleven players in Section 2. A very light and distant-sounding *p* must be maintained. Bowed vibraphones highlight the four pitches of the motive and, by nature of the bowing, will sound later than the beginning of each beat. This produces an additional "eerie" effect.

Both the score and parts are a little confusing to the eye in these repeated segments. Pencil brackets and numbers over the repetitions will eliminate some uncertainty in the rehearsals and in performance.

The last three repetitions of the *ostinato* (mm. 150-155) leave the "answer" phrase suspended. A small *diminuendo* can add to the "solemn" indication. A slight re-articulation at the beginning of each of the last four measures is all that is necessary. Any type of accent or emphasis may destroy the mood. A quick breath before the last measure may be taken, if needed, to ensure complete control of the final *diminuendo*. The wind players and contrabasses should perform the *decrescendo* so that it disappears into the percussion-piano decay without an abrupt cut-off of the tone. It is important here that no one moves until the conductor releases the effect after the very last sound has stopped in the hall.

ENSEMBLE SET-UP:

The composer conceived *From a Dark Millennium* as an interaction between three separate choirs – woodwind, brass, percussion – with the amplified keyboards as a unifying element. The score does not contain a preferred set-up or any discussion as to placement of any instruments. With the numerous inherent balance and ensemble problems presented in this work, any stage arrangement will be a compromise of solutions.

Certainly extra-musical factors such as size of stage, size and amount of reverberation in the hall, and experience of the performers are to be considered in the choice of set-up.

Listed below are three alternative seating arrangements, each with its own pro's and con's. The conductor can assess his or her own circumstances and preferences in choosing one of these or creating his or her own.

This set-up is from a verbal description the composer gave me in 1981. The three choirs are presented visually, and the separation of brasses and woodwinds gives an antiphonal effect to many sections in the score, including the singing and whistling choruses. Placing the piano/celesta center solidifies the *ostinati* as did the harpsichord in the center of the Baroque orchestra. Percussion surrounding the ensemble gives them both visual importance as well as room to work.

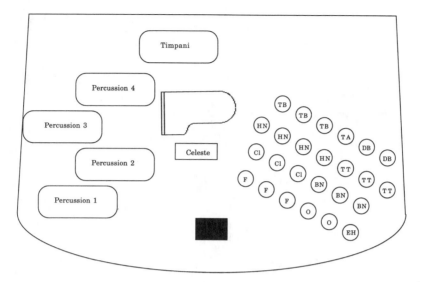

A major problem lies in the ability of the woodwind section to balance the brass. This set-up may eliminate the woodwind sound from *tuttis* or cause the brass to over-suppress their volume.

Less-experienced percussion sections may have difficulty because of their separation. For a smaller stage, this gives the percussion section more room and certainly a visual importance. The balance between brass and woodwinds is much improved through reinforcement. The balance between winds and percussion is now a concern as is the "time of attack" problem mentioned at the beginning of this discussion.

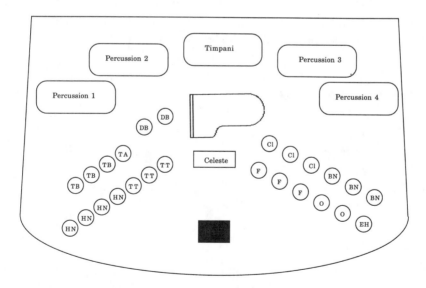

This is more of a traditional set. The visual separation of the instrumental choirs is eliminated and the keyboards are no longer in the center of the ensemble. Most balances are more easily handled.

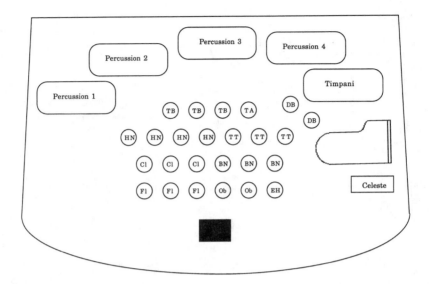

AMPLIFICATION:

A word about amplification is in order here. The piano and celesta should never sound as though they are truly amplified; their projection should only be reinforced.

The piano microphone, whether a PZM type placed on the underside of the piano lid or a microphone on a boom stand over the strings, should not be placed too close to the hammer mechanism. The "after-ring" of the strings held by the *sostenuto* pedal is the main focus of the reinforcement.

The celesta will need just enough boost to balance with the piano. Speakers for both the piano and celesta should be placed close to the actual instruments in order for the sound to appear to come from them. Caution must be taken to prevent either microphone from picking up other instruments in any set-up.

Unit 8: Suggested Listening

Joseph Schwantner:
   A Sudden Rainbow
   Aftertones of Infinity
   and the mountains rising nowhere
   Elixir
   In Evening's Stillness
   Music of Amber
   New Morning of the World
   Sparrows

Unit 9: Additional References and Resources

Renshaw, Jeffrey. "Conducting Analysis: Joseph Schwantner's *and the mountains rising nowhere*." *The Instrumentalist*, IVV January 1991.

Renshaw, Jeffrey. "Conducting Analysis: Joseph Schwantner's *From a Dark Millennium*." *The Instrumentalist*, IVIV September 1989.

Renshaw, Jeffrey. "Interview with Joseph Schwantner," *The Instrumentalist*, IVV May 1991.

Contributed by:

Jeffery Renshaw
Director of Bands
University of Connecticut
Storrs, Connecticut

Teacher Resource Guide

"In Praise of Winds," Symphony for Large Wind Orchestra

Gunther Schuller
(b. 1925)

Unit 1: Composer

Gunther Schuller was born on November 22, 1925, in New York. He was raised in a musical family; his paternal grandfather was a bandleader in Germany before immigrating to America; his father was a violinist for the New York Philharmonic. Schuller studied at the St. Thomas Choir School and also received private instruction in theory, flute, and horn. He became so proficient on horn that he soon began playing professionally in orchestras, such as the New York City Ballet Orchestra, the Cincinnati Symphony, and the Metropolitan Opera Orchestra, all before he was twenty years old. At the same time, he became fascinated with jazz. Schuller played horn in a combo led by Miles Davis and also began to compose jazz pieces. He began to compose a variety of works for orchestras and ensembles of varying instrumentation and has created more than 160 original compositions in virtually every musical genre. In the late 1950s, Schuller coined the term "third-stream" in reference to music that was a fusion of jazz and "classical" styles. In the early 1970s, he premiered reorchestrations of works by Scott Joplin with the New England Conservatory Ragtime Ensemble and began the "ragtime revival." Schuller has received a number of honorary doctorate degrees and awards, including Grammy Awards, Guggenheim Fellowships, a MacArthur Foundation Grant, the William Schuman Award, and the 1994 Pulitzer Prize. He has taught at several schools of music and served as president of the New England Conservatory of Music. He has gathered a lifetime of observations on conducting in his book, *The Compleat Conductor* (1997). Schuller's original works for band include *Symphony for Brass and Percussion* (1950), *Meditation* (1963), *Diptych for Brass Quintet and Band* (1964), *Study in Textures* (1967), *Fanfare for St. Louis* (1968), *Tribute to Rudy Wiedoeft* (1978), *Eine Kleine Posaunenmusik for Trombone and Wind Ensemble* (1980), *On Winged Flight* (1989), *Song and Dance for Violin and Band* (1990), *Festive Music* (1992), *Blue Dawn into White Heat* (1996).

Unit 2: Composition

In Praise of Wind was completed on January 29, 1981. The work was commissioned by the University of Michigan School of Music and the University of Michigan Bands for the Centennial Celebration of the University of Michigan School of Music.

In Praise of Winds demands an enormous ensemble. The expanded woodwind, brass, and percussion sections are extremely effective in demonstrating the desire of a distinguished composer to praise an orchestra of winds. The work's four movements resemble the formal design of a traditional symphony, particularly the last three movements. The second movement is a slow *ternary* form; the third movement is a *scherzo* that is an AABA form; the fourth movement is a *rondo*. The first movement, beginning with a slow section leading to an *allegro*, is suggestive of a *sonata-allegro* movement. This first movement, however, is not in *sonata* form but is written in a continuous developmental style. Schuller uses diverse twentieth century compositional techniques in a work with eighteenth century formal designs. These contemporary compositional techniques combined with challenging performance techniques create a formidable work for even the most advanced ensembles. Performance of the four movements totals approximately twenty-seven minutes in length: Movement I (6:30), Movement II (10:00), Movement III (3:30), and Movement IV (7:00).

Unit 3: Historical Perspective

In Praise of Winds was premiered on February 13, 1981, in Hill Auditorium by the University of Michigan Symphony Band, H. Robert Reynolds conducting, as part of the twenty-first national convention of the College Band Directors National Association.

Composers have been contributing symphonies to the repertoire of the large band since the classical period and the years of the French Revolution. Louis E. Jadin wrote his *Symphonie for Band* in 1794. Hector Berlioz composed *Symphonie Funébre et Triomphale* in 1840. Significant symphonies of the twentieth century include Paul Robert Fauchet's *Symphony in B flat* (1926), Paul Hindemith's *Symphony in B flat* (1951), Morton Gould's *Symphony for Band* (1952), Vincent Persichetti's *Symphony No. 6* (1956), and Vittorio Giannini's

Symphony No. 3 (1958). These twentieth century symphonies for band all use traditional classical forms, as does Schuller's symphony. There is considerable contrast, however, between these symphonies and Schuller's *Symphony for Large Wind Orchestra* in compositional style. The works cited above are abundantly influenced by the Romantic style period. The substantial use of twentieth century compositional ideas and techniques in Schuller's symphony is fundamental to its style.

Schuller wrote the following notes for a 1984 performance of the symphony:

> I chose the form of the "symphony" for this work because I believe, in contradistinction to much of what one was told in recent decades by leading composers and tastemakers about the obsolescence of many 19th century forms, that the four-movement symphony is still a viable form and vehicle, far from exhausted. This is actually my third symphony, No. 1 being my early *Symphony for Brass and Percussion* (1949-1950). My second is a work entitled *Symphony* (1965) for full orchestra; and *In Praise of Winds* is No. 3, with No. 4 on the way, a four-movement *Symphony for Organ* – perhaps the first of its kind since Sowerby's *Organ Symphony* of 1936.
>
> It is not that the symphony and sonata form types were "inherently" obsolete and dead; it is rather that much of the music the professional avant-gardists of the 1950's and 1960's were writing and promoting did not fit these forms. The conclusion reached was that the forms were at odds with the new styles of language when actually the reverse was true. It was much of the new music, coming out of Darmstadt and Warsaw and the Cageian philosophy, that was stillborn; but it was difficult to convince anyone of that in those days. In any event, the symphonic forms seemed to me appropriate for a work of major size (both in instrumentation and duration) and one worthy of the occasion of its premiere: the celebration of the 100th anniversary of the School of Music at the University of Michigan.

Unit 4: Technical Considerations

The composition is atonal and highly chromatic. *In Praise of Winds* uses a twelve-note tone row, but Schuller exercises a remarkable degree of freedom from serialism throughout the work. Prominent melodic passages and chordal structures are derived from the row. Melodic fragments throughout the four movements exhibit diatonic characteristics representing a variety of keys and appear in some sections of polytonality. The work overflows with a multitude of rhythmic challenges. The rhythmic notation includes dotted notes (with up to three dots), groupings of thirty-second notes in tens, and groupings of sixteenth notes in fives and sixes. The fourth movement includes notations of rhythms that are beamed across measure lines (indicating the approximate rhythmic placement of pitches), notes with slanted beams (indicating a change in speed of articulation), and note heads with no stems (indicating specific pitch without specific rhythms). The *allegro* of the first movement is a continuous flow of meter changes, with forty-six changes in its first sixty measures. Diverse intricate rhythmic patterns are begun on various parts of different beats. Movement II, which contains some of the most expressive and serene passages of the symphony, has some of the most complex polyphonic sections. During mm. 44-50 are simultaneous rhythms of twos, threes, fours, fives, sixes, and notes displaced from the beat! The *scherzo* of Movement III, performed at one beat per measure, contains entrances placed on various parts of different beats.

Multiple tonguing is required of brass players (e.g., triple tonguing in m. 89 of Movement I and double and triple tonguing in the fanfare motive of Movement IV). Advanced techniques in tonguing, including flutter tonguing, are also demanded from woodwind players (as in Movement I at m. 163, m. 42 in Movement II, and mm. 85-90 in Movement IV). A variety of mutes are necessary for the brass. Trumpets need straight, Harmon cup, plunger, and whisper mutes. Trombones, euphoniums, and tubas need straight mutes, and there are sections for trombones with solotone mutes.

The greatest challenge for performing ensembles is the instrumentation. The score lists separate parts for three piccolos, three flutes, alto flute, three oboes, English horn (with parts divided), E-flat clarinet, four B-flat clarinets, two alto clarinets (divided for four players in Movement II), two bass clarinets, two contralto clarinets, two contrabass clarinets, two bassoons, contrabassoon, soprano saxophone, two alto saxophones, two tenor saxophones, baritone sax, eight horns, five trumpets (parts divided and with one trumpet in C or D), four trombones, two baritones, three tubas, two contrabasses, two timpanists, six percussion, harp, piano, and celesta. With the necessary doubling for balance concerns, an ensemble of ninety-five to one hundred players is essential for performance.

Unit 5: Stylistic Considerations

The tempi marked are as follows: Movement I, quarter note = 80 and then quarter note = 116; Movement II, quarter note = 74; Movement III, dotted-half note indicated as the beat with no metronome marking; Movement IV, quarter note = 126. The introduction of Movement I, marked *andante*, provides a plodding, somewhat somber and portentous opening. A careful growth in tempo and momentum will provide an exciting and seamless transition into the *allegro*. Movement II, marked *tranquillo*, is mostly slow and serene. The long-line expressive passages require careful balance between the few instruments that play these flowing passages. In these homorhythmic sections, the quartal harmonies require an equal balance of sound. Movement III, the

"Scherzo," is marked *presto*. Without a specific metronome marking, the tempo chosen by the conductor must be fast enough to provide a *scherzo* spirit without being so fast as to obliterate the virtuosic lines. Movement IV, the "Rondo," through its form, requires careful consideration by the conductor of the styles used in the rondo's contrasting sections: fanfare-like, waltz-like, and up-tempo jazz-like. Throughout all movements, Schuller provides very specific articulation markings. These markings undoubtedly will assist conductors in preparation for performance. Care must be taken to choose a specific style of each marking and to be sure the players are consistent in their performance of the markings.

Unit 6: Musical Elements

Schuller's four-movement symphony is an atonal work containing melodic lines and harmonic structures derived from a twelve-note tone row. As the beginning of Movement I illustrates, Schuller uses a remarkable degree of freedom in his use of the tone row. Pitches are used out of row order and sometimes in reverse order. The entire row does appear in m. 104 in the 1st clarinet. The row in original form is g-sharp, a, d, f, b, c, e, f-sharp, d-sharp, c-sharp, a-sharp, g. Throughout the work Schuller uses divisions of the row that are groupings of seven and five pitches. The flute line in m. 25 is a melodic motive based on the first seven pitches. The last five pitches of the row appear as a vertical sonority on the downbeat of m. 40. Movement I exploits the many different choirs and timbres of the large ensemble in light-textured passages that contrast with full-powered climaxes using the entire ensemble. The sweeping melodic lines in this movement and throughout the work sometimes appear to sound as strings of improvisatory passages. The opening chords of Movement II are configured so that all twelve chromatic pitches are sounded in every three different four-voice sonorities. These chords are arranged in quartal harmonies. Schuller manipulates these chords to repeat this procedure in the opening measures. Although this second movement contains some of the thickest textures and complex polyphony of the entire work, the long-line expressive passages in the solos for trumpet and horn are the essence of the movement. Movement III is the most homogenous of the four movements. The tempo is constant, eighth notes predominate, and the textures are less contrasting than those within the other movements. Contrasting sections are plentiful in Movement IV through Schuller's use of *rondo* form. The opening refrain is a fanfare for the brass, with multiple complex rhythms and articulations. Special effects such as trombone *glissandi*, stopped horn, and flutter tonguing are used along with pointillistic effects. The opening sonorities of the fanfare suggest polytonality in this passage, with D minor in the trumpets and A-flat major in the horns. The first episode (m. 39) is marked "very smoothly," creating a *legato* line that sharply contrasts with the articulated opening. The second episode is a waltz (m. 97). The third episode is an up-tempo jazz section containing the composer's instruction for a jazz drummer on drum set. This final movement closes with a slow *crescendo* to the thickest texture of the work and concludes with a thunderous mass of sonority that exhibits the full aggregate force and power of the winds.

Unit 7: Form and Structure

SECTION	MEASURE	EVENT AND SCORING
Movement I:		
Introduction	1-34	A slow building of sound
(*allegro*)	35-61	Pointed rhythmic figures in woodwind and brass choirs
	62-77	Woodwind soli over clarinet murmur
	78-94	Fuller scoring of pointed rhythmic figures
	95-113	Fast melodic lines in upper woodwinds above long lines in low woodwinds
	114-147	Add brass chords
	148-162	Full ensemble with long lines in low ranges
	163-176	Long lines in saxophones and low woodwinds in the midst of quivering pedals in the upper woodwinds and trombones
	176-207	A series of upward sweeps of sound, with brass fanfares in the full ensemble
Movement II:		
A	1-20	Tranquil homorhythmic passages for pairs of woodwinds voiced in fours
	21-39	Muted trumpet solo with brass
B	40-43	*Crescendo* of woodwind texture
	44-51	Full ensemble with ten lines in polyphonic texture
	52-55	*Diminuendo* of woodwind texture
	56-70	Tranquil passage in pairs of flutes with harp (D-sharp minor tonality)
	71-83	Rhythmic polyphony in woodwinds moving to homophony with percussion
A´	84-102	Tranquil homorhythmic passages for pairs of brass voiced in fours
	103-127	Horn solo with woodwinds

SECTION	MEASURE	EVENT AND SCORING
Movement III:		
A	1-3	Introductory hexachords
a	4-21	Woodwind use of tone row material in upward sweeps over brass accompaniment
b	22-33	Consequent section
a′	34-44	Rising woodwind sweeps
c	45-67	Sustained chords in *Klangfarben* style
	68-70	Hexachords and repeat of A
B	71-89	Pointed rhythmic figures similar to Movement I
	90-108	Consequent section
A′	109-111	Hexachords
a	112-129	In thicker texture
b	130-141	In thicker texture
a′	142-150	In thicker texture
d	151-158	Shortened chords in coda
Movement IV:		
A	1-10	Woodwind sweeps
	11-38	Fanfare in brass with pointillistic effects
B	39-68	Broad *legato* motion in woodwinds
A	69-96	Fanfare in brass (transposed) with added woodwind pointillistic effects
C	97-133	Waltz variant of B
A	134-136	Abbreviated fanfare
D	137-216	Up-tempo jazz variant
Coda	217-240	Woodwind sweeps and final chords

Unit 8: Suggested Listening

Jere Hutcheson, *Chromophonic Images* (1978), work for large ensemble
Gunther Schuller, *Symphony* (1965), *Symphony for Organ* (1981), other
  works for band

Unit 9: Additional References and Resources

Baker, Theodore. *Baker's Biographical Dictionary of Musicians*. 8th ed., rev.
  Nicolas Slonimsky. New York: Schirmer, 1992. S.v. "Gunther Schuller."

Carnovale, Norbert. *Gunther Schuller*. Westport, CT: Greenwood Press,
  1987.

Hopkins, Stephen. "Analysis: Gunther Schuller's *In Praise of Winds*." *Journal of Band Research*, 24:1 Fall 1988, 28-43.

Margun Music, Inc. 167 Dudley Road, Newton Centre, MA, 617-332-6398.

Rehrig, William H. *The Heritage Encyclopedia of Band Music*. Westerville, OH: Integrity Press, 1991.

Smith, Norman and Albert Stoutamire. *Band Music Notes*. Lake Charles, LA: Program Note Press, 1989.

www.schirmer.com/composers/schuller

www.wpi.edu/~miranda/schuller.html

Contributed by:
Kenneth Kohlenberg
Director of Bands, Professor of Music
Sinclair Community College
Dayton, Ohio

Teacher Resource Guide

Konzertmusik für Blasorchester, Op. 41

Paul Hindemith
(1889–1963)

Unit 1: Composer

In an autobiography submitted for the Second Donaueschingen Festival (1922), Hindemith succinctly expressed his desire to be known primarily by his art rather than by lengthy discourse on his background, philosophy, or other nonmusical matters. Nonetheless, his significance as a major composer of the twentieth century requires a more detailed examination than perhaps Hindemith would have approved. Born in Hanau, Germany, in 1895 of a working-class family, Hindemith began his formal study of music on violin around age ten. He attended the Hoch Conservatory in Frankfurt on full scholarship until 1917. While at the conservatory, Hindemith studied composition with Bernhard Sekles and counterpoint with Arnold Mendelssohn. Toward the end of World War I, Hindemith was drafted into the Army, where he was assigned to a regimental band and performed in a string quartet for the entertainment of officers. He played bass drum in the band and also distinguished himself as an accomplished performer on clarinet and viola.

During the early years of the Donaueschingen Music Festival, Hindemith's compositions were selected for inclusion on festival programs several times. So highly regarded was his work that he was asked to become a member of the Donaueschingen selection committee in 1923. His influence would have an increasingly profound impact on the artistic direction of the festival. In 1924, Hindemith proposed that music be commissioned for neglected musical mediums, thus setting the stage for the military band emphasis of 1926.

Hindemith was identified as a "staunch anti-Nazi," who left the country in 1935, first to Turkey and then to Switzerland in 1937. In an attempt to explain (for his students) contemporary music writing, Hindemith produced the two-volume work, *The Craft of Musical Composition*, which was published in 1937. He moved to New York in 1938 and eventually obtained a professorship at Yale University, where he stayed until 1953. He returned to Switzerland that same year, where he accepted a position at the University of Zurich. During the ensuing years, Hindemith made numerous conducting appearances throughout Europe and in the United States. He died in Frankfurt, Germany, in 1963. Frankfurt has since become the location of the Paul Hindemith Institute and Archive.

As a result of his residence in the United States, Hindemith had a major influence on the development of art music in this country, not only through the exposure provided for his music but also through the training he provided for many significant American composers.

Unit 2: Composition

Konzertmusik für Blasorchester, Op. 41, was written for the 1926 Donaueschingen Music Festival and was premiered by the military band stationed in Donaueschingen with the 14th Infantry Regiment of the German army. The premiere was conducted by noted contemporary music exponent Hermann Scherchen, to whom the work was dedicated. The music was so difficult that the military band posted in Donaueschingen had to be augmented by a virtuoso trumpet and trombone player to adequately cover the parts. The original manuscript of *Konzertmusik für Blasorchester* is missing according to both the proprietors of the Hindemith Archive in Frankfurt and Schott Publishers. The critical reviews of *Konzertmusik* were essentially positive. One critic, however, suggested that even though the variations of the second movement were perhaps the best that had been written since Reger, Hindemith should rescore the movement for a different group of instruments, implying that the military band was unworthy of such exceptional music.

Unit 3: Historical Perspective

In 1924, the selection committee for the Donaueschingen Music Festival in Donaueschingen, Germany, decided to commission new music for mediums that had been neglected by composers of serious art music. In those days, a commission simply represented a call for new composition and a guarantee of performance. For the 1926 Donaueschingen Music Festival, the selection committee identified the military band as a neglected ensemble, among others, and thereby issued a commission for musical works of artistic merit for that medium. The initial call for original compositions for military band was not productive, which led the committee to instigate the commissioning of specific composers for the project. The commissions produced four works that were performed at the July 24, 1926 concert that served to welcome guests to the festival. Those works included *Konzertmusik für Blasorchester, Op. 41*, by Paul Hindemith; *Drei Marsche für Militärorchester, Op. 44*, by Ernst Krenek; *Kleine Serenade für Militärorchester*, by Ernst Pepping; and *Spiel für Militärorchester, Op. 39*, by Ernst Toch. Famous modernist conductor Hermann Scherchen led the premieres of three of the four compositions. A fifth work, *Promenademusik für Militärorchester*, by Hans Gal, was evidently performed at a "replay" concert on the Monday evening following the conclusion of the festival. That work was not considered to be successful. Several other composers well known in Germany at the time were contacted by the committee but evidently did not follow through on the commission, although a composition entitled "Wake Up," by Paul Dessau, is mentioned in correspondence.

Newspaper and magazine reviews of the July 24 concert provided much insight into the reception given to the works for band. Generally, opinions were mixed, but the prevailing view indicated that the performances and the compositions were not of the highest caliber. More recent scholarship has identified three of the works, the compositions by Krenek, Toch, and Hindemith, as important works for wind band. The composition by Pepping, which is now available through Georg Bauer Musikverlag, was rediscovered in 1989 and carefully edited for publication. *Promenademusik für Militärorchester*, by Gal, has been recently published through Schott and edited by Wolfgang Suppan.

Unit 4: Technical Considerations

This work was intended for a one-on-a-part, military band of regimental size (approximately twenty-four players). The instrumentation of the military band in Donaueschingen included E-flat clarinet, tenor horns, and baritone. Hindemith's instrumentation also called for two flugelhorns. Clarinet parts have considerable technical demand, particularly in the first movement. The *tessitura* for flugelhorn is quite high and requires confident, secure players. Very competent principal trumpet and trombone performers are also needed, particularly in the first movement, which features a very challenging duet. The tenor horn part was intended for a small bore, treble clef, B-flat brass instrument of bright quality, while the baritone was a bass-clef brass instrument of larger bore. Hindemith's intention was to define his polyphony with contrasting timbres in those particular parts. In view of the flugelhorn range and the availability of tenor horns, Hindemith offers substitutions of soprano and tenor saxophone, respectively, as reflected in the cover notes to the Schott publication of *Konzertmusik*. If the goal is authenticity, however, a euphonium may substitute for the baritone and a small-bore baritone may substitute for the tenor horn. To obtain the desired transparency, players must be aware of the composer's coloristic goals. Percussion demands are minimal.

Unit 5: Stylistic Considerations

Konzertmusik für Blasorchester, Op. 41, is a prime example of the neoclassical movement of the 1920s in Western European art music. The use of a neotonal harmonic language framed in forms derived from the classical and, particularly, the baroque style periods was characteristic of composers who were reacting against the excessive emotionalism of late romanticism and the harshness of atonality. As with many baroque-period instrumental works, the three-movement macro-form was used as a rather standard format, with the typical fast-slow-fast configuration. A primary way of developing melodic material within any extant form, particularly in the works of German composers, would be the use of counterpoint. Polyphonic textures abound in this and other musical compositions which evolved during the neoclassical period in central Europe. Additionally, parody and experimentation were common features of this style of music writing.

Unit 6: Musical Elements

OVERVIEW:

Outside of the sheer technical demand that makes *Konzertmusik* one of the most difficult compositions to perform in the wind band repertoire, there are several basic elements to be considered. First, the overall texture of the work is polyphonic, which is characteristic of the German approach to neoclassicism. Great care must be given to clarity of line and precision of rhythmic placement. A key factor in the definition of the polyphony is the use of contrasting timbres. Furthermore, it seems to be Hindemith's intention that *Konzertmusik* be performed by only one player per part. Doubling of instrumentation, or performance by a larger ensemble than originally intended, would only serve to obfuscate the desired transparency.

Another important consideration has to do with the neotonal harmonic language. As might be expected, tonal centers are not established by traditional common practice means. Rather, tonal centers are the result of numerous different methods such as *ostinato*, repetition, and leading tone motion. Conductors need to concern themselves carefully with the development of tension through repetition, textural change, stretto, and dissonance. Through control of dynamic movement and tempo, it is possible to achieve powerful arrivals at moments of repose.

Each movement represents a musical form utilized in earlier musical style periods. The first movement combines a slow introduction, from which motivic ideas are extracted, with a clever Concerto Grosso form. One of the most wonderfully crafted theme and variations forms of the twentieth century occurs as the second movement. The final movement follows the traditional form of minuet-trio, but in duple instead of triple meter.

One final element to be considered is more psychological than technical.

During the Weimar Republic in Germany (1919-33), the performing arts enjoyed a certain amount of freedom of expression. As a result, there was quite a bit of experimentation and questioning of societal values. Art music tended to be parodistic and sometimes cynical. The element of parody in *Konzertmusik* is found in the use of march-like quotes featuring traditional oom-pah accompaniment in unexpected places, the presentation of march-like material by unusual instrumentation, the absence of traditional march accompaniments in the march section and in the use of a traditional folk song that tells the story of a military hero. Simultaneously, Hindemith pays homage to and satirizes military music in a composition that has the craft and subtlety of a great art work.

MOVEMENT 1: "OVERTURE"

The overture is developed through the use of rhythmic *ostinati* and imitative counterpoint. It opens in 9/8, dotted-quarter note = 69 beats per minute. The initial statement is a loud, rhythmic unison in upper voices with an imitative entrance of a pedal tri-tone in the tuba and 2nd and 3rd trombones. The voicing of the chord on beat two in m. 1 is similar to the voicing of a harmonic series beginning on the second partial. The basic harmonic materials contain a large number of tri-tones and major/minor seconds creating a very terse, dissonant impression. Chromaticism abounds in the early measures. In m. 3, the low voices begin their imitation of the opening motive, but it is displaced in the measure to beat one instead of beat three as in the initial statement, creating a displacement of three beats. In m. 5, the imitation begins on beat two, displaced two beats, and then at [A] (m. 7), the imitation occurs with a one-beat displacement. This texturally creates the first climax which resolves into a soft fantasia figure in 1st clarinet. While eighth-note figurations derived from m. 2 continue in the tuba in octaves at m. 9, the clarinets and upper woodwinds have doubled the values, producing demand for virtuosity. Underneath, middle brass parts provide harmonic underpinning with ascending progressions centered around d minor and g minor. A second climax occurs at m. 12 that resolves with an eighth note figure that descends in fourths to a soft B-flat concert. Horns provide an open-fifth pedal (B-flat and F) that creates harmonic security in the section from [B] to [C]. The clarinets reinforce the horn pedal with an undulating figure in the upper chalumeau. The primary melodic interest is found in the tenor horn/baritone group which plays an expanding, somewhat chromatic, lyrical line over fragments from the opening. This continues to build into a recapitulation of the beginning at m. 28 at the same pitch level. At letter [D], the clarinet fantasia figure occurs again, but it is accompanied differently. After the texture thins and slows slightly, a new section in 2/4 time begins with an "animated quarter note." The basic melodic interest is found first in trumpet, tenor horn, and second horn, and then in upper woodwinds. Although the orchestration and melodic writing is fragmentary, the effect achieved is a complicated and colorful polyphonic texture. Ending in a *tutti* rhythmic unison, mm. 39-58 proceed as a series of imitative duets, most significantly between trumpet and trombone. *Tutti* interjections of material from either mm. 39-40 or 41-42 serve to provide continuity to the section. At [H] the trumpet/trombone duet perform an accompaniment figure to a new duet between clarinet and flugelhorn. In the flugelhorn line, at m. 160, may be found an example of writing to the extremes of the tessitura, certainly something that likely caused consternation to the players in the Donaueschingen military band. The trumpet/trombone duet resumes at letter [J], with one additional interjection by the flugelhorn at m. 153. While the duet counterpoint continues at a following distance of an eighth note at m. 158, the clarinet enters with an *ostinato* figure as a harmonically stabilizing accompaniment. At m. 169, E-flat clarinet and 1st clarinet use the theme from mm. 39-40 as an *ostinato*. Leading to a recapitulation of m. 39, all winds play a *tutti* transition based upon the motive first introduced by clarinet solo at [H]. The recapitulation occurs at letter [N], and until letter [O], it is almost exactly the same. The trumpet/trombone duet then develops the motive from mm. 41-42 in imitative counterpoint which *diminuendos* into the closing section beginning at m. 216. There, a simple eighth note accompaniment, which is stacked above a G-flat *ostinato* in the tubas, underlays more trumpet/trombone duet. The trumpet material is based upon the clarinet solo motive from [H], while the trombone develops the primary motive from m. 39. Dialogue continues until the end where the trumpet and trombone together have final say, holding a fermata while the other instruments have finished. The final interval is a perfect twelfth, an E over an A displaced by an octave, with the G-flat *ostinato* hiding discretely in the background. Hindemith gives the instruction that there should be no break between movements.

MOVEMENT 2: SECHS VARIATIONEN ÜBER DAS LIED
    "PRINZ EUGEN, DER EDLE RITTER"
The second movement of *Konzertmusik* is in theme and variation form. Beginning in the key of B-flat major, this is the only place where a key signature may be found in the composition. Perhaps that is because the very diatonic "Prinz Eugen" (pronounced *Oy-gain*) folk song upon which the movement is based is quoted literally except for the last note of m. 8 and without the traditional repeat of the last half of the melody. Hindemith found this tune to be quite suitable for a number of reasons. First, the song was well traveled and well known by many Germans. It would be an ideal basis for a set of variations that would "entrap" the Donaueschingen listeners. Second, it was appropriate because the song's lyrics told a story about a military campaign. Hindemith must certainly have considered the content of the words as he concerned himself with producing quality music for the military band. Could

it be that Hindemith was demonstrating that in the hands of a craftsman art may be produced out of questionable materials for an unlikely medium? Finally, one of the subjects of concern in the lyrics had to do with Prinz Eugen building a bridge to cross the Donau (Danube) river. The connection with Donaueschingen is rather obvious.

Metrically, "Prinz Eugen" is much like many folk songs of the central European region in that its phrases are irregular. In the one notated version located in an old songbook, the time signature is 5/4. This is combined with several fermatas to achieve a rather free-sounding meter. Hindemith captures the feel by alternating between 3/4 and 4/4. There is no tempo marking at the beginning of the second movement, perhaps because the song was so well known. On the song version, the expressive marking is *Nicht zu langsam und nachdrücklich* (Vigorously and not too slow). The movement lasts six minutes and forty-one seconds.

The thematic presentation, which is stated in trumpet and upper woodwinds, occurs within a mild polyphonic texture created by low voices and the interplay of sixteenth notes in various other voices. Of particular interest is the *tutti* B-flat chord on beat one of m. 10 and the two-one suspension in the horns. The first variation begins at m. 11 in 3/4 time, *l'istesso* tempo. The two phrases of "Prinz Eugen" become the primary motivic material for this section, which is scored for a quintet of woodwinds: flute, oboe, and the three B-flat clarinets. Development of the variation is achieved through the handing off of the two mentioned phrases which have been melodically and rhythmically mutated. The second phrase is presented first in the oboe, m. 11, and the first phrase occurs in 2nd clarinet, m. 12. The interplay continues until m. 23, where a transition using the rest of the original tune is presented, albeit altered. Besides being highly polyphonic, the music is moderately chromatic and follows a dynamic arch that climaxes at the introduction of the remaining portion of "Prinz Eugen." This variation concludes at m. 31 on an A-flat major chord. Variation two begins on the pick-ups to m. 32. The varied melody is initially presented in the 1st trumpet in the original key. Development is achieved through the alternation of a countermelodic figure that is stated by oboe/E-flat clarinet/1st B-flat clarinet (mm. 32-35). After the altered melody is played for four measures (the first half of "Prinz Eugen") by 1st trumpet, the low brass repeats the figure while the horn group takes a turn at the countermelody. Upper woodwinds provide counterpoint in mm. 36-39 based upon the same figures initially played by 2nd and 3rd trumpets underneath the 1st trumpet. The same sequence of development occurs for the second half of the 'Prinz Eugen' melody. Percussion make their first appearance since the theme presentation with a simple beat/afterbeat accompaniment. A woodwind line, with baritone, of flowing eighth notes serves as an introduction to the third variation at [E]. The melodic derivative is stated in the flugelhorn and trumpet in its most altered form yet. With alternating time signatures, the whole variation is a gentle *diminuendo*, as can been seen in the reduction of instruments on the melody until only one flugelhorn is left at the end of the variation in m. 64. The written instruction at the end requests a gradual slowing down.

The fourth variation begins with the pick-ups to m. 65. Hindemith used only brass and percussion in this variation, which melodically and harmonically is the most obtuse of the movement. The most clear derivative of the melody may be found in the tuba part beginning at [G]. Technically and in terms of *tessitura*, this variation provides perhaps the greatest challenge in the composition for the brass. The conclusion of the section is played by the first trombone on a high G, which serves as a dominant pivot into the C minor of the next variation.

Texturally, variation five is the simplest, consisting of two linear lines with accompaniment. The theme is in the trombone section, with counter-melodic material occurring in upper woodwinds. Written in 12/8 time, the tempo and expressive indication at [H] indicates that the variation should be played "in the style of a slow stepping march." Variation six begins at m. 93 and is the most complicated and extensive variation of the set. It is in 3/8 time, and Hindemith's instructions indicate that the tempo should remain the same as before. This, of course, places the pulse at one beat per measure. Initially, the 1st trumpet presents the theme which functions as the subject for a *fugato*. Pitched in concert C, it is twelve measures long. The next statement is by baritone, which is ten measures long in F concert. Clarinets follow in E-flat concert for twelve measures, and then the flutes perform what might best be described as a bridge for seven measures. The next fugue subject occurs in flute/oboe in D concert for ten measures. In terms and pitch relationships, Hindemith has constructed a very unconventional *fugato* which culminates in a short coda, mm. 169-171. At m. 172, the music should proceed "a little more tranquilly" as the texture thins. In this section, Hindemith uses fragmentation of materials from the *fugato* theme to develop an accompaniment for the finale to the set of variations which begins in the muted 1st trumpet, who Hindemith instructs to play out a little at m. 190. Here, the theme, which is in G-flat concert, is the most literal since the initial presentation. Much of this portion has the flavor of a scherzo, but the joke, however, is that the theme is written out of time. The "out of timeness" is caused by writing the theme in duple against the triple accompaniment by grouping the rhythms with ties across bar lines. In anticipation of the "grand finale," Hindemith thins the texture and orchestration through letter [O], using a technique of rhythmic and harmonic *ostinato* that will also be employed in the coda. With the pick-ups to m. 234, Hindemith has made the most massive thematic statement using tuba, baritone, second tenor horn, and trombone. Like the 1st trumpet at m. 191, it is also written out of time and in D-flat concert. The contrapuntal density is at its greatest in mm. 234-257 with the appearance of the *fugato* subject as a countermelodic figure above the main theme. The first four measures of the *fugato* theme is also used as material for the coda, which begins at letter [S] (m. 258). By using that phrase fragment as a rhythmic and harmonic *ostinato*, Hindemith anticipated the same technique he would use in the codas of the first and third movements of *Symphony in B Flat*. The figure is stated first in upper, then middle, and finally in low winds, creating a powerful drive to the final measures. At m. 270, the last four chords define a D-flat major concluding sonority, but not without disagreement from the trombones who insist four times upon B and C, written as a difficult-to-play, descending major seventh. The most arrogant moment in the entire composition occurs at the very end when the trumpet section plays B, F-sharp, E at maximum volume, thus destroying any feeling of finality or stable tonal center. Since it is so unexpected, the trumpet declaration provides one of the most delightful, and probably controversial, surprises of the work. As at the end of the first movement, Hindemith instructs that there should be no break going into the third movement.

MOVEMENT 3: "MARSCH"
The third movement is the shortest, lasting only two minutes and twenty seconds. Centered around a B-flat tonality, it is in a minuet-trio (ABA) form that facsimiles traditional European march form, and it also is in traditional 2/4 time, but without the usual march accompaniment rhythms. Although it is more homophonic than any other movement, it also contains significant examples of linear counterpoint. The first four measures are *forte* and lead into a harmonically obtuse but obviously militaristic trumpet call punctuated by tonally ambiguous *tutti* chords in the ensemble (open B-natural/F-sharp underneath an F dom. 7 structure). The harmonic structure centers around B-flat concert, but B-natural, F-sharp, and C-sharp all play prominently in the chosen vocabulary. Great care has been given to development of material through presentation in varying instrumental colors. Full *tutti* sounds occur occasionally. In a typical march strain, dynamic alteration would happen with relative infrequency, but in Hindemith's march there are six changes in the first section alone, which is repeated at m. 16. A strong chromatic element in the melodic material continues throughout. In m. 21, a more polyphonic texture appears as the woodwinds play against tuba/baritone, but that only lasts briefly as it transitions back into the material from m. 1 at m. 27, only this time it is presented a perfect fourth lower along with a counterpoint in the horn and tenor horn group and a descending chromatic line in bass voices. At m. 31, the trumpet call is reiterated one whole step higher than before. Whereas the cadence in mm.15-16 resolves to an F tonality, the cadence at mm. 36-37, which is also the *Fine* ending, resolves to a B-flat tonality, albeit missing a D and containing a suspended E-flat. One of the most interesting features of the march is the woodwind sextet that forms the trio, consisting of

three B-flat clarinets, E-flat clarinet, flute, and oboe. Since the typical military march usually modulates to the subdominant, E-flat in this case, Hindemith chose to open the trio with three E-naturals in the oboe, while changing the time signature to 3/4 for the one measure. He was just kidding. The dynamic range requested in the trio is wide and fast-changing. The basic texture is polyphonic with some interesting treatments, especially from mm. 49-53 where there are separate lines doubled in octaves: flute with 2nd B-flat clarinet, oboe with 3rd B-flat clarinet, and E-flat clarinet with 1st B-flat clarinet. Measures 40-48 are repeated at mm. 58-67, after which there is a *da Capo al Fine*.

Unit 7: Form and Structure

SECTION	MEASURE	EVENT
Movement I (5:30)		
A	1-12	*Tutti* fanfare; 9/8 time signature; *maestoso* tempo (dotted-quarter note = ca. 69); running clarinet figure; ascended figure announced by 1st flugelhorn
B	12-24	*Tremelo*-like clarinet accompaniment; lyrical material in tenor horn/baritone
A	25-38	Return of fanfare; running clarinet figure and transition into second section of movement; *concerto grosso* form
Ripieno	39-52	2/4 time signature; animated quarter note (ca. 112); primary motive in m. 39
Concertino	59-77	Trumpet and trombone; sixteenth note figure related to opening fanfare material
Development	78-104	Considerable fragmentation and development of ideas by both *concertino* and *ripieno*
Ripieno	105-124	Derivative idea introduced by clarinet and imitated by flugelhorn
Concertino	125-152	Trumpet and trombone develop idea; f irst presented at m. 105
Ripieno/ Concertino	153-179	All main motive ideas are presented in counterpoint
Ripieno	180-183	Closing section and reference to *maestoso* material in m. 183

SECTION	MEASURE	EVENT
Ripieno	184-199	First statement of *ripieno*; mm. 39-55 repeated almost literally
Concertino	200-215	Trumpet and trombone play fragments of *ripieno* motives
Coda	216-252	*Ostinato* eighth note accompaniment underneath *concertino* trumpet performing *ripieno* motive from m. 105 and trombone performing *ripieno* motive from m. 39

Movement II (6:41)
Theme and Variation form

Theme A	1-10	Presentation of main melodic material in trumpet against polyphony in clarinets and bass voices
A´	11-31	3/4 time signature; *l'istesso* tempo; development of melodic ideas for a quintet of woodwinds
A´´	32-45	4/4 time signature; l'istesso tempo; new countermelody in oboe, E-flat clarinet, and 1st clarinet; varied melody in *staccato* notes in brass
A´´´	46-64	Alternating 3/4 and 2/4 time signatures; flowing accompaniment in woodwinds, and altered theme in trumpet and flugelhorn
A´´´´	65-81	Majestic; brass and percussion only; most obtuse thematic presentation
A´´´´´	82-92	Shortest and simplest variation; 12/8 meter; in tempo of slow stepping march; trombones have the altered theme
A´´´´´´	93-257	3/8 time signature; *l'istesso* tempo; *fugato* texture; more tranquil at m. 172; first tempo at m. 233 with most of the brass section playing the theme in the most literal form of any variation against materials derived from the *fugato*

Section	Measure	Event
Coda	258-278	Concluding section based upon a repeated, four-measure figure derived from the *fugato*, ending on a unison, three-note trumpet fanfare of defiance

Movement III (2:20)
Minuet-Trio in duple meter

Minuet a,a	1-16	2/4 time signature, repeated; march-like section
Minuet b	17-26	*Staccato* passages alternating between brass and woodwinds; some chromaticism
Minuet a	27-38	Altered first section material transposed down a perfect fourth
Trio	39-67	Begins with a single 3/4 time signature, then returns to 2/4; woodwind sextet; slight *ritard.* at the end, *da Capo al fine*
Minuet a,b,a	1-38	*Fine* ending

Unit 8: Suggested Listening

Ernst Krenek, *Drei Marsche für Militärorchester, Op. 44*
Ernst Pepping, *Kleine Serenade für Militärorchester*
Igor Stravinsky, *Octet for Wind Instruments* (1923)
Ernst Toch, *Spiel für Militärorchester, Op. 39*

Unit 9: Additional References and Resources

Carmichael, John C. *The Wind Band Music of Hindemith, Krenek, Pepping, Toch and Others from the 1926 Donaueschingen Music Festival: An Analysis of Historical and Artistic Significance*. Ann Arbor, MI: UMI, 1994.

Kemp, Ian. *Hindemith*. London: Oxford University Press, 1978.

Paulding, James E. "Paul Hindemith (1895-1963) A Study of His Life and Works." Ph.D. Dissertation. University of Iowa, 1974.

Skelton, Geoffrey. *Paul Hindemith*. New York: Crescendo Publishing, 1975.

Contributed by:

John C. Carmichael
Director of Bands
Western Kentucky University
Bowling Green, Kentucky

Teacher Resource Guide

Niagara Falls
Michael Daugherty
(b. 1954)

Unit 1: Composer
Born in 1954 in Cedar Rapids, Iowa, Michael Daugherty is the son of a dance-band drummer and the oldest of five brothers, all professional musicians. Daugherty has received numerous awards for his music, including recognition from the American Academy and Institute of Arts and Letters, and fellowships from the Guggenheim Foundation and the National Endowment for the Arts. His music is published exclusively by Peermusic, New York, and is represented in Europe by Faber Music, London. He is currently an Associate Professor of Composition at the University of Michigan.

Unit 2: Composition
A gateway between Canada and the United States, Niagara Falls is a mecca for honeymooners and tourists who come to visit one of the most scenic waterfalls in the world. The Niagara River also generates electricity for towns on both sides of the border, where visitors are lured into haunted houses, motels, wax museums, candy stores, and tourist traps, as well as countless stores that sell "Niagara Falls" postcards, T-shirts, and souvenirs.

This composition is another souvenir, inspired by Daugherty's many trips to Niagara Falls. It is a ten-minute musical ride over the Niagara River with an occasional stop at a haunted house or wax museum along the way. Its principal musical motive is a haunting chromatic phrase of four tones corresponding to the syllables of "Niagara Falls," and repeated in increasingly gothic proportions. A pulsing rhythm in the timpani and lower brass creates an undercurrent of energy to give an electric charge to the second motive, introduced in canons by the upper brass. The saxophones and clarinets introduce another level of counterpoint in a "bluesy" riff with a film noir edge. *Niagara Falls* is Daugherty's meditation on the American Sublime.

Niagara Falls is scored for piccolo, flutes, oboes, English horn, E-flat clarinet, B-flat clarinets, bass clarinet, alto saxophones, tenor and baritone saxophones, bassoons, contrabassoon, horns, trumpets, trombones, euphoniums, tubas, six percussion, timpani, organ, harp, and double bass. (Piano or synthesizer with harp patch could be substituted for harp if necessary.)

Niagara Falls was commissioned by the University of Michigan Bands for their centennial anniversary. The first performance was given in Hill Auditorium, Ann Arbor, on October 4, 1997, by the University of Michigan Symphony Band conducted by H. Robert Reynolds.

Unit 3: Historical Perspective

Daugherty's music is very much based on American icons. In *Desi*, his first piece exclusively for winds, Daugherty based the music on the American icon Desi Arnez, acknowledging that in a very direct way in the title. Daugherty states that he was just beginning to think about what his influences were, emotionally and aesthetically, around the time he was composing *Desi*. He is definitely unique in that perspective, and it is something that is very important to him. It has people acknowledging that it's kind of his thing. Since the writing of *Desi*, Daugherty's titles definitely reflect the American icon palette, including *Metropolis Symphony*, *Dead Elvis*, *Bizarro*, *Jackie-O*, *Motown Metal*, *Niagara Falls*, and others. He employs the use of alternating large textures and chamber music textures in his large works.

Unit 4: Technical Considerations

All metronome markings are accurate and should be adhered to. Daugherty is very precise with dynamics and articulations. They should be followed with accuracy. Because of Daugherty's use of polyrhythms, the piece becomes a highly technical challenge because of the way the rhythmic blocks must be played with a sense of individuality but with a systematic interlocking to create the complex counterpoint. Technical accuracy is paramount.

Unit 5: Stylistic Considerations

Daugherty calls for all of the indicated falls in the piece to be played in a jazz style. Also, he is very insistent on muted brass play with real plungers when indicated. Saxophones are asked to perform with jazz mouthpieces to achieve a more cutting, strident sound.

Unit 6: Musical Elements

All motives and themes are introduced in some fashion during the introduction of the piece (mm. 1-27). Polyrhythmic counterpoint is a characteristic found throughout *Niagara Falls*. Counterpoint generates harmonies by the stacking of single lines. This layering effect becomes more dominant as Daugherty writes for the large texture sections of the piece. He also tends to write in rhythmic blocks that stack on top of each other. Daugherty employs the techniques of *glissando* or jazz falls as a play on the name and action of *Niagara Falls*.

The piece is built around three different themes and one thematic motive. Theme I is referred to as the Niagara Falls theme. It is a haunting chromatic phrase of four tones corresponding to the syllables of "Niagara Falls." Theme II is first heard in horns, euphonium, trumpets, and trombones. It is a short, punctuated theme built around fourths and tri-tones. Theme III is set in the woodwinds. It is a rhythmic theme that, when lines are stacked, creates a sort of cluster jazz chord reminiscent of modern jazz of the 1960s.

Daugherty describes the thematic motive that he uses throughout the piece to create yet another layer of counterpoint as a "bluesy" riff with a film noir edge. Daugherty develops all of the themes through orchestration, augmentation, key center changes, and rhythmic layering with contrasting motion, chromatic interruption, and stretto technique. Theme I (Niagara Falls) serves as the binding element of the piece. He also manipulates the whole-tone scale to serve as transitional material nostalgic of 1950s film scores.

Unit 7: Form and Structure

SECTION	MEASURE	THEME
Introduction	1-27	Theme I (Niagara Falls)
A	28-57	Theme II; m. 32: horns, euphonium, trumpets, trombone; m. 46: heard in canon
B	58-81	Theme III; m. 72: woodwinds; Theme I (NF), trumpets
C	82-87	Theme I (NF)
D (transition)	88-116	Whole-tone scales
E	117-129	Bluesy film noir motive; Theme II; m. 126: horns
Introduction 1	130-145	Theme I (NF); upper woodwinds: Straussian, chromatic movement
C1	146-155	Theme I (NF); chromatic build
B1	156-192	Bluesy film noir motive; Theme II, augmented in saxophones

SECTION	MEASURE	THEME
C2	193-200	Theme I (NF); bluesy film noir motive
Transition	201-223	
A1	223-237	Theme II; bluesy film noir motive; major key feel
E1	238-251	Transition to coda (canons)
Coda	252-end	Multiple tempo feel; stretto; m. 278: Theme II, bluesy film noir motive

Unit 8: Suggested Listening

Michael Daugherty:

    Bizarro, Argo CD Metropolis Symphony (452 103-2), Baltimore Symphony, David Zinman, Conductor.

    Desi, Argo CD Dance Mix (444 454-2), Baltimore Symphony, David Zinman, Conductor.

    Motown Metal, Argo CD American Icons (458 145-2), London Sinfonietta, David Zinman, Conductor.

    Niagara Falls, Mark Custom Recording (2697 MCD), The University of Texas Wind Ensemble at Carnegie Hall, Jerry F. Junkin, Conductor.

Unit 9: Additional References and Resources

Spede, Mark James. "Michael Daugherty's Red Cape Tango: A Transcription for Band." Diss., The University of Texas, 1998.

Contributed by:

Kevin L. Sedatole
Associate Director of Bands
The University of Texas at Austin
Austin, Texas

Teacher Resource Guide

Parable IX, Op. 121
Vincent Persichetti
(1915–1987)

Unit 1: Composer

Vincent Persichetti was one of the most universally admired American composers of the twentieth century. Persichetti began his musical life at the age of five, first studying piano, then organ, double bass, tuba, theory, and composition. By the age of eleven, he was paying for his own musical education, supporting himself by performing professionally as an accompanist and church organist. His earliest works, written at age fourteen, exhibit true mastery of form and style. By age twenty, Persichetti was simultaneously head of the Theory and Composition Departments at the Combs College of Music, studying conducting with Fritz Reiner at the Curtis Institute of Music, and studying piano with Olga Samaroff at the Philadelphia Conservatory. He received a Diploma in Conducting from the Curtis Institute, and Master of Music and Doctor of Musical Arts degrees from the Philadelphia Conservatory.

Persichetti was appointed head of the Theory and Composition Departments at the Philadelphia Conservatory in 1941. In 1947, he joined the faculty of the Julliard School of Music, where he taught for the next forty years, assuming chairmanship of the Composition Department in 1963. He was the recipient of three Guggenheim Fellowships; grants from the National Foundation on the Arts and Humanities, and the National Institute of Arts and Letters; the Julliard Publication and Symphony League Awards; The Blue Network and Columbia Records Chamber Music Awards; and citations from the American Bandmasters Association and the National Catholic Music Educators Association.

Unit 2: Composition

Parable IX, Op. 121, was composed in 1972 on a commission from the Drake University College of Fine Arts for performance during the opening year of its Fine Arts Center. The work, written in one, sixteen-minute movement, was first performed in Des Moines, Iowa, by the Drake University Symphonic Wind Ensemble on April 6, 1973. The ninth in a series of twenty-five "Parables" written for various solo instruments and ensembles, *Parable IX* dramatically embodies its definition: "a short, fictitious story that illuminates a moral attitude or a religious principle." In *Parable IX,* Persichetti explores the duality of human nature. The music is at once passive as well as aggressive; lyrical as well as angular; amiable as well as angry; and, at its most basic level, portrays the conflict that continues in every individual between good and evil. The "gracious and gritty" clash, quarrel, and challenge is a work of supreme compositional mastery.

Parable IX is crafted in nine segments, or "parables," many related by tempo, style, or theme. Throughout the work, solo instruments challenge entire sections of the ensemble, set against a dramatic percussive commentary. Lyricism of melodic line contrasts with a vigor of rhythm, and solo or soli instruments link each of the parables with combinations of sophisticated beauty and crude enthusiasm. *Parable IX* begins and ends with trombone statements of the "threat motif," a dark and macabre pattern dominating the texture. Poignantly, while the work constantly explores the contradistinction between good and evil, it is good which ultimately prevails.

Unit 3: Historical Perspective

Persichetti composed for nearly every musical medium, publishing over 120 works. He devoted a significant portion of his creative output to repertoire for winds. From *Serenade for Ten Wind Instruments, Op. 1,* to *Chorale Prelude: O God Unseen, Op. 160,* Persichetti provided a wealth of literature of unparalleled excellence. Included among his thirteen works for band are *Divertimento, Op. 42* (1950); *Psalm, Op. 53* (1952); *Pageant, Op. 59* (1953); *Symphony No. 6, Op. 69* (1956); *Masquerade, Op. 102* (1965); and *Parable IX, Op. 121* (1972).

Donald Morris and Jean Oelrich quoted Persichetti, in their article for *The Instrumentalist* magazine, that he considered bands to be worthy of his artistic efforts:

> The concert band is a medium of expression distinct from, but not subordinate to, any other medium. More and more young American composers are turning to it now. You can get lots of things out of a band that you just can't get out of an orchestra.

The wind music of Persichetti has been influential on all composers who have chosen to explore this medium. Musicians of all ages and abilities should be given the opportunity to study his music.

Unit 4: Technical Considerations

This major opus is a compendium of musical colorings, demanding virtuoso technique from all players. The work is scored for standard band instrumentation; however, several sections are split into more parts than are normally found in most band pieces. Included in the score are parts for two piccolos, four flutes, English horn, nine B-flat clarinets, six trumpets, two euphoniums, and two tubas, in addition to the normal division of instruments. The alto clarinet is a separate, crucial part in the work, as is the contrabass clarinet part. The piece requires four multi-percussionists.

Persichetti did not write "down to bands." He is quoted as saying this about *Parable IX*:

> There are many excellent bands in this country that play as well as the fine orchestras. My *Parable for Band*, a compendium of musical colorings demanding virtuoso technique and flexible shaping phrases, has had countless first-rate performances. Every musician is asked to play meaningfully and skillfully, even the second bassoonist and second alto saxophonist – and they do!

Many musicians believe *Parable IX* to be Persichetti's most challenging work for winds. The writing for clarinet is formidable, with separate parts for nine soprano clarinets. The clarinets have many instances of sectional-solo passages throughout the work. The highly lyric, and notably technical, passages are among the most arduous in band literature. The melodic, harmonic, and rhythmic writing requires virtuoso playing from all performers. Persichetti explores the extremes in dynamics, tempos, and range, and presents technical challenges for both soloists and sections. There are extended solos for English horn, bassoon, and alto saxophone.

Unit 5: Stylistic Considerations

Characteristic of Persichetti's style, *Parable IX* makes wide use of bitonality, percussive interjections, extreme timbrel changes, widespread layering of instrumental colors, simultaneity, and "dots of sound." He varies the scoring thickness throughout and constantly searches for unique color combinations. Performers must be comfortable with playing angular melodic material, with non-traditional chordal and rhythmic accompaniment. As intervals are stacked within various harmonic passages, each musician must be confident in performing his or her pitch against dissonant tones from other performers. Persichetti's use of space and rhythmic variety will also challenge each section of the ensemble. The parts are clearly notated with articulations, phrase markings, and dynamics that are crucial to the performance of the work. Ensemble members are required to play contrasting styles simultaneously, as well as between each section. As is typical of Persichetti's writing, the percussion scoring is tastefully written and is crucial to the overall performance of the work.

Persichetti has been quoted as saying this about his compositional style: "My music varies, it goes from gracious to gritty very often. Sometimes it has a lot of serial in it; other pieces have less of that and are more tonal. It's a mixture." *Parable IX* certainly exploits, within one work, both the "gracious and gritty" sides of Persichetti's compositional style.

Unit 6: Musical Elements

While this work is considered very contemporary in nature, the musical elements found are common to compositions from throughout music history. The piece is, in many ways, truly a Romantic work. *Parable IX* includes a "cantus firmus," which expresses the two sides of the composition (and human nature) – "gracious and gritty" – and is found in both the beginning and ending sections. The use of polytonality, a hallmark of Persichetti's style, is ever present. Donald Morris, in his dissertation about the work of Persichetti, mentions that among the manuscript materials Persichetti used in composing this work was found a cover sheet marked "Materials" that included a twelve-tone row and several "Hexas," variations of the row, along with some thematic transformations. There is a strong sense of organic unity in the work, as the nine sections are interconnected into a larger work. The last section of the piece includes a "simultaneous recapitulation" of all the themes presented throughout the work.

Unit 7: Form and Structure

SECTION	MEASURE	EVENT AND SCORING
I	1-10	4/4 meter (quarter note = 69); four-count chords from various sections *crescendo* and *decrescendo* leading to the clarinet section soli; trombone "threat motive" briefly introduced in m. 4
	11-17	Quick bursts of sounds throughout the ensemble, ending with full brass section statement, and an answer in saxophones and low reeds
	18-24	4/4 to 3/4; more relaxed lyrical statements in an interlude featuring the horns and trumpets
	25-41	Back to 4/4, eventually alternating with 3/4; trombone "threat motive" in m. 25; crucial chime part, along with short, quick, sixteenth and thirty-

SECTION	MEASURE	EVENT AND SCORING
		second note statements from all sections; concludes with trills in the woodwinds, followed by the brass, to set up closing English horn cadenza
II	42-55	4/4 meter (quarter note = 76); begins with clarinet section solo, answered by flutes, oboes, English horn, and saxophones, with light percussion interjections
	56-60	Piccolo, flute, English horn, and alto clarinet lyrical melody
	61-68	Alto saxophone solo followed by clarinet section, muted trumpet and trombone *soli*
III	69-76	4/4 meter (quarter note = 76); English horn and clarinet section *soli*, with sixteenth note accompaniment from the piccolo, flutes, and tambourine; horns take over melody at m. 74
	77-81	Sixteenth note build-up through the entire ensemble, with the exception of the euphonium and tuba sections who play a melodic statement; sixteenth note group then basically flows back down to m. 81
	82-88	Full ensemble builds tension through trills and sixteenth and thirty-second note runs, leading to an eighth note statement from most of the ensemble in m. 85; section concludes with a melodic statement in the horns
IV	89-107	3/4 meter (quarter note = 161); piccolo and flute exchange with percussion; culminating in m. 93 where the clarinets lead into a decisive statement from the trumpets and horns; this continues until a unison theme statement from most of the woodwinds, horns, and euphoniums in m. 105
	108-116	Melodic material is segmented and passed around the clarinets, trombone, euphoniums, tubas, horns, and trumpets

Section	Measure	Event and Scoring
	117-125	Clarinet section soli statement eventually passed to the piccolos and flutes, then to the trumpets, before ending with the clarinets
	126-136	Sixteenth note build-up beginning in alto, bass, and contrabass clarinets, eventually moving through the entire woodwind section; percussion accompaniment; xylophone has crucial melodic fragments to contribute
	137-153	Horn section melodic material, with rhythmic interjections from the trumpets, upper woodwinds, and percussion; this section ends with melody in the low flutes
V	154-164	4/4 meter (quarter note = 69); bassoon solo with horn counterline; melody passed to clarinet section, then saxophone section, and back
	165-169	Clarinet section soli
	170-179	Chime-like bell tones in upper woodwinds, ending with low woodwind melodic statement and descending sixteenth note lines in the horns and euphoniums
	180-188	Rhythmic ascending build-up beginning in contrabass clarinet extending through to piccolos; "bird-like" chirps in piccolos and flutes
	189-204	Melodic material in brass and percussion with sustained chords in the woodwinds, ending with trumpet, horn, and chime statements
VI	205-211	4/4 meter (quarter note = 160); rhythmic "chatter" from all sections
	212-223	Rhythmic interjections with melodic material in upper woodwinds, and counterline in trumpets
	224-228	Percussion statement, with strong timpani presence

SECTION	MEASURE	EVENT AND SCORING
	229-242	Melodic material passed from muted trumpet solo, to flute and clarinet sections, to horns
	243-249	Trumpet section soli with horns leading to bell-tone effects in the woodwinds
	250-261	Clarinet section wanders, with ascending and descending slurred eighth notes; flute section soli at m. 255
	262-271	Low reed melodic material, moving to trumpet section in m. 267; this section ends with a short oboe melodic fragment
VII	272-276	3/4 meter (quarter note = 69); oboe and alto saxophone duet with clarinet and bassoon interjections
	277-286	Soft clarinet section soli
	287-294	Loud ensemble build-up leading to full ensemble in m. 290; culminates with thirty-second note rhythmic statement in trumpets, horns, and percussion in m. 293
	295-305	Theme in woodwinds, then passed to horns with counterline in tenor saxophone and euphoniums
VIII	306-313	4/4 meter (quarter note = 160); rhythmic interplay between upper woodwinds, trumpet, and xylophone; leads to sustained melodic material for all woodwinds
	314-321	Simultaneous recapitulation of all melodic material; full ensemble, *forte* and *fortissimo*
	322-332	Rhythmic build-up throughout the ensemble, culminating in loud percussion statements
	333-337	*Tutti* rhythm for almost entire ensemble with xylophone interjections
IX	338-339	4/4 meter (quarter note = 69); coda; alto saxophone cadenza
	340-342	English horn, bassoon, alto saxophone trio

SECTION	MEASURE	EVENT AND SCORING
	343-351	Begin building chords to the end; trombone "threat motive" appears in extended form in mm. 344-345; ensemble *crescendos* to *fortississimo* (*fff*) twelve-tone chord at the end

Unit 8: Suggested Listening

Vincent Persichetti:
  Divertimento
  Masquerade
  Pageant
  Psalm
  Symphony No. 6

The Compositions of Vincent Persichetti. Robert E. Foster, University of Kansas Symphonic Band. Golden Crest ATH-5054, 1978.

Imagination & Beyond. Eugene Corporon, University of Northern Colorado Wind Ensemble. Soundmark R990 BSCR, 1983.

The Music of Vincent Persichetti. Vincent Persichetti, Tennessee Tech University Symphonic Band. USC KM-1558, 1977.

Soundscapes. Eugene Corporon, North Texas Wind Symphony. Klavier KCD-11099, 1999.

Unit 9: Additional References and Resources

Fennell, Frederick. *The Band's Music - Volume One*. Traverse City, MI: Village Press Publications, 1992.

Morris, Donald Alan. "The Life of Vincent Persichetti, with Emphasis on his Works for Band." Ph.D.diss., The Florida State University, 1991.

Morris, Donald and Jean Oelrich. "Vincent Persichetti Remembered: Music from Gracious to Gritty." *The Instrumentalist*, Vol. 47, No. 4 (November 1992), 30-36/74-76.

Rasmussen, Richard Michael. *Recorded Concert Band Music, 1950-1987*. Jefferson, NC: McFarland Press, 1988.

Rehrig, William H. *The Heritage Encyclopedia of Band Music*. Edited by Paul E. Bierley. Westerville, OH: Integrity Press, 1991.

Smith, Norman and Albert Stoutamire. *Band Music Notes*. Third edition. San Diego, CA: Kjos West, 1982.

Theodore Presser Company. "Vincent Persichetti, 1915-1987." Informational brochure from Elkan-Vogel, Inc., a subsidiary of Theodore Presser Company, which includes a biography; list of works and premier performances; reference lists; discography; and commentary.

Workinger, William. "The Band Sound of Vincent Persichetti." *The Instrumentalist*, Vol. 28, No. 9 (April 1973), 44-46.

Contributed by:

James Popejoy
Doctoral Conducting Associate
University of North Texas
Denton, Texas

Teacher Resource Guide

Scenes

Verne Reynolds
(b. 1926)

Unit 1: Composer

Verne Reynolds was born in Lyons, Kansas, on July 18, 1926. In addition to horn, Reynolds also studied violin and piano at the Cincinnati Conservatory of Music, where he received his Bachelor of Music Degree in Composition in 1950. After receiving his Master of Music Degree in Composition from the University of Wisconsin in 1951, he went to London as a Fulbright Scholar at the Royal College of Music. Before joining the faculty of the Eastman School of Music in 1959, Reynolds taught at the University of Wisconsin and Indiana University. As a performer, he has been a member of the Cincinnati Symphony Orchestra, the American Wind Quintet and, from 1959 to 1968, principal horn of the Rochester Philharmonic. After a long and distinguished teaching career, Reynolds retired from the Eastman School of Music in 1995. He is known worldwide for his music for wind and brass ensembles, as well as for his method books, etudes, and transcriptions for horn.

Unit 2: Composition

Scenes was composed in 1971 for Donald Hunsberger to celebrate the twentieth anniversary of the Eastman Wind Ensemble. It is a virtuosic work scored for an expanded orchestral wind section, piano, celesta, timpani, and four percussionists. The wind instrumentation is as follows: four flutes (3rd and 4th doubling piccolo), four oboes (4th doubling English horn), three B-flat clarinets, three bassoons, five horns, four B-flat trumpets, three trombones, and tuba.

    Scenes was followed in 1977 by *Scenes Revisited* and in 1979 by *Last Scenes*, a concerto for horn and wind ensemble. Taken together, they comprise a trilogy which are related in compositional style, level of difficulty, and even by certain pitch relationships. Once available for purchase, *Scenes* is now available only on rental from G. Schirmer. The duration of *Scenes* is approximately seventeen minutes.

Unit 3: Historical Perspective

Like many of Reynolds' works for wind ensemble, *Scenes* employs twelve-tone rows and serial procedures. Most of the time the usage is not strict and rows are rarely manipulated beyond transpositions of the prime. By the composer's admission, the rhythmic style of the fast sections of the entire "Scenes" trilogy is influenced by the atonal jazz of Dizzy Gillespie.[1] Thus, although certain passages in *Scenes* are quite difficult, the desired effect is one of freedom and "looseness." These seemingly disparate influences can be linked through listening examples and appropriate instruction from the conductor.

Unit 4: Technical Considerations

This work is essentially a concerto for wind ensemble, with the flutes, clarinets, horns, and trumpets having the most difficult passages. Many of the difficult passages do not particularly "lie well" for the instruments, thus even very good players will need time to achieve ownership of the music. Control at extremes of the dynamic spectrum is also absolutely necessary for the entire ensemble. The opening section requires the accurate realization of complex, interlocking rhythms at the level of thirty-second notes. The fifth section is an extended solo for an offstage English horn which requires a very mature performer. The final section requires multiple tonguing from all brass players.

Unit 5: Stylistic Considerations

Scenes requires mastery of virtually every aspect of instrumental performance (tonal control, technical virtuosity, rhythmic understanding) and musical maturity. The work runs the dynamic gamut from very quiet to extremely loud and intense music. It is important to remember that the loud music is never intended to be ugly, merely powerful, intense, and dramatic.[2] The perceived modernness of the music should not influence quality of sound demanded from the players.

Unit 6: Musical Elements

The harmonic language of *Scenes* is post-tonal. Reynolds employs twelve-tone rows serially and in a more free manner, having stated that "one hopes that the music exists on its own quite apart from its theoretical aspects."[3] The primary row of the work is eventually presented sequentially by the horns in mm. 344-380, almost as if the composer were "leaving the answer in the back of the book." Working in reverse, one can find that row imbedded in the brasses in the very opening of the piece. Although serial, the work can be said to have a pitch center. The primary row begins on C-sharp, which is also the first and last pitch of the piece. The work also employs aleatoric techniques, in which multiple tempi must be performed independently of the conductor.

Unit 7: Form and Structure

Six distinct sections may be discerned in *Scenes*. Each section has a different character that could be likened to a dramatic scene, if one wishes to use that approach.

1ST SCENE   BEGINNING TO REHEARSAL 5
       Maestoso, quarter note = 56; dramatic and intense; complex composite rhythms distributed among the ensemble

2ND SCENE   REHEARSAL 5 TO REHEARSAL 12
       Allegro, quarter note = 138; section soli for horns and trumpets, very difficult flute and clarinet soli

3RD SCENE   REHEARSAL 12 TO REHEARSAL 13
       Aleatoric music, quarter note = 138, 100, 72, 60, and 50; tone-row music, quarter note = 50; twelve-tone row is repeated at six different pitch levels over an aleatoric background which intensifies with each repetition

4TH SCENE   REHEARSAL 13 TO REHEARSAL 15
       Quarter note = 60; trumpet section soli using whispa mutes over a very soft and sustained series of chords in the ensemble

5TH SCENE   REHEARSAL 15 TO REHEARSAL 16
       Quarter note = 60; offstage English horn solo

6TH SCENE   REHEARSAL 16 TO THE END
       Presto, quarter/dotted-quarter note = 160; multiple tonguing for all brass; very difficult trumpet section soli; extended horn section soli

Unit 8: Suggested Listening

Verne Reynolds:
 Concerto for Band
 Concerto for Piano and Wind Ensemble
 Last Scenes
 Scenes Revisited

Unit 9: Additional References and Resources

Faust, Randall E. "Composer Profile: Verne Reynolds," *Journal of the National Association of College Wind and Percussion Instructors*, Spring, 1987. Vol. XXXV, No. 3, pp. 41-42.

Forte, Allen. *The Structure of Atonal Music*. New Haven: Yale University Press, 1973.

Rahn, John. *Basic Atonal Theory*. New York: Schirmer Books, 1980.

Reynolds, Verne, *Scenes*. The Tokyo Kosei Wind Orchestra, Frederick Fennell, Conductor. Kosei Compact disc KOCD-3569.

Reynolds, Verne, *Scenes Revisited*. The Miami University Wind Ensemble, Gary A. Speck, Conductor. Stevens Recorded Performances, Compact disc 920002.

Strauss, Joseph N. *Introduction to Post-Tonal Theory*. Englewood Cliffs, NJ: Prentice-Hall, 1990.

Contributed by:

Gary A. Speck
Wind Ensemble Conductor
Miami University
Oxford, Ohio

---

1 Conversation with the composer, 13 April 1992.
2 Conversation with the composer, 13 April 1992.
3 Conversation with the composer, 13 April 1992.

Teacher Resource Guide

Skating on the Sheyenne
Ross Lee Finney
(1906–1997)

Unit 1: Composer

Ross Lee Finney was born on December 23, 1906, in Wells, Minnesota, to a musically talented family. His mother was an accomplished pianist who gave piano lessons to all of the family members. Finney began lessons on the cello at age six with a local violinist in Valley City, North Dakota. In 1919, Finney began studying harmony and counterpoint with Donald Ferguson at the University of Minnesota. He later transferred to Carleton College, where he received his Bachelor of Arts Degree in 1927. That same year, Finney received a scholarship from the Johnson Foundation to study with Nadia Boulanger in Paris. He returned to the states the following year, where he worked for the Tilton School for Boys in New Hampshire until accepting a faculty position at Smith College in 1929. In 1932, Finney spent the winter semester in Vienna studying with Alban Berg. While there, Berg introduced him to serialism, which he did not use until much later in his career. In 1936, Finney applied for the Guggenheim Fellowship to work on his compositions in Europe. The following year with notification of his fellowship in hand, Finney also was given the Pulitzer Scholarship in music.

In 1944, Finney was drafted into the Army but failed the health examination and later that year joined the Office of Strategic Services. He was transferred to France, where he met Walter Hinrichsen on the way to Leipzig. He was going to recover music manuscripts and engraving plates from the old C.F. Peters publishing house, which he successfully relocated to New York City. In 1949, Finney was offered a full-time position as Professor of Composition and Composer-in-Residence at the University of Michigan, where he would establish a Composition Department at the School of Music. During his tenure at the University of Michigan, several gifted students began their formal training with Finney, including George Crumb, Roger Reynolds, Leslie Bassett, Sydney Hodkinson, and William Albright. Finney began teaching only one semester per year in 1965 so he could spend more time composing. He then retired from the University of Michigan in 1973 and continued composing full-time. He later accepted an appointment to a newly endowed faculty chair at the University of Alabama for the 1982-83 school year. Finney's other works for band include *Fanfare* (1964), *Summer in Valley City* (1969), *Concerto for Alto Saxophone and Winds* (1974), *Spaces* (1986 transcription of orchestral work), and *Small Town Music* (1987). He died at the age of ninety on February 4, 1997.

Unit 2: Composition

Skating on the Sheyenne is a three-movement work completed in 1977 under a commission by the Brooklyn College Symphonic Band. It received its premiere on May 20, 1978, under the direction of Dorothy Klotzman. This descriptive work draws upon Finney's childhood in North Dakota. The first movement, "Figure Eights," evokes an image of a skater on the frozen North Dakota river, creating geometrical shapes on the ice. The second movement, "Northern Lights," captures the splendor of the Aurora Borealis in all of its glory. The final movement, "Crack the Whip," is full of joyous childhood memories that bring the work to a delightful conclusion. Finney discusses the work and its conception in his autobiography, *Profile of a Lifetime*:

> When Brooklyn College asked me to compose a work for their concert band, I accepted the commission because I had developed very strong ideas about the band as a symphonic organization. I first decided on the largest volume of sound available (the *tutti*) and made a musical form that took shape from the dynamic and tonal points of the work. In between these points were soloistic sections that exploited the wonderful color of the wind instruments. My first work for band had been *Summer in Valley City*, and this new work also drew on my childhood experience in North Dakota. I remembered the fun we used to have ice skating and I decided to call my piece *Skating on the Sheyenne*.

Finney goes on to offer a short program for the work:

> The first movement, "Figure Eights," is filled with all kinds of musical circles, right side up and upside down, like one skates a figure eight. The second movement, "Northern Lights," tries to capture that awesome experience. "Crack the Whip," which ends the work, is funny.

The work is available by rental only and is twelve minutes in duration.

Unit 3: Historical Perspective

Descriptive works of music have long since held a prominent role in Western Art music. A "program" offered by the composer sometimes communicates impressions to an audience far better than the music simply standing alone. Yet, the tone poems of Richard Strauss, the *Sixth Symphony* of Beethoven, and Hector Berlioz's *Symphonie Fantastique* all illustrate the positive effect a program can have to quality music. Without the program, the music of these great composers would still stand on its own. Composers of wind band music in this century also use this device with varying degrees of success. For example, the music of Karel Husa, though not programmatic, possesses an added poignancy when the listener is familiar with the composer's inspiration (i.e., *Music for Prague 1968*, *Apotheosis of the Earth*, *Les Couleurs Fauves*). Too often, composers rely on the "message" to deliver an otherwise modest musical experience. Finney's program in *Skating on the Sheyenne* helps the listener to visualize the composer's impressions from childhood. This information will only add to the understanding and enjoyment of the well-crafted composition.

Unit 4: Technical Considerations

Movement I: "Figure Eights"
The movement begins with a light and punctuated rhythmic figure that occurs throughout the movement. The meter changes to fit the rhythmic intent of the composer. There are numerous range issues and technical passages for horns and woodwinds. The demands placed on the solo bass clarinet and tuba require advanced players with great control of the extended range. Other solo lines include B-flat clarinet, oboe, piccolo, and alto saxophone. The expanded instrumentation of this work includes the addition of English horn, alto flute, contrabassoon, multiple percussion, and piano/celesta.

Movement II: "Northern Lights"
There are few technical demands in this movement. Alto flute must begin the solo on a low C. Other soloists include piccolo, flute, oboe, English horn, celesta, and piano.

Movement III: "Crack the Whip"
This movement contains many challenges for all players. The woodwinds begin immediately with difficult sixteenth note combinations. Multiple meter changes and staggered entrances throughout the movement demand attention. Difficult solo lines begin with piccolo and move through the woodwind section during the first cadenza. Articulation of rhythmic motives presents multiple problems for brass when performed at the indicated tempo.

Unit 5: Stylistic Considerations

MOVEMENT I: "FIGURE EIGHTS"
Understanding the descriptive nature of this work will help in preparing each movement for performance. The first movement contains numerous "musical circles" that are supported by a light and buoyant rhythmic motive. The solo first presented in the bass clarinet contains the "circles" separated by a long "glide" between each entrance. Ascending and descending lines help draw the picture for the listener. The unmeasured cadenza areas present conducting concerns when cueing additional groups of instruments.

MOVEMENT II: "NORTHERN LIGHTS"
The second movement has a transparent quality introduced by major triads within instrument groups. Sound color and texture are conveyed through muted brass and extremely soft woodwind sonorities. Using the alto flute and the celesta as solo instruments add to the iridescent quality often found in French Impressionism. The unmeasured and sequential material that opens the movement requires careful attention.

MOVEMENT III: "CRACK THE WHIP"
The last movement is highly energetic with the required extreme technical demands. The "swirling of snow" must come through to the listener without noticeable attention to notes. This will be attained with proper connection and release of melodic fragments between instrument groups. Staggered entrances by woodwinds must be connected smoothly, as they depict cascading snow. Trombones should exaggerate the *glissando* to attain the proper comic effect. Tempo changes and transitions present minor conducting concerns.

Unit 6: Musical Elements

MOVEMENT I: "FIGURE EIGHTS"
The first movement requires careful attention to contrasting sections primarily viewed as ensemble versus solo cadenza. The transitions between the many free-measured soli and the motivic variations create conducting concerns that may disrupt the musical continuity of the work. Accurate tempi through shifting meters and sudden mood changes will convey the composer's intent of a winter landscape. The proper balance and layering of entrances should be exaggerated between instrument groups throughout the movement. Sensitive solo work along with attention to dynamic contrast will deliver the beauty of this tonal picture.

MOVEMENT II: "NORTHERN LIGHTS"
The second movement is the most beautiful and reflective of the work. The tonal colors and textures written by Finney create the breath-taking imagery that surrounds you when experiencing the Aurora Borealis of the Northern

skies. The unmeasured entrances of major triads by saxophones, clarinets, and muted brass must add only texture beneath the alto flute solo. The notes should be connected to produce a seamless background for the melodic colors found in the solo woodwind and celesta lines. Care should be taken to produce a gentle motion with the beginning of the metered section. Accordingly, the movement should never go beyond a dynamic level of *piano*.

MOVEMENT III: "CRACK THE WHIP"
The final movement possesses the unbridled exuberance of swirling snow during a sleigh ride across the hills of North Dakota. The conductor must avoid allowing the technical demands of this movement to overshadow the inherent musical considerations. Proper balance must be achieved between the sixteenth notes of the woodwinds and the short, punctuated brass and percussion fragments. The declamatory rhythmic statements by both brass and percussion must play a prominent role while woodwinds flurry about. As with the cadenzas in the previous movements, technical demands on the soloists must not detract from the "effect" intended by Finney. Cascading woodwinds in the first cadenza and a comical trombone in the second cadenza must be prevalent. The *accelerando* after the second cadenza must be gradual up to the coda, where a very bright tempo will help create the vivacious energy that will conclude the work.

Unit 7: Form and Structure

SECTION	MEASURE	EVENT AND SCORING
Movement I: "Figure Eights"		
A	1-12	Low winds motivic statement
	Cadenza 1A	Bass clarinet solo; oboe/B-flat clarinet duet
	13-17	Motivic fragment as transition
	Cadenza 1B	Piccolo solo, tuba solo, horn duet, bass clarinet solo, B-flat clarinet solo
	18-19	Motivic fragment as transition
	20-24	Trumpet variation and motivic fragment
B	25-35	6/8 triple contrasting section with horns and trumpets
A	36-39	Return of motivic statement in low winds
	40-44	Ascending transitional material with woodwinds
	Cadenza 1C	Alto saxophone solo; clarinet *tutti*
C	47-60	3/4 waltz

SECTION	MEASURE	EVENT AND SCORING
	Cadenza 1D	Tuba solo with percussion/trumpet trills
	61-68	Instrument pairs as transition material
A	69-73	Theme returns with variation
	74-79	Variation
	80-89	Variation
	Cadenza 1E	Layered soli beginning with xylophone
Coda	90-99	Layered entrances and releases

Movement II: "Northern Lights"

SECTION	MEASURE	EVENT AND SCORING
A	Unmeasured 1	Triads providing color and texture
	2	Alto flute solo
	3	Flute/piccolo duet with alto flute and woodwinds
	4	Celesta and percussion provide transitional material
B	Measured 1-8	6/8 celesta and percussion
	9-16	3/4 transition with woodwinds staggered entrances
A	17-20	Alto flute solo returns
Coda	21-25	Piccolo duet

Movement III: "Crack the Whip"

SECTION	MEASURE	EVENT AND SCORING
A	1-9	Ascending and descending woodwinds and accented brass through *accelerando*
	10-19	More woodwind flurry with brass punctuated lines
	20-37	*Tutti* section of "swirling and drifting snow"
	Cadenza 3A	Staggered woodwind solo entrances
	38-42	Trombone and timpani *glissandi* used as transition
B	43-60	Brass melodic fragment presented and varied
	Cadenza 3B	Trombone *glissando* solo with fragmented interjections
	61-68	Transition
	Cadenza 3C	Trombone solo with shimmering chordal effect
A	69-79	*Tutti* ascending and descending with accented brass
	80-86	More woodwind flurry with brass punctuated lines

SECTION	MEASURE	EVENT AND SCORING
B1	87-106	Augmented melodic fragment from B theme
	107-138	Woodwinds present augmented B theme with ascending-only lines in *tutti* ensemble
Coda	139-153	*Tutti*

Unit 8: Suggested Listening

Ludwig van Beethoven, *Symphony No. 6* (Pastoral)
Hector Berlioz, *Symphonie Fantastique*
Michael Colgrass, *Winds of Nagual*
Claude Debussy, *La Mer*
Paul Dukas, *The Sorcerer's Apprentice*
Ross Lee Finney, *Summer in Valley City*
Gustav Holst, *The Planets*
Richard Strauss, *Don Juan*

Unit 9: Additional References and Resources

Borroff, Edith. *Three American Composers*. Lanham, MD: The University Press of America, 1986.

Camus, Raoul F. "Band Music: by Donald Erb, Ross Lee Finney, Jere Hutcheson, Robert Jager, Alfred Reed." Notes: *Quarterly Journal of the Music Library Association*, September 1983, 156-158.

Cooper, Paul. "The Music of Ross Lee Finney." *The Musical Quarterly*, January 1967, 1.

Finney, Ross Lee. *Profile of a Lifetime: A Musical Autobiography*. New York: C. F. Peters, 1992.

Goossen, Frederic, ed. *Thinking About Music: The Collected Writings of Ross Lee Finney*. Tuscaloosa: The Alabama Press, 1991.

Hitchens, Susan Hayes. *Ross Lee Finney: A Bio-Bibliography*. Westport, CN: Greenwood Press, 1996.

Oderdonk, Henry. "Aspects of Tonality in the Music of Ross Lee Finney." *Perspectives of New Music*, Spring-Summer 1968, 125.

Sadie, Stanley, ed. *The New Grove Dictionary of Music and Musicians*. 20 Vols. London: Macmillan, 1980. S.v. "Ross Lee Finney," by Edith Borroff.

Slonimsky, Nicolas. "Ross Lee Finney," *Baker's Biographical Dictionary of Twentieth-Century Classical Musicians*. Edited by Laura Kuhn, associate editor Dennis McIntire. New York: Schirmer Books, 1997.

Contributed by:
Rich Lundahl
Assistant Director of Bands
Delta State University
Cleveland, Mississippi

Teacher Resource Guide

Spiel für Blasorchester, Op. 39

Ernst Toch
(1887–1964)

Unit 1: Composer

Ernst Toch has been identified as one of the most significant and most performed composers of the first half of the twentieth century. He was born in
Vienna on December 7, 1987. As the son of a leather merchant, he did not
receive encouragement for the study of music. He did receive piano lessons,
however, in accord with standard middle-class upbringing. His first composition teachers were the scores of Mozart string quartets and Bach's
Well-Tempered Clavier, and he began to compose works for various ensembles
as a young teenager. Believing a career as a composer to be unfeasible, Toch
pursued medical studies at the University of Vienna from 1906-09. This did
not curtail his composition of music, however, and in 1909, he won the prestigious Mozart Prize of the city of Frankfurt, along with a scholarship to study
music formally for the first time at the Hoch Conservatory in Frankfurt. While
there, he studied piano with Willy Rehberg and composition with Iwan Knorr.
It was at the Hoch Conservatory where Toch, then twenty-one, met a
fourteen-year-old Hindemith. Through this early connection, Toch and
Hindemith later became good friends, especially in the 1920s.

Toch won the Mendelssohn Prize in 1910 and four consecutive Austrian
State Prizes for his compositions. In 1913, he became a teacher of composition
at the Mannheim Musikhochschule. During World War I, he served in the
Austrian army from 1915-18. After the war, he resumed his teaching career.
Finding the theory books of the day to be unusable as they dealt with melody,
Toch decided to focus on the issue in his Ph.D. document at Heidelberg
University in 1921. The published form of that dissertation became his famous

book on melody, *Melodielehre*. Toch, who was known as a profound and sophisticated thinker, continued to write throughout his career, culminating his thoughts on music in his best-known literary work, *The Shaping Forces of Music*.

The friendship with Hindemith led to Toch's involvement with the Donaueschingen Music Festivals, to which he became a regular contributor after 1922. When the Nazis came to power in 1933, Toch, who was Jewish, was compelled to immigrate to the United States. While in America, Toch did not promote himself as did some of the other displaced European composers. Although he had received a certain acclaim for his film music and had even received a Pulitzer Prize for his *Third Symphony* in 1956, he felt that he was the most forgotten composer of the twentieth century. He taught composition at the University of Southern California in Los Angeles from 1937 to 1948, and after living in Switzerland for eight years and taking several concert tours of Europe, he returned to Los Angeles, where he died in 1964.

Unit 2: Composition

Spiel für Blasorchester, Op. 39, was written for the 1926 Donaueschingen Music Festival and was premiered by the military band stationed in Donaueschingen with the 14th Infantry Regiment of the German army. The premiere was conducted by noted contemporary music exponent Hermann Scherchen, to whom the work was dedicated. The original manuscript of *Spiel für Blasorchester* is missing according to Schott Publishers. A photocopy of the original movement from *Bacchae*, an earlier work written by Toch and used as a basis for the second movement of *Spiel*, is in the Toch archives at UCLA. It was meant to be performed by a one-on-a-part ensemble of wind and percussion instruments of the following instrumentation: [original rental version] piccolo/flute, flute, oboe, bassoon, E-flat clarinet, four B-flat clarinets, four C trumpets, two flugelhorns, four horns, tenor horn, baritone, three trombones, tuba, three percussion, timpani, [new Schott edition, SHS1003] piccolo/flute, flute, oboe, bassoon, E-flat clarinet, three B-flat clarinets, three B-flat trumpets, four horns, three trombones, two flugelhorns, tenor horn, baritone, tuba, three percussion, timpani. It was the largest of the works composed for the 1926 Donaueschingen Music Festival. The critics were divided in their criticism of *Spiel*. One described it as being inferior to Toch's other works, while another backhandedly indicated that *Spiel* would be easily understood by the uninitiated to military bands playing more serious music. *Spiel* was also described as being expertly put together, even though the content was rather light. Perhaps the most complimentary statement implied that *Spiel* was a bridge between alienating, self-engrossed, avant-garde art music and music that could be enjoyed by a broader public.

Unit 3: Historical Perspective

In 1924, the selection committee for the Donaueschingen Music Festival in Donaueschingen, Germany, decided to commission new music for mediums that had been neglected by composers of serious art music. In those days, a commission simply represented a call for new compositions and a guarantee of performance. For the 1926 Donaueschingen Music Festival, the selection committee identified the military band as a neglected ensemble, among others, and thereby issued a commission for musical works of artistic merit for that medium. The initial call for original compositions for military band was not productive, which led the committee to instigate the commissioning of specific composers for the project. The commissions produced four works that were performed on the July 24, 1926 concert that served to welcome guests to the festival. Those works included *Konzertmusik für Blasorchester, Op. 41*, by Paul Hindemith; *Drei Marsche für Militärorchester, Op. 44*, by Ernst Krenek; *Kleine Serenade für Militärorchester*, by Ernst Pepping; and *Spiel für Militärorchester, Op. 39*, by Ernst Toch. Famous modernist conductor Hermann Scherchen led the premieres of three of the four compositions. A fifth work, *Promenademusik für Militärorchester*, by Hans Gal, was evidently performed at a "replay" concert on the Monday evening following the conclusion of the festival. That work was not considered to be successful. Several other composers well known in Germany at the time were involved but evidently did not follow through on the commission, although a composition entitled "Wake Up," by Paul Dessau, is mentioned in correspondence.

Newspaper and magazine reviews of the July 24 concert provided much insight into the reception given to the works for band. Generally, opinions were mixed, but the prevailing view indicated that the performances and the compositions were not of the highest caliber. More recent scholarship has identified three of the works, the compositions by Krenek, Toch, and Hindemith, as important works for wind band. The composition by Pepping, which is now available through Georg Bauer Musikverlag, was rediscovered in 1989 and carefully edited. *Promenademusik für Militärorchester*, by Gal, has been recently published through Schott and edited by Wolfgang Suppan.

Unit 4: Technical Considerations

This work was intended for a one-on-a-part military band of regimental size. Toch's composition requires a larger compliment of players than any of the other military band compositions from the 1926 Donaueschingen Music Festival. Because *Spiel* was written for military band instrumentation, one might expect problems finding an appropriate substitute for the tenor horn. The solution offered by Hindemith for *Konzertmusik* may also be used in *Spiel*: substitute tenor saxophone for tenor horn and soprano saxophones for flugelhorns. A better, more authentic solution might be obtained by using a small-bore baritone instead of a tenor horn and by substituting a large-bore euphonium for the baritone. Use flugelhorns as indicated.

The most technically difficult section of *Spiel für Militärorchester* is found in the first movement where Toch uses melodic displacement and hemiola to achieve an interesting rhythmic effect. It is strongly suggested that a metronome set at a first-level division be used in the rehearsal of this movement, particularly mm. 9-20.

Unit 5: Stylistic Considerations

Spiel für Militärorchester, Op. 39, is a good example of the neoclassical movement of the 1920s in Western European art music. The use of a neotonal harmonic language framed in forms derived from the classical and, particularly, the baroque style periods was characteristic of composers who were reacting against the excessive emotionalism of late romanticism and the harshness of atonality. The use of parody and experimentation were also common features of this music. The three-movement macro-form was a rather standard format, consistent with the typical fast-slow-fast organization of baroque instrumental works. Although this work does not reflect parody, it is essential that clarity be achieved in the polyphonic texture. Players must use a light, precise articulation style in combination with perfect vertical alignment of rhythmic figures. Because the work is intended to be performed by one player on a part, balance was a key consideration for Toch and the other Donaueschingen band composers. Careful dynamic projection of sequential melodic ideals against accompaniment properly placed in the background is critical to obtain transparency. Toch's style of writing, however, is much less imitative than what is found in *Konzertmusik für Blasorchester, Op. 41*.

Unit 6: Musical Elements

MOVEMENT 1: "OUVERTÜRE"
The first movement, "Ouvertüre" (2:06), begins in 2/4 time, quarter note = 132 mm., and is in an ABA form. The opening instruction requests a very light and flexible, precise *staccato*. Starting with a pick-up to the anacrusis in m. 1, Toch sets the stage for a rhythmically complex and metrically varied movement. Use of an accented rest on the downbeat of *Spiel* is a device of Toch's that illustrates a tenet of *The Shaping Forces in Music*. The initial melodic material is presented by clarinets and flute, and its irregular phrase lengths and hemiola create interest above a generally uninteresting accompaniment of eighth notes. Although it begins in the key of C major, chromaticism and dissonant harmonies are present throughout. A repeat of the opening measures occurs at m. 21 but with a different accompaniment figure in the brass. The instruction in the score calls for "clean harmony" in the brass section. The melodic reiteration is followed by a mixed meter passage that features a call/response between woodwinds and brass, and serves as a

closing section. At m. 38 begins a contrasting lyrical portion of the move-ment, metrically more regular than that which proceeded it. It is accompanied by a rather traditional rhythmic figure in trumpets and flugelhorns, and deco-rated by a brilliant woodwind *obligato* which is performed in parallel first-inversion chords for a portion of its duration. The principal melody is in horn, tenor horn, baritone, and 1st and 2nd trombone, and is centered in the key of F. After a short bridge where oboe and E-flat clarinet share melody with horn, the original lyrical melody returns at m. 62 but with a different voicing. Now trumpets, flugelhorns, and horns have the lead. The accompaniment is also different, with a simple oom-pah figure in tuba/bass trombone (perhaps an example of parody) and a clever borrowing of the accompaniment rhythms used with the original melody in mm. 21-23, now placed in upper woodwinds and spliced in with portions of the earlier *obligato*. Although the melody is dis-tinctly diatonic, the accompaniment in the upper woodwinds moves chromatically. This section ends with a *dal segno* back to m. 2. As in the other Donaueschingen military band compositions, the percussion section is used sparingly. Toch, however, breaks with convention and adds a single triangle note on beat one of m. 62 for delightful effect. Dynamically, most of the movement is soft, with louder volumes happening only at the beginning and in a few other places for either projection of woodwind parts or special effect.

MOVEMENT 2: "IDYLL"

The second movement of *Spiel* originated as part of the incidental music for a stage play entitled *Bacchae*, which was completed in early 1926. It is the only movement of music from the play to survive. The first version was originally for woodwind quintet, so Toch had to make a few changes by enriching har-monies, doubling parts, and adding triangle to adapt it for the larger military band instrumentation. Not all of the instruments of the band, however, were used for "Idyll." The flugelhorns, tenor horn, baritone, 3rd and 4th trumpets, and the battery percussion are tacet. Clearly notated in G major, "Idyll" (4:01) is in 6/8 time, with eighth note = 116 mm. After one measure of accompani-ment, the oboe enters with perhaps the most lyrical and memorable melody of the Donaueschingen band music. In the original rental score version (an apparent copy of the manuscript), at mm. 4, 12, 34, and 42, the bassoon and accompaniment figures do not seem to agree when the harmony changes. Upon first glance, this would seem to be a mistake, but the fact that it occurs four times with only one slight difference in m. 12 would seem to indicate intent. In the more recently published *Schott Harmonie Series* score (SHS1003), the noted irregularity has been adjusted for harmonic agreement. At m. 6, the bassoon initiates a short duet with the oboe that produces linear counterpoint while exploring rather sudden harmonic shifts. The oboe returns with the original melody at m. 10, but after four measures the oboe modulates into a new key area. At m. 19, 1st and 2nd clarinet take over with a more somber and angular melodic idea. An imitative entrance at a different pitch level by flute at m. 24 seems to indicate imitative counterpoint but is only the beginning of a brief development section in mm. 25-29. The clarinet then returns at m. 30 with a closing figure that foreshadows the return of the original melody in the oboe. After a short *ritard* and a brief hemiola (3/4 against 6/8) in m. 31, the oboe again performs its melody, but this time with a countermelody by horns. Instructed to play "very tenderly," the first two horns alternate the countermelody with the bassoon and then clarinet, producing Toch's finest linear counterpoint of the composition. The oboe is told to "hold back" at m. 45 as it performs an extension of the melody that moves into the closing section beginning at m. 48. In m. 46, the trombones make their first contribution of the movement – an accompanying chord progression in almost a somber, religious affectation that moves from G major to a quartal structure. Above a repeated G-major chord, the melody gradually fragments and disappears after stating, finally, its first three notes. Then at m. 55, Toch provides a clever little side trip away from the G tonality, creating some tension while arriving at the loudest moment of the movement at m. 59. In one measure, the music delicately and evaporatively returns to G as the triangle signals the end of the movement. Structurally, this movement is an ABA form with a proportionately long coda section. In the older version of *Spiel*, there are some missing accidentals in the clarinet parts from m. 55 to the end. All of the notated Gs should be natural. This has been corrected in the new version.

MOVEMENT 3: "BUFFO"
Buffo is in 2/4 time throughout except for the last few measures, and quarter note = 132-138 mm. Even though it is the most chromatic of the three movements, the tonal center seems to be C, as prepared by the last note of the introduction (G) and as indicated by some melodic figures. The introductory material is derived from the first theme, an extracted dotted-rhythm figure which is performed in octaves that outline a G-flat major chord which abruptly resolves to G. Above a standard accompaniment figure, the clarinets, horn, and trumpet vigorously introduce the first melodic theme, which is eight bars long and moves downward in chromatic increments. It is restated, also at *forte*, in upper woodwinds above a completely different, more pointillistic accompaniment. A glockenspiel appears for the first time in any of the Donaueschingen military band compositions. By comparison, Toch's percussion writing is by far the most colorful. At m. 21, a second eight-bar theme which had been foreshadowed by the accompaniment figure in mm. 13-19 appears in the woodwinds. For the theme's reiteration at m. 29, it is voiced even more brilliantly with brass instruments providing accompaniment. Cymbal is played with a wooden stick during this and other later sections. The introduction figure returns at m. 37, leading into another appearance of the

first theme, this time voiced in horn, baritone, tenor horn, and trombone against a new countermelodic figure in horn and trumpet. So far the effect has been true to the "clownish" implication of the movement title. The new countermelody, according to Toch, is to be played "tenderly." It is quite lyrical and grows to be more dominant at m. 49 on its repeat, while the first theme diminishes. At m. 55, the countermelody disappears in a curious flurry of augmented triads while the first theme reappears, fragmented by instrumental timbre and in imitation of itself at a one-measure interval. The overall effect is to move downward through the voices for eight measures, only to return upward for the following eight, culminating in a short closing figure similar to that at mm. 11-12, emphatically landing in a C tonal center. Linear counterpoint is the primary means of composition from mm. 41-68. Measures 73-79 are transitional, leading to a new melodic idea at m. 80. Even though the intervallic structures are different, there is economy in the use of rhythmic materials as evidenced by the appearance of the dotted figure in the new line and the facsimile of a transitional motive at m. 93 from m. 74. The second figure being developed is rhythmically derived from the accompaniment at m. 21. Fragmentation and timbre variation continue through a thinly orchestrated development section that is harmonically ambiguous. At m. 109, Toch closes the previous section with a line of triplets against eighth notes that moves back to a C major chord, but not without an ascending chromatic by clarinet above it.

Continuing the triple division as an accompaniment figure, Toch repeats the melodic idea from m. 80 with melodic extensions following the dotted rhythms. The trumpet signals an impending recapitulation with a fanfare figure at m. 128 that, rather than building to a climax, fades away with a whimper in bassoon to a short *caesura*. Following the accented rest on beat one of m. 144, the woodwinds explode into the introduction music from m. 1, only this time there is imitative material in some brass voices on beat two in m. 145. The first melody is orchestrated in horn and flugelhorn, with both accompaniment figures from the first two statements of the theme in this movement used simultaneously. For the second statement of the theme, the second half of the countermelody is brought back as counterpoint. At m. 165, the dotted-figure theme is fragmented and used imitatively to create a polyphonic texture similar to that in m. 57, only with a slightly different instrumentation. Above, the piccolo and flute, and then the clarinets, provide a kind of *obligato* accompaniment. After an ascending C major scale figure at m. 179, the original theme returns one last time in a 3/2 measure which is used to frame an eighth note expansion of the principal motive. Woodwinds have one last interjection with a Poulenc-like ascending figure of ambiguous harmonic content that they are instructed to play strongly. The movement finishes in C, but not without a little dissonant "bite" occurring on the sixteenth notes just before the last C major chord. Although Toch was not as thickly polyphonic in his composition as were Hindemith and Pepping of the Donaueschingen military band composers, he does use, to a significant extent, linear counterpoint to develop melodic ideas. Furthermore, he has a tendency to mix colors on melodic material more than any of the other 1926 Donaueschingen band composers. His use of percussion is decidedly more creative and colorful.

As noted earlier, a new published version of the *Spiel* has been made available for purchase through the *Schott Harmonie Series*. Here are some additional differences between the older rental score and this one that should be mentioned. First, the new score has ad-lib parts for alto and bass clarinet. which do not exist in the older version. Also, the older version has four C trumpet parts and four B-flat clarinet parts, but the newer one has only three of each, and the trumpets are in B-flat. The newer version is more clear, however, in the listing of every percussion instrument to be used.

Unit 7: Form and Structure

SECTION	MEASURE	EVENT
Movement I: "Ouvertüre" (2:06)		
A (a, b, a, c)	1-37	
a	1-8	Melodic material in flute, E-flat clarinet, and 1st clarinet; simple accompaniment by chromatically descending eighth notes
b	9-20	Complicated hemiola of five 3/8 groupings over four 2/4 measures beginning after an eighth rest, ending in a cadence and occurring twice
a	21-28	Thicker texture than first "a" but softer dynamic presentation
c	29-37	Dialogue between lower brass voices and upper woodwinds; alternates 3/4 and 3/8 measures for interesting rhythmic effect; ends with strong cadence to C major
B (a, b, a)	38-75	
a	38-53	Contrasting lyrical section in horn, baritone, and tenor horn; accompanied by trumpets and flugelhorns with upper woodwinds playing a sixteenth note *obligato* derived in part from A section material

SECTION	MEASURE	EVENT
b	53-61	Bridge-like melody in woodwinds and horn; chordal accompaniment in trombone and flugelhorn; C pedal in 3rd trombone and 3rd and 4th horn
a	62-75	Lyrical melody returns in horn and trumpet; *staccato* accompaniment in clarinet and flute
A (a, b, a, c)	76-112	Written-out *da capo*
a	76-83	Same as mm. 1-8
b	84-95	Same as mm. 9-20
a	96-103	Same as mm. 21-28
c	104-112	Literal restatement of mm. 29-37; strong cadence to C major

Movement II: "Idyll" (4:01)

A	1-18	Simple accompaniment in bassoon, clarinet, and horn; lyrical melody in oboe; G major; some countermelodic interest in the bassoon
B	19-31	Clarinet lead echoed by flute six measures later; B minor; rapid modulation; figure derived from melody in m. 2 acts as an elision back to A section
A	32-47	Nearly exact repeat of first A section with the exception of an added horn countermelody; mm. 43-47 represent new melodic material in oboe with clarinet countermelody
Coda	48-60	Repeated melodic fragment in oboe used as a closing figure; deceptive departure from key center by flute, clarinet, and brass; moves abruptly to a V7-I cadence in horn at end

Movement III: "Buffo" (2:32)

Introduction	1-4	Establishes a G minor center
A	5-21	Descending chromatic melody; altered orchestration for second statement of melody

SECTION	MEASURE	EVENT
B	2-39	Contrasting *staccato* figure in upper woodwinds, second statement considerably thicker with added brass; G major
Introduction	37-40	Stronger statement than at beginning of movement; G minor
A	41-60	Descending chromatic melody voiced darkly; new countermelodic material in 3rd and 4th horns and 3rd trumpet
A′	61-72	Original melody serves as a basis for imitative counterpoint; second phrase ascends rather than descends; material from B section used to accompany; ends in C tonality (the subdominant)
Trio introduction	73-79	Fragmented dialogue between wood winds and brass; anticipates figures to be used in trio
Trio a	80-96	Chromatically expanding melodic line in trumpet and flugelhorn, later in oboe and E-flat clarinet; accompanied by sixteenth note-eighth note groupings from trio introduction
b	97-111	New melody in flugelhorn that starts with large intervals that contract; first homage to tradition march with trombone afterbeats in accompaniment; second half of section features a fragmented dialogue between brass and woodwinds; triplets are introduced for first time at mm. 109-111
a	112-128	Chromatically expanding melodic line in upper woodwind; triplet accompaniment provided by clarinet, triangle
c	128-143	Closing passage featuring a military-like trumpet call
Introduction	144-148	A powerful reiteration of the original introduction at beginning of "Buffo"
A	149-172	Descending chromatic melody as in beginning but with ascending accompaniment in upper woodwind for contrast

SECTION	MEASURE	EVENT
A´	173-179	Chromatic melody ascending
Coda	180-182	Derived from initial descending melody; extensions of rhythmic grouping; ends in C major

Unit 8: Suggested Listening

Paul Hindemith, *Konzertmusik für Blasorchester, Op. 41*
Ernst Krenek, *Drei Marsche für Militärorchester, Op. 44*
Ernst Pepping, *Kleine Serenade für Militärorchester*
Igor Stravinsky, *Octet for Winds* (1923)

Unit 9: Additional References and Resources

Carmichael, John C. *The Wind Band Music of Hindemith, Krenek, Pepping, Toch and Others from the 1926 Donaueschingen Music Festival: An Analysis of Historical and Artistic Significance.* Ann Arbor, MI: UMI, 1994.

Gray, Winfried. *Music für Blasorchester 1926.* Schweiz: Neue Musik Serie, 1995.

Johnson, Charles Anthony. "Part I: The Unpublished Works of Ernst Toch. Part II: Chronology of Compositions and Thematic Catalog." Ph.D. Dissertation. University of California, Los Angeles, 1973 (UMI 73-28, 717).

Toch, Ernst. *The Shaping Forces of Music.* New York: Criterion Music Corporation, 1948.

Contributed by:

John C. Carmichael
Director of Bands
Western Kentucky University
Bowling Green, Kentucky

Teacher Resource Guide

Symphonies of Wind Instruments

Igor Stravinsky
(1882–1971)

Unit 1: Composer

Igor Stravinsky is generally considered to be one of the most original and out-standing composers of the twentieth century. Stravinsky was born in what is now Lomonosov, Russia, in 1882 and died in New York in 1971. He was a Russian composer, later of French (1934) and American (1945) nationality. Stravinsky's life, career, and compositional style were rich and varied.

Stravinsky's early training in piano, harmony, and composition was encouraged by his father, Fydor, a bass singer with the Imperial Opera Theater. As a teenager Igor was introduced to his friend's father, Nicolai Rimsky-Korsakov, who became an important teacher and mentor to Stravinsky. Rimsky-Korsakov had a seminal influence on his compositional and orches-trational style.

Stravinsky's music can be grouped into three distinct style periods: the Russian period (1905-20), the neoclassical period (1920-52), and the serial period (1952-71). Stravinsky's music was strongly influenced by his cultural surroundings and artistic and intellectual influences. He formed a close asso-ciation with the impresario Sergey Dyagilev, founder of both the *World of Arts* movement in Russia and the *Ballet Russe*. Dyagilev provided Stravinsky with his first commissions, including the ballets *The Firebird*, *Petrushka*, and *The Rite of Spring*. The seeds of Stravinsky's uniquely creative voice in his treat-ment of rhythm, orchestration, and harmony are already clearly in evidence in these highly acclaimed works. Music from this period is imbued with Stravinsky's stylized use of Russian folk song material and demonstrates an awareness of his Russian contemporaries, including Rimsky-Korsakov,

Tchaikovsky, and Glazenov as well as the French composers Dukas, Debussy, and Ravel.

Symphonies of Wind Instruments was written at the end of a period of exile in Switzerland during World War I. It exemplifies a move by Stravinsky to the use of smaller forces, sparer textures, more succinct forms, and emotional detachment as a precursor to his neoclassical period. Important works from this time include *L'Histoire du soldat*, *The Wedding*, *Reynard*, and *Three Pieces* for string quartet.

Stravinsky's neoclassical compositions spanning the years 1920-39 in France and 1939-52 in the United States reference the gestures and manners of the eighteenth century and neobaroque formal discipline. Major works from this period include *Symphony of Psalms*, *Pulcinella*, *Piano Concerto*, *Oedipus Rex*, *Persephone*, *Symphony in C*, and *The Rake's Progress*. The last period of Stravinsky's life began a close association with Robert Craft, whose enthusiasm for the Second Viennese School influenced Stravinsky. This interest precipitated an assimilation of serial technique into Stravinsky's style in a highly personal manner. *Canticum sacrum*, *Agon*, *Threni*, and his final work, *Requiem Canticles*, written with his own approaching death in mind, are all from this period.

Stravinsky left us with three major works for winds, including *Symphonies of Wind Instruments*, *Piano Concerto*, and *Octet*, as well as several smaller works, including *Circus Polka* commissioned by the Barnum and Bailey Circus Band, an arrangement for winds and percussion of the *Song of the Volga Boatman*, and a memorial for Rimsky-Korsakov that Stravinsky lost. Other works that use wind and/or percussion instruments extensively are *Symphony of Psalms*, *Reynard*, *L'Histoire du soldat*, *Rag-time for 11 Instruments*, *Elegy for J.F.K.*, *Epitaphium*, and *Mavra*.

Unit 2: Composition

Symphonies of Wind Instruments was composed in 1920 and was significantly revised in 1947. It was called by the composer an "austere ritual which is unfolded in terms of short litanies between different groups of homogeneous instruments."[1] The term "symphonies" thus refers to the earlier term "sinfonia," a shorter sectional and intermittently contrapuntal instrumental work of contrasting timbres and textures. *Symphonies of Wind Instruments* is dedicated to the memory of Claude Debussy. The original memorial was composed first and appears in the concluding chorale.

Symphonies of Wind Instruments was premiered by Koussevitsky at the conclusion of a Romantic program and was met by a mixed audience response. Stravinsky soon withdrew the work, criticizing the conductor and the score, citing problems in harmony, texture, and meter. In 1945, during a period of intense revision of many of his earlier works, Stravinsky reworked the *Symphonies of Wind Instruments*, changing instrumentation (deletion of alto flute and alto clarinet, use of B-flat trumpets), chord voicings and articulations, rebarring, and limiting interpretive decisions by performers and conductors. The result was an altogether different work. Although Stravinsky described the 1920 version as inferior and the revision as definitive, the original version is well worth investigating.

Symphonies of Wind Instruments is scored for three flutes, two oboes, English horn, three clarinets in B-flat, two bassoons, contrabassoon, four horns in F, three trumpets in B-flat, three trombones, and tuba. It contains elements of Stravinsky's Russian period in his stylized use of Russian folk song and dance, and the formal structure and emotional detachment of his neoclassical period. The *Symphonies of Wind Instruments* is highly organic in that most of the germinal ideas are presented in the first twenty-eight measures. The work is cast in three sections, beginning with an exposition which includes several Russian folk melodies. The second section is a wild Russian dance, and the third and final section is the austere and beautiful chorale memorializing Debussy.

Unit 3: Historical Perspective

Stravinsky was enamored with Claude Debussy's music during a period when cultural exchange between France and Russia was particularly strong. Stravinsky was introduced to Parisian artistic circles by Dyagilev and became friendly with Debussy and Ravel. Stravinsky's *The Nightingale* borrows musical ideas from Debussy's *Nuages*. Debussy's experimentation with harmony opened the door to a new tonal vocabulary which included pandiatonicism, extended tertian harmony and modality, new scale structures including whole-tone and pentatonic scales, and a move away from the traditional tonic-dominant relationship. *Symphonies of Wind Instruments* was composed two years after Debussy's death in 1918.

Symphonies of Wind Instruments reflects a new aesthetic perspective at the beginning of the twentieth century. Stravinsky and his contemporaries rejected what they considered the expressive excesses of the symphonic composers of the German Romantic tradition. This also reflects the trauma experienced during World War I. Arnold Schoenberg's *Pierrot lunaire* had a strong impact on Stravinsky. Its scoring, succinct form, and theatrical impact can be seen reflected in Stravinsky's *L'Histoire du soldat* from this period. Stravinsky became fascinated with wind timbres and their ability to directly convey expression without the emotional excesses of large string sections. *Octet* (1923) and *Piano Concerto* (1924) were written in rapid succession and reflect this aesthetic.

Unit 4: Technical Considerations

Symphonies of Wind Instruments is musically demanding especially in terms of precise rhythmic execution. The constantly shifting meters make reading difficult. Control of tempo and the ability to anticipate tempo change through the understanding of tempo relationship is key to successful performance. A feel for the smallest unit of subdivision is necessary throughout the work.

Unique instrument pairings and sonorities require a careful attention to balance and color. The occasional use of upper ranges (especially bassoon in mm. 8-9 and mm. 38-39), melodies that are unpredictable, and sudden changes of style and tempo make *Symphonies of Wind Instruments* difficult to negotiate. The tuning of open intervals, dissonances, and extended tertian harmonies require careful attention. Widely spaced chords in the horns are difficult to tune.

Tonal control and sensitivity to ensemble are required, as is flexibility of timbre. The "wild dance" requires aggressive playing with a firm and *secco* articulation style, while the chorale calls for a well-controlled *sostenuto*. Very little doubling occurs in *Symphonies of Wind Instruments* and soloistic playing abounds.

Unit 5: Stylistic Considerations

Symphonies of Wind Instruments bears all three of the stylistic trademarks of Stravinsky's mature style: 1) the stylized use of Russian folk song and dance and the permutation of a melodic cell, 2) stasis as a closing gesture and structural device, and 3) internal rhythmic organizational logic based on tempo relationships connected by a small rhythmic unit.

Symphonies of Wind Instruments marks a transition between Stravinsky's Russian and neoclassical periods. An overt Russian influence can be heard in the use of two folk songs in the exposition and the wild Russian dance, while a logical, formal design and the extended use of two-voiced counterpoint foreshadows the works of his neoclassical period.

The utmost clarity of texture and formal balance must be achieved by the conductor. A wide range of articulation styles and dynamics are demanded of the players. The bar line exists to fit the musical gesture and should not get in the way of performance. Individual contribution is great, and each part must be performed with confidence, without being overly expressive. The final chorale must receive the most musical weight. Stravinsky's attempt to limit performance choices has provided many of the interpretive clues to idiomatic performance.

Unit 6: Musical Elements

The intervals of the second, third, and fourth are used both melodically and harmonically throughout *Symphonies of Wind Instruments*. The harmonic and melodic vocabulary draws upon an early twentieth century language that includes pandiatonicism, modality, bitonality, extended tertian harmony, and whole-tone, diatonic, chromatic, and octatonic scales. Repeated dissonance is used as a harmonic anchor (mm. 1-2, 4-5 and mm. 6-9, 38-39). Tonal centers are not arrived at via traditional means. The long-range tonal motion is from G in the opening measures to a final arrival on C major9.

Melodies are generally conjunct, simple, and repetitive, and encompass a small range usually within a perfect fifth. They are straightforward and almost "primitive" in nature. Textures are both polyphonic (mm. 14-26), and homophonic (mm. 47-56, 65-end). Rhythm is an important formal element in *Symphonies of Wind Instruments*. There are three interrelated tempi. The first is quarter note = 144, the second is one-third as fast as the first, and the third tempo is twice as fast. The final chorale moves twice as slowly as the first tempo.

Symphonies of Wind Instruments is a singular work that was undervalued for many years. It has recently been recognized as a seminal composition in Stravinsky's output and is cited as an important influence on composers such as Karlheinz Stockhausen since World War II.

Unit 7: Form and Structure

SECTION	MEASURE	EVENT AND SCORING
Movement I: "Exposition"		
A (*a tempo* I)	1-7	Pointillistic accompaniment; declamatory octatonic clarinet melody in the third register; intervals: major second, minor third, augmented fourth
b	8-13	Static *tutti* octatonic chord open position; long-short articulation followed by a *legato* melody; intervals: minor second, major third, perfect fourth; foreshadows chorale
a	14-18	Shortened recapitulation
c	19-21	Sixteenth note subdivision (double-time feel); oboe, English horn fifths; foreshadows "Wild Dance"
b	22-27	Return, *legato* melody mutated
Closing	28-29	*Legato* oboe, English horn closing gesture; intervals: major second, minor third, perfect fourth
B (*a tempo* II)	30-39	Pastoral: diatonic flute melody, static dissonant flute accompaniment
b	40-46	Bassoon melody on three pitches in extreme upper register, static dissonant flute accompaniment
A (*a tempo* I)	47-52	Shortened recapitulation of A

SECTION	MEASURE	EVENT AND SCORING
b	53	
Closing	54	
C (tempo II)	55-70	*Pesante* trombone diads from A b; *sforzando* long-short clarinet and horn dissonant chords, diatonic *staccato* trumpet, oboe melody; melodic and harmonic material features the major second and perfect fourth
D a	71-99	Extended passage of two- and three-voice counterpoint between flute and two clarinets; mostly diatonic and conjunct
C + D	100-122	*Staccato* melody from C stated in the oboes and English horn
Closing	123-124	Austere closing gesture featuring a descending perfect fourth in the English horn with bassoons
A a	125-129	Shortened recapitulation
b	129-132	
Closing	133-134	English horn and bassoons
D a	135-151	Shortened recapitulation
C + D	152-169	
Closing	170-171	English horn and bassoons
A a	172-174	
B b	175-181	
A a	182-186	
Closing	187-188	Oboe and English horn
Codetta	195-200	*Sostenuto* short-long gesture; starts with anacrusis in woodwinds and horns and anticipates chorale; bitonal: A-flat/F to E-flat/D-flat
Transition:		
Chorale fragment	201-205	Trumpet, trombone, tuba anacrusis; harmonic stasis: G7(b9) second inversion
Codetta	206-207	*Sostenuto* short-long gesture; begins with anacrusis in bassoon and horn; anticipates "Wild Dance"; fermata on open position chord built on major second, minor third, and perfect fourth

SECTION	MEASURE	EVENT AND SCORING
"Wild Dance" fragment	208-212	Trumpet, trombone, tuba *secco* and dissonant eighth notes
Codetta	213-216	*Sostenuto* short-long in flute, clarinet, and bassoon; intervals: second, third, fourth
Movement II: "Wild Dance"		
A (tempo III)	217-243	Eighth note *staccato* melodic fragments; intervals: minor second, fourth, fifth octatonically derived
B	244-270	Alternation between bassoon, oboe and English horn, horn and tuba; rapidly changing meter, sudden dynamic contrast; becomes more emphatic with *tutti* scoring, *fff*, brass melody with woodwind punctuation
Transition:		
Chorale (tempo I)	271-274	Brass-anacrusis, short-long; G7(b9) second inversion
Codetta (tempo II)	275-280	Flute, oboe, clarinet, bassoon
Wild Dance + codetta (tempo III)	281-305	Codetta material in "Wild Dance" style
Codetta (tempo II)	306-310	Flute, oboe, clarinet, bassoon
Movement III: "Chorale"		
Tempo I (1/2)	311-371	Long-short gesture, harmonic stasis on G7(b9) second inversion; alternating choirs: brass, double reeds, and horn; ends with soft dynamic, harmonic progression: emi7-dmi9-Cmajor 9

Unit 8: Suggested Listening

Claude Debussy:
   Nocturnes
   Prelude to the Afternoon of a Faun
   The Sunken Cathedral
Paul Hindemith, *Six Chansons*
Darius Milhaud, *La creation du monde*
Maurice Ravel, *Rhapsodie Espagnole*

Nicoli Rimsky-Korsakov, *The Golden Cockerel*
Arnold Schoenberg, *Pierrot lunaire*
Igor Stravinsky:
   Circus Polka
   The Firebird
   In memoriam Dylan Thomas
   L'Histoire du soldat
   Mavra
   Octet
   Petrushka
   Piano Concerto
   Pulcinella
   The Rake's Progress
   Renard
   Requiem Canticles
   The Rite of Spring
   Symphonies of Wind Instruments (1920)
   Symphony in C
   Symphony of Psalms
   Three Pieces for string quartet
Edgard Varese, *Octandre*

Unit 9: Additional References and Resources

Andriessen, Louis, and Elmer Schonberger. *The Appolonian Clockwork-On Stravinsky*. New York: Oxford University Press, 1989.

Cone, Edward T. *Perspectives on Schoenberg and Stravinsky*. New York: W.W. Norton and Company, 1972.

Craft, Robert, and Igor Stravinsky. *Themes and Episodes*. New York: Alfred A. Knopf, 1966.

Craft, Robert. "On the Symphonies of Wind Instruments." *Perspectives of New Music* 22 (1984): 448-55.

Craft, Robert. *Stravinsky-Glimpses of a Life*. New York: St. Martin's Press, 1982.

Spittal, Robert J. "The 1920 and 1947 *Symphonies of Wind Instruments* by Igor Stravinsky." Doctoral diss., Cincinnati College-Conservatory of Music, 1995.

Stravinsky, Igor. *An Autobiography*. New York: W.W. Norton and Company, 1962.

Stravinsky, Igor. *Circus Polka*. Eugene Corporon and the Cincinnati College-Conservatory of Music Wind Symphony, 1994. Compact disc KCD-11059.

Stravinsky, Igor. *Symphonies of Wind Instruments* (1920). Robert Craft and the Orchestra of St. Luke's, 1992. MusicMasters Classics Compact disc: "Igor Stravinsky the Composer," Volume III.

Stravinsky, Igor. *The Poetics of Music*. New York: Harvard: University Press, 1942.

Stravinsky, Igor. *Themes and Conclusions*. London: Faber and Faber, 1972.

Stravinsky, Vera, and Robert Craft. *Stravinsky in Pictures and Documents*. New York: Simon and Schuster, 1978.

Tyra, Thomas, "An Analysis of Stravinsky's *Symphonies of Wind Instruments*." *Journal of Band Research* 8 (Spring 1972): 6-39.

Walsh, Stephen. *The Music of Stravinsky*. London: Routlege, 1988.

Watkins, Glenn. *Soundings*. New York: Schirmer Books, 1988.

Weisberg, Arthur. *Performing Twentieth-Century Music*. New Haven and London: Yale University Press, 1993.

White, Eric Walter. *Stravinsky: The Composer and His Works*. 2nd ed. Berkeley: University of California Press, Inc., 1984.

Contributed by:

John P. Lynch
Associate Director of Bands
Northwestern University
Chicago, Illinois

---

1   Eric Walter White, *Stravinsky: A Critical Survey*, (London, 1947) p. 96.

Teacher Resource Guide

Third Symphony
James Barnes
(b. 1949)

Unit 1: Composer

James Barnes, a member of both the band and theory-composition faculties at the University of Kansas, teaches orchestration, arranging, composition, band, and orchestral literature courses. He conducts the wind ensemble and the concert band. His numerous works for concert band are extensively performed in the United States, Canada, Europe, and the Pacific Basin. He has twice received the American Bandmasters Association Ostwald Award for outstanding contemporary wind band music, as well as numerous ASCAP awards and the Kappa Kappa Psi Distinguished Service to Music Medal.

Unit 2: Composition

The *Third Symphony* was commissioned by the United States Air Force Band in Washington, DC, and was completed on June 25, 1994. Barnes began the work after the death of his baby daughter, Natalie. In the preface to the score Barnes states, "This symphony is the most emotionally draining work that I have ever composed. If it were to be given a nickname, I believe that 'Tragic' would be appropriate."

The work progresses from the deepest darkness of despair all the way to the brightness of fulfillment and joy. The first movement is a work of much frustration, bitterness, despair, and despondency – Barnes' personal feelings after losing his daughter. The *scherzo* (second movement) has a sarcasm and bitter sweetness about it, representing the pomposity and conceit of certain people in the world. The third movement is a fantasia which represents a farewell to his daughter. The finale (fourth movement) represents a rebirth of spirit and reconciliation. The second theme of the last movement is based on an old Lutheran children's hymn, "I Am Jesus' Little Lamb," which was sung at his daughter's funeral.

Unit 3: Historical Perspective

The term symphony is now normally taken to signify an extended work for band or orchestra. The symphony became the chief vehicle of orchestral music in the late eighteenth century, and from the time of Beethoven came to be regarded as one of music's highest and most exalted forms.

Unit 4: Technical Considerations

MOVEMENT 1:

The first movement begins with extensive soli for the tuba, English horn, and bassoon. The tuba and English horn soli are quite long, at times only accompanied by a 6/4 motive in the timpani. Much of this movement is based on the polymetric opposition of 2/2 against 6/4. Harp and celesta are used to establish an important harmonic pedal point at several times. The saxophone scoring includes soprano saxophone and the flute scoring includes alto flute.

There is extensive unison passage work for both the woodwinds and brass that link several important thematic sections. There is also much unison doubling of principle themes. The beginning of the development section employs changing irregular meters at a fast tempo. There is much rhythmic and technical demand for all instruments.

MOVEMENT II:

The second movement is a *scherzo*, with a tempo of *allegro moderato*. It opens with a three-part bassoon *ostinato* which accompanies two very demanding soli, one for bass clarinet and one for baritone saxophone. There is also an extensive clarinet solo. This opening woodwind section is concluded with some very nice percussion ensemble writing which features the xylophone. The middle B section (for brass) is march-like in character. This section features much divisi writing for choirs of trumpets, horns, and trombones. The A section reappears with an exciting saxophone quartet feature. The brass, woodwind, and percussion themes reunite at the end of the movement.

This movement is light and, with the exception of the solo passages, not technically demanding. Celesta and harp are again important in this movement.

MOVEMENT III:

The third movement is a beautiful and slow (quarter note = 56) lament. There is, again, a great demand for solo playing. There are soli and duets for oboes, English horn, alto saxophone, soprano saxophone, tenor saxophone, horn, and bassoon. The opening contains a large cadenza for both the baritone saxophone and the English horn. There are three main thematic sections. The first theme is scored for solo instruments and accompaniment. The second, and longest, thematic section builds in thickness of texture. This is the section in which the movement reaches a penultimate climax (m. 66). The third thematic section features duets for the oboe and English horn, and soprano and alto saxophones. The restatement of the B section is rescored with the addition of a lyrical countermelody and a sixteenth note "motor" figure in the woodwinds. This movement concludes with a brief coda which features choirs of horns, double reeds, and saxophones.

MOVEMENT IV:
The finale is a bright and challenging movement in 6/8. The tempo is marked *Allegro giocoso* (dotted-quarter note = 120). Two themes dominate this movement. The first theme is a fast and rhythmic melody, and it eventually passes between all of the voices. The theme is often accompanied by woodwind runs or brass fanfare motives. The second theme (m. 116) is based on the childhood hymn, "I Am Jesus' Little Lamb," and is introduced by the woodwinds. After an exciting development section, both themes return in a simultaneous recapitulation (m. 371).

Unit 6: Musical Elements

Barnes freely draws on all the harmonies and textures available to a composer at the end of the twentieth century but contains them within the traditional forms for the movements of a symphony. The first movement, in C minor, is a modified sonata form, with an extended coda. The second is an ABA form in the subdominant F minor. The outer "A" sections are scored for woodwinds and percussion, with the "B" section scored for muted brass. Both themes return scored for the full band at the end of the movement. Exquisite in its simplicity, the hauntingly beautiful third movement is a fantasia in D-flat in the form ABCABC-Coda. Balancing the entire work, the fourth movement, C major, is again in sonata form. The first theme is stated by the horns and the second theme, as previously mentioned, is the tune of the children's hymn.

Unit 7: Form and Structure

SECTION	MEASURE	EVENT AND SCORING
Movement I:		
Exposition		
Opening Theme a	1-33	Theme in tuba solo; 6/4 triplet motive in timpani
Ascending Theme b	34-54	Ascending theme in oboe solo
Variation of Theme a	54-62	Variation in bassoon solo
Ascending motive	62-73	Ascending motive develops through woodwinds

Section	Measure	Event and Scoring
Transition	74-82	Descending scalar passage motive
Restatement of Theme a	83-95	Full restatement in trumpets and woodwinds with extension of descending scalar motive
Restatement of 6/4 motive	96-113	Restatement in low brass; continued unison passage work
Theme a	114-133	Theme a restated in woodwinds and horns in opposition against 6/4 motive in trumpets; builds to climax in m. 128
Codetta	134-161	Extended flute solo
Development		
6/4 motive fanfare	162-173	Fanfare in brass
Theme a	173-187	Trombones and euphoniums
Theme C	188-210	*Allegro* – changing meter; compounding brass scoring beginning with horns
Theme D	211-221	New theme in trumpets
Return of triplet motive	222-230	Variations of triplet motive in all voices
Variation of Theme D	231-240	Canon between low and high voices
Theme A motive	241-288	Return of minor ninth motive developed through all voices
Full restatement of Theme A	289-331	Restatement of entire Theme A with unison passage extension to climax in mm. 330-331
Transition	332-345	Unison passage work
Recapitulation		
Ascending Theme B	346-355	Theme B in woodwinds, fugal, and euphoniums
Theme A (6/4 motive)	356-361	Theme A restated with opposing 6/4 triplet motive
Extension	362-378	Extension to final statement
Finale statement	379-397	Final climactic statement of main theme
Coda	398-443	Alto flute and English horn soli, interjecting triplet motive in trumpets
Movement II:		
A section	1-24	Three part bassoon *ostinato*
(woodwinds only)	25-37	Bass clarinet solo
	48-56	Oboes/saxophones continue *ostinato*; baritone/saxophone solo
	57-60	Percussion interlude

Section	Measure	Event and Scoring
	61-77	Flutes/clarinets play the first woodwind Theme a; percussion/bassoons continue *ostinato*
	75-85	Oboes/saxophones continue theme
	86-93	Clarinet solo against the continued woodwind theme
	94-113	Percussion only – featuring the xylophone
	114-116	Short segue to B section
B section (brass only)	117-124	Brass Theme b in three-part French horn
	125-134	Cornets/trombones continue theme
	135-153	Brass continue thematic dialogue
Transition	154-175	Lyrical eighth note passage transitions from brass to woodwinds
A section	176-201	Trombones/bassoons now share *ostinato*
	202-207	Piccolo/bass clarinet duet
	208-214	Flute/contra-alto clarinet duet
	215-228	Saxophone section feature
	229-231	Transition to brass
	232-253	Restatement of brass Theme b
	254-268	Restatement of woodwind Theme a
Coda	269-287	Lyrical transition material interspersed with Theme f fragments

Movement III:

Section	Measure	Event and Scoring
A section	1 - 9	Accompaniment *ostinato* in harp, celesta, and percussion
	10-17	Oboe/English horn solo dialogue
	18-21	English horn cadenza
	22-28	Baritone saxophone cadenza
B section	29-33	Accompaniment *ostinato* in woodwinds and percussion
	34-41	French horn solo
	42-65	B section continued and developed toward climactic moment
	66-69	Climax of B section and transition to C section
C section	70-77	Oboe/English horn duet
	78-90	Soprano/alto saxophone duet
	91-93	Short transition to restatement of A section

SECTION	MEASURE	EVENT AND SCORING
A section	94-99	Accompaniment *ostinato*
	100-104	Short oboe solo
B section	105-112	Theme B reintroduced in tenor saxophone
	113-137	B section developed with addition of countermelodies and running sixteenth notes
	138-148	Climax of B section and a substantially longer transition
C section	149-161	Bassoon duet
Coda	162-172	Choir of horns, double reeds, and saxophones trade past thematic material
Movement IV:		
Introduction	1-36	Brass fanfares; running woodwind lines
Exposition	37-44	Theme A introduced in horns
	45-52	Theme A continued in trumpets
	53-60	Connective motive in woodwinds
	61-68	*Tutti* Theme A
	69-76	Theme A continued in trombones
Transition	77-115	Introductory material used as transition
Theme B	116-164	Theme B material traded between choirs of woodwind and brass
Development	165-316	Development of thematic material from introduction, Theme A, and Theme B
Recapitulation	317-324	Horns reintroduce Theme A
	325-332	Trumpets continue theme
	333-340	Connective motive in brass and woodwinds
	341-348	*Tutti* Theme A
	349-370	Transition through development of Theme A
	371-410	Simultaneous recapitulation of Themes A and B; Theme A in woodwinds; Theme B in brass
Coda	411-445	Coda utilizes motives from introduction, Theme A, and Theme B

Unit 8: Suggested Listening

James Barnes:
Centennial Celebration Overture
Invocation and Toccata

Unit 9: Additional References and Resources

Dvorak, Thomas L., Robert Grechesky, and Gary Ciepluch. *Best Music for High School Bands*. New York: Manhattan Beach Music, 1993.

Contributed by:

Ryan Nelson
University of North Texas
Denton, Texas

Appendix

Selected Compact Disc Survey

Compiled by Edwin C. Powell
Director of Bands
McLennan Community College

Introduction

It was a very pleasant surprise to find that literally thousands of wind recordings are available worldwide. It is not the intention of this survey to be a complete discography but rather to show a representative snapshot of what is available for each of the grade four, five, and six compositions in the GIA series. Events like all-state band concerts and high school band festival recordings were left off unless they were one of the only recordings available. This survey primarily lists readily available discs by professional, collegiate, and military bands. At the time this survey was completed, there were only ten works in the GIA series unrecorded. This is a rather impressive fact considering that there are now three hundred pieces discussed in the three volumes. It is a strong testament to the hard work and dedication of hundreds of professionals worldwide.

A complete set of the grade two and three works are available through a three-volume anthology recorded by the North Texas Wind Symphony and sponsored by GIA Publications. Also soon to be released will be a collection of grade one works recorded by the University of Wisconsin-Milwaukee.

A few of these recordings can only be obtained through publishers or the United States Military. The recordings of the United States Military Bands are not for sale. They may be easily found in both college and public libraries. It is possible to obtain these recordings by writing the respective military branch and requesting them officially through your school. Generally, they will send them with the understanding that they become the property of the school and are used for educational purposes.

Three primary sources were consulted while putting together this survey. They were Shattinger Music's "Resource Guide," the West Coast Music

Service Catalog, and the Mark Custom Recording Catalog. Special thanks should go to Jim Cochran of Shattinger Music for his constant updates. Happy listening!

Following is contact information for each of the three sources; they would surely welcome your business:

Shattinger Music
Contact: Jim Cochran
1810 South Broadway
St. Louis, MO 63104
(800) 444-2406-Voice
(888) 621-2408-Fax
jcresource@aol.com
http://www.shattingermusic.com

West Coast Music Service
Contact: Tommy or Helyn Ferlazzo
P.O. Box 3501
North Ft. Myers, FL 33918
(888) 422-6323-Voice
(941) 731-0565-Fax
bandcd@earthlink.net

Mark Custom Recording
Contact: Mark Mouret
P.O. Box 406
Clarence, NY 14031
(716) 759-2600-Voice
(716) 759-2329-Fax
Markcustom@aol.com

Volume I, Grade IV

Title	Composer	Recording Group	Recording No.	Page Ref.
Allerseelen [8:00]	Richard Strauss/Davis/Fennell	North Texas Wind Symphony Tokyo Kosei Wind Orchestra	GIA CD-490 KOCD-2811	pg. 218
Amazing Grace [5:00]	Frank Ticheli	Cincinnati Wind Symphony KeyStone Wind Ensemble Michigan State	KCD-11060 MCD-1530 MCD-2744	pg. 222
Caccia and Chorale [7:00]	Clifton Williams	Arkansas State University North Texas Wind Symphony Texas All State	MCD-1938 GIA CD-490 TMEA93 MCD-1260	pg. 225
Chorale and Alleluia [5:00]	Howard Hanson	KeyStone Wind Ensemble	CTD-88111	pg. 229
Chorale and Shaker Dance [10:00]	John Zdechlik	Northshore Concert Band North Texas Wind Symphony	4-4104-2 GIA CD-490	pg. 234
Chorale and Toccata [5:30]	Jack Stamp	KeyStone Wind Ensemble	MCD-1332	pg. 238
English Folk Song Suite [11:00]	Ralph Vaughan Williams	Cleveland Symphonic Winds Keystone Wind Ensemble London Wind Orchestra RNCM Wind Orchestra Tokyo Kosei Wind Orchestra	TELARC CD-80099 GIA CD-490 LWO-588 CHAN 9697 KOCD-3563	pg. 241
Fantasia in G Major [5:30]	J. S. Bach/Goldman and Leist	Cleveland Symphonic Winds North Texas Wind Symphony	CD-8038 GIA CD-490	pg. 247
First Suite in E-flat [10:30]	Gustav Holst	Cleveland Symphonic Winds Eastman Wind Ensemble Keystone Wind Ensemble North Texas Wind Symphony	CD-8038 SK-47198 CTD-88127 GIA CD-490	pg. 251

TITLE	COMPOSER	RECORDING GROUP	RECORDING NO.	PAGE REF.
First Suite in E-flat (continued)		RNCM Wind Orchestra Tokyo Kosei Wind Orchestra	CHAN 9697 KOCD-3576	
Irish Tune from County Derry [5:00]	Percy Grainger	London Wind Orchestra North Texas Wind Symphony Tokyo Kosei Wind Orchestra University of Houston University of Illinois University of Illinois	LWO-629 GIA CD-490 KOCD-3566 MCD-1086 MCD-1210 MCD-1458	pg. 255
Liturgical Music, Op.33 [10:30]	Martin Mailman	IUP Symphony Band North Texas Wind Symphony	Bands of IUP GIA CD-490	pg. 259
Night Dances [8:00]	Bruce Yurko	North Texas Wind Symphony	GIA CD-490	pg. 263
Old Home Days [8:30]	Charles Ives/Elkus	Cincinnati Wind Symphony University of Miami, Ohio	KCD-11042	pg. 267
Pageant [7:30]	Vincent Persichetti	DePauw University Band KeyStone Wind Ensemble North Texas Wind Symphony Northern Illinois University Winds of the London Symphony	MCD-2271 CTD-88132 GIA CD-490 HSB-003 HMU-907092	pg. 271
Prelude, Siciliano, and Rondo [7:00]	Malcolm Arnold/Paynter	Northwestern University North Texas Wind Symphony	Vol. 6 GIA CD-490	pg. 276
Scenes from "The Louvre" [10:30]	Norman Dello Joio	1990 New York All State Band KeyStone Wind Ensemble	MCD-815 CTD-88132	pg. 282
Second Suite in F [11:30]	Gustav Holst	Cleveland Symphonic Winds Keystone Wind Ensemble London Wind Orchestra	CD-80038 GIA CD-490 LWO-588	pg. 286

Title	Composer	Performer	Recording	Page
Shadows of Eternity [7:30]	Thomas Stone	RNCM Wind Orchestra	CHAN 9697	pg. 294
		Tokyo Kosei Wind Orchestra	KOCD-2304	
		Tokyo Kosei Wind Orchestra	KOCD-3563	
		Tokyo Kosei Wind Orchestra	KOCD-3576	
Sinfonia V [8:00]	Timothy Broege	DePauw University Band	MCD-2271	pg. 300
		Honor Band of America	Volume V, 1995	
		North Texas Wind Symphony	GIA CD-490	
		CSU Fullerton Wind Ensemble	GIA CD-490	
		North Texas Wind Symphony		
		UNC Greensboro Wind Ensemble		
Variations on a Korean Folk Song [7:00]	John Barnes Chance	North Texas Wind Symphony	GIA CD-490	pg. 304
		Tokyo Kosei Wind Orchestra	KOCD-2302	

Volume I, Grade V

Title	Composer	Performer	Recording	Page
Canzona [5:00]	Peter Mennin	KeyStone Wind Ensemble	Not yet released	pg. 309
Children's March [7:00]	Percy Grainger/Erickson	East Texas State University	TMEA93 MCD-3	pg. 313
		Eastman Wind Ensemble	432 019-2	
		Michigan State	DE-3101	
		United States Marine Band	MW93 MCD-9	
		University of Houston	MCD-1523	
		University of Illinois	MCD-1210	
		University of Illinois	MCD-1457	
Colonial Song [6:00]	Percy Grainger	Australian Wind Orchestra	MW93 MCD-27	pg. 316
		BBC Philharmonic	CHAN-9493	
		Michigan State	DE-3101	
		University of Houston	MCD-1086	
		University of Illinois	MCD-1210	

Title	Composer	Recording Group	Recording No.	Page Ref.
Divertimento [11:00]	Vincent Persichetti	Tokyo Kosei Wind Orchestra Winds of the London Symphony	KOCD-3076 HMU-907092	pg. 319
Fantasies on a Theme by Haydn [12:00]	Norman Dello Joio	Tokyo Kosei Wind Orchestra USAF Tactical Air Command Band	KOCD-3571	pg. 323
George Washington Bridge [9:00]	William Schuman	Cincinnati Wind Symphony Tokyo Kosei Wind Orchestra USAF ACC Heritage Band of America	KCD-11048 KOCD-3562	pg. 326
La Fiesta Mexicana [23:00]	H. Owen Reed	Cincinnati Wind Symphony Dallas Wind Symphony Tokyo Kosei Wind Orchestra University of Illinois	KCD-11048 RR-38CD KOCD-2814 MCD-1649	pg. 330
Overture in C [7:00]	Charles Simon Catel/ Goldman and Smith	United States Marine Band		pg. 334
Overture to "Candide" [4:30]	Leonard Bernstein/Grundman	Cincinnati Wind Symphony	KCD-11048	pg. 341
Overture, Op. 24 [8:00]	Felix Mendelssohn-Bartholdy/ Boyd	Tokyo Kosei Wind Orchestra University of Illinois USAF AETC Band of the West	KOCD-3566 MCD-3566	pg. 337
Sketches on a Tudor Psalm [12:00]	Fisher Tull	KeyStone Wind Ensemble North Texas Wind Symphony	CTD-88108 KCD-11070	pg. 345
Suite Francaise [16:30]	Darius Milhaud	Cincinnati Wind Symphony London Wind Orchestra Tokyo Kosei Wind Orchestra United States Army Field Band	KCD-11058 LWO-629 KOCD-3101	pg. 349
Suite of Old American Dances [18:30]	Robert Russell Bennett	Cincinnati Wind Symphony Tokyo Kosei Wind Orchestra	KCD-11060 KOCD-2302	pg. 357

Title	Composer	Ensemble	Recording	Page
Symphony No. 3 [23:00]	Vittorio Giannini	United States Air Force Band		pg. 365
		University of Illinois		
		USAF Strategic Air Command Band	MCD-1649	
Symphony No. 6, Op. 69 [17:00]	Vincent Persichetti	Dallas Wind Symphony	RR-52CD	pg. 361
		Eastman Wind Ensemble	434 320-2	
		Northwestern University	Vol. 4	
		USAF ACC Heritage of America Band		
Toccata and Fugue in D minor [9:00]	J. S. Bach/Leidzen	Baden Wurtemburg Wind Ensemble	MAS 337	pg. 369
		Cincinnati Wind Symphony	KCD-11047	
		Eastman Wind Ensemble	432 754-2	
		Tokyo Kosei Wind Orchestra	KOCD-3076	
		Tokyo Kosei Wind Orchestra	KOCD-3101	
		USAF Tactical Air Command Band		
Trauermusik [8:30]	Richard Wagner/Votta/Boyd	Eastman Wind Ensemble	SK-47198	pg. 372
		Tokyo Kosei Wind Orchestra	KOCD-2815	
		Tokyo Kosei Wind Orchestra	KOCD-7507	
		Indiana State University	BOCD-7507	
		Wisconcin Wind Orchestra	MCD-2483	
Variants on a Medieval Tune [11:00]	Norman Dello Joio	Austin Symphonic Band	MW89 MCD-23	pg. 378
		Dallas Wind Symphony	RR-52CD	
		USAF ACC Heritage of America Band	MCD-856	
Variations on "America" [7:30]	Charles Ives/Rhoads	Cincinnati Wind Symphony	KCD-11060	pg. 382
William Byrd Suite [18:00]	Gordon Jacob	Eastman Wind Ensemble	MERC D-125361	pg. 385
		Tokyo Kosei Wind Orchestra	KOCD-3563	
		United States Air Force Band		

Volume I, Grade VI

TITLE	COMPOSER	RECORDING GROUP	RECORDING NO.	PAGE REF.
Armenian Dances, Part 1 [10:30]	Alfred Reed	Senzoko Gakuen Symphonic Winds Tokyo Kosei Wind Orchestra Tokyo Kosei Wind Orchestra UNCG Wind Ensemble University of Illinois	WFR-140 KOCD-3016 KOCD-3502 CD-104 MCD-1210	pg. 390
Carmina Burana [25:00]	Carl Orff/Krance	Northern Illinois University University of Northern Iowa	HSB-005 UN of NI	pg. 394
Emblems [11:30]	Aaron Copland	Cincinnati Wind Symphony Tokyo Kosei Wind Orchestra USAF ACC Heritage of America Band	KCD-11030 KOCD-3073	pg. 400
Hammersmith [14:00]	Gustav Holst	Dallas Wind Symphony Eastman Wind Ensemble European Wind Orchestra Keystone Wind Ensemble London Wind Orchestra North Texas Wind Symphony RNCM Wind Orchestra Stockholm Wind Orchestra Tokyo Kosei Wind Orchestra Tokyo Kosei Wind Orchestra United States Air Force Band University of Illinois	RR-39CD 432 009-2 TROY-120 CTD-88127 LWO-588 KCD-11070 CHAN 9697 CAP 21415 KOCD-3073 KOCD-3576 MCD-1651	pg. 403
Heroes, Lost and Fallen [11:00]	David Gillingham	Cincinnati Wind Symphony University of Illinois Koninklijke Militaire Kapel	KCD-11042 MCD-1458	pg. 407
Lincolnshire Posy [16:00]	Percy Grainger	Baylor University Cleveland Symphonic Winds	TMEA95 MCD-4 CD-80099	pg. 410

Title	Composer	Ensemble	Recording	Page
Masquerade, Op. 102 [12:00]	Vincent Persichetti	Eastman Wind Ensemble	432 754-2	pg. 415
		Eastman Wind Ensemble	SK-47198	
		North Texas Wind Symphony	KCD-11079	
		Tokyo Kosei Wind Orchestra	KOCD-2818	
		United States Air Force Band		
		University of Houston	MCD-1086	
		University of Illinois	MCD-1210	
		University of Illinois	MCD-1866	
		USAF ACC Heritage of America Band		
Music for Prague 1968 [21:00]	Karel Husa	Cincinnati Wind Symphony	KCD-11066	pg. 420
		Texas A&M-Commerce	MCD-2704	
		Tokyo Kosei Wind Orchestra	KOCD-3562	
		Winds of the London Symphony	HMU-907092	
		Baylor University	TMEA95 MCD-4	
		Eastman Wind Ensemble	MK-44916	
		University of Illinois	MCD-1866	
Passacaglia (Homage on B-A-C-H) [11:00]	Ron Nelson	Cincinnati Wind Symphony	KCD-11058	pg. 435
		Dallas Wind Symphony	RR-76CD	
		Tokyo Kosei Wind Orchestra	KOCD-2402	
		UNCG Wind Ensemble	MCD-1810	
		United States Marine Band	MW93 MCD-9	
		University of Illinois	MCD-1458	
		University of Wisconsin-Milwaukee	VAWB-1134	
		USAF AETC Band of the West		
Passacaglia and Fugue in C minor [12:30]	J. S. Bach/Hunsberger	Dallas Wind Symphony	RR-43CD	pg. 429
The Passing Bell [14:00]	Warren Benson	No Known Compact Disc Recording		pg. 441
Piece of Mind [21:00]	Dana Wilson	Cincinnati Wind Symphony	KCD-11051	pg. 444
		Tokyo Kosei Wind Orchestra	KOCD-3569	

Title	Composer	Recording Group	Recording No.	Page Ref.
A Postcard to Meadville [5:30]	Frank Ticheli	Cincinnati Wind Symphony Michigan State University University of Georgia University of Wisconsin-Milwaukee	KCD-11058 MCD-2744 UN of GA VAWB-1134	pg. 450
Sinfonia No. 4 [6:00]	Walter Hartley	Tokyo Kosei Wind Orchestra	KOCD-3569	pg. 456
Sinfonietta [19:30]	Ingolf Dahl	Cincinnati Wind Symphony Tokyo Kosei Wind Orchestra	KCD-11030 KOCD-3571	pg. 461
Symphony in B-flat [17:30]	Paul Hindemith	Cincinnati Wind Symphony European Wind Orchestra Tokyo Kosei Wind Orchestra Tokyo Kosei Wind Orchestra Tokyo Kosei Wind Orchestra University of Georgia University of Illinois University of Wisconsin-Milwaukee US Coast Guard	KCD-11059 C 197 891 A KOCD-7506 KOCD-2304 KOCD-3314/15 UN of GA MCD-1648 VAWB-1134 MW91 MCD-8	pg. 465
Symphony No. 4 "West Point" [20:00]	Morton Gould	Cincinnati Wind Symphony Eastman Wind Ensemble Tokyo Kosei Wind Orchestra	KCD-11042 434 320-2 KOCD-3311	pg. 469
Terpsichore [22:00]	Bob Margolis after Michael Praetorius	Cincinnati Wind Symphony University of Houston	KCD-11058 MCD-1875	pg. 476
Theme and Variations, Op. 43a [11:30]	Arnold Schoenberg	Australian Wind Orchestra Cincinnati Wind Symphony University of Illinois	MW93 MCD-27 KCD-11047 MCD-1648	pg. 482
Zion [10:00]	Dan Welcher	North Texas Wind Symphony University of Texas Arlington	KCD-11070 TMEA95 MCD-1	pg. 488

Volume II, Grade IV

Africa: Ceremony, Song and Ritual [9:00]	Robert W. Smith	George Mason University	EL9748CD	pg. 284
Autumn Walk [6:00]	Julian Work	Northern Arizona University		pg. 289
Color [6:20]	Bob Margolis	St. Olaf Band	STO-986	pg. 293
Dreamcatcher [12:00]	Walter Mays	North Texas Wind Symphony	KCD-11089	pg. 298
Elegy for a Young American [6:00]	Ronald LoPresti	Tokyo Kosei Wind Orchestra Northern Illinois University	KOCD-3562 HSB-002	pg. 304
Four French Songs [7:30]	Robert Hanson	No Known Compact Disc Recording		pg. 308
Fugue G Minor [3:30]	Johann Sebastian Bach	Tokyo Kosei Wind Orchestra University of Georgia	KOCD-2815 UNGA	pg. 313
Hymn of St. James [5:30]	Reber Clark	IUP Symphony Band	IUP/1997	pg. 317
Japanese Tune [6:00]	Soichi Konagaya	Fukuoka Wind Orchestra 1992 Indiana All-State Band	MC-20897CD MCD-1080	pg. 321
Kaddish [8:00]	W. Francis McBeth	Texas Tech University Tokyo Kosei Wind Orchestra USAF AETC Band of the West	MWFM-396 KOCD-2818	pg. 325
Masque [7:15]	W. Francis McBeth	No Known Compact Disc Recording		pg. 332
Of Dark Lords and Ancient Kings [5:00]	Roland Barrett	No Known Compact Disc Recording		pg. 339
Satiric Dances [7:30]	Norman Dello Joio	USAF Strategic Air Command Band		pg. 344
Sea Songs [4:00]	Ralph Vaughan Williams	Cleveland Symphony Winds	CD-80099	pg. 349

781

Title	Composer	Recording Group	Recording No.	Page Ref.
Sea Songs (continued)		Tokyo Kosei Wind Orchestra United States Air Force Band	KOCD-7504-1	
A Solemn Music [5:30]	Virgil Thomson	No Known Compact Disc Recording		pg. 353
Suite on Greek Love Songs [8:00]	Henk van Lijnschooten	UTSA Wind Ensemble	MCD-5/9	pg. 356
Three Chorale Preludes [9:00]	William P. Latham	Belwin Concert Band Northern Illinois University	BCB-877 NIU-732	pg. 364
Toccata [4:00]	Girolamo Frescobaldi, et al.	Tokyo Kosei Wind Orchestra	KOCD-3573	pg. 370
Trail of Tears [6:15]	James Barnes	No Known Compact Disc Recording		pg. 378
Watchman, Tell Us of the Night [15:00]	Mark Camphouse	Deutsche Blaser-Philharmonie KeyStone Wind Ensemble	98-SS09 CTD-88128	pg. 381
Volume II, Grade V				
Al Fresco [8:30]	Karel Husa	Czech Army Central Band University of Florida	CQ-0016-2 MAS-330	pg. 386
American Salute [5:00]	Morton Gould	Cincinnati Wind Symphony Northshore Concert Band Washington Winds	KCD-11060 4-4104-2 EL9752CD	pg. 391
Chester [6:00]	William Schuman	Cincinnati Wind Symphony Northern Illinois University	KCD-11048 NIU-732	pg. 431
Dance of the Jesters [4:30]	Peter Ilyich Tchaikovsky/Cramer	Indiana University The Symphonic Band / Belgian Navy United States Coast Guard Band University of North Texas	VAWB-941 CURN-1078 MW91-MCD-8 MCD-3144	pg. 437

Title	Composer	Ensemble	Recording	Page
Exaltations, Op. 67 [8:00]	Martin Mailman	University of Texas No Known Compact Disc Recording	MCD-2697	pg. 442
Festivo [5:30]	Edward Gregson	DePauw University Band RNCM Wind Orchestra	MCD-2271 DOYCD-043	pg. 447
Four Scottish Dances [10:00]	Malcolm Arnold	Dallas Wind Symphony Northwestern University Royal Air Force University of Illinois	RR-66CD VOL-6 QPRM-117D MCD-1651	pg. 452
Illyrian Dances [10:00]	Guy Woolfenden	Ithaca College RNCM Wind Orchestra	MCBS-35891 DOYCD-042	pg. 461
Incantation and Dance [7:00]	John Barnes Chance	KeyStone Wind Ensemble Northern Illinois University UNGC Wind Ensemble	CTD-88132 HSB006 CD-103	pg. 469
"Lads of Wamphray" March [8:30]	Percy Aldridge Grainger	Eastman Wind Ensemble RNCM Wind Orchestra University of Houston University of Illinois	SK-47198 CHAN-9549 MCD-1350 MCD-1210	pg. 473
Movement for Rosa, A [11:30]	Mark Camphouse	KeyStone Wind Ensemble UNGC Wind Ensemble	CTD-88111 MCD-1810	pg. 479
Orient et Occident Grande Marche [8:00]	Camille Saint-Saëns	United States Marine Band		pg. 483
Outdoor Overture, An [9:30]	Aaron Copland	Cincinnati Wind Symphony Tokyo Kosei Wind Orchestra	KCD-11048 KOCD-3562	pg. 408
Paris Sketches [14:30]	Martin Ellerby	James Madison University RNCM Wind Orchestra	VAWB-1169 SERCD-2400	pg. 487

Title	Composer	Recording Group	Recording No.	Page Ref.
Ricercare a 6 [6:30]	Johann Sebastian Bach	No Known Compact Disc Recording		pg. 492
Russian Christmas Music [12:00]	Alfred Reed	Tokyo Kosei Wind Orchestra	KOCD-3502	pg. 497
Solitary Dancer, The [6:30]	Warren Benson	United States Marine Band University of Georgia	MW93-MCD-9 UNGA	pg. 502
Soundings [15:00]	Cindy McTee	North Texas Wind Symphony	KCD-11084	pg. 508
Symphony No. 1, "The Lord of the Rings" [40:00]	Johan de Meij	Amsterdam Wind Orchestra Dutch Royal Military Band United States Air Force Band	900101CD OTR-C18924	pg. 513
Toccata Marziale [5:00]	Ralph Vaughan Williams	Eastman Wind Ensemble Keystone Wind Ensemble RNCM Wind Orchestra Kneller Hall All-Star Band Tokyo Kosei Wind Orchestra Tokyo Kosei Wind Orchestra	MK-44916 CTD-88127 CHAN 9697 VBEB-1034 KOCD-2811 KOCD-3576	pg. 522

Volume II, Grade VI

Title	Composer	Recording Group	Recording No.	Page Ref.
and the mountains rising nowhere [12:30]	Joseph Schwantner	Eastman Wind Ensemble North Texas Wind Symphony University of Calgary University of Illinois	SK-47198 KCD-11079 UC-CD9503 MCD-1865	pg. 529
Aspen Jubilee [11:00]	Ron Nelson	Cincinnati Wind Symphony Dallas Wind Symphony IUP Wind Ensemble	KCD-11065 RR-76CD	pg. 541
Bacchanalia [5:30]	Walter S. Hartley	No Known Compact Disc Recording		pg. 544

Title	Composer	Ensemble	Catalog	Page
Blue Shades [11:00]	Frank Tichelli	Michigan State North Texas Wind Symphony University of Georgia University of Florida	MCD-2744 KCD-11091 MCD-2550 MCD-2792	pg. 547
Celebration [6:30]	Edward Gregson	Cincinnati Wind Symphony RNCM Wind Orchestra	KCD-11047 DOYCD-043	pg. 552
Circus Polka [3:30]	Igor Stravinsky	Cincinnati Wind Symphony Tokyo Kosei Wind Orchestra USAF ACC Heritage of America Band	KCD-11059 KOCD-3074	pg. 555
Concerto for Twenty-Three Winds [16:00]	Walter S. Hartley	Canticum Winds Cincinnati Wind Symphony Eastman Wind Ensemble Tokyo Kosei Wind Orchestra	CSCD-102 KCD-11065 432-754-2 KOCD-7506	pg. 559
Dance Movements [20:00]	Philip Sparke	North Texas Wind Symphony United States Air Force Band	KCD-11084	pg. 569
Dance of the New World [9:15]	Dana Wilson	North Texas Wind Symphony University of Maine	KCD-11079 TROY-206	pg. 577
Divertimento in "F" [15:45]	Jack Stamp	KeyStone Wind Ensemble UNCG Wind Ensemble	CTD-88108 CD-103	pg. 584
Fantasy Variations on a Theme of Paganini [15:15]	James Barnes	Tokyo Kosei Wind Orchestra United States Marine Band	MW88-MC-6	pg. 588
Fiesta Del Pacifico [9:00]	Roger Nixon	Dallas Wind Symphony USAF Tactical Air Command Band	RR-38CD	pg. 592
Gazebo Dances [14:45]	John Corigliano	North Texas Wind Symphony	KCD-11083	pg. 598
Huntingtower Ballad [6:45]	Ottorino Respighi	Royal Military Band of the Netherlands	DHM-1007.3	pg. 606

Title	Composer	Recording Group	Recording No.	Page Ref.
Huntingtrower Ballad (continued)		Tokyo Kosei Wind Orchestra United States Air Force Band	KOCD-3037	
Leaves Are Falling, The [9:00]	Warren Benson	Eastman Wind Ensemble	CRC-2014	pg. 615
Profanation [7:45]	Leonard Bernstein	UNCG Wind Ensemble University of Georgia University of Illinois	CD-102 UNGA MCD-1456	pg. 620
Shakata [8:00]	Dana Wilson	UNCG Wind Ensemble University of Florida Wind Ensemble	CD-103	pg. 627
Symphonic Metamorphosis [20:30]	Paul Hindemith	North Texas Wind Symphony Tokyo Kosei Wind Orchestra University of Illinois	KCD-1107 KOCD-3020 MCD-1456	pg. 630
Tunbridge Fair [4:45]	Walter Piston	Cincinnati Wind Symphony United States Marine Band	KCD-11030	pg. 639
Winds of Nagual [25:00]	Michael Colgrass	Cincinnati Wind Symphony Ohio State University	KCD11065	pg. 644

Volume III, Grade IV

Title	Composer	Recording Group	Recording No.	Page Ref.
Ballad [8:30]	Morton Gould	North Texas Wind Symphony Tokyo Kosei Wind Orchestra University of Illinois USAF ACC Heritage of America Band USAF AETC Band of the West	KCD-11070 KOCD-3562 MCD-1648	pg. 296
Cajun Folk Songs II [11:00]	Frank Ticheli	Michigan State University	MCD-2744	pg. 304

Title	Composer	Ensemble	CD	Page
Colors and Contours [8:30]	Leslie Bassett	North Texas Wind Symphony University of Miami Ohio	KCD-11091	pg. 310
Dream of Oenghus, The [21:00]	Rolf Rudin	North Texas Wind Symphony	KCD-11089	pg. 316
Elegy [8:15]	John Barnes Chance	Tokyo Kosei Wind Orchestra University of Illinois	KOCD-3566 MCD-1457	pg. 322
Fantasia in G [5:00]	Timothy Mahr	KeyStone Wind Ensemble Northern Illinois University St. Olaf Band UNCG Wind Ensemble	CTD-88128 HSB-004 WCD-29633 MCD-1810	pg. 336
Festal Scenes [7:30]	Yasuhide Ito	Tokyo Kosei Wind Orchestra	KOCD-2904	pg. 340
First Suite in F [11:00]	Thom Ritter George	Southern Music Promotional CD	Vol. 8	pg. 344
Gum-Suckers March, The [3:30]	Percy Grainger	Cincinnati Wind Symphony Michigan State Wind Ensemble United States Coast Guard Band University of Illinois	KCD-11065 DE-3101 MW91MCD-8 MCD-1865	pg. 352
Laude [13:00]	Howard Hanson	Tokyo Kosei Wind Orchestra USAF ACC Heritage of America Band	KOCD-3578	pg. 357
Medieval Suite [18:00]	Ron Nelson	University of Calgary USAF AETC Band of the West	UC-CD9401	pg. 383
Molly on the Shore [4:15]	Percy Grainger	Michigan State Wind Ensemble RNCM Wind Orchestra Tokyo Kosei Wind Orchestra University of Houston University of Texas	DE-3101 CHAN-9549 KOCD-3566 MCD-1086 MCD-2697	pg. 389
Of Sailors and Whales [16:30]	W. Francis McBeth	Arkansas State University	MCD-1938	pg. 394

Title	Composer	Recording Group	Recording No.	Page Ref.
Of Sailors and Whales (continued)		USAF AETC Band of the West		pg. 399
Original Suite, An [10:00]	Gordon Jacob	Arkansas State University Keystone Wind Ensemble Kneller Hall All-Star Band Tokyo Kosei Wind Orchestra	MCD-1938 CTD-88137 VBEB-1034 KOCD-1938	
Secular Litanies, Op. 90 [7:45]	Martin Mailman	IUP Wind Ensemble	IUP/1996	pg. 413
Suite Provençale [7:00]	Jan Van der Roost	Dutch Royal Military Band Royal Netherlands Air Force	DHM-2006.3 DHM-10.001-3	pg. 419
Symphonic Songs [14:00]	Robert Russell Bennett	Eastman Wind Ensemble KeyStone Wind Ensemble Tokyo Kosei Wind Orchestra United States Air Force Band University of Illinois	432-009-2 CTD-88132 KOCD-3562 MCD-1649	pg. 427
Three London Miniatures [8:30]	Mark Camphouse	No Known Compact Disc Recording		pg. 435
Variations on a Bach Chorale [10:00]	Jack Stamp	Concordia University Indiana State University Keystone Wind Ensemble	MCD-2381 ISU CTD-88140	pg. 439

Volume III, Grade V

Title	Composer	Recording Group	Recording No.	Page Ref.
Circuits [5:30]	Cindy McTee	Cincinnati Wind Symphony UNCG Wind Ensemble University of Florida	KCD-11042 CD-102	pg. 446
Country Band March [4:30]	Charles Ives/Sinclair	Eastman Wind Ensemble Northern Illinois University Tokyo Kosei Wind Orchestra	SK-47198 HSB-005 KOCD-3562	pg. 451

Title	Composer	Ensemble	Recording	Page
Danza de los Duendes [9:30]	Nancy Galbraith	UNCG Wind Ensemble University of Georgia	CD-103 UNGA	pg. 457
Daughter of the Stars [11:30]	Warren Benson	North Texas Wind Symphony	KCD-11089	pg. 461
Divertimento [11:00]	Roger Cichy	The Washington Winds	KCD-11070	pg. 468
Early Light [5:00]	Carolyn Bremer	North Texas Wind Symphony Texas A&M-Commerce	KCD-11083 MCD-2704	pg. 477
Festive Overture, Op. 96 [6:30]	Dmitri Shostakovich/Hunsberger	Eastman Wind Ensemble University of Illinois	SK-47198 MCD-1211	pg. 481
Galactic Empires [10:30]	David Gillingham	The Colony H.S. Band	MW98-MCD	pg. 487
Grande Symphonie Funèbre et Triomphale [36:00]	Hector Berlioz	Montreal Symphony and Chorus Musique des Gardiens de la Paix The Wallace Collection	WALL-903	pg. 492
Hound of Heaven, The [17:30]	James Syler	Northern Illinois University	HSB-003	pg. 500
In Evening's Stillness [12:00]	Joseph Schwantner	North Texas Wind Symphony	KCD-11084	pg. 506
Morning Music [17:00]	Richard Rodney Bennett	RNCM Wind Orchestra	DOYCD-037	pg. 517
Sea Drift [18:00]	Anthony Iannaccone	Clarion Wind Symphony	TROY-280	pg. 529
Short Ride in a Fast Machine [4:30]	John Adams/Odom	Cincinnati Wind Symphony Netherlands Wind Ensemble	KCD-11058 CHAN-9363	pg. 537
Sounds, Shapes, and Symbols [12:00]	Leslie Bassett	University of Illinois	MCD-1865	pg. 543
Symphony in B-Flat [28:30]	Paul Fauchet	Wisconsin Wind Orchestra	MCD-2483	pg. 548

Title	Composer	Recording Group	Recording No.	Page Ref.
Symphony No. 19, Op. 46 [26:00]	Nikolai Miaskovsky	Stockholm Concert Band / Tokyo Kosei Wind Orchestra	CHAN-9444 / KOCD-3574	pg. 557
Symphony No. 3, "Shaker Life" [20:00]	Dan Welcher	North Texas Wind Symphony	KCD	pg. 566
Symphony No. 3, "Slavyanskaya" [14:00]	Boris Kozhevnikov	Koninklijke Militare Kapel / UNCG Wind Ensemble / United States Marine Band	KMK-002 / CD-102	pg. 573
Variations for Wind Band [15:00]	Ralph Vaughan Williams/Hunsberger	Eastman Wind Ensemble	SK-44916	pg. 580

Volume III, Grade VI

Title	Composer	Recording Group	Recording No.	Page Ref.
Apotheosis of This Earth [24:00]	Karel Husa	Kerkrade Nederland		pg. 612
Arctic Dreams [24:30]	Michael Colgrass	New England Conservatory	CRC-2288	pg. 621
Awayday [6:30]	Adam Gorb	North Texas Wind Symphony	KCD-11091	pg. 632
Caricatures [23:30]	Jere Hutcheson	North Texas Wind Symphony	KCD-11091	pg. 639
Child's Garden of Dreams, A [32:00]	David Maslanka	Cincinnati Wind Symphony	KCD-11030	pg. 592
Dialogues and Entertainments [20:00]	William Kraft	North Texas Wind Symphony	KCD-11083	pg. 647
Dionysiaques, Op. 62 [11:00]	Florent Schmitt/Duker	Cincinnati Wind Symphony / Kunitachi College Blasorchester / Musique des Gardiens de la Paix / Stockholm Wind Orchestra / University of Illinois / USAF ACC Heritage of America Band	KCD-11066 / CAP-21384 / MCD-1457	pg. 652

Title	Composer	Ensemble	CD	Page
El Salon Mexico [12:30]	Aaron Copland/Hindsley	Baylor University Cincinnati Wind Symphony Northern Illinois University	TMEA91-3CD KCD-11048 HSB-004	pg. 659
Fantasy Variations [8:15]	Donald Grantham	North Texas Wind Symphony University of Texas	KCD MCD-2697	pg. 666
For Precious Friends... [20:15]	Martin Mailman	North Texas Wind Symphony	KCD-11083	pg. 671
From a Dark Millennium [12:30]	Joseph Schwantner	Baden Wurtemburg Wind Ensemble Ithaca College North Texas Wind Symphony	MAS-279 MCBS-35891 KCD-11089	pg. 682
Konzertmusik, Op. 41 [15:00]	Paul Hindemith	Eastman Wind Ensemble Furman Civic Wind Ensemble North Texas Wind Symphony Tokyo Kosei Wind Orchestra	MK-44916 CRS-9051 KCD-11110 KOCD-3073	pg. 706
Niagara Falls [9:45]	Michael Daugherty	North Texas Wind Symphony Univerisity of Texas	KCD MCD-2697	pg. 718
Parable IX, Op. 121 [18:00]	Vincent Persichetti	North Texas Wind Symphony Winds of the London Symphony	KCD HMU-907092	pg. 722
Scenes [16:45]	Verne Reynolds	Tokyo Kosei Wind Orchestra	KOCD-3569	pg. 731
Skating on the Sheyenne [12:00]	Ross Lee Finney	University of Kansas	GR-95701	pg. 735
Spiël, Op. 39 [8:45]	Ernst Toch	Baden Wurtemburg Wind Ensemble Canticum Winds Furman Civic Wind Ensemble North Texas Wind Symphony Northwestern University	MAS-330 CSCD-102 CRS-9051 KCD-11079 Vol. 4	pg. 743

Title	Composer	Recording Group	Recording No.	Page Ref.
Symphonies of Wind Instruments [9:00]	Igor Stravinsky	Detroit Chamber WInds Laval University London Sinfonietta Netherlands Wind Ensemble Orchestra of St. Luke's Symphonic Band of the Belgian Guides	3-7211-2H1 VBEB-1051 SK-45797 SWE-NWE-1194 0162-67103-2 SBBG-1024	pg. 754
Symphony, "In Praise of Winds" [20:00]	Gunther Schuller	No Known Compact Disc Recording		pg. 698
Symphony No. 3 [39:00]	James Barnes	United States Air Force Band		pg. 763

Index by Title for Teaching Music through Performance in Band: Volumes 1, 2, 3

Index by Publisher for Teaching Music through Performance in Band: Volumes 1, 2, 3

Index by Composer, Arranger, Transcriber for Teaching Music through Performance in Band: Volume 3

Index by Title for Teaching Music through Performance in Band: Volume 3

810